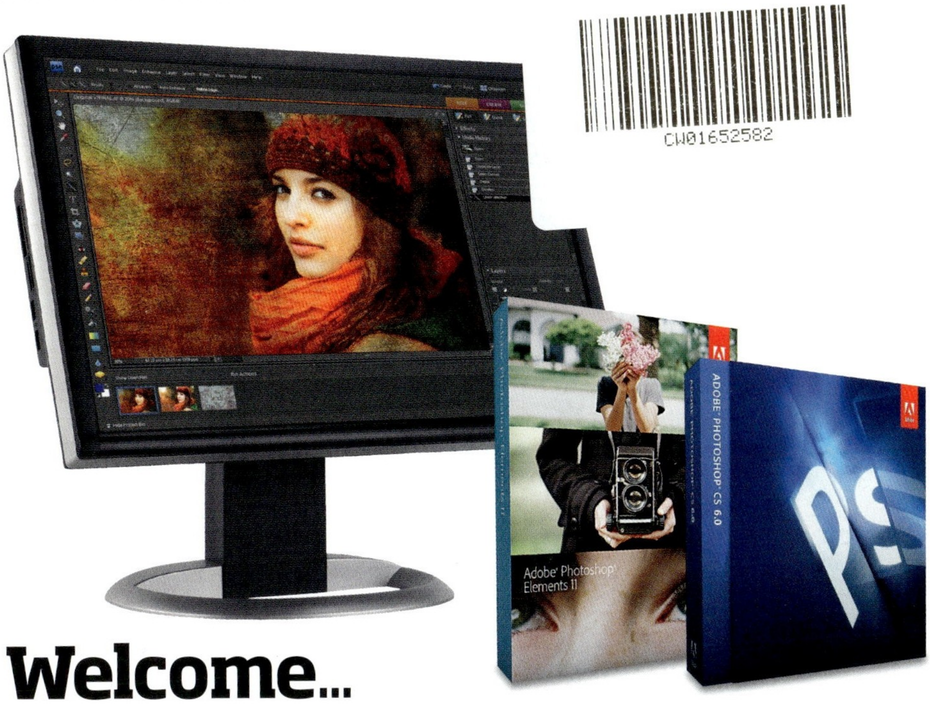

Welcome...

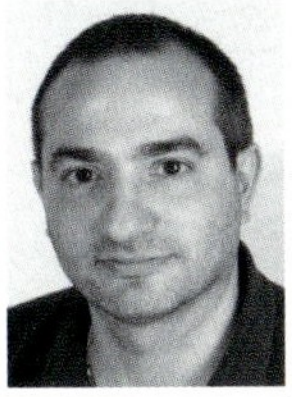

"The very best photographers have always been those with skills in capturing pictures with their camera and producing great results in post-production. In the past, this was by using film, which was processed and printed in the darkroom, today it's by shooting digitally and manipulating images on the computer, usually using Photoshop as the software of choice. Regardless of the type of digital camera you use, once you have your images on your PC or Mac, Photoshop allows you to experiment, enhance and manipulate to your heart's content. Whether using Adobe's affordable Photoshop Elements package or the more powerful Creative Suite, there are countless ways to improve or transform your photographs. Of course, such a sophisticated tool requires time and effort to master, which is where *The Photographers' Guide to Photoshop* will help. Produced by photographers for photographers, this guide is the perfect introduction to Photoshop, guiding you through the key features and tools that you need to use, as well as providing you with a variety of techniques geared towards helping you make the most of your digital images. By following the jargon-free advice given by our team of experts, you can look forward to mastering key Photoshop techniques, while having fun as you learn new skills along the way. We've covered various techniques, from basic skills that enhance images to more advanced options that transform them. All the best!"

DANIEL LEZANO, EDITOR

Meet our team of Photoshop experts

All our experts are team members or regular contributors to *Digital SLR Photography* magazine. For more expert advice and inspiration, pick up the latest issue available on the second Tuesday of every month. For further information visit the magazine's website at www.digitalslrphoto.com

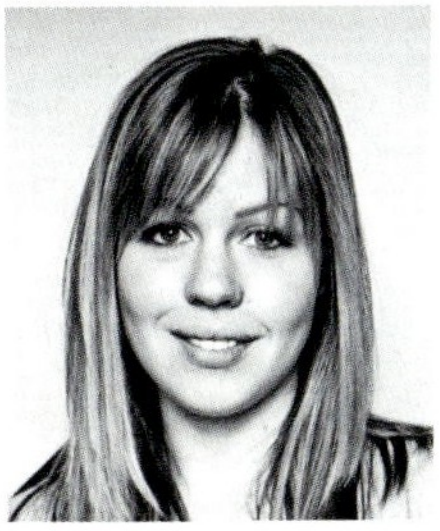

CAROLINE WILKINSON
An avid enthusiast photographer for several years, Caroline uses her in-depth knowledge of Photoshop and creative skills in post-production to add extra impact and polish to pictures.

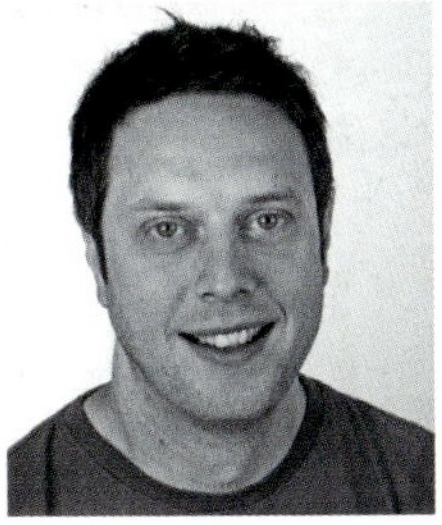

LUKE MARSH
A keen DSLR photographer, Luke's also the creative genius behind the look of *Digital SLR Photography* magazine and this MagBook, as well as a Photoshop expert.

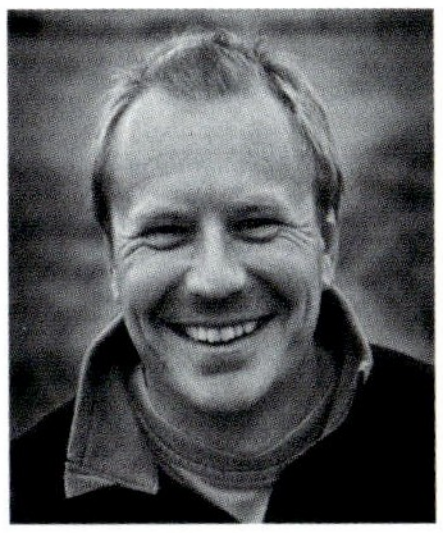

LEE FROST
A professional photographer and writer for two decades, Lee regularly combines his in-camera skills with Photoshop to get the very best from his images. *www.leefrost.co.uk*

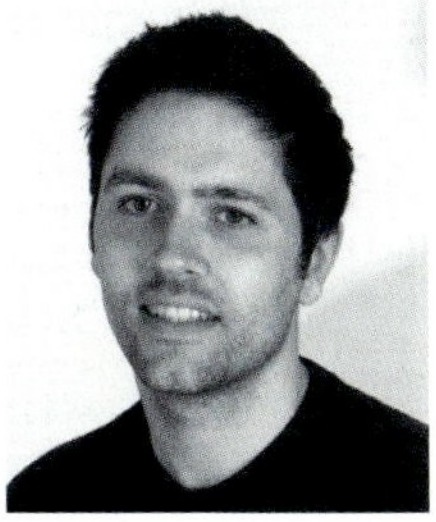

JORDAN BUTTERS
With his roots in shooting motorsport, Jordan's passion for photography has evolved to include Photoshop. He is highly skilled in creating stunning images in post-production.

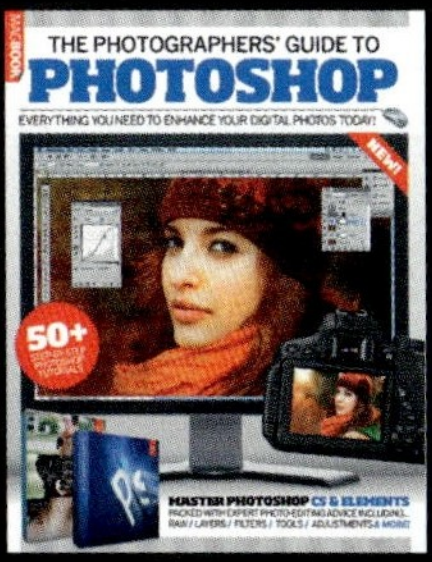

The Photographers' Guide to Photoshop (Vol.5)

Produced by *Digital SLR Photography* at:
6 Swan Court, Cygnet Park,
Peterborough, Cambs PE7 8GX
Phone: 01733 567401. Fax 01733 352650
Email: enquiries@digitalslrphoto.com
Online: www.digitalslrphoto.com

Editorial

To contact editorial phone: 01733 567401
Editor **Daniel Lezano**
daniel_lezano@dennis.co.uk
Art Editor **Luke Marsh**
luke_marsh@dennis.co.uk
Deputy Editor **Caroline Wilkinson**
caroline_wilkinson@dennis.co.uk
Senior Features Writer **Jordan Butters**
jordan_butters@dennis.co.uk
Designer **Luke Medler**
luke_medler@dennis.co.uk
Editorial Co-ordinator **Jo Lezano**
jo_lezano@dennis.co.uk
Editorial contributors:
Brett Harkness, Ross Hoddinott, Paul Stefan, Bjorn Thomassen, Paul Ward & Donna Willingham

Advertising & Production

Display & Classified Sales: 020 7907 6651
Group Advertising Manager **Alex Skinner**
alex_skinner@dennis.co.uk
Production Controller **Daniel Stark**
daniel_stark@dennis.co.uk
Digital Production Manager **Nicky Baker**
nicky_baker@dennis.co.uk

Management

MAGBOOK PUBLISHER **DHARMESH MISTRY**
OPERATIONS DIRECTOR **ROBIN RYAN**
MD OF ADVERTISING **JULIAN LLOYD-EVANS**
NEWSTRADE DIRECTOR **DAVID BARKER**
COMMERCIAL & RETAIL DIRECTOR **MARTIN BELSON**
PUBLISHING DIRECTOR **JOHN GAREWAL**
CHIEF OPERATING OFFICER **BRETT REYNOLDS**
GROUP FINANCE DIRECTOR **IAN LEGGETT**
CHIEF EXECUTIVE **JAMES TYE**
CHAIRMAN **FELIX DENNIS**

The Photographers Guide to Photoshop ISBN 1-78106-163-7

Licensing & Syndication: To license this product please contact Carlotta Serantoni on +44 (0) 20 7907 6550 or email carlotta_serantoni@dennis.co.uk. To syndicate content from this product please contact Anj Dosaj Halai on +44 (0) 20 7907 6132 or email anj_dosaj-halai@dennis. co.uk

Printed at Benham Goodhead Print (BGP)

CONTENTS

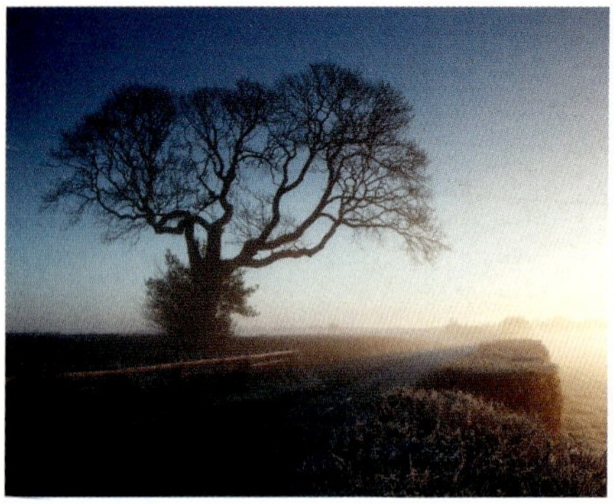

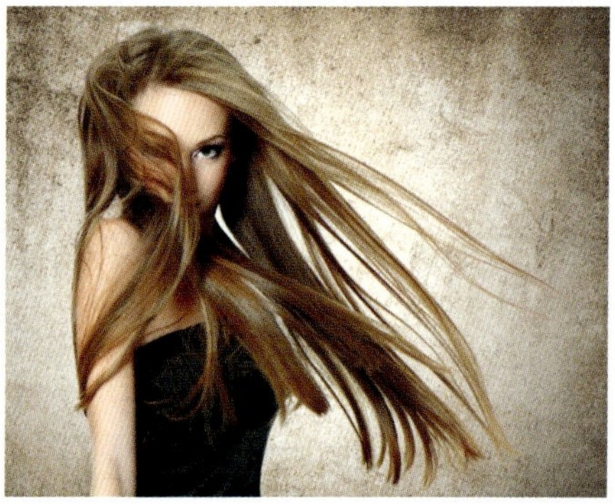

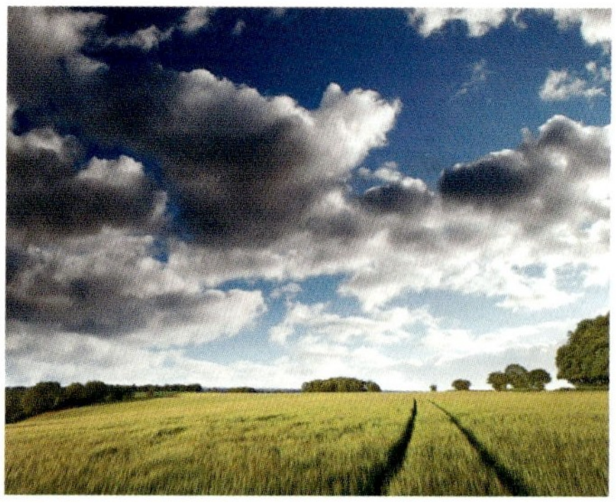

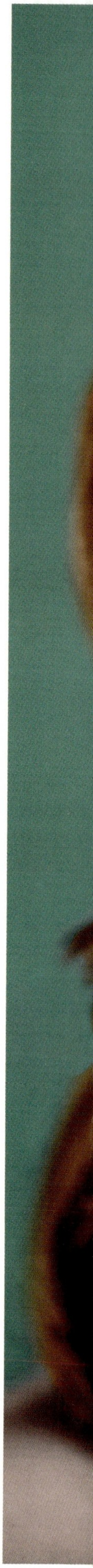

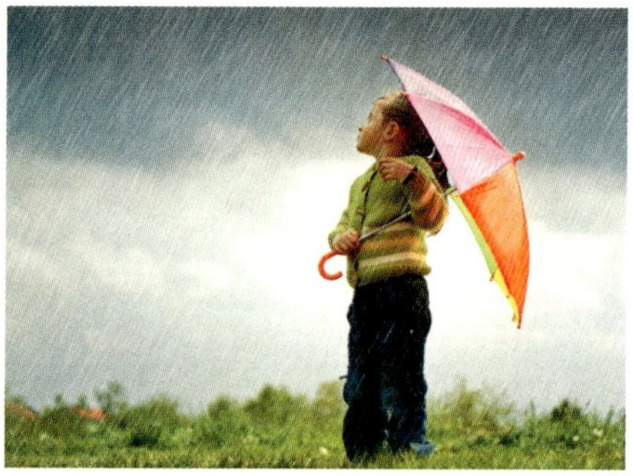

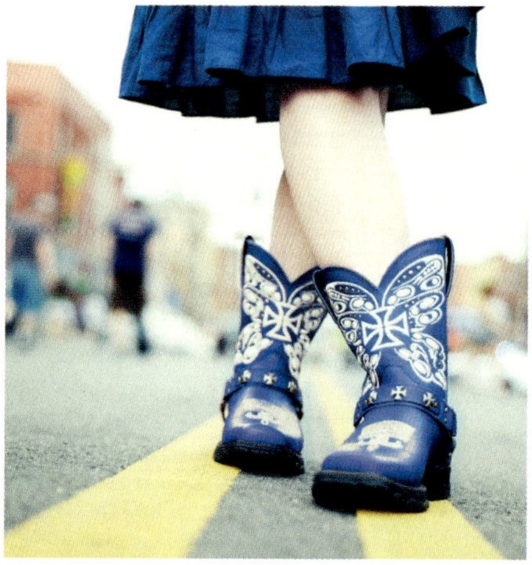

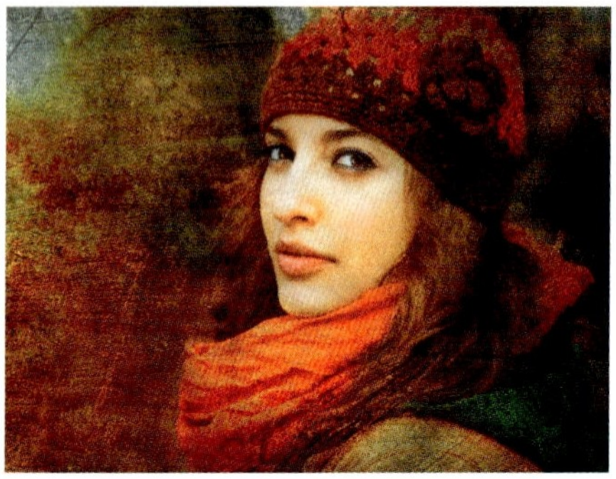

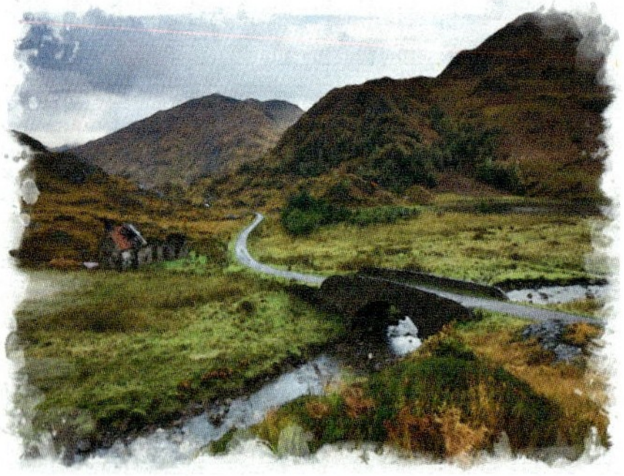

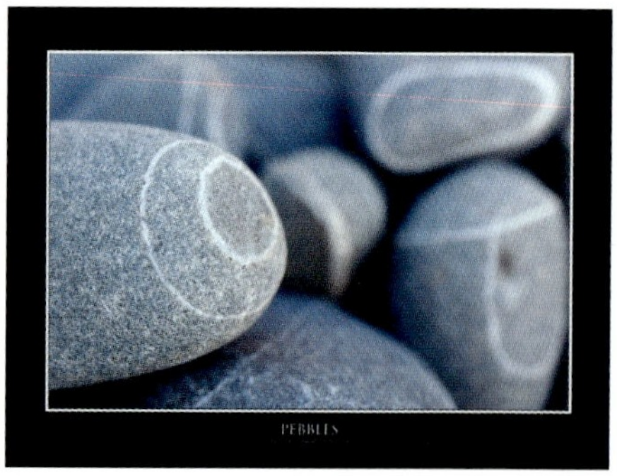

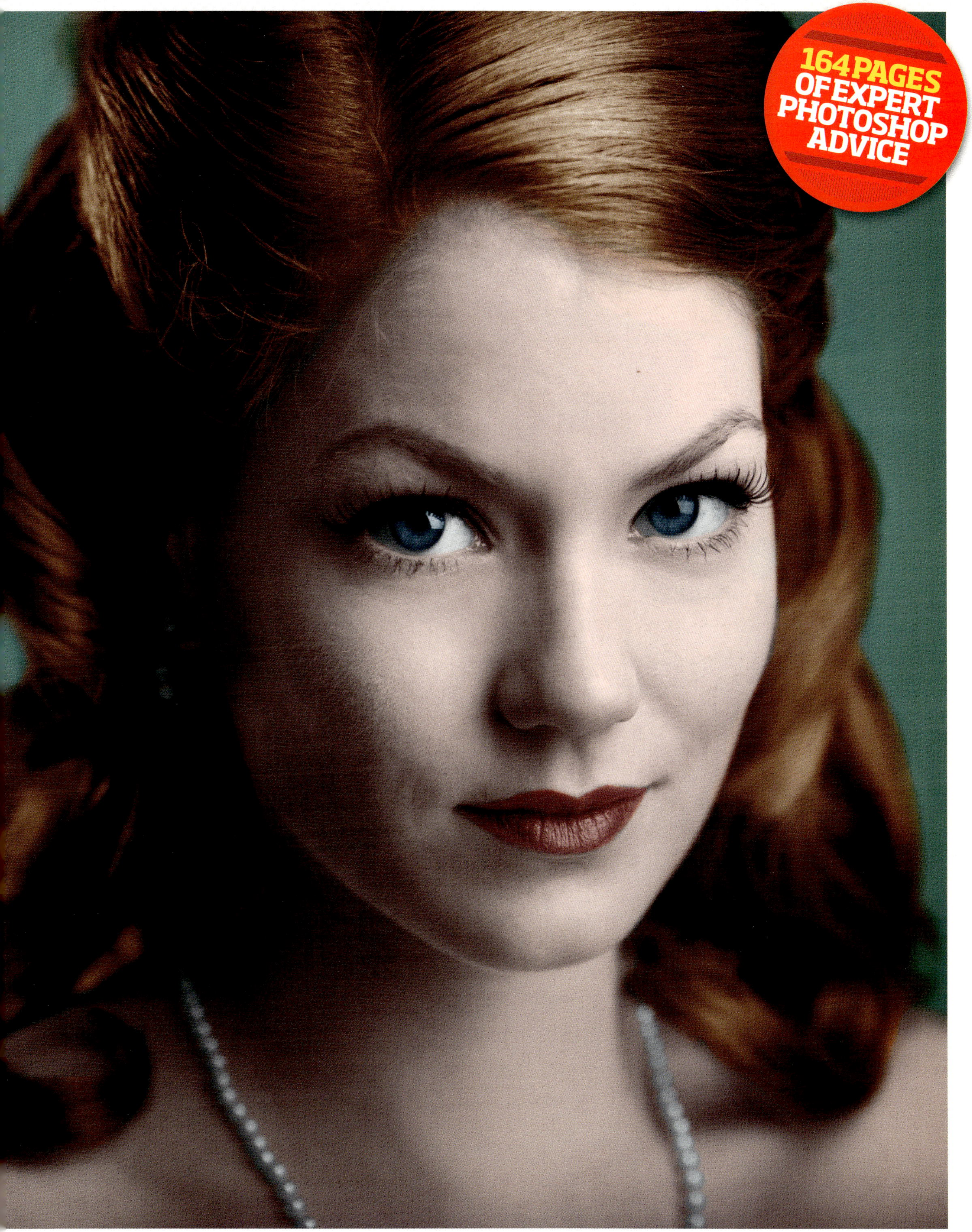
164 PAGES
OF EXPERT
PHOTOSHOP
ADVICE

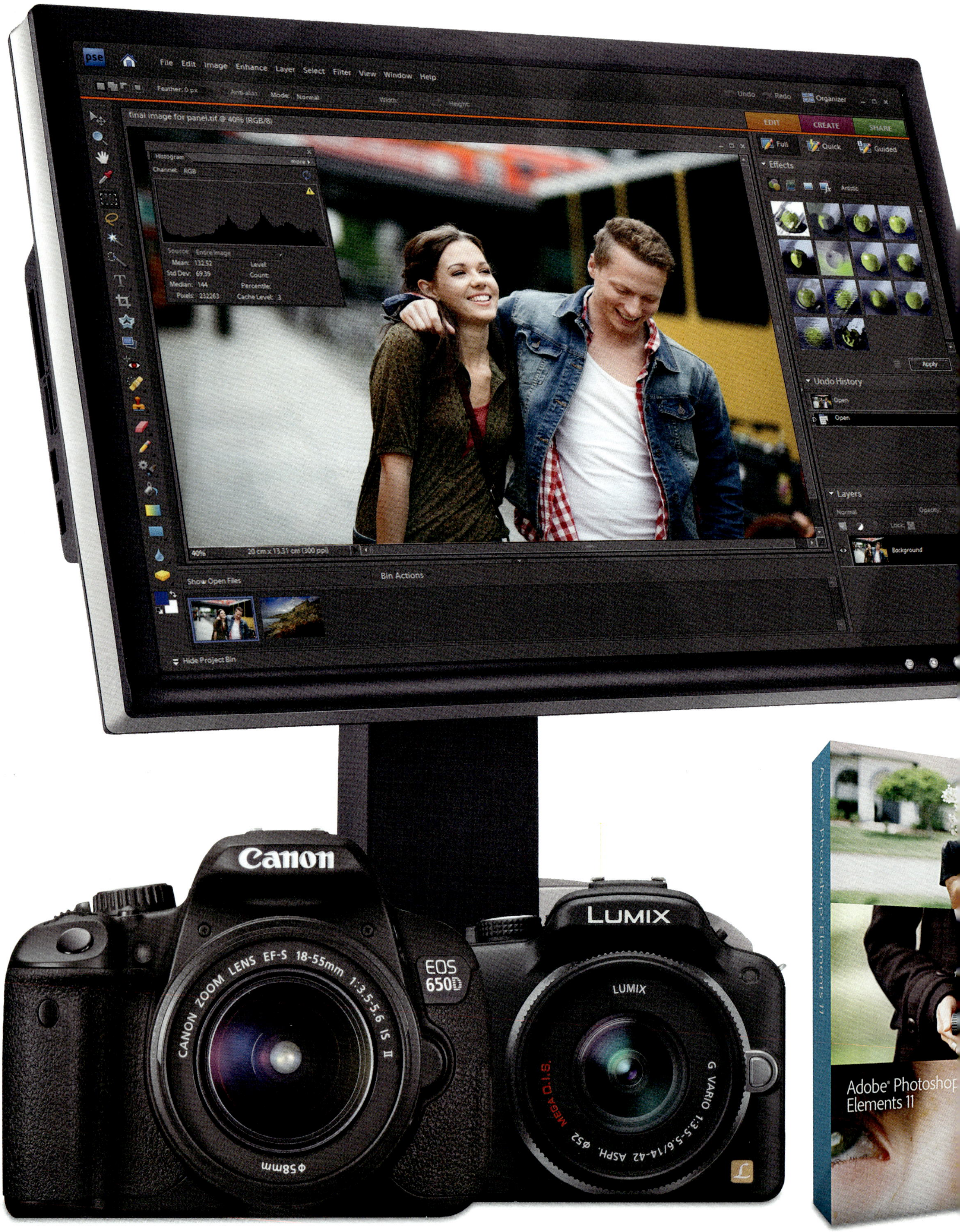
pse
File Edit Image Enhance Layer Select Filter View Window Help
final image for panel.tif @ 40% (RGB/8)
EDIT
CREATE
SHARE
Full
Quick
Guided
Effects
Undo History
Layers
Show Open Files
Bin Actions
Hide Project Bin
Canon
EOS 650D
CANON ZOOM LENS EF-S 18-55mm 1:3.5-5.6 IS II
φ58mm
LUMIX
LUMIX
G VARIO 1:3.5-5.6/14-42 ASPH. φ52
MEGA O.I.S.
Adobe Photoshop Elements 11
Adobe® Photoshop Elements 11

PHOTOSHOP. THE DIGITAL PHOTOGRAPHERS' CHOICE!

PHOTOGRAPHY IS ABOUT creativity, always has been. Since its inception, photographers haven't simply been content to document their surroundings but have sought to enhance, embellish, beautify and distort their imagery, be it via the darkroom or with in-camera techniques. Photoshop is just another tool in the creative arsenal, though it happens to be a damn good one – the best possible. Everything that was done in the film darkroom can be recreated in Photoshop, and far more besides. Images that are now appearing in this digital age are really pushing the boundaries of the imagination. So if you haven't already jumped on the Photoshop bandwagon, it's really time to take that leap. You're missing out on the chance to really explore your creative self. Even if your ambitions are a little more modest, you'll find that there isn't an image in the world that can't be improved by Photoshop in some manner, even if it's a matter of a simple contrast tweak or basic blemish removal. And the best way to learn is just to get stuck in. After, of course, you've familiarised yourself with the basics in our feature-packed guide to the best imaging software on the planet! Here are our favourite reasons for using Photoshop...

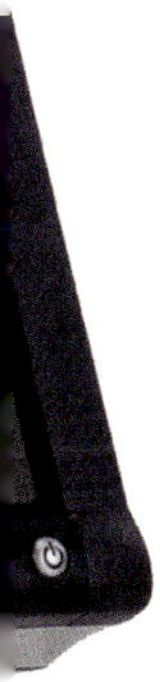

1) Raw conversion: All digital cameras come with their own brand software to help convert Raw files into an editable image state (ie JPEG or TIFF). However, not all are straightforward to use. Photoshop and Photoshop Elements come with their own Raw converter, Adobe Camera Raw (ACR), which just happens to be rather good at the job. Most people tend to plump for the Adobe engine rather than the camera manufacturer's own, not least because of its seamless integration with Photoshop.

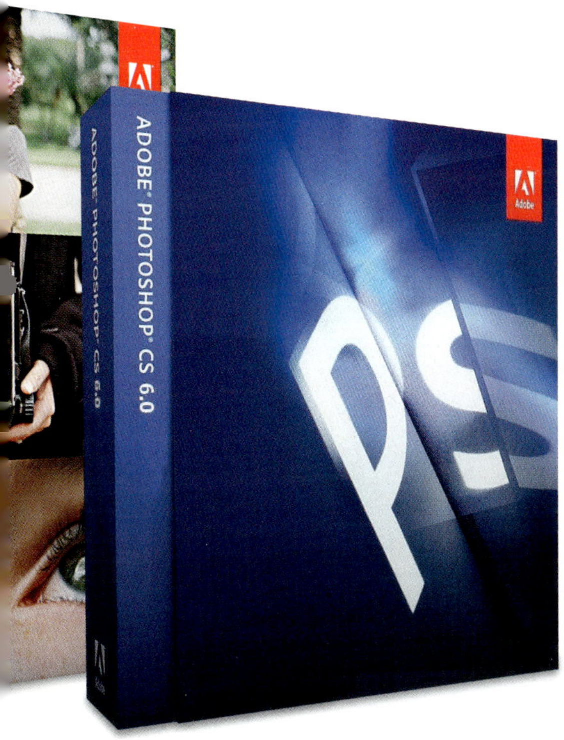

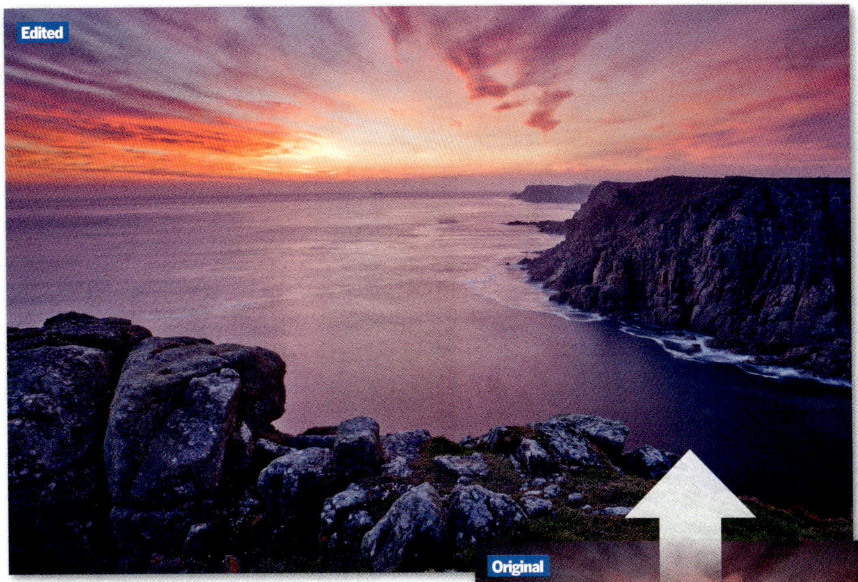

2) Exposure control: Photoshop gives you the kind of control over exposure that darkroom enthusiasts could have only dreamed of. Not only can you lighten or darken the image as a whole, but you can work on specific tones, lightening the highlights or darkening shadows, for example. You can also work on specific areas to 'dodge' and 'burn' in the traditional darkroom manner – darkening a sky perhaps, or bringing out a bit more detail in a landscape foreground.

3) Colour control: We're not just talking about warming things up or cooling them down. You can tweak colours in any way imaginable and locally as well as globally, changing the colour of someone's eyes, hair, or perhaps the colour of a particularly bad tie. And you can control colour saturation as well as hue, so you can make those sunsets really burn.

4) Better black and white: Yes, you can shoot black and white in camera but, no, it won't do. First, you'll be shooting JPEG and secondly, all you're doing is performing a basic desaturation, which means you'll be discarding vital information. Anyone who's printed in the traditional darkroom knows there's a bit more to mastering monochrome. Photoshop lets you control specific colour channels in the way that black and white filters did for film cameras.

5) Blemish removal: On a basic level, this means polishing portraits a little by removing spots, moles and wrinkles, but this process can be extended to pretty much anything with the clever combination of Clone Stamp and Healing Brush Tools. You can remove a telegraph pole from an otherwise picture-perfect landscape, an unwanted reflection from a window, and so on.

6) Montage: Layers allow you to montage (otherwise known as composite) different images, in the same way that you might have once cut and pasted family photos. But Photoshop allows you to go that extra mile. You can change a cloudy sky for a clear one, add trees where there were none, or even place a person in a completely different background scene. This type of montage is also known as compositing and has grown in popularity with amateur users and professionals alike.

7) Subject enhancement: As well as taking out aspects you don't really like and sticking in stuff that wasn't really there, you can also enhance what you've already got. Aside from the colour and exposure controls for whitening teeth or pulling out grey hairs, you could change the shape and size of parts of your image with various Transform commands. And yes, that can mean slimmer hips and bigger biceps, but it could also mean ironing out the converging verticals of a tall building or scaling down a hand that's too close to a wide-angle lens.

8) Web preparation: If you want to post your photos in a forum, an online gallery or your own website, Photoshop is certainly going to come in handy. You can resize them, sharpen them, convert them to sRGB mode and save them with the appropriate JPEG quality setting.

9) Special Effects: Photoshop has a massive array of filters to enable you to achieve special effects. Turn photos into watercolour paintings, add frames and borders, add rain to a cloud scene, the list goes on.

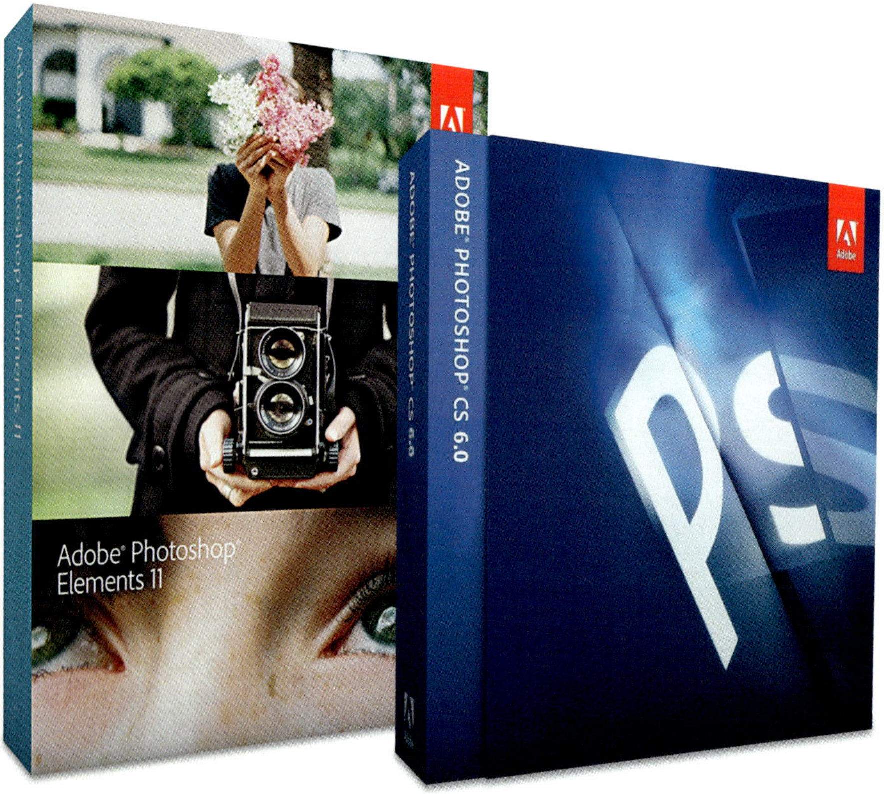

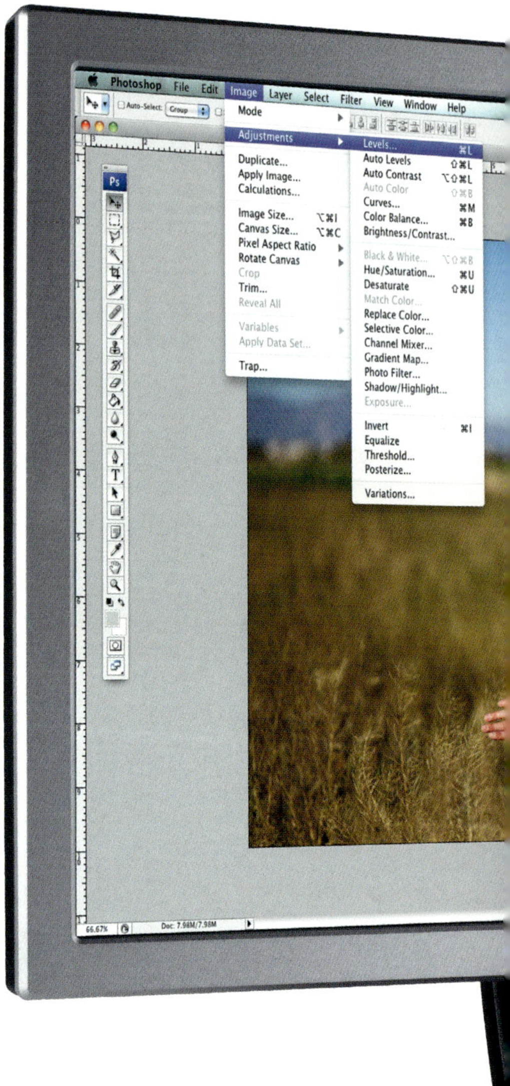

Which Photoshop: Elements or CS?

PHOTOSHOP COMES in two distinct flavours. You have the full-blown professional version, running from the original in 1990 all the way to Photoshop 7, then Creative Suite, CS2, CS3, CS4, CS5, CS6 and now CC, or Creative Cloud. Previous versions of Photoshop were available as stand-alone software to purchase, however CC is a monthly subscription-based service. At the time of print, it is still possible to purchase CS6 from Adobe, if you prefer. Also available is the beginner-friendly, consumer version called Photoshop Elements, now at version 11. To give you an idea of the price difference, Photoshop CC costs between £9 and £18 per month, and Photoshop CS6 costs between £660 and £945 as a one-time purchase, whereas you can buy the latest version of Elements for around £80. Unless you're planning complex composites involving the extraction of intricate shapes, you'll be fine with Elements. If you're good enough to be doing detailed cut-outs, you'll probably already have access to the full-blown Photoshop. Most, if not all, basic edits can be done in Elements along with a few intermediate edits, especially as Elements 9 onwards features Layer Masks. As a first-time buyer, the only occasion you might want CS is if you plan on using retouching as part of a semi- or fully professional workflow or have ambitions for advanced retouching. In this case, it's perhaps wise to familiarise yourself with Photoshop from the start to save making the transition later on.

While the Elements interface is a little different from that found on Creative Suite, there are enough similarities so that photographers migrating from one to the other won't find it too alien.

Which Photoshop: New or old?

If you're a first-time buyer, there's little incentive to buy earlier versions of either Photoshop or Photoshop Elements as there is little difference in price and you have the added compatibility problems with newer digital cameras (for which updates are often only released for the latest versions). Owners of older versions may be forced to upgrade their copies for this reason. If you're not planning to invest in the latest and greatest digital camera and already own a copy of CS, CS2, CS3 or CS4, you'll have to weigh the upgrade price against new features.

It's worth noting that there's nothing spectacular that you couldn't be without in earlier versions. Many of the new features are quite gimmicky, though the Photomerge advancements were a big improvement for panoramic enthusiasts in CS3, CS4's Clone Stamp Tool overlay and CS5's Content-Aware Fill function alone make the upgrade worth considering if you do a lot of clean-up work. Also, the addition of Layer Masks in Elements 9 is a big bonus. Of course, with cloud-based Photoshop CC just launched, many may prefer to own a DVD-based CS version than pay a monthly subscription.

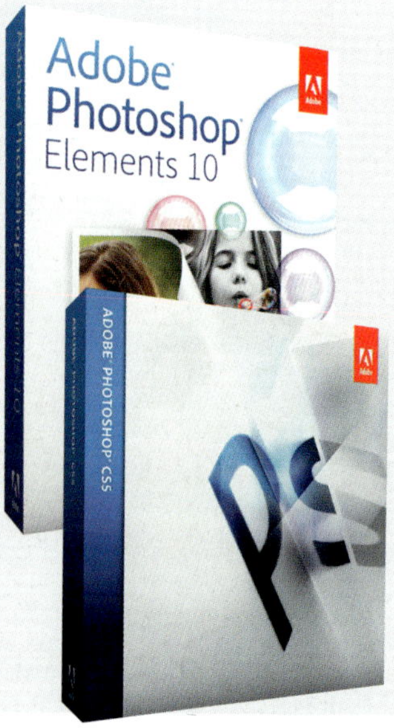

File formats

Check out the File Format drop-down list in the Photoshop Save As dialogue and get a shock at the multitude of options available. Panic not, though; there are only really four formats worth discussing.

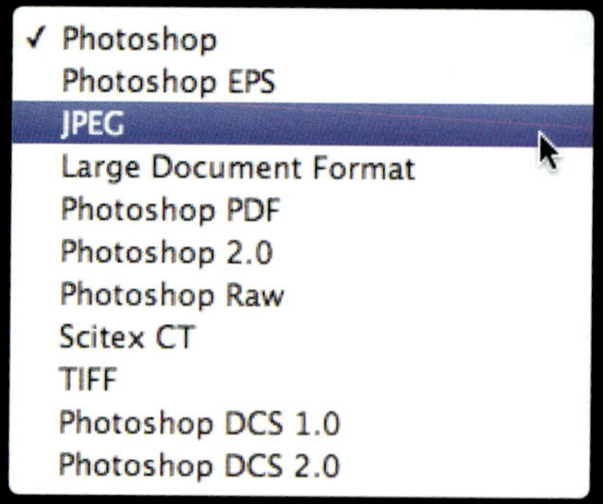

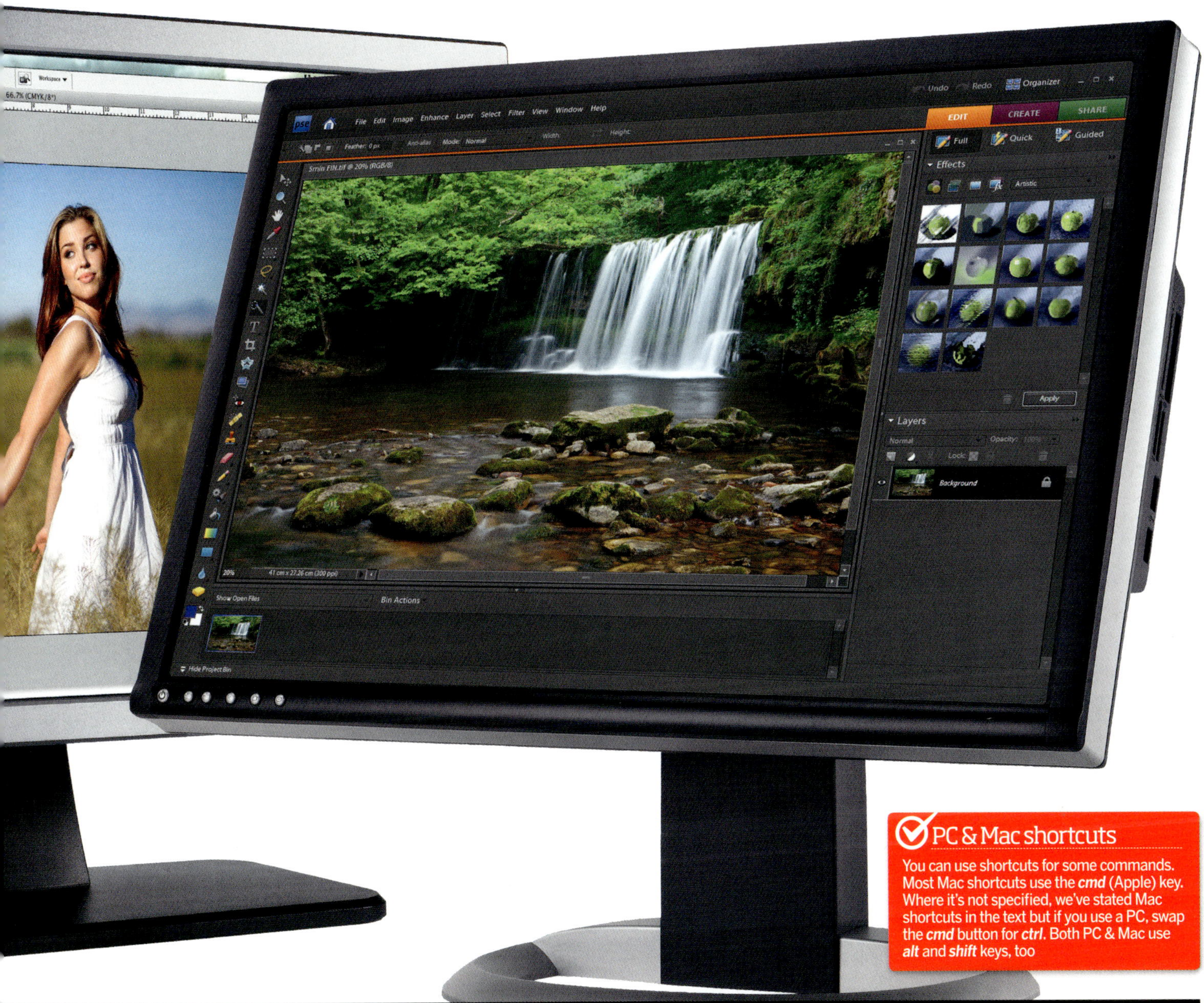

PC & Mac shortcuts

You can use shortcuts for some commands. Most Mac shortcuts use the ***cmd*** (Apple) key. Where it's not specified, we've stated Mac shortcuts in the text but if you use a PC, swap the ***cmd*** button for ***ctrl***. Both PC & Mac use ***alt*** and ***shift*** keys, too

RAW

This is the catch-all term given to the different proprietary file formats that come directly out of a digital camera when shooting in Raw (a Canon EOS 5D Mk II Raw file, for example, has the extension .CR2). These files need converting into editable information via a Raw converter, such as Adobe Camera Raw (ACR), which comes packaged with both Photoshop and Elements. Shooting Raw allows access to the full range of information recorded by the camera sensor, giving more room to correct for exposure mistakes and to make edits to your image without chancing visible degradation. Raw files give you access to 16-bits of information, as opposed to a JPEG's 8-bits.

PSD

The PSD file is a Photoshop format that allows all Photoshop information, such as layers and saved selections, to be easily stored and re-accessed at a later date. It's an uncompressed format and maintains the full 16-bits of information. While TIFF files do give you the option of including Photoshop layers, the file size increases disproportionately, making PSD the file format of choice for editing your images. When the image is finally flattened, it can be saved as a TIFF or JPEG, although it's always a good idea to keep the PSD file with all the layers work you've done in case you need to make any additional changes at a later date.

JPEG

The JPEG is a compressed file format, designed to keep file size as low as possible with as little quality loss as possible. It uses what's termed a 'lossy' version of compression, meaning image information is thrown away for good. The amount discarded depends on the compression setting. A JPEG file retains only 8-bits rather than 16-bits of information, making it less useful as a format for image editing; the decrease in available information can produce signs of degradation if adjustments are pushed particularly hard. The reduced file size makes JPEGs great for web reproduction, email and even magazine reproduction, with a quality setting of 9 or more.

TIFF

The TIFF is generally an uncompressed file format (though there is a 'lossless' compression option), and an alternative to the JPEG for distributing images once you've made all your edits in Photoshop and flattened the layers. File sizes are considerably bigger than JPEGs, so it's used as a maximum quality option if you're prepared to distribute images on a CD or upload them via FTP – forget email! Those without a copy of Photoshop are normally able to open a TIFF file without any problems. It can hold 16-bits of information, but as it's not generally used for editing, it's better to convert your images to 8-bits before saving as a TIFF to keep down the file size.

The Toolbar

Photoshop's tools are generally quick and easy to understand as their descriptions usually outline their function well. A small black arrow to the bottom right of a tool icon indicates a sub-menu with further tools accessed by clicking and holding.

Move Can be used to move pixel information on a layer, text or an active selection. Just click and drag.

Zoom Click to zoom in, or ***alt*** and click to zoom out. You may also choose to use ***ctrl*** (PC) or ***cmd*** (Mac) plus the **+** or **–** keys.

Hand Used for moving around your image when zoomed in. Access quickly by holding down the ***spacebar*** instead.

Eyedropper Select a colour from your image by clicking on the areas or hold it down to reveal any of the three tools housed underneath, including Ruler.

Marquee Use these tools to make a selection based on a shape such as a rectangle or ellipse. Simply drag to size.

Lasso Draw your own custom selections with this tool, either freehand or using magnetic polygon points.

Quick Selection Houses both the Quick Selection and Magic Wand Tool for semi-automated selections. Use by adjusting the Tolerance in the Options bar.

Text Type text directly onto your image using any of the installed fonts. Type horizontally or vertically and create selections based on your type.

Crop Crop out unwanted aspects from the edges of your image. Set a specific width-to-height ratio if needed in the Options bar.

Healing Brush Replace blemishes with nearby clean pixel information and have it blend in with surrounding pixels. Also houses the Spot Healing Brush Tool, Patch Tool and Red Eye in CS4/5.

Clone Stamp Allows you to copy and paste pixels from one area to another without the blending of the Healing Brush.

Eraser Remove pixel information manually or in a semi-automated manner using the Background or Magic Eraser Tool.

Brush One of the tools used most often, particularly for painting information in and out of an image when combined with a Layer Mask. You control its Opacity and edge Hardness via the Options bar. The Pencil Tool and Color Replacement Tool sit underneath.

Gradient Draw gradients directly onto layers or their masks. Also houses the Paint Bucket Tool for single colour fill.

Blur Soften selected areas of your image or sharpen and smudge them with the two other useful tools housed underneath Blur.

Shape Draw shapes or lines using any one of the default shapes, or choose another with the Custom Shape Tool.

Dodge & Burn The Dodge Tool lightens and the Burn Tool darkens depending on the Exposure level set in the Options bar. You can choose whether to focus on Shadows, Mid-tones or Highlights and there's also a Sponge Tool for increasing or decreasing colour saturation.

History Brush (CS4/5 only) Go back in time by painting previous states into your image in conjunction with the History palette.

Pen (CS4/5 only) Allows the user to create curved as well as straight-edge selections to accurately outline solid-edge subjects.

Direct Selection (CS4/5 only) This tool and the one it hides are for selecting and moving paths created with the Pen and Shape Tool.

Quick Mask Mode (CS4/5 only) View selections as a translucent red mask rather than marching ants. When active, you can paint onto your image with a Black or White brush to add or subtract from the selection. Press ***Q*** to turn it on and off.

Menus, tools and palettes

THE PHOTOSHOP WORKSPACE can be a daunting place at first, with its vast array of features. However, once you grasp a basic understanding of just a few key areas, you'll be up and running in no time. Here we'll be looking at the workspace of Photoshop Elements and although there are differences between this interface and that of CS3, CS4 or CS5, Adobe does a great job with crossing over packages to encourage a progression for users as they become more experienced. The three key areas to understand are the Toolbar (which runs vertically on the left side and incorporates the Options bar running horizontally above it), the Menu bar (which runs horizontally along the top of the workspace), and, finally, the palettes. All these items can be hidden or made visible via the Window tab, allowing users to customise the workspace to their individual needs.

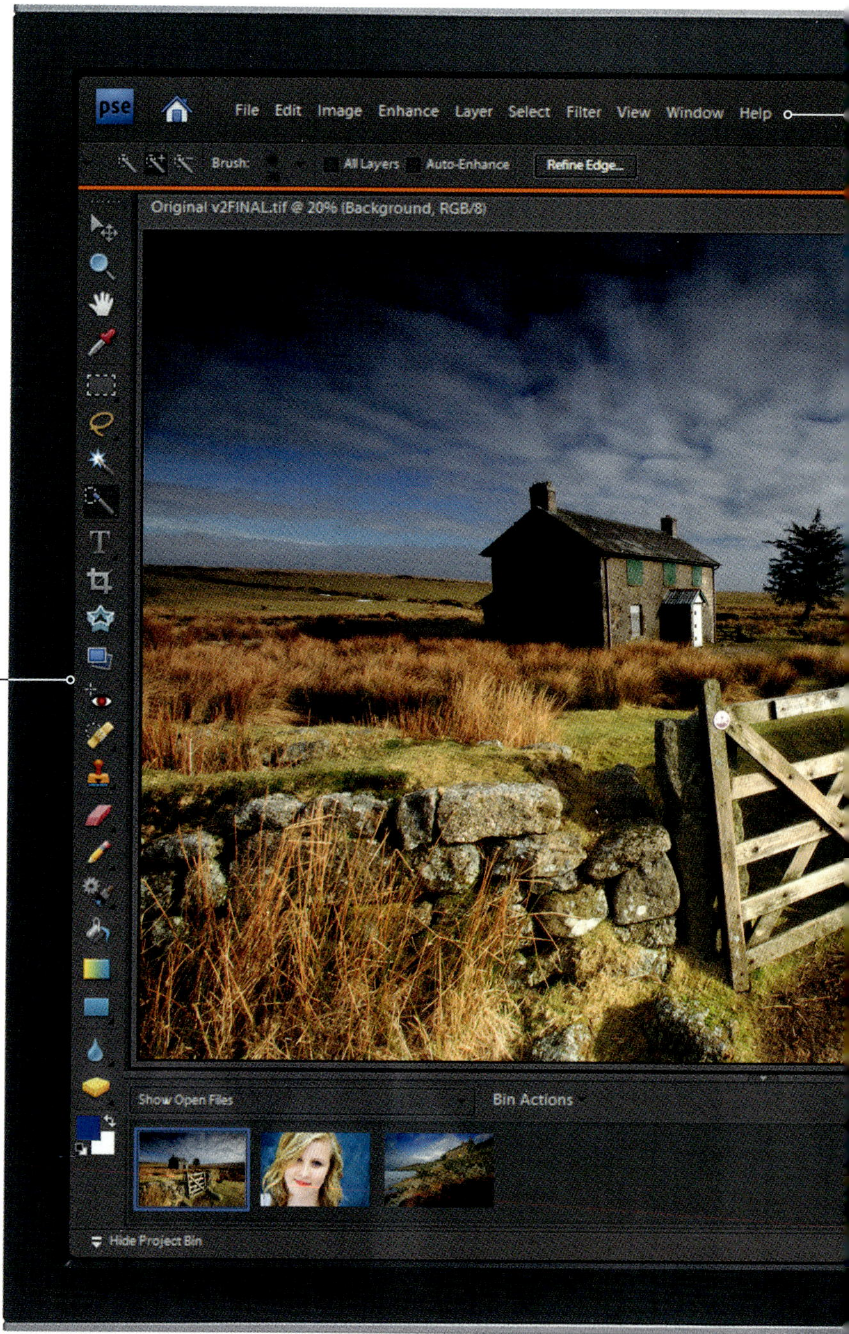

The Menu bar

EDIT As well as hosting options for general preferences and keyboard shortcuts, the Edit menu is home to Cut, Copy and Paste, though all these are accessed easier via their keyboard shortcuts. The Transform commands are located here, too, allowing you to perform things such as Scale, Rotate and Skew.

IMAGE All the popular image adjustments such as Levels and Curves can be found here, though usually you'll want to add these as Adjustment Layers via the button in the Layers palette, rather than applying them directly to pixel information. The Image menu also lets you alter size via the Image Size command.

LAYER The Layer menu is home to popular layer-based commands like Convert to Smart Object, Merge Layers and Flatten Image, and you can also add Adjustment Layers from here. In truth, virtually everything here is better accessed by keyboard shortcuts or buttons on the Layers palette itself.

SELECT Everything to do with selections is here, such as Select All, Deselect and Select Inverse. You can also modify selections via this menu with commands like Expand, Contract and, most commonly, Feather. This menu also gives access to the very useful Transform Selection and Color Range commands.

FILTER Along with being home to a variety of special-effects filters, the Filters menu also includes two of the most often used filters in Photoshop – Unsharp Mask and Gaussian Blur. These two filters are integral to much of the work done in Photoshop and can be employed for a variety of purposes.

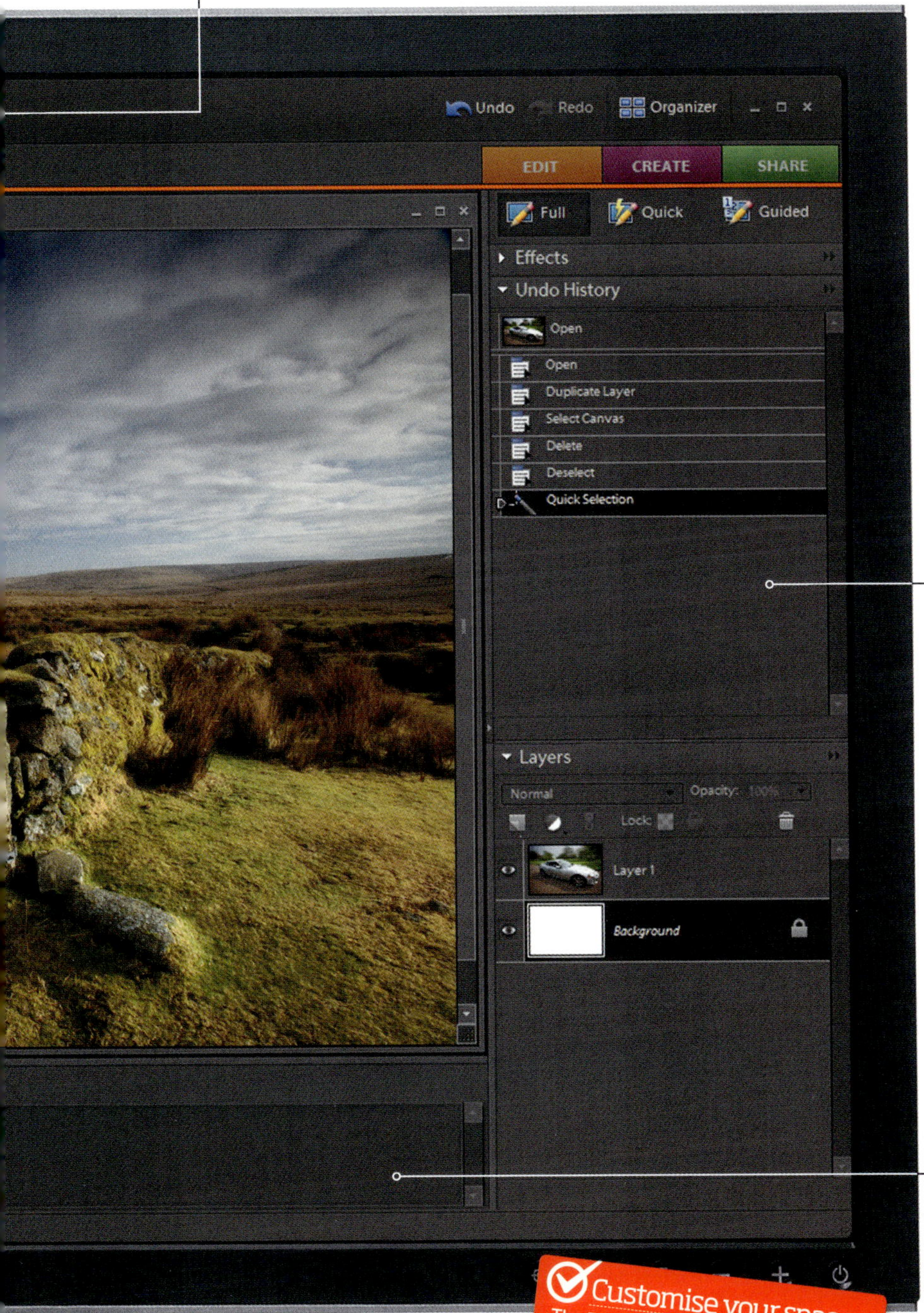

Palettes

There are several interchangeable palettes accessed in the Window tab of the menu including Colour Swatch, Histogram, Info, Navigator, Styles and Effects. Here are two you won't be able to live without...

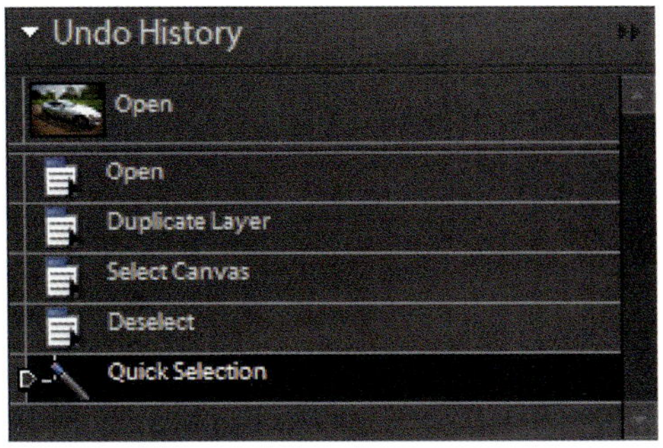

History Everything you do in Photoshop, whether it be applying a brush stroke, filter or deleting a layer, is recorded in the History palette. The number of steps kept in memory is specified in the Preferences palette (the default is 20, but 40 is safer). To go back step by step through your history, click ***cmd+alt+Z*** (Mac) or ***ctrl+Z*** for PC users.

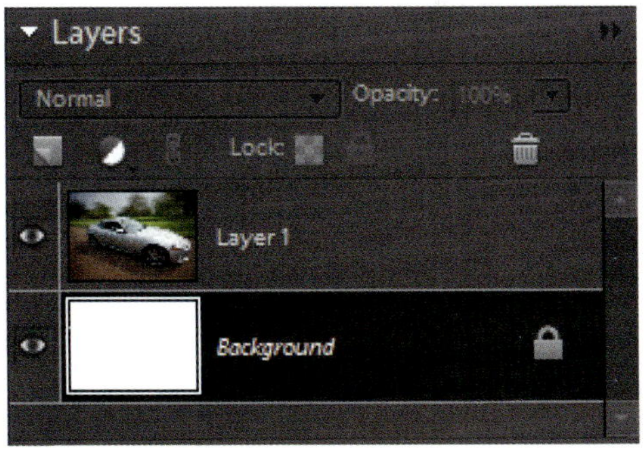

Layers This palette contains all your pixel, vector and Adjustment Layers, as well as their masks. You can reorder and delete these layers at any time, organise layers into groups, turn them on and off with the visibility icon and, of course, add Layer Styles from the palette itself. There's also a context menu for more layer commands, such as Flatten Image.

Photo Bin (Elements)

The Photo Bin in Photoshop Elements is an organisational tool that shows thumbnails of all the files you have open in the workspace. Underneath the thumbnail you'll see the file name, and when you click on a thumbnail, that file becomes the active document. A right-click on a thumbnail gets you to a shortcut menu where you can minimise, close or rotate the image, create a duplicate file or access the image's original camera data.

Customise your space

The Photoshop interface is fully customisable. If there are palettes you don't use, simply hide them in the Window menu. Also, you can drag and drop them into positions that suit you!

Selection tools

The various selection tools available in Photoshop vary in difficulty and control, but are generally used for the same purpose: to copy areas of an image and for making localised adjustments. Find out how...

THE ABILITY TO MAKE isolated selections within your image is a key aspect of using Photoshop. There are several different ways to make selections from those that are done manually, such as the Polygonal Lasso, to those that are semi-automated like the Magic Wand or Quick Selection tools. Once made, the selection area is defined by a series of moving black and white pixels widely referred to as 'marching ants'. Each of the selection tools comes with a number of options that you'll find located in the Tool Options Bar that's located by default under the menus at the top of the screen. Among the most important are the New Selection, Add Selection (or press shift while making selection), Subtract Selection (or press alt while making selection), and Intersect Selection buttons (the Quick Selection Tool doesn't have the latter). These determine how multiple selections interact together. Here's a quick look at the selection tools and the way in which they function.

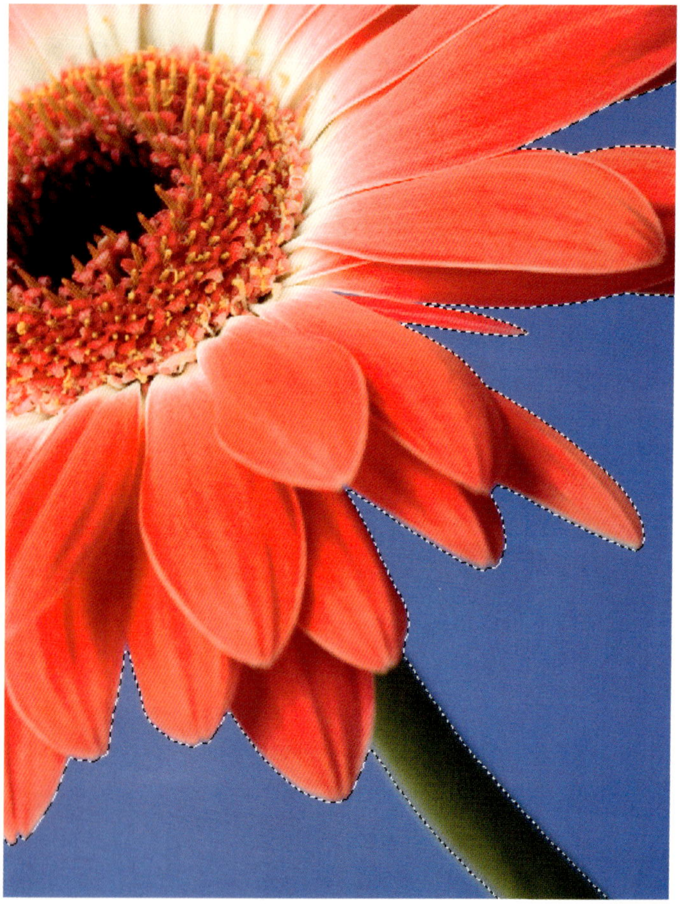

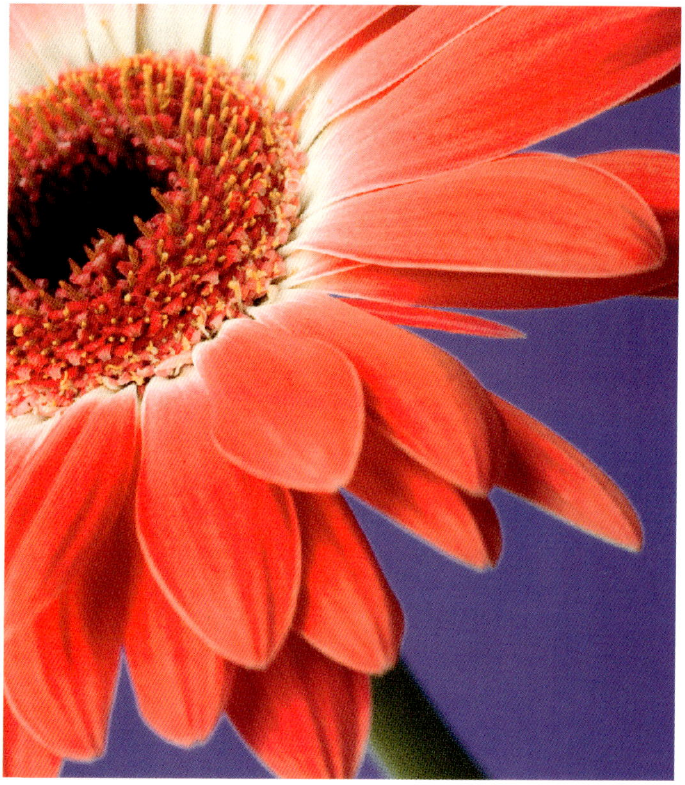

Natural selection: This image is perfect for the Magic Wand Tool as there is high contrast between colours. Due to the large areas of solid colour, we can set the Tolerance to 100 pixels in the Options bar, then select the blue of the background by clicking it. Next, while holding the shift key, we select the remaining blue areas to add them and then alter the background as we see fit.

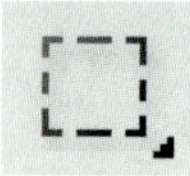

RECTANGULAR MARQUEE

Allows you to create a selection based on a rectangular shape of any size or proportion. Simply click and drag to size. If you hold down the ***shift*** key you can also constrain the proportions, allowing you to create an exact square selection. This tool is great for selecting easy, solid edges.

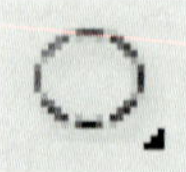

ELLIPTICAL MARQUEE

The Elliptical Marquee Tool allows you to create a selection based on an ellipse, again of any size or proportion. Click in your image and drag to get the size and shape to suit. Hold down ***shift*** to draw a perfect circle. This tool has less practical selecting applications than Rectangular Marquee.

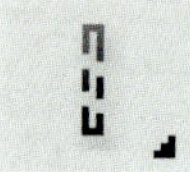

SINGLE COLUMN MARQUEE

Works in the same way as the Single Row Marquee Tool, only it creates a vertical selection rather than a horizontal one. The selection is just one pixel wide and is useful for cleaning up straight-edged subjects masked or pasted via selections that are showing unwanted pixels.

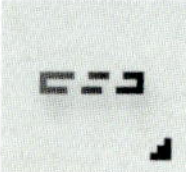

SINGLE ROW MARQUEE

The Single Row Marquee Tool creates a row-type selection that measures just one pixel in height. It can prove useful for cleaning up the edges of a previous selection that are showing stray colours of pixels that shouldn't be there – the top edge of an added doorway, for example.

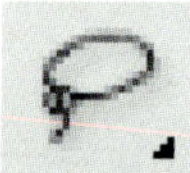

LASSO

The Lasso Tool enables you to draw a selection freehand. As it's virtually impossible to trace around a subject freehand with 100% accuracy, it tends to be more useful for drawing rough selections that you plan to modify further down the line or for selecting areas that require erasing.

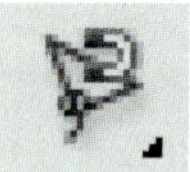

MAGNETIC LASSO

Works in the same manner as the Polygonal Lasso Tool in the sense that anchor points are used to draw straight-edge shapes, only this time the anchor points are placed automatically by Photoshop as you move around an image edge. You can also plot points manually.

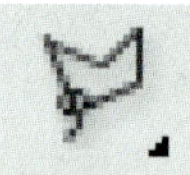

POLYGONAL LASSO

This tool allows you to draw your own selection manually, and has a distinct advantage for accuracy over the straight Lasso Tool as it works by plotting anchor points to create polygonal-based shapes. It can only draw straight lines, though; use the Pen Tool for curved-edge selections.

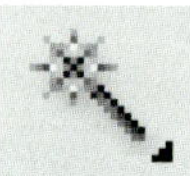

MAGIC WAND

The Magic Wand Tool was the original semi-automated tool, allowing you to simply click into an area and let Photoshop guess the area to be selected. As with the Magnetic Lasso and Quick Selection tools, you can control factors like Tolerance via the Tool Options Bar, but it's also best left for simple tasks.

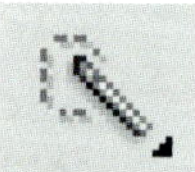

QUICK SELECTION

Introduced in CS3, this tool allows you to quickly 'paint' a selection. As you click and drag, the selection expands and automatically finds and follows defined edges in the image. It's another semi-automated tool, like Magnetic Lasso and Magic Wand, that offers varying degrees of success.

Crop Tool

PC & MAC QUICK SELECT KEY FOR PHOTOSHOP CS & ELEMENTS = C

Cropping will likely be one of the first things you learn to do in Photoshop. Here's how to best use the Crop Tool…

THE CROP TOOL is possibly the most widely used tool amongst digital photographers as composition is the key to a great image. As its name suggests, the Crop Tool allows you to select a specific area of an image and discard all information outside this area. Although cropping reduces the dimensions of an image, it is not the same as resizing as the process does not reduce the pixel quality. There's no easier tool to use in Photoshop! Firstly you need to drag the cursor to create a crop preview area, then resize if needed by moving any of the corner points and finally apply the crop by pressing the return key or double-clicking inside the active crop area. Simple! The crop preview can be rotated as well as resized by moving outside the active crop area until the cursor changes to indicate rotate is enabled. If you wish to crop and resize your image in one go, you can type in a specific size into the Crop Tool options bar before making a preview selection.

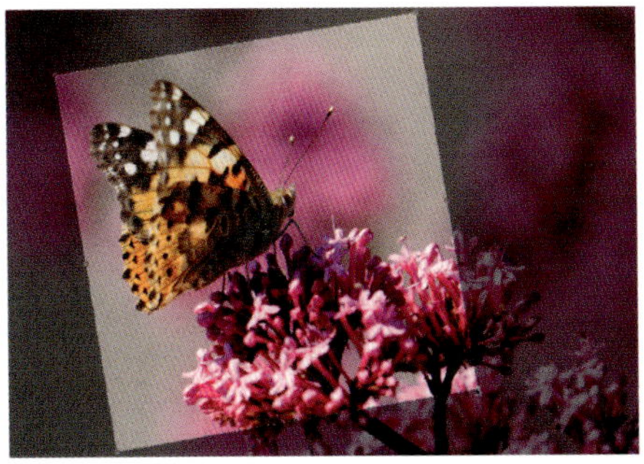

Moving, scaling & rotating: You can make as many alterations as you wish before applying the crop. Move the crop area by clicking and dragging, resize by moving any corner point or scale by holding *shift*. You can also rotate by moving the cursor outside the crop frame until the cursor changes, indicating that rotate is enabled.

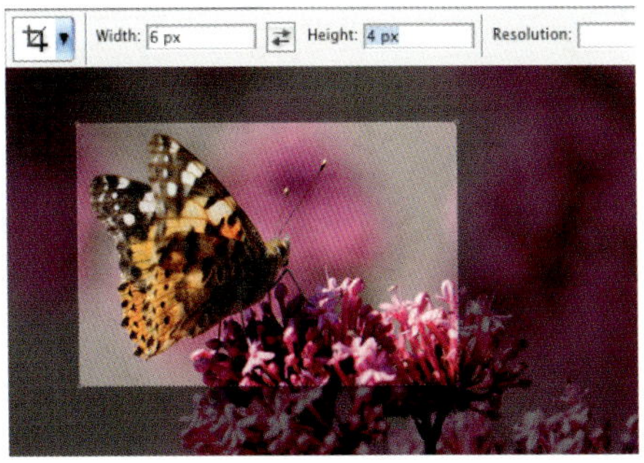

Using the Crop Tool info bar: Before you make your initial crop selection, you are able to type in width and height to create the precise size of your image once the crop is applied. Once the crop preview is active, the info bar changes with options to control the preview shield. You can turn it off, change its colour or adjust its opacity.

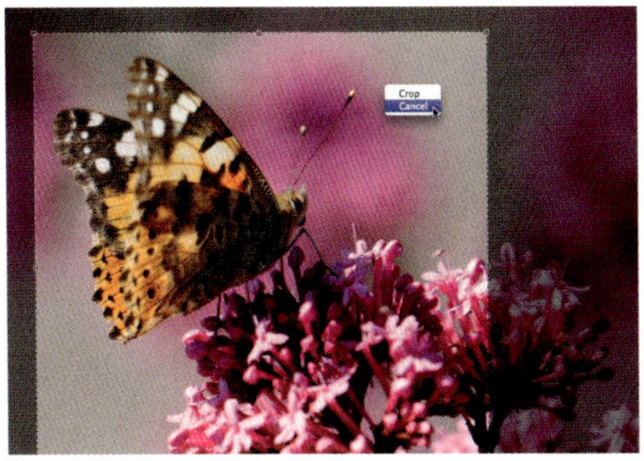

Applying the crop: Once you're happy with the crop preview, it's time to apply the crop. To do this you can either go to *Image>Crop* in the menu bar or you can simply double-click inside the crop area. Better still, press the *return* key. If you decide to exit the crop preview, use right-click and select *Cancel*. If you're not happy, press *ctrl+Z* to undo.

Sharpening

OWING TO THE WAY that image sensors work, digital images all need to be sharpened at some point, be this in-camera or afterwards in Photoshop or Elements. Put simply, you can break down 'sharpness' into two components. The first is resolution – the amount of detail a lens and sensor are able to resolve between them. Unfortunately there is nothing you can do to enhance this aspect in post-processing. The second is acutance – the amount of edge contrast in a picture. This is the part of sharpness we *can* enhance.

There are many tools to do this in Photoshop's Filter>Sharpen menu, but the only two worth bothering with are Unsharp Mask and Smart Sharpen (found in the Enhance menu in Photoshop Elements).

Unsharp Mask lets you adjust the edge contrast so an image appears sharper (in reality you don't have any more resolution than you did before). There are some simple rules of thumb: set the *Amount* to *100%* and the *Threshold* to *0*. Work out the correct *Radius* setting by dividing the intended output resolution by *200*. In other words, if you are printing at 300ppi, sharpen with a *Radius* of *1.5*; if you are outputting to the web, where people will look at your work on screens with a resolution of about 100ppi, the correct *Radius* here is *0.5*. Be warned, though, go too far with the Radius control and you'll see nasty-looking halos around the edges in your picture.

Smart Sharpen (*Filters>Sharpen>Smart Sharpen* in Photoshop or *Enhance>Adjust Sharpness* in Elements) does the same job but in a slightly more refined manner. Select *Lens Blur* from the *Remove* menu to have the filter only sharpen edges and not areas of continuous tone (like skies) that don't need it.

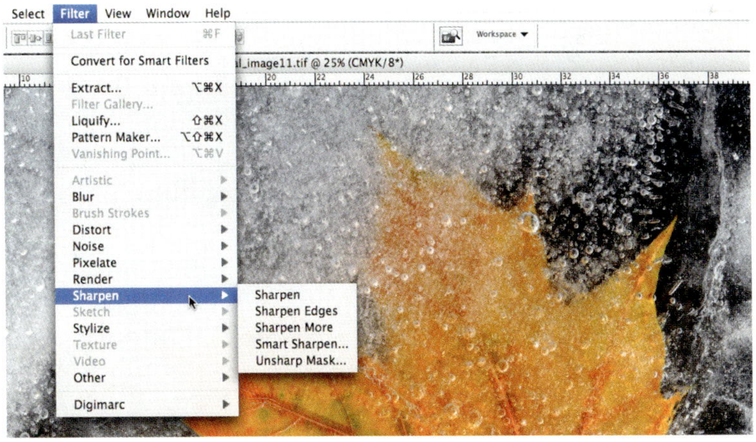

Many photographers do not realise the benefits (and dangers) of using the Sharpen tool. Try making an A4 print with and without sharpening applied and note the detail. Take care not to oversharpen as this can have an adverse effect on image quality. If you're submitting images to magazines or stock libraries, check if they prefer unsharpened or sharpened images as most prefer you not to have applied any sharpening.

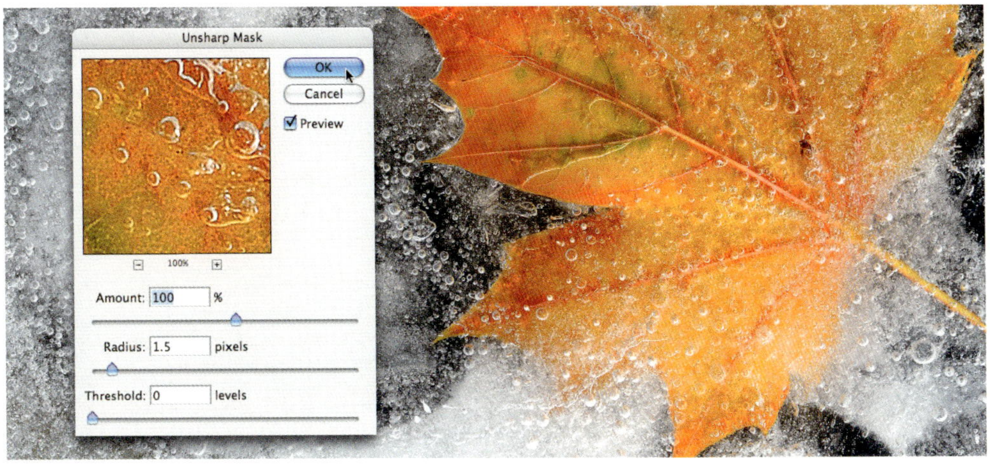

Clone Stamp Tool

PC & MAC QUICK SELECT KEY FOR PHOTOSHOP CS & ELEMENTS = S

Find out the hidden secrets of the Clone Stamp Tool that will make replacing pixels that much easier

THE CLONE STAMP TOOL is one of the most powerful retouching tools in Photoshop's arsenal. And while it can get rid of distracting elements in a photograph, it can also add parts to an image to make it more interesting. The Clone Stamp Tool works by sampling pixels from a source layer and applying them to a target layer (the target layer can be the same layer or a different layer). To make a source sample, click alt and click on the area you want to replace. It's a powerful tool that, rather than masking the area like other retouching tools, copies and replaces pixels. Before you start any retouching, create a new layer (Layer>New) and select Sample: All Layers in the top toolbar. By cloning to a new layer, you protect the original image pixels so you can reverse any changes you make.

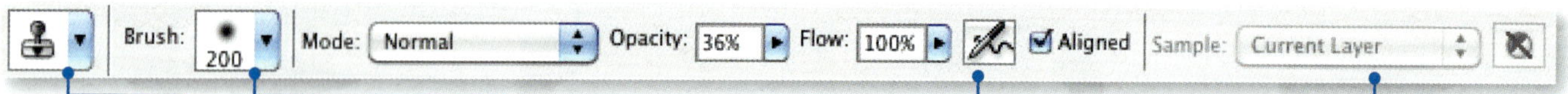

Tool preset picker: Click the arrow to show a list of preloaded Clone Tool presets.

Brush preset picker: Here you can select brush presets and control its Size and Hardness.

Adjustments: Alter the way the cloning sample interacts with the target layer.

Clone sample mode: Select what layer is used to take your cloning sample from.

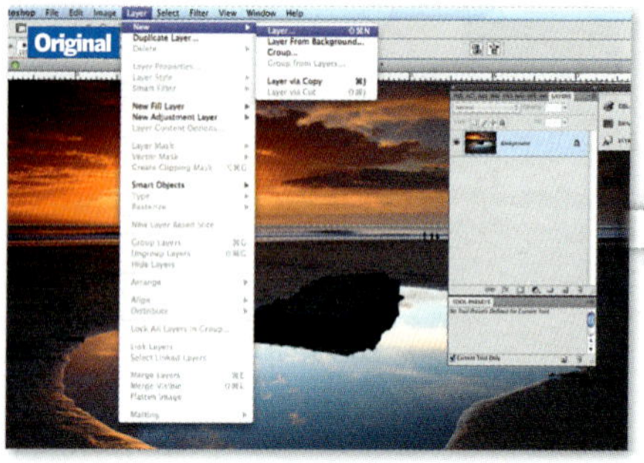

1 Create a new layer (*Layer>New*) and select the *Clone Stamp Tool* and *All Layers* from the *Sample* menu in the Options toolbar. Zoom into the area to clone out and set the *Opacity* to *100%*.

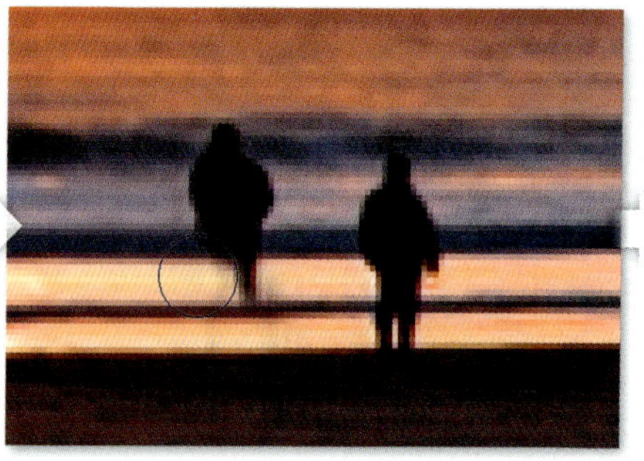

2 Take a source sample of pixels from near the target area by holding *alt* and brush over the target area using small stroking motions to avoid leaving signs of clicking the mouse.

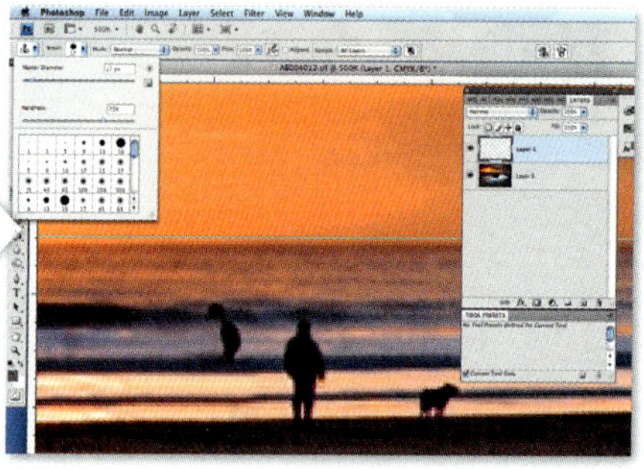

3 The edges of cloning can look quite harsh, so reduce the brush's *Hardness* to *20%*, leaving the *Opacity* at *100%*. Also try adjusting the *Flow* for more subtle control over the cloning.

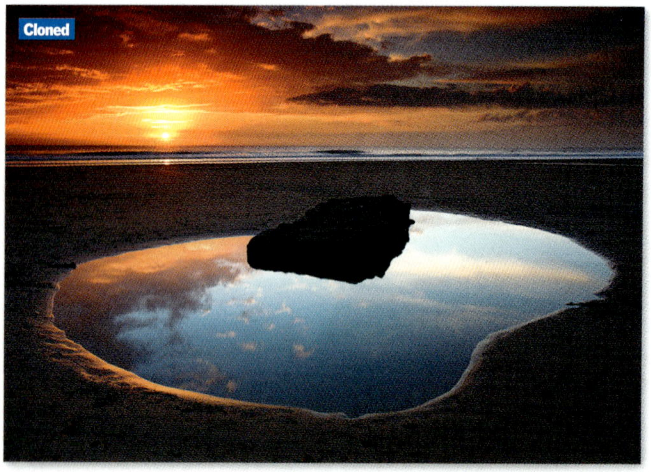

4 Cloning in a different area can create a repeat pattern if the sample is too close to the target. If this happens, undo your changes and then clone from an area further away from the target but on the same plane of focus.

HOT KEY

Brackets

Brushes are accessed via the top toolbar or via *Window>Brushes*. While you're working on an image, if you need to alter the size of your brush, press the right or the left square brackets (next to the letter P).

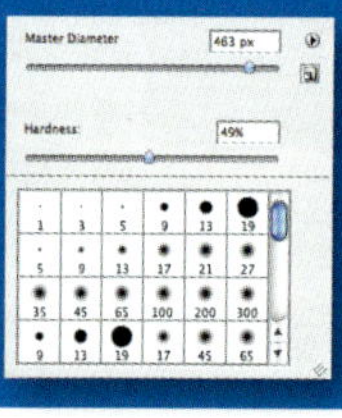

☑ CLONE TIP: CLONE FROM ANOTHER IMAGE

USE: ADD ELEMENTS TO AN IMAGE

Open the source image and the target image in Photoshop and then align the documents side by side, by dragging one off the other. Now select the *Clone Stamp Tool* and tick the *Aligned* box in the top toolbar. Select a soft brush and take a selection from the sample picture, in this case the clouds, and then paint the source where you want it on the target image. You may find adjusting the *Opacity* helps improve the results.

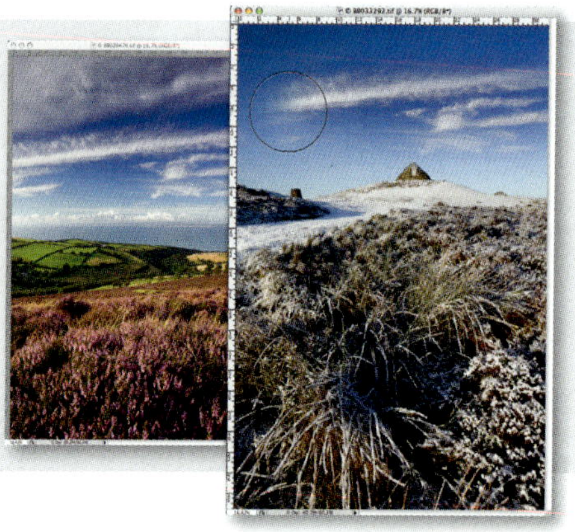

Secrets unlocked

☑ WORKFLOW ASSISTANCE

1) Create a 'shadow' window

Click *Window>Arrange>New Window for [filename]* to create a shadow image. Now you can zoom into the working image and have the shadow image open to see the overall effect, saving you from zooming in and out.

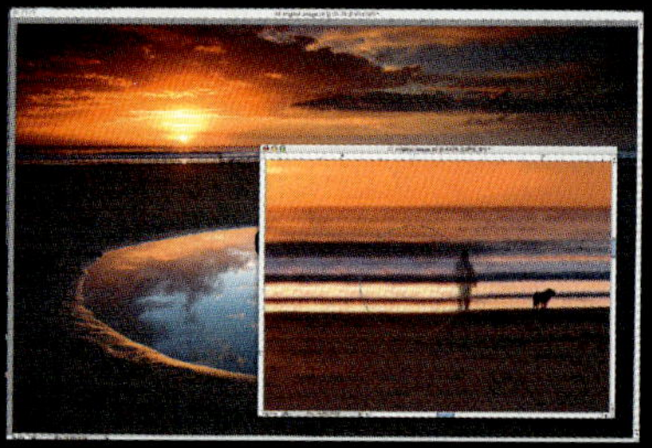

2) Create a preview overlay

Activate the *Show Overlay* and the *Clipped* checkbox in the Clone Source panel (*Window>Clone Source* or *shift+alt*) to see an overlay of the image as you clone it.

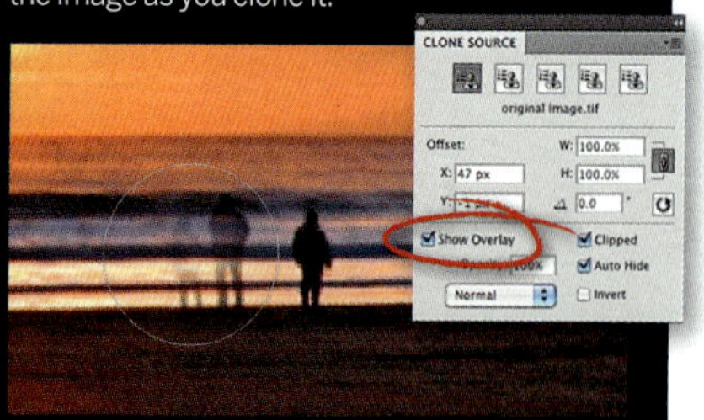

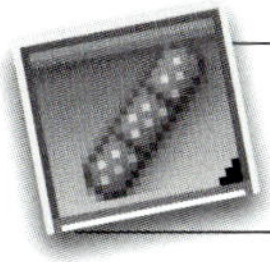

Healing Brush Tool

PC & MAC QUICK SELECT KEY
FOR PHOTOSHOP CS & ELEMENTS = J

Learn how to use the Healing Brush Tool and its various sub-tools to improve your retouching techniques

IMAGES OFTEN HAVE unwanted marks – such as imperfections like spots or wrinkles on portraits – that all need minimising. The Healing Brush Tool is the main device for doing this kind of retouching, but there are several sub-tools such as the Patch Tool and Spot Healing Brush Tool that do the same thing: hiding unwanted elements, but working in different ways and having different effects. The Healing Brush Tool works by matching the texture, luminosity and colour of the sample with the target area, so it blends with the pixels around it. As the Healing Brush spreads, it's useful to use a hard-edged brush. The tool also struggles on edges or areas of high contrast as it does not know how to blend tones, and it doesn't have the Opacity setting found on the Clone Stamp Tool.

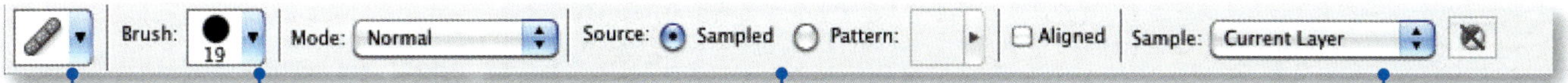

Tool preset picker: Click the arrow to show a list of preloaded Healing Brush presets.

Brush preset picker: Here you can select brush presets and control its Size and Hardness.

Set source: When doing retouching, make sure Sampled is selected as the source.

Clone sample mode: Select what layer is used to take your cloning sample from.

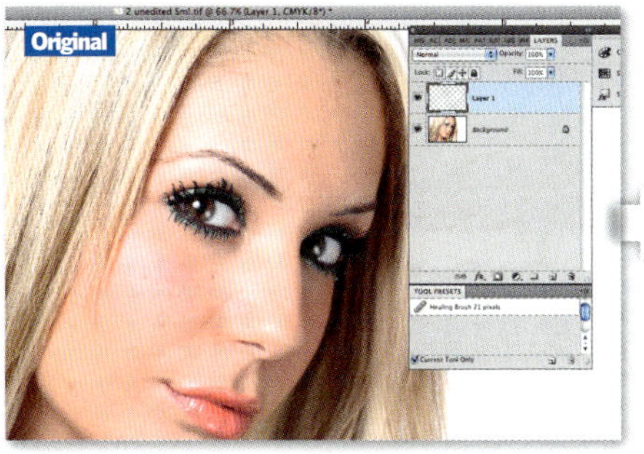

1 Create a new layer (*Layer>New*), select the *Healing Brush Tool* and a hard-edged brush, and click *All Layers* from the *Sample* menu in the top toolbar. Zoom into the areas you want to clean up.

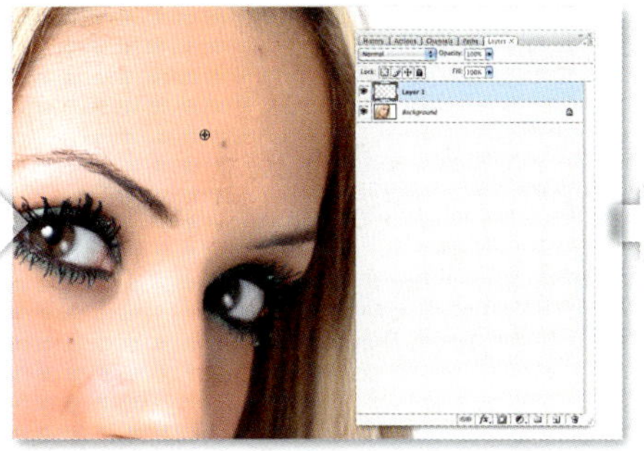

2 Take a sample from close to the area that you want to clear up by clicking *alt/Option*. Brush over the areas with the blemishes and alter the *Size* and *Hardness* of the brush as you go along.

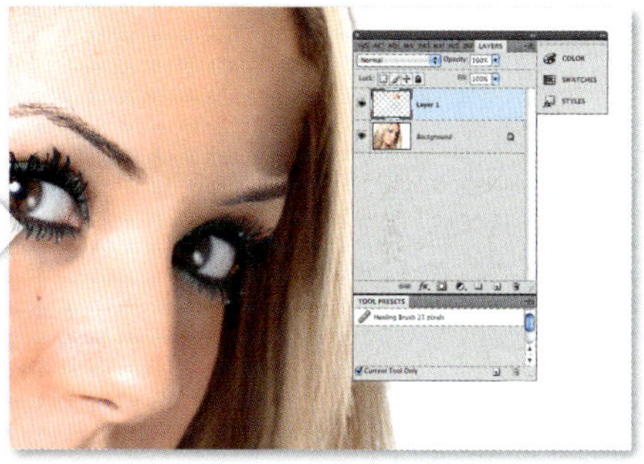

3 As the Healing Brush Tool brushes over an area of contrast, it can smudge as it struggles to match the varying tonality. It's best to take samples close to the target area.

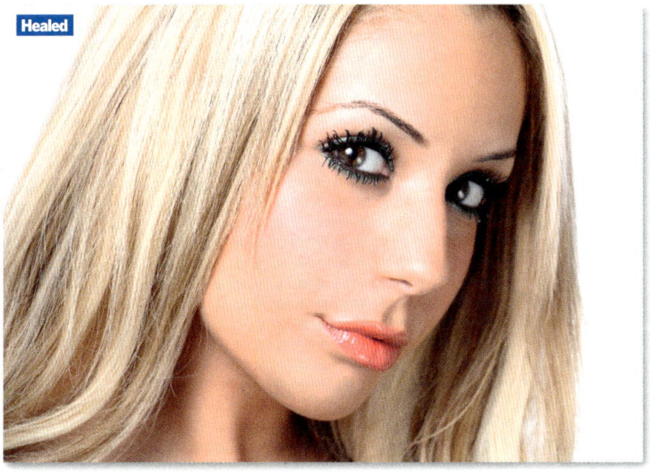

4 Be careful not to overdo the Healing Brush Tool's effect: you don't want to eliminate all imperfections as your subject will look like a porcelain doll. To avoid this, vary the opacity by clicking *Edit>Fade Healing Brush*.

HOT TIP

Aligned

When this option is ticked in the top toolbar, the sample points are aligned with the tool as it moves. This means every time you release the mouse you need to take a new sample. When *Aligned* is deselected, the original selection is locked in and used for every new stroke.

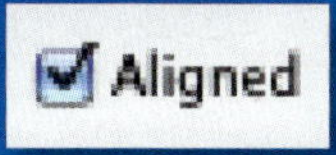

Secrets unlocked

CONTENT AWARE FILL

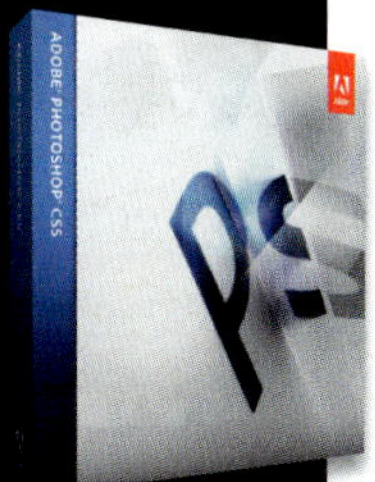

If you want easy, clean removal of unwanted photo elements, then you need to try Photoshop's Content-Aware Fill option, which automatically removes objects by filling the area with the pixels around it, matching the lighting, tone and noise of the surrounding area. It can be achieved by either using the *Spot Healing Brush Tool* and ticking the *Content-Aware Fill* option in the top toolbar, or by making a selection using a tool such as the Lasso Tool, then clicking *Edit>Fill>Content Aware Fill*.

SUB TOOL: SPOT HEALING BRUSH

USE: CLEAN UP DUST SPECKS

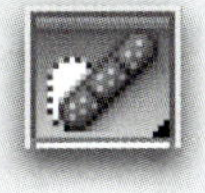

This tool works best on areas of low detail as it lacks the user control of the other retouching tools. Instead of being able to take a sample, you click on the area you want to hide and this tool will automatically take a sample of the pixels around it to match the target area. It's ideal for cleaning up dust specks.

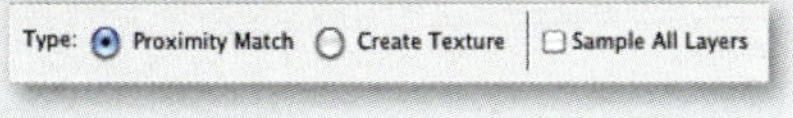

SUB TOOL: PATCH TOOL

USE: BE MORE SELECTIVE

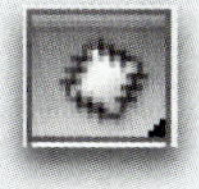

One of the more intelligent tools, the Patch Tool uses a selection instead of a brush. There are two ways you can apply this tool: draw a selection of a good area and drag it on top of a damaged area and select *Destination* in the top toolbar; or select a bad area and drag it on to a good area and select *Source* in the toolbar.

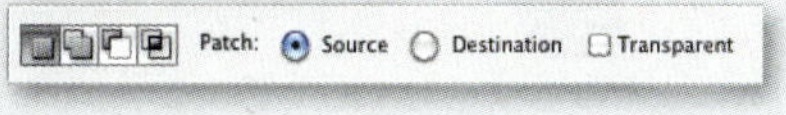

SUB TOOL: RED-EYE TOOL

USE: CORRECT RED-EYE

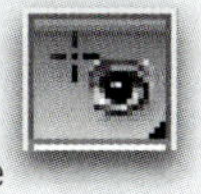

When a subject looks directly into a camera's on-camera flash it often causes them to get red-eye (where the pupils are rendered red). To correct this and return the subject's eye colour back to normal, select the *Red-Eye Tool*, zoom in to the subject's eye and click on the red pupil once to see the colour disappear.

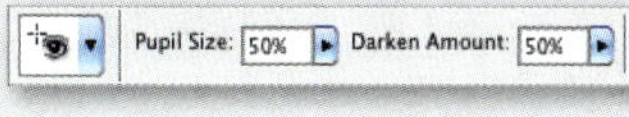

Layers & Layer Masks

Working with Layers is not essential for basic image editing, but for those photographers who want to take their images to the next level, they are a fundamental part of your editing workflow

LAYERS ARE THE BUILDING blocks of nondestructive image editing, giving you the opportunity to construct an image in stages and the flexibility to make any edits at any time. With this in mind, hopefully by the end of this feature you'll have a better understanding of how to get the most from Layers so your editing can become more selective and sophisticated whether using Elements or CS.

When you open an image in Photoshop, your image automatically becomes the Background layer in the Layers palette (accessible via Windows>Layers), which is located via the Tools menu. You cannot edit the Background layer as it's locked, but you can make it editable by double-clicking on the padlock symbol. Most of the time it's advisable to keep this Background layer locked and, instead, create a duplicate layer (Layer>Duplicate Layer) to work on. By doing this, it means at least one layer of your image still retains the unedited, original pixels, so if you make a mistake and want to start again, all you need to do is delete the extra layers and you're back where you started.

It's best to think of layers as clear sheets of acetate stacked on top of each other, each featuring a part of your image (object or effect) that, when merged together, create your final picture. The three types of layers we'll be covering here are transparent layers (layers without any pixels) that you can add pixels to, image layers that contain duplicate pixels from the original image or parts of a different photo, and Adjustment Layers, which we'll cover in depth later on. Layers allow you to combine parts of different photos, but for basic photography editing, this usually doesn't stretch further than replacing a sky in a dull landscape, adding a few extra people to a street scene or switching frowning faces in a group shot for smiles. However, there are some photographers and digital artists that take it to a higher level, using multiple layers and objects from different images to literally construct their picture from scratch. We'll only cover the basics here, but the internet and Adobe's website is bursting with more advanced techniques if you wish to delve in to this realm called compositing.

HOW TO CREATE A NEW LAYER

If you want a transparent layer, either click the *Create a new layer* icon at the bottom of the Layers palette or go to *Layer>New>Layer*. If you want a layer with the same pixels as your original image, you can duplicate the Background layer by dragging it down to the *Create a new layer* button or by clicking *Layer> Duplicate Layer*. To copy parts of one image on to another, you first need to make your selection from the source image and then press *ctrl/ cmd+C* to copy it. Revert back to your destination image and press *ctrl/cmd+V* to paste it on the image. Or using the *Move Tool*, click and drag the selection from the source image to the destination image (press *ctrl/ cmd+A* to move the whole picture). The new image will immediately create a new layer above the destination image. Then use the *Move Tool* to reposition your selection.

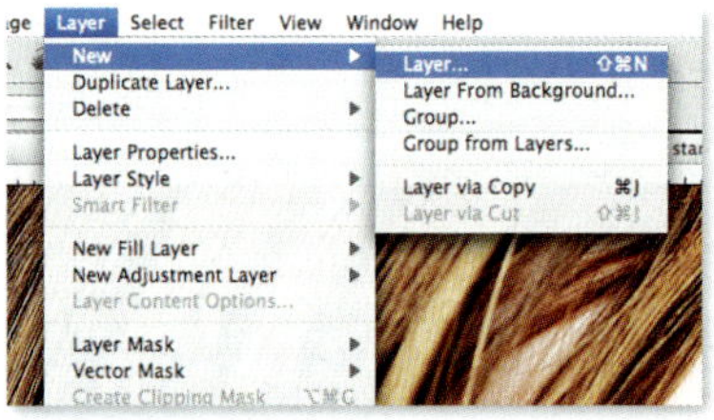

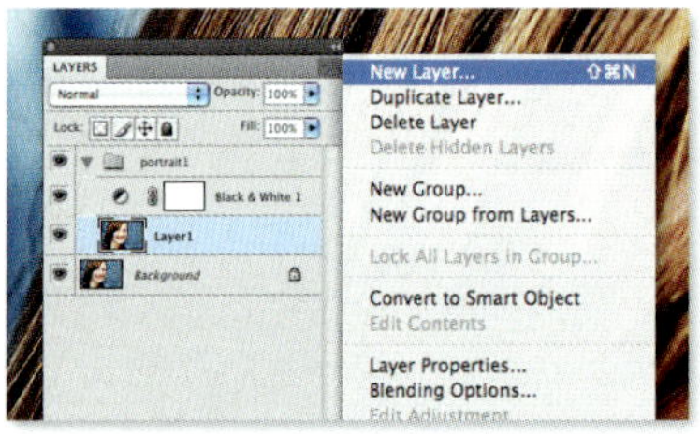

HOW LAYER ORDER WORKS

Every new layer that's created automatically sits on top of the layer before it in the Layers palette and its effect or pixels will affect every layer that's underneath it. Use the *Move Tool* to reorder the layers.

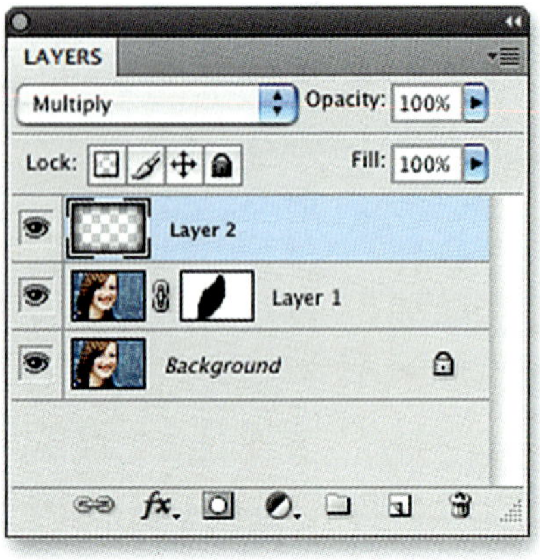

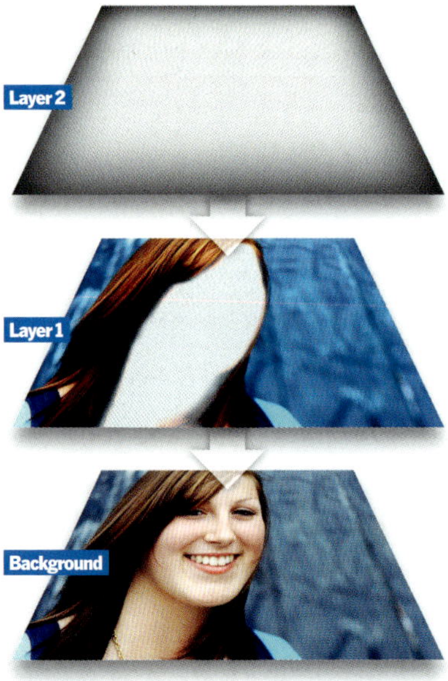

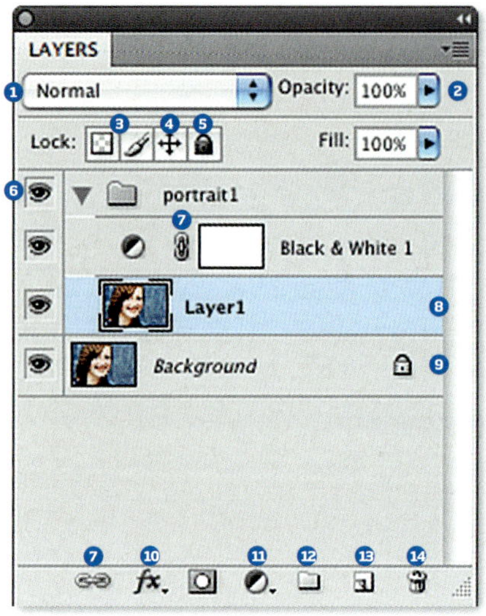

THE LAYERS PALETTE

1) Blend Mode This accesses the drop-down menu of layer Blend Modes that control how the layers interact with one another.

2) Opacity Use this slider to adjust the transparency of the layer, controlling how much of the layer beneath it shows through.

3) Lock transparent pixels/image pixels These two buttons enable you to lock an individual layer so only image or transparent pixels can be edited respectively.

4) Lock position Use this to prevent your image from moving rank in the Layers palette. Click once to lock and again to unlock.

5) Lock all Apply this lock to any layer that you want to protect from editing. If you want to unlock a layer, highlight it and press the lock button again.

6) Layer visibility Click the eye icon to make the adjacent layer invisible. Click it again to make the layer visible.

7) Link Use this option to link multiple layers together.

8) Select layers You can tell which layer you've got selected by whether it's highlighted blue. Select multiple layers by holding down *cmd* (Mac) or *ctrl* (PC) and clicking on each to select them.

9) Background layer This is your original image. Keep it locked so it cannot be edited.

10) Add Layer Style Access a variety of styles from Blend Modes to drop shadows and outer glows. They're special effects that work well with objects and text.

11) New Adjustment Layer Click here to access a list of all the Adjustment Layers.

12) Create New Group Use this to group layers together into a folder to contain your editing to those selected layers.

13) Create New Layer Click to apply an empty, transparent layer. Or click and drag an image layer down on to the icon to duplicate it.

14) Trash Can Highlight the layer, or Layer Mask, and click the bin to delete it or, alternatively, click and drag them on to the Trash Can.

Workflow tools

✓LAYER MASKS

Layer Masks are extremely powerful editing tools as they enable you to localise your edits to specific parts of an image. You can apply them to any layer – Adjustment Layers have one already attached (see next page for more details) – and use the *Brush Tool* to 'paint' areas in or out of the layer that you want to make visible in your final image. Layer Masks were a new feature to Elements 9 and are accessible in the same way as CS via the ***Add a mask*** icon at the bottom of the Layers palette or *Layer>Layer Mask>Reveal All* or *Hide All*. When added, a Layer Mask appears next to the layer it's linked to in the Layers palette. As its default, or when set to *Reveal All*, a Layer Mask appears white and doesn't affect any pixel until you paint on it. When set to *Hide All*, a Layer Mask is filled with black and will hide all the pixels in the image layer until you use white paint on the mask to reveal the pixels. It's a forgiving process for editing your layers, although it does take practice and requires you to adjust the Size and Hardness of your brush to get a smooth, accurate finish. Another way is to select and refine the area you want to keep visible, then apply the Layer Mask. You can do this by clicking *Layer>Layer Mask>Reveal Selection* or *Hide Selection*, if it's the area you want invisible.

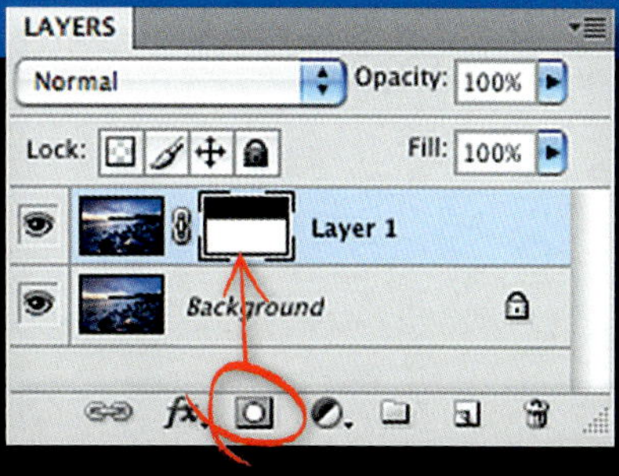

Secrets unlocked

✓LAYER MASK HOTKEYS

SHIFT To temporarily disable a mask, hold *shift* and click on the *Layer Mask thumbnail* so a red cross appears through it. Click the thumbnail again to restore it.

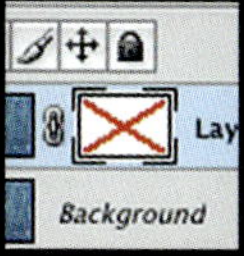

ALT The Layer Mask thumbnail gives a small indication of what you're painting on the mask. To see an image-sized version, hold down *alt* and click on the thumbnail.

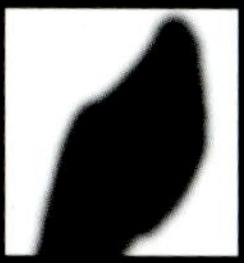

COMMAND Once you've painted the areas you want to adjust on the Layer Mask, hold *cmd* and click on the mask to convert the area into a selection.

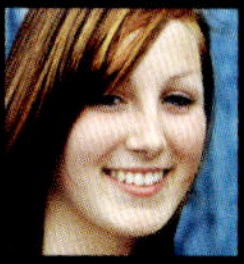

Editing images using Layers and Layer Masks

Learn to improve your photos post-capture by replacing unwanted parts with something more appealing

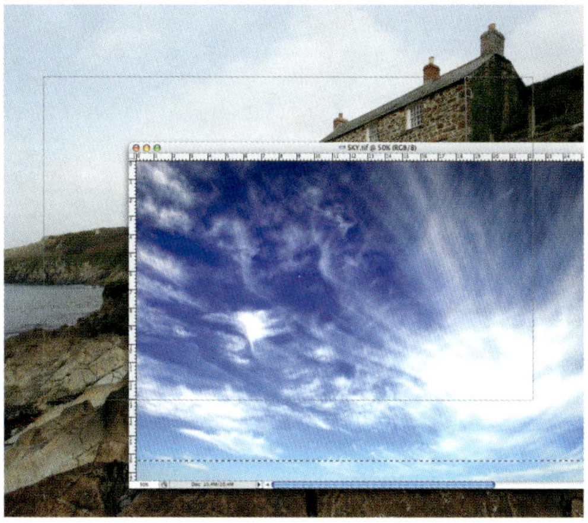

1 Here, we have a landscape image with a dull sky but an impressive foreground. By exchanging the sky for one with more interest, it should dramatically improve the image. Open both images in Photoshop and, using the *Move Tool*, drag the landscape image on top of the sky picture.

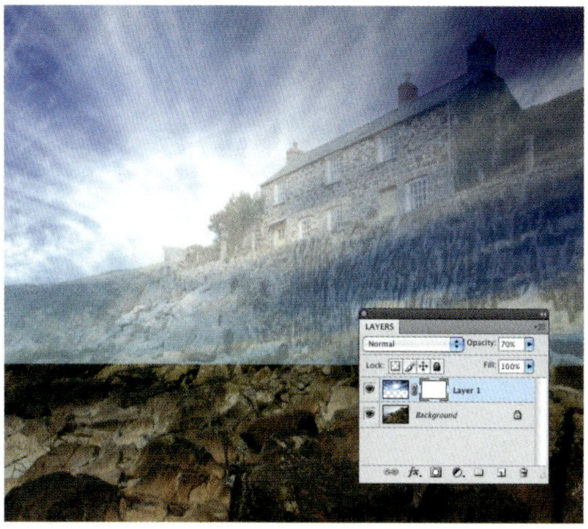

2 The sky image now features two layers in its Layers palette, with the landscape picture on top. With that layer selected, apply a Layer Mask by clicking on the *Add layer mask* icon at the bottom of the Layers palette. Reduce the *Opacity* of the top layer so the sky image shows through.

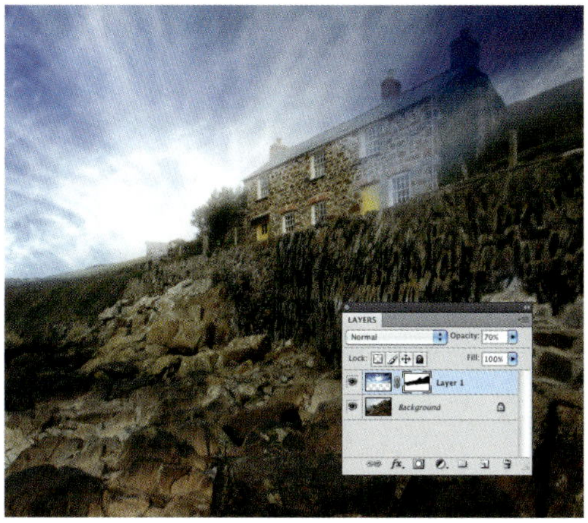

3 Move the image so the new sky covers the old one entirely. Now select the *Brush Tool* and reduce the *Hardness* to below *10%* to give it a soft edge, and select *Black* as your *Foreground Color*. With the *Layer Mask* selected, paint on the image to hide the old sky and reveal the new one.

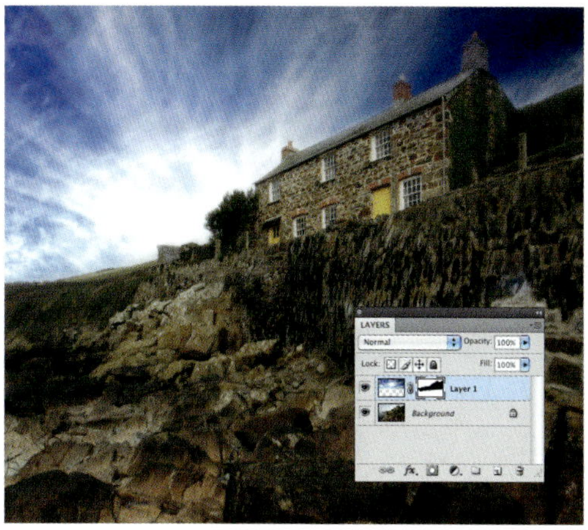

4 Once you've finished and roughly gone around the objects on the horizon, increase the layer's *Opacity* back to *100%*. Now zoom in to the horizon and, using a smaller brush, go around the areas of the landscape you might have missed. Use *White* paint to restore any foreground.

HOW DO I...

Delete a Layer Mask?

Click on the link (looks like a paperclip icon) in between the image and Layer Mask thumbnail. This will unlink the two so you can click and drag the Layer Mask in to the trash at the bottom of the Layers palette. Or hold ***ctrl*** and click the ***Layer Mask*** to access a menu with ***Delete Layer Mask***.

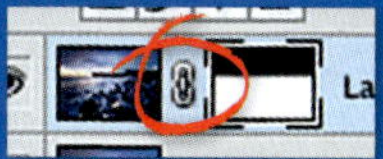

HOT KEY

To decrease or increase the size of your brush, click *[* or *]* respectively. To toggle between Black and White paint, to hide or reveal detail, simply press ***X***.

HOT TIP

By default, the Layer Mask button in the Layers palette creates a Reveal All mask. If you want to add a Hide All Layer Mask, hold down ***alt*** while clicking the same button.

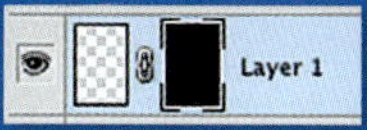

Adjustment Layers

For nondestructive editing, you can't beat Adjustment Layers for ease of use and flexibility. Here, we explain the basics to using these invaluable layers so you can be more selective with your editing

BEFORE ADJUSTMENT LAYERS were introduced, photographers would have to duplicate the Background layer to avoid editing or damaging the original image. While you can still do this, Adjustment Layers allow you to apply adjustments like Curves, Levels or Hue/Saturation as a separate layer that you can refine, change or delete at any time during your editing process.

The alternative would be to apply an adjustment command via Image>Adjustments directly to a duplicated image layer, but this won't give you the flexibility of editing the effect after you've committed to it. Plus, if you want to get rid of the adjustment's effect, you'll have to delete the whole image layer, which can be frustrating if you've applied different adjustments to the image layer you need to delete. Most of the usual adjustment commands are available as an Adjustment Layer, making it a much more favourable way to edit pictures, but it's still worth checking out the Adjustments menu for those commands you can't access as a separate layer.

Being able to control how an adjustment affects your image post-application means you're not committed to any adjustment command you use, making the process a lot more forgiving and fluid. Not only can you reverse or delete an adjustment, you can temporarily hide them the same way you would an image layer, you can apply a Blend Mode or fine-tune the effect by changing the Opacity and you can restrict the effect using Layer Masks.

An Adjustment Layer can be created in one of three ways: by clicking Layer>New Adjustment Layer and selecting your required adjustment; clicking on the Adjustment icon (half black/half white circle) at the bottom of the Layers palette to access the same list of options; or by opening the Adjustments panel via the Windows menu. Any of those work, but some are quicker than others and offer you more options: you just need to find the one you work with the most efficiently.

ADJUSTMENT LAYERS PANEL

By opening the Adjustments panel, you get immediate access to all adjustment presets and the 15 core Adjustment Layers at the click of a button. When you select an Adjustment Layer from the panel, the Adjustments panel converts into a control panel for the command with the tools to refine the effect. Click back on to the Layers palette to close and convert the control panel back to the Adjustments panel. Have a go to see what we mean…

1) Add an adjustment: Click on the half white/half black icon at the bottom of the Layers palette to access Adjustment Layers. Click on the adjustment you want to apply.

2) Presets: Click the drop-down menus of each of the Adjustment Layers to access their loaded presets, normally located at the top of the specific Adjustment Layer's control panel.

3) Expand View: Click here to enlarge the Adjustment panel. It can be useful if you're working with Curves or Levels and need a larger area to view the adjustment graphs.

4) Clip the Adjustment Layer: Click here to clip an Adjustment Layer to the layer directly below it in the Layers palette so it's the only one that's affected by the adjustment.

5) Layer visibility: Click on the eye to temporarily switch off the Adjustment Layer. It's useful to toggle between visible and invisible to see the effect of the Adjustment Layer on the original image.

6) Review: If you re-edit an Adjustment Layer, click and hold this button to revert back to the Adjustment Layer's original state to see whether your re-editing has improved or worsened the overall effect of your image.

7) Reset: Click here to reset the Adjustment Layer back to its default settings.

8) Delete: Click the trash can to delete the current Adjustment Layer.

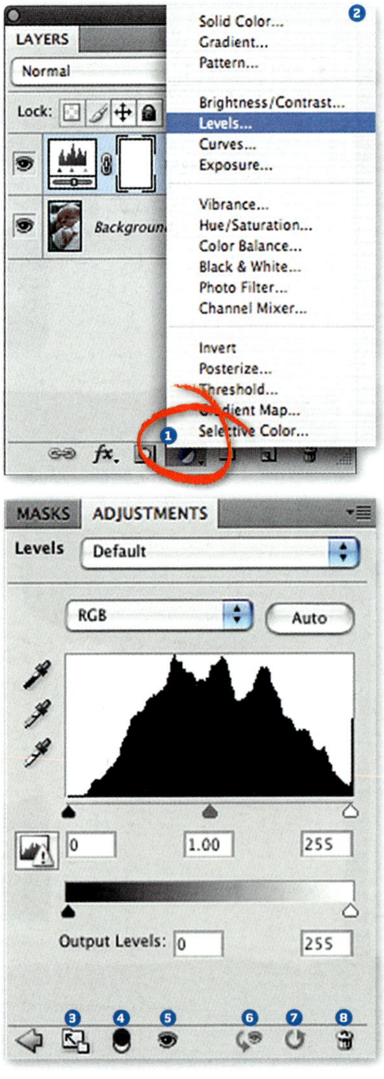

Secrets unlocked

GROUPING LAYERS

If you want your Adjustment Layer to affect, say, two of the layers in your image, you can group them by clicking the ***Create a New Group*** button at the bottom of the Layers palette so it contains them in a folder. Click and drag the layers you want to group in to that folder, add your Adjustment Layer to the folder, too, and change the ***Blend Mode*** from ***Pass Through*** to ***Normal***. The adjustment will only be applied to that group.

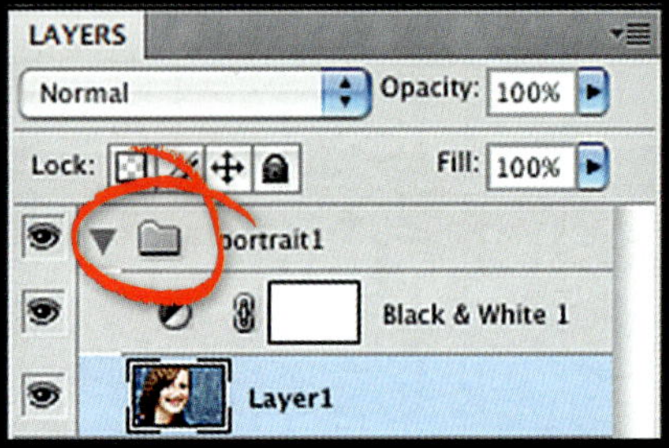

Software highlights

ELEMENTS

Elements features Adjustment Layers and they're accessible the same way as they are in CS via the Layers palette. However, you only have access to a small proportion of the adjustments found in CS4 onwards. You have the basic Levels, Brightness/Contrast, Hue/Saturation and Solid Color along with seven others, but you lack the versatility of Exposure, Selective Color, Black & White, Curves and many others. Elements is fine for basic adjustments, but if you want to get in to more complex and sophisticated editing, then you may want to upgrade to Photoshop.

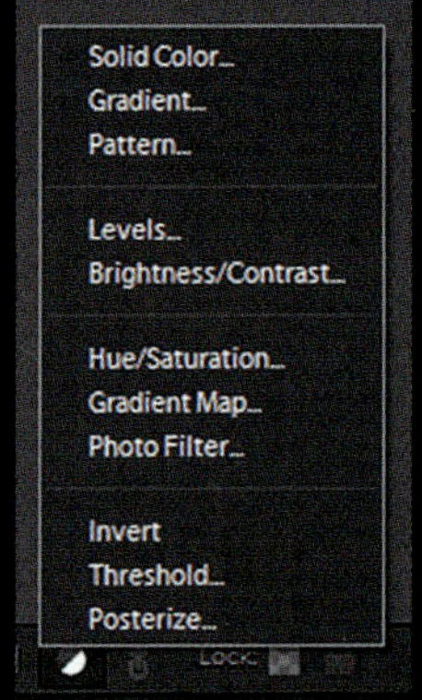

HOW TO... SAVE LAYERED IMAGES

When you apply multiple layers to your image, be it image layers or Adjustment Layers, the size of your file will increase accordingly. To compress the image for printing or web use, once you're happy with the final edited image, go to *Layer>Flatten Image* to merge all the layers back in to the Background layer. Then save the image as a JPEG or TIFF. It's a good idea to always keep a Photoshop version of your image (.PSD), which retains the various layers in your image, so that you have the option of re-editing the picture differently later if you need to.

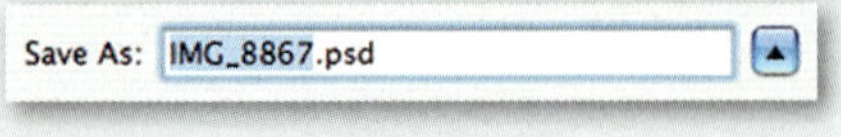

Using an Adjustment Layer with a Layer Mask

Learn how to selectively control the effects of an Adjustment Layer by 'painting' on a Layer Mask

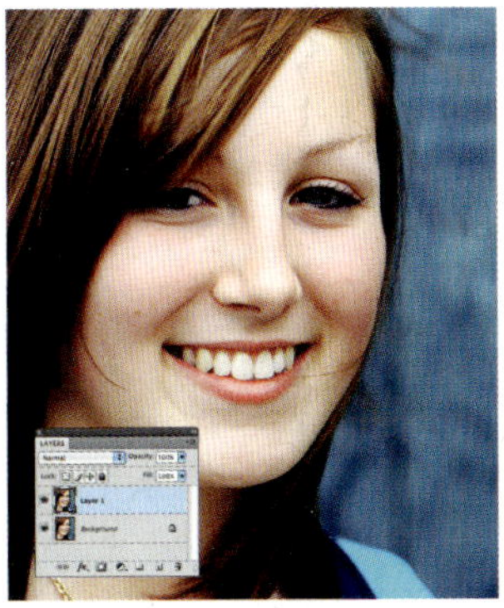

1 Open your image in Photoshop and then duplicate the Background layer so you're working on a copy (*Layer>Duplicate Layer*). Now apply an *Adjustment Layer* of choice. Here we've chosen Hue/Saturation.

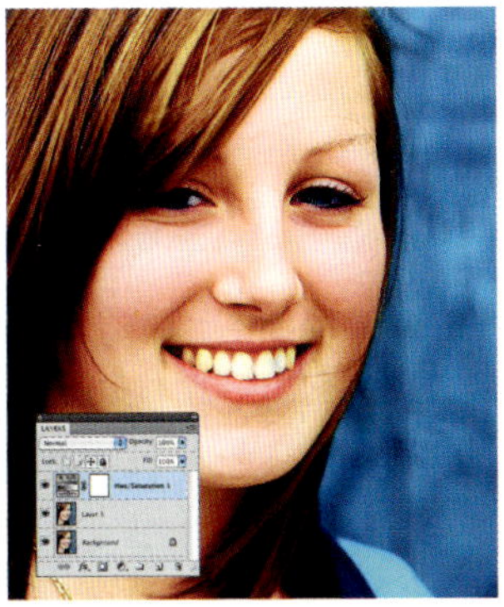

2 Make your necessary adjustments. We've boosted the colour in this portrait but, as you can see, it also makes the skin tones very unnatural. We need to neutralise the colour on the face while retaining the saturation elsewhere.

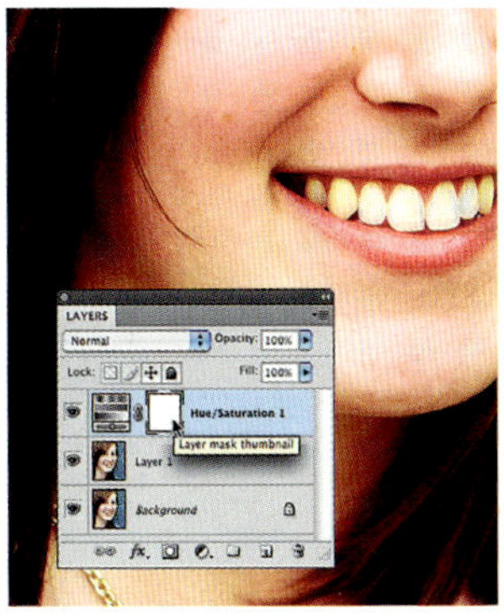

3 Attached to the Adjustment Layer in the Layers palette is a Layer Mask, which looks like an empty white box. Click on it to make it active. Then select your *Brush Tool* from the toolbar, with a soft-edge medium-sized brush set to *Black*.

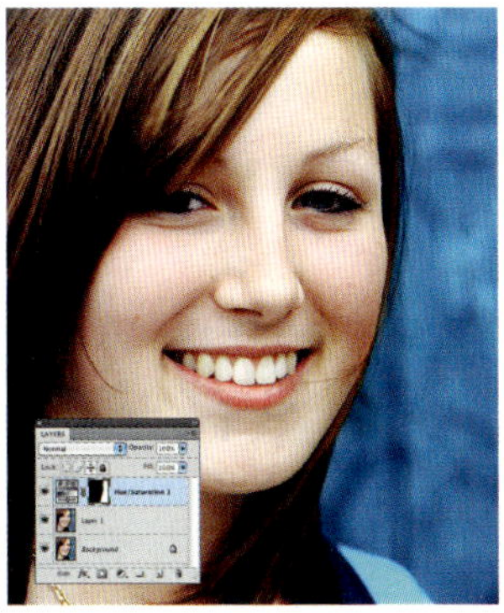

4 Using the *Brush Tool*, 'paint' over the areas of the image you want to revert back to their original state, varying the *Opacity* to control by how much. The Layer Mask turns black where you're painting. Use *White* paint to reverse the effect.

Three more ways for you to use an Adjustment Layer

For more precision editing, master these three techniques for improved results and added flexibility

1 REDUCE THE ADJUSTMENT

CONTROL THE EFFECT'S STRENGTH

However you apply an Adjustment Layer, you'll notice the full extent of its effect on your image instantly. Sometimes, though, this effect is too strong for the finish you want. An easy way to control the strength of the effect on the image is to reduce the *Opacity* of the Adjustment Layer. Once you've made your adjustments, select the Adjustment Layer so it's highlighted blue and drag the *Opacity* slider at the top of the Layers palette gradually down from 100% until you reach the desired strength.

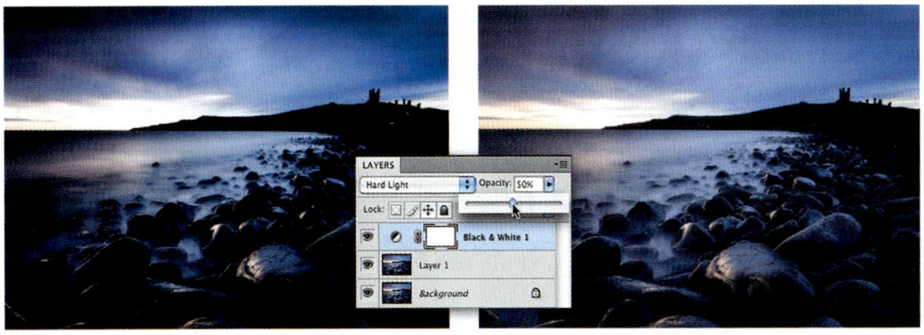

2 BE SELECTIVE

MAKE LOCALISED ADJUSTMENTS

For a slightly more advanced but precise way to selectively apply an adjustment to an area of an image using an Adjustment Layer, simply create the selection and refine the edge (see pages 38-45 for more details on how to do this.) Here, we've used the Quick Selection Tool. Then apply the *Adjustment Layer* of choice. This instantly fills the attached Layer Mask with black, blocking any adjustments that you then might make in areas other than what you have selected.

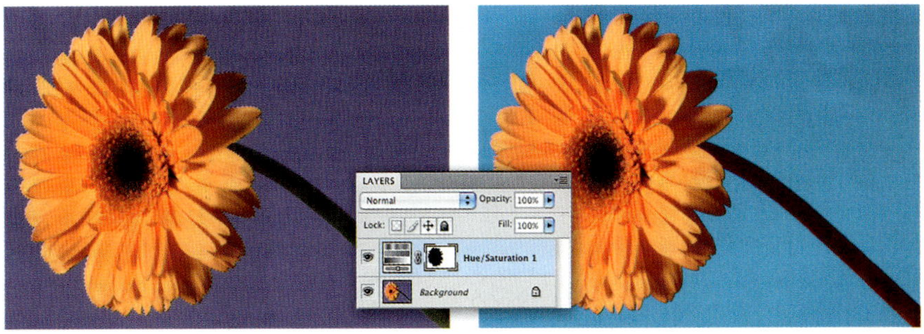

3 CLIP LAYERS TOGETHER

APPLY TO ONLY CERTAIN LAYERS

Clipping an Adjustment Layer means that it affects only the layer directly beneath it in the Layers palette. It's handy if you have an image made up of multiple layers with separate components, but you want to apply an Adjustment Layer to only one of them. You can clip the layers together by either pressing the *Clip* button at the bottom of the Adjustments panel or by holding down *alt* while you click on the line that separates the two layers in the Layers palette.

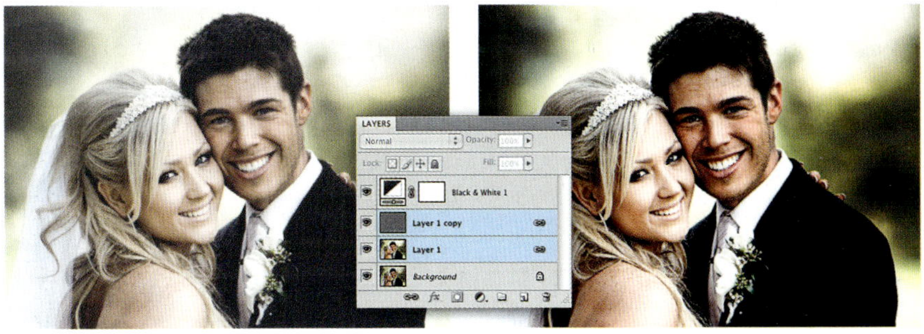

Layer Blend Modes

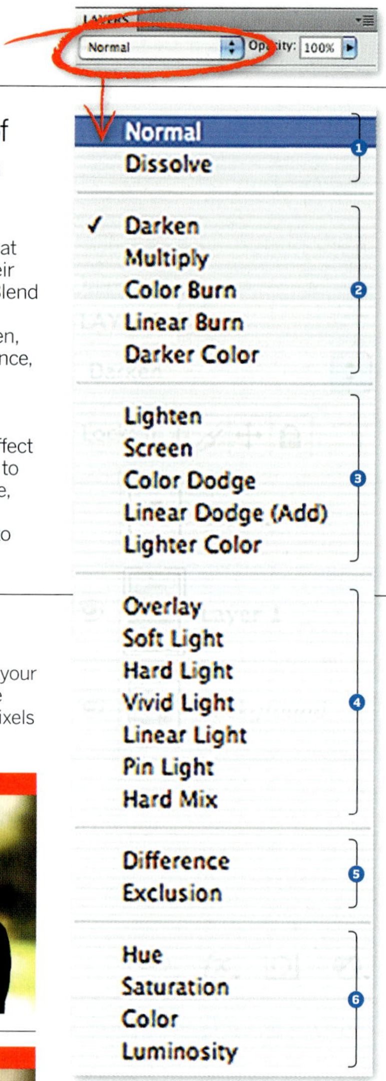

Along with Layers and Adjustment Layers, Blend Modes are essential parts of Photoshop's editing arsenal. Knowing how and when to use them can open a world of creative possibilities, especially when combined with Layer Masks

NOW YOU'VE GOT to grips with the principles of Layers and Adjustment Layers, it's a good place to introduce Blend Modes. They allow you to control how the content of a layer blends with the layer or layers directly below it. When you add a new layer to the Layers palette, by default the Blend Mde is set to Normal, which hides the lower layer with the content in the layer above it.

Without using a Blend Mode, the only way to merge layers together is to reduce the Opacity or Fill of any layer so the layer underneath shows through, but this alone doesn't yield very effective results.

There are 27 Blend Modes, which are all accessible from a drop-down menu at the top of the Layers palette, each affecting the way pixels interact. They're divided into six groups: Normal and Dissolve; Darken; Lighten; Contrast; Comparative; and HSL. While we advise that you play about with all the modes to get a feel for their effects, in real editing terms there are only a dozen Blend Modes that a photographer might need to use on a regular basis for image editing. These are Darken, Multiply, Lighten, Screen, Overlay, Soft Light, Difference, Luminosity and Color.

You can apply a Blend Mode to any layer or Adjustment Layer. For instance, you could use Luminosity with an Adjustment Layer so it doesn't affect the colour components of the image. As a quick way to preview the effects of the various modes on an image, making sure the Brush Tool isn't selected, the shift button can be held down and the + and – keys used to scroll up and down the list of Blend Modes.

FOUR BASIC WAYS TO USE BLEND MODES

To help you understand how Blend Modes work, here are four commonly used modes and ways to apply them to your images. Overlay superimposes the top layer on the base layer, while preserving the highlights and shadows of the bottom layer; Color replaces the hue and saturation of the base layer with the top layer; Darken replaces lighter pixels from the base layer with darker ones from the top layer; and Lighten is the opposite.

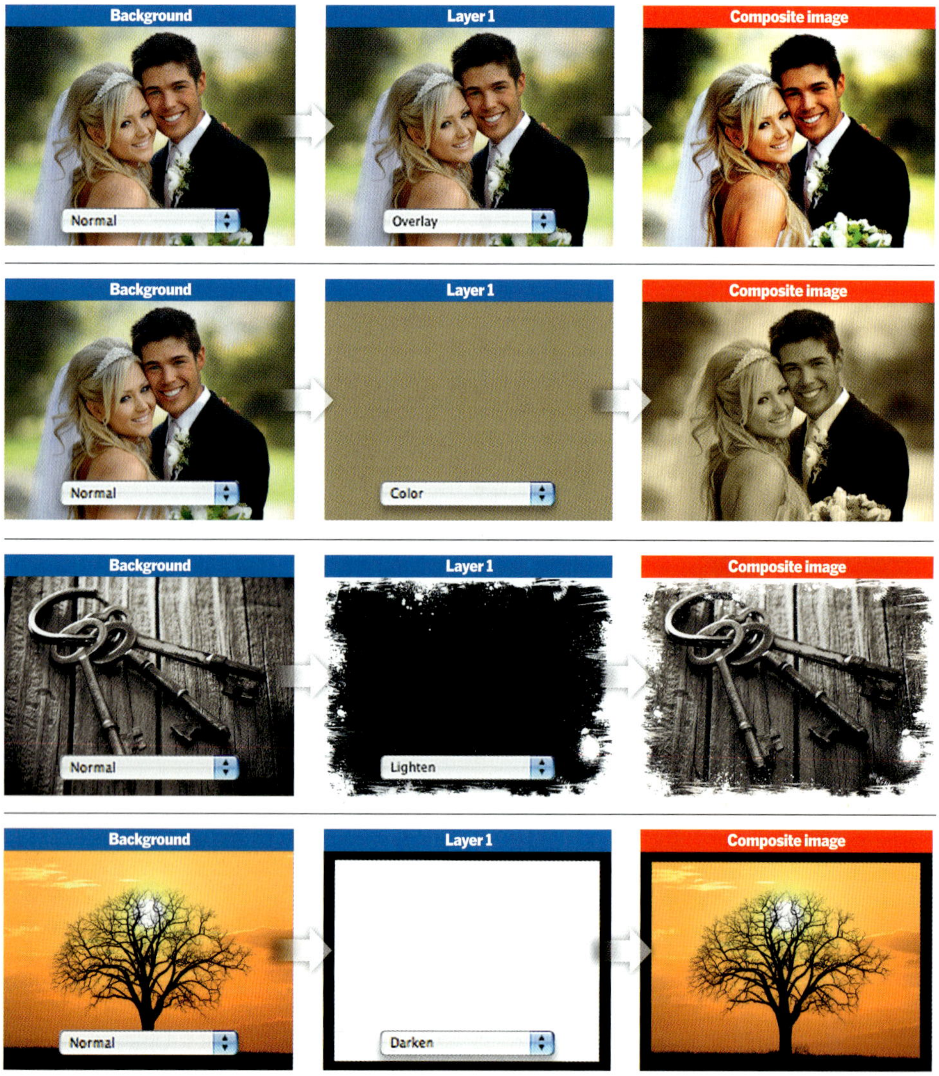

1) Normal and Dissolve: In Normal mode, the top layer is not affected by the layer beneath unless Opacity is less than 100%. The Dissolve mode turns some pixels of the top layer transparent.

2) Darken modes: Darken, Multiply, Color Burn, Linear Burn, Darker Color. These modes give prominence to dark-coloured pixels at varying degrees.

3) Lighten modes: Lighten, Screen, Color Dodge, Linear Dodge (Add), Lighter Color. These modes give prominence to light-coloured pixels for different effects.

4) Contrast modes: Overlay, Soft Light, Hard Light, Vivid Light, Linear Light, Pin Light and Hard Mix. These modes vary in strength when it comes to boosting your image's contrast.

5) Comparative modes: Difference and Exclusion. These modes create colours based on the difference between the top and base layer.

6) HSL modes: Hue, Saturation, Color, Luminosity. These modes replace the base layer pixels with the top layer pixels, depending on which mode is chosen.

Three ways Blend Modes can enhance your images

Here are a few ways of working with some of the most popular Blend Modes during photo editing

1 HIGH CONTRAST
USE IT TO DESATURATE

By blending a black & white image with a colour version using Hard Light, grey will be added to the resulting colour causing the image to become slightly desaturated. This mode also blends the colour from the base layer with the monochrome layer, darkening and lightening the shadows and highlights to boost the contrast.

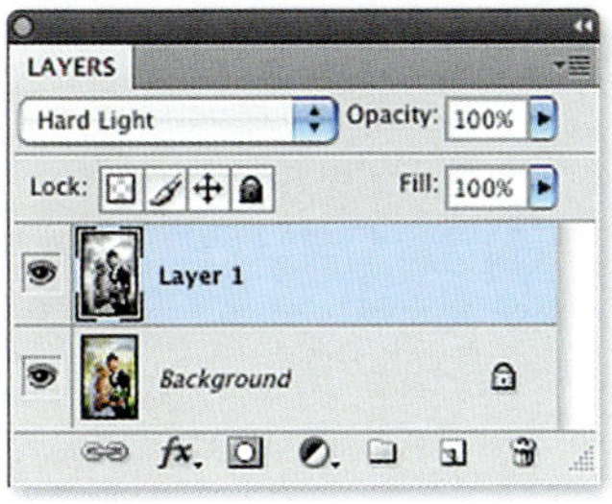

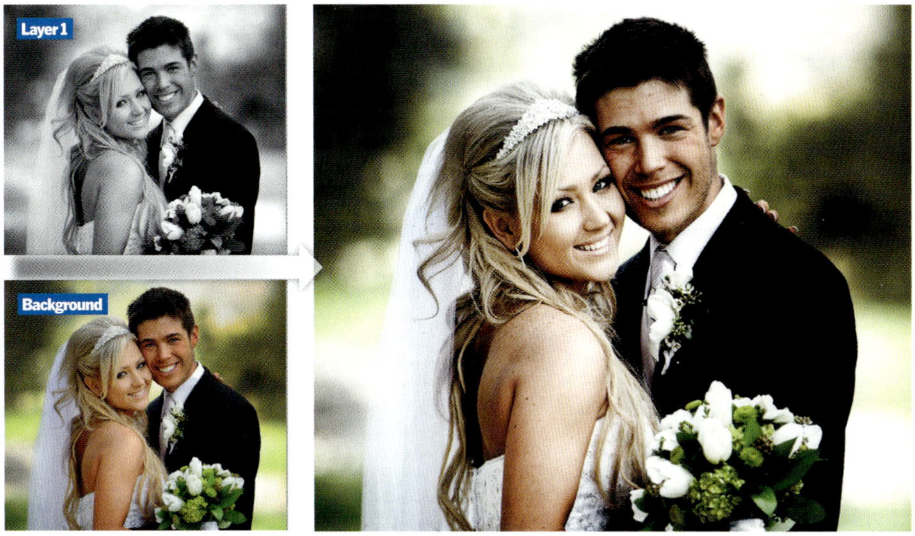

2 APPLY TEXTURE
USE IT TO ADD INTEREST

Soft Light works in the same way as Hard Light and Overlay, but delivers much gentler results. By blending this image of wood over the top of the still-life image, the texture shows through subtly by darkening the blending pixels that are more than 50% grey and lightening those that are less than 50% grey.

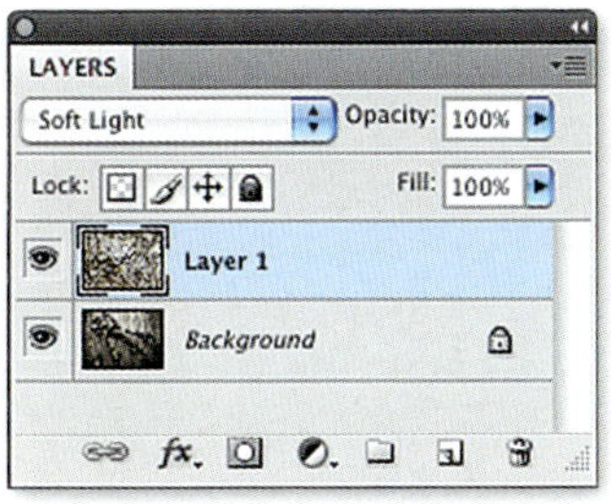

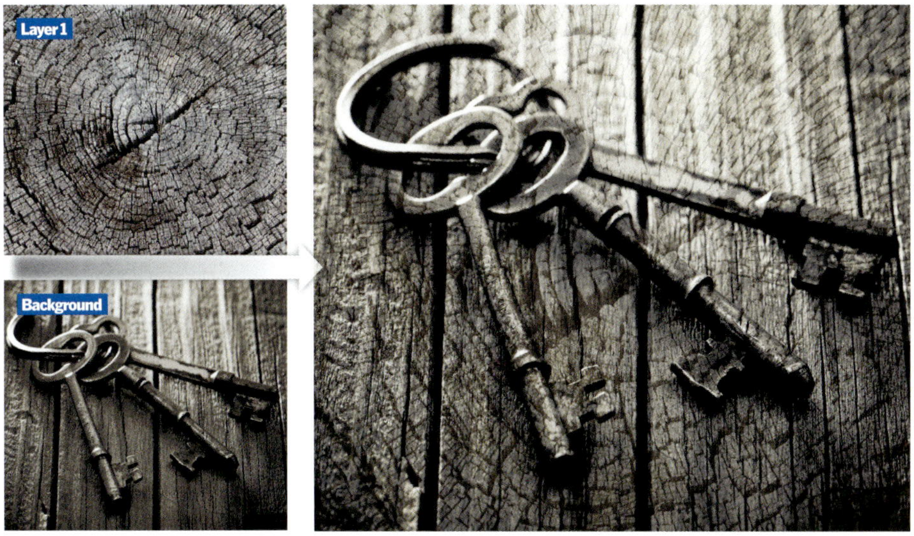

3 MERGING IMAGES
USE IT TO REPLACE A SKY

Multiply works by multiplying the base colour with the top colour to get the resulting colour. Every pixel gets darker, except for white, which remains unchanged. It's great for darkening overexposed areas and building up detail. Here, the white pixels are discarded and replaced with darker pixels, filling in the sky.

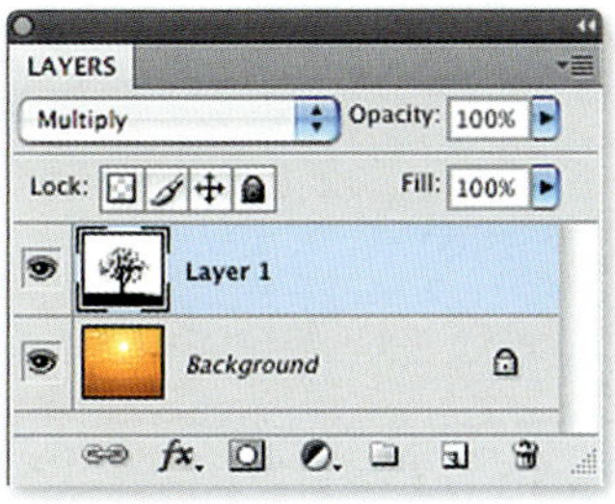

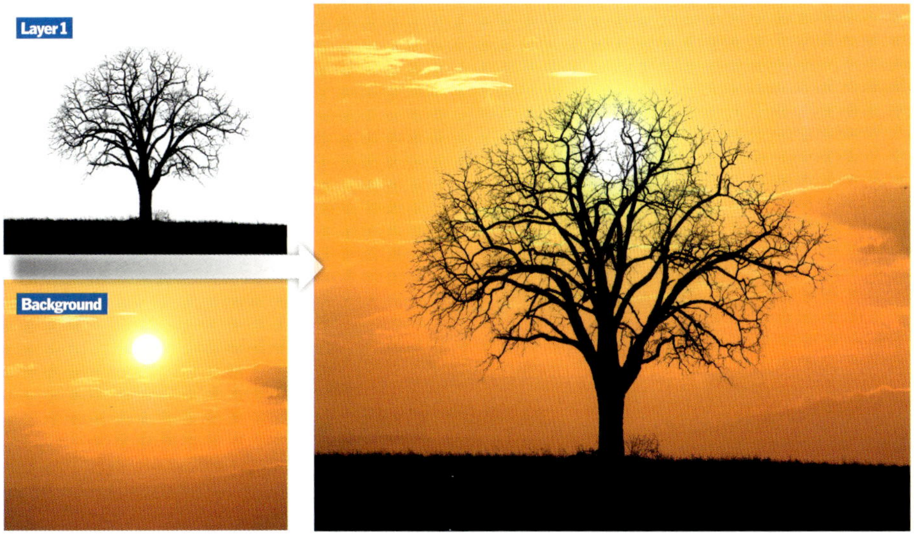

Levels

PC QUICK SELECT KEY FOR PHOTOSHOP CS & ELEMENTS = ctrl L

MAC QUICK SELECT KEY FOR PHOTOSHOP CS & ELEMENTS = ⌘ L

Boost the contrast and correct the colour of your images using one of the most popular adjustments in the Photoshop arsenal: Levels

LEVELS CONTROLS THE histogram, which holds all the exposure and colour detail in an image. Its primary role is to adjust the luminosity of a picture; its brightness, darkness, contrast and colour. It's a subset of Curves and a step up from Brightness/Contrast, allowing for more precision in your adjustments. Levels is available as an image adjustment that directly affects an image's pixels (Image>Adjustments) or as an Adjustment Layer, which gives you the same experience, but is a veneer over the image. It's advisable to use the latter option whenever you can, as it's non-destructive and gives you the flexibility to edit and revisit changes or to delete them at a later date, giving you a lot more creative control. You can select an Adjustment Layer from the Layers palette or by clicking Layer>New Adjustment Layer.

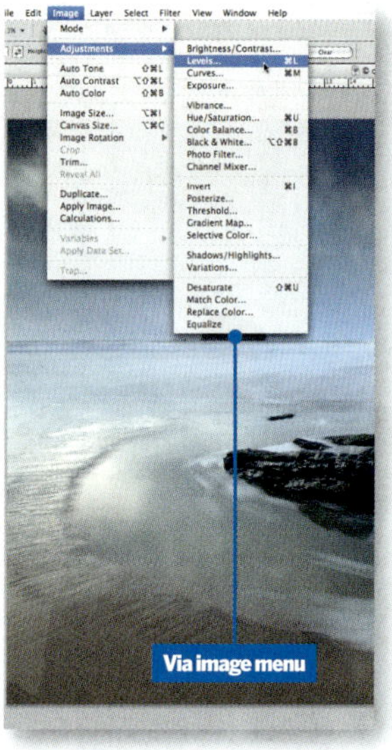

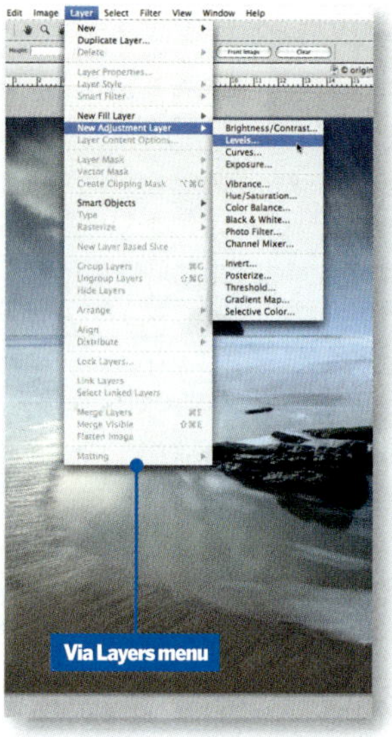

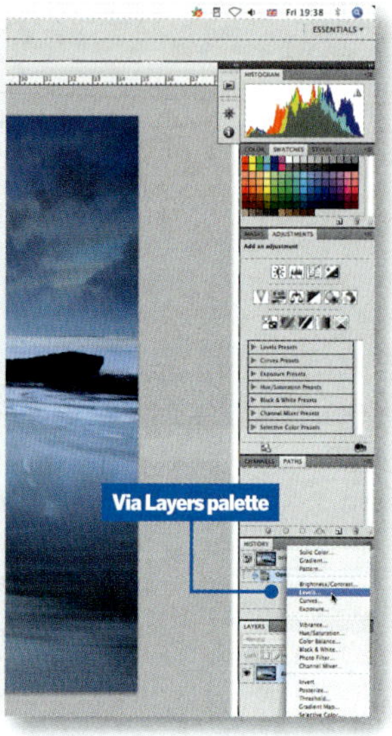

THE LEVELS DIALOGUE BOX

1) Auto The Auto function takes a look at the image and maps points from black to white to try to give the best tonal range.

2) Presets These functions are there to get you started quickly and easily, but while they work, they're not perfect. It's advisable to manually adjust the histogram using the sliders instead.

3) Histogram This black bumpy mound reflects the distribution of tones in your photograph. It shows the brightness range from dark to light and the peaks and troughs reflect how many pixels have that particular level of brightness. A well-exposed image should have an even spread of peaks and troughs.

4) The eyedroppers The real power of Levels is in the three eyedroppers – they can set the black, mid-tone and the white point in the histogram, by clicking them on the darkest and lightest part of the image. The grey eyedropper also has the power to alter colour balance.

5) Input slider By far the most popular method of adjusting the histogram. Moving the three little triangles allows you to manually adjust the shadows, mid-tones and highlights to get a very balanced exposure.

6) Output levels Adjusts the output shadows and highlights. Leave this alone unless you deliberately want to adjust the output contrast, such as when working with a grayscale image.

7) Options Click to open the Auto Color Corrections Options dialogue box. It gives you different options for adjusting the colour in a less precise manner than the grey eyedropper, but it will go some way to correcting a colour cast.

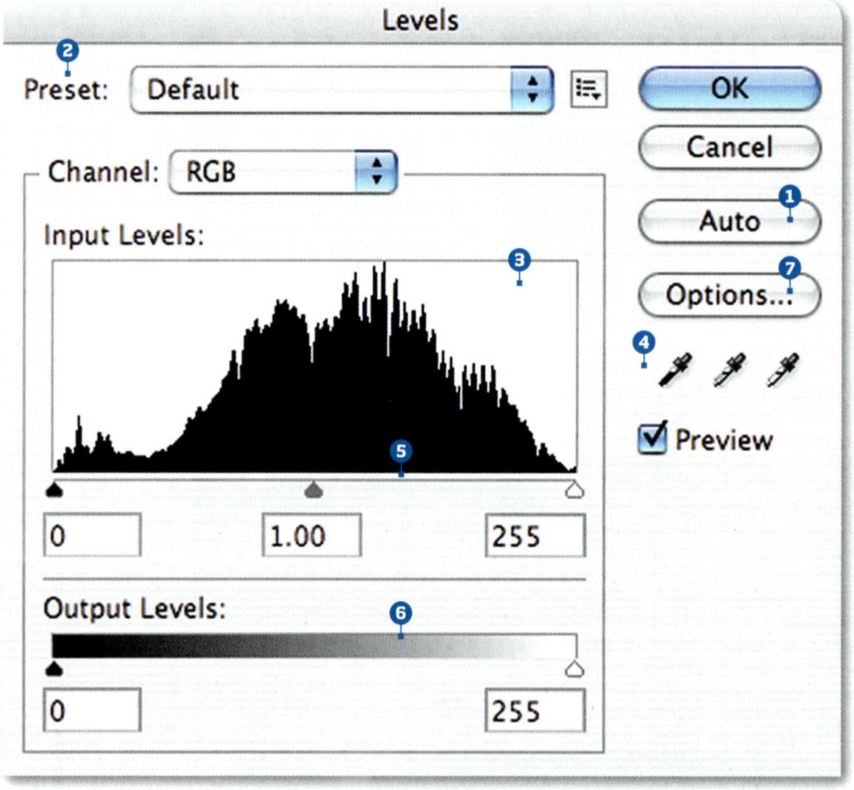

☑ LEVELS TIP: WHITE POINT

USE: PERFECT PRODUCT SHOTS

Product shots look great on a white backdrop, but more often than not the backdrop can render as off-white or grey, even if the image is correctly exposed. Levels has a quick and easy way to correct this: using the white eyedropper, click on the greyest part of the background. This will turn it white, leaving the product relatively unaffected. Carefully adjust the midpoint and black sliders to bring any lost detail back in to the product. Great for ebay!

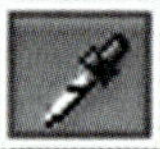

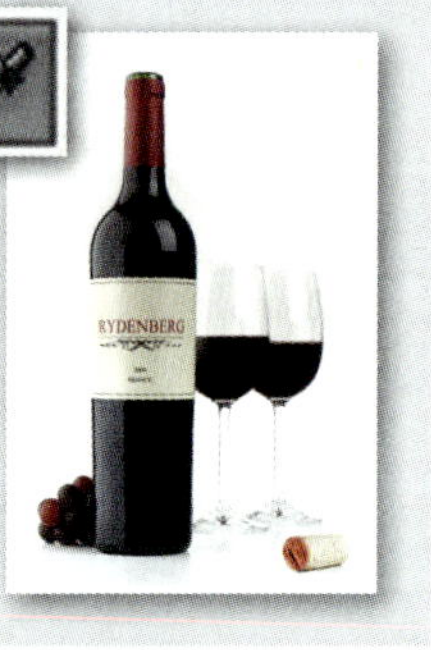

Secrets unlocked

✔ HIGHLIGHT WARNING

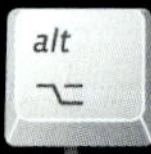

As you adjust the sliders, it can be easy to lose detail in either the highlights or shadows, known as clipping. To check for clipping, hold down ***alt*** while clicking on the black or white slider triangle. The image will change to show a threshold view with hotspots that indicate where detail has been lost.

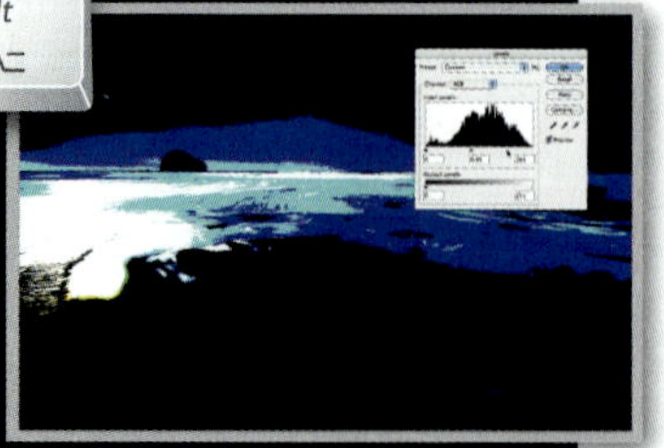

Three ways to use Levels

As you gain Photoshop experience and want to have more control over colour correction and contrast, different ways of applying the adjustments are available to suit your ability level and need for control

1 USE THE AUTO OPTION
ONE-CLICK AUTOMATIC RESULT

Once you open Levels, you'll be presented with a histogram. Pressing the *Auto* button is a good place to start as it takes a look at the image and maps points from black to white to get the best tonal range. A lot of the time, if you have an under- or overexposed image, Auto will make it look a lot better. If you hold ***alt***, while clicking on *Auto*, the Auto Color Corrections Options dialogue box will appear, giving you options to adjust the colour balance.

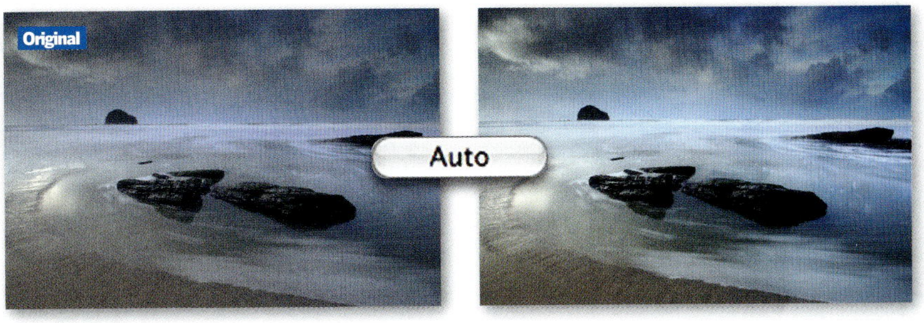

2 EYEDROPPER
AUTOMATED WITH USER INVOLVEMENT

These can set a picture's tonal range by clicking on the image directly. To set black, click on the darkest area of the image with the black eyedropper. If it's lighter than any other part, you'll find the whole image will darken to compensate. The reverse happens with the white eyedropper if you do not select the lightest part of the image. The grey eyedropper selects the midpoint, but can also correct colour casts, depending on what neutral area you click on.

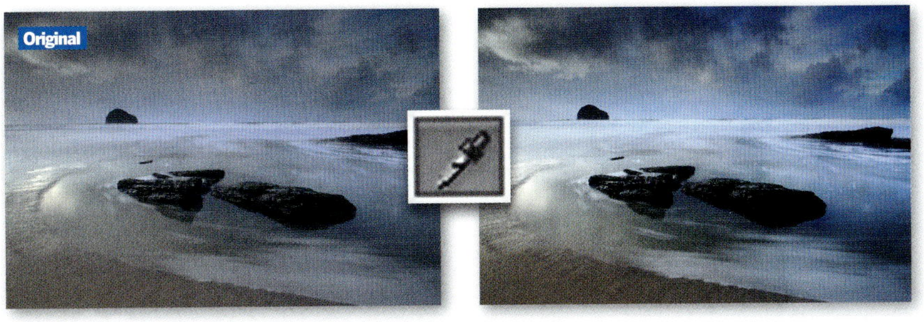

3 SLIDERS
FULL CONTROL FOR THE EXPERIENCED USER

On the Input Levels slider, you have three triangles: black for shadows; grey for Gamma, which controls the relative image brightness between the shadows and highlights; and white for the highlights. The idea is to move these triangles to expand the contrast without losing any detail in either the shadows or highlights (known as 'clipping'). The first thing to do is bring the black and white triangles in to align with the edges of the histogram – this will automatically move the Gamma slider, too. To intensify the highlights or shadows, move the *Gamma* slider and then use the grey eyedropper to correct any colour cast.

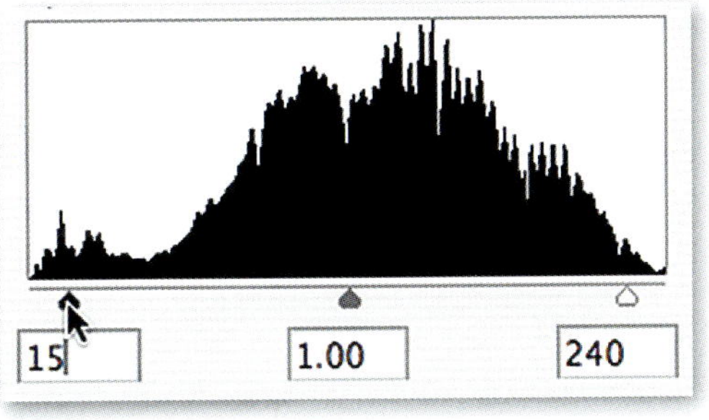

HOT KEY
alt ⌥

Alt to reset

If you hold down ***alt***, the Cancel button in the dialogue box will change to Reset so you can revert back to the original image and start again. This will work for most of the dialogue boxes you use.

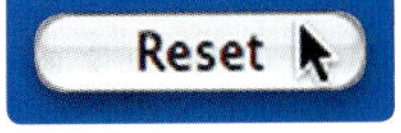

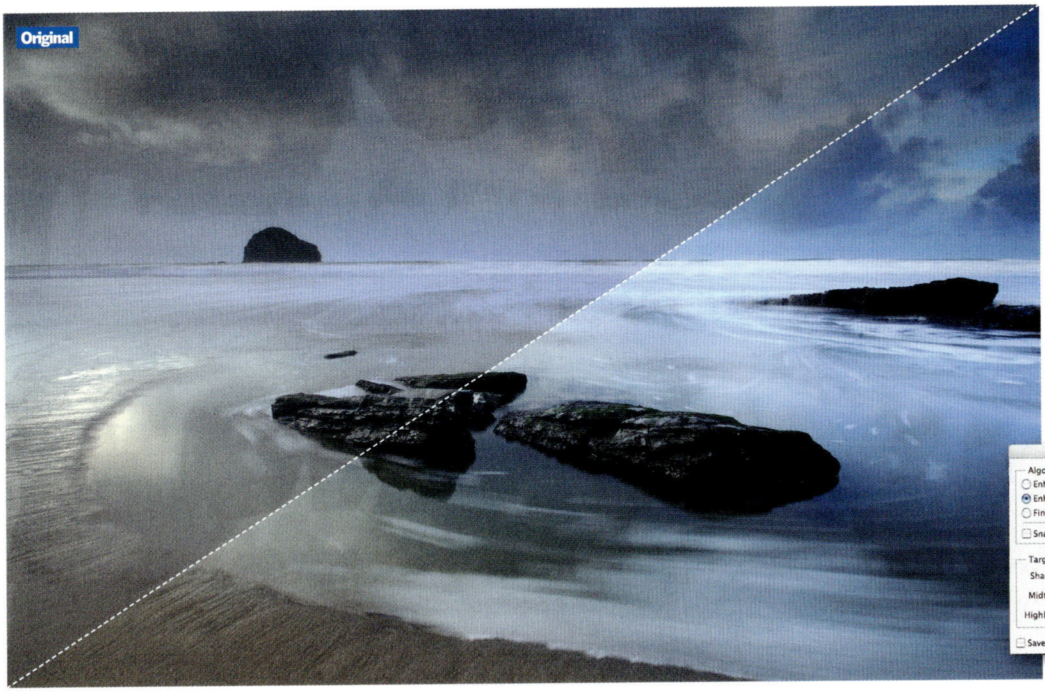

OPTIONS

Controlling colour

To access the Auto Color Correction Options in an Adjustment Layer, you need to click ***Auto*** while holding down ***alt***. To adjust the colour, click ***Snap Neutral Midtones*** and then experiment with the algorithms to find what works best.

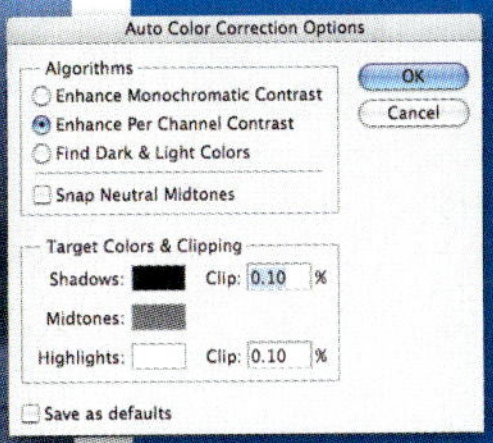

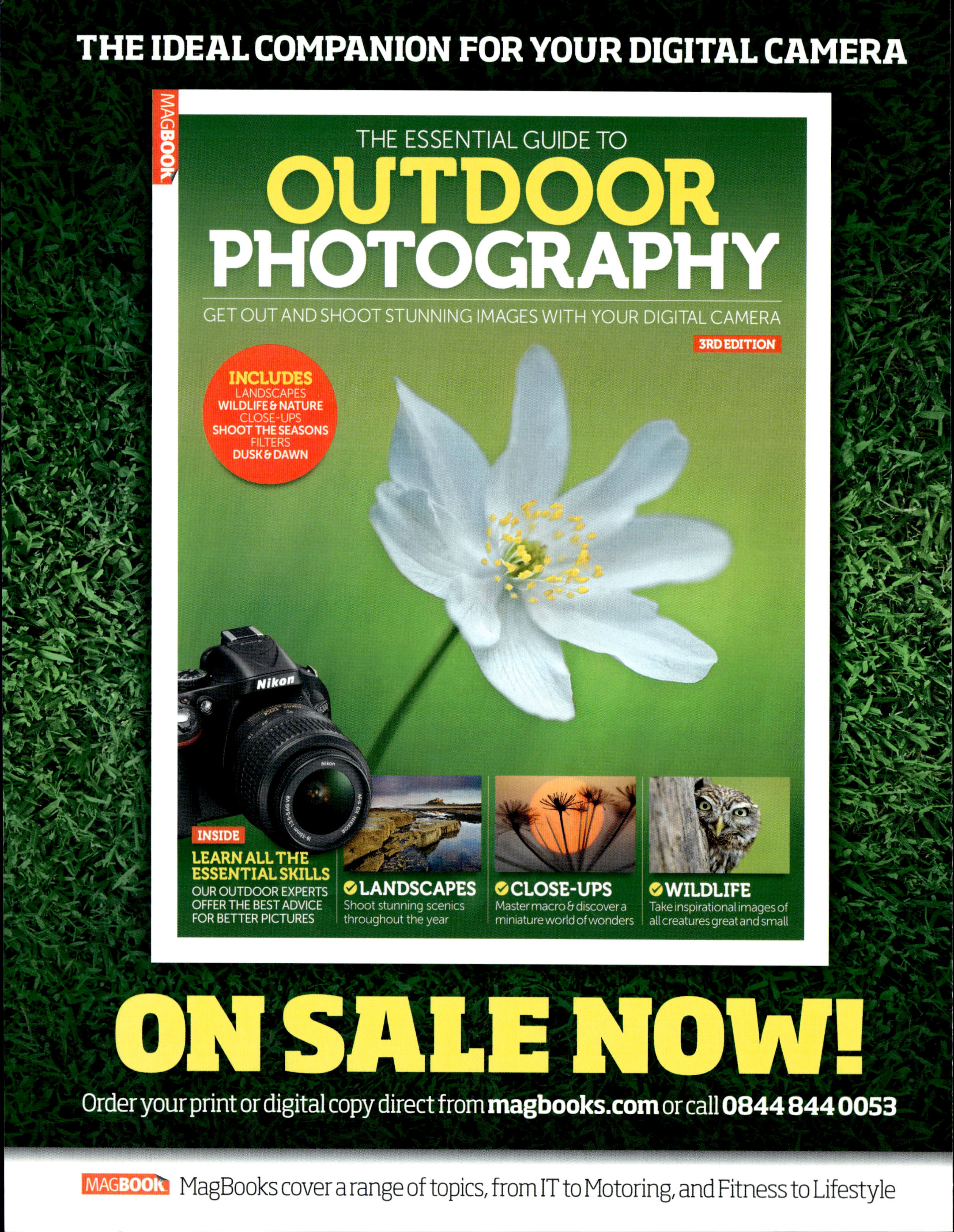
THE IDEAL COMPANION FOR YOUR DIGITAL CAMERA
MAGBOOK
THE ESSENTIAL GUIDE TO
OUTDOOR PHOTOGRAPHY
GET OUT AND SHOOT STUNNING IMAGES WITH YOUR DIGITAL CAMERA
3RD EDITION
INCLUDES
LANDSCAPES
WILDLIFE & NATURE
CLOSE-UPS
SHOOT THE SEASONS
FILTERS
DUSK & DAWN
Nikon
INSIDE
LEARN ALL THE ESSENTIAL SKILLS
OUR OUTDOOR EXPERTS OFFER THE BEST ADVICE FOR BETTER PICTURES
LANDSCAPES
Shoot stunning scenics throughout the year
CLOSE-UPS
Master macro & discover a miniature world of wonders
WILDLIFE
Take inspirational images of all creatures great and small
ON SALE NOW!
Order your print or digital copy direct from magbooks.com or call 0844 844 0053
MAGBOOK MagBooks cover a range of topics, from IT to Motoring, and Fitness to Lifestyle

Curves

PC QUICK SELECT KEYS = ctrl M   **MAC** QUICK SELECT KEYS = ⌘ M

If you want more control over contrast, then get familiar with Curves and your images are sure to improve

CURVES IS PROBABLY the most powerful adjustment feature in Photoshop and also one of the most advanced, but once you've got to grips with it you'll find yourself using it time and time again. Just like Levels, Curves can be applied as an Adjustment or an Adjustment Layer (Layer>Adjustment Layer>Curves) and affects the tonal range of your image. Unlike Levels, you have far more control and many more features and methods of use – all of which could fill a book of their own – so we'll just be covering the basics here.

When you open the Curves adjustment panel, you'll be presented with a similar set-up to Levels but this time there's a diagonal line across the histogram: it's this line you'll need to move to adjust tonality. There are two adjustment points at either end of the line, which are the equivalent to Level's Shadow and Highlight sliders. The additional control Curves offers comes from being able to click anywhere along this line to create as many adjustment points as you want to target specific areas of the histogram/tonal range. The whole idea behind using a curve is that tones are altered gradually, avoiding problems such as posterisation.

By moving the end points at the top and bottom, you also gain control of the darkest and lightest points of your image, which effectively does the same as the white and black Input and Output sliders in Levels. Pretty much everything you can do in Levels, you can do in Curves (although the reverse isn't true), so it's down to personal preference as to which you use for specific tasks, but Curves is definitely an upgrade in control.

How to create an 'S' curve

Using Curves can get complicated, but here's a useful technique that's highly effective and easy to do

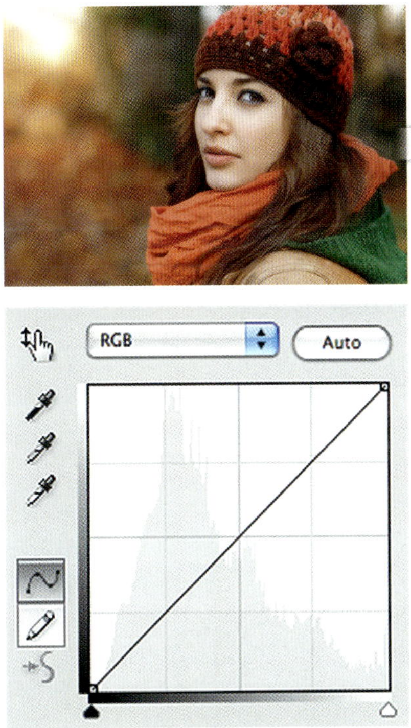

1 First of all, select ***Show Clipping for Black/ White Points*** from the panel menu in the top-right corner. Then set the black and white points to the edges of the histogram as you would in Levels. Or hold down ***alt*** as you drag the black or white ***Input*** sliders to preview the clipping.

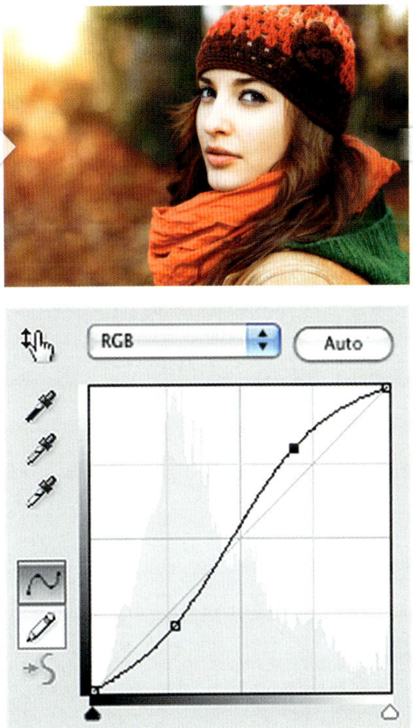

2 Click about a quarter of the way down the diagonal line and drag the point up slightly to brighten highlights. Click about a quarter of the way up the line from the bottom and drag the point down to darken the shadows. The steeper the curve is, the stronger the contrast will be.

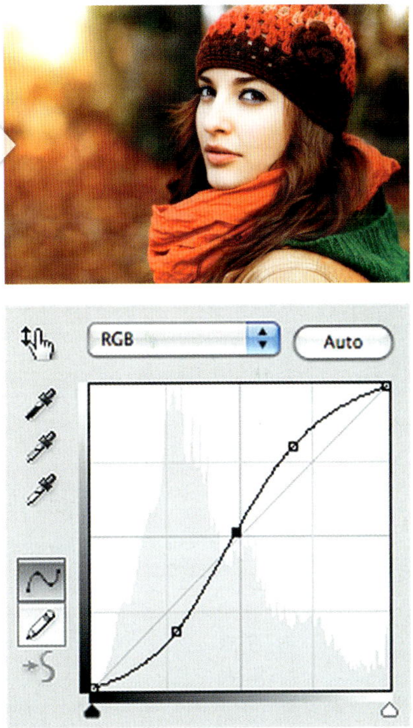

3 To target the mid-tones, place a point in the centre of the line and then drag the line up or down depending on whether you want to brighten or darken the mid-tones. You can change the colour of an image, too, using Curves, see *Secrets unlocked* below for more details.

Secrets unlocked

✔TARGET MODE

Instead of manually adjusting the line in the Curves chart, click on the hand icon in the top left of the control panel. You can now click on an area of the image you want to adjust, and click and drag the cursor up (to brighten) or down (to darken) for more intricate control.

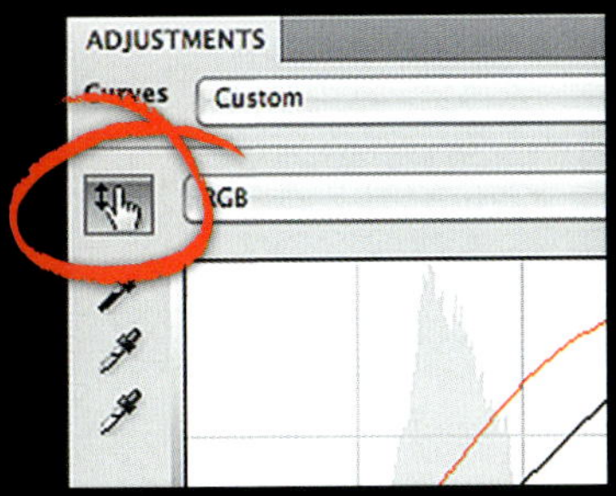

Secrets unlocked

✔ADJUST THE CHANNELS

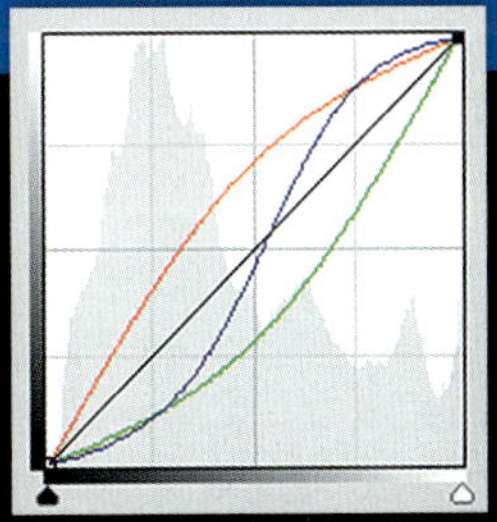

Curves is capable of adding colour casts by moving the individual colour channels, located in the drop-down menu at the top of the panel. You could add a blue cast to shadows (or remove one for that matter) and a red cast to highlights, for example, simply by moving the Curves line as you would to adjust the global contrast. One of the best ways to do this is to set a middle point on the curve and to drag it slightly up or down to add or reduce the colour channel in the image respectively.

Brush Tool

PC & MAC QUICK SELECT KEY FOR PHOTOSHOP CS & ELEMENTS = B

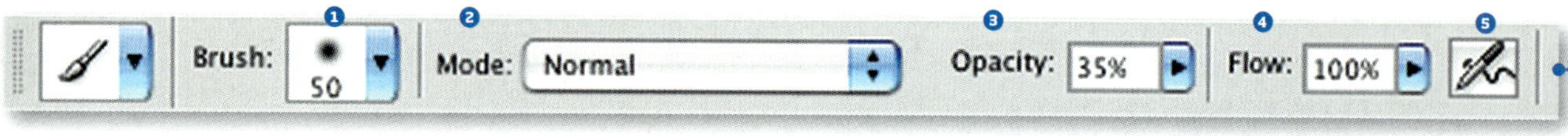

Access the hidden secrets of the Brush Tool and find out how it can help you retouch and selectively adjust your image's colour, exposure and contrast

THE BRUSH TOOL has some of the most diverse and useful applications for post-processing images. Designed to replicate the effect of a paintbrush, the tool's primary purpose is to apply colour to an image specified via clicking on the colour palette at the bottom on the toolbar. But it has many more sophisticated uses than just 'painting' colour on a canvas – for example, you can use it to edit the tonality of pictures by using it in conjunction with a Layer Mask, to retouch pictures and skin tones and to make selections (see page 34 for more details).

The Brush Tool's options are overwhelming, especially in CS5 onwards. While you can alter the shape, size and style of your brush in CS4, as well as the Flow and Opacity of the paint, in CS5 onwards you also have more bristle-tip types to choose from to improve your control, accuracy and creative potential. You can select various types of flat and round brushes as well as setting parameters like how thick and long each bristle is, depending on the type of brush stroke you want to replicate, and the wetness and paint load. As a photographer who is really only interested in editing their pictures, on a day-to-day basis you'll probably only graze the surface of the Brush Tool's potential and have little need to even access the crammed Brush Panel (see below) for the advanced parameters. The options, however, are well worth exploring in case you fancy getting into digital art or want to apply a creative design to one of your pictures.

❶ **Brush palette:** Selects the size, shape, texture and hardness of your brush to suit your adjustment.
❷ **Mode:** Determines how pixels in the image are affected by the Brush Tool and its paint.
❸ **Opacity:** Controls the density of the paint and its level of coverage.
❹ **Flow:** Controls the liquidity of the paint and the speed it's applied.
❺ **Airbrush:** When switched on, you can build the paint up depending on how long you hold your mouse or pen down for, not by how many strokes you take.

THE BRUSH PANEL

While shortcuts and the Options panel will usually quickly provide you with the brush you need, if you want to explore your control over the Brush Tool, look towards the Brush Panel. To open it, go to *Window>Brushes* or right-click *ctrl* and click on the image, and you'll be able to change the tip's style, as well as other more detailed settings such as preset shapes and textures. Rarely would a photographer need this much power – it's intended more for digital artists – but if you get into creative painting and digital illustrations, it's worth checking out.

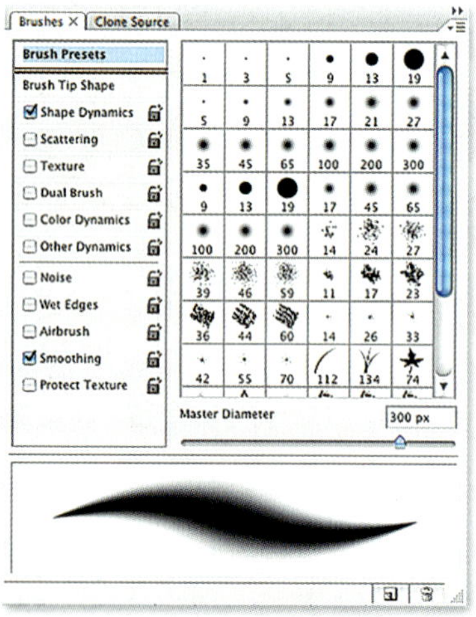

BRUSH TOOL BLEND MODES

1) Normal: This is the default mode. It paints/edits each pixel to turn the base colour (the layer you're applying it to) in to the blend colour (the colour loaded on the brush).

2) Behind: Paints/edits only on transparent areas of an image. It only works on layers that have Lock Transparency deselected.

3) Clear: Paints/edits pixels to make them transparent, similar to an eraser. It only works on layers that have Lock Transparency deselected.

4) Soft Light: Darkens or lightens the base colour, depending on what blend colour is used. The effect is similar to shining a diffused light on the image. If the brush's colour is lighter than 50% grey, the image is lightened as if it were dodged. If the brush's colour is darker than 50% grey, the image is darkened as if it were burned in. Painting with pure black or white produces a distinctly darker or lighter area, but does not result in pure black or white, and other colours will leave a light tint on the image.

5) Hue: Creates a resulting colour from the luminance and saturation of the base colour combined with the hue of the blend colour.

6) Saturation: Creates a resulting colour from the luminance and hue of the base colour combined with the saturation of the blend colour.

7) Color: Creates a resulting colour with the luminance of the base colour and the hue and saturation of the blend colour. This is useful if you want to turn part of an image black & white or you're tinting an image.

8) Luminosity: Creates a resulting colour with the hue and saturation of the base colour and the luminance of the blend colour. This mode creates the inverse effect of Color mode.

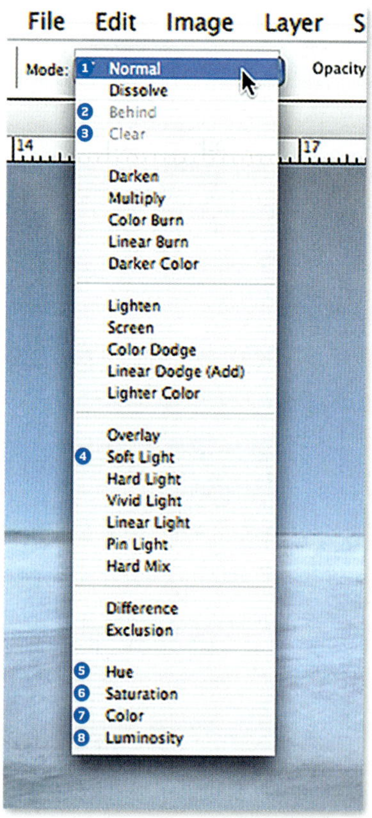

HOT KEY

Brackets

Brushes can be accessed via the Options bar or via *Window>Brushes*. However, if you're working on an image, and want to alter the brush's Size, press the right or the left square brackets (next to the letter P).

Secrets unlocked

HISTORY & ART HISTORY BRUSH

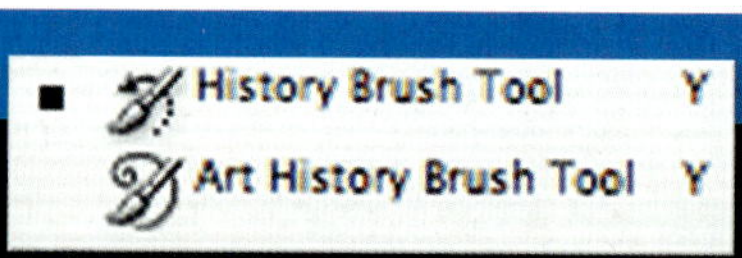

The History Brush Tool can be used to partially undo any adjustment, filter or tool. With the tool selected, click on the History Panel (*Window> History*) and click in the box next to the step you want to revert back to. This will select it as your source state. Now you can go back to the image and paint selectively to take the area back to the reverted state. You can go back as far as the History Panel allows: the default is 20 states but you can extend this via the *Preferences>General panel.* The Art History Brush works in a similar way but has the power to add an Impressionist look to your picture, similar to CS5's Mixer Brush and Element's Impressionist Brush. The biggest mistake people make with this tool is using too large a brush so the edges blur and diminish detail.

HOT KEY

Number keys

To alter the paint's opacity, press **4** for ***40%, 7*** for ***70%*** etc, unless you're working with the airbrush, in which case this affects the Flow. Hold ***shift*** and press a number to affect the opacity of the airbrush.

Uses for the Brush Tool

Learn how to correct skin tones and reduce blemishes in portraits. Plus we show you an easy way to correct problems with exposure

1 SKIN RETOUCHING
USE IT TO EVEN OUT SKIN TONE

An easy way to get rid of dark bags, or to reduce wrinkles and blemishes, is to take a sample of skin tone and paint it over the area with a low-opacity brush. It's always better to gradually build the colour up to the tone you want with multiple brush strokes.

- Zoom in to the image so you have a close-up view of the area you want to retouch. Select a medium-sized brush (no bigger than the area you're planning to retouch), with a ***Hardness*** of around ***0-10%***, and the ***Opacity*** set to around ***10%***.
- Hold down the ***alt*** key (Mac) or ***cmd*** (PC) so the brush cursor turns into an eyedropper, then click on an area of colour near the area you want to retouch. This loads the colour on the brush. Now brush over the area to even out the skin tone. Take a new colour sample from next to each area you retouch to ensure the colours are similar in tone.

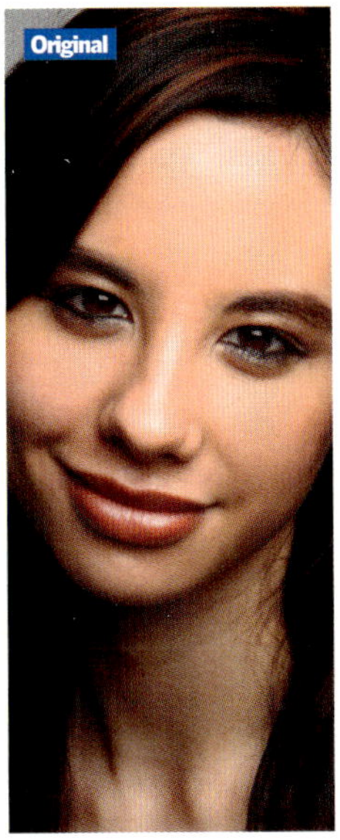

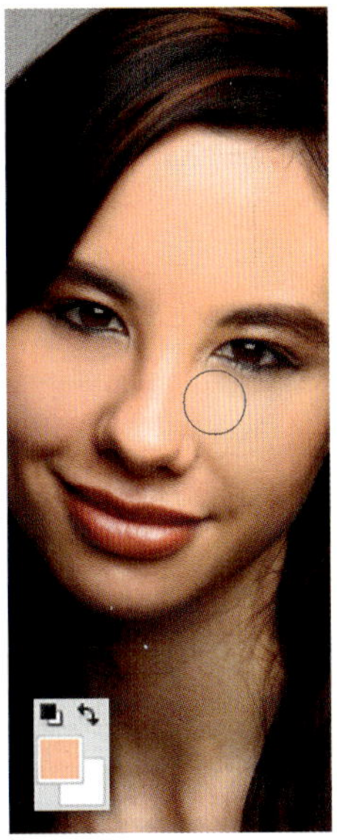

2 TONAL ADJUSTMENTS
USE IT TO CORRECT EXPOSURES

If parts of an image are under- or overexposed, there's an easy, nondestructive way to selectively correct ill-exposed areas with the help of the Brush Tool and Layer Masks. This technique can be applied to contrast or colour changes by simply using a different adjustment layer.

- Add an Exposure adjustment layer (***Layer>New Adjustment Layer>Exposure***) and adjust the sliders until the area you want to amend is correctly exposed.
- Each Adjustment Layer has a Layer Mask attached. Select the mask, then set the ***Foreground Color*** to ***Black*** and pick a soft, round brush with an ***Opacity*** of ***100%***. Paint over the area that's now poorly exposed to bring back the detail from the original image.
- If you make a mistake, switch the ***Foreground Color*** to ***White*** and brush the area back in on the Layer Mask.

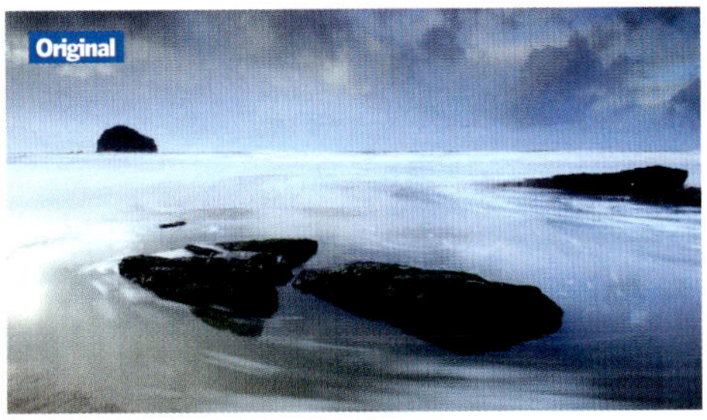

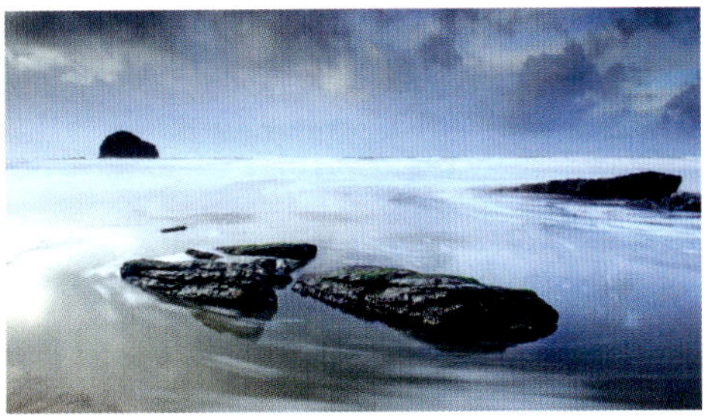

Software highlights

✓SPECIALITY BRUSHES

While the Brush Tool in Elements 9 and 10 works in the same way as in CS4, it also offers speciality brushes that paint shapes like stars, flowers and butterflies. Elements 9 also features the Impressionist Brush that blurs and blends the edges of the objects in your image to resemble an Impressionist painting. It's tricky to get a handle on, but it can yield interesting results. Try using it on a duplicate layer and then reduce the layer's opacity to see what happens.

✓SMART BRUSH TOOL

While this brush can be used to make selections in Elements 9 and 10, like the Quick Selection Tool, it also edits your image. Found underneath the Paint Brush Tool, you can use it to make selective adjustments by brushing over an area to change the colour, adjust the exposure, apply special effects or convert it to black & white among other Smart Paint options.

✓MIXER BRUSH IN CS5 ONWARDS

This ingenious tool is designed to work like an actual paintbrush, with a variety of bristle tips, the ability to adjust the amount of paint loaded on the brush and its wetness – the same way you'd work if you were applying paint to a real canvas. The real showstopper is the Mixer Brush, which enables you to literally mix the colours in your photograph by controlling its Mix value and Wetness. It takes practice, so don't be discouraged if your picture looks like a five-year-old's finger painting rather than a Rembrandt masterpiece at first.

Tools of the trade

✓USING A GRAPHICS TABLET

A Wacom tablet is really handy when using the Brush Tool as brush movements are much more natural. You can also adjust the Opacity and the Size of the brush based on your pressure points. If your tablet's pen has barrel rotation, you can also change the angle of your brush intuitively rather than have to specify the angle in the brush palette.

The Brush Tool and Layer Masks

Find out how painting on Layer Masks can be used to hide or reveal image information

By adding a Layer Mask to a layer (*Layer>Layer Mask>Reveal All/ Hide All*), be it an image layer or an Adjustment Layer, you can use the Brush Tool to mask off areas of an image so it's not affected by an adjustment.

For example, set the brush's colour to *Black*, and select the Layer Mask, then brush over the adjusted areas that you want to hide.

White paint does the reverse and grey partially does both, leaning towards one or the other depending on how dark or light the tone is. The process is nondestructive; delete the Layer Mask to undo any edits.

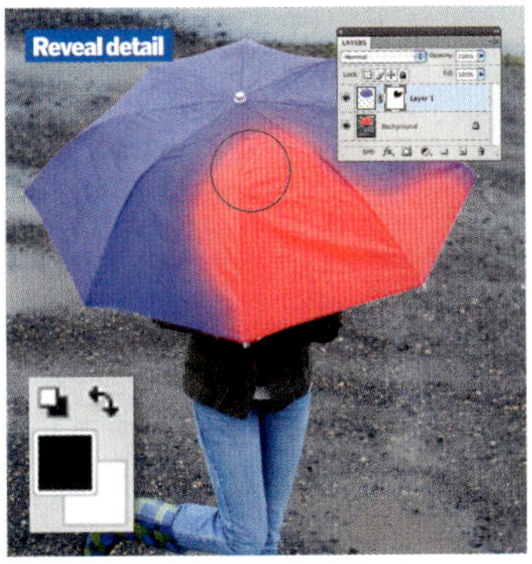

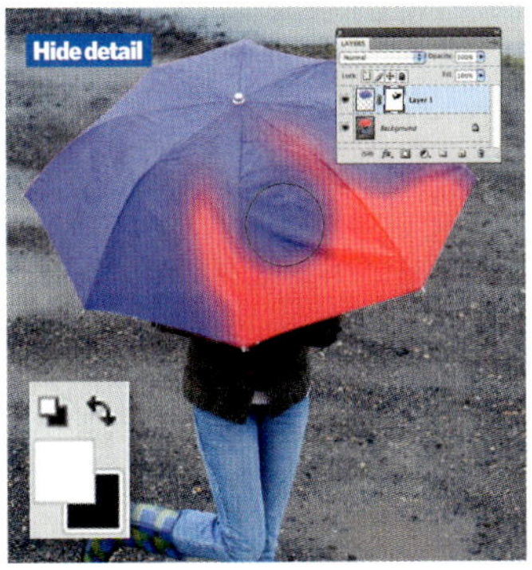

HOT TIP

You can download a variety of brushes from www.adobe.com or from the web for free. Then add them to your Brush Panel by clicking on the small arrow in the top-right corner to access a drop-down menu, then clicking *Load Brushes* to save them to your palette. Under the same menu you'll also find different preloaded brush types that you can add to your palette.

Black & White adjustment layers…

Learn how to take control over your black & white conversions to maximise detail, tonal range and creative effect

THERE'S NO DENYING that colour can be beautiful, but black & white is often classic, elegant and can be very powerful with the right kind of scene or subject. It's a favourite with most photographers, whether of the film or digital age, as we can all appreciate its compelling charisma. So, how can you craft a tonally rich black & white image post-capture?

When working with film, photographers used to rely on colour filters to modify a scene's tonal range: for modest adjustments, they'd use the yellow or orange filter; and for a dramatic difference, a red filter. A red filter lightens every red tone in the scene and darkens everything else. It was very popular with portrait photographers as it lightened skin tones, and with landscape photographers as it made blue skies darker and more dramatic.

In essence, this is how a Black & White adjustment layer works: once you apply the Adjustment Layer (Layer>New Adjustment Layer>Black & White…) the image will instantly be converted to mono. You'll be faced with a dialogue box that allows you to adjust the various colours in the image to improve and control the tonal range, the same way you would when applying a colour filter to your camera.

The fact it's an Adjustment Layer means any alterations you make are nondestructive, you can delete or edit the layer at any time, and it gives you precise control over the colour channels. Above all, though, it's one of the easiest, most versatile and quickest routes to turning a colour image into a punchy black & white masterpiece.

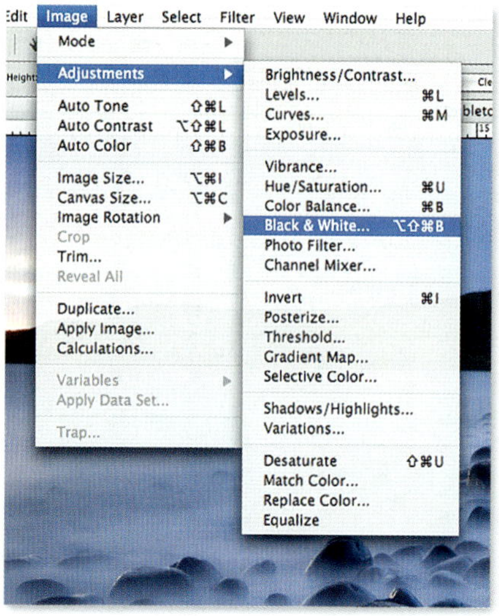

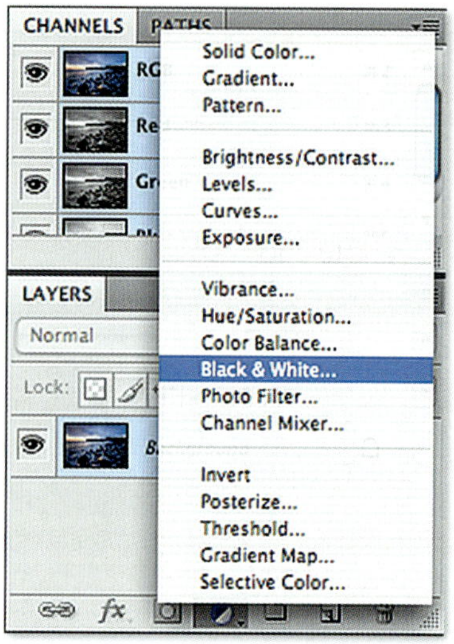

Secrets unlocked

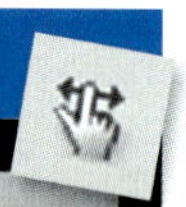

✔ TARGET MODE

Rather than use the sliders, if you click on the Hand Tool in the top of the dialogue box, you can click on any area of the image to target a specific colour that you want to modify. Then, when the hand cursor appears, click and drag it left or right to decrease or increase its strength.

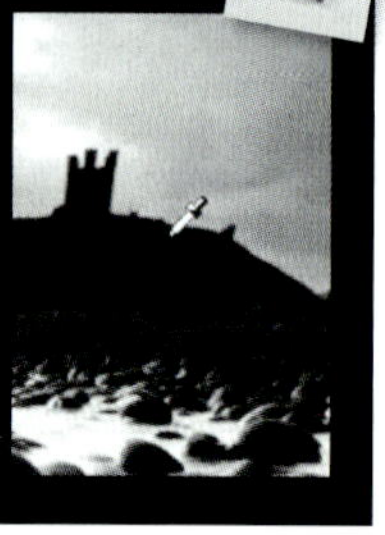

NAVIGATING THE MENU

1) Preset: Select a predefined grayscale mix or a previously saved grayscale mix.

2) Target mode: Use this optional tool with an Adjustment Layer to make changes directly on an image (see box, left). It's an automatic facility with *Image>Adjustments*.

3) Tint: Check this box and select a colour to add a duotone tint to your picture.

4) Auto: Sets a grayscale mix based on the image's colour values. Use it as a starting point, then tweak the tone using the colour sliders.

5) Colour channels: These sliders affect the grayscale tone of each colour in the picture.

6) Clip: Use this to link the adjustment layer to the layer/s beneath it to limit its effect. It's useful if you're working with multiple layers but don't want to affect them all.

7) Reset: Click this icon to revert all the sliders back to their default position.

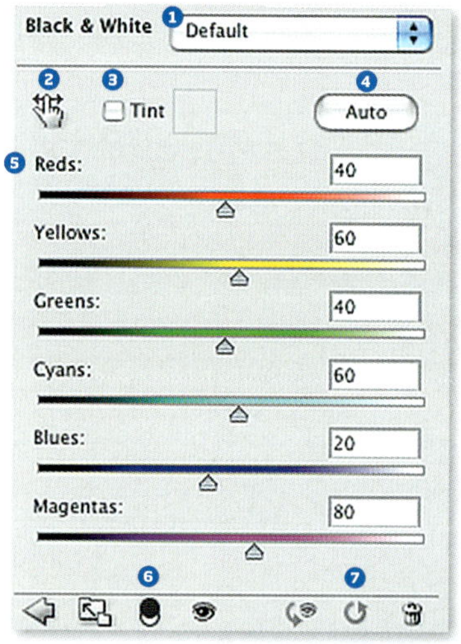

✔ TRY USING… BLEND MODES WITH A BLACK & WHITE ADJUSTMENT LAYER

You can change the tone and contrast of your colour image using Blend Modes.

By applying a Black & White adjustment layer and then using a Blend Mode to control how the layer interacts with the colours of the original image beneath, you can get some interesting and appealing results. The three key Blend Modes worth looking at are Soft Light and Overlay for contrast, and Luminosity for colour. If the effect is too strong, you can simply reduce the opacity of the Black & White adjustment layer. The beauty of doing this is that you can adjust the brightness of the image's individual colours by moving the Adjustment Layer's colour sliders.

Overlay: Boosts the contrast of a colour image by darkening and lightening tones.

Soft Light: Has a gentler but similar effect to Overlay blend mode.

Luminosity: This mode allows you to adjust the luminance and brightness of each colour without altering the saturation.

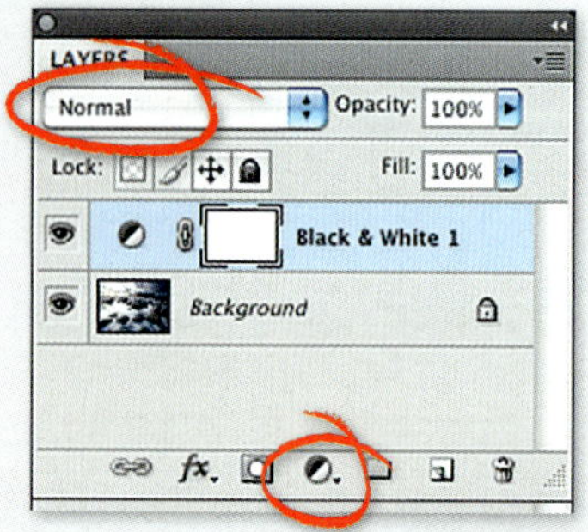

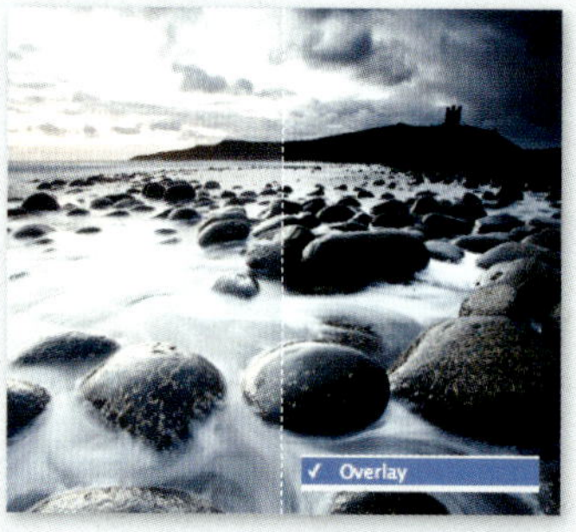

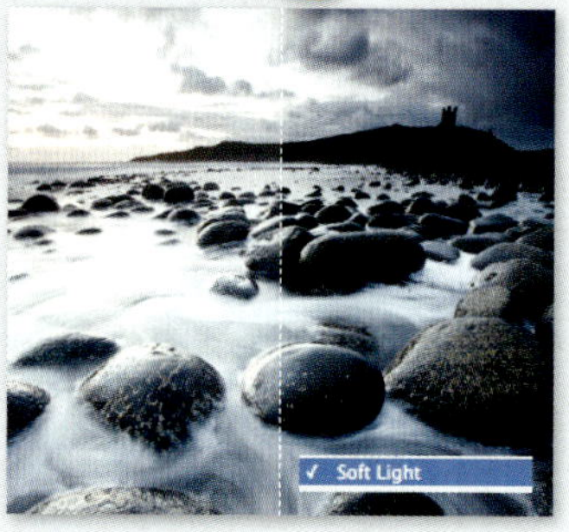

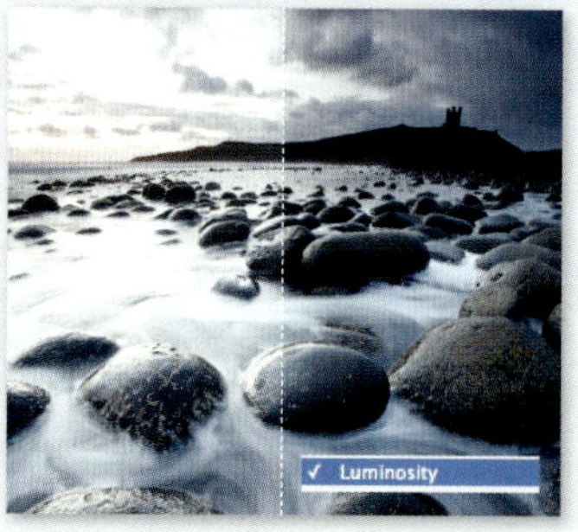

HOT TIP

Black & White in Elements

Duplicate the original layer and go to ***Enhance>Convert to Black & White*** and pick the conversion preset you want to use. You can then adjust the intensity of the tones using the Red, Green, Blue and Contrast colour sliders.

HOT KEY

Hide layer

To temporarily view your image before your previous change in the Adjustment Layer, hold down the \ key. It's a useful way to see how your latest adjustment affected your image.

Three ways to use Black & White on your images

The Black & White adjustment layer can be used for more than just a simple monochrome conversion. Read on to find out how to selectively colour and tint your image with the help of a Layer Mask

1 TURN AN IMAGE BLACK & WHITE

LEARN TO CONTROL THE TONALITY OF YOUR MONOCHROME CONVERSION

To convert a colour image to black & white, first go to *Layer> New Adjustment Layer>Black & White...* or access the Adjustment shortcut from the b&w circle icon at the bottom of the Layers palette. Your image will instantly turn black & white. Now click *Auto*; this will create a fairly accurate tonal conversion that you can then refine to your liking later. Alternatively, select one of the filters or effects from the *Preset* drop-down menu. Either way, once you have a basic conversion, use the colour sliders to target individual grayscale tones. At this point, it may help to flick back to your original image to judge the colours you want to refine by clicking the **eye** icon, next to the Adjustment Layer in the Layers palette.

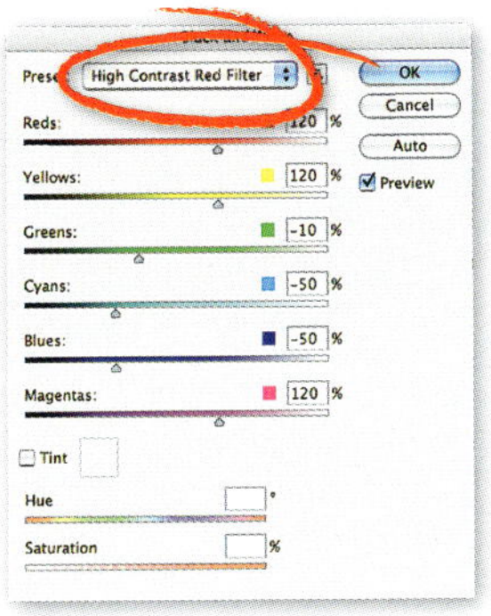

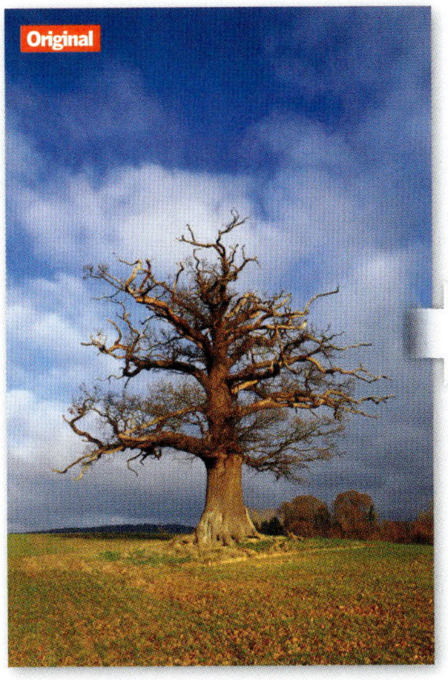

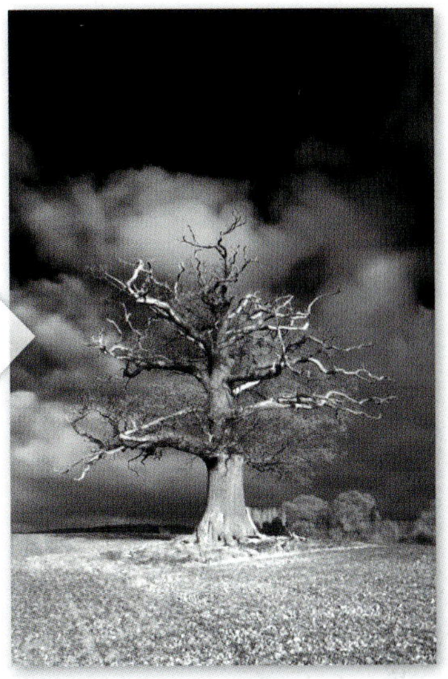

2 TINT AN IMAGE USING BLACK & WHITE

CREATE A DUOTONE PHOTOGRAPH

Before you tint your picture, use a *Black & White* adjustment layer to get the contrast you want. Then create a new *Black & White* adjustment layer and clip it to the Adjustment Layer beneath it, so you've created one Adjustment Layer for your b&w conversion and another for tinting, which comes in useful later. Check the *Tint* box and double-click on the coloured box next to it to open the colour picker. Once you've selected the coloured tint you want by using the gradient or colour library, you may find that the colour is too strong for your picture and you want to reduce the cast. As you're working on a new Adjustment Layer, you can reduce the layer's *Opacity* by moving the slider in the Layers palette to tone down the effect without revealing the original image underneath, as you would do normally.

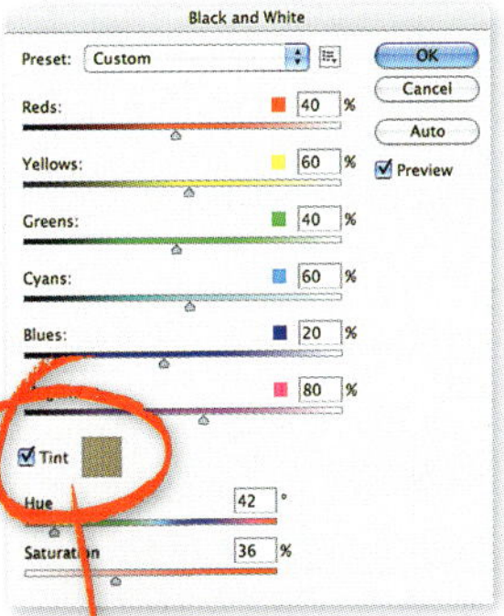

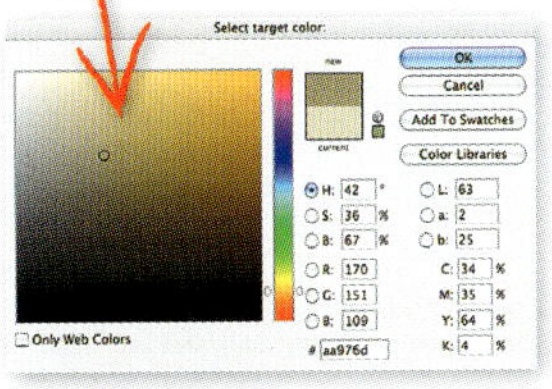

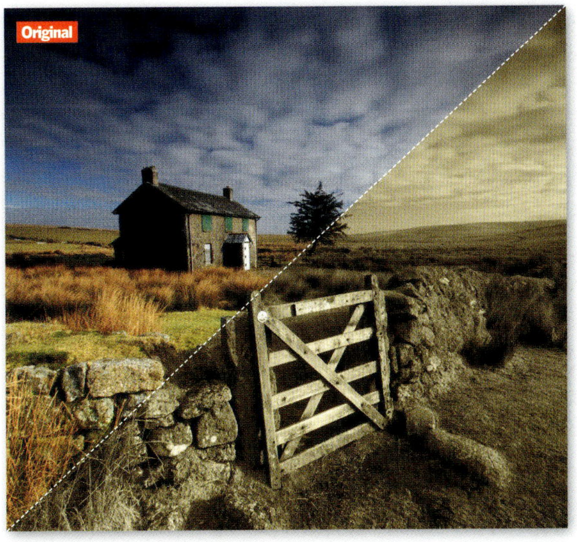

3 SELECTIVE COLOURING USING BLACK & WHITE

ADD IMPACT TO YOUR MONO PICTURES

Convert your image to black & white. Then add a Layer Mask to the Adjustment Layer by clicking *Layer>Layer Mask*. At this point, decide if you want most of your image colour with a touch of black & white or a black & white picture with a touch of colour, and then pick *Hide All* or *Reveal All*, respectively. Here, Reveal All was used as the majority will be black & white. Now select the *Brush Tool* and set the paint colour to *Black*. With the Layer Mask selected, paint over the area you want to turn to colour using a soft brush that's smaller than the area you're painting. If you make a mistake, switch the paint colour to *White* and zoom in to the image for more precision and paint the areas you want to return to b&w. To delete the Layer Mask, click the grey link on the Adjustment Layer and drag the Layer Mask in to the trash at the bottom of the Layers palette.

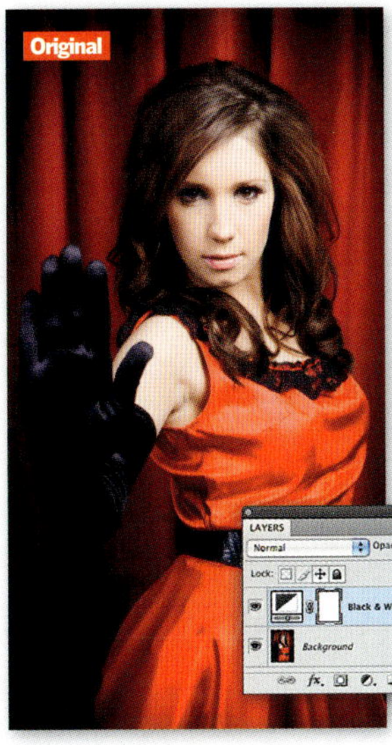

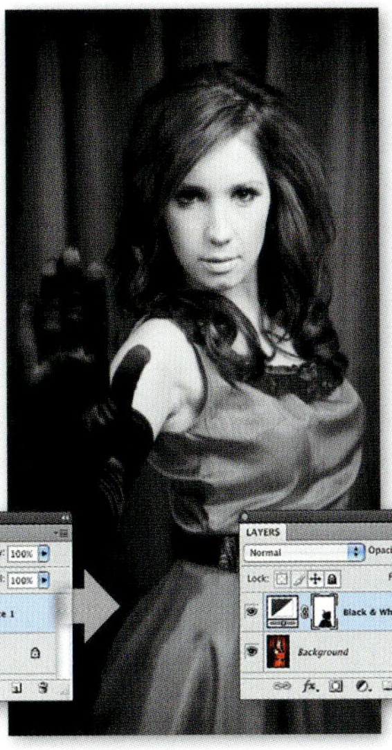

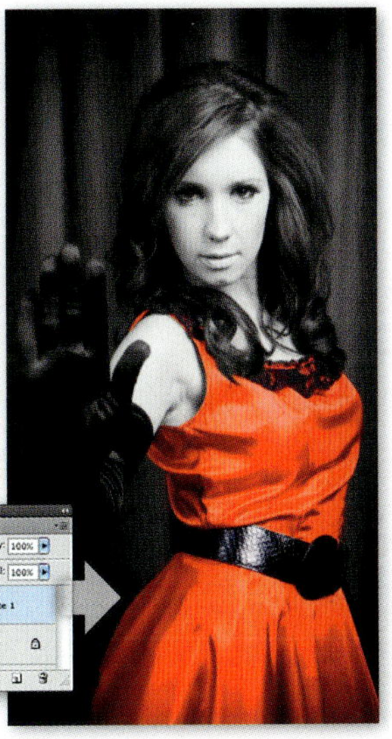

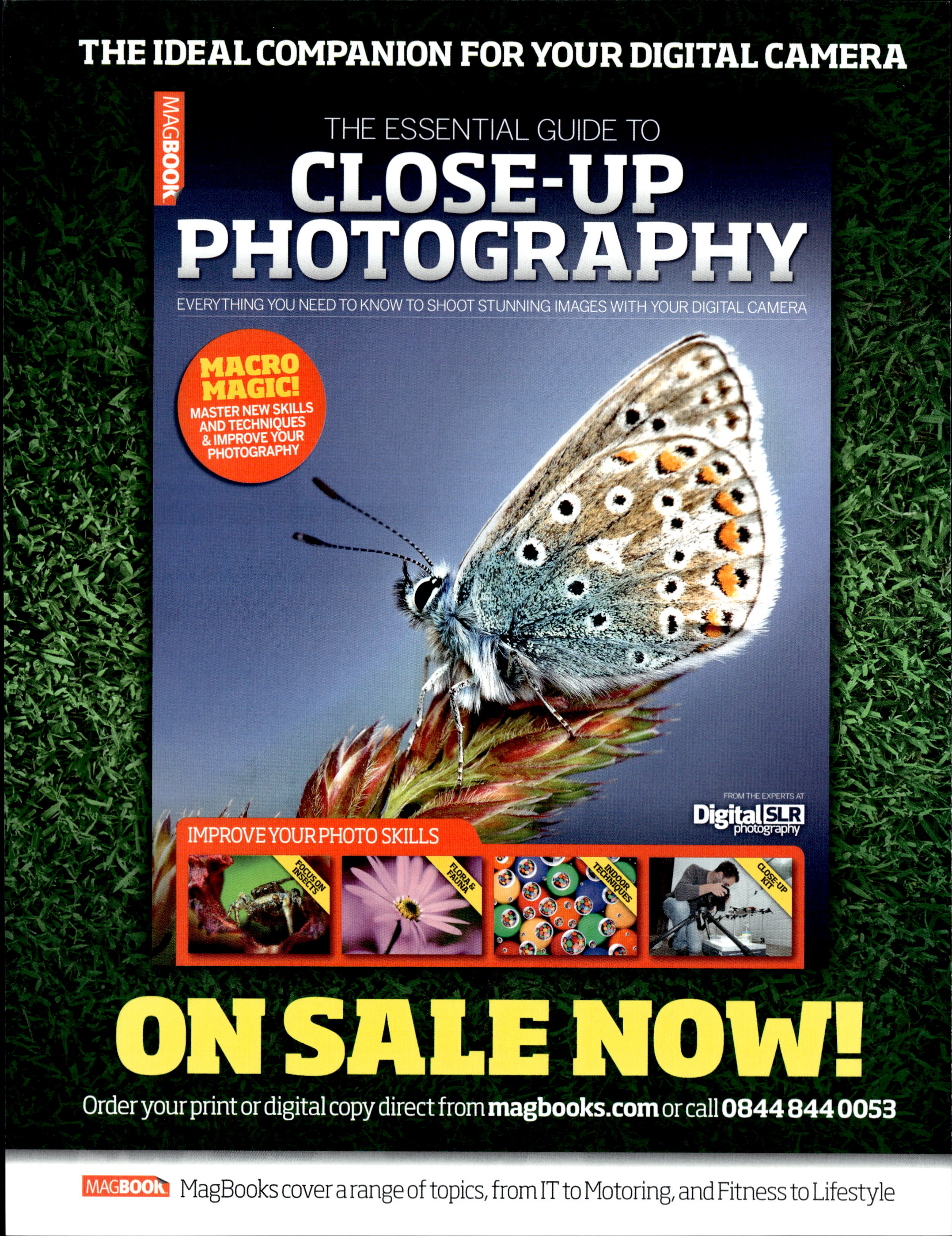
THE IDEAL COMPANION FOR YOUR DIGITAL CAMERA
MAGBOOK
THE ESSENTIAL GUIDE TO
CLOSE-UP PHOTOGRAPHY
EVERYTHING YOU NEED TO KNOW TO SHOOT STUNNING IMAGES WITH YOUR DIGITAL CAMERA
MACRO MAGIC!
MASTER NEW SKILLS AND TECHNIQUES & IMPROVE YOUR PHOTOGRAPHY
FROM THE EXPERTS AT
Digital SLR photography
IMPROVE YOUR PHOTO SKILLS
FOCUS ON INSECTS
FLORA & FAUNA
INDOOR TECHNIQUES
CLOSE-UP KIT
ON SALE NOW!
Order your print or digital copy direct from magbooks.com or call 0844 844 0053
MAGBOOK
MagBooks cover a range of topics, from IT to Motoring, and Fitness to Lifestyle

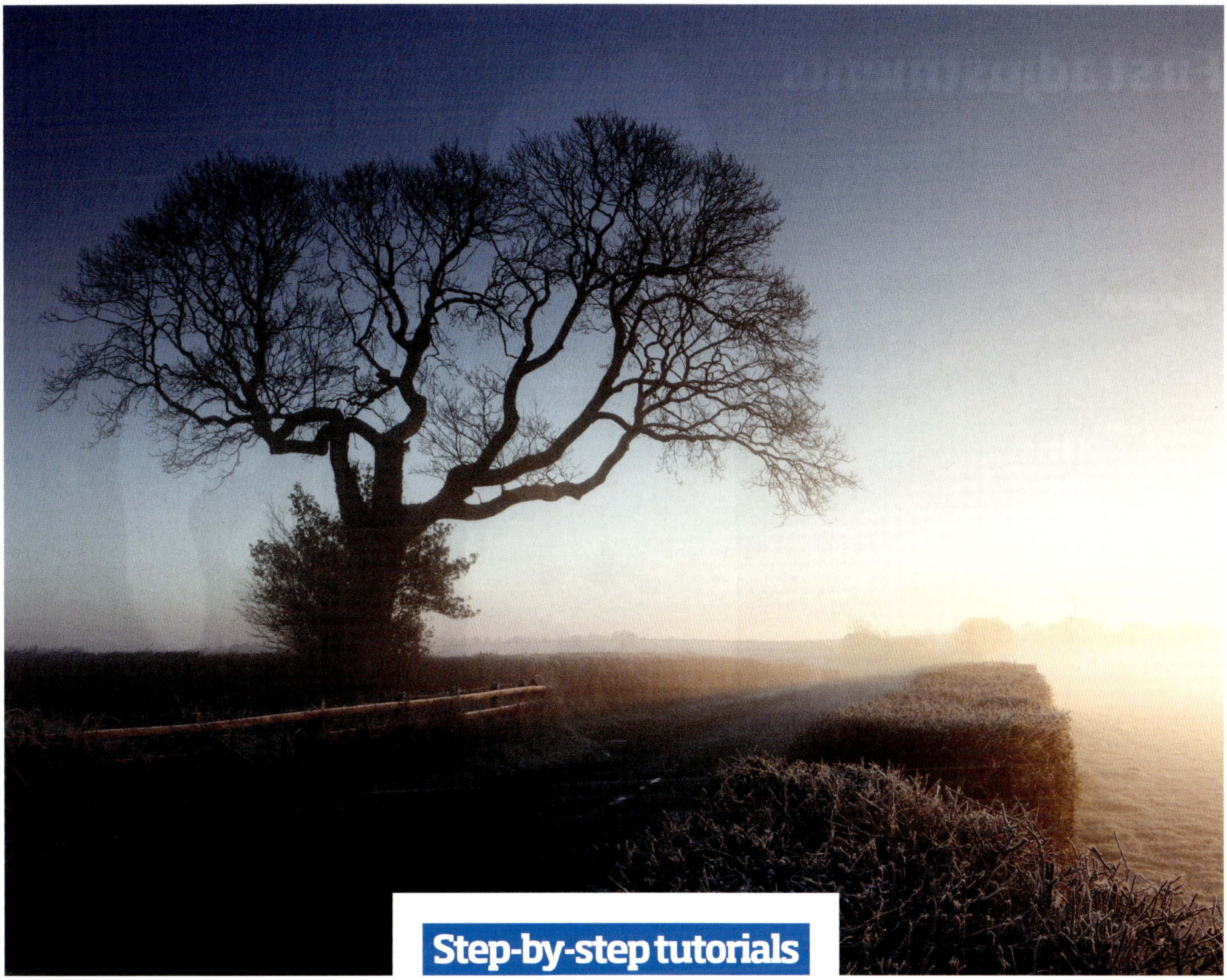

Step-by-step tutorials

BASIC TECHNIQUES

Transform your pictures with minimal effort using our favourite Photoshop skills

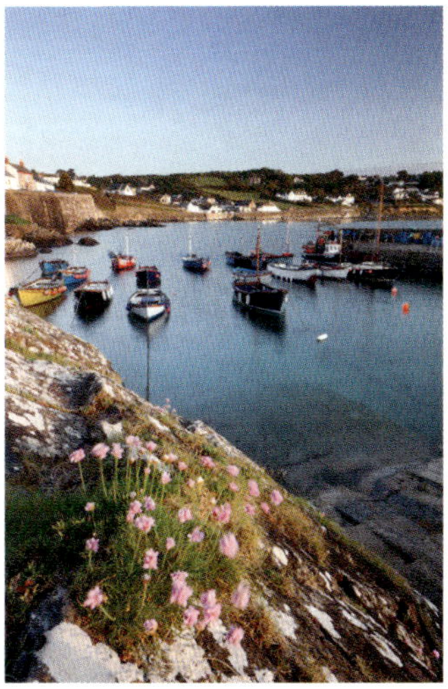

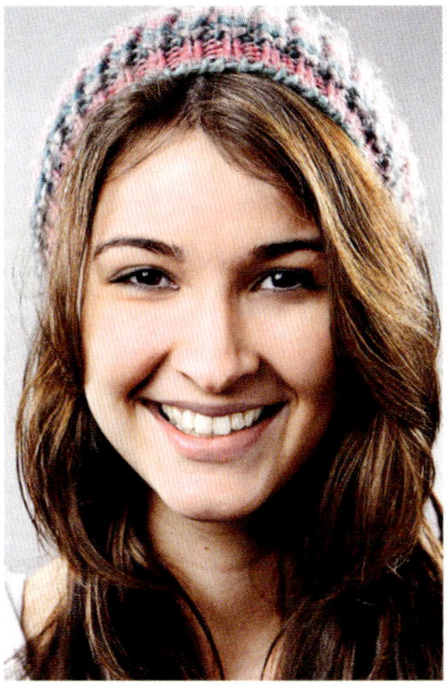

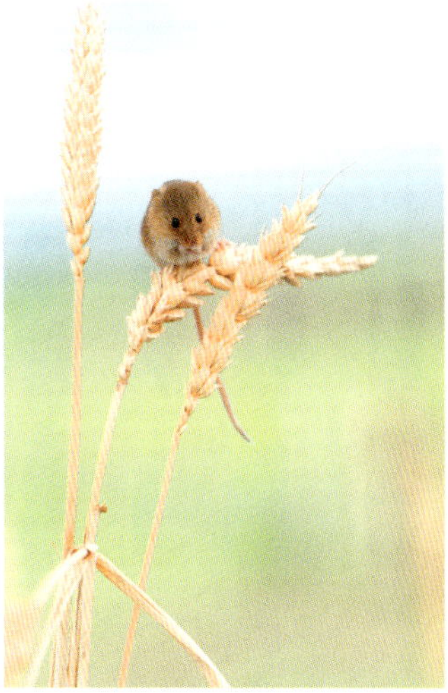

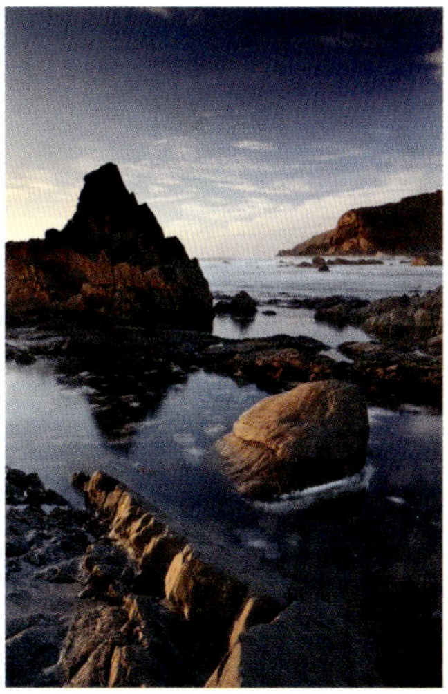

First adjustments

The first changes you may need to make to an image is correcting any distortions and to crop. Here are a selection of techniques and tools to help you with these initial edits

REFORMAT

The Crop Tool is more versatile than you might think and should be your first step for reformatting images. Select the *Crop Tool* from the toolbar (or press the *C* key), then click and drag over the area that you wish to include in the composition. You don't have to get it right first time; the changes aren't applied until you commit to them. You can use the anchor points around the bounding box to expand or contract the crop as needed. If you would like to maintain your image's aspect ratio, hold down the *shift* key when making your initial selection or you can preset the size or ratio using the *Width* and *Height* input boxes in the top toolbar. You can also use the Crop Tool to rotate an image by hovering your cursor outside one of the corner points: the cursor will change to a curved arrow and you can then click and rotate the selection. Finally, commit to your crop by clicking on the green *tick* or by pressing *Enter*.

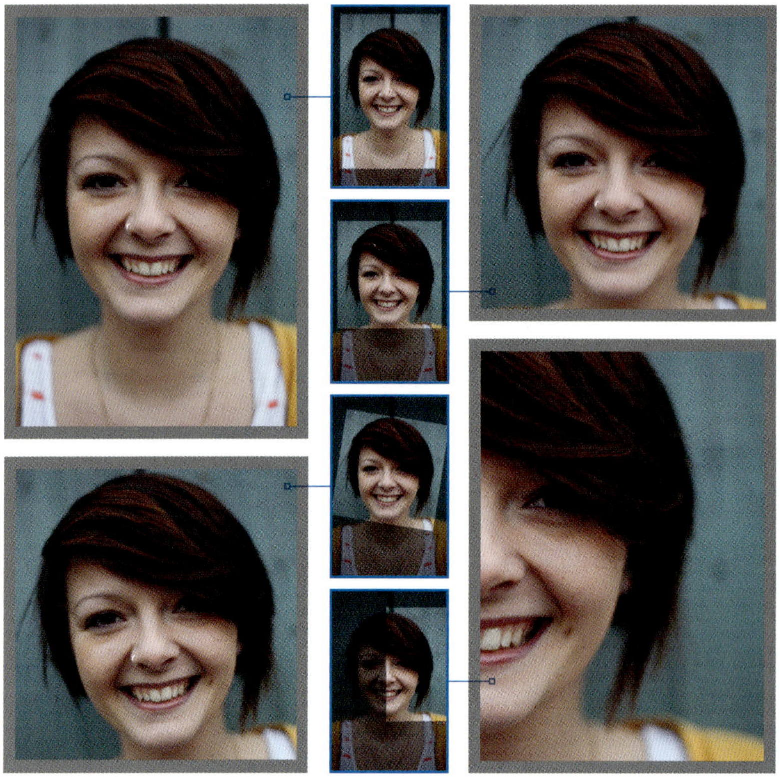

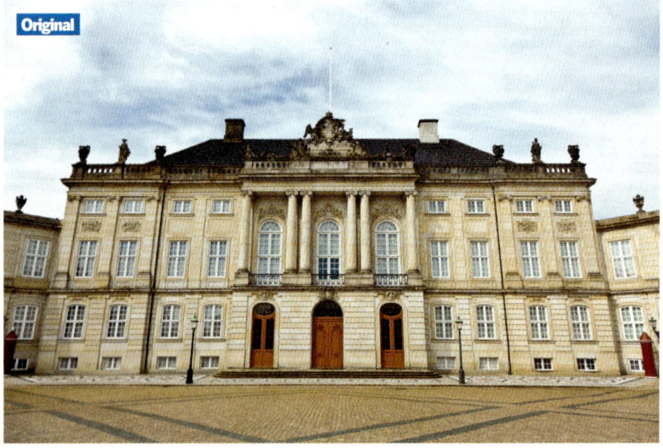

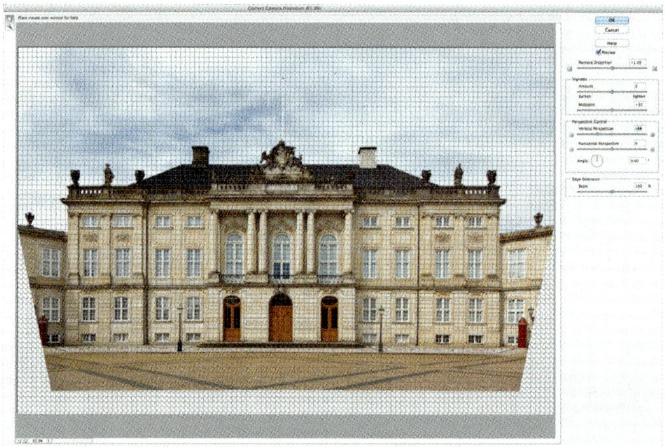

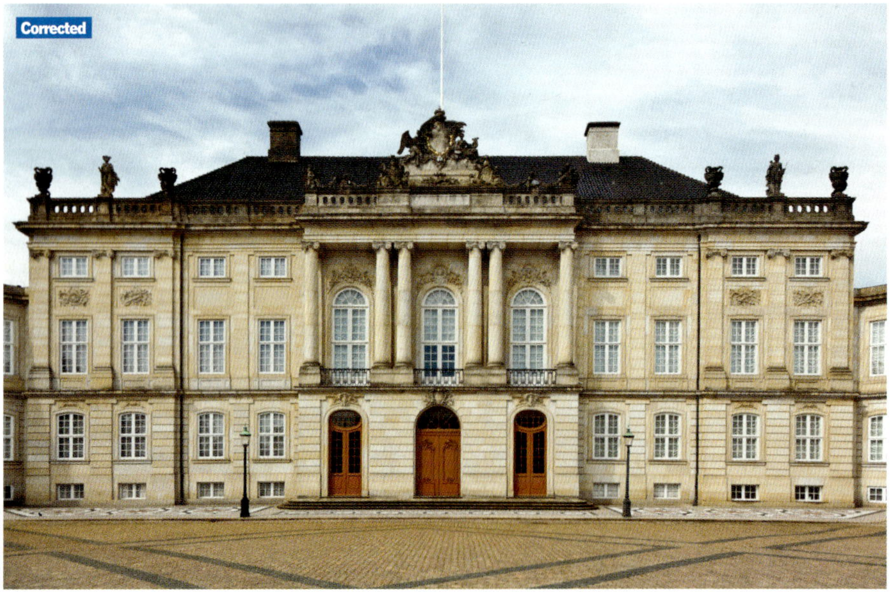

ISTOCKPHOTO

CORRECT DISTORTION

When you capture an image using a wide-angle lens, pictures can often suffer from distortion. One telltale sign that your image is distorted is converging verticals, which is more obvious when the image contains straight lines. By going to *Filters>Correct Camera Distortion* you can fix distortion, remove vignetting, correct perspective and even rescale your image. Your preview image allows you to easily assess any changes made. Use the *Remove Distortion* slider to correct barrel or pincushion distortion. Move the *Amount* slider to adjust the edges' tonality and the *Midpoint* slider to select the size of the area to be affected. Use the *Perspective Control* sliders for correcting any vertical or horizontal tilting and the *Vertical Perspective* slider to correct images taken from a low angle. Finally, use the *Scale* slider under *Edge Extension* to resize your image to remove any empty areas created by the corrections.

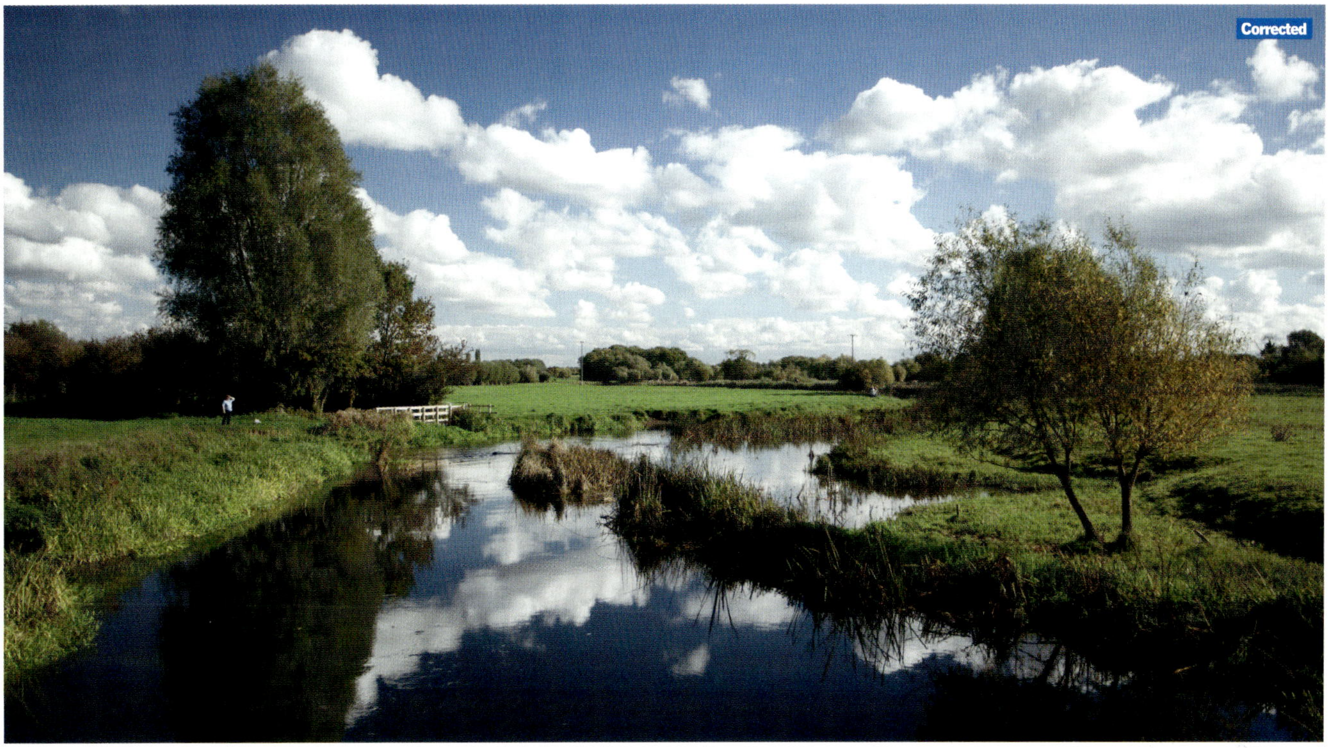

☑STRAIGHTEN

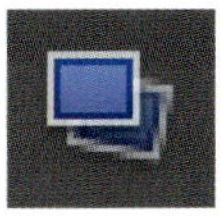

A wonky horizon is an error that's hard to ignore, but it's also easy to correct. The Straighten Tool allows you to level out your images with a simple drag-and-drop action. To do this, select the *Straighten Tool* from the toolbar (or press the *P* key) and then make your choice of three Canvas Options from the top toolbar. *Grow or Shrink Canvas to Fit* rotates the image and then increases or decreases the size of the canvas to fit the area. *Crop to Remove Background* rotates the image while cropping out excess background. *Crop to Original Size* rotates the image while keeping the original dimensions. Once you have chosen your method, click and drag along the image's horizon. Hold *shift* to restrict the adjustment to 45° increments to rotate an image. If you're not sure if your image needs horizon correction, go to *View>Grid* to activate guidelines – you'll immediately see if it's straight.

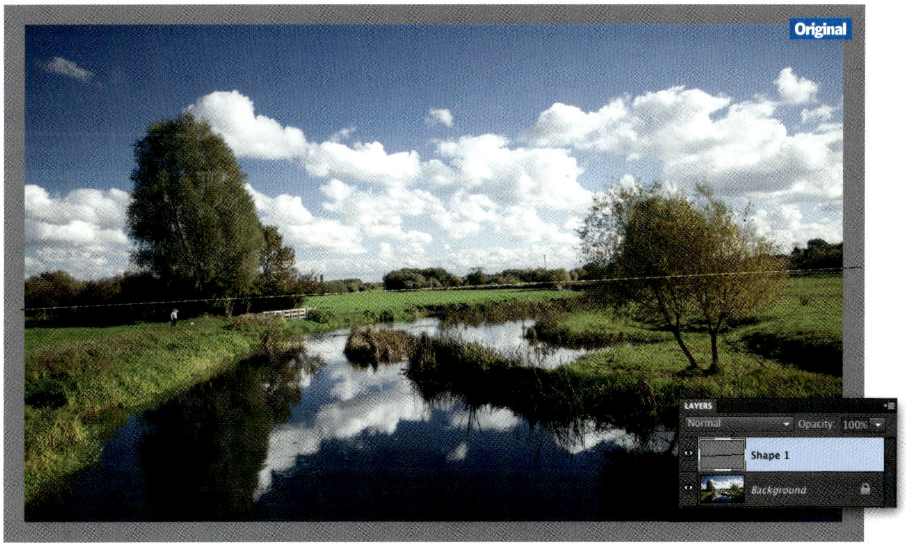

Other software

☑PHOTOSHOP CS5

A step up from the correction tools in Elements, CS5 offers all the Transform tools plus Warp Tool, which allows you to manipulate different parts of your image independently. You can also correct converging verticals by selecting the ***Perspective*** option in the top toolbar when using the ***Crop Tool***.

☑LIGHTROOM 4

The same adjustments can be made in Lightroom as they can in Elements and CS. As well as manual settings to correct distortion, Lightroom also allows you to apply the exact correction needed via ***Lens Correction>Profile***, and selecting the camera and lens you used.

☑TRANSFORM

If you want to be able to access most of these corrective functions at once, you can use the Transform commands for precise, manual adjustments. To access them, go to *Image>Transform>Free Transform* (or press *cmd/alt* and *T*). You can then use the anchor points around the bounding box, along with a shortcut key, to do a range of actions such as perspective alterations, skew and distortion. As Free Transform can be tricky to master, though convenient once you do, we suggest you select each command (*Skew*, *Distort* and *Perspective*) individually via the *Image>Transform* menu. You can also rotate or flip your picture via the *Image>Rotate* menu. As the Transform commands affect image pixels, every time you apply a transformation you degrade the quality. To minimise this damage, make all your adjustments before committing to them.

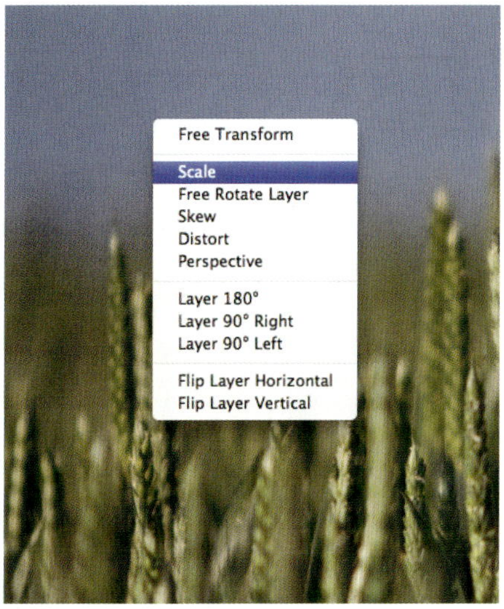

Speed up your selections

Elements offers so many different selection tools that it can often be difficult to know the best one to use. Time to get hands-on…

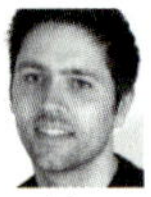

Jordan Butters: Each of Element's selection tools has its pros and cons, depending on what you want to select. Smart selection tools require some guidance, but they also monitor nearby pixels and make an educated assessment on what you do and don't want included.

The Magnetic Lasso Tool, for example, looks for high-contrast edges to attach to, while the Magic Wand Tool selects pixels of similar colour and tone, based on a Tolerance value you set. The higher the Tolerance, the wider the tonal range selected. The Quick Selection Tool works in a similar way to the Magic Wand Tool, except that you brush to select, rather than click. It's the simplest way to make a selection if the area comprises different colours and tones – it saves time when you're editing, and is often as effective as making a manual selection. Our guide should help you decide which tool to use depending on the job in hand.

Useful tools

✔SMART BRUSH TOOL

This is similar to the Quick Selection Tool but the Smart Brush allows you to choose from a list of artistic and practical presets such as Blue Sky, White Teeth and Sketch effect. The Smart Brush Tool can only be used with these effects and cannot be used to make a selection for any other purpose.

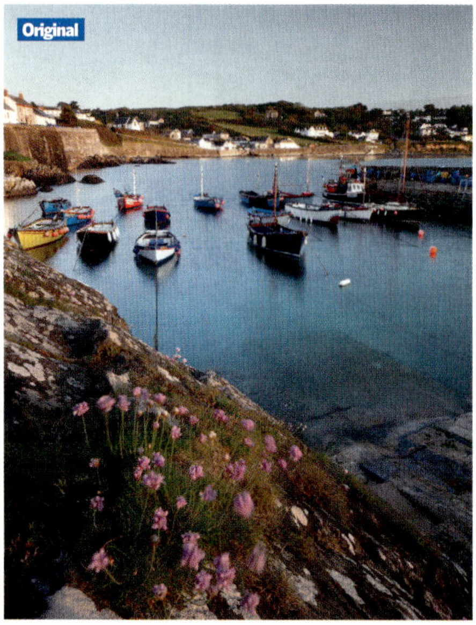

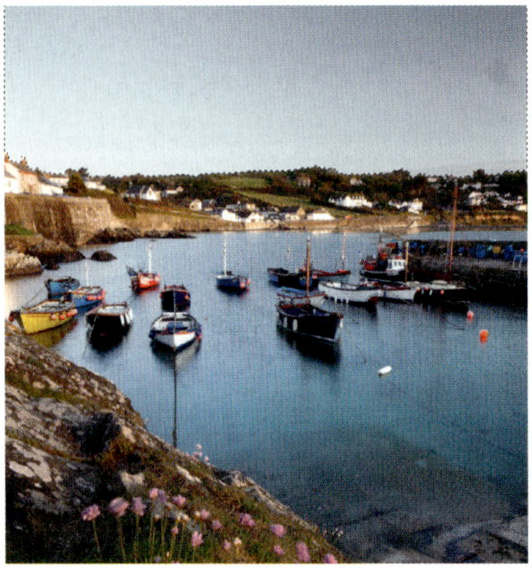

1 Use the Magic Wand To boost the saturation in the sky, select the ***Magic Wand Tool*** and click on the sky. If the entire area isn't selected first time, hold down the ***shift*** key and click on the additional areas to be selected. If you select an area by mistake, hold the ***alt*** key and click on these areas again to deselect them.

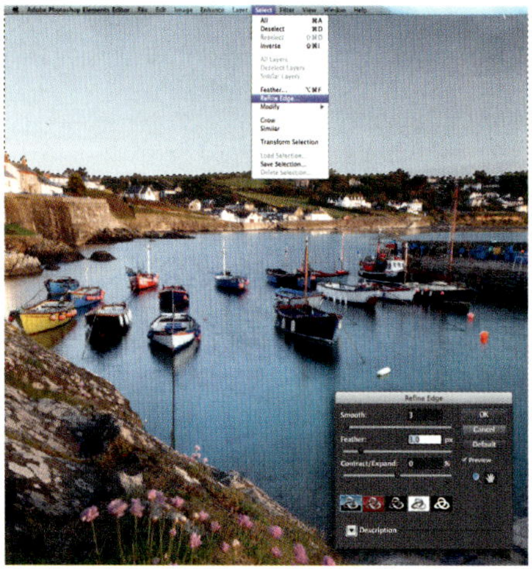

2 Refine the selection The selection will be highlighted by a running-ant line flashing around the edges. With your selection made, go to ***Select>Refine Edge*** and, in the Refine Edge box, increase the ***Feather*** to ***3.0px*** and click ***OK***. This will smooth the edges of the selection and get rid of any jagged edges.

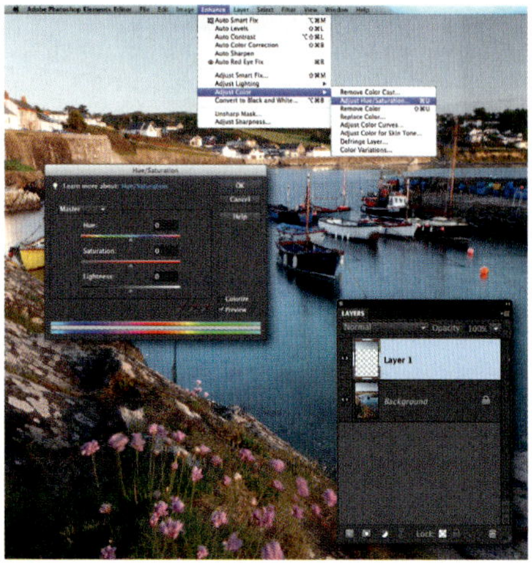

3 Adjust the saturation To boost the blue in the sky, go to ***Layer>New>Layer via Copy*** which will create a new layer using this selection. Then go to ***Enhance>Adjust Color>Adjust Hue/Saturation***. In the Hue/Saturation palette, increase the ***Saturation*** slider accordingly to suit your image and once done, click ***OK***.

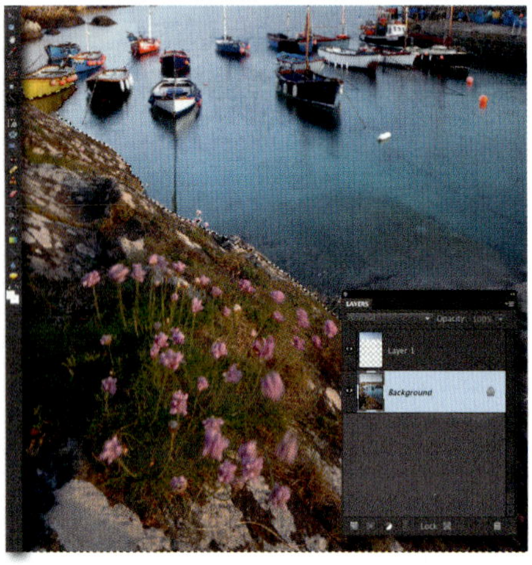

4 Use the Quick Selection Tool The foreground could do with a slight boost in brightness and contrast. First select the ***Background layer*** in the Layers palette and then click on the ***Quick Selection Tool***. Use the ***[*** and ***]*** keys to decrease or increase the brush size and brush over the area that you want selected.

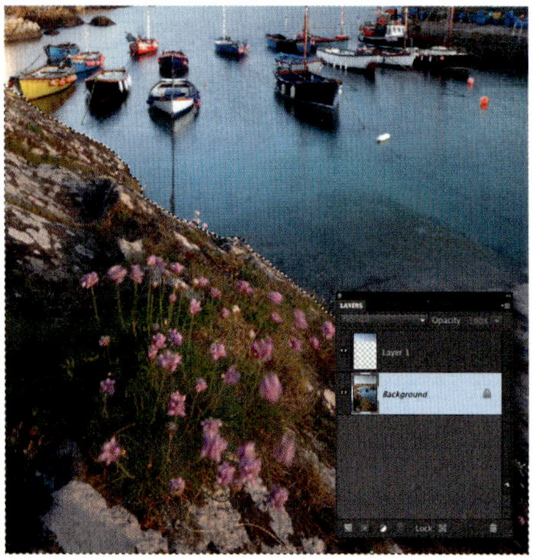

5 Correct the selection If the tool selects any unwanted areas, first reduce the brush size and then hold down the ***alt*** key while brushing back over these areas you wish to deselect. You may find that some back and forth is needed to select only the areas required. Refine the edge as before by going to ***Select>Refine Edge***.

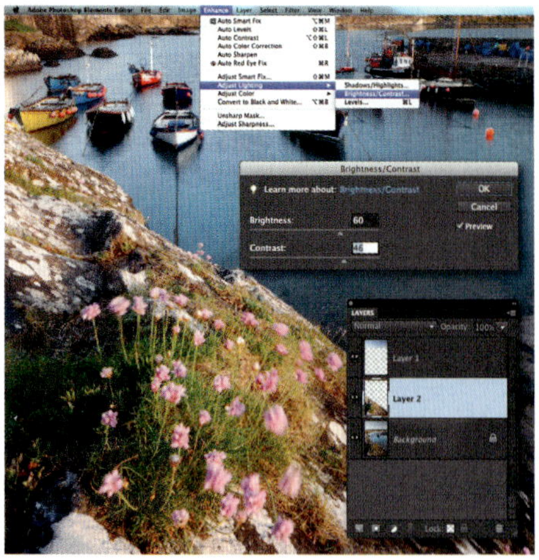

6 Enhance the lighting Go to ***Layer>New> Layer via Copy*** to create a new layer again using this selection and this time go to ***Enhance> Adjust Lighting>Brightness/Contrast***. In the Brightness/Contrast adjustment panel, increase the ***Brightness*** and ***Contrast*** accordingly to suit your image and click ***OK***.

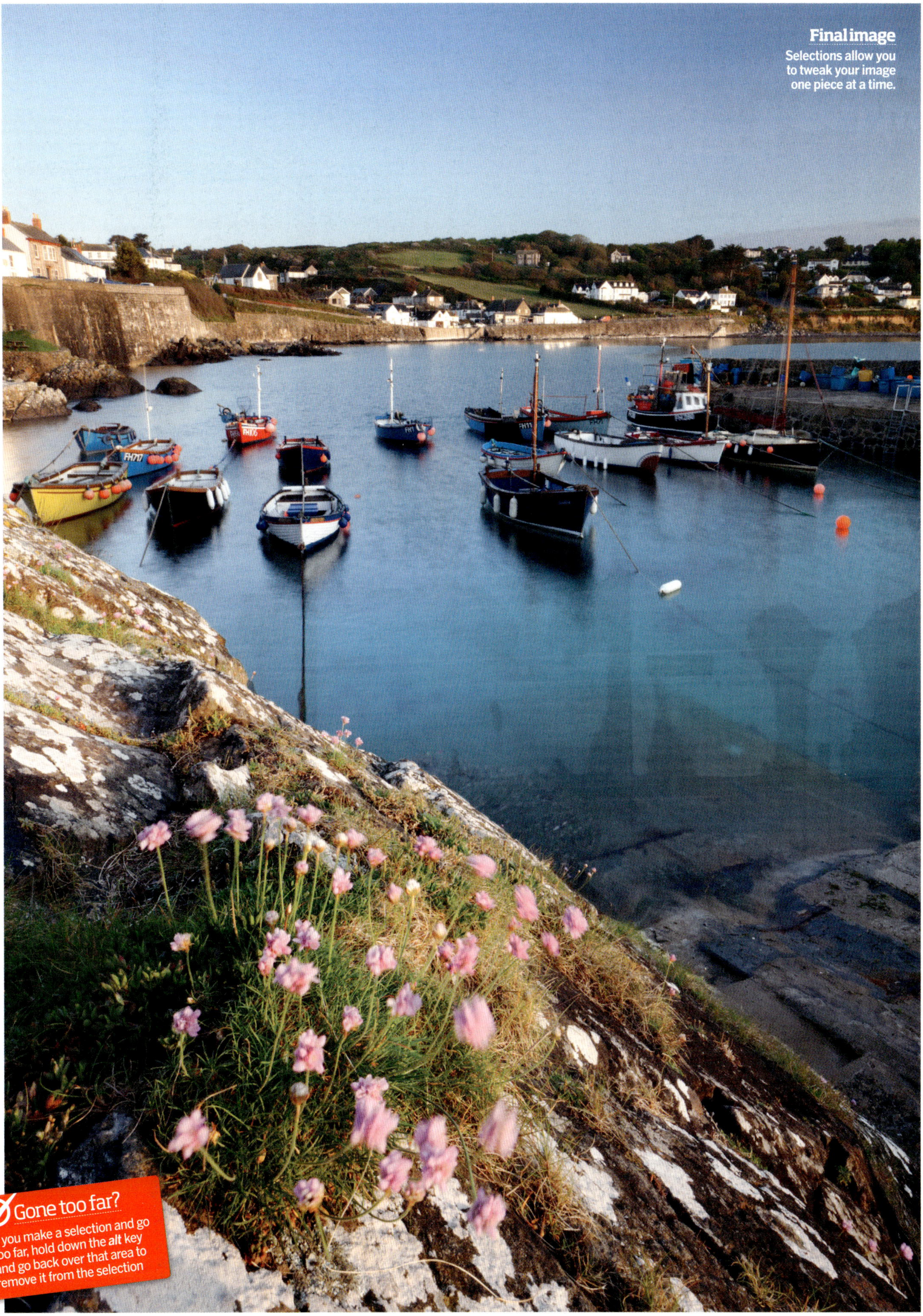

Final image
Selections allow you to tweak your image one piece at a time.

Gone too far?
If you make a selection and go too far, hold down the **alt** key and go back over that area to remove it from the selection

Mastering masking

The real power of Elements is evident when using multiple layers and adjustments. Power is nothing without control and this is where Layer Masks help...

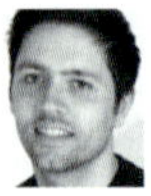

Jordan Butters: The world of multiple layers and masking can be a daunting one if you've never dabbled in them before. However, in reality, the concept of using Layer Masks is incredibly simple – they do exactly as their name implies – they act as a mask in front of a layer, which you can edit and manipulate to reveal as much or as little of the layer as you want. On the surface, masking might sound very similar to using the Eraser Tool – it is, but with one crucial difference: Layer Masks are nondestructive, so any changes you make can be undone without altering the original image.

Layer Masks can be applied to Adjustment Layers, to selectively adjust your image or, depending on the version of Elements that you're using, they can be applied directly to image layers – highly useful when combining two or more exposures, or creating a composite image. Early versions of Elements unfortunately didn't offer this functionality, but see the panel above for a workaround.

Secrets unlocked

✔ MASKING IN EARLIER VERSIONS

Elements 8 and earlier sadly do not offer Layer Masks. There is a workaround, though, which works like this: place your image layer directly on top of a Levels adjustment layer and go to *Layer>Create Clipping Mask*. Then edit the Levels' Layer Mask using the *Brush Tool*. The mask will be applied to both layers, but as no Levels adjustments were made, only the image layer is masked.

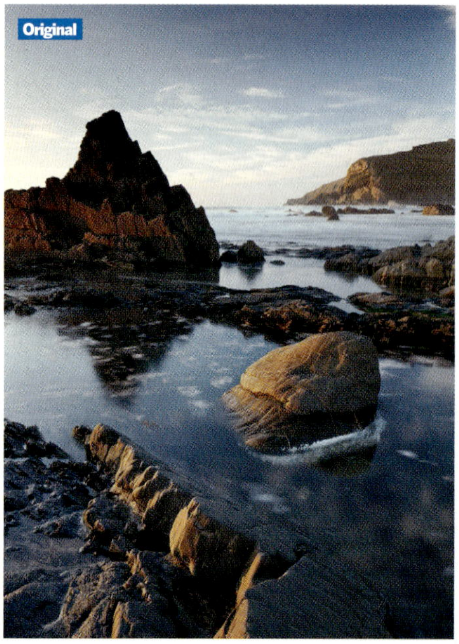

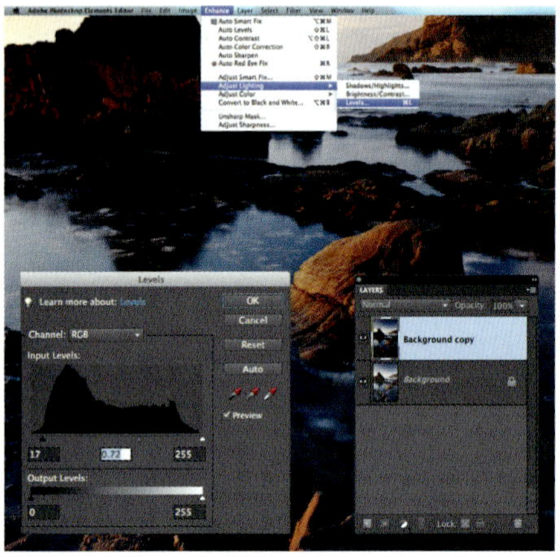

1 Duplicate the image I want to boost the contrast in the sky and water without affecting the rocks in my image. First go to ***Layer>Duplicate Layer***. Then select ***Enhance>Adjust Lighting>Levels*** and tweak the ***Black, Grey*** and ***White*** points to boost the contrast in the image. Once you're done, click ***OK***.

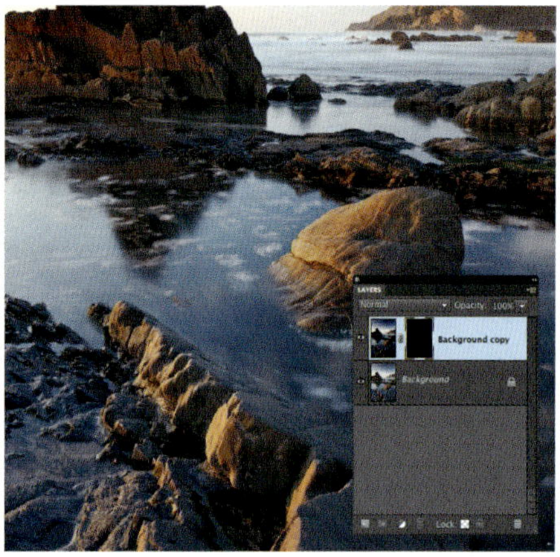

2 Add the Layer Mask Hold down the ***option*** key (Mac), or ***alt*** key (PC) and click on the ***Add layer mask*** button in the Layers palette to add a Hide All Layer Mask – the layer will then be completely hidden. Conversely, if you select the ***Add layer mask*** button without holding down the key, you add a Reveal All Layer Mask.

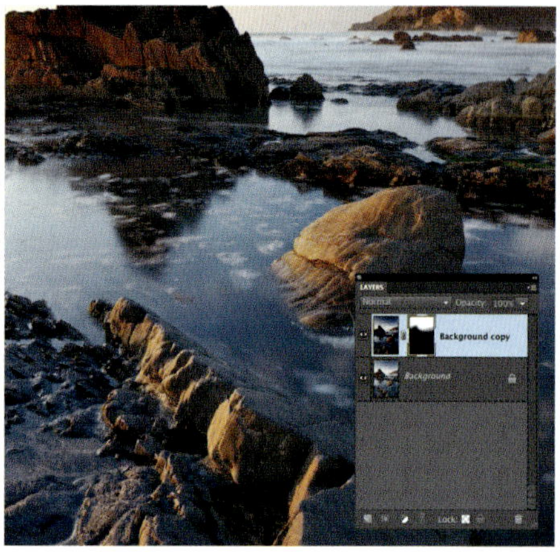

3 Brush onto the mask Select the ***Brush Tool*** and set ***White*** as your ***Foreground Color.*** Use the top toolbar to set the brush ***Size*** and ***Hardness*** and start to brush the sky back in. Use the top menu again to lower the brush ***Opacity*** when approaching the horizon to blend in the higher contrast layer.

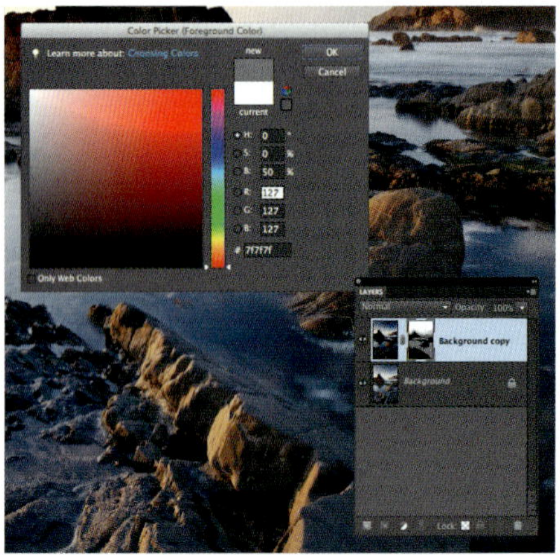

4 Reveal parts of the image Layer Masks can be used to partly reveal a layer at a lower opacity, too. Change your ***Foreground Color*** to a mid-grey and brush onto your image again. Here, I have chosen to use 50% grey on the water in my image to add some of the contrast back in, without going over the top.

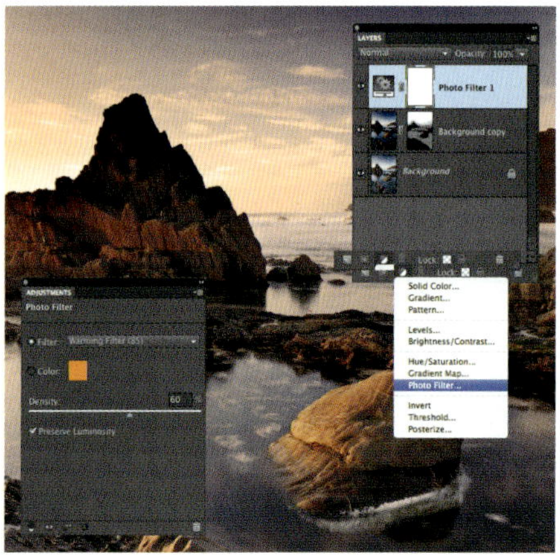

5 Add an Adjustment Layer Layer Masks can also be used with Adjustment Layers. Click on the ***Create new fill or adjustment layer*** button in the Layers palette and then select ***Photo Filter***. I'm going to use a Warming filter to enhance the orange glow on the rocks. Adjust the ***Density*** of the filter to suit your image.

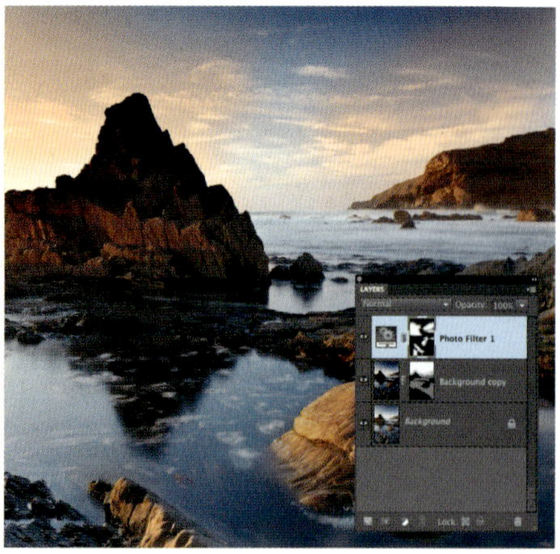

6 Mask the adjustment A Reveal All Layer Mask is automatically added to any Adjustment Layer. Select the ***Brush Tool*** and set ***Black*** as your ***Foreground Color***. Brush over any areas where you don't want the adjustment to be applied – such as the sky, water and shadow areas of the rocks in my image above.

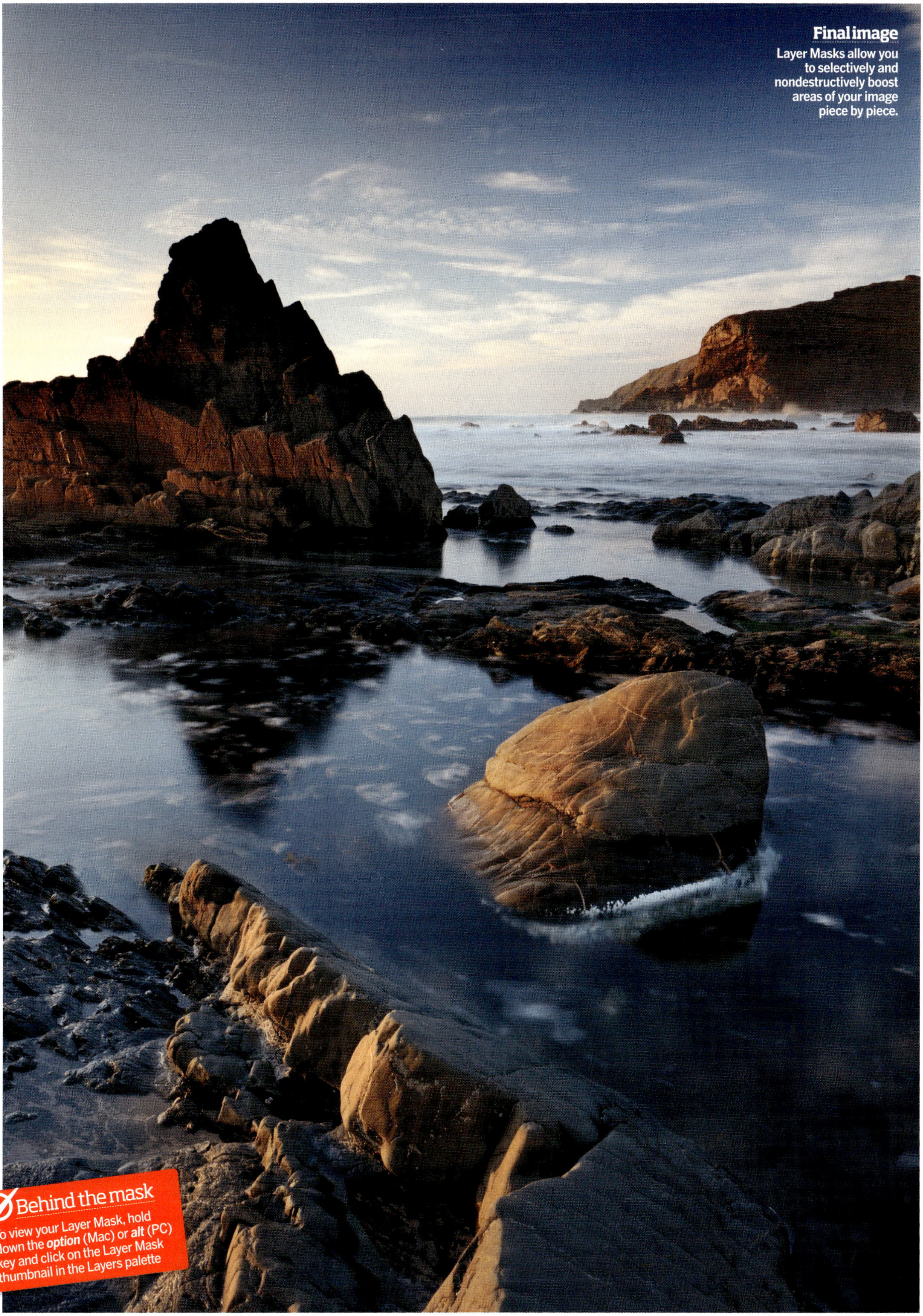

Final image

Layer Masks allow you to selectively and nondestructively boost areas of your image piece by piece.

Behind the mask

To view your Layer Mask, hold down the **option** (Mac) or **alt** (PC) key and click on the Layer Mask thumbnail in the Layers palette

Understanding Levels

Levels: the simple secret to improving contrast and colour. Find out how to master this trouble-free tool to transform your images

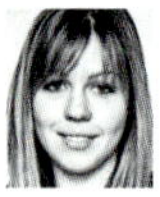

Caroline Wilkinson: If you're new to digital editing you may not have heard of Levels, which is a useful tool to improve the contrast, tweak the exposure and enhance the colours of your images. Levels is an all-in-one solution for these basic adjustments – and it does a great job of it, too. This tutorial presumes that you want to edit a well-exposed JPEG, not a Raw file, which is best done using Raw conversion software to maximise on the detail and dynamic range (see our Raw section on page 80). JPEGs carry less information than Raw files, so they greatly reduce your scope for rescuing an exposure and making edits without damaging image quality. The fewer tweaks to JPEGs, the better.

You may be tempted to use Elements' Quick Edit features, but I suggest bypassing this section and going straight into the Full editing suite to use Adjustment Layers. The Quick Edit one-click adjustments take the hassle out of editing but rarely produce the best results; often blowing highlights to open up shadows or making highlights muddy for the sake of deepening shadows. They also target your image's pixels so the effects are irreversible.

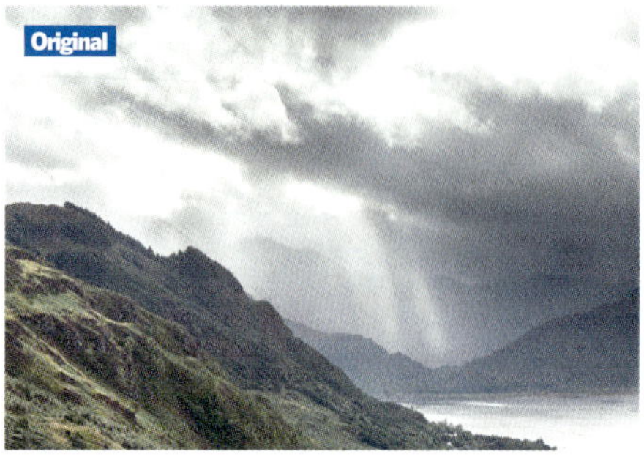

An Adjustment Layer, on the other hand, gives you the flexibility to erase your adjustments at any time, leaving the original pixels untouched and image quality the best it can be. You can also selectively adjust areas of your image using the Adjustment Layer's Layer Mask; it's a slightly more advanced option, requiring more control and judgement over editing decisions, but once you get the hang of working in Elements, it's a technique worth having in your arsenal for images that need a bit more attention before print.

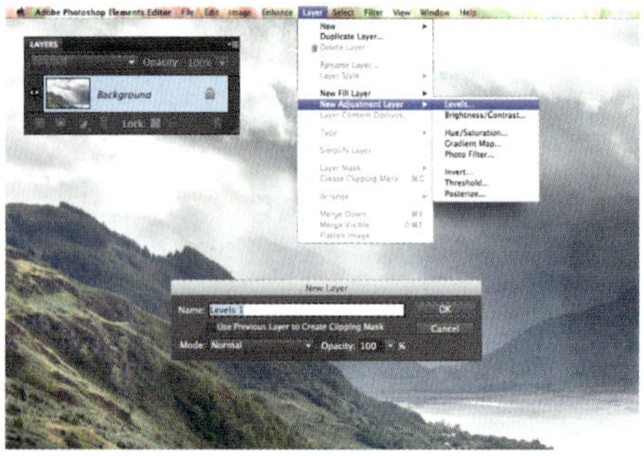

1 Access Levels You'll need your Layers palette open (***Windows>Layers***). Now add a Levels adjustment layer (***Layer>New Adjustment Layer>Levels***), when the New Layer dialogue box appears, click ***OK***. You should not only see a new layer appear in your Layers palette but a large dialogue box displaying a histogram – this is the exposure histogram for your image; the same as you would see on your camera's LCD.

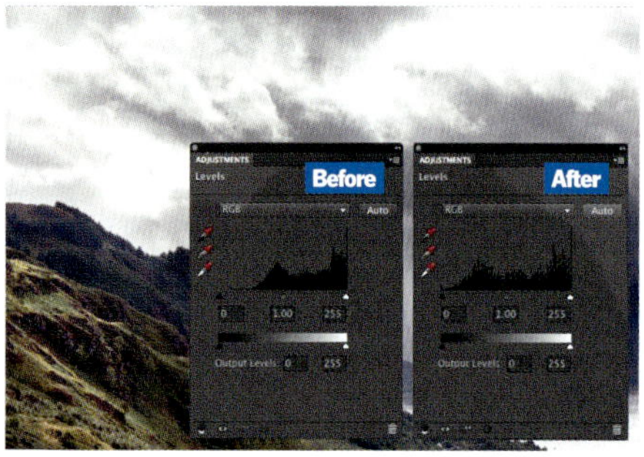

2 Assess your image For an average scene that doesn't bias the shadows or highlights, you want a histogram that runs from the far right to the far left, so your blacks are true black and your whites are true white. The 'Before' histogram doesn't look like this, causing the image to be flat and colours dull. Click ***Auto*** to see how it changes your image. Our 'After' shot shows the shadows and highlights more evenly spread.

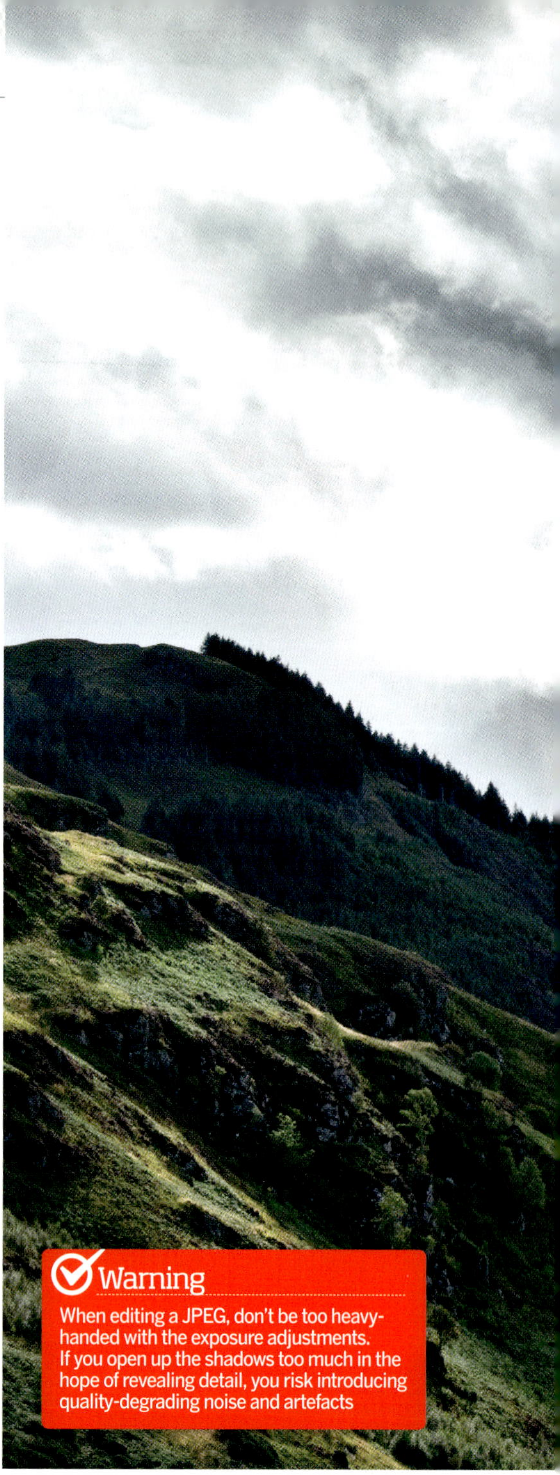

Warning

When editing a JPEG, don't be too heavy-handed with the exposure adjustments. If you open up the shadows too much in the hope of revealing detail, you risk introducing quality-degrading noise and artefacts

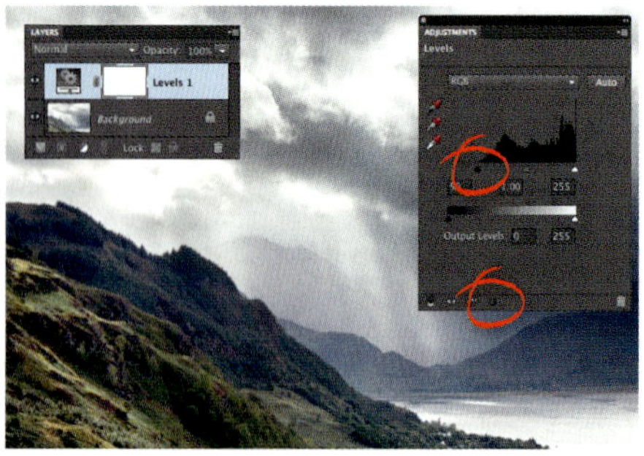

3 Take control If Auto improves the contrast and colour sufficiently, you could close the dialogue box and leave your editing there. If not, click the ***Reset to adjustment default*** button at the bottom of the Adjustment panel and move the black slider to the right so it's at the edge of the histogram and the white slider similarly to the left; you should see an instant improvement to the tonal range and depth of the colours.

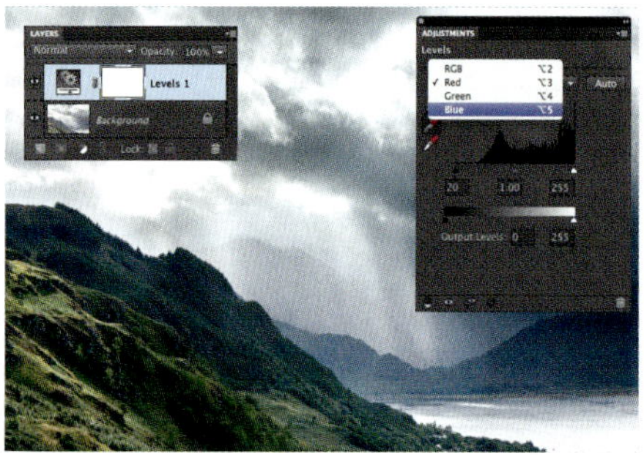

4 Target colour If your image has taken on a slight colour cast, or you want to adjust the colours in your image, you can also do this using Levels. One way is to select the middle ***Eyedropper tool*** and to click on an area of grey/mid-tone to set the White Balance. Alternatively, you can target the tonality of Red, Green and Blue independently via the ***Channel*** drop-down menu, which as default will show as RGB.

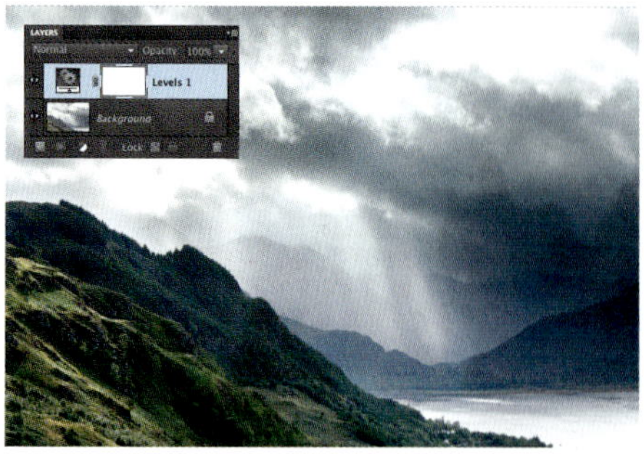

5 Take the next step Beginners might find this level of editing sufficent and want to finish the tutorial at step four; others may find these advanced steps worth mastering. If you have an image like this one, where making the sky stronger leaves the foreground underexposed, or vice versa, you can use the Layer Mask attached to the Levels adjustment layer in your Layers palette to edit your adjustment to affect only one or the other.

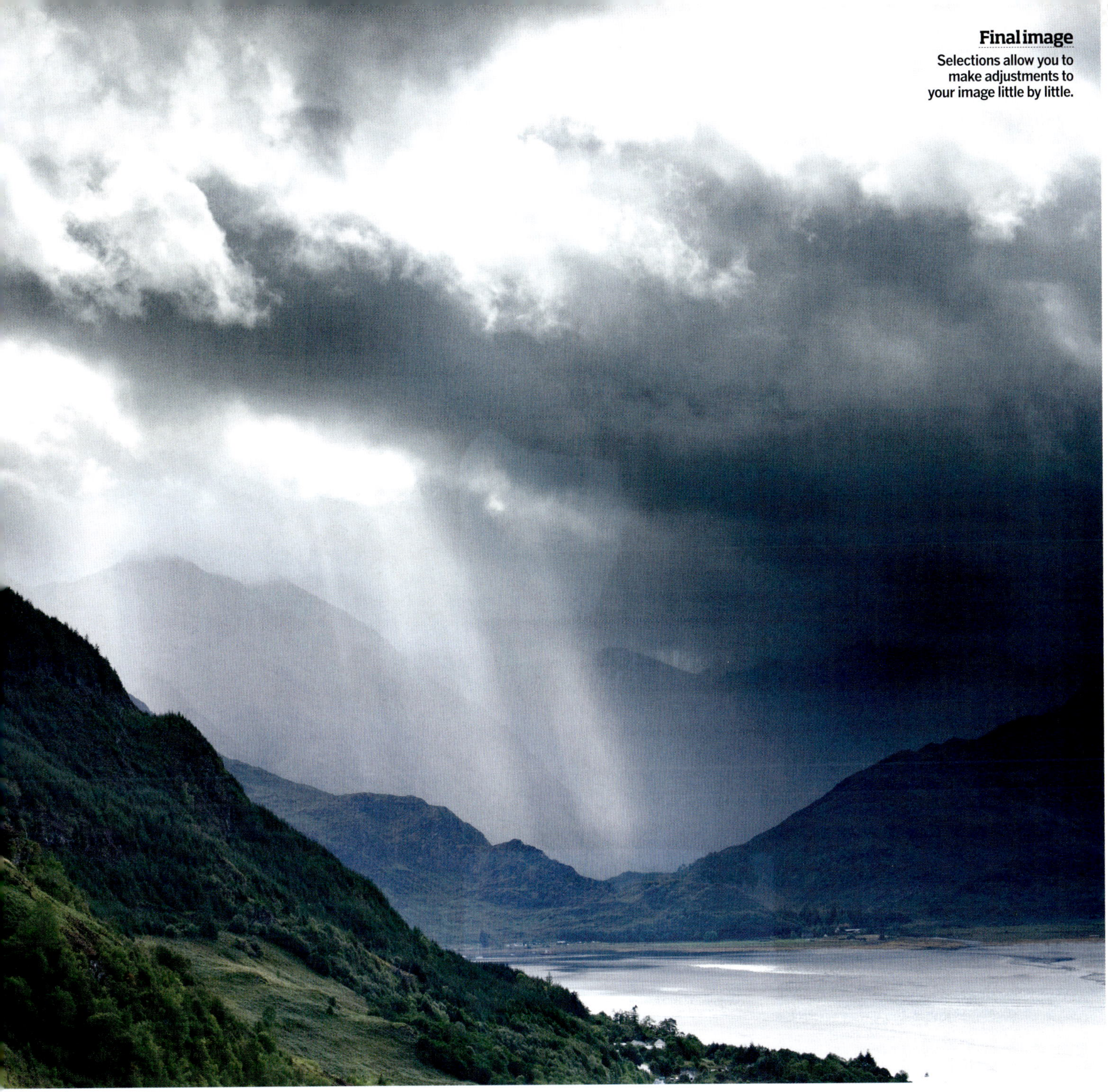

Final image
Selections allow you to make adjustments to your image little by little.

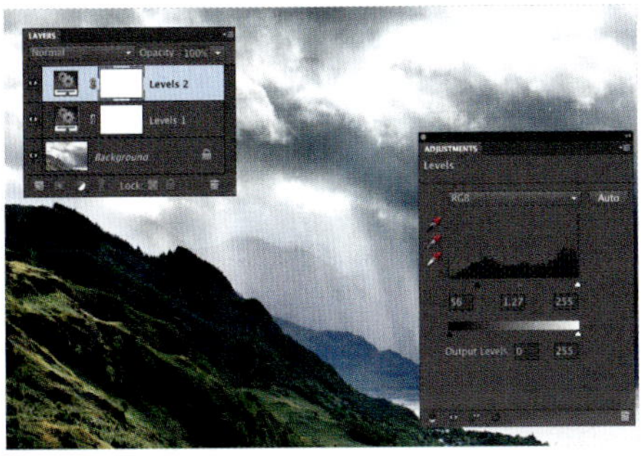

6 Use the Layer Mask Here, the tonality of the foreground has been improved but the sky and misty background could look better in areas. To target the sky separately, add a new ***Levels*** adjustment layer and tweak by only focusing on this section, ignoring any effect on the foreground. Once you're happy, select the ***Brush Tool***, make sure ***Foreground Color*** is set to ***Black***, the edges are soft and ***Opacity*** is ***100%***.

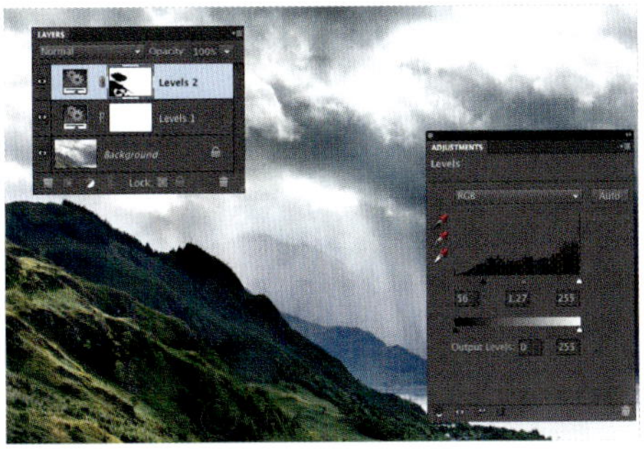

7 Edit the sky Click on the ***Layer Mask*** next to your new Adjustment Layer to activate it, and then start to brush over the foreground to reveal your first Levels-adjusted image. When you come to the edges of where the foreground and sky meet, try lowering the ***Opacity*** slider to ***40-50%***, zooming into the image and selecting a smaller brush to ensure your editing creates a smooth graduation between the two sections.

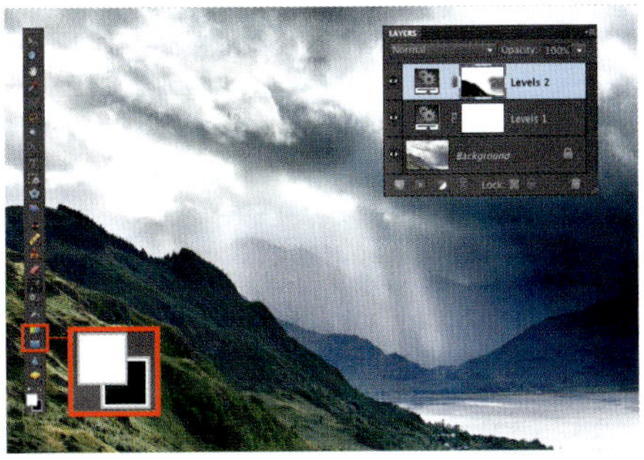

8 Adjust your process Repeat this process for as many parts of the image that need individual attention. For better control, use a low ***Opacity*** brush. If you make a mistake at any point, switch the ***Color*** from ***Black*** to ***White*** and go over the area again on the Layer Mask to restore the original state. You can delete the Adjustment Layers if they're no longer needed or double-click on them to re-edit the histogram.

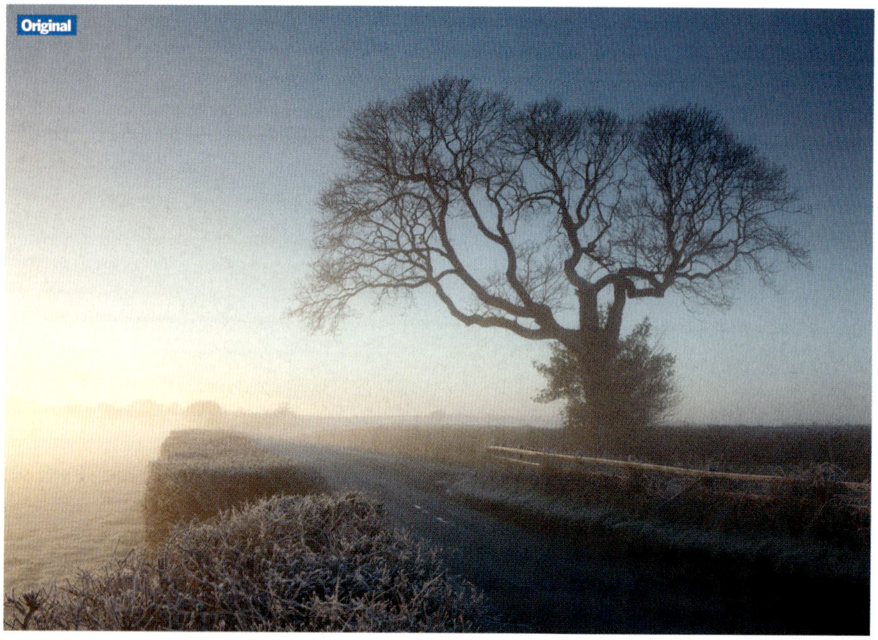

Increase contrast using Adjustment Layers

Are your images in need of a contrast boost? Find out how to add extra punch to colours using Adjustment Layers and Blend Modes

Jordan Butters: Mist and fog add a wonderful atmosphere to images. Nothing quite conveys the mood of a chilly autumn or winter morning like the early morning sun piercing through a beautiful heavy haze.

More often than not, though, misty landscapes are hindered by a lack of contrast. Not to worry, though, as with the addition of an Adjustment Layer and some experimentation with Blend Modes, you can apply the punch to your misty landscape images. While this tutorial has been done in Elements 10, the same features and methods can be applied to images being worked on in Photoshop CS as well. Similarly, some CS tutorials in this guide can be done in Elements, too.

Nondestructive editing

✓ ADJUSTMENT LAYERS

We usually advise duplicating your original image layer before you start editing, just in case you make a mistake. However, a major benefit of Adjustment Layers is that they are nondestructive, meaning any changes you make do not affect the original image data. What's more, the parameters and values of an Adjustment Layer can be tweaked in the Adjustment palette at any time throughout the editing process, or if you're not entirely happy with the effect, you can simply delete that Adjustment Layer and start afresh.

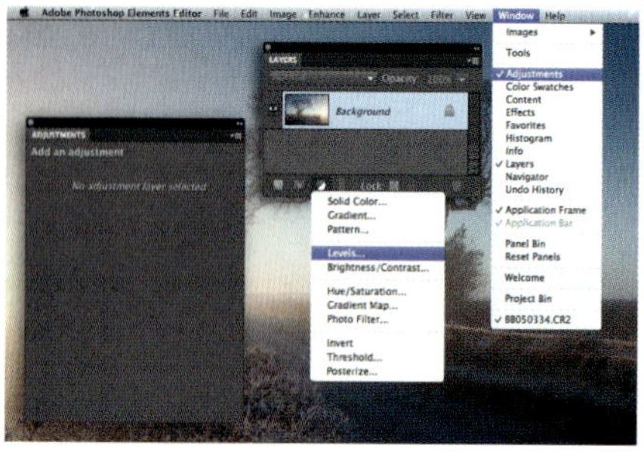

1 Add an Adjustment Layer You'll need the Layers and Adjustments palettes visible, so first go to the ***Window*** menu and make sure that both ***Adjustments*** and ***Layers*** are ticked. Then click on the ***Create new fill or adjustment layer*** button at the bottom of the Layers palette and, in the drop-down menu that appears, select ***Levels***.

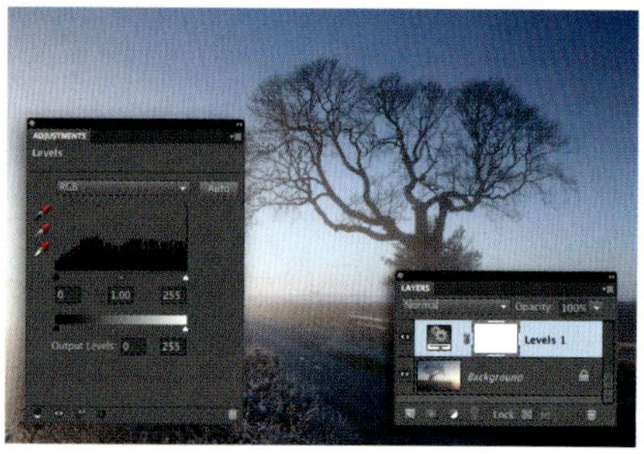

2 Try the Auto feature In the Adjustments palette, first try using the ***Auto*** button to allow the software to decide which adjustments should be made to your image. This works better on some images than it does on others. The Auto levels tool adjusts each of the Red, Green and Blue channels independently so you may notice a colour cast appear in your image.

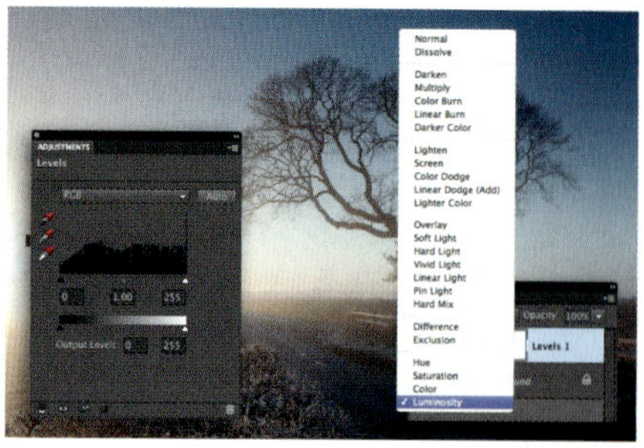

3 Correct the colour To correct the colour cast, make sure that the ***Levels*** layer in the Layers palette is selected and, using the Blend Mode menu at the top, change the ***Blend Mode*** of the layer to ***Luminosity***. This will remove the image's colour cast by ensuring that the Adjustment Layer only affects the contrast in the image below it and not the colours.

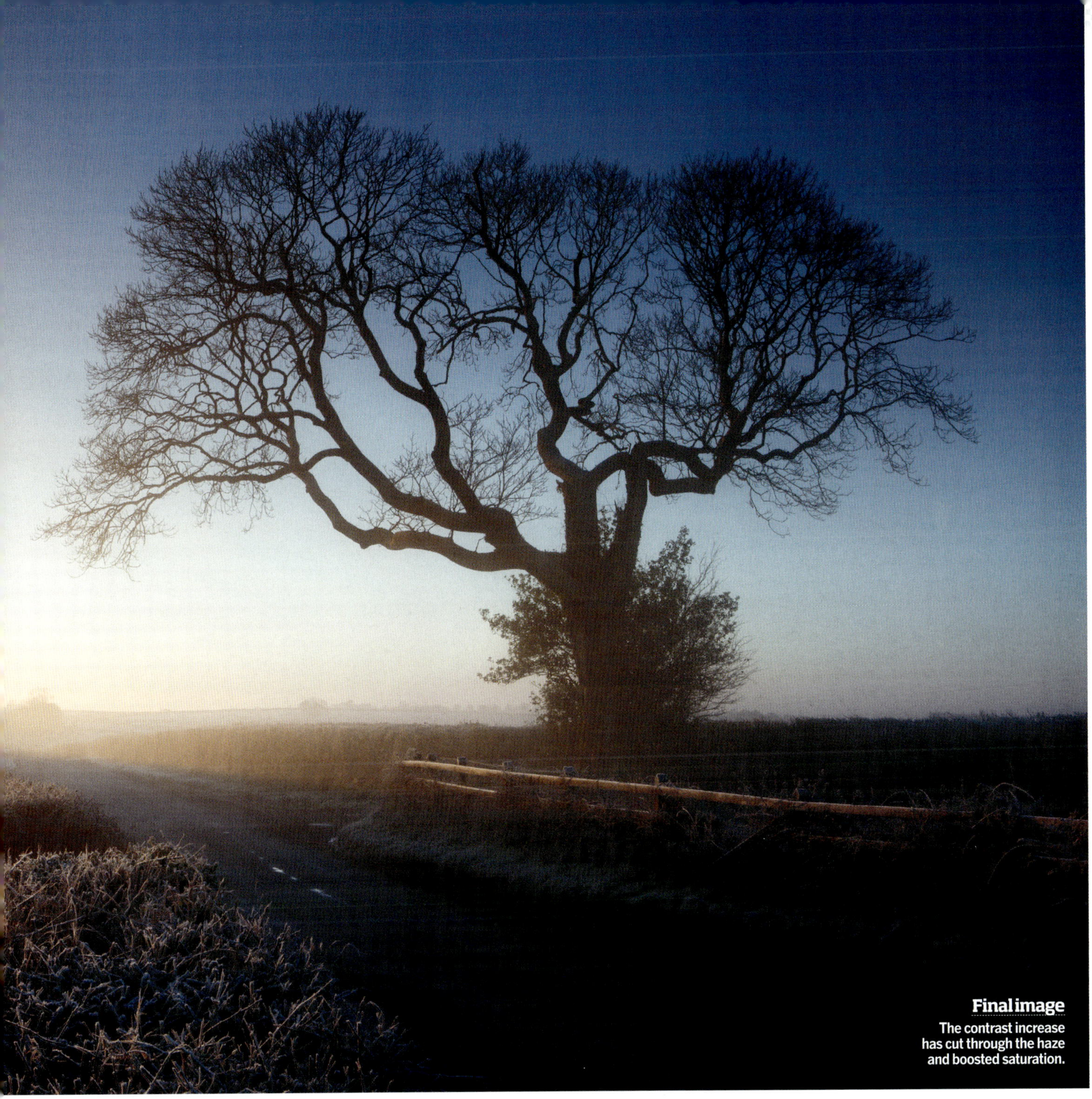

Final image
The contrast increase has cut through the haze and boosted saturation.

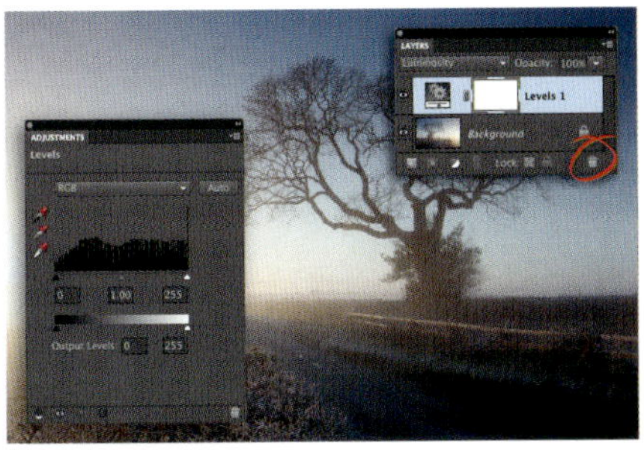

4 Try a manual adjustment If you aren't happy with the effect from using Auto levels, delete your Adjustment Layer by clicking on it in the Layers palette and dragging it to the ***Delete layer*** icon at the bottom; this reverts the image back to its original state. Add another Adjustment Layer by clicking on the ***Create new fill or adjustment layer*** button and selecting ***Levels***.

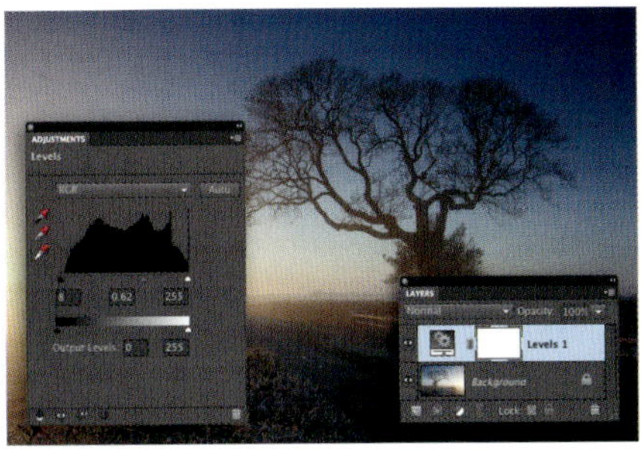

5 Manually set Levels This time, rather than using the Auto adjustment, click and drag on the ***black***, ***grey*** and ***white*** point sliders in the Adjustments palette to tweak the contrast of your image. Be careful how far you push the black and white points so you don't clip the shadows and highlights and lose detail. You can be more liberal with the grey slider for the mid-tones.

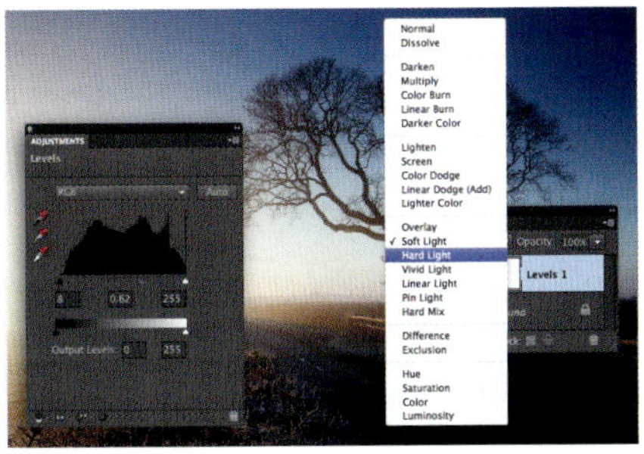

6 Experiment with Blend Modes Back in the Layers palette, experiment with the different ***Blend Modes*** to alter the effect. ***Overlay, Soft Light*** and ***Hard Light*** will all offer slightly different effects. You can also use the ***Opacity*** slider at the top of the Layers palette to weaken the effect or you can revisit the Adjustment palette at any time to tweak the parameters.

Target colour casts & improve saturation

Increasing the vibrancy of your shots is an easy task in Photoshop and in this tutorial we reveal a simple method for making improvements to colour

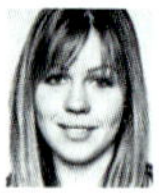

Caroline Wilkinson: When was the last time one of your photos looked as good – or even better – on screen as it did in the flesh? Can't remember? That's no surprise. Each camera produces colour and contrast differently and it depends how you set them up as to how accurate or saturated the colours are. Even the cameras with superb colour rendition can produce images lacking vitality – especially in Raw format where no in-camera presets have been applied. This is why tone and colour adjustments are the main reasons photographers post-process their images as the smallest adjustments can draw life out of a picture and make a huge difference to its impact.

A colour cast is very common and is usually the first thing that gets corrected. You can get one if you've used the wrong White Balance for the light temperature, shot in mixed lighting or had light reflect off a coloured surface – you might not even realise you have one until you come to correct it, which is why it's my first step in this tutorial. After that you'd probably adjust your tonal contrast using Levels or Curves, but I say focus on the colour. By improving saturation and your image's vibrance, you might find that you don't have to increase tonal contrast as much. Contrast adjustments will also increase colour saturation, so if you want to give your colour more attention, tackle this independently first for best results.

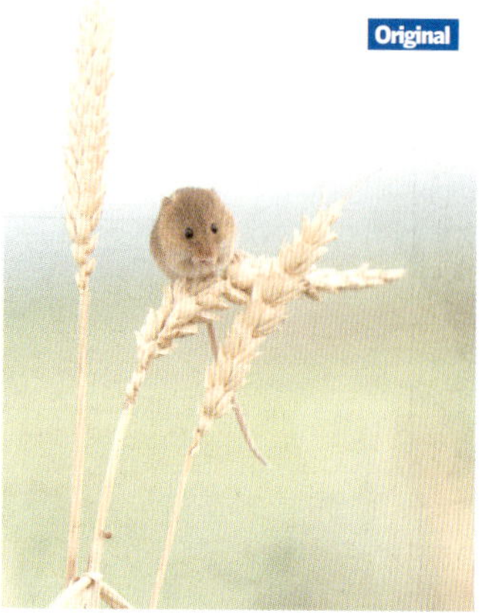

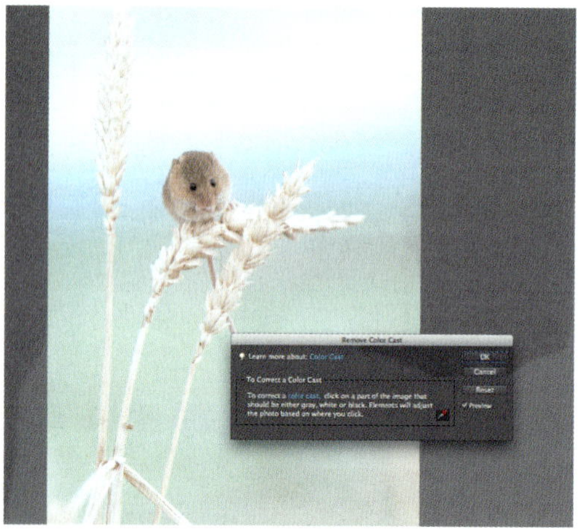

1 Remove any colour casts Before you can start intensifying the colour in your images, you need to make sure you've got the base colours that you want to work with correct and that means getting rid of any colour casts. If you've shot in Raw, I'd advise changing the White Balance in Adobe Camera Raw, but if you've shot in JPEG, go to ***Enhance>Adjust Color>Remove Color Cast*** and use the eyedropper to click on an area of white, grey or black to get the colour temperature that you want.

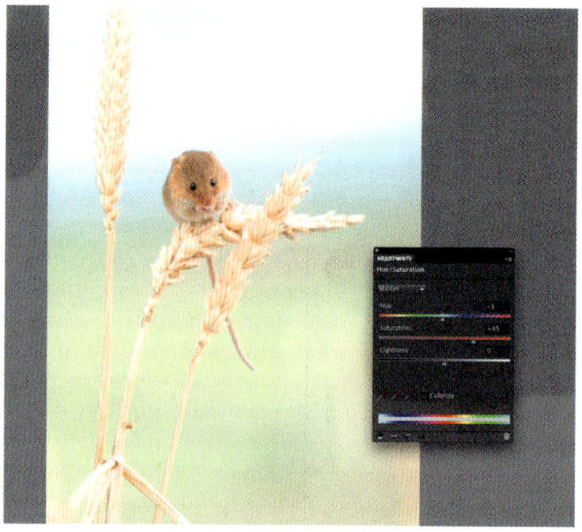

2 Adjust saturation Now with your base image correct, go to ***Layer>New Adjustment Layer>Hue/Saturation***. When possible, it's always best to use an Adjustment Layer rather than apply an adjustment directly to an image as it means that you can go back to re-edit the Adjustment Layer at any time. Move the ***Saturation*** slider as far as you want to the right. Don't be concerned if certain areas get oversaturated – this can be corrected later – at this stage aim to have most of the image at an ideal saturation.

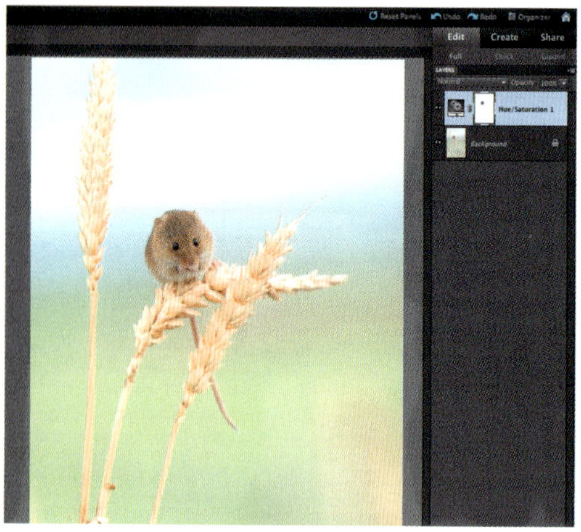

3 Edit the adjustment Once you're happy, close the Adjustment panel. In the Layers palette you'll see the Adjustment Layer has a Layer Mask attached. Select the ***Brush Tool*** and ***Black*** paint, an appropriate sized brush, and take the ***Opacity*** down to ***30-40%***. With the ***Layer Mask*** selected, brush over where you want to reduce the intensity of the colour. In this case, the dormouse. Use ***White*** paint to put colour back in. Then select both layers and press ***cmd, alt, shift*** and **E** to merge into a new layer.

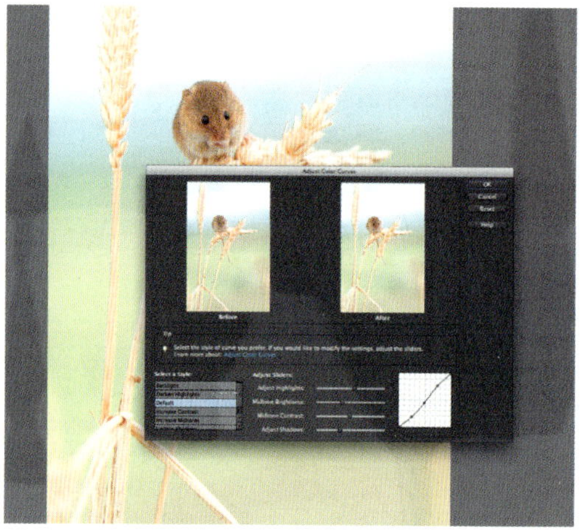

4 Adjust contrast With the new layer selected, go to ***Enhance>Adjust Color>Adjust Color Curves...*** This feature is there to help you improve your colour tones by targeting highlights, mid-tones and shadows. You can use one of the presets or adjust the sliders for custom settings – personally I get better results using the sliders as they offer more control. If you wanted to target a specific area of your image, select it using a selection tool before accessing ***Color Curves***. When you're happy, press ***OK***.

Presets

Elements 10 has a selection of preset treatments, one of which is ***Saturated Slide Film Effect***. To access it, click on the ***Guided*** tab under ***Edit*** and then the ***Photography Effects*** drop-down menu to select the effect to apply. Each effect comes with a brief user guide, but in many respects they're one-click wonders offering little control. In the case of Saturated Slide Film Effect, all you need to do is click ***Apply*** as many times as you want to intensify the effect. To see the before and after image, change the ***View*** preset in the bottom left-hand corner of the screen. Click ***Done*** when you're happy. Back at ***Edit>Full*** you'll see that each time you clicked ***Apply*** you added a new image layer to the Layers palette; you can now delete layers or use Layer Masks to edit the effect as you see fit.

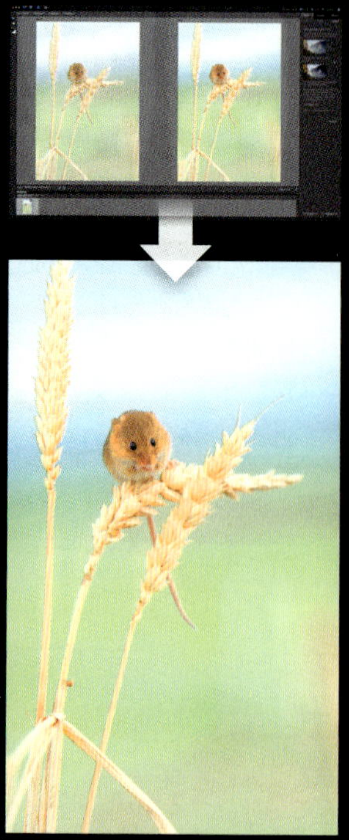

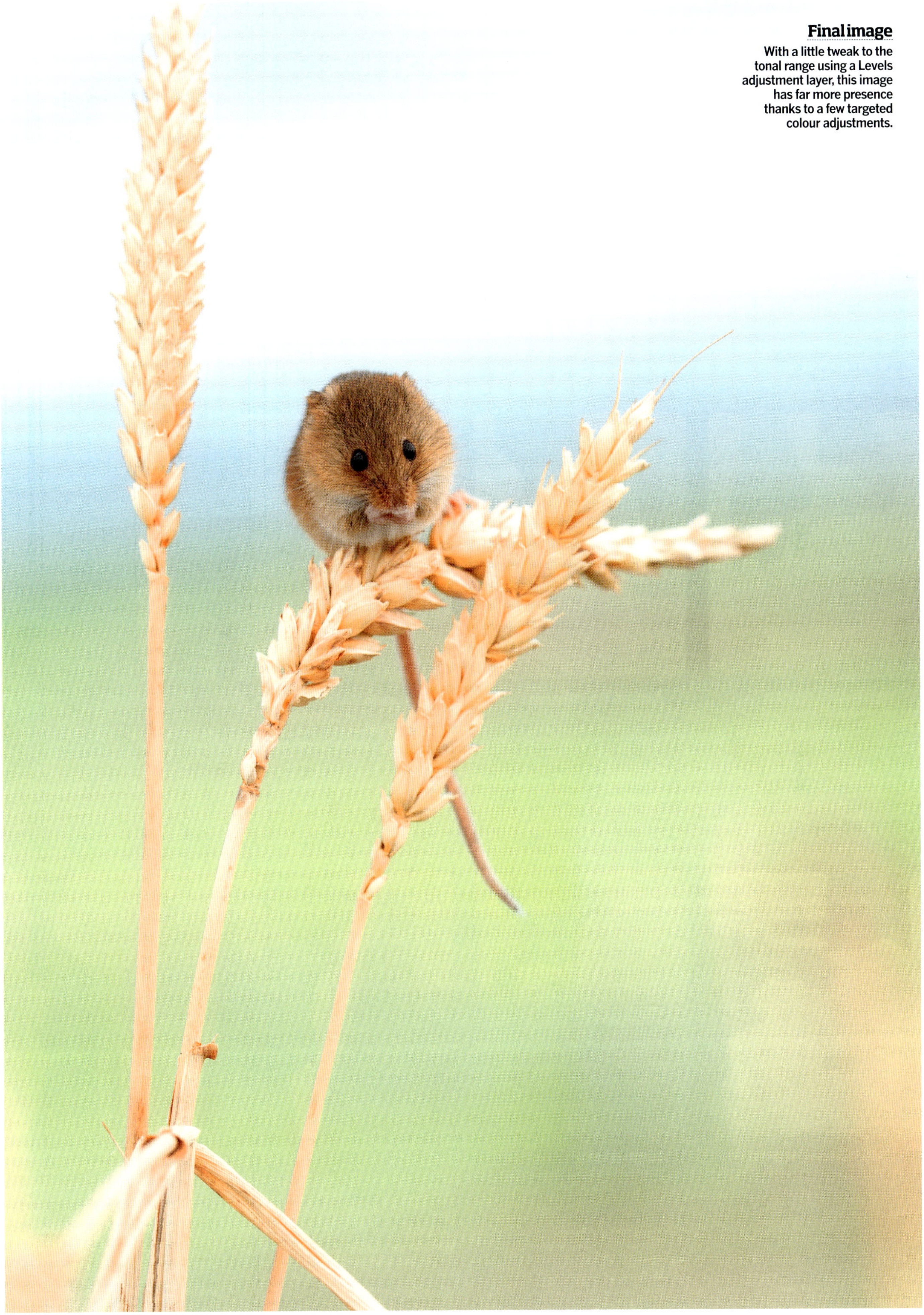

Final image

With a little tweak to the tonal range using a Levels adjustment layer, this image has far more presence thanks to a few targeted colour adjustments.

Simple steps to a punchy black & white

Puzzled by how to make your images more powerful and full of impact? Fear not. We've got some easy steps to show you the secrets of contrast…

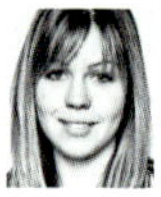

Caroline Wilkinson: Without bright sunshine to give a scene contrast, many outdoor photographs look lacklustre straight out of camera, with a bias to the mid-tones; not what you often want for a punchy image. You need brilliant whites and rich blacks, with an even distribution of mid-tones, to avoid dull and lifeless images. Obviously some images suit more highlights than shadows and vice versa – depending on personal taste and the style of picture – but here we'll assume that we want a range of tones and punchy contrast.

There are many ways to add contrast in post-production, and it's easy to go over the top – so watch out for detail being lost in the shadows and highlights. You'll have much more flexibility if you shoot in Raw, rather than JPEG, because of the amount of information stored in the file: but that doesn't mean you shouldn't get the exposure right in-camera as much as possible first. ACR is a great place to develop your base image, but don't leave your editing there. Open it in Elements to refine the contrast selectively and use tools like Levels and Shadows/Highlights for more control. Brightness/Contrast is good for final tweaks, not major adjustments.

Contrast is never more important than with a black & white image as it relies on strong tones for impact. For this reason, while these techniques can be applied to colour photos, I've added a black & white conversion to the tutorial so that you know how to create beautiful mono images, too.

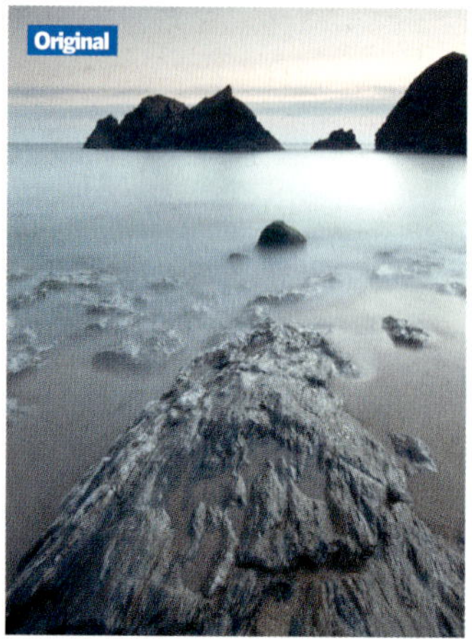

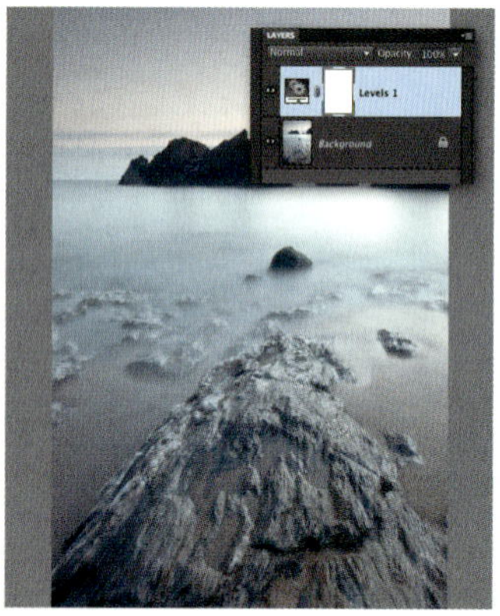

1 Inspect the histogram Once you've opened your image in Elements, add a Levels adjustment layer (***Layer>New Adjustment Layer>Levels***) to evaluate the exposure using the histogram. As you can see here, the histogram is weighted to the left, so the image has more highlights than shadows and looks a little dull, so could benefit with a contrast boost.

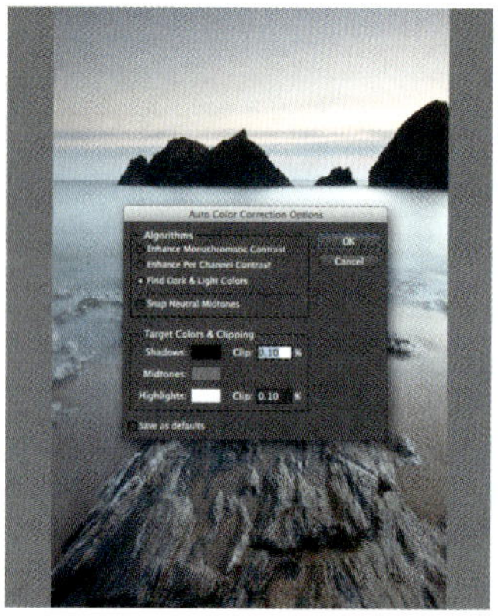

2 Improve the exposure For a scene with a balanced tonal range, the pixels should stretch across the full length of the histogram, rather than bunch at either end. If they sit just in the centre, the picture will probably look quite dull and will be lacking in contrast. Click ***Auto*** now – it's the first step you should take to improve the image's contrast, exposure and colour.

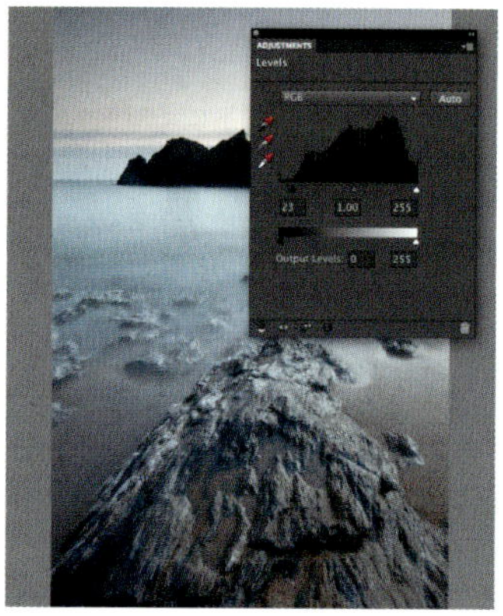

3 Use Levels When clicking ***Auto***, if you hold down ***cmd/option*** you can access further edits that allow more control over the automatic function. If you want to manually control Levels, click on the black triangle and move it to the left until it's in line with the first peak, or just before you start to lose detail in the shadows. Do the same with the white triangle if needed.

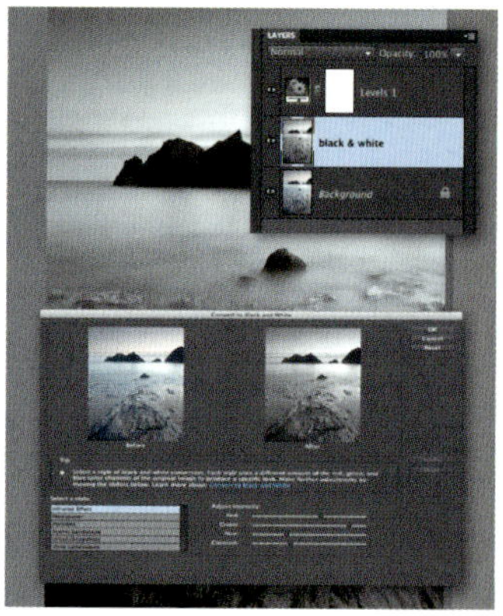

4 Convert to mono Duplicate the image (***Layer>Duplicate Layer***) so you're not working on the original pixels, and name it something suitable, such as Black & White. Go to ***Enhance>Convert to Black & White*** to open the monochrome control panel. You can pick a preset or manually control the contrast by altering colour channels (***Red, Green, Blue*** sliders) and the ***Contrast*** slider.

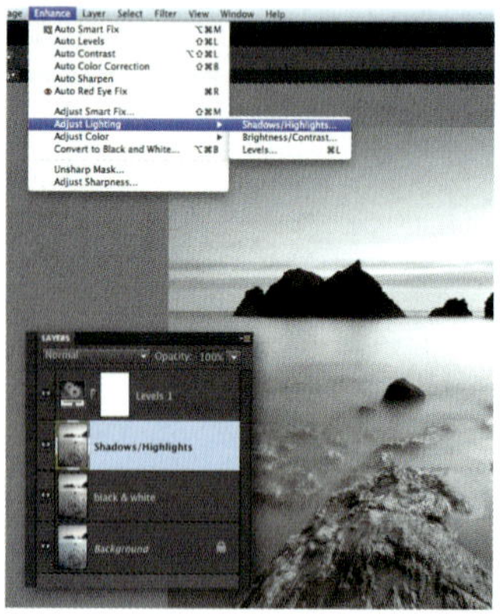

5 Apply Shadows/Highlights By boosting the contrast you may find that areas of your image lose detail in the shadows or highlights, so a little bit of selective editing may be needed if the rest of the image looks fine. For this, first duplicate your black & white layer (***Layer>Duplicate Layer***) and then go to ***Enhance>Adjust Lighting>Shadows/Highlights***.

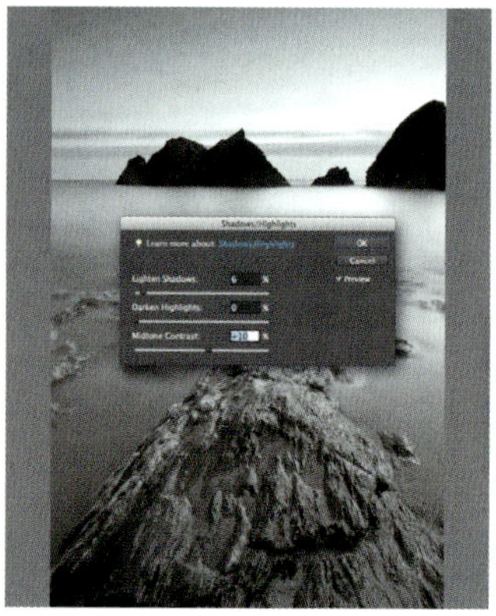

6 Target an area If there are areas that could be improved, target them now. To reveal detail in the distant rocks, adjust the sliders – ignoring the effect on the rest of the image. ***Lighten Shadows*** reveals shadow detail, while ***Darken Highlights*** reveals highlight detail. Use ***Midtone Contrast*** only if the contrast doesn't look right after using Shadows and Highlights.

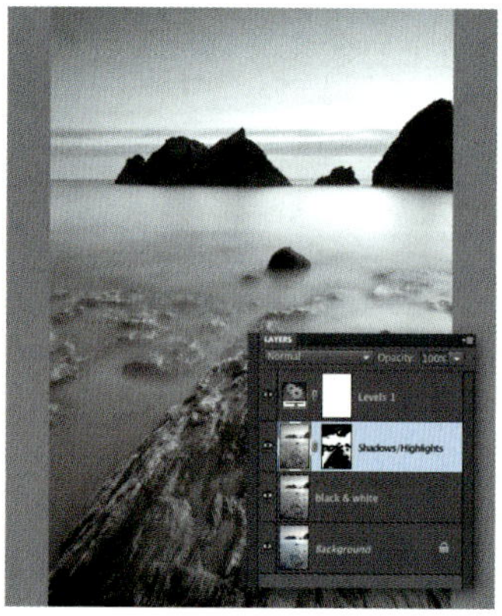

7 Use a Layer Mask Once you're happy with the adjustments you've made, click ***OK***, then click on the ***Add new Layer Mask*** icon at the bottom of the Layers palette. Select the ***Brush Tool***, ***Black*** paint, and an appropriate ***Hardness*** and ***Size*** for the area/s you want to target. Brush over the areas of the image that you don't want affected by the Shadows/Highlights adjustment.

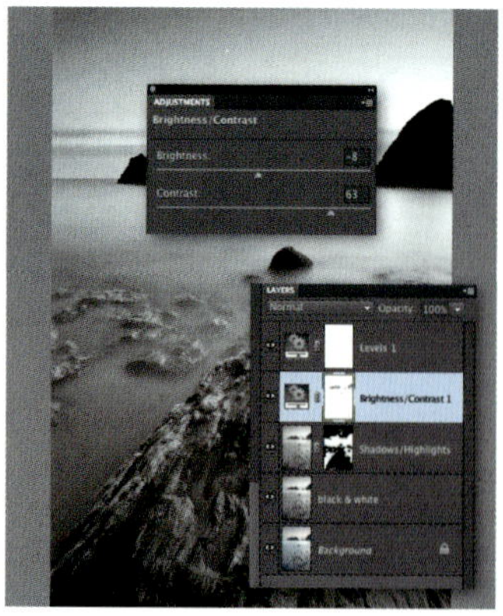

8 Extra boost If you feel that your image needs an extra punch in contrast, you can add a ***Brightness/Contrast*** adjustment layer (just a different method of exposure control) or double-click on your ***Levels*** adjustment layer to re-edit it. Both come with a Layer Mask attached, so you can repeat step seven to selectively reduce the contrast where you feel it's necessary.

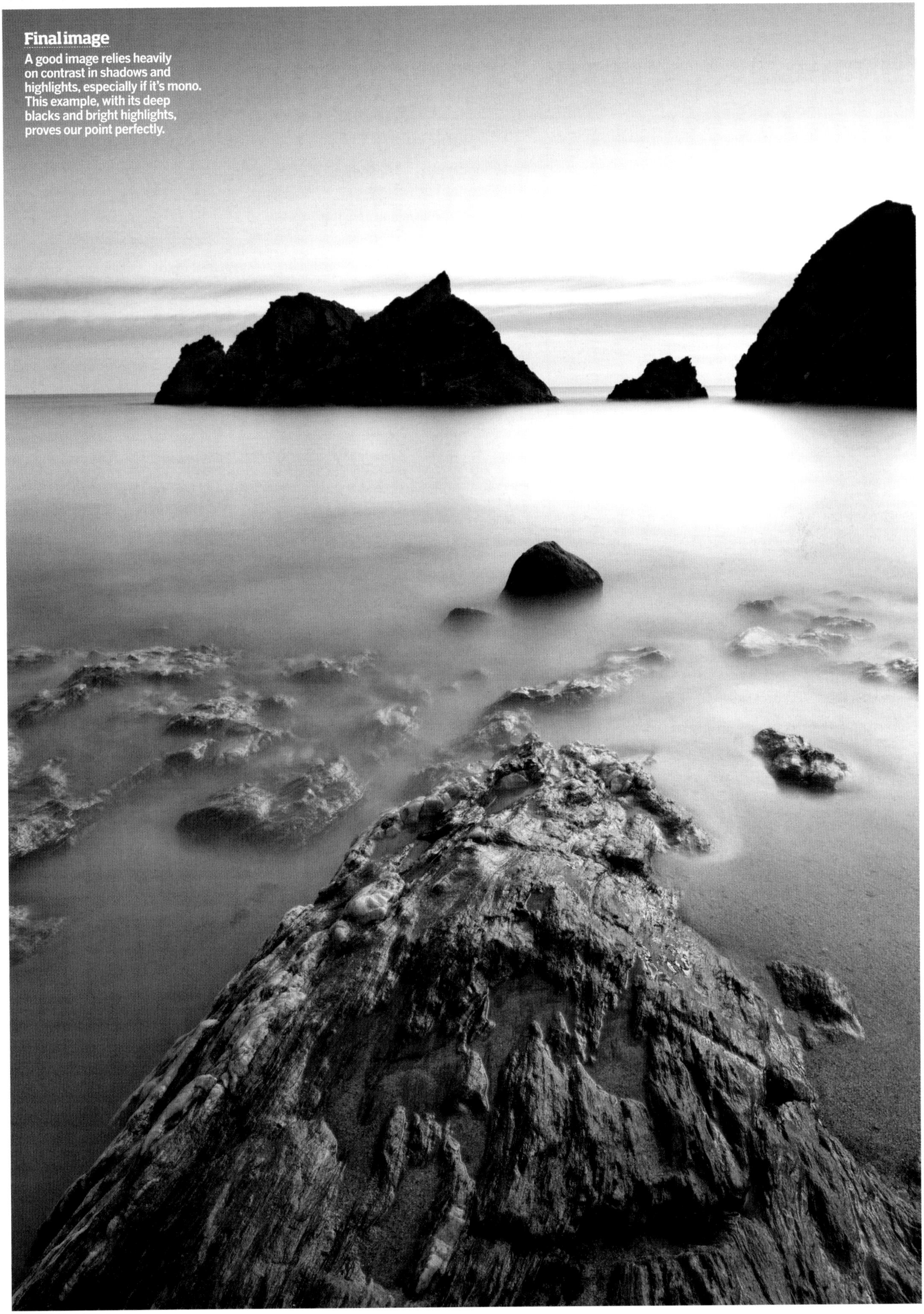

Final image

A good image relies heavily on contrast in shadows and highlights, especially if it's mono. This example, with its deep blacks and bright highlights, proves our point perfectly.

Six steps to better portraits

Find out how being smart with your portrait retouching in Photoshop Elements 10 can make your editing easier than ever

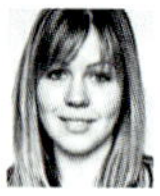

Caroline Wilkinson: Retouching portraits is usually the one editing tutorial photographers yearn to know more about. With mountains of megapixels in our modern DSLRs, the detail they capture is incredible and somewhat unforgiving. Unless you're photographing one of the rare few with a flawless complexion, every portrait you shoot will need some degree of retouching if you want a flattering, more attractive image. Faces wear the sins of our night-before antics, hectic schedules and junk-food diets, but with a little Photoshop help you can make your subject look the glossy and healthier version of themselves, and give you a more pleasing image.

Elements 10 has really made portrait retouching easy for you. Its Smart Brush and Detail Smart Brush Tools offer you several actions that can make editing simple. It's worth exploring these tools to see what features they offer to benefit your other images, too, but for the sake of this article we'll concentrate on the Portrait presets.

Useful tools

✓QUICK ACCESS

Coloured icons appear on your image when you make a new edit. If you click on one it will navigate you to the corresponding layer and Layer Mask – it's a really useful tool if you end up with dozens of layers.

Personally, I prefer the Detail Smart Brush as you can paint the adjustment on to the face, whereas the Smart Brush Tool creates a selection. Try both to see which you prefer. When you make an adjustment with these tools, it automatically creates an Adjustment Layer and Layer Mask, which means any edits you make don't affect the original image and are fully editable at any point during the process. The Smart Brush Tools are divided into three: New Selection, Add Selection and Subtract from Selection. As default, it will be set to Add Selection, but if you wish to undo one of your edits, simply switch to Subtract from Selection in the top toolbar and brush back over the area. Before you start any retouching, though, apply exposure or contrast adjustments to create a solid base image. Now off you go…

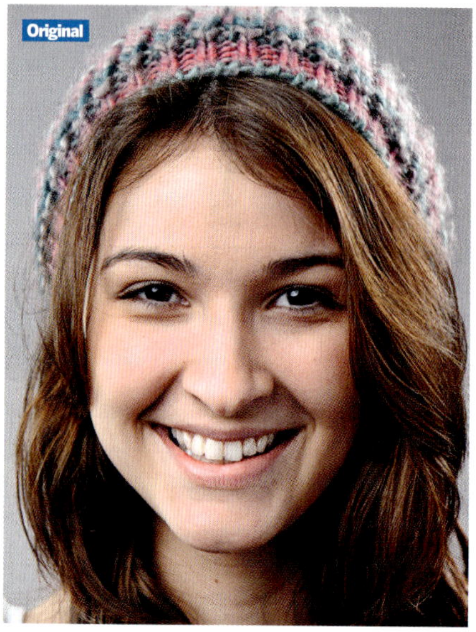

ISTOCK PHOTO

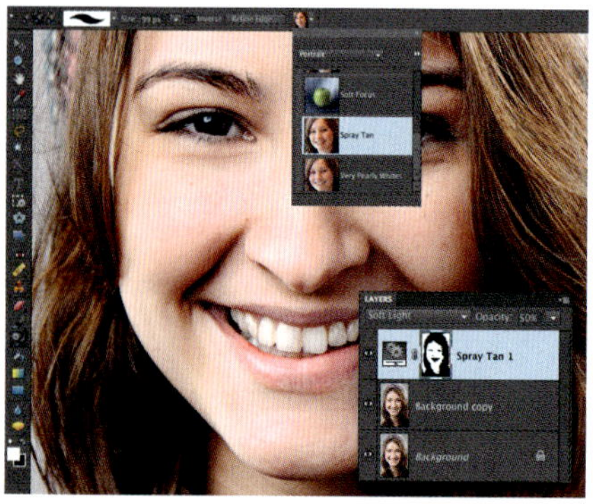

1 Access the tools Use the ***Spot Healing Brush Tool*** to remove any obvious blemishes from the skin. Now click on the ***Smart Brush Tool*** in the toolbar and select the ***Detail Smart Brush Tool*** underneath. In the far right of the top toolbar, click on the white picker arrow (by the picture box) to access features. Click the ***All Purpose*** drop-down menu and select ***Portrait***.

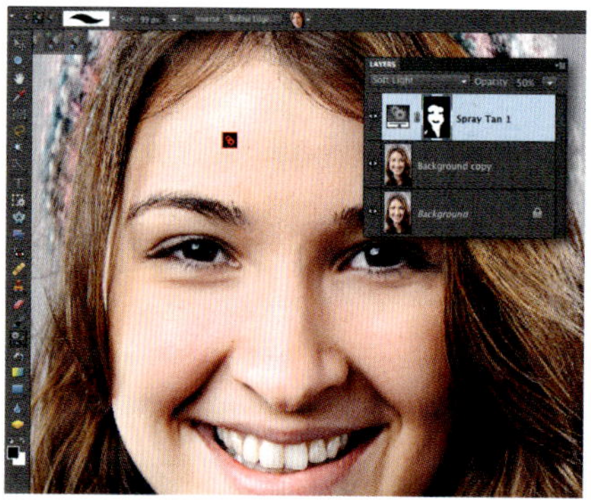

2 Adjust skin tone To apply a healthy glow to the skin, select ***Spray Tan***. As you hover over the face you'll see a small cursor appear to brush the effect over the skin. Use ***Size*** in the top toolbar to adjust the size of your brush. As default, the effect is set to ***50% Opacity***. To strengthen or weaken the effect, drag the layer's ***Opacity*** slider higher or lower respectively.

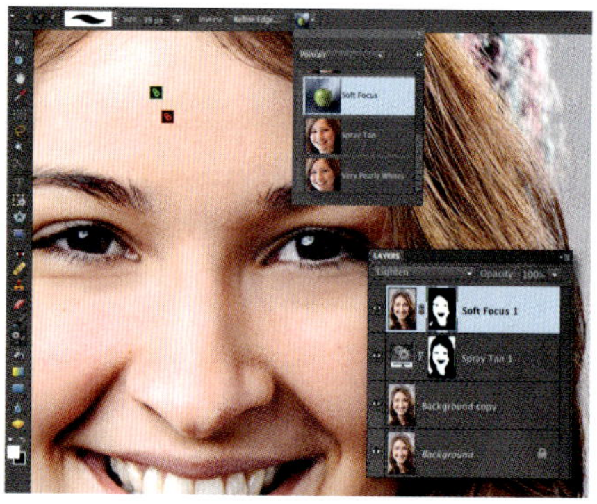

3 Smooth skin Before you apply the next adjustment, click on the ***Background layer*** in the Layers palette to deselect the previous adjustment. If you don't, you'll override the Spray Tan adjustment. This time select ***Soft Focus*** and brush over the skin to soften it, trying to avoid features like eyes, eyebrows and lips. Adjust ***Opacity*** to control the effect's strength.

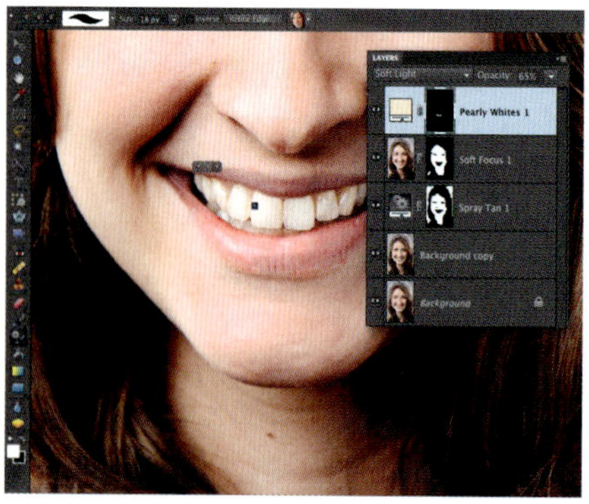

4 Brighten eyes & teeth Click the ***Background layer***. Now select ***Pearly Whites*** from the drop-down menu and brush over the teeth: adjust the layer's ***Opacity*** to control the effect. Deselect the adjustment and pick ***Brighten Eyes***. Zoom into the eyes and brush in the adjustment. Refine with the ***Subtract from Selection*** brush and set ***Opacity*** lower than ***40%***.

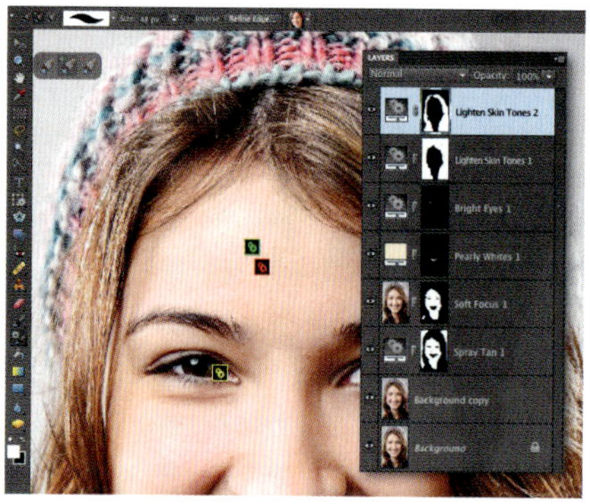

5 Add shine to the hair Deselect the adjustment and then pick ***Lighten Skin Tones***. Avoiding the skin, brush over the hair to enhance the highlights and shine. You may find going over other areas of the image can help improve the impact, too, like I've done here to brighten the background as well as her hat. To exaggerate the shine, repeat this step again.

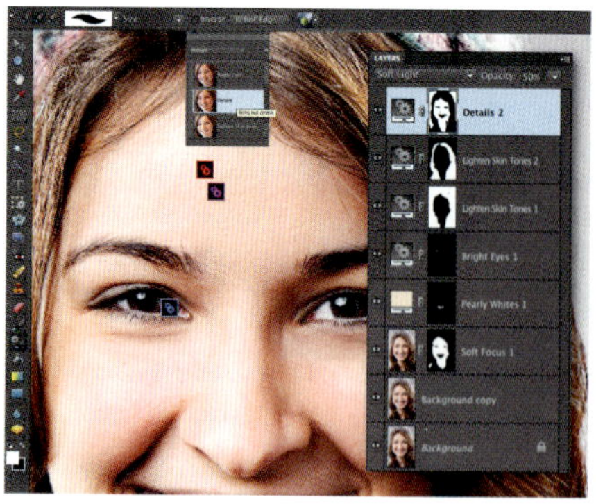

6 Enhance details For your next adjustment, click ***Detail***; this works in a similar way to sharpening, allowing you to increase the clarity of certain areas. Use this feature on the eyes, teeth, hair and eyebrows, but stay clear of the skin; you don't want to undo all that flattering skin softening. Now save your image as a TIFF file to keep the layers.

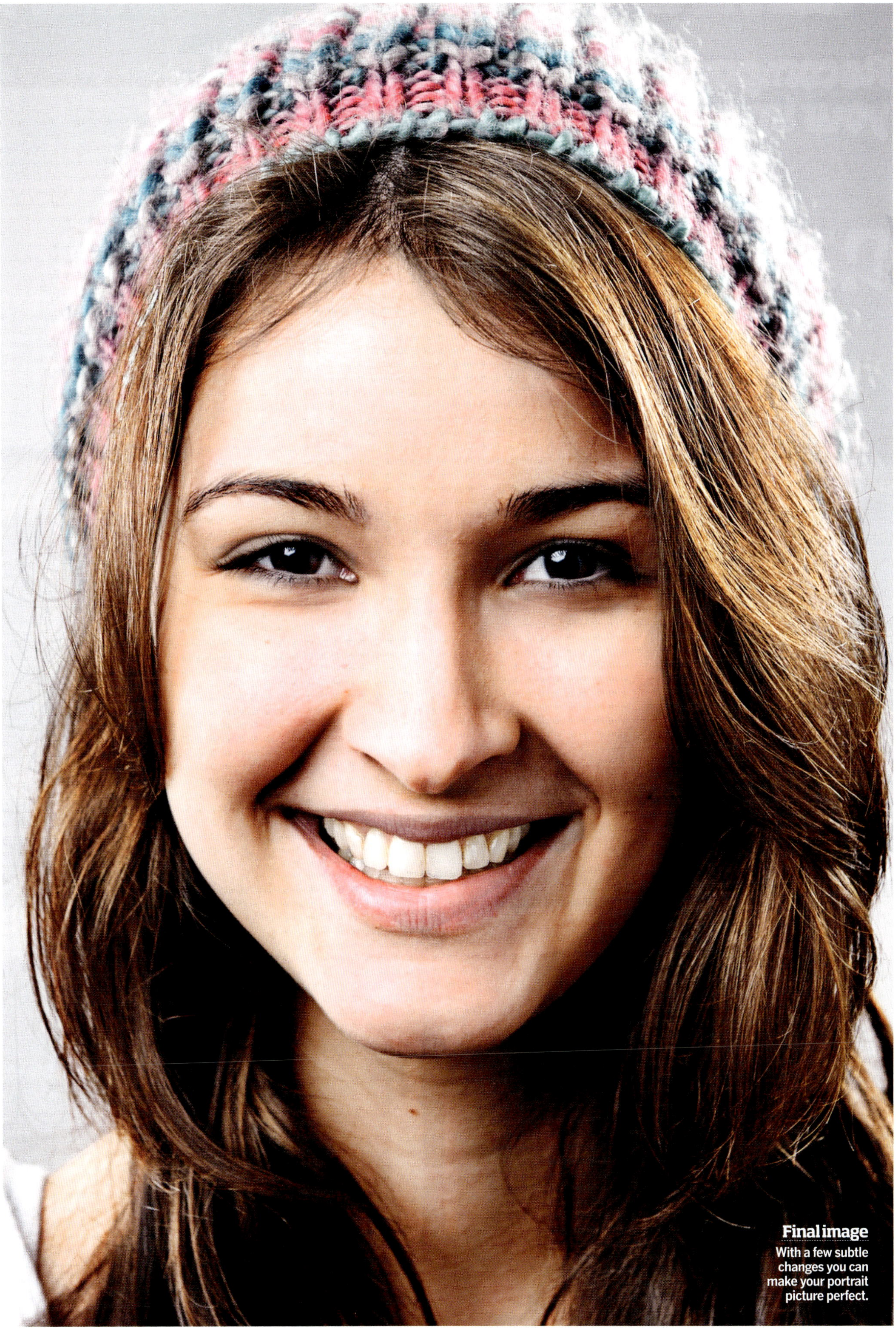

Final image
With a few subtle changes you can make your portrait picture perfect.

Recompose your images

Simple steps to changing the composition of your images and removing distractions

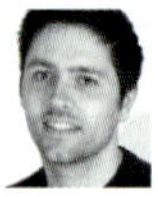

Jordan Butters: The ideal scenario in photography is always to get as much right in-camera as possible. Unfortunately, there are many components that are outside of your control that can mean your images will never be as perfect as you'd like them to be. The Recompose Tool in Elements 10 can be powerful when used correctly, although it isn't ideal for all situations. Depending on exactly what it is you want to remove and the end result you are trying to achieve, you may have to also use a combination of the Recompose Tool and either the Spot Healing Brush, Healing Brush or Clone Stamp Tool to finish tidying up.

I want to recompose this landscape-format image into portrait format. However, I'm keen to retain some of the background and surroundings while ideally bringing the subjects closer together. It sounds like there is a lot of healing and cloning work to be done, but the Recompose Tool makes light work of the task.

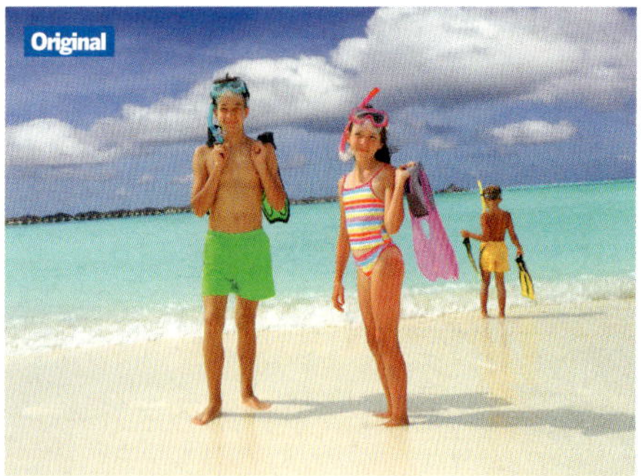

ISTOCK PHOTO

Useful tools

✔ HEALING BRUSH

For removing larger items from your images, click and hold the ***Spot Healing Brush Tool*** to reveal the ***Healing Brush Tool***. Select your brush ***Size*** from the top menu bar, press ***alt*** and click on the area of your image that you want the tool to sample. Brush to blend the sample area with the pixels surrounding your selection.

✔ CLONE STAMP

The Clone Stamp Tool is similar to the Healing Brush Tool, except that rather than blending pixels, it creates a carbon copy of your sample area – useful for removing items against a strong pattern or where there are defined edges nearby. Select the tool by clicking on the icon in the menu bar and holding down ***alt*** to select your sample area as before. You can then adjust the brush variables in the top menu bar.

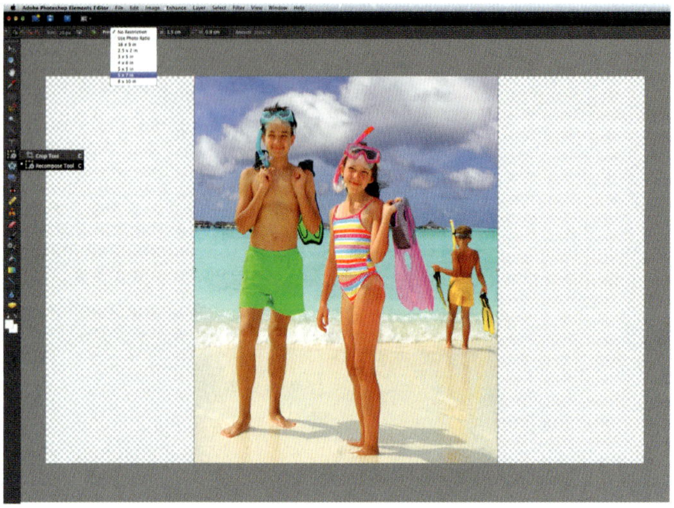

1 Recompose the image Click and hold the ***Crop Tool*** to reveal and select the ***Recompose Tool***. Select the ***5x7in*** preset and the software identifies the vital areas, bringing the children in the foreground together and compressing the backdrop. This is often all you need to do, but I want to remove the child in the background, so I revert to the original image.

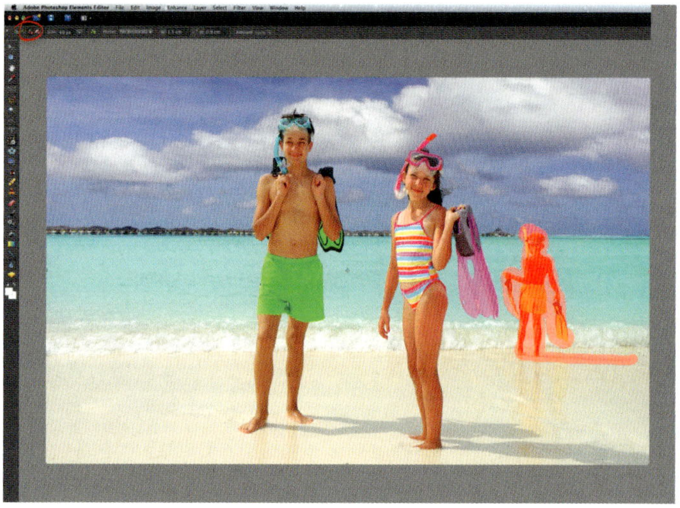

2 Mark areas for removal The child on the far right is distracting and the composition is off-centre. In the top menu bar, select ***Mark for Removal*** and adjust the brush ***Size*** using the brush options or by pressing the ***[*** or ***]*** keys. Pressing the ***Escape*** key will return your image to its original form. Brush over any area you want removed upon recomposition.

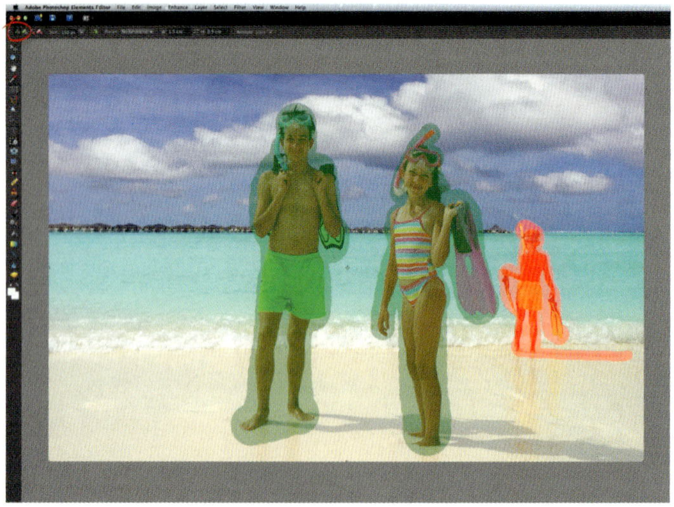

3 Mark areas for protection You can also mark any areas for protection by clicking on the ***Mark for Protection*** button in the top menu and roughly brushing in these areas, too. Once marked, repeat the first step to recompose the image and, when you're happy, commit by clicking on the green ***tick*** in the lower right corner or by pressing ***Enter***.

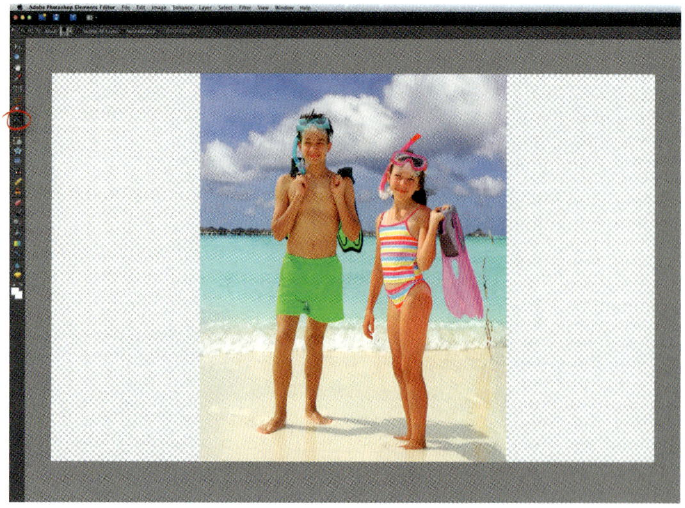

4 Tidy up There may be some areas that need tidying up. Select the ***Spot Healing Brush Tool*** and, in the top menu bar, choose your brush ***Size*** and select ***Content-Aware*** from the ***Type*** options. Brush along any areas of your image that need tidying up and the tool will sample nearby pixels to determine the best content to fill the space with.

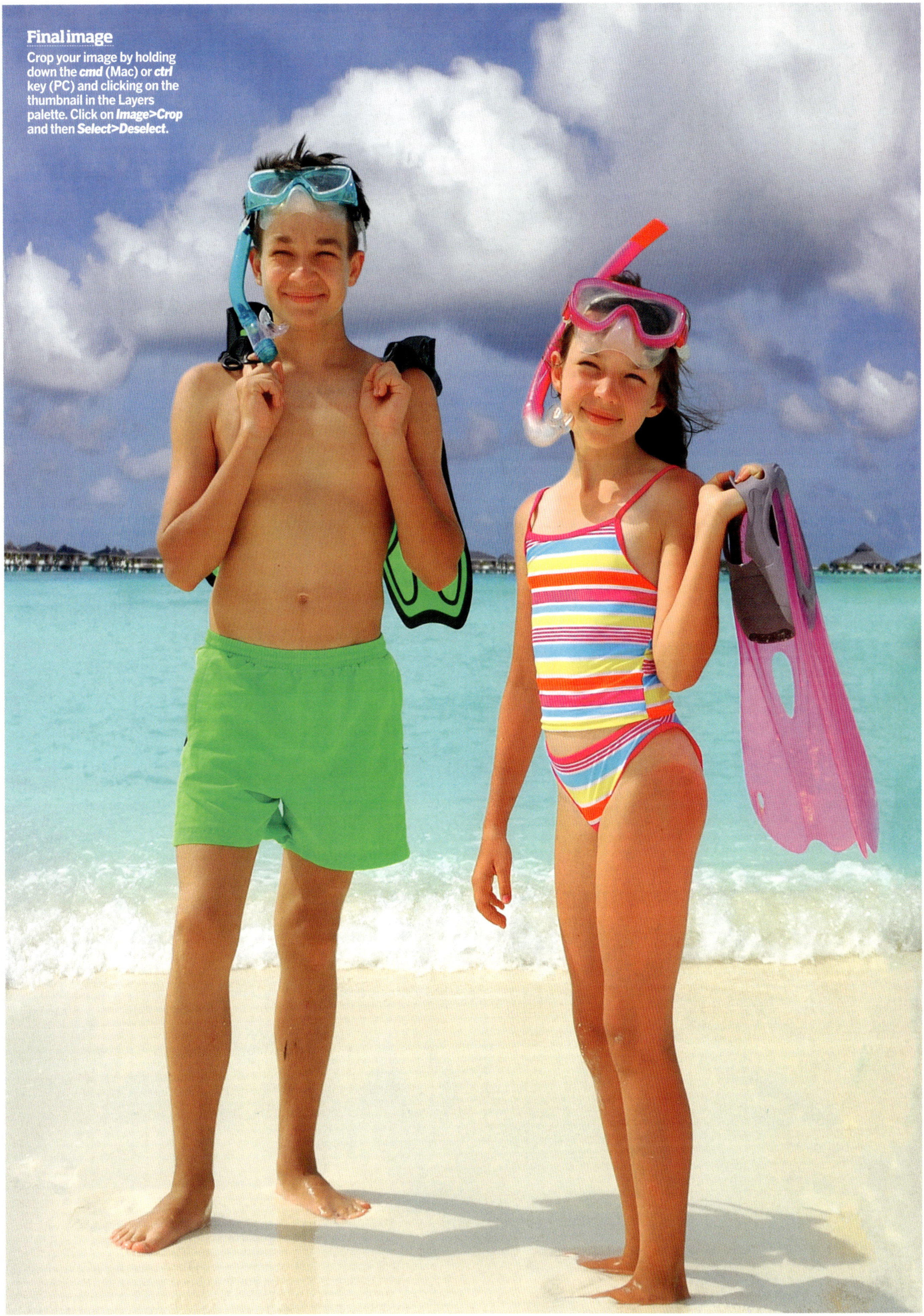

Final image

Crop your image by holding down the ***cmd*** (Mac) or ***ctrl*** key (PC) and clicking on the thumbnail in the Layers palette. Click on ***Image>Crop*** and then ***Select>Deselect***.

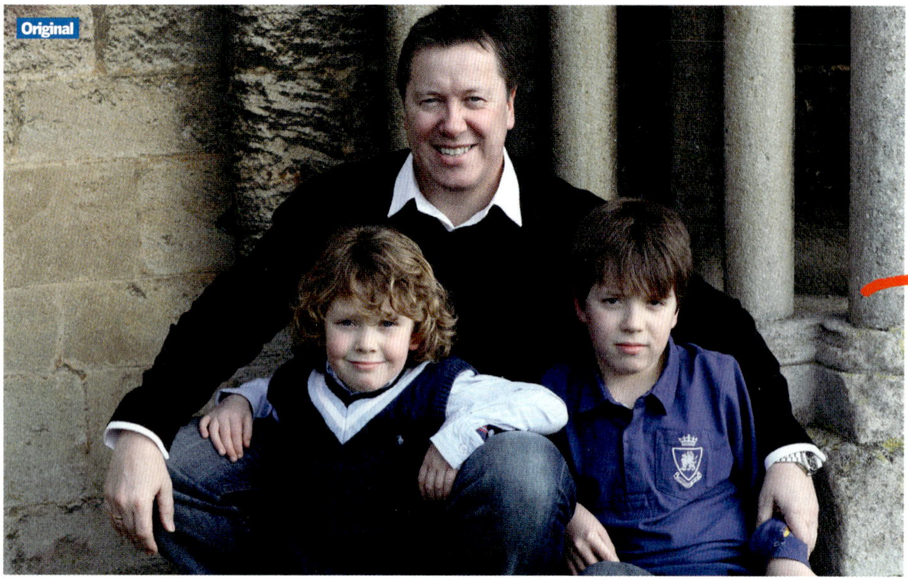

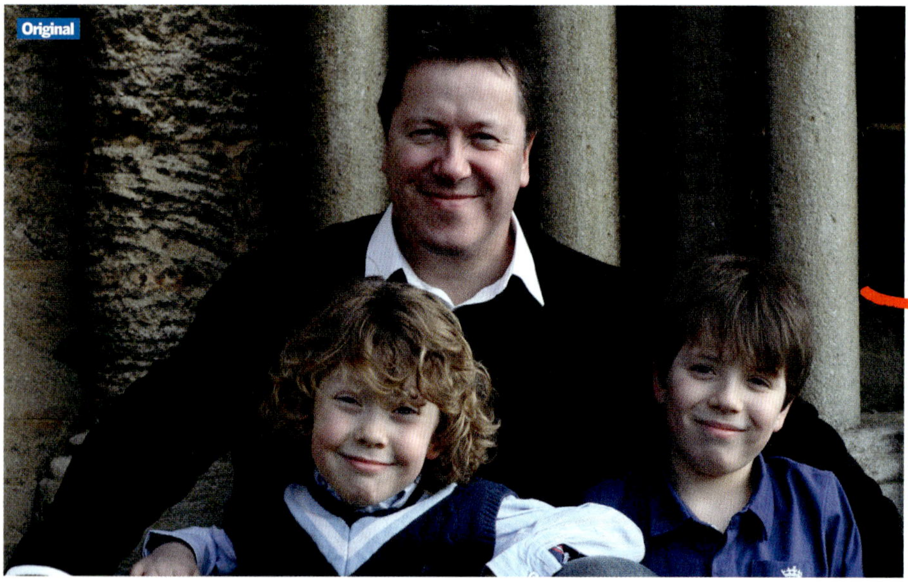

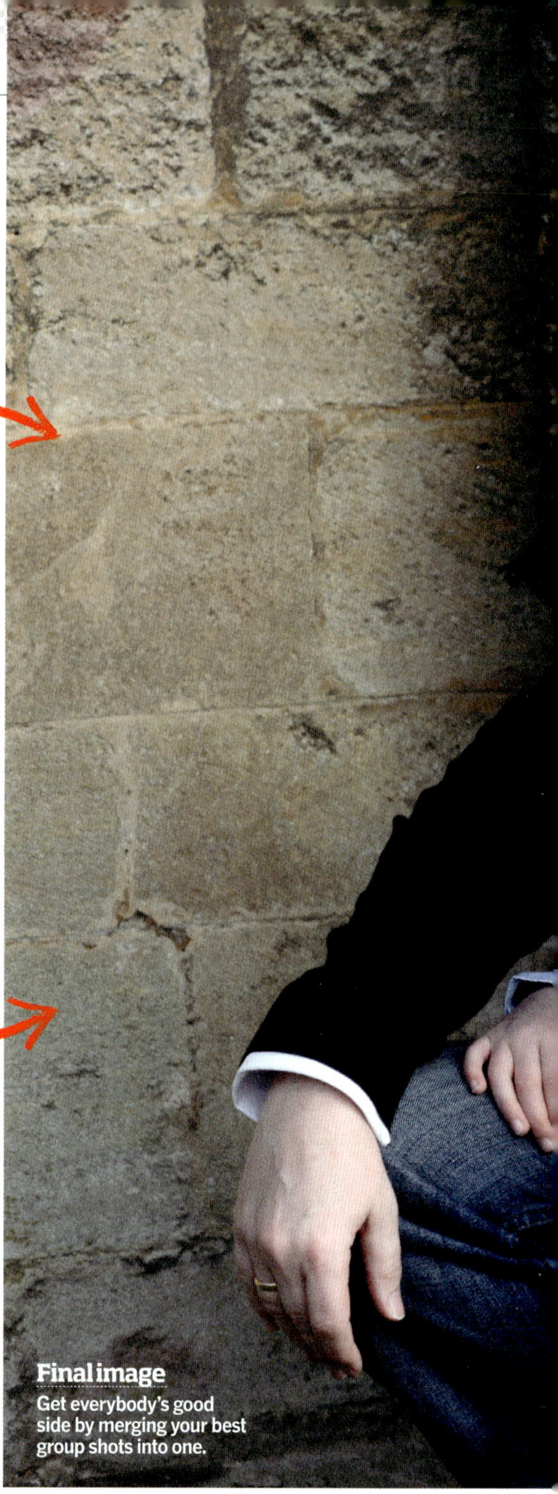

Final image

Get everybody's good side by merging your best group shots into one.

Quick steps to face swapping

Getting frustrated when a group portrait isn't going your way? Then combine the best shots you have of everyone into one image

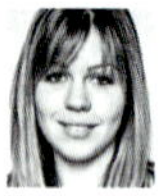

Caroline Wilkinson: If you've ever tried taking a family or group photograph, you'll know it's almost guaranteed that you'll capture at least one person looking the wrong way, pulling a peculiar face or with eyes shut. But instead of yelling and filling your memory card with dozens upon dozens of frames in a vain attempt to get everyone working with you, stop stressing and use Elements instead. With this technique you can take the best shots of each person and merge them in one frame.

For the best result, and ease of use, try to keep the background the same in each frame, as well as your angle and perspective, to avoid having to do too much manipulation using the Transform tools. Limit yourself to taking three to five frames of your group shot in the hope that you'll get each person looking perfect in at least one picture, then follow this step-by-step to bring them together.

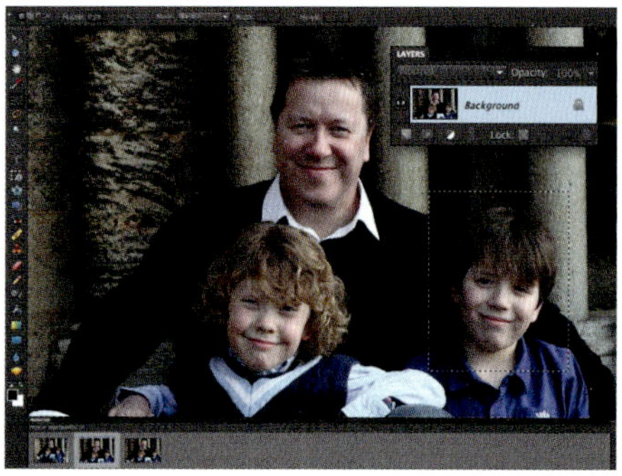

1 Open your images In Elements Edit, sort through the images in your Project Bin at the bottom of the screen to source your best image: this will become your background image for any new faces. Next, click on the image with the first face you want to transfer. Use the ***Rectangular Marquee Tool*** to select around the head and then go to ***Edit>Copy***.

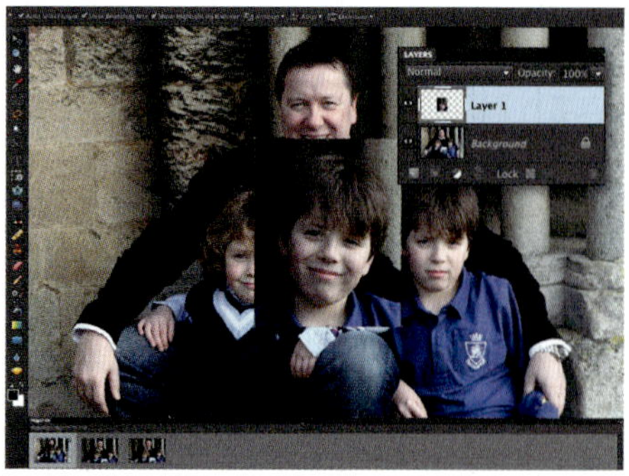

2 Position the head Click back on your background image and go to ***Edit>Paste*** to see the new head appear. Use the ***Move Tool*** and ***alt*** to resize the selection proportionally and drag it on top of the face you want to replace to align it. Try to match the size and angle as close as possible using the ***Transform*** commands and the ***Opacity*** slider.

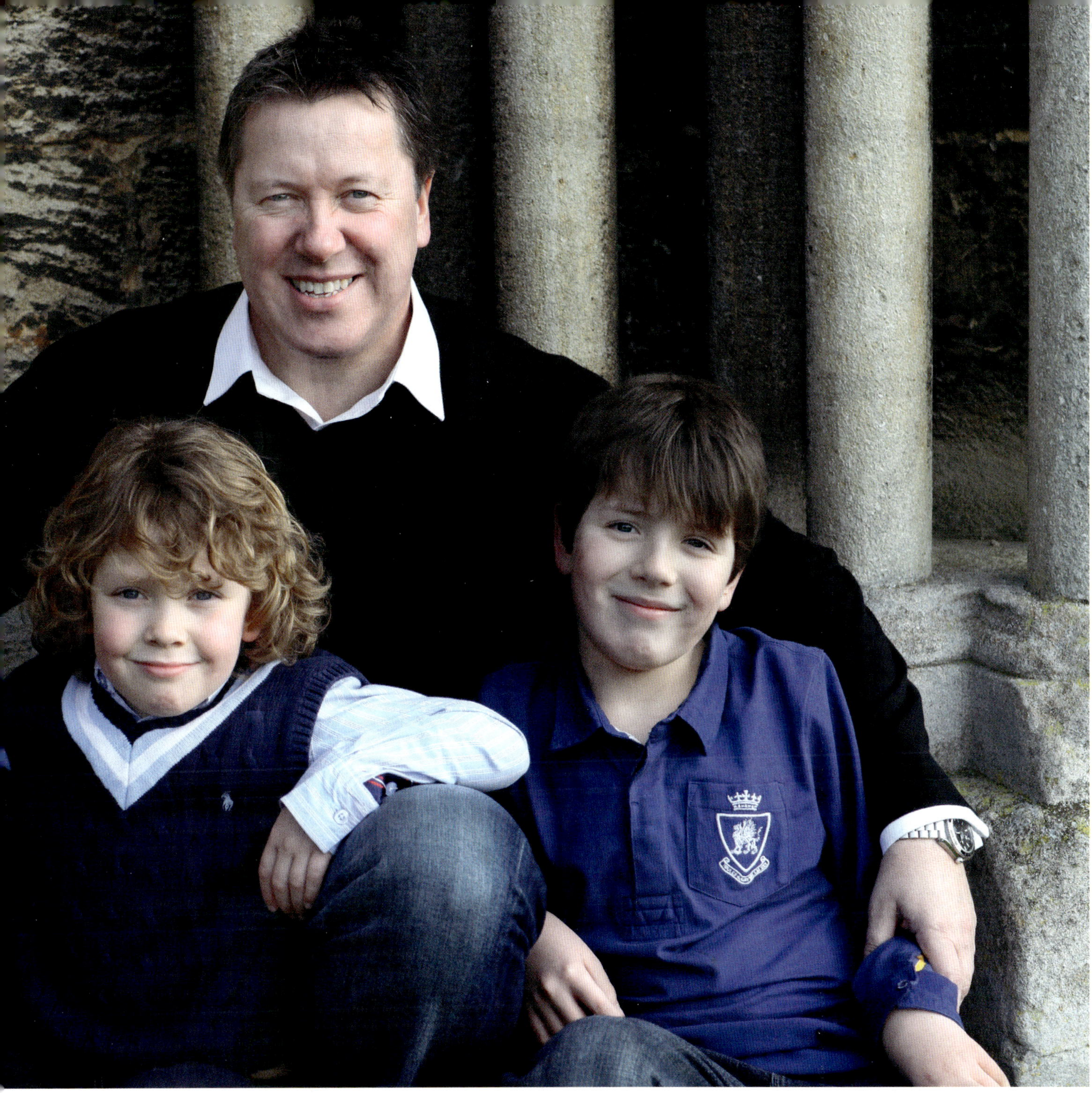

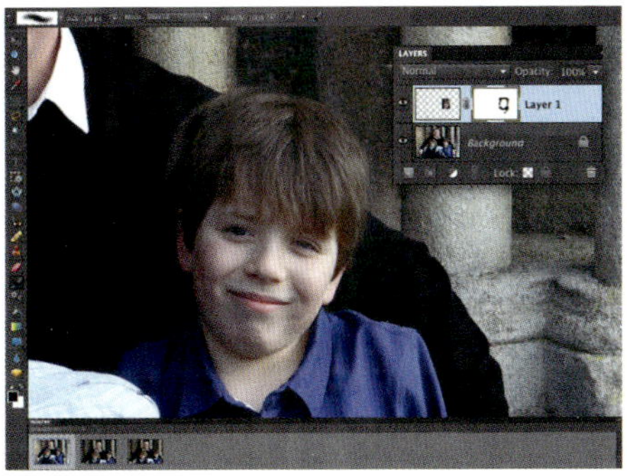

3 Use a Layer Mask If some areas of the new image don't line up with the background image, don't worry – it's the face that's important. Click the ***Add layer mask*** icon in the Layers palette and use the ***Brush Tool*** and ***Black*** paint to hide areas of the new image, revealing the background image. Be careful not to go over the face.

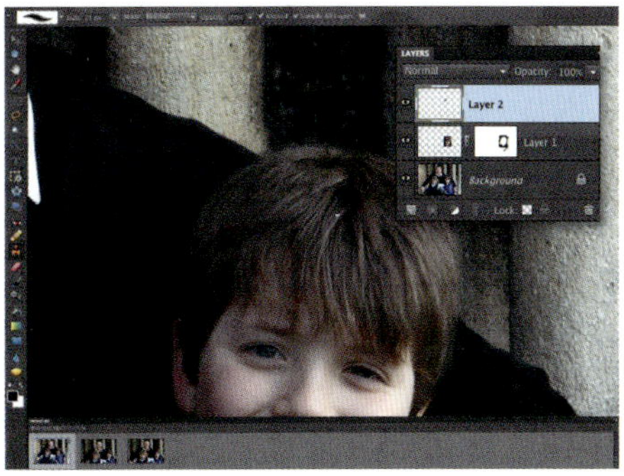

4 Use the Clone Stamp Tool By blending two layers together, you might find that too much of the background is revealed. For instance, the boy's hair from the original image doesn't line up. To sort this, add a new empty layer, zoom into your image and use the ***Clone Stamp Tool*** with a soft brush and ***Opacity*** on ***100%*** to get rid of these areas.

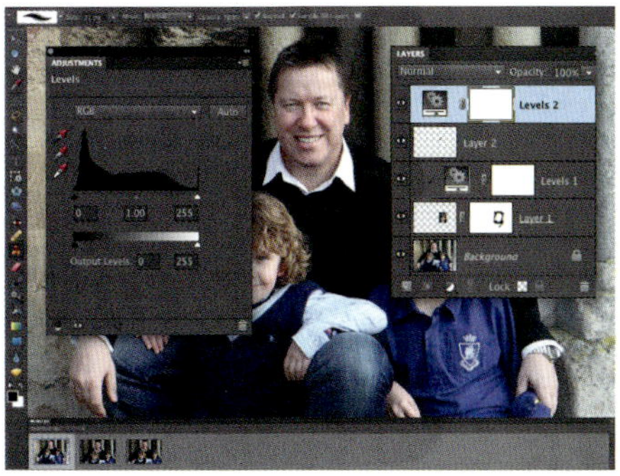

5 Adjust the lighting If the lighting changed between shots, the tonality of the new face may not match the others. Go to ***Layer>New Adjustment Layer***, and click and drag that layer above the layer with the new face. Click on the line between the layers while pressing ***alt*** to link them. Now any adjustment you make only affects the new face.

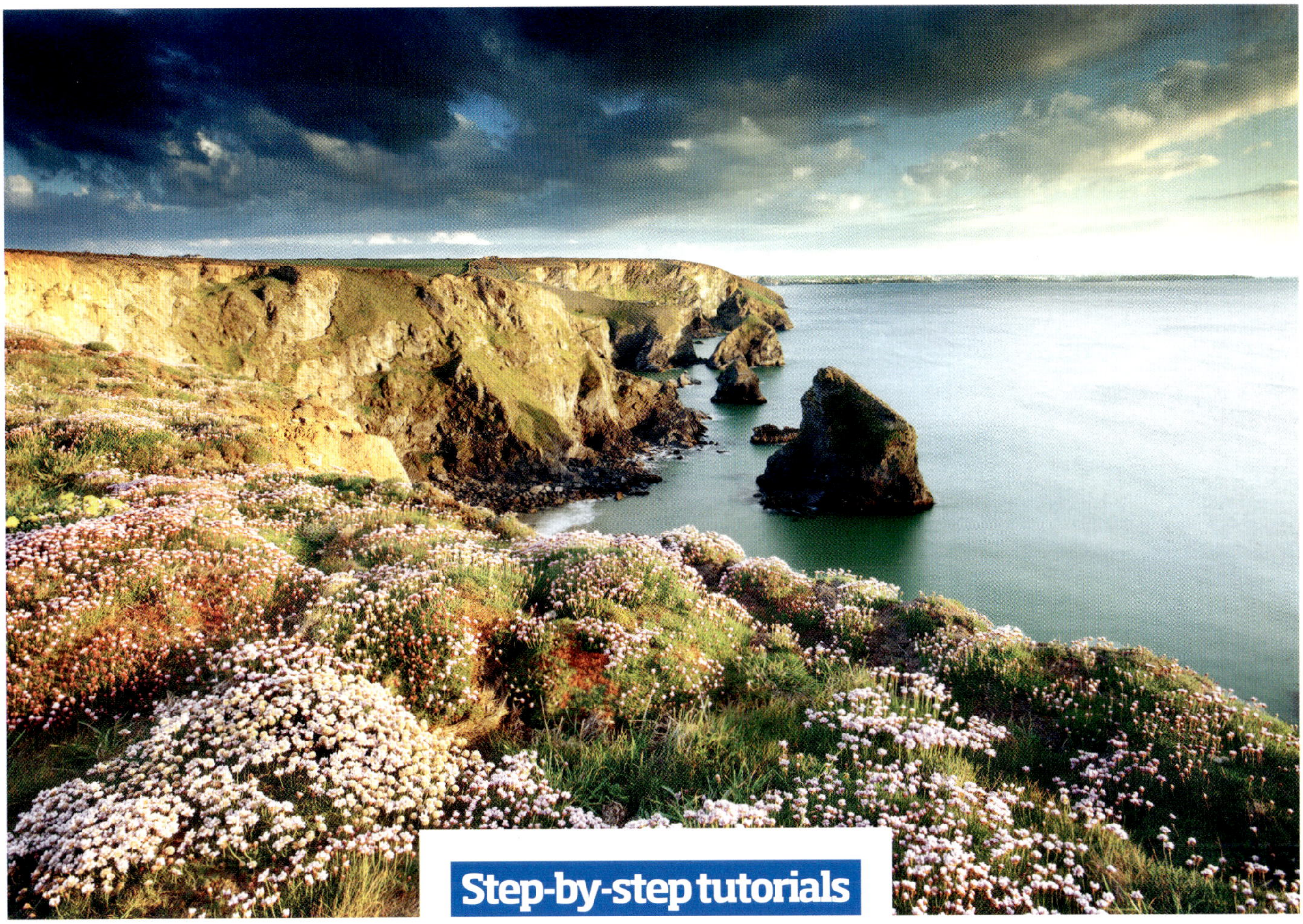

Step-by-step tutorials

PRACTICAL PHOTOSHOP

To get the most from your images, you need to know the basics of post-production...

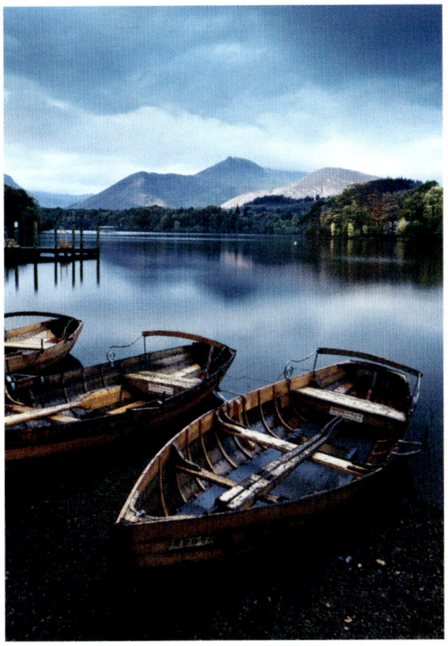

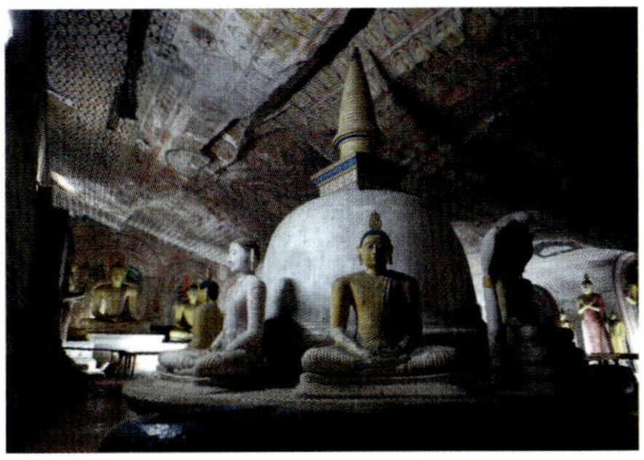

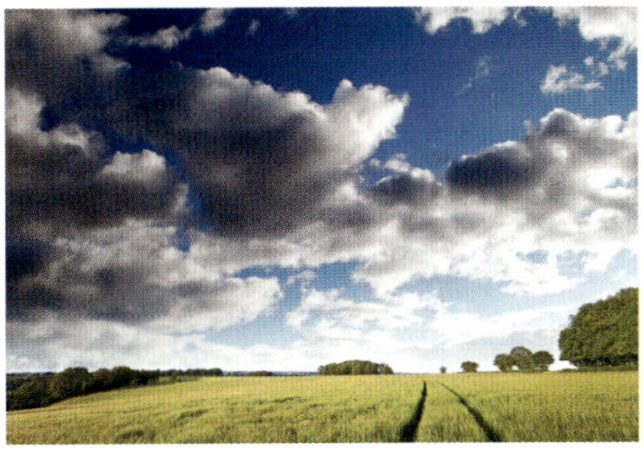

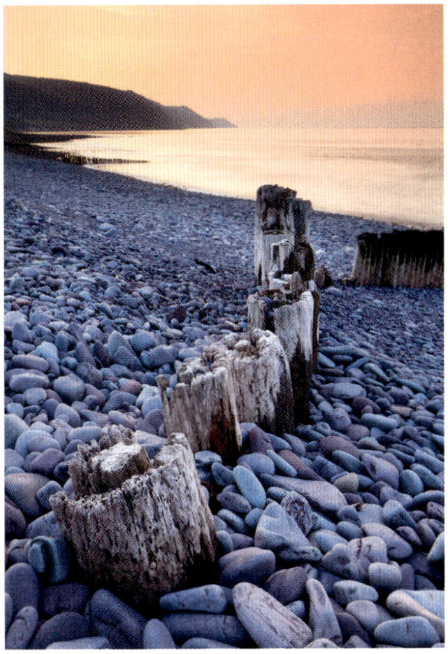

Making manual selections

Smart selection tools are quick and convenient, but when control is paramount, manual selections are usually the best solution

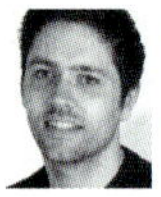

Jordan Butters: While smart tools can select areas of colour (see page 34 for our Elements guide), what happens when you need to select something that isn't a distinctive colour or is an awkward shape? That's where manual selection tools come into play. They take a bit more time to use than the smart tools as you'll be tracing the area that you wish to select, but it's a good way to make an accurate selection.

For instance, I want to create a dramatic, high-contrast, desaturated final image of this scene. However, as some areas are already high contrast, I only want to boost contrast on specific areas, such as the boardwalk and sky. As the boardwalk has defined edges with sand in between, I'm going to need to use both the Lasso and Polygonal Lasso Tools to make an accurate selection.

Alternative tools

☑ THE PEN TOOL

The Pen Tool is an advanced selection method. Rather than create a selection, the Pen Tool creates a Path. Paths follow vector lines rather than pixel edges, so are ideal for situations when precision is paramount, although the tool takes some time and practice to master.

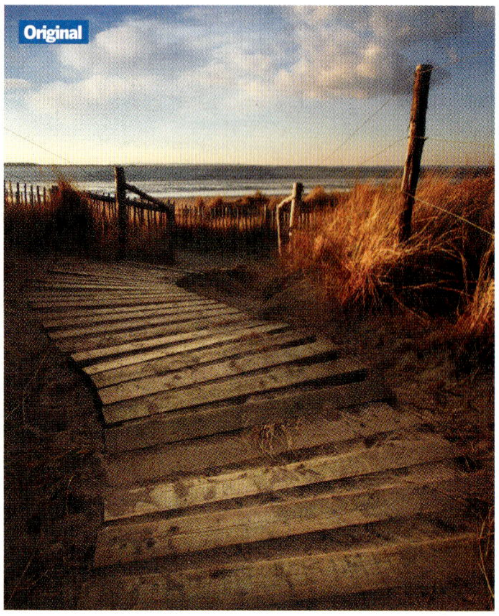

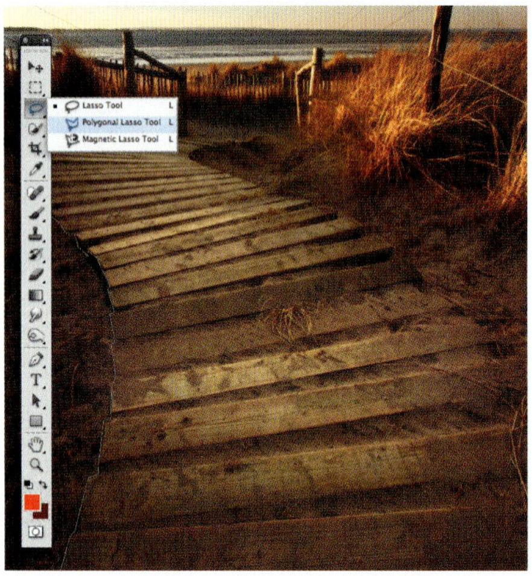

1 Make your first selection Click and hold on the *Lasso Tool* in the toolbar to choose the *Polygonal Lasso Tool*. Click once on your image to set the start of your selection before moving the cursor and clicking to set the next anchor point, aligning the line with the straight edges of the subject that you want to select.

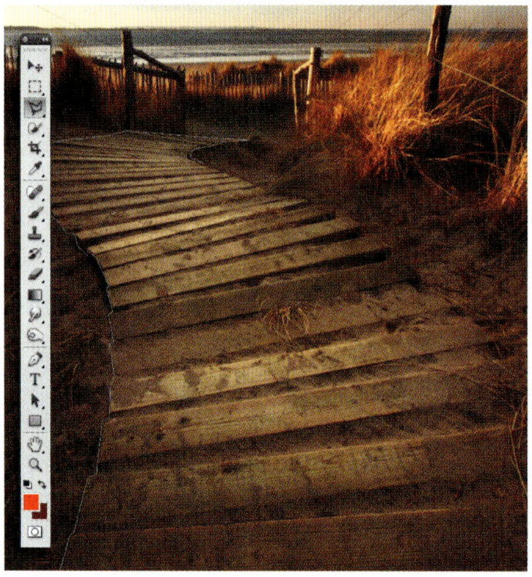

2 Switch between the Lasso Tools If you come to an area that requires more fluidity, hold down *alt* to switch to the *Lasso Tool* and trace the cursor around your shape. Release the *alt* key to switch back to the *Polygonal Lasso Tool*. Once done, double-click near your selection start point to close your selection.

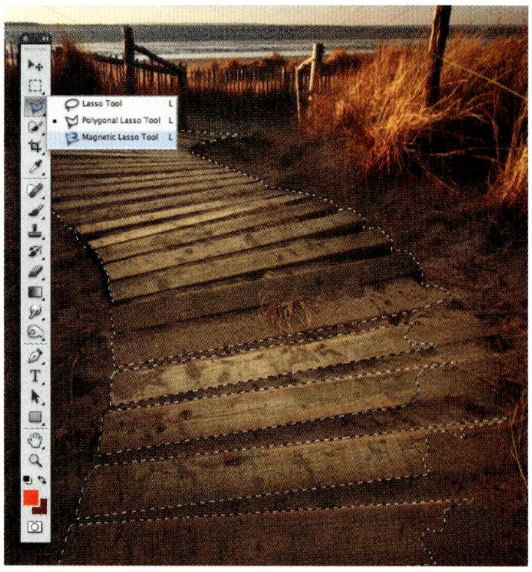

3 Subtract areas To subtract the areas of sand between the boards, hold down the *alt* key and select these areas one by one. Upon closing off each selection, that area will be removed from your original selection. Once done, click and hold on the *Polygonal Lasso Tool* in the toolbar to select the *Magnetic Lasso Tool*.

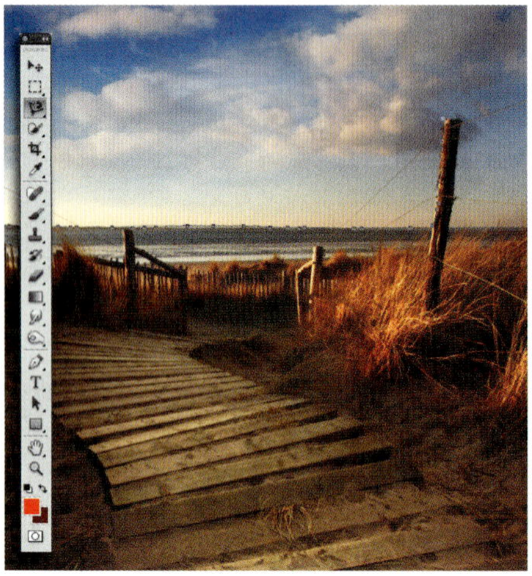

4 Add to your selection Hold down the *shift* key to add to the selection and click to set the first anchor point. Trace along the horizon and the tool will anchor to any edges of contrast. If the tool struggles at any point, click once to set a new anchor point along that edge. If it places an anchor incorrectly, press the *backspace* key.

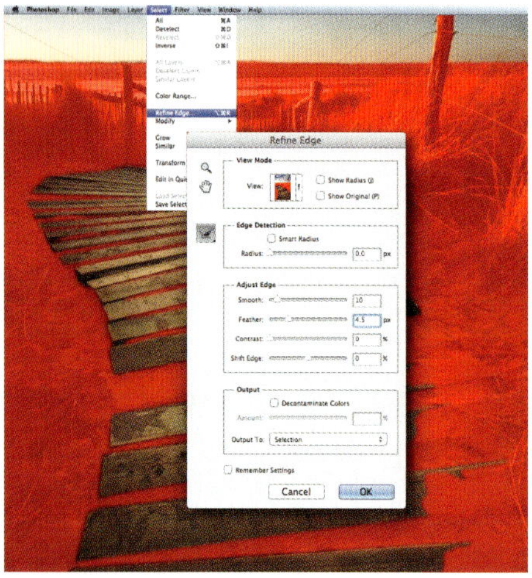

5 Refine the selection With the horizon traced, hold down the *alt* key again and click around the edges of the image to close off the selection around the sky. Then go to *Select>Refine Edge* and, in the Refine Edge box, increase the *Feather* to *6.0px* and change *Smooth* to *10*. This will smooth and blur the edges of your selection.

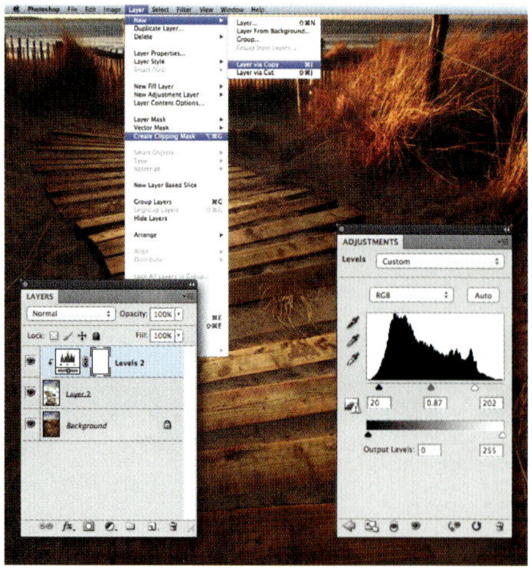

6 Add the adjustments Create a Pixel Mask by going to *Layer>New>Layer via Copy*. Add a *Levels* adjustment layer and before making any adjustments, go to *Layer>Create Clipping Mask*. Then, in the Adjustments palette, tweak the black, grey and white point sliders to boost contrast in your selected areas only.

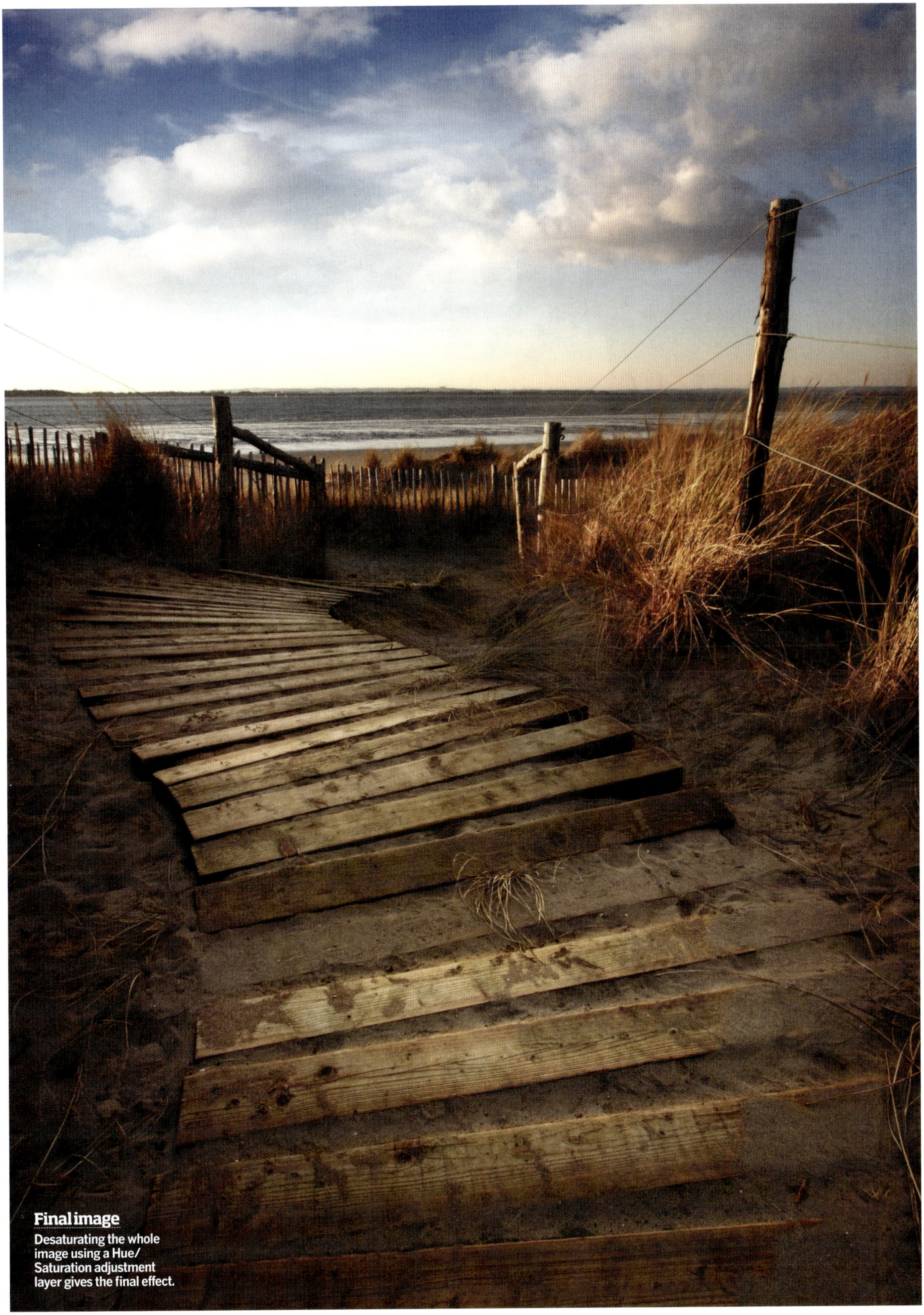

Final image
Desaturating the whole image using a Hue/Saturation adjustment layer gives the final effect.

Learn how to be selective

Global adjustments are often not enough to maximise detail and add impact, which is when you should treat an image in sections with more precise adjustments using the following techniques

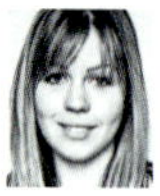

Caroline Wilkinson: You went out shooting without your filters and, as a result, you've got images where the exposure and impact of your images leave you wanting. Perhaps you've already processed the Raw file to try to get a half-decent result, but there are still areas that you think could be improved and you need to do this selectively. Or, perhaps, you didn't shoot in Raw at all and instead have JPEGs that can't benefit from the healing power of Adobe Camera Raw. Either way, this step-by-step guide could help as mastering the art of using Adjustment Layers enables you to make nondestructive edits that target individual areas of your image.

You could select the area you want to address first using the Quick Selection or Lasso Tool, with the Feather set to about 20px, then add an Adjustment Layer. Alternatively, you could apply the Adjustment Layer and then use the Brush Tool with either White or Black paint to edit the attached Layer Mask and, consequently, the effect. I'll show you both ways here so that you can choose your preferred method, but remember that this style of editing can be used not just for exposure, but selective colour edits, too – you just need to choose different Adjustment Layers.

There are two ways that you can select Adjustment Layers: at the bottom of the Layers palette is a black/white icon labelled 'Add a new fill or adjustment layer' – click on it and select from the list. Alternatively, go to Layer>New Adjustment Layer. It can also help to remember that when the Layer Mask is white, the effect is visible, in which case use Black paint to hide the edits on the image. If the Layer Mask is black, the effect you've applied is completely hidden and you will need to use White paint to reveal the edits.

To turn your Layer Mask black, click on the mask in the Layers palette and press cmd + I or go to Image>Adjustments>Invert. You can also adjust the Opacity slider of the Brush Tool if you want to reduce the amount that you reveal or hide. Depending on the size of the area you want the edits to affect, you may find one of these methods easier to use than the other – try them out to discover what works for you.

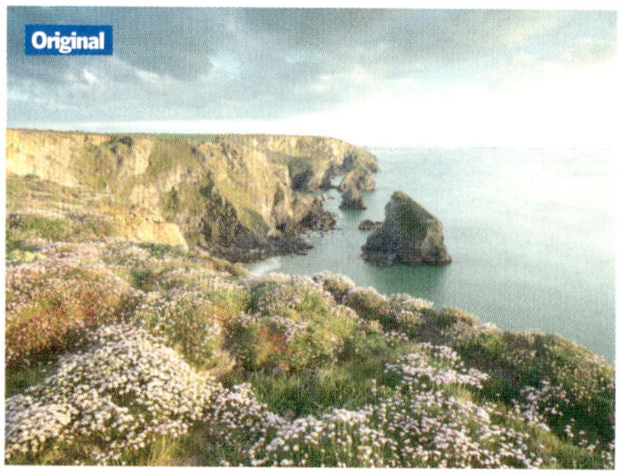

ROSS HODDINOTT

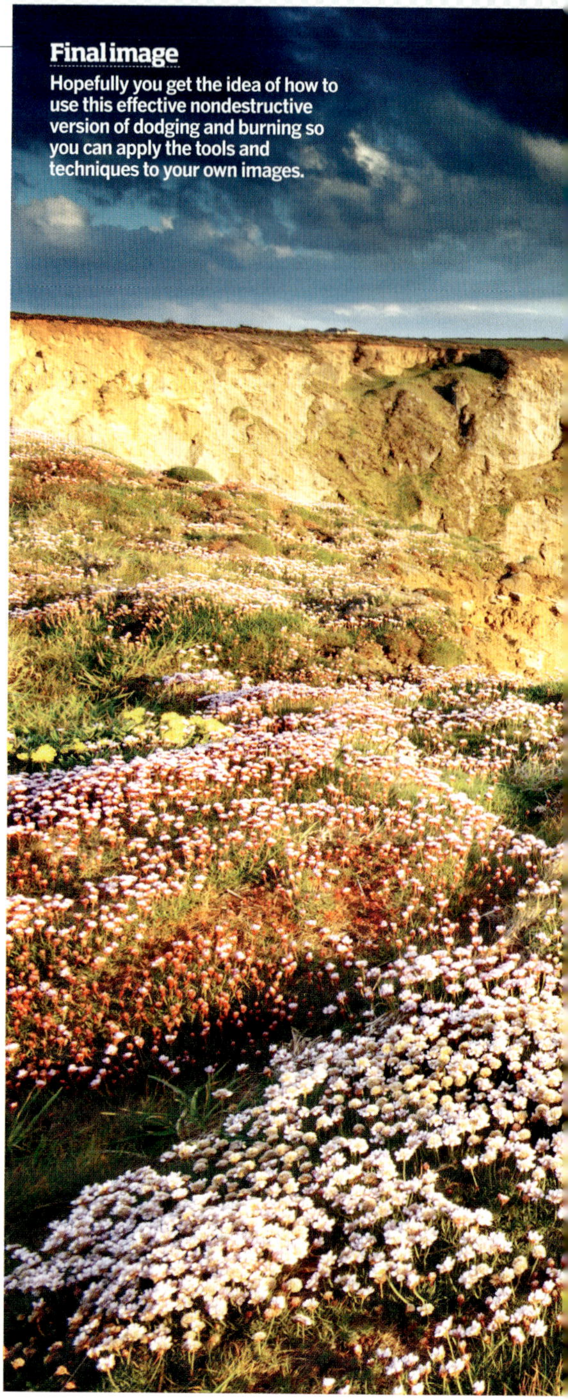

Final image
Hopefully you get the idea of how to use this effective nondestructive version of dodging and burning so you can apply the tools and techniques to your own images.

Secrets unlocked

☑ ADJUSTMENT LAYERS

The beauty of Adjustment Layers is that you can add as many as you want – for each adjustment you make to as many different areas of the image that suit you – without ever affecting the original image. This means that if you make a wrong or unnecessary adjustment, you can not only re-edit the Adjustment Layer or use the Layer Mask to refine the areas edited or the strength of existing edits, but you can delete the adjustment completely at any point during your editing process. To do this, simply click and drag on the ***Adjustment Layer*** in the Layers palette down to the trashcan icon, or press the ***backspace*** key to delete.

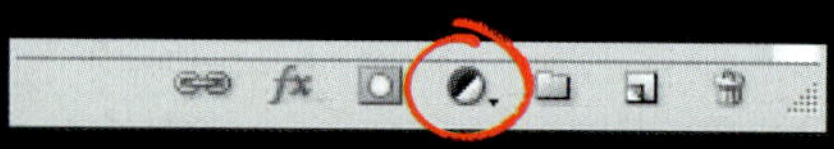

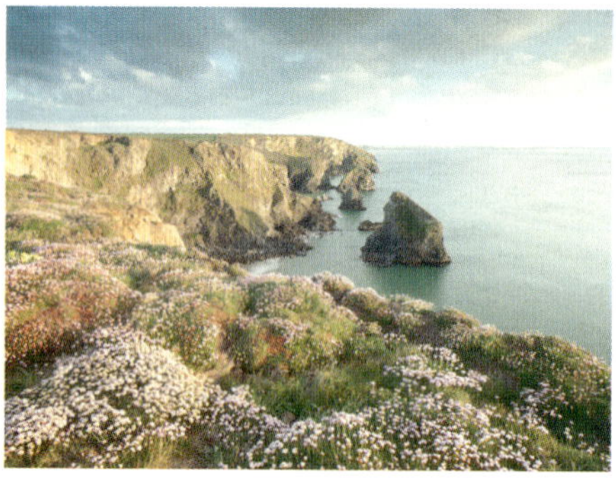

1 Open your image Presuming you've edited your image in Adobe Camera Raw already or you're working with a JPEG, open your image in Photoshop. As you can see in this image, the sky lacks detail and punch along the horizon, which can easily be enhanced by adjusting its exposure slightly. However, if you do this with a global adjustment, you'll find the landscape becomes too dark and you lose detail in the shadows.

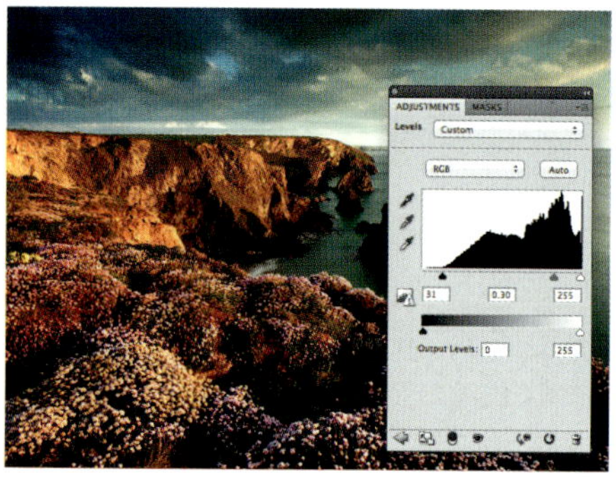

2 Adjust the sky's exposure Add a Levels adjustment layer and move the sliders until you're happy with the level of detail recovered in the sky, ignoring the effect on the foreground. I found the mid-tone and shadow slider the most effective as the sky has been slightly overexposed in-camera. You can use Levels for this technique or Exposure, Brightness/Contrast or Curves – whichever works best for you.

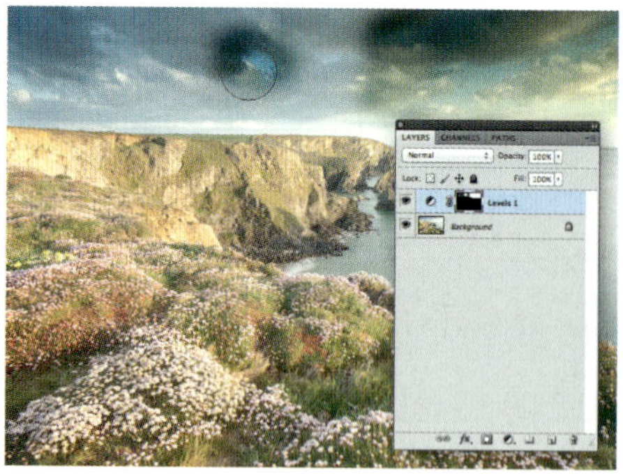

3 Edit using a Layer Mask With more foreground in the image than sky, it's easier to hide the entire effect and then paint it in where needed. Click on the Levels adjustment layer's ***Layer Mask*** and click ***cmd*** to fill it with black, then use the ***Brush Tool*** and ***White*** paint to reveal the darker sky. Lower the ***Opacity*** and brush ***Size*** as you approach areas you don't want affected to avoid overlapping and halos.

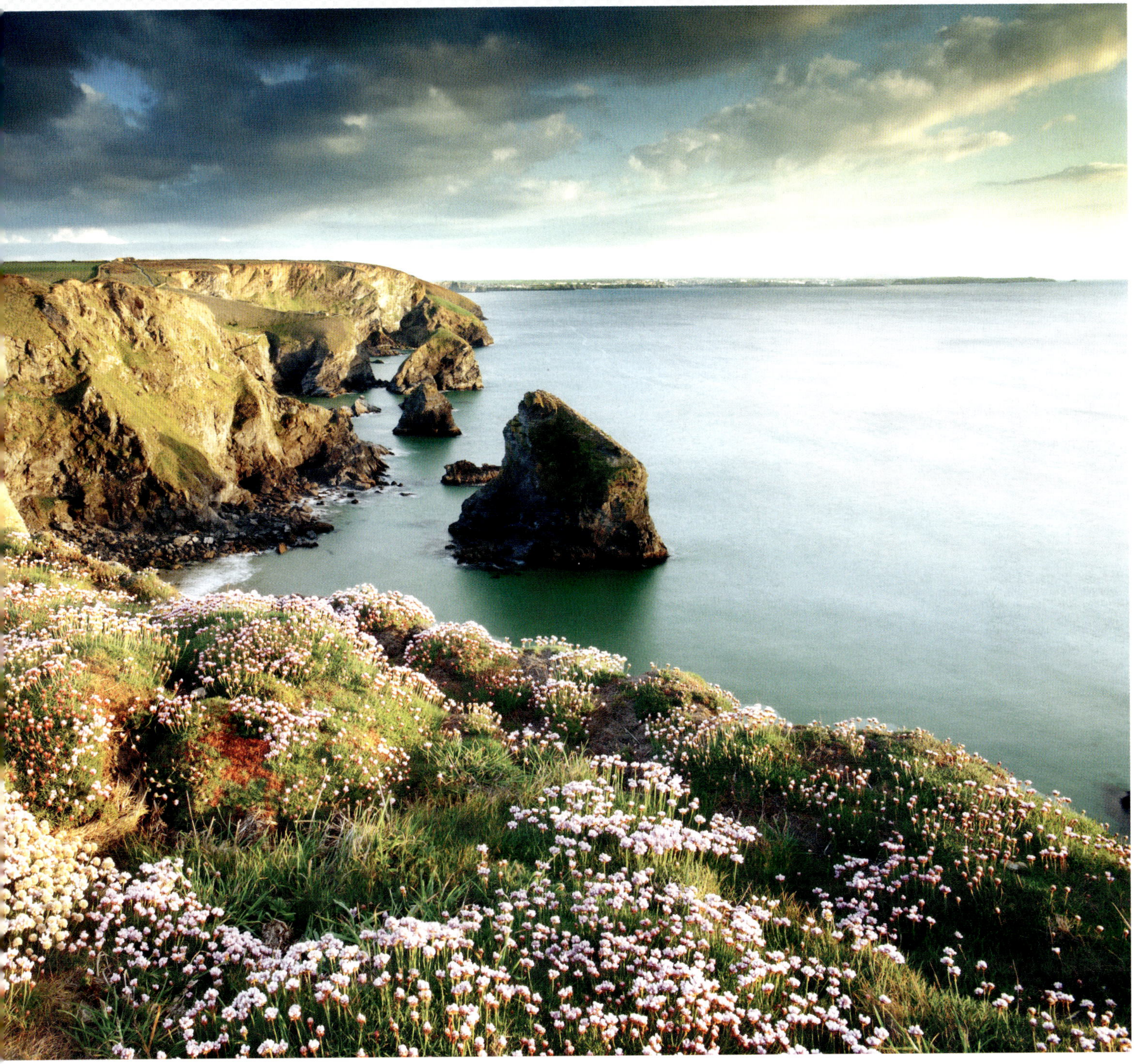

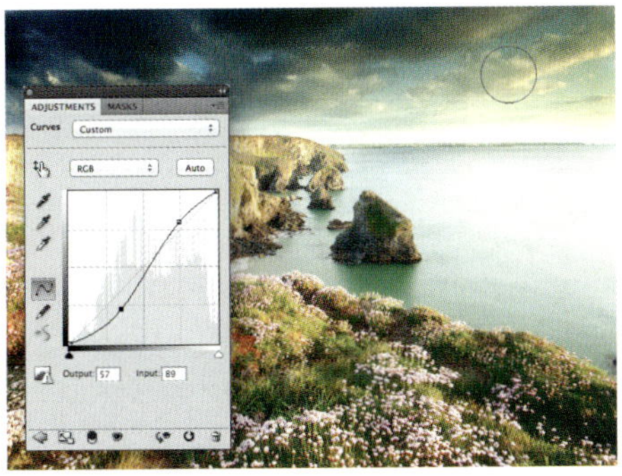

4 Use Curves To target the foreground in your image, add a ***Curves*** adjustment layer and create a soft 'S' shape with the curve line to improve the contrast. In the process of improving the tonality of the foreground, you'll affect the sky, too, so once again, using the ***Brush Tool*** and an appropriate-sized brush, you'll need to hide the new adjustment, but this time using ***Black*** paint on the Layer Mask.

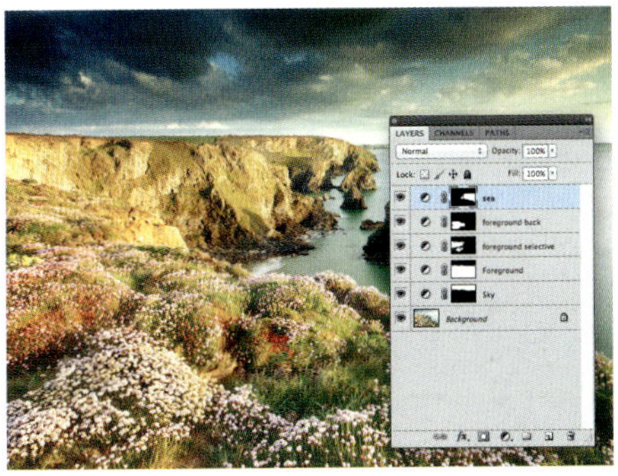

5 Concentrate on the details If some areas are still too dark or light, target your focus more selectively. Use a new adjustment layer for each area you target in case you want to delete an edit. Use the ***Lasso Tool*** with the ***Feather*** set to ***20px*** and ring around your target area, apply an adjustment layer and edit using the Layer Mask as needed. Repeat for different areas, tackling shadows and highlights separately.

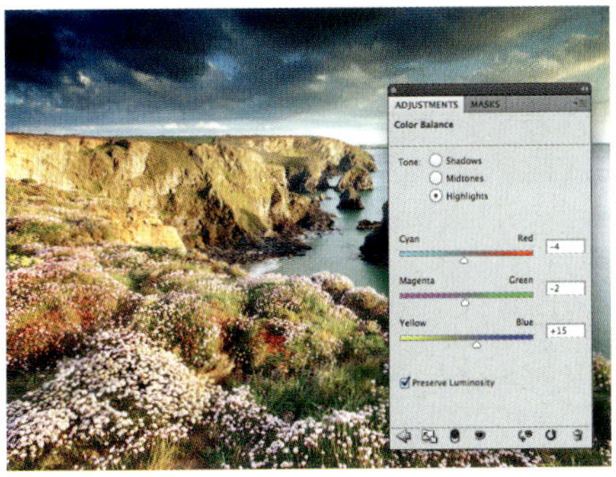

6 Address the colour Often when you boost contrast, you in turn increase the saturation and boost any colour casts there may be. As this image was taken shortly after sunrise, there's a slight red/yellow cast enhanced by the other adjustments. While I don't want to lose all the warmth here, the image could benefit from a ***Color Balance*** adjustment layer, increasing the ***Blue*** slider slightly to cool the tones.

Behind the mask

Combining Adjustment Layers and Layer Masks opens up a world of options for selectively tweaking and perfecting your shots

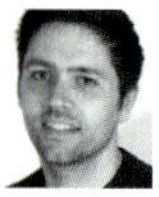

Jordan Butters: Without a doubt, one of the most powerful features of Adobe Photoshop CS is the ability to selectively edit your images in a nondestructive manner using Adjustment Layers and Layer Masks.

Adjustment Layers offer a series of effects and adjustments, each with adjustable parameters to suit your images. Furthermore, they can be applied to the entire image at once, clipped to just a single layer or applied selectively using a Layer Mask.

Layer Masks, as the name suggests, mask the layers that they are applied to, allowing you to edit or affect only selected parts of your image at a time. If you've been using Photoshop but haven't yet delved into the world of Layer Masks and Adjustment Layers, you're missing out on myriad options for improving your images and it's time to harness the full power of CS.

Alternative method

LAYER MASKS

Layer Masks can be applied to image layers as well as Adjustment Layers. For images that have two or more layers present, select the layer you wish to mask and click the ***Add vector mask*** button in the Layers palette. Then use the ***Brush Tool*** to brush over and mask your image. Just remember that White reveals the layer, while Black masks it.

TOP TIP

To apply an adjustment to a single layer rather than the whole image, select the ***Clip to layer*** button in the Adjustments palette.

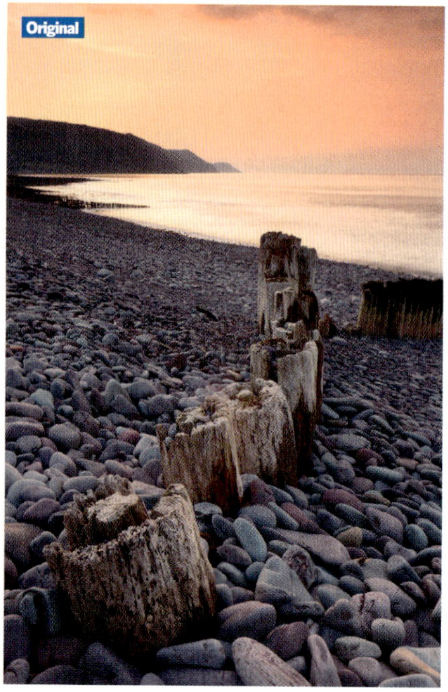

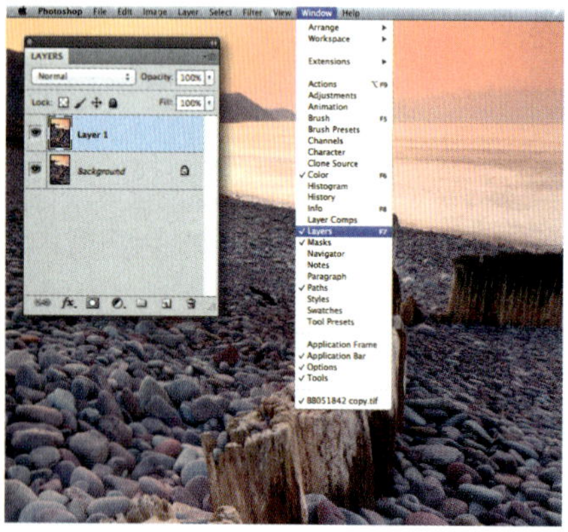

1 Show the Layers palette With your image loaded in Photoshop, make sure the Layers palette is visible by going to ***Window>Layers***. In the Layers palette you will only see a Background layer at present. Duplicate this layer by going to ***Layer>Duplicate Layer***, or by pressing ***Cmd+J*** if you're on a Mac or ***Ctrl+J*** if you're using a Windows-based PC.

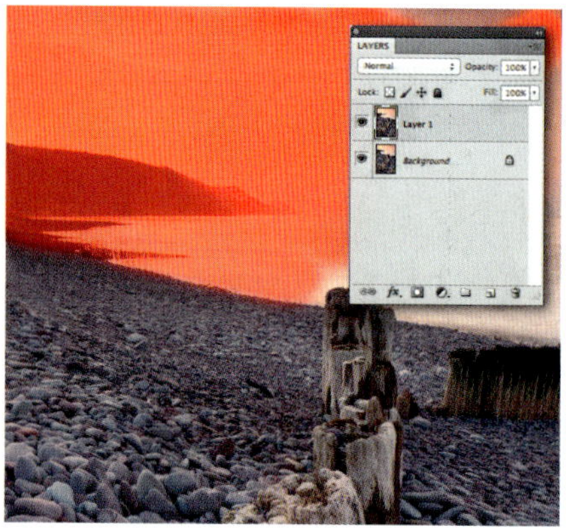

2 Add a Quick Mask I want to retain the warm tones in the sky but add a neutral tone to the foreground. Press the ***Q*** key to enable Quick Mask mode, select the ***Brush Tool*** and use the top menu to customise the brush to suit. Brush over the area you wish to remain unaffected by any changes. If you make a mistake, press the ***X*** key and brush back over to remove the mask.

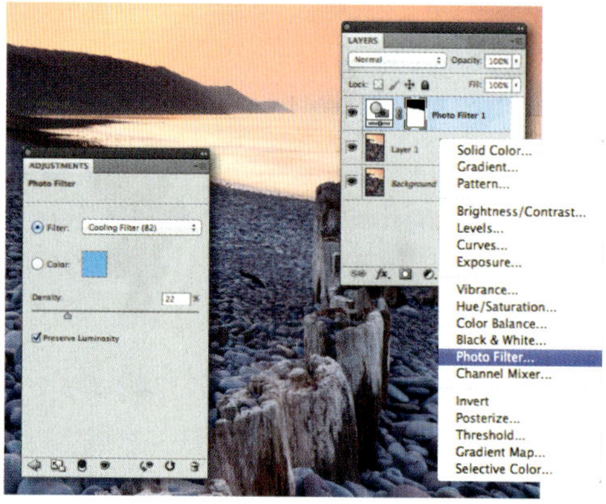

3 Add an adjustment With your area masked off, press the ***Q*** key again to turn this mask into a selection and, in the Layers palette, click on the ***Create new fill or adjustment layer*** button and select ***Photo Filter*** from the drop-down menu. In the Adjustments palette, select one of the three preset ***Cooling Filters*** and adjust the ***Density*** slider to alter its effect.

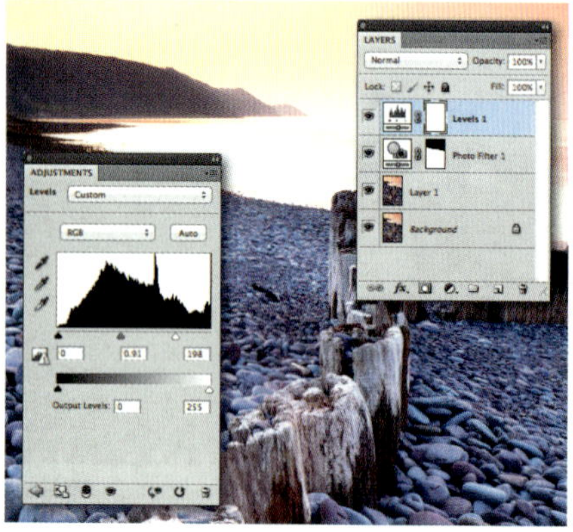

4 Add another adjustment To bring out detail in the foreground, click on the ***Create new fill or adjustment layer*** button again to create a new adjustment and this time select ***Levels***. In the Adjustments palette, adjust the sliders until you are happy with the effect. These changes will be applied to just the foreground in the next step, so don't worry about the sky for now.

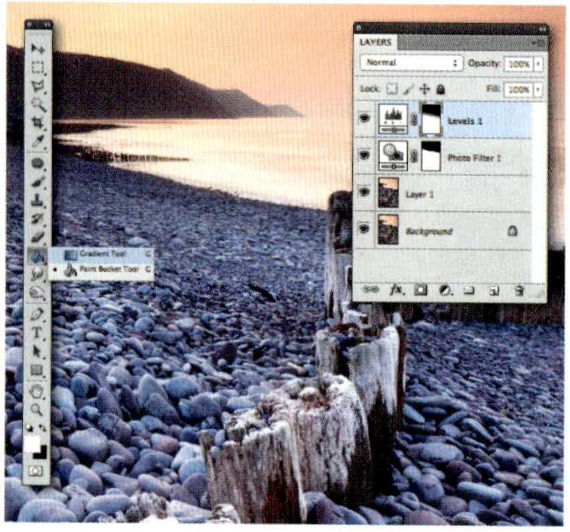

5 Apply a gradient mask Click and hold on the ***Paint Bucket Tool*** to select the ***Gradient Tool*** and press the ***D*** key to make sure that your colour palette is reset. In the top menu, make sure that the ***Mode*** is set to ***Normal***. Click and drag on your image in the direction of foreground to background to apply the mask. The longer the line, the softer the gradient.

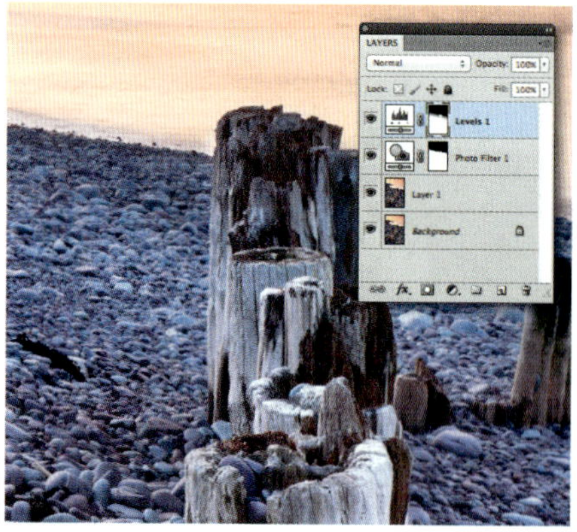

6 Tweak the mask Don't worry if you don't get the gradient right first time, you can click and drag as many times as you need to get the right transition. The gradient cuts through the final wooden post in my image and doesn't look natural. Select the ***Brush Tool*** and, with ***White*** set as your ***Foreground color***, paint in the post. If you go too far, press ***X*** to paint back over.

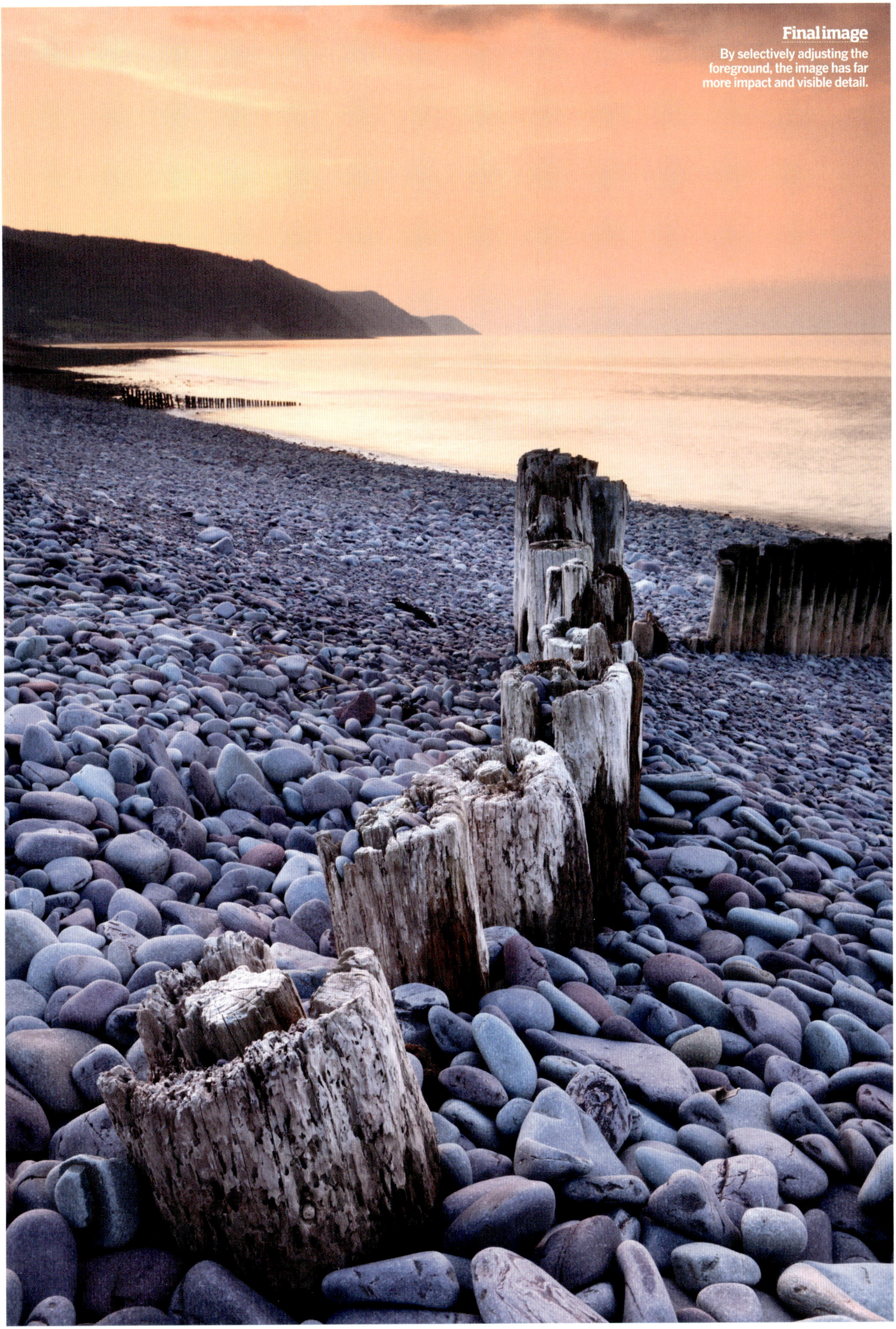

Final image

By selectively adjusting the foreground, the image has far more impact and visible detail.

Breathe life into flat photos

Want to create an HDR effect but don't have Raw files or a set of bracketed exposures? Don't despair! Use Shadows & Highlights…

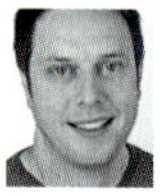

Luke Marsh: We all have images that didn't quite render the scene how you remember it. Maybe the sky's not as moody, or the ground is too dark, or maybe the overall appearance of the image lacks contrast or is badly exposed. Well, Shadows & Highlights can resurrect these images. This nifty adjustment is a fantastic photographic tool, which is often overlooked by users since dedicated HDR software like Photomatix and Photoshop actions became available from third-party companies. In the simplest terms, the adjustments allow you to recover detail from over- or underexposed areas by adjusting the Highlights or Shadows controls respectively, or you can improve the overall tonal range using the Midtone Contrast slider. It's really very simple.

The key to success with Shadows & Highlights is subtlety. As with any process that plays with tonal range, HDR included, Shadows & Highlights can produce photographic Frankensteins if used too eagerly. So why not give it a go? The controls may seem daunting at first, but after a little experimentation and with a better understanding of what can be achieved, you may find you'll be using this feature regularly.

HOT KEY

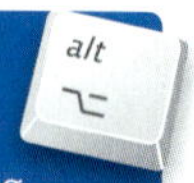

Alt to reset

When working in Shadows & Highlights, hold down ***alt*** to change the Cancel button to a Reset button in case you want to take the filter back to its default settings. You can also uncheck ***Preview*** to toggle between the blurred and original image.

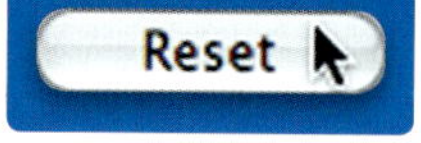

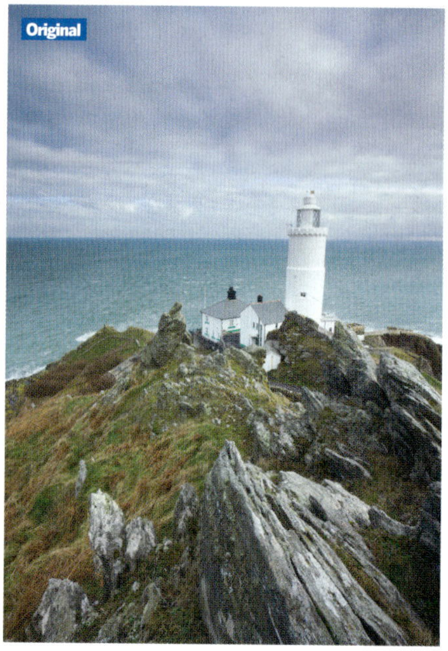

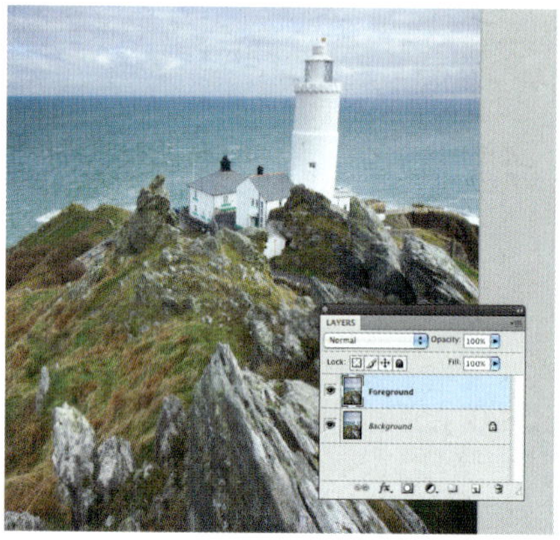

1 Duplicate original Our chosen image is a bit lifeless, yet clearly has potential texture in the sky and detail in the foreground that could be pulled out using Shadows & Highlights. First, create a duplicate layer from the original by going to ***Layer>Duplicate Layer…***, naming the layer accordingly for reference later.

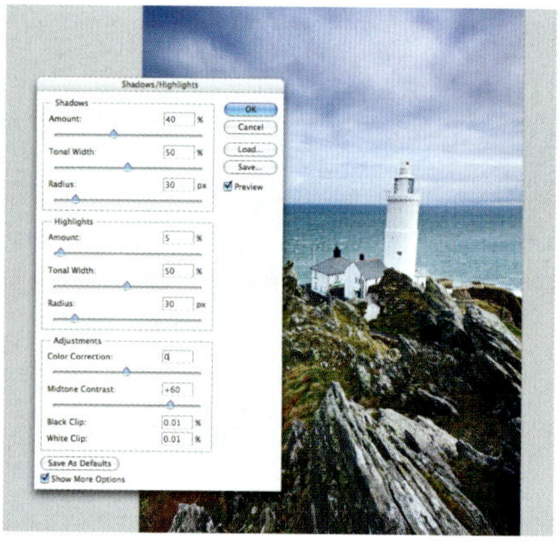

2 Shadows & Highlights On the duplicate layer go to ***Image>Adjustments>Shadows & Highlights…*** As the image is generally flat, concentrate on the ***Shadows*** and ***Midtone Contrast***, with only minor adjustments to the ***Highlight*** field. At this stage you want to be focusing more on getting the foreground right.

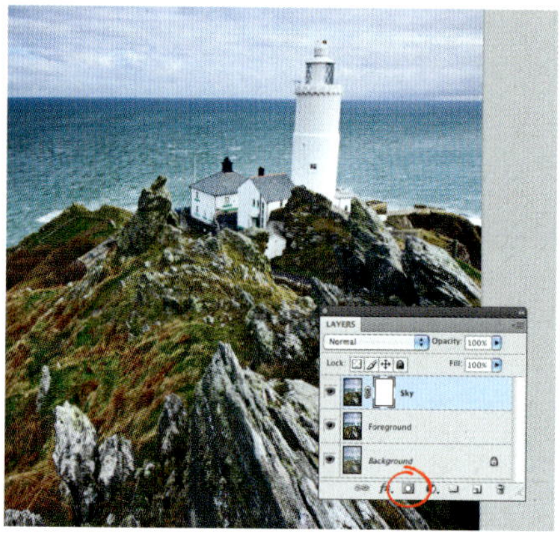

3 Duplicate adjusted layer Now duplicate this edited layer with ***Layer>Duplicate Layer…*** Then add a Layer Mask by going to ***Layer>Layer Mask>Reveal All*** or by clicking on the ***Add Layer Mask*** icon at the bottom of the Layers palette (circled). The purpose of the Layer Mask is so that the next edit only affects the sky area of this layer.

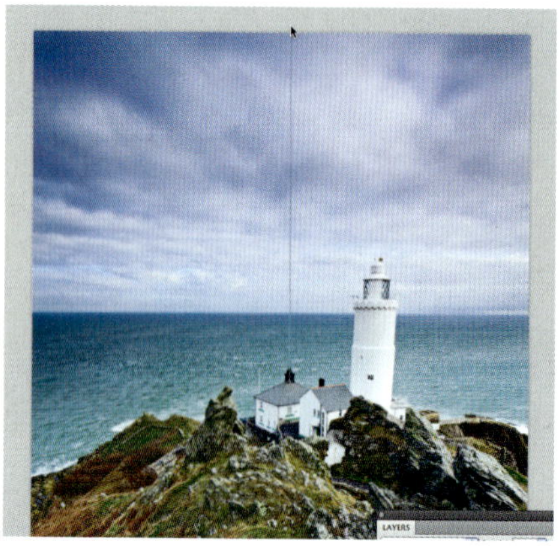

4 Add a gradient Click on the ***Layer Mask*** thumbnail and select the ***Gradient Tool***, ensuring the ***Foreground*** and ***Background Color*** are set to the default ***Black*** and ***White***. With the ***shift*** key held down to ensure a straight line, click near the horizon and drag, letting go at the top of the image. This adds a gradient to the mask.

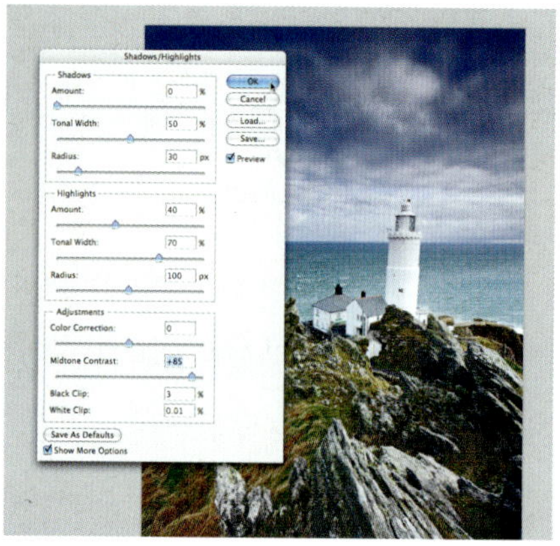

5 Create a stormy sky With the mask in place, any work done will only affect the sky area. Open ***Shadows & Highlights*** as instructed in step two, but this time work mainly on the ***Highlights*** and ***Midtones Contrast*** to pull all the detail back into the sky. You may want to increase the ***Black Clip*** to improve the overall contrast.

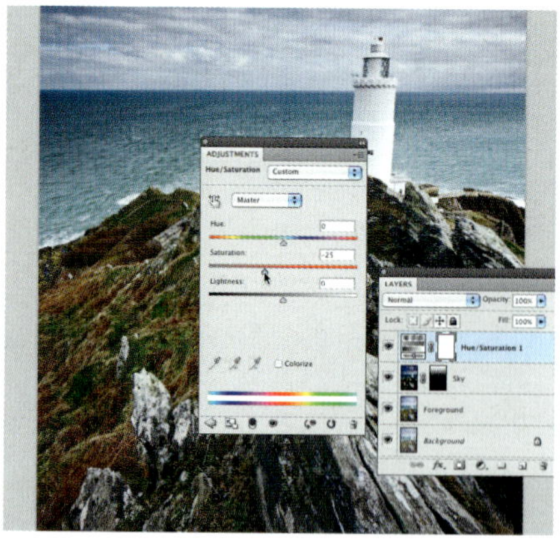

6 Reduce the saturation One final tweak is to remove some of the colour to enhance the storm-like appearance of the image. With the top layer still active, go to ***Layer>New Adjustment Layer>Hue/Saturation…*** and reduce the ***Saturation*** slider by around ***20%***, then click ***OK***. Now save as a ***PSD***, to preserve all the layers.

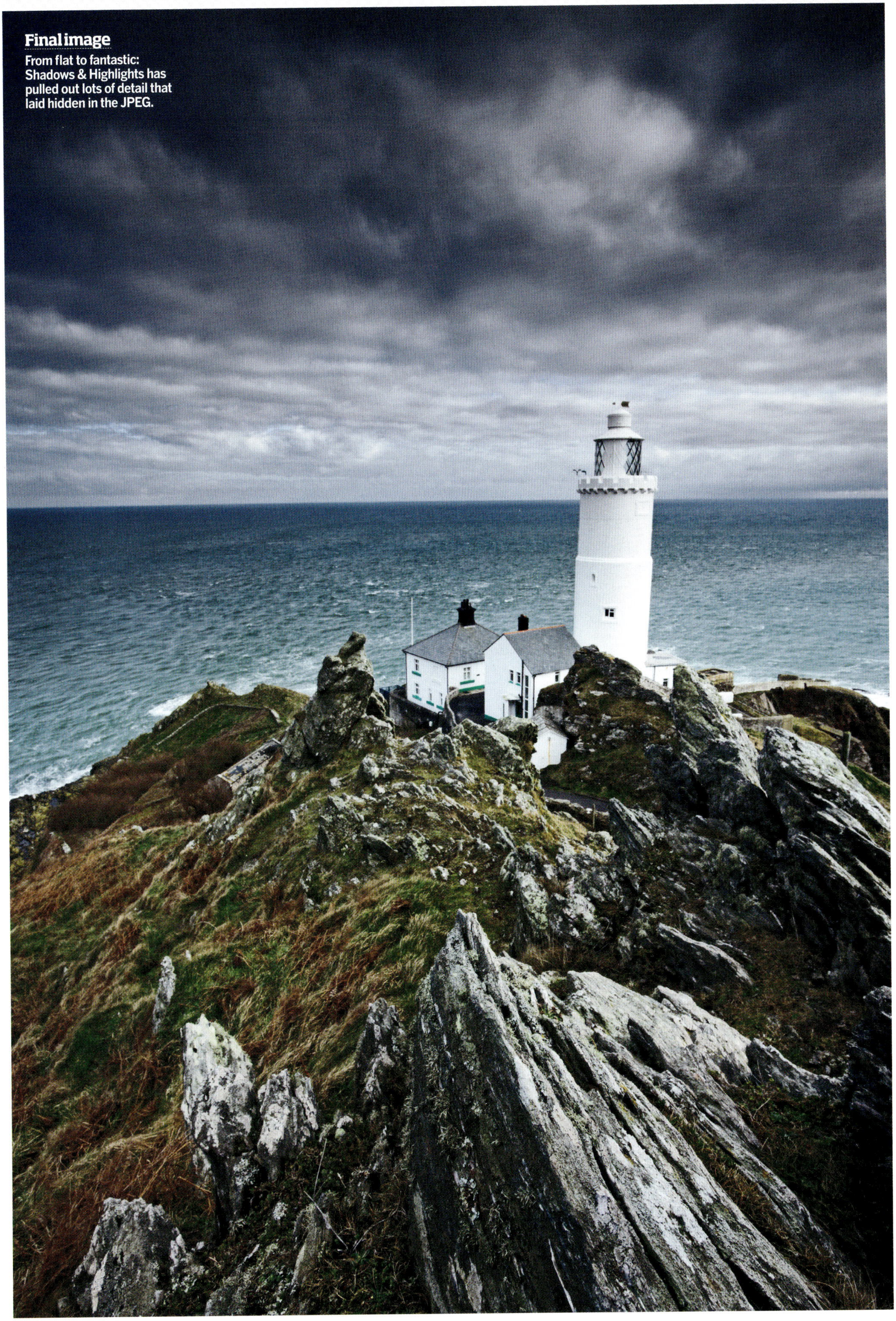

Final image

From flat to fantastic: Shadows & Highlights has pulled out lots of detail that laid hidden in the JPEG.

Boost contrast and colour with Blend Modes

Learn how to add punch to your pictures using Blend Modes and a Black & White adjustment layer

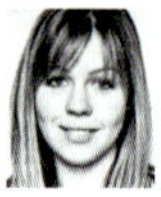

Caroline Wilkinson: Blend Modes are a quick and easy way to merge two layers: be it an Adjustment Layer with an image layer, a coloured layer with an image or two image layers, like texture and a portrait, for creative effect. Each mode – there are 27 in total – determines how the top layer interacts with the layer directly beneath it in the Layers palette.

As default, the Blend Mode menu (located at the top of the Layers palette or via Layer>Layer Style>Blending Options) is set to Normal to stop any layers from merging. The Blend Modes are grouped together, separated by a line in the menu. You have your modes that darken, lighten, adjust contrast to varying degrees, modes that decide colour based on the difference between the layers, and HSL modes, which replace the base-layer pixels with top-layer pixels. It might all sound very complicated, but have a play with the different modes to get a sense of their effects. For most photographic purposes, it's Multiply, HSL (Hue, Saturation, Luminosity) and the various contrast modes that you'll use the most.

Out of all the contrast modes, Overlay, Soft Light, Hard Light, and maybe Vivid Light, prove the most practical – each altering contrast and colour to varying degrees of strength, so it's largely a matter of taste which one you choose. For this technique, I'll show you a really easy way to dramatically boost contrast and how to manually control its results using the colour channels in a Black & White adjustment layer. We go in-depth with Layer Masks on pages 16-17, so they've not been mentioned extensively here – but remember that if there are areas that are rendered too dark or colour saturation is too bright, you can always use the Brush Tool with the Foreground Color set to Black, and a low Opacity, to reduce the effect using your Layer Mask to reveal the original detail.

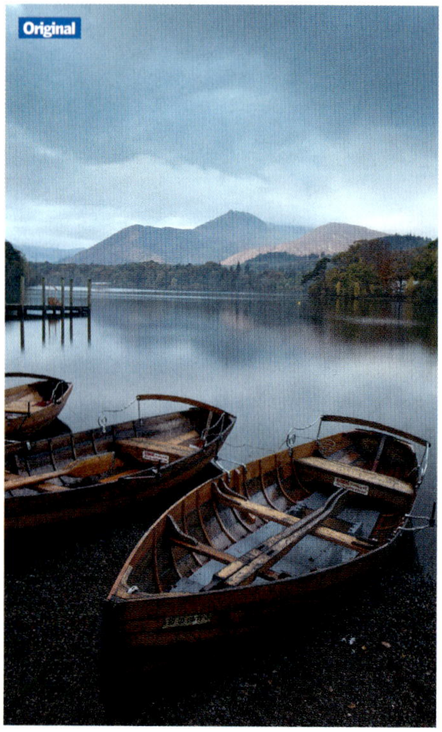

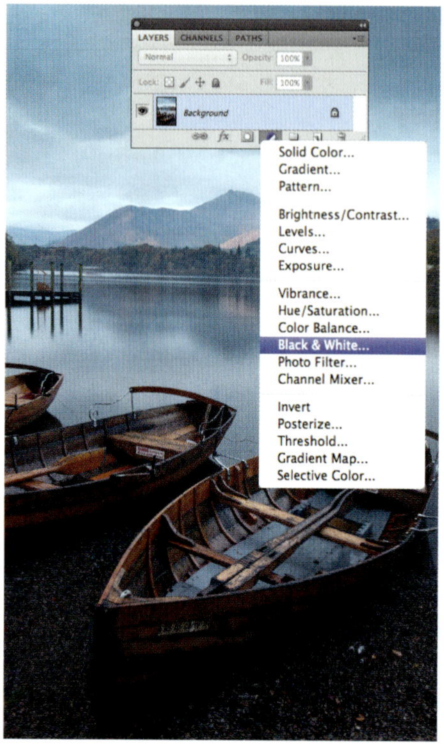

1 Access your Layers palette Open your image and make sure the Layers palette is visible (***Window>Layers***). Click the ***Add adjustment layer*** icon at the bottom of the Layers palette and choose ***Black & White***.

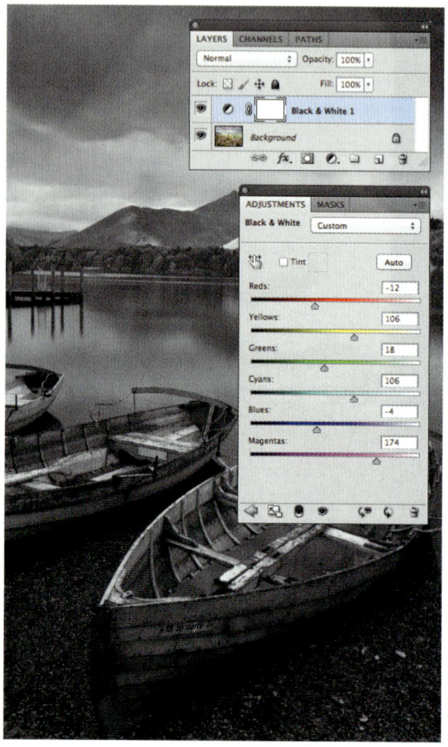

2 Edit the colours in your mono image In the ***Adjustments*** panel, use the colour sliders to edit the contrast of your b&w image. Some will work better than others, so set the slider to ***0*** if you want to return it to its default setting.

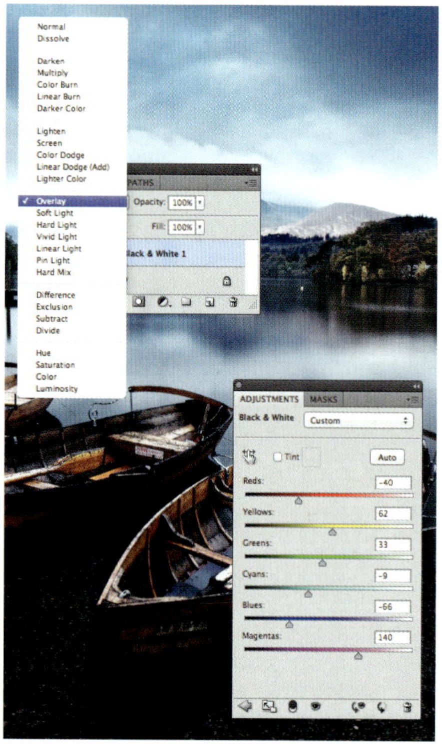

3 Apply a Blend Mode To recolourise your image, change the ***Blend Mode*** to one of the contrast modes (***Overlay*** is usually best) by clicking on the ***Blend Mode*** drop-down menu at the top of the Layers palette.

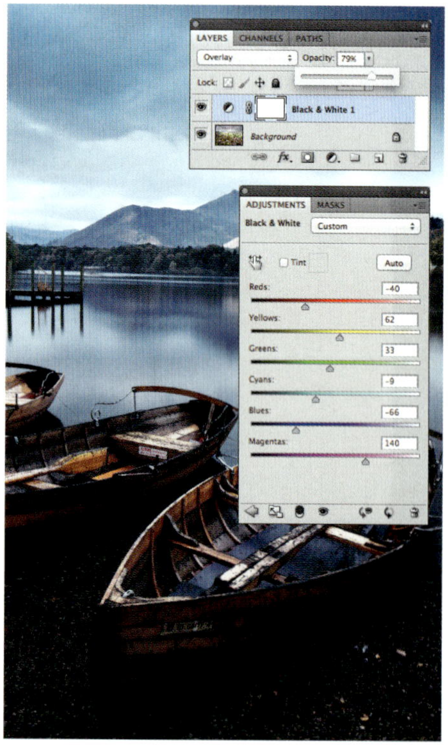

4 Tweak the results At this stage you may want to readdress the sliders to make certain colours pop. Or you might want to create a subtler effect, in which case reduce the ***Opacity*** slider at the top of the Layers palette; here it's set to 79%.

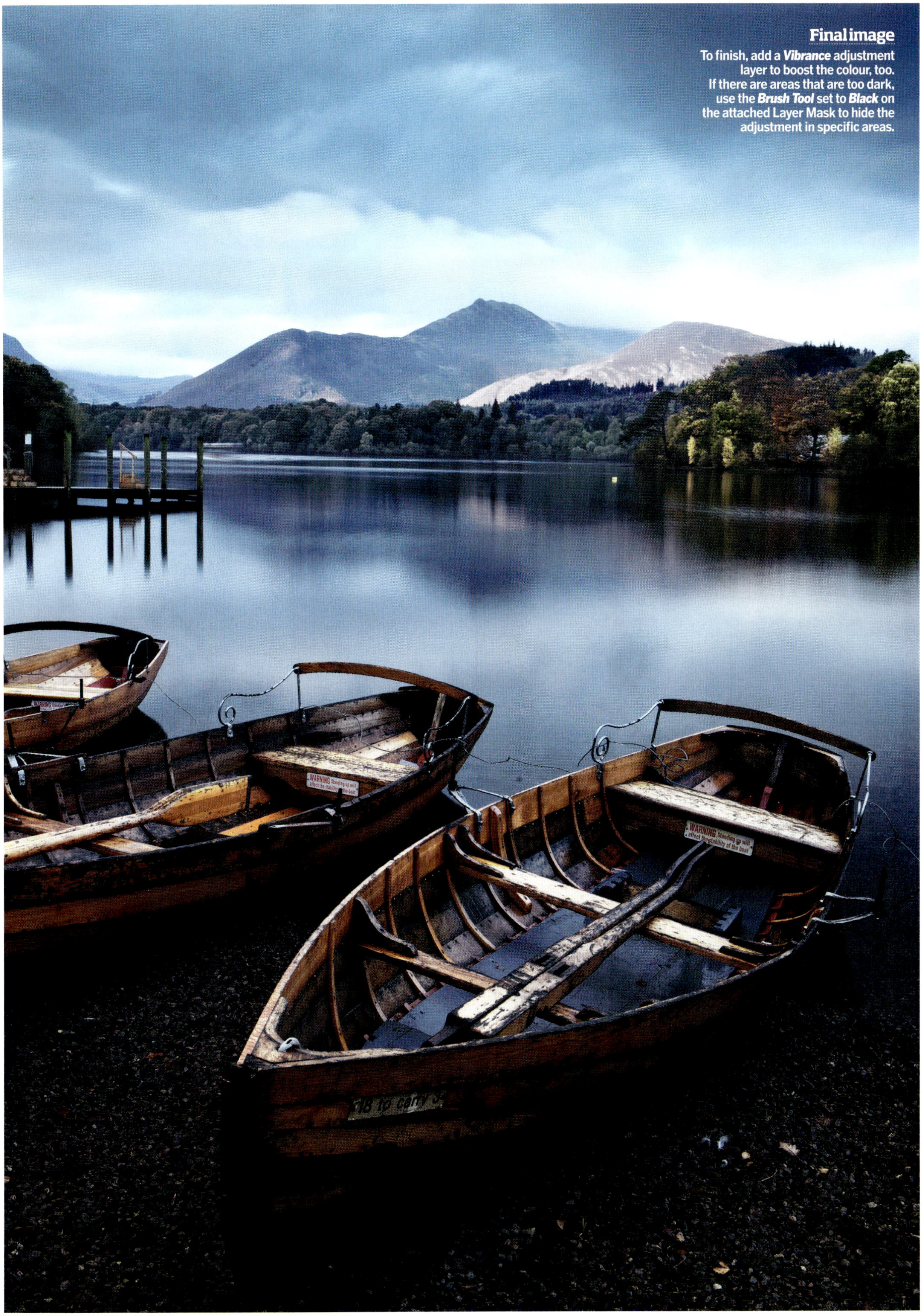

Final image

To finish, add a ***Vibrance*** adjustment layer to boost the colour, too. If there are areas that are too dark, use the ***Brush Tool*** set to ***Black*** on the attached Layer Mask to hide the adjustment in specific areas.

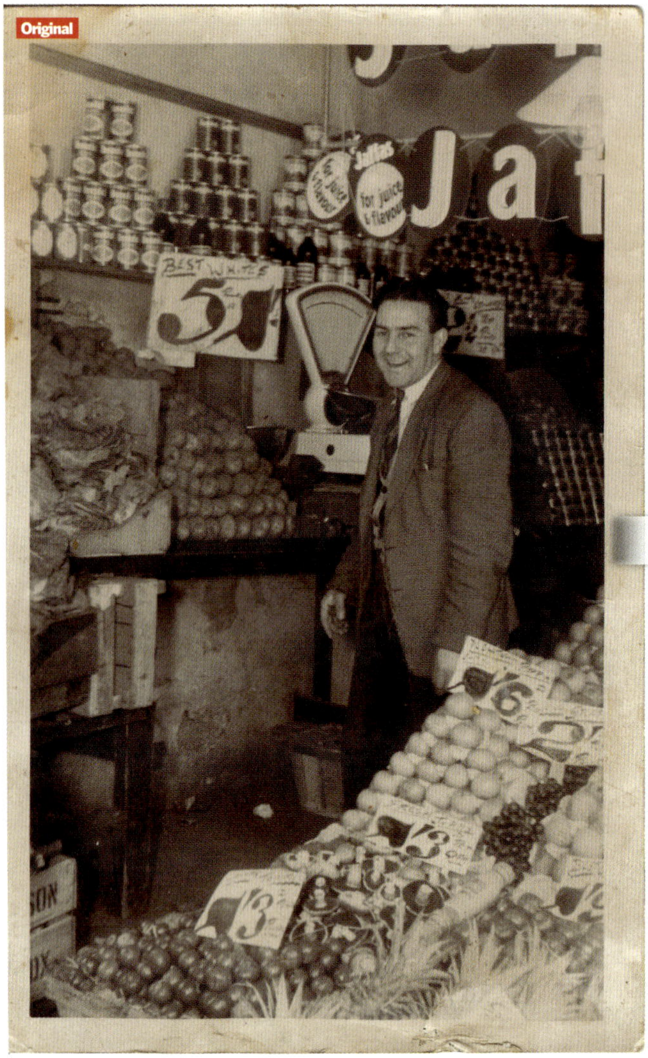

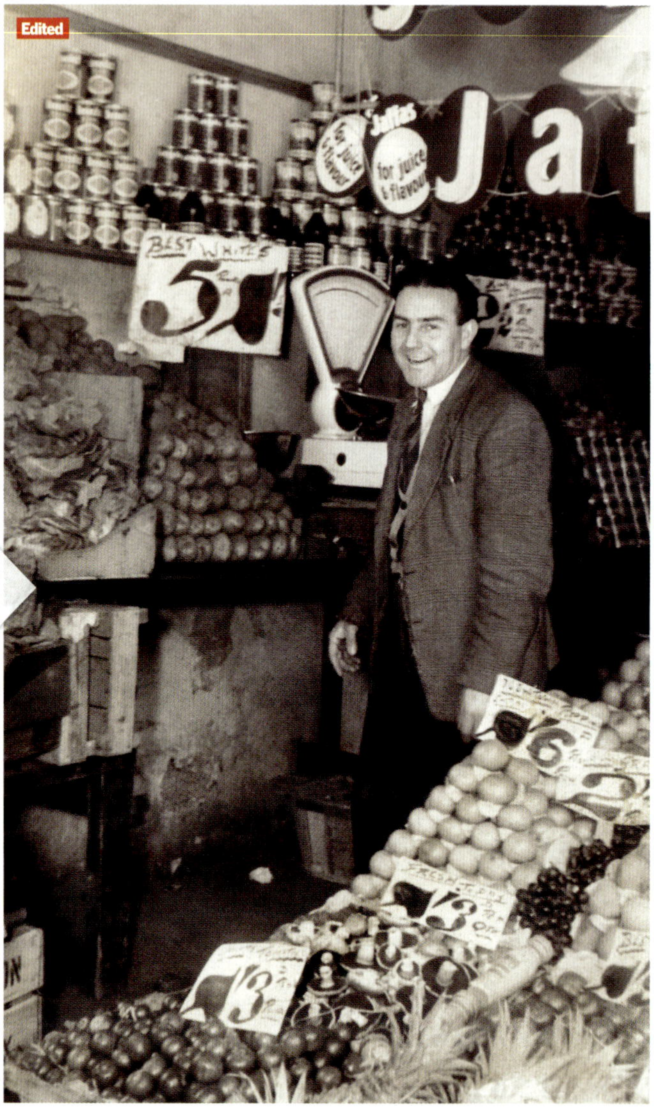

Learn how to revive your old photographs in a few steps

Restoring images is a doddle, it's retaining their charm that's the challenge. Here's all you need to know to make yours look like new

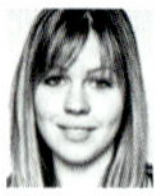

Caroline Wilkinson: Most of us would admit to having family photos, generations old, gathering dust in a drawer, too damaged to display. Before they get beyond repair, take the time to digitalise them by scanning the prints into a computer to do some restoration work. Then burn them to a disc, save them to your hard drive, put the old prints into archival protective sleeves and frame the new images. It's a lengthy process, but you'll be preserving the memories for generations to come.

Before I go further, we advise you don't cut corners on the printing of your new images. Use archival quality inks and papers to avoid discolouration and fading over time. Files corrupt and formats change, so make sure you have quality hard copies, too. If your archived images never made it into prints, remaining as 35mm slides or negatives, you can still digitalise the pictures by using a flatbed scanner.

You may be tempted to convert old prints to black & white, but part of the charm is their aged, sepia cast. It can cause images to look dull and flat, so reducing any cast will be a benefit, but getting rid of it entirely isn't restoring the images sympathetically.

Here, I used Selective Color to reduce yellow and red tones in the colour channels, Whites and Neutrals (mid-tones), but you could try Color Balance or Hue/Saturation. Dust, scratches, creases and stains are common with old photos; most can be cleared up using the Dust and Scratches command, but at the expense of softening details, which is why sharpening the image is another crucial step. You can then use the Healing Brush Tool for minor damage and the Clone Stamp Tool for areas of major restoration.

How to scan the image

If you have Photoshop, you can import your image directly.

✔1) IMPORT:

In Photoshop, go to ***File*** and choose ***Import>Twain Acquire*** (Mac) or ***WIA Support*** (PC) to open the scanning software. Make sure ***Open Acquired Images*** is selected and choose ***Adjust the Quality of The Scanned Picture***.

✔2) SETTINGS:

Select the appropriate dpi by estimating the scan resolution. The minimum resolution you should set when scanning an image for print is 300dpi and for every doubling in print size, double the dpi – ie if you scan a 4x6in print but want to print the image, double the size (8.5x11in) and double the resolution (300dpi to 600dpi). Also scan the image in at 200% to improve image quality when the picture is enlarged. Saving the file as a TIFF will also help. Press ***Preview*** to trial the scan and use the selection tool to crop the image to the proper size, ready for the actual scan.

✔3) CROP:

In Photoshop, use the ***Crop Tool*** to do any cropping and straightening.

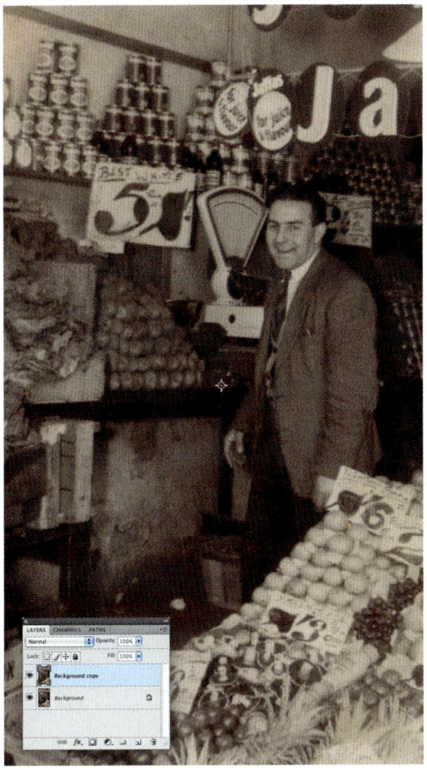

1 Prepare your picture With your image imported and cropped in Photoshop, duplicate the image by dragging the ***Background layer*** down to the ***Create a new layer*** icon at the bottom of the Layers palette (accessible via ***Windows>Layers***).

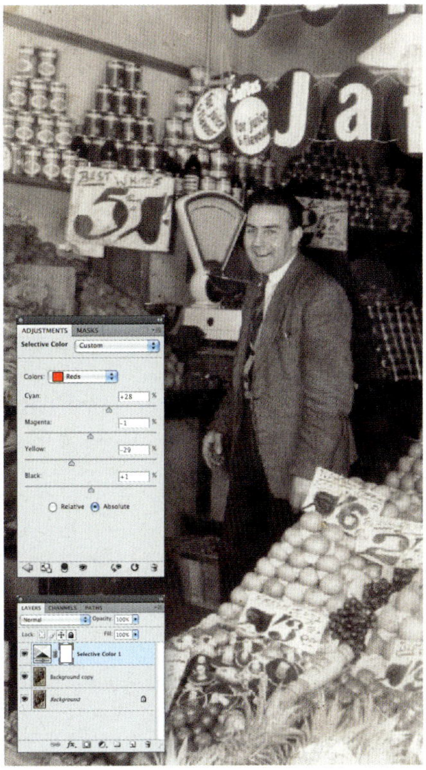

2 Adjust the colour Add a Selective Color adjustment layer (***Layer>New Adjustment Layer>Selective Color***) and then in the ***Colors*** drop-down menu, select ***Reds*** and adjust the sliders to reduce the sepia tint. Do the same for ***Neutral*** and ***Whites***.

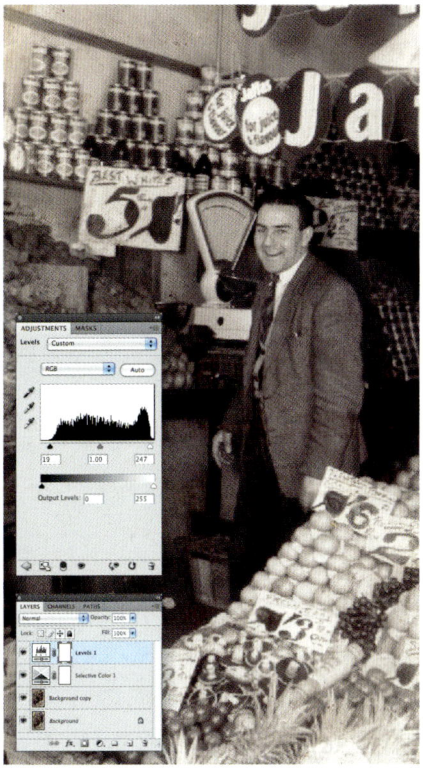

3 Adjust the contrast Use a ***Levels*** adjustment layer to improve the tonal range globally. Next, click on a duplicate image layer and use the ***Dodge*** and ***Burn*** tools to make localised tonal adjustments, keeping the ***Exposure*** below ***10***, the brush's ***Hardness*** to ***0*** and vary the ***Range***.

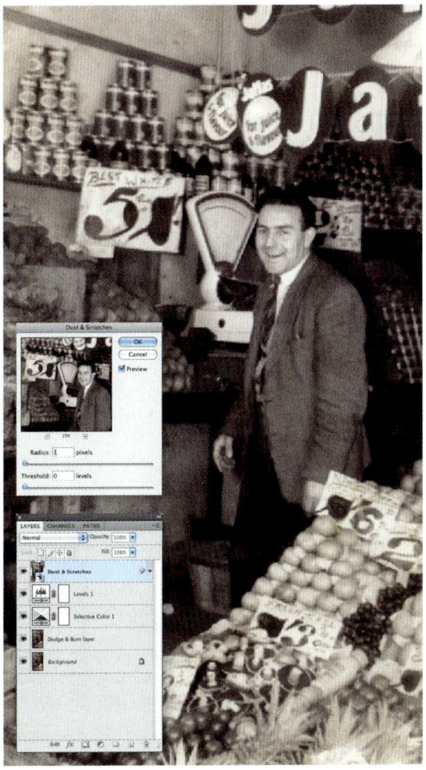

4 Retouch marks Select all the layers by holding down ***shift*** and clicking on each. Then press ***cmd + alt + shift + E*** to create a combined layer. Go to ***Filter>Convert to Smart Filters***, then ***Filter>Noise>Dust and Scratches***. Keep the ***Radius*** to ***1px*** and ***Threshold 0***.

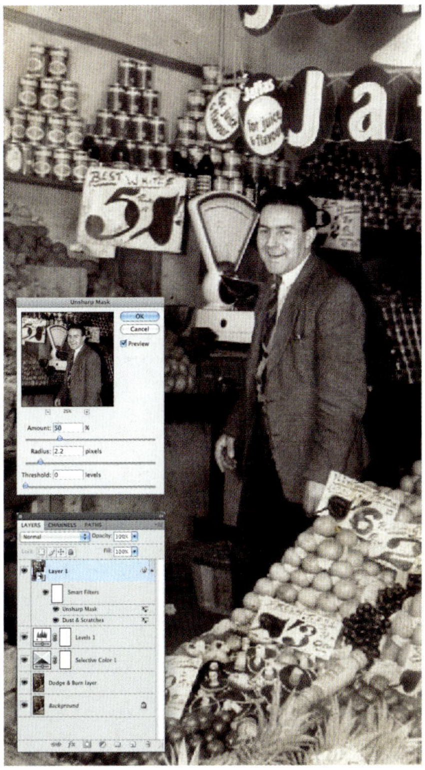

5 Sharpen the image As scanning and Dust and Scratches softens a lot of the detail, you need to sharpen the image slightly. With the 'combined' layer selected, go to ***Filter>Sharpen>Unsharp Mask*** and adjust the ***Radius*** slider, being watchful of artefacts affecting image quality.

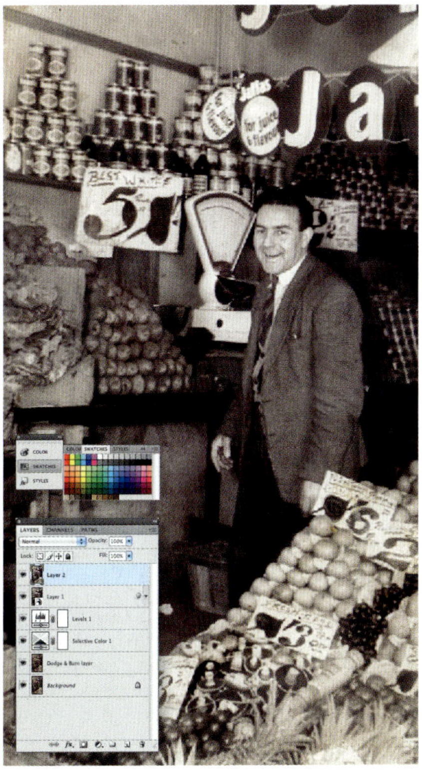

6 Clone and Heal Duplicate the 'combined' layer by dragging it down to the ***Create New Layer*** icon in the Layers palette. Now zoom into the image 100% and work your way around using the ***Healing Brush*** to get rid of any marks or stains. Use the ***Clone Stamp*** on edges to avoid blurring.

Eliminating distractions

Here's how to use CS5's cloning and healing tools to best effect…

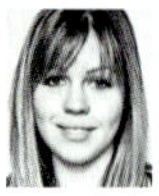

Caroline Wilkinson: While removing unwanted objects from your scene before you shoot can certainly help you at the editing stage, it's not always possible to do so, which is why these tools and techniques are invaluable. From the odd blemish on a subject's face, to phone lines, bins and the annoying person hanging around in the background, these tools can help. You could even use them to strengthen the composition of a scene: you want to move the focal point or to add a subject from a different shot? The Clone Stamp Tool is great for this.

There are dozens of preferred workflow methods when using these tools – some like the Healing Tool, others Spot Healing with Content Aware switched on, some the Patch Tool and others the Clone Stamp Tool with a low Opacity. Throw in the choices you have if you change the Blend Mode and you've lots of different options to experiment with. If you're an Elements 10 user, then you'll be happy to know that the same techniques and tools apply to you as well as CS5 users. If you'd like to know how these retouching tools work, see our panel, otherwise here's a step-by-step on how to use them.

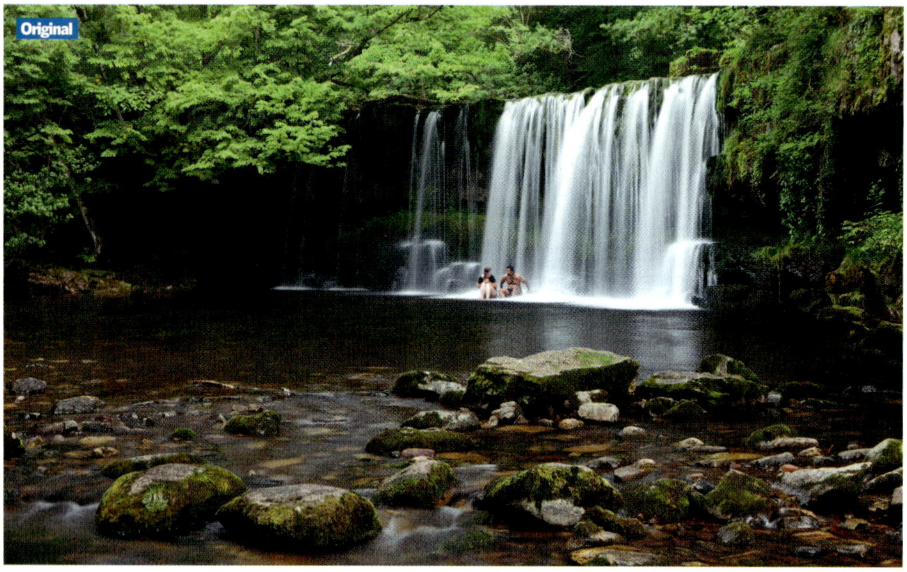

ADAM BURTON

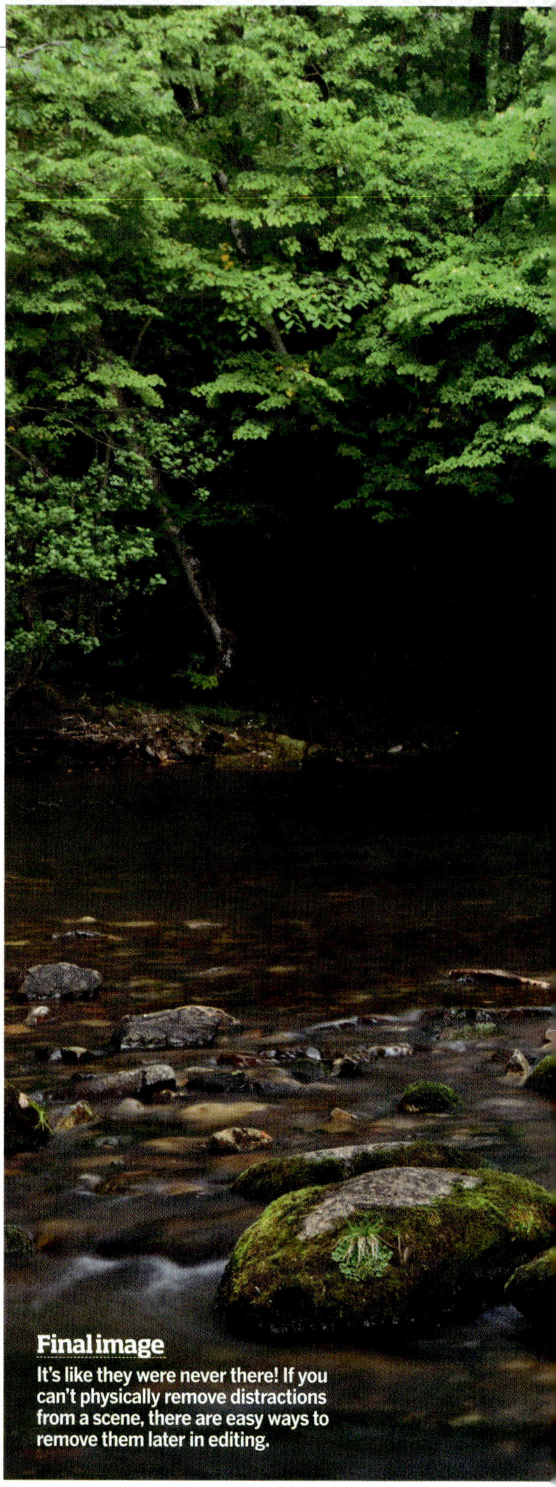

Final image

It's like they were never there! If you can't physically remove distractions from a scene, there are easy ways to remove them later in editing.

Types of brushes

CLONE STAMP: Use to duplicate objects or remove defects. Set ***Size***, ***Hardness*** and ***Opacity***, then holding ***alt/option***, click on a sample area, release and paint over the area you want to replace.

HEALING BRUSH: Blend imperfections by painting with sampled pixels from an image. It matches texture, lighting and shading of the sampled pixels to the pixels being covered.

SPOT HEALING BRUSH: This selects the source point for you, but works like the Healing Brush. Select ***Content Aware***, the brush ***Size*** and ***Hardness*** for the area you want covered and click on the spot.

PATCH: Select around the area you want to replace – click and drag that selection on to the area you want to sample, selecting ***Destination*** in the Options bar. Select Source to reverse the method.

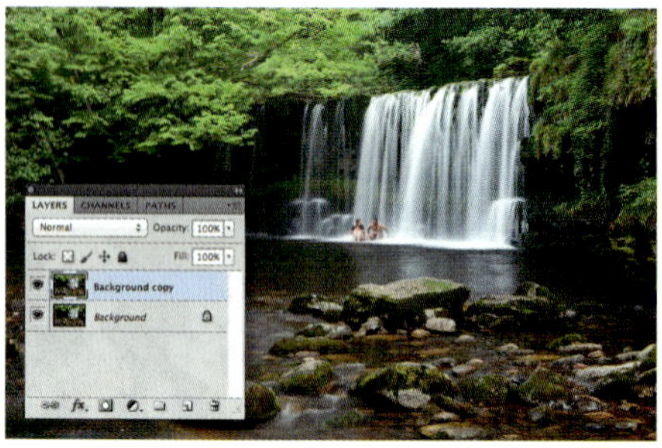

1 Duplicate image This would be a picturesque scene if not for the two people in the waterfall. Before starting to remove elements, duplicate the image layer so you can revert back to the original image if you make a mistake. Drag the layer down to the ***Create new layer*** icon at the bottom of the Layers palette.

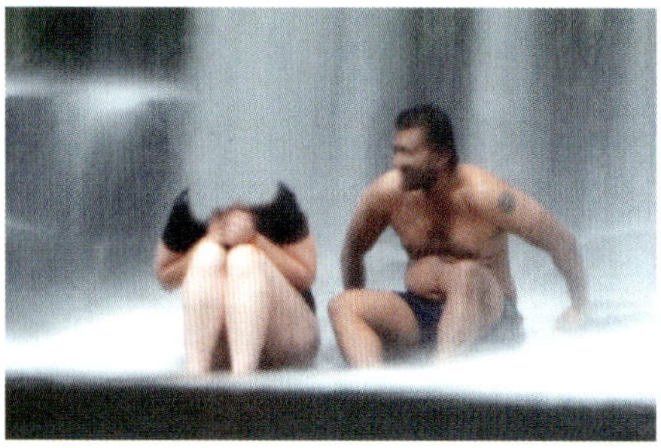

2 Zoom in to objects When working on a small area, it's best to zoom in to make the target area as big as possible. Do this via the ***View*** menu or pressing ***cmd/ctrl*** and + (press – to zoom back out). Select the ***Clone Stamp Tool*** and an appropriate size brush set to ***100% Opacity*** to copy the water's texture precisely.

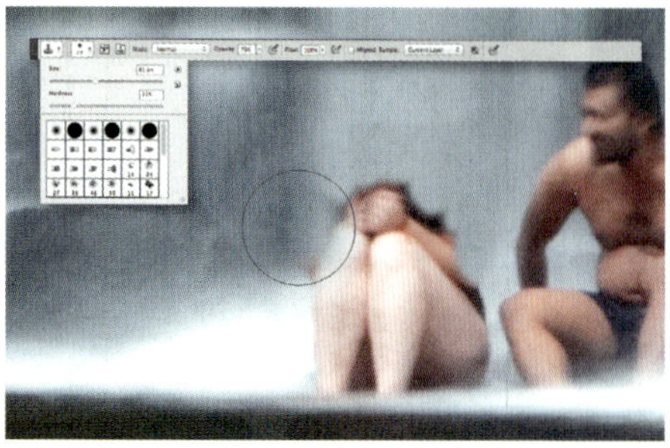

3 Blend over objects Take a sample of the waterfall – hold down ***alt*** and carefully brush downward, extending the waterfall. Vary the ***Size*** of the brush, the ***Hardness*** and ***Opacity***, depending on the area that you're working on. As this area needs to blend a little, I use a low Opacity and build up the area using a soft brush.

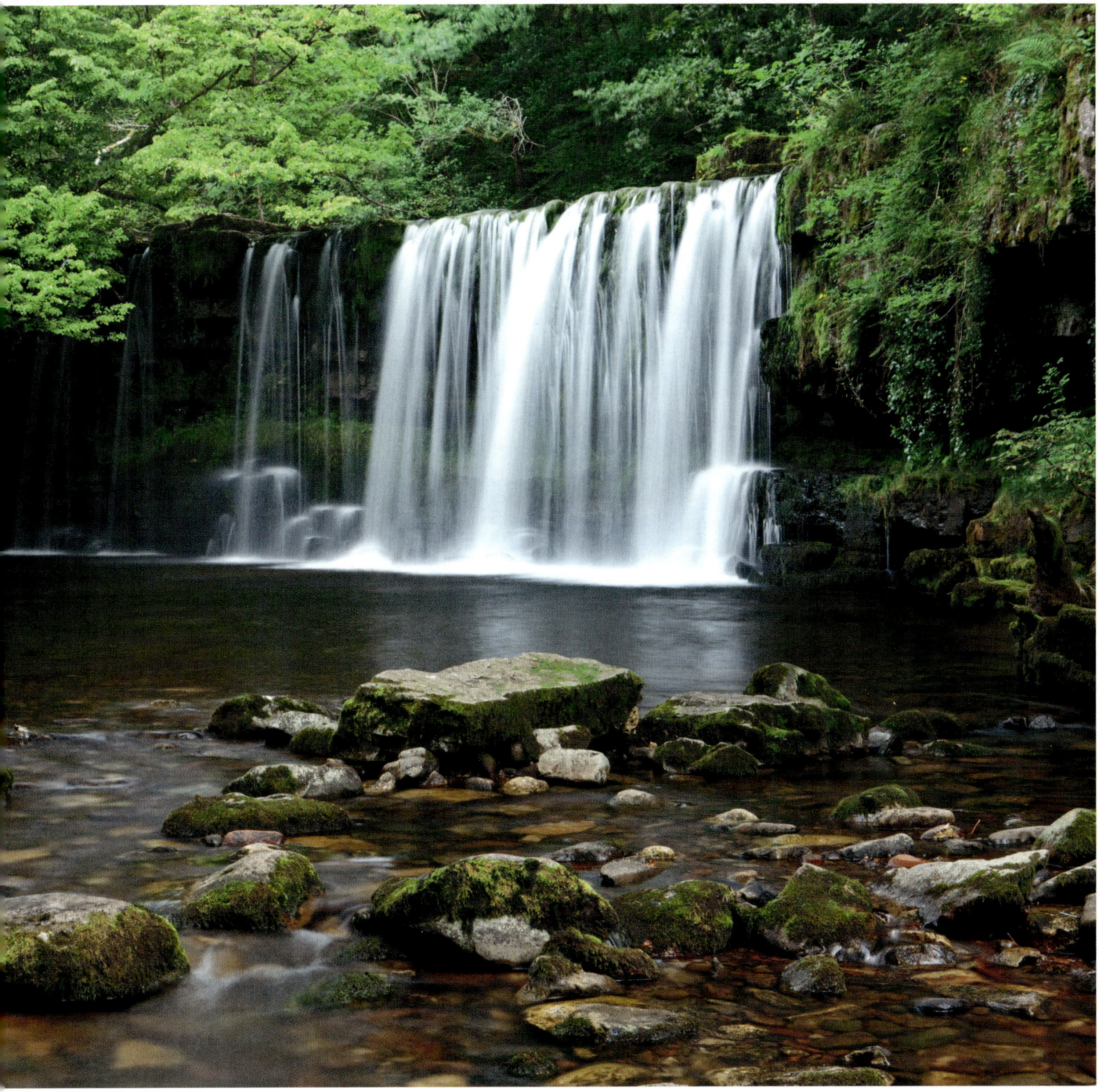

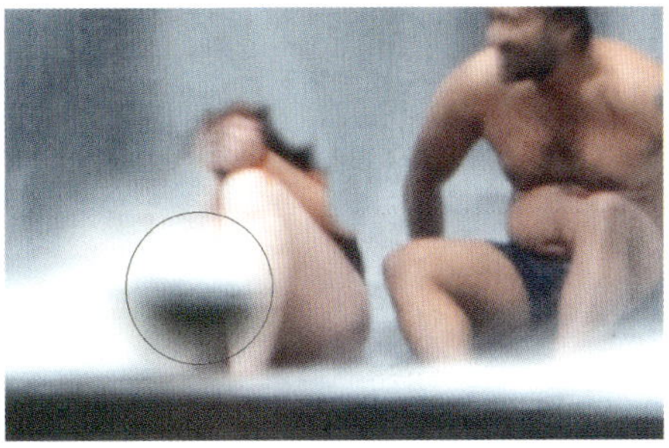

4 Reduce Hardness When Hardness is set high, there's a defined edge to the cloned area. For smooth results, keep ***Hardness*** below ***20%*** and ***Opacity*** at ***50-60%***, except if you are cloning defined edges, when ***Opacity*** should be ***70-100%***. Use the overlay image to align the sampled edges with the target area.

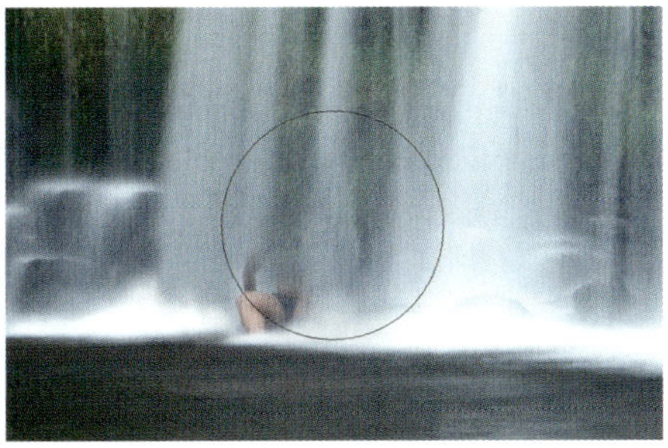

5 Clone large areas While working on small areas with a small brush can suit intricate cloning, large areas can also be cloned, but care must be taken for it to look natural. Use a large brush, ***Hardness*** still set to around ***10%*** and the ***Opacity*** set to ***95%***, take a cloning sample and use the overlay to align any edges.

Options explained

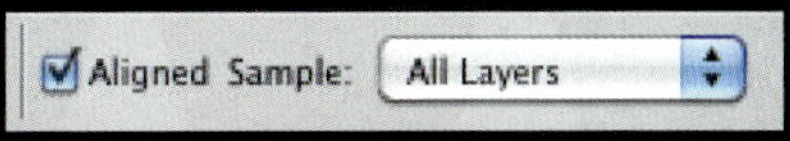

ALIGNED: Sample pixels continuously without losing the current sampled point, even if you release the mouse, by 'aligning' the source and target point. Deselect ***Aligned*** to reset the source point each time you release and click again.

SAMPLE: Select ***Sample: All Layers*** from the toolbar to clone one area of an image layer on to a different layer image, using the techniques seen here. By not selecting All Layers, you can only take pixel samples from the layer you're working on.

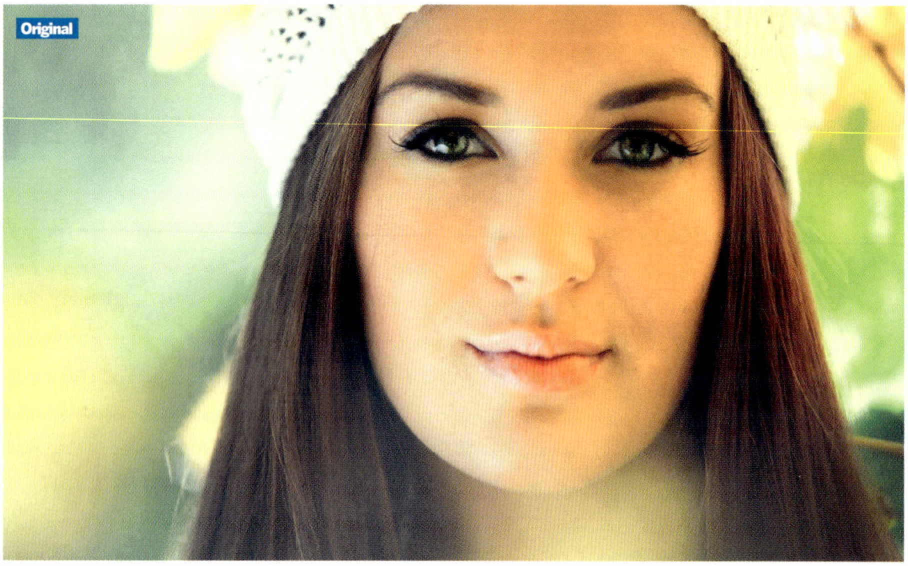

ISTOCK PHOTO

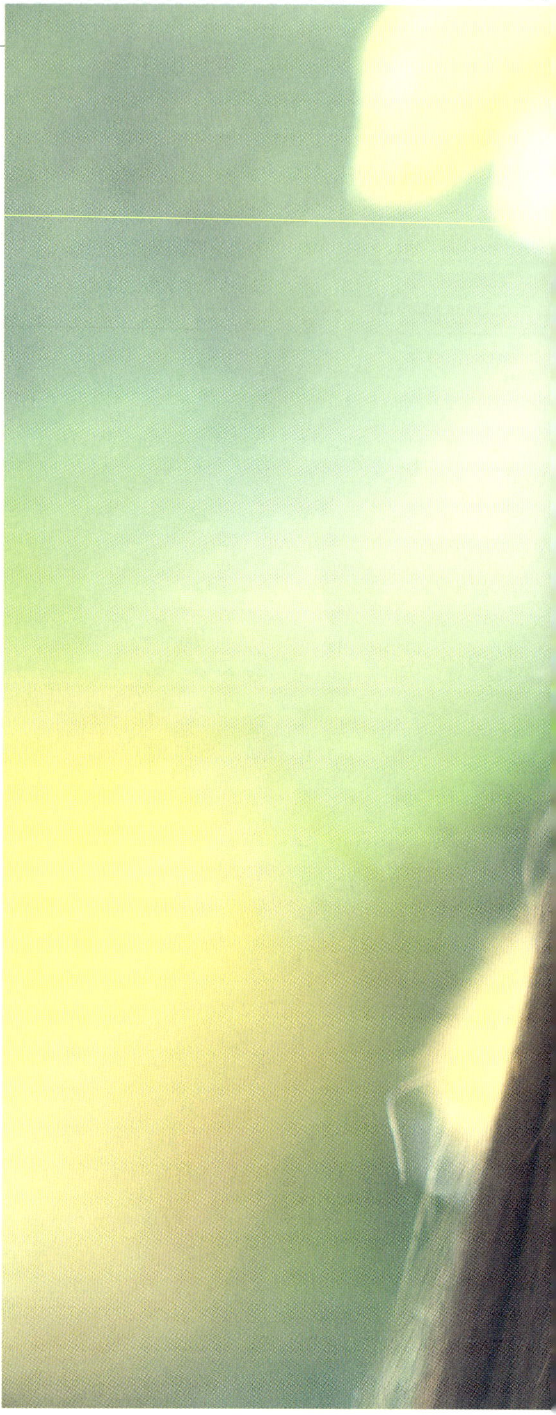

The smart way to sharpen

It's easy to get wrong: the slightest under- or over-sharpening can be detrimental to image quality. Here's how to do it properly…

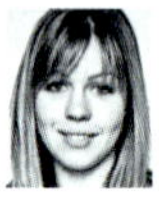

Caroline Wilkinson: Every image needs sharpening – even JPEGs that have already been sharpened in-camera – but how do you do it and, more importantly, what's the best way to approach it? There are many, many ways, which is why it's probably the most complex and avoided part of post-production, as it's easier to get wrong than it is right. You have to think of your type of image: what level of sharpening has already been applied in-camera? Do some areas need sharpening more than others? And what's your output going to be? You don't need to sharpen half as much for a low-res web file as you will for a high-resolution print.

With so much to consider, not to mention the many ways to execute the treatment, I'm going to make it very easy for you: use Smart Sharpen, and if your version of Photoshop doesn't have it, use Unsharp Mask (both accessible via Filter>Sharpen). Unsharp Mask has been the preferred method for years, but Smart Sharpen offers more control and better results, due to being able to address specific types of blur and to isolate shadows and highlights. Whichever method of sharpening you opt for, however, I can't advocate enough the role of re-editable Smart Filters. Like an adjustment layer, converting your image layers to a smart object via Smart Filter will allow you to adjust any sharpening at any stage of editing. Otherwise, when you apply any effect from the Filter menu, it directly affects the image pixels and it's much more complicated to reverse the effects. I've used a portrait for this technique, as it's a good example of when you often need to selectively sharpen to draw the detail out in the features, as opposed to globally which will also alter the smoothness of the skin.

The dialogue box has two options: Basic and Advanced. Start with Basic and use Advanced to reduce any artefacts in the shadows or highlights. While Unsharp Mask targets Gaussian blur, Smart Sharpen allows you to target Lens Blur, too; a type of blur that's more common in images than Gaussian. By reducing lens blur during editing, you can reduce halos and reveal finer details.

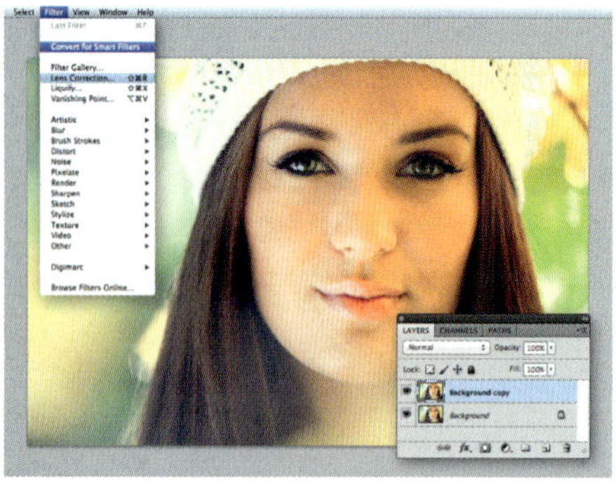

1 Duplicate your image layer Go to ***Layer>Duplicate Layer***, click on the new image layer and go to ***Filter>Convert to Smart Filters***. Click ***OK*** if a dialogue box appears. The top layer in your Layers palette should now be a smart object, identifiable by an icon in the bottom right of the layer's image: double-click on the layer to re-edit any filters that you apply at any point in editing.

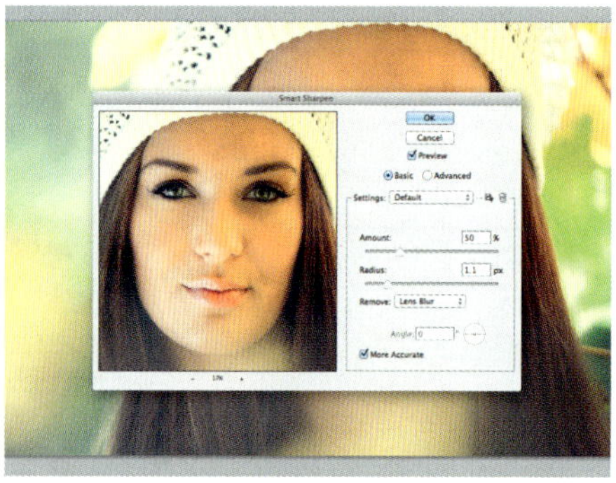

2 Add Smart Sharpen filter With the Smart Filter layer selected, go to ***Filter>Sharpen>Smart Sharpen***. Click on the ***Remove*** drop-down menu to select ***Lens Blur*** and check ***More Accurate*** as this will help you target only the areas that need sharpening. Generally, for best results, keep the ***Radius*** within ***2px*** and adjust the ***Amount*** slider to between ***50-100%***.

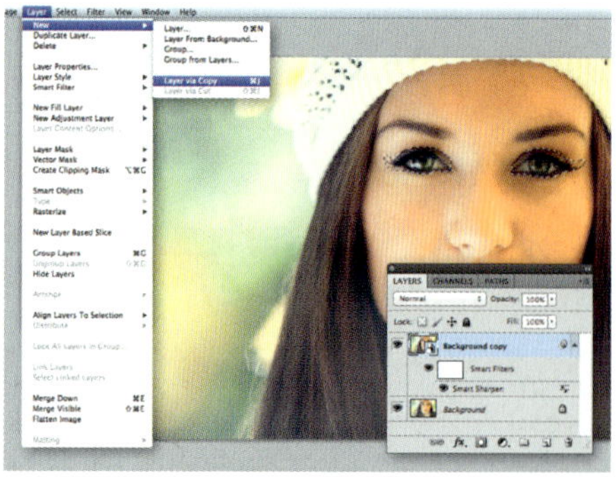

3 Selectively sharpen On some images, you may need to sharpen some areas more than others. A portrait, for instance, usually needs crisp features but soft skin – unless you want every line, pore and wrinkle visible. With the image layer selected, use the ***Quick Selection Tool*** to draw around the area you want to target – in this case the eyes – then go to ***Layer>New>Layer via Copy***.

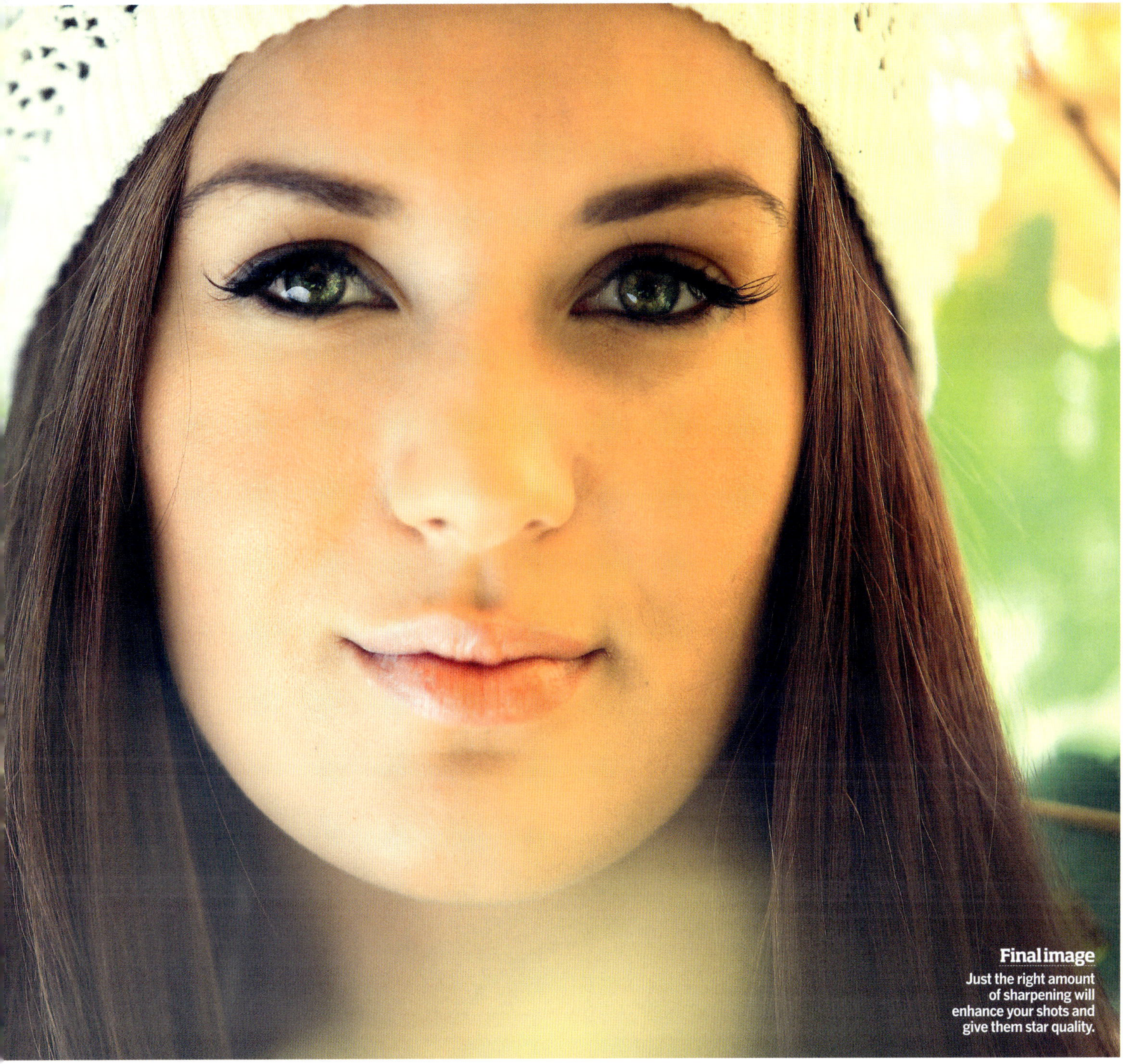

Final image
Just the right amount of sharpening will enhance your shots and give them star quality.

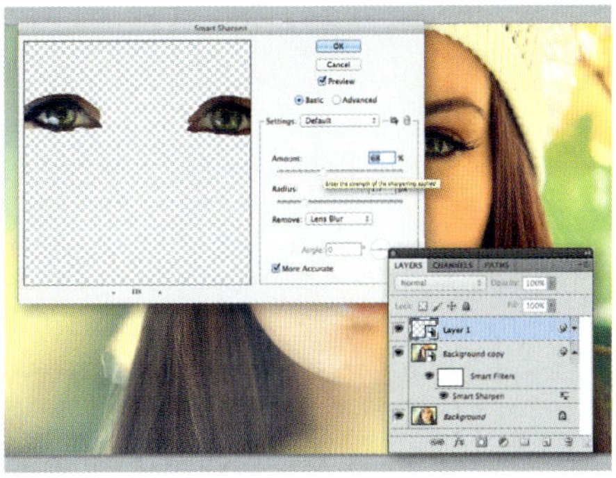

4 Make adjustments Convert the new layer to a Smart Filter as in step one, and again apply the ***Smart Sharpen*** filter as in step two. I increased the Radius to 2px and the Amount. Once you're happy, click ***OK***. Enlarge the preview by clicking on the small **+** to see the effects better and to look for artefacts. To compare the sharpening to the original pixels, click and hold on the preview image.

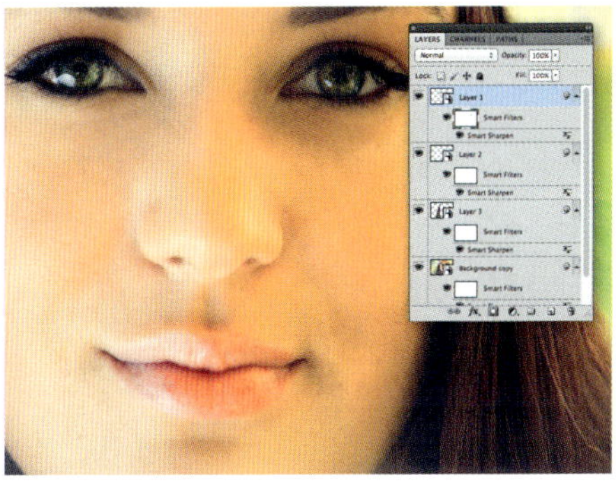

5 Refine the sharpening You can repeat these steps as many times as you want to target different areas of the image that need different amounts of sharpening. If you want to edit any sharpening in the selections, you can do it two ways: either by double-clicking on the Smart Filter or using the attached Layer Mask and Black paint to hide any areas you mistakenly affected.

Common errors

✓ OVER-SHARPENING

It's easy to over-sharpen an image once you notice the details it's revealing, but sometimes you can do more harm than good if you don't recognise the telltale signs of destruction. You need to watch that areas of colour or tonal range don't become pixelated, that artefacts (black and white marks) don't appear or halos form around the areas being sharpened – if this happens, pull back on the adjustment; easy to do if you're working with a Smart Filter.

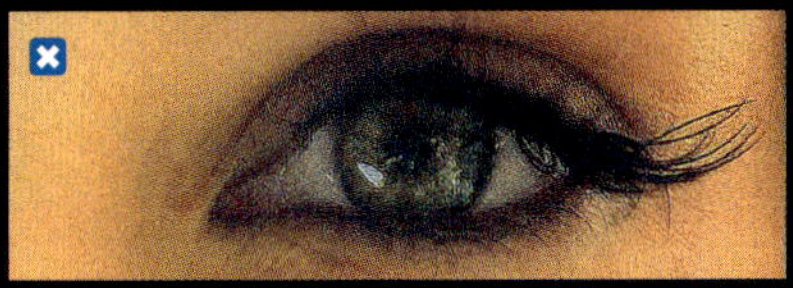

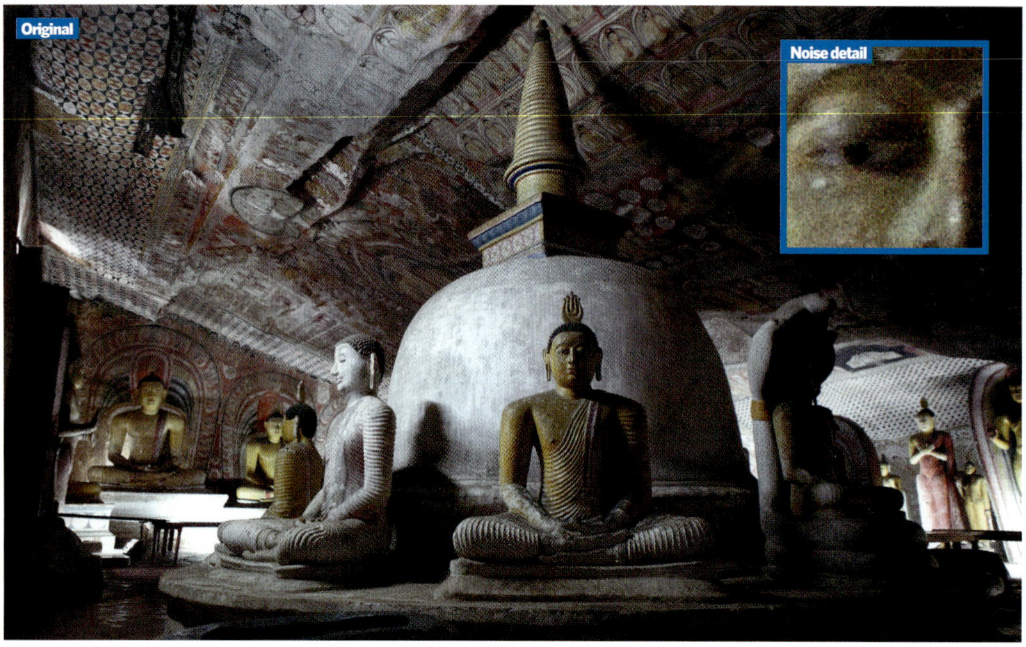

JORDAN BUTTERS

Noise reduction

Effective noise reduction in Photoshop is fairly simple, but it's easy to go too far. Get it right here

Jordan Butters: Recent generations of DSLRs handle noise a lot better than they used to. Shooting at high ISO ratings was previously avoided at all costs unless you wanted to make it look as if you were photographing in a snowstorm. Rarely did you push above ISO 800 unless you absolutely had to. However, thanks to advances in both camera and software technology, cranking up the ISO to shoot in low light no longer confines your images to the trash. Of course, using a high ISO isn't the only cause of noise – it can also be affected by long exposures or by over-zealous editing and exposure manipulation.

Photoshop offers some excellent controls that allow you to alter the grain in your images. The temptation, though, is to wind the sliders all the way across to eliminate all noise, but it's important to use the controls with restraint. Go too far and you end up reducing image sharpness and losing detail and texture. This is especially noticeable when shooting portraits as excessive noise reduction glazes the skin and can make people look mannequin-esque. When applying noise reduction, compare both the full image and a 100% zoomed-in selection; the sample area will allow you to assess the effect that the changes have on the noise, whereas the full image will give you an indication of when you've gone too far.

Secrets unlocked

The Advanced tab within the Reduce Noise tool is useful if you only have noise on one or two colour channels. First, set the ***Strength*** and ***Reduce Color Noise*** sliders to ***0*** and click on the ***Advanced*** box and the ***Per Channel*** tab. Assess the Red, Green and Blue channels using the grayscale preview to see which channels need noise reduction applying before applying it using the sliders.

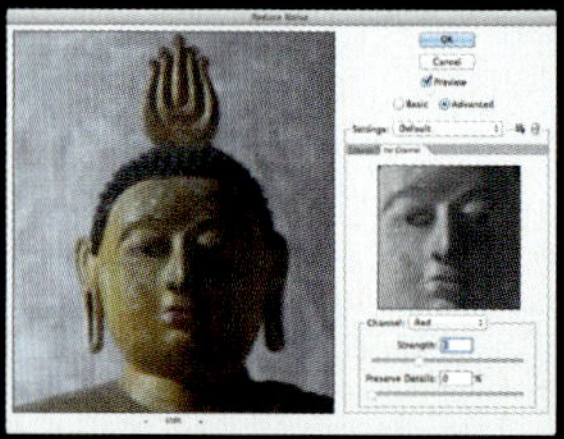

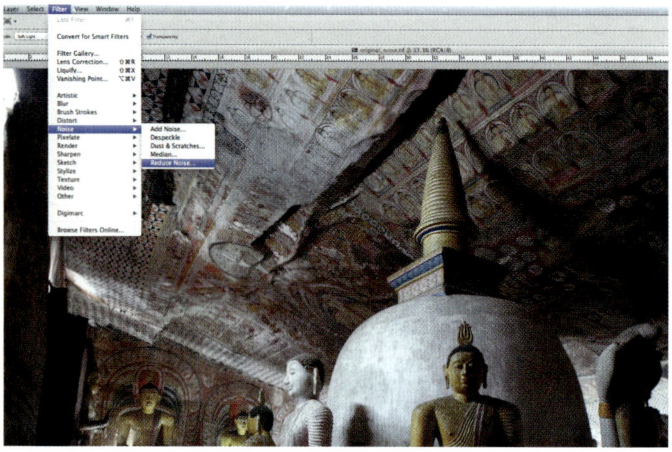

1 Open the image Open your image in Photoshop and go to ***Filter>Noise>Reduce Noise***. The Reduce Noise dialogue box will appear, presenting you with a number of parameters to adjust and a 100% zoomed preview window to assess the changes. Click on your main image in the area that you want to preview before making any adjustments.

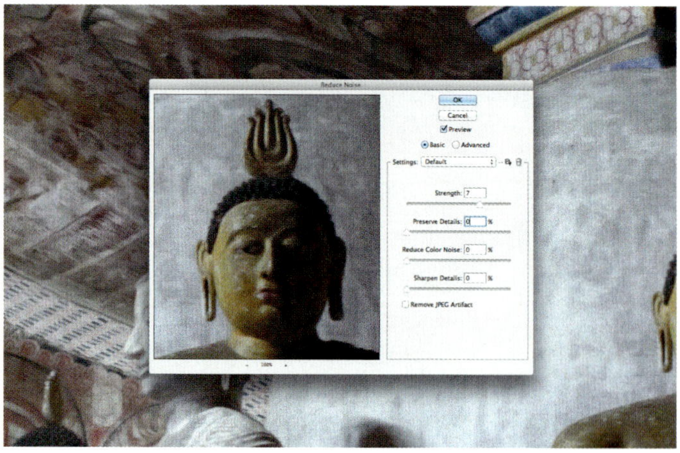

2 Preserve the details By default the Preserve Details slider will be set to 60%. Preserving detail is an important part of noise reduction, but for now move this slider down to ***0%*** as it can also preserve noise too. You should also move the ***Sharpen Details*** slider down to ***0%*** as well, as image sharpening is best done in the final stages of processing.

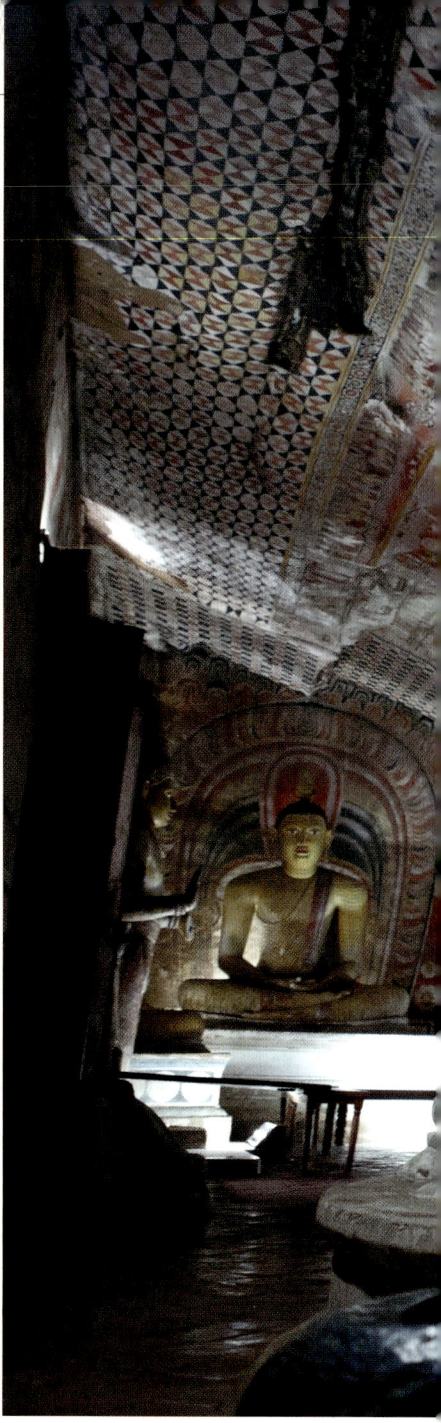

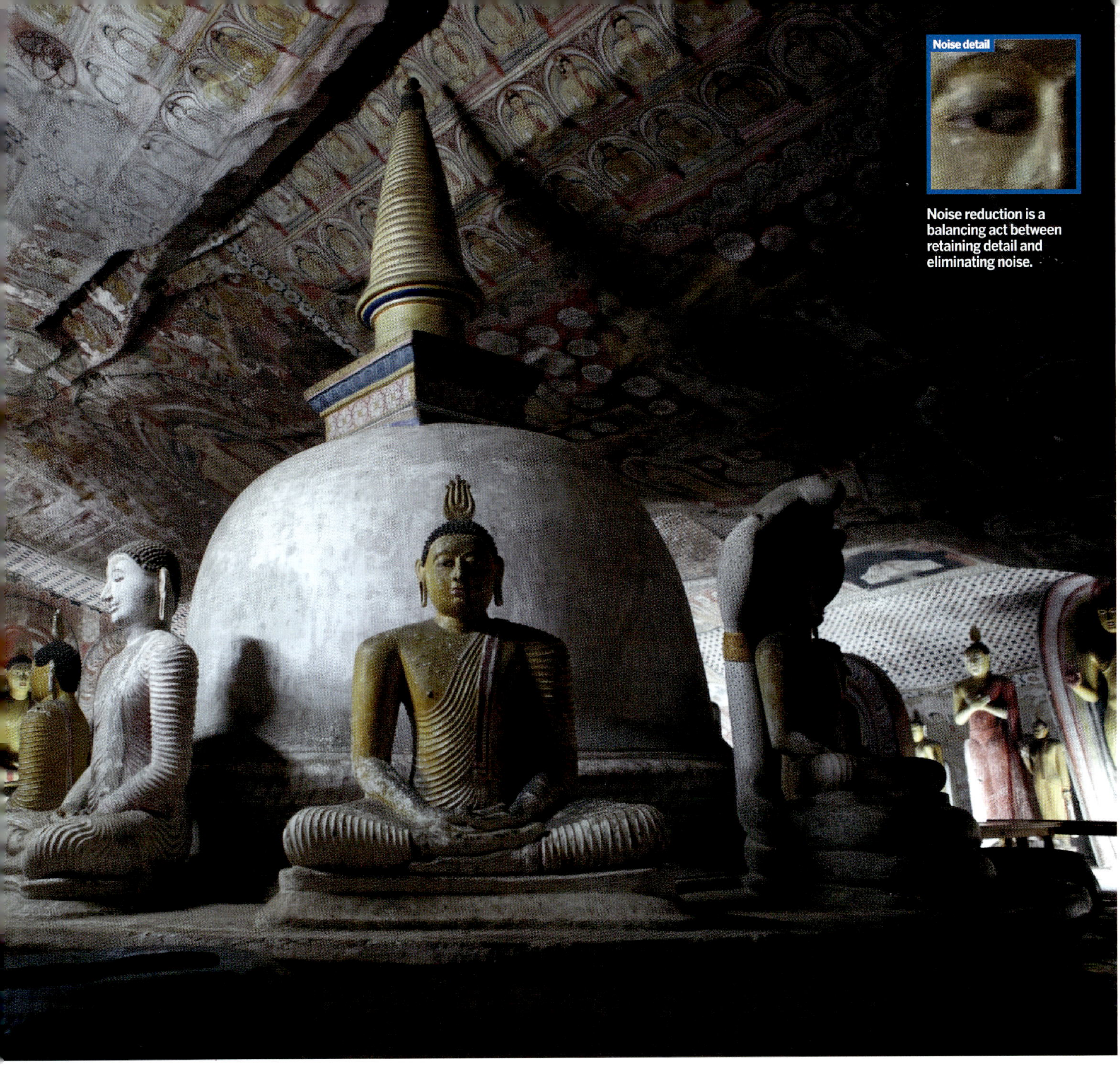

Noise reduction is a balancing act between retaining detail and eliminating noise.

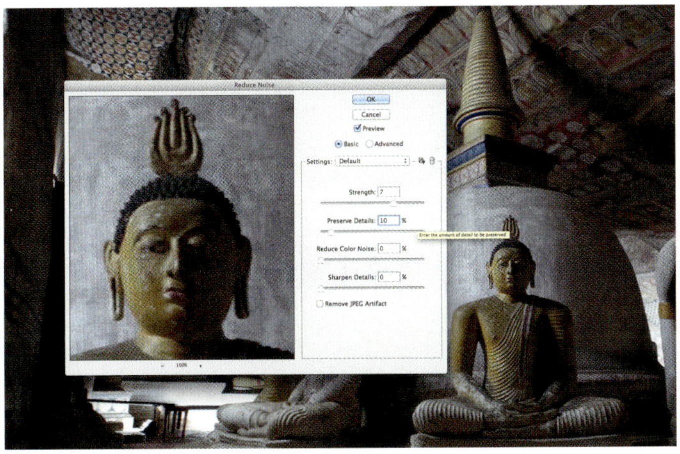

3 Reduce the noise Adjust the ***Strength*** slider to apply noise reduction. Keep a careful eye on the preview window to apply the right amount, being careful not to go too far. Once happy with your selection, start increasing the ***Preserve Details*** slider to bring back lost details, but not going so far that you start to reintroduce the noise.

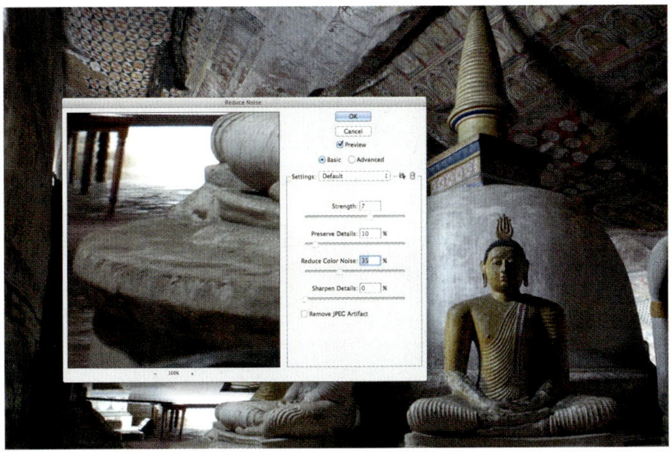

4 Reduce colour noise The ***Reduce Color Noise*** slider can be particularly useful if you have areas of coloured artefacts in your image. As before, use it sparingly as too much colour noise reduction can desaturate your image. The ***Remove JPEG Artefacts*** checkbox can also be used for getting rid of noise caused by JPEG compression.

Bland to beautiful: learn how to replace a sky

Improve your landscape images ten-fold with this simple technique where you can swap an uninspiring sky for one with more drama

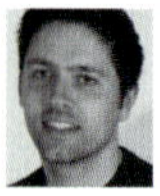

Jordan Butters: The British weather is well known for not doing quite what you want it to and rarely do all of the elements play ball when it comes to landscape photography. You can be perched above a beautiful vista, camera-ready on a tripod and remote in hand, but the one thing you can't do much about is a bland sky. All is not lost, though: in a few simple Photoshop steps you can replace the sky and transform your landscapes from drab to dramatic. You'll need to find a replacement sky to swap in, of course, and it's worth keeping a small library of skies in a folder on your computer for such occasions.

Try to shoot a range of different skies from different times of the day: the benefit of this is that it makes it a lot easier when the sky you are replacing is of a similar colour and time of the day to the replacement. You'll often find that trial and error is the key to finding the right sky for your scene.

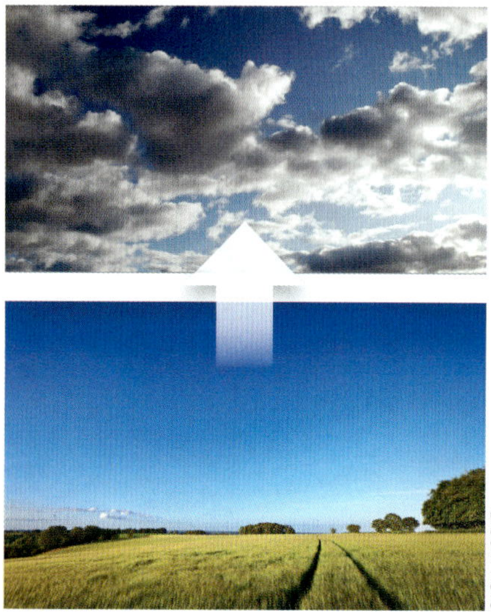

ISTOCK PHOTO

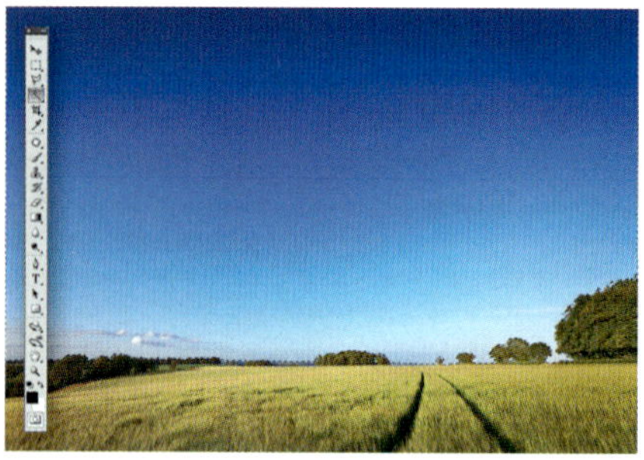

1 Select the sky Open your image, choose the ***Quick Selection Tool*** and begin painting across the sky. If your image contains objects on the horizon, as ours does, you will need to zoom in and adjust your brush ***Size*** in the options toolbar to make a more accurate selection. If you select an area by mistake, simply hold down the ***alt*** key and erase the selection. Once happy with your selection, go to ***Select>Inverse***.

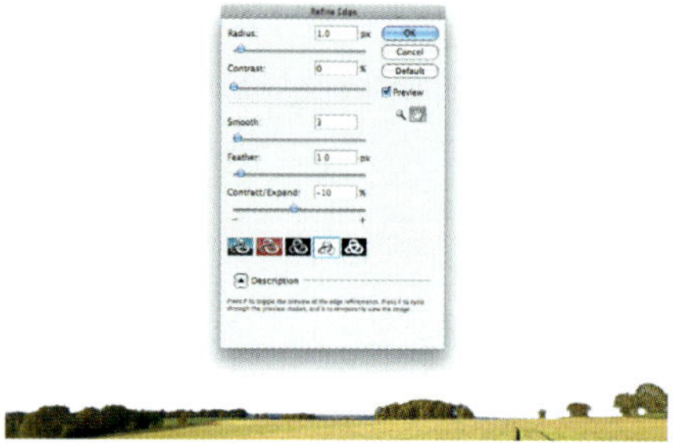

2 Refine the selection Go to ***Select>Refine Edge*** to bring up the ***Options*** window. Click ***Default*** and the sky will appear white. Using the ***Contract/Expand*** slider, adjust the selection so that it closely follows the lines of the horizon. You can alter the preview that you see by selecting one of the preview options at the bottom. Once done, click ***OK***. Then go to ***Select>Inverse*** again and press the ***backspace*** key to remove the sky.

New horizons

The sky typically gets brighter the closer to the horizon it is. Bear this in mind when applying your gradient – if the gradient is too low or too hard, then the effect will lack realism

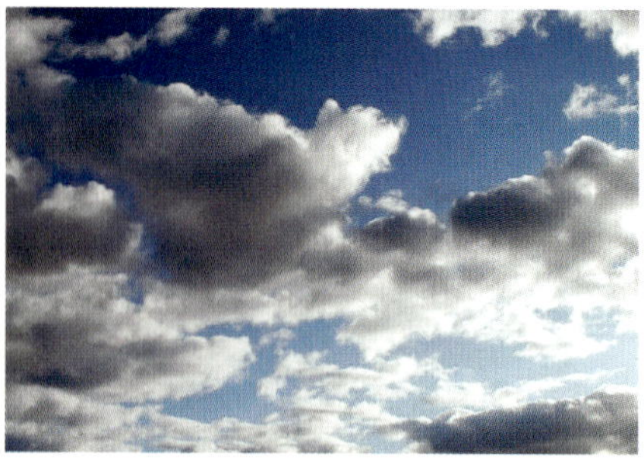

3 Bring in the new sky Open your replacement sky image in a new window and, using the ***Rectangular Marquee Tool***, select the sky only. Copy your selection by going to ***Edit>Copy*** and close your sky image without saving. Head back to your original image and paste the sky in by going to ***Edit>Paste***. It's very unlikely that your new sky will fit your image straight away, so don't worry if this is the case.

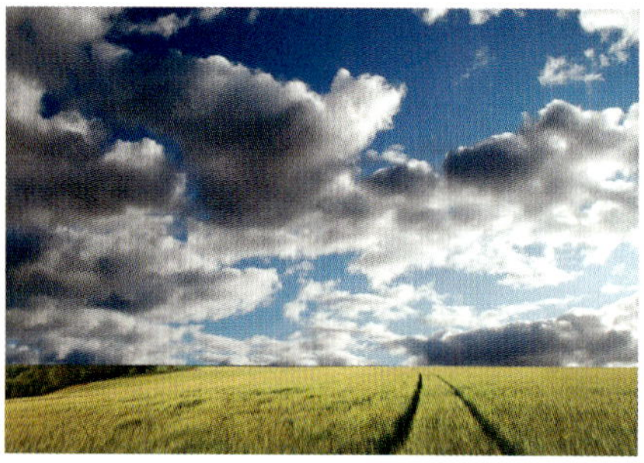

4 Adjust the proportions Go to ***Edit>Transform>Scale*** and, holding down the ***shift*** key, drag the corners of the sky image out to match the width of your landscape. Once happy, click on the ***tick*** at the top, or press the ***enter*** key. Use the ***Move Tool*** to line the sky up so that it completely covers the white area of the image. Don't worry about any overlap onto the horizon at this point.

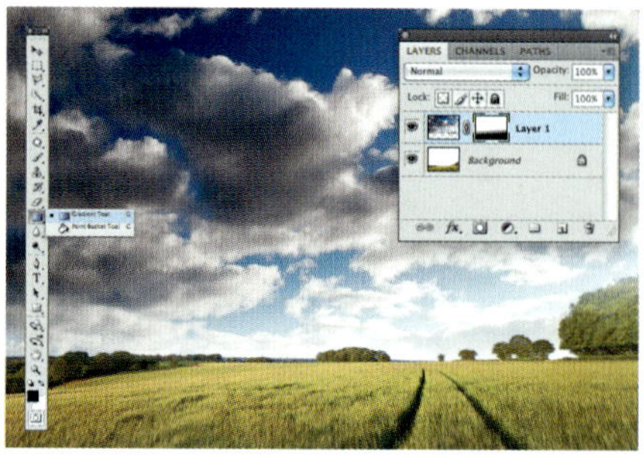

5 Create a gradient Click on the ***Add Vector Mask*** button in the Layers palette. Select the ***Gradient Tool*** and, at the top of the screen, make sure that the black to white gradient is selected. On the image, click and drag the line from just below the horizon towards the top of the sky, then release the button. This part involves some trial and error, but you can repeat as many times as you need to until you are happy with the effect.

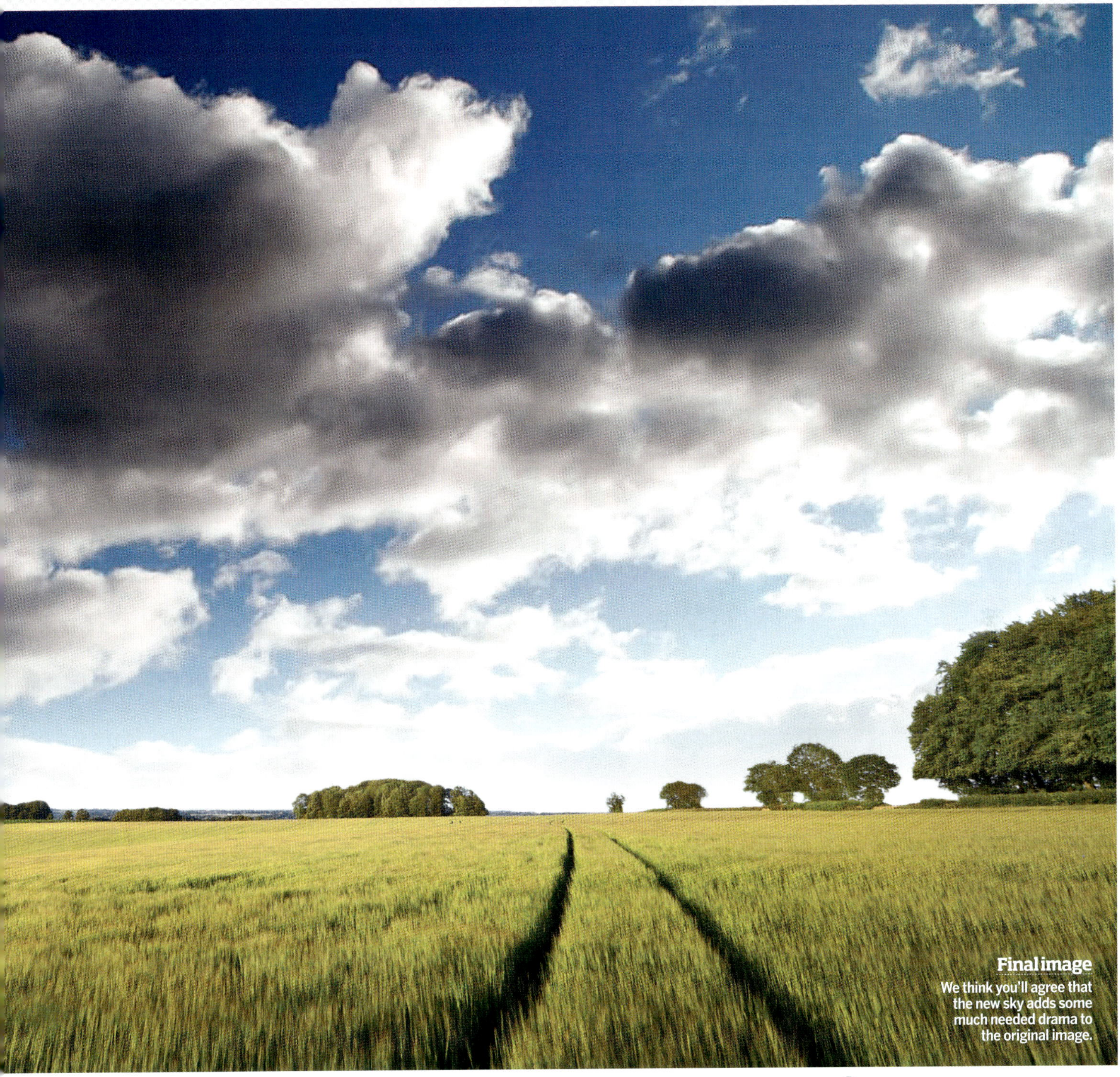

Final image
We think you'll agree that the new sky adds some much needed drama to the original image.

ISTOCK PHOTO

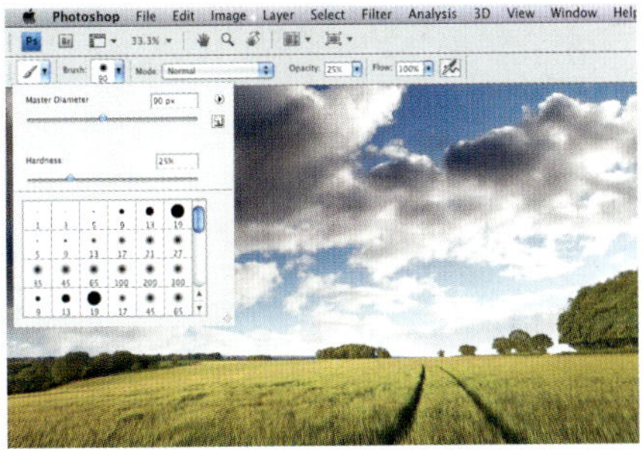

6 Tidy up the horizon Some of your new sky will still overlap onto the landscape, so to tidy this up, select the ***Brush Tool***, lower the ***Opacity*** to ***25%*** and set the brush's ***Hardness*** to ***25%*** in the brush options toolbar. Select ***Black*** as your ***Foreground Color*** and brush over the horizon, building up areas that you wish to reveal. If you go too far or make a mistake, simply select ***White*** as your ***Foreground Color*** and brush back over.

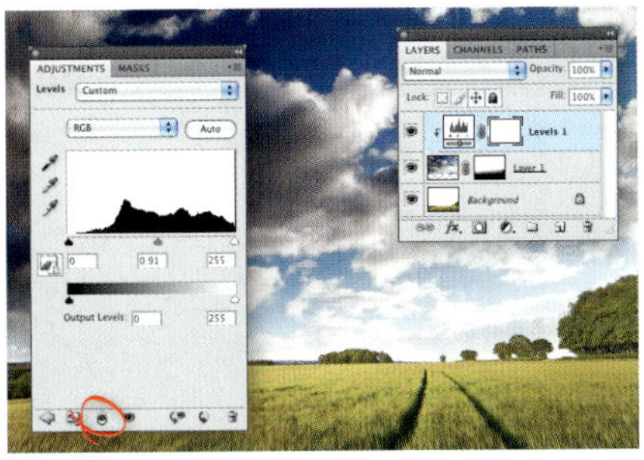

7 Adjust the contrast In the Layers palette, click on the ***Create new adjustment layer*** button and select ***Levels*** from the menu. First make sure that the adjustment is clipped to the layer below only by clicking the button at the bottom of the Adjustments palette. Then adjust the contrast of your sky to match the rest of the image using the middle (mid-tones) level slider. Once done, save your image using ***File>Save As***.

Secrets unlocked

✓ QUICK SELECTION

The Quick Selection Tool was released with the launch of Photoshop CS3 and Elements 6, and has featured in all versions since. It works by detecting contrast differences, and makes a selection based on this; ideal for separating skies from horizons. Just be aware of horizons with low cloud or mist cover, as the tool may struggle to separate them accurately.

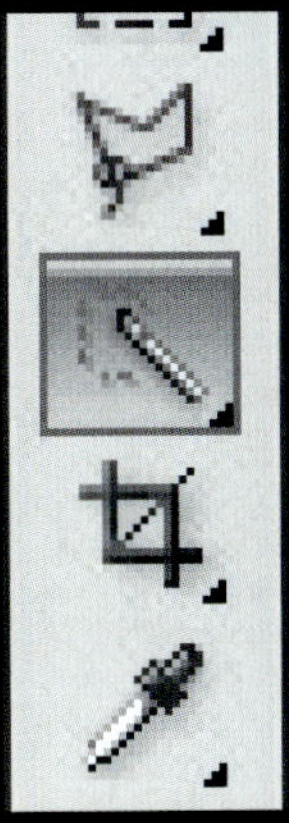

Extend a background

Changing the aspect ratio of an image is often akin to fitting a round peg into a square hole. Extend the background to make life easier

Jordan Butters: Extending a background is an incredibly useful technique. It can be used to change the aspect ratio of an image without resorting to awkwardly cropping your image and either drastically altering the composition or, even worse, cropping out part of your subject. It's also a widely used technique in publishing when overlaying copy on an image.

There's no one-size-fits-all approach to extending a background and quite often you'll find that a combination of different methods works best – see our box-out for alternative ways to do it. The general rule of thumb is that the more complicated and less uniform the background, the trickier the process becomes. Clear and uncluttered backgrounds with a solid, uniform tone are the easiest; for example, those shot against a single-colour backdrop.

In this example, I want to resize my 6x4in image to fit neatly within a 9x7in photo frame. If I was to simply crop the image I would end up cropping out either part of the subject's head or feet – not ideal. By first making sure that my entire subject is included in the frame, I can extend the background at each side to fill the missing areas. The following four steps will show you how…

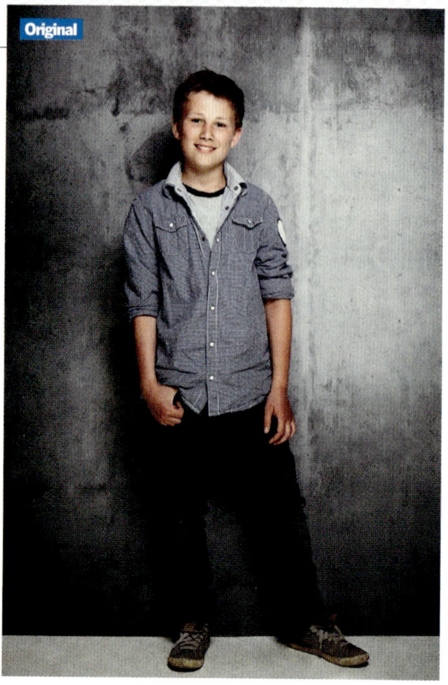

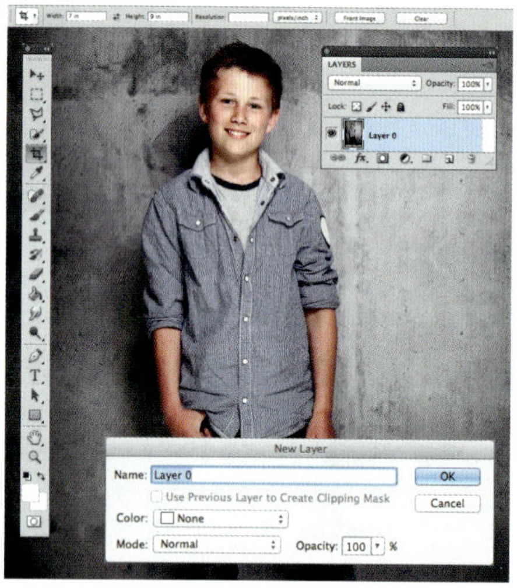

1 Select the ratio First you need to unlock the Background layer; double-click on the layer in the Layers palette. In the dialogue box that opens up, click ***OK***. Select the ***Crop Tool*** and, in the menu bar at the top, enter the new aspect ratio that you wish your image to take; in my case, 7in Width by 9in Height.

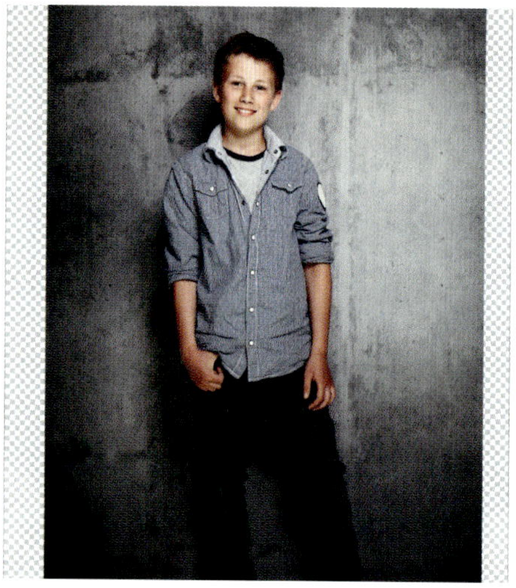

2 Crop your image Click and drag to make your initial selection. At this point the tool won't allow you to select past the edges of the existing image. Release the mouse and then click on one of the corner anchor points and drag outwards, off the edge of the image. Press the ***Enter*** key to commit to the crop.

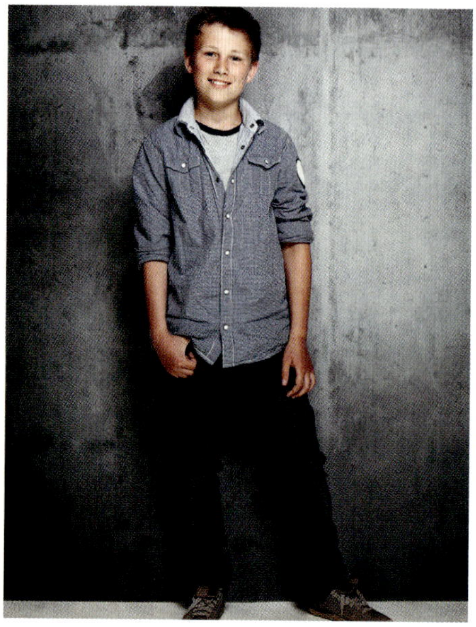

Above: Applying a 9x7in crop without extending the background crops the subject.

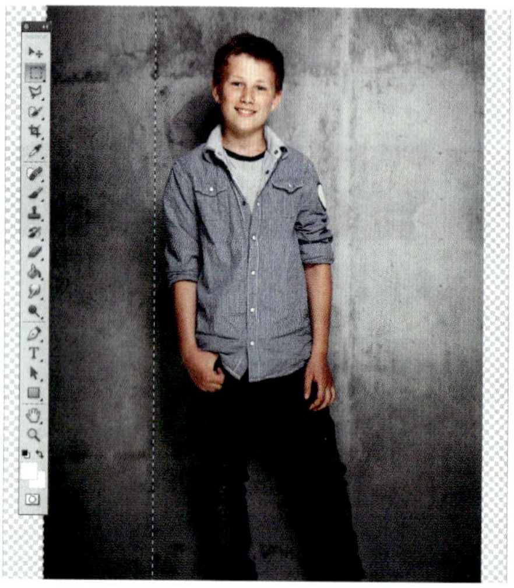

3 Select the background To fill the empty space on either side of your image, select the ***Rectangular Marquee Tool*** and click and drag on your image to select as much of the background as possible to one side of your subject. Be careful not to select the edges of your subject at all or they will distort in the next step.

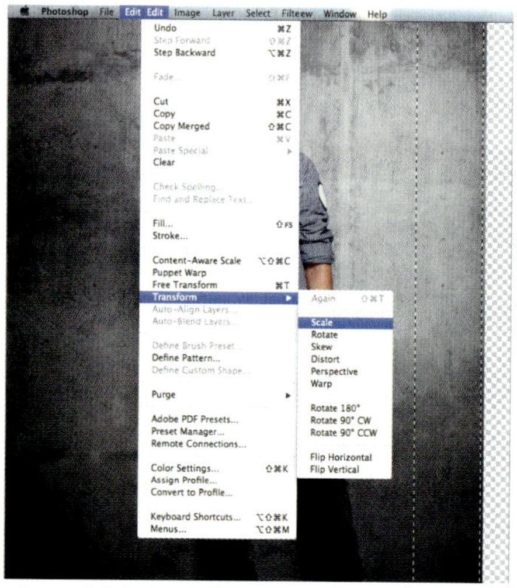

4 Extend the background With your selection made, go to ***Edit>Transform>Scale*** and use the side anchor point to stretch your background to the edge of the frame. Press the ***Enter*** key to commit to this transformation. The other side of the image will then need the same treatment, so repeat steps three and four for that side, too.

Secrets unlocked

If your background distorts when using this method, try one of these alternative techniques. The first two steps remain the same no matter which method you choose.

- ✔ **CONTENT AWARE SCALE** Go to ***Edit>Content Aware Scale.*** Drag the anchor points outwards, keeping an eye on your subject to make sure they don't distort.
- ✔ **CONTENT AWARE FILL** Select the empty space on either side of your image with the ***Rectangular Marquee Tool***. Go to ***Edit>Fill*** and select ***Content Aware*** – Photoshop will try to choose the best content for the space.
- ✔ **CLONE STAMP TOOL** Use the ***Clone Stamp Tool*** to sample the background and brush them in place in the empty spaces.
- ✔ **COPY AND PASTE** With the ***Rectangular Marquee Tool***, select areas of the background and ***Copy*** and ***Paste*** them in to the empty spaces. Use the ***Clone Stamp Tool*** to hide any joins.

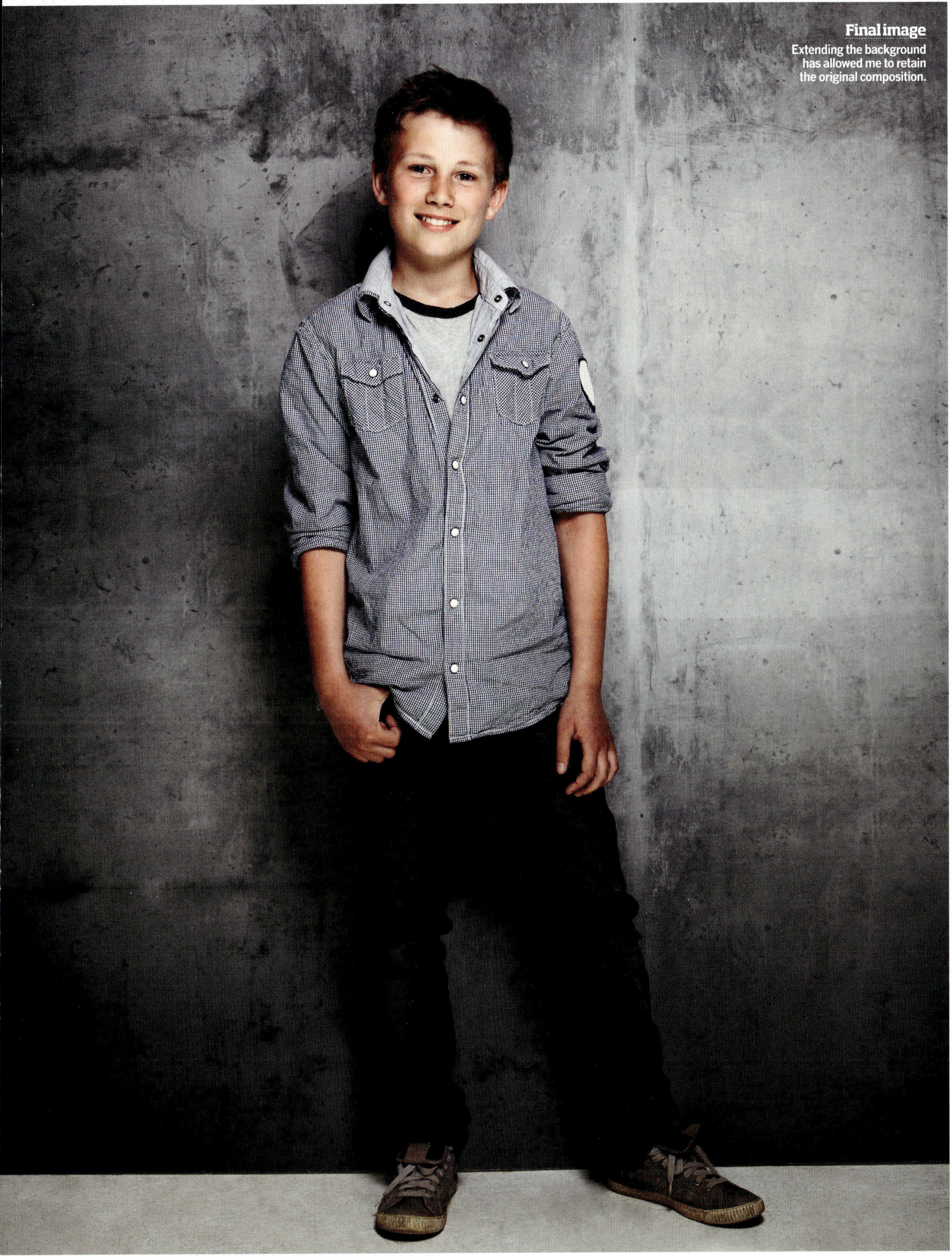

Final image

Extending the background has allowed me to retain the original composition.

Convert images to black & white

Sometimes images need help to convert well to mono – adjusting tones separately will often give a better result than a simple straight conversion

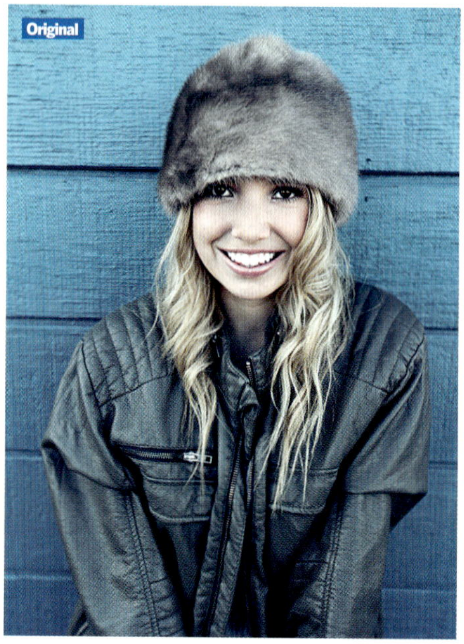

Caroline Wilkinson: The strength of a monochromatic portrait depends largely on its tonal range, form and composition. If you're stripping an image of colour, you need to ensure the raw components are strong enough to give impact. Knowing the different grayscale shades of certain colours can help you identify if your image has the potential to be successful as a black & white portrait, or only works in colour; for instance, yellows are highlights and deep reds and purples often render as shadows, while greens and certain shades of blue can look like mid-tones. You need a range of these tones for a strong black & white to create contrast and a good balance across the image to stop the viewer's eye from lingering too long on heavy dark and light areas. Imagining a colour image in black & white is one way to do it, another is to do a quick temporary conversion in Photoshop to assess its potential. A good indication to its success is the level of tonal separation between the background and subject – if your subject is wearing a blue coat against a green bush, you know there will be limited tonal separation between these two mid-tones, making the image look flat. However, if you've got a dark blue coat against a bright blue or overexposed sky, you've probably got something to work with. Or, if you know you've got a dark or mid-toned background, opt for a blonde model rather than a brunette for that tonal distinction.

There are lots of ways to convert an image to black & white in Photoshop, not to mention creative plug-ins from the likes of Nik Software's Silver Efex Pro 2 or Power Retouche's Black & White Studio. But here you'll learn one of the best ways: the Gradient Map adjustment layer.

Secrets unlocked

THREE OTHER WAYS TO CONVERT TO BLACK & WHITE USING PHOTOSHOP

☑ **Black & White adjustment layer** Go to ***Layer>New Adjustment Layer>Black and white***. The image instantly turns mono and you can adjust the coloured sliders to darken or lighten the different tones for exquisite contrast control.

☑ **Channel Mixer** Choose ***Image>Adjustments>Channel Mixer*** and tick the ***Monochrome*** box. Now use the colour channel sliders: ***Red***, ***Green*** and ***Blue*** to adjust contrast, making sure they all amount to ***100%***.

☑ **Desaturate** You can do this either via ***Image>Adjustments>Desaturate*** or using a ***Hue/Saturation*** adjustment layer and dragging the ***Saturation*** slider to ***0***. It offers no control over contrast, but you could use ***Levels*** afterwards.

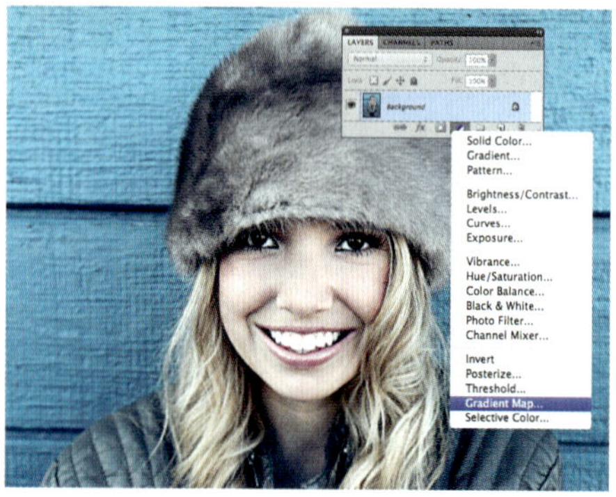

1 Open your colour image With your image open, make sure the Layers palette is visible (***Window>Layers***) and then click on the ***Add new adjustment or fill layer*** button at the bottom of the Layers palette and select ***Gradient Map***.

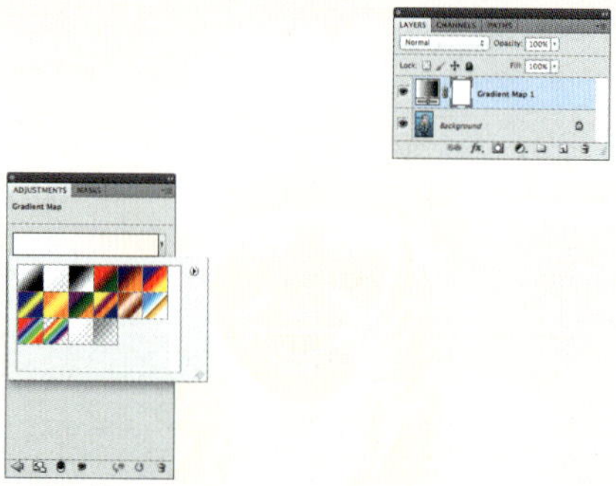

2 Add a Gradient Map With the Gradient Map accessed, you'll notice the colours might not be black & white yet. Click on the gradient in the adjustment panel to access the ***Gradient Map Editor*** and select ***Black to White***.

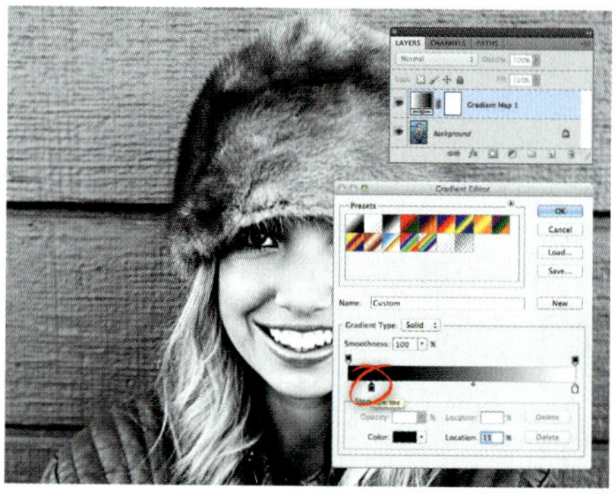

3 Edit the contrast With the Gradient Map Editor open, you can use the sliders under ***Gradient Type*** to set the black and white point in your image. This can give your picture beautiful deep blacks and really bright whites.

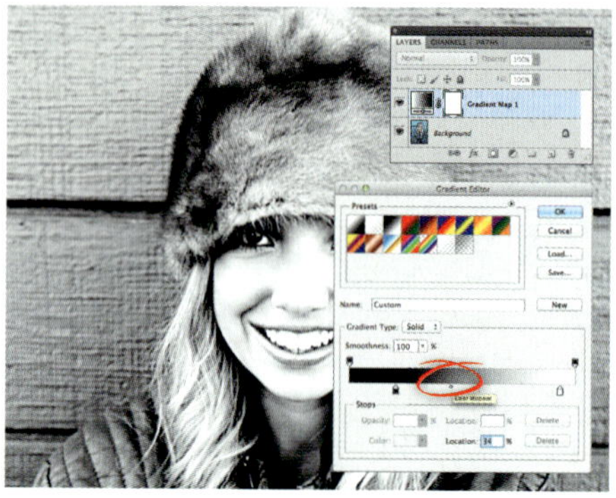

4 Adjust the transition To control the gradient transitions between the two stops, move the ***Color Midpoint***, as circled in the palette above, to steepen the transition towards the nearest colour stop.

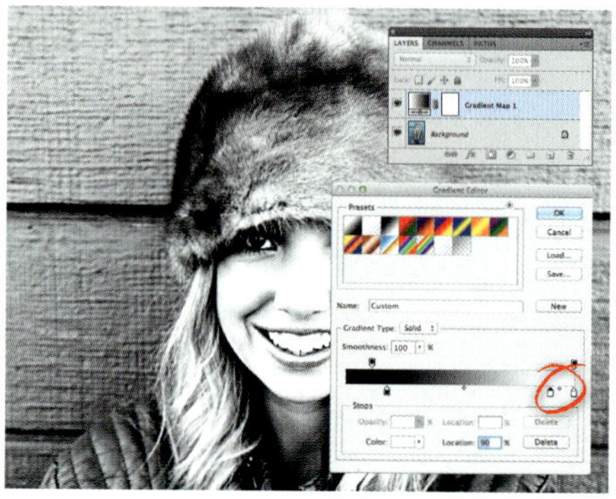

5 Add a stop or two You can edit as intricately as you want by creating new colour stops and transitions by clicking where you want them within the gradient. If you get stuck, click ***alt*** to turn the ***Cancel*** button to ***Reset*** or ***delete*** to remove the stop.

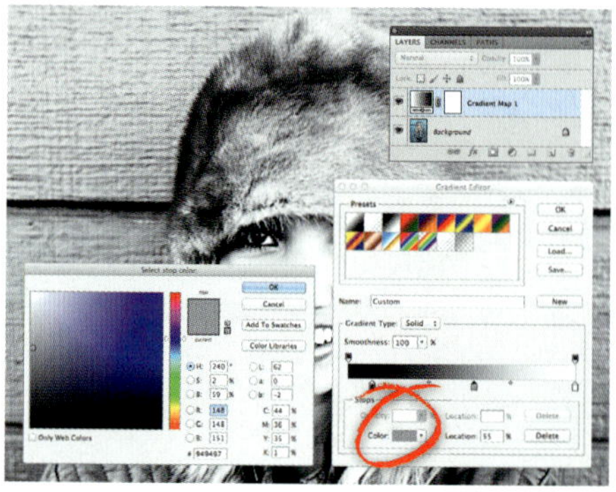

6 Add colour By adding a stop and changing its colour via the ***Color*** box, you can create some interesting effects, like this silvery conversion, or even a sepia effect by selecting a deep orange. Have a play to see what works.

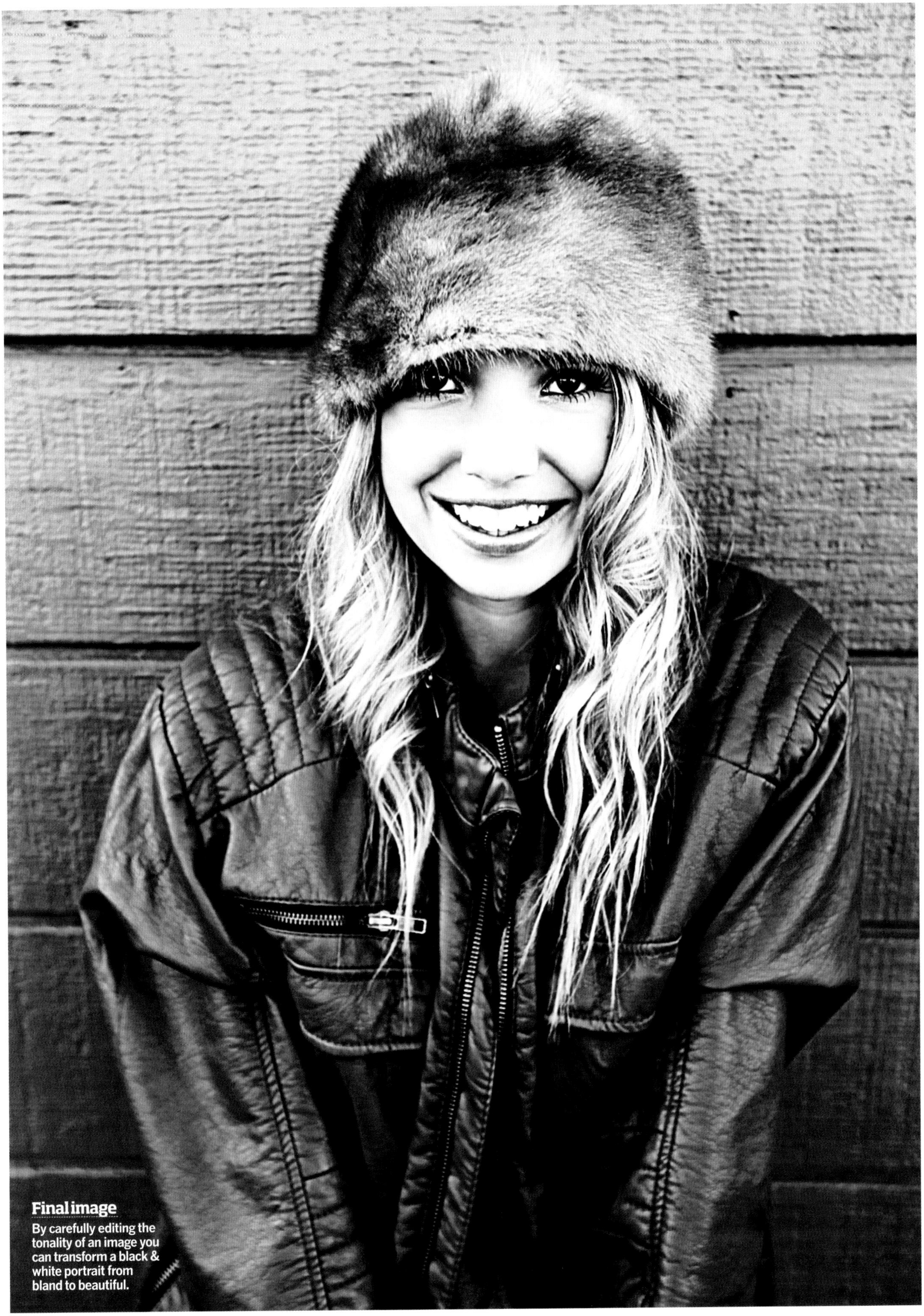

Final image

By carefully editing the tonality of an image you can transform a black & white portrait from bland to beautiful.

Advanced retouching skills

Want professional retouching results? This tutorial may take time and an eye for detail, but your portraits will reap the rewards

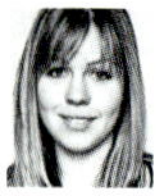

Caroline Wilkinson: It's easy to cake a face in blur or paint over skin for a porcelain finish; the difficulty comes when you want to keep the natural texture but even out and improve the tone. Portrait professionals do it with ease and keep their methods close to their chest, but we have a few secret techniques that we're more than willing to share. Some of you will probably already use quick-fix techniques to smooth skin and reduce imperfections, and it will be all you need for a while, but more seasoned Photoshoppers might be ready to move on to this more thorough and advanced technique. Yes, dedicated software helps you get flawless results, but why spend the money when you already have Photoshop? Layers, Adjustment Layers and Layer Masks are essential here, so make sure you understand how they work as we're skipping the basics. Be prepared for lots of layers, lots of selections and employ your eye for detail, as you'll have to target specific areas – no one-stop-shop global adjustments here! So grab a cuppa, your latest portrait and get ready for a couple of hours' work – the aim is amazing but undetectable editing. Here we go…

How to use...

✔ LAYER MASKS

A Layer Mask allows you to hide detail from the layer it's applied to, revealing the image beneath without erasing it. Select the Layer Mask, then add ***Black*** to the mask to hide image detail and change to ***White*** to restore detail. Use ***X*** to switch between the colours.

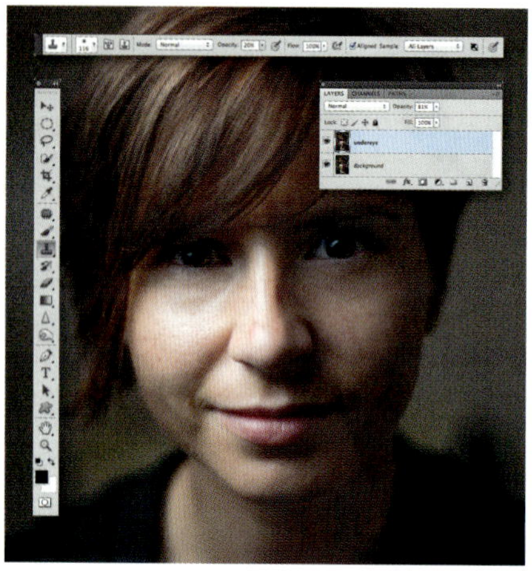

1 Cover up dark circles Under-eye shadows can make a subject look unduly tired. The easiest way to brighten a complexion is to minimise these shadows and even out the skin tone. Duplicate your image layer (***Layer>Duplicate Layer***) and select the ***Clone Stamp Tool***, set its ***Opacity*** to around ***20%*** and lightly blend in the new skin. Be careful not to hide all the shadow as you can make the subject look unnatural. If you go too far, use a Layer Mask (***Layer>Layer Mask***) to pull back the effect (see box-out above).

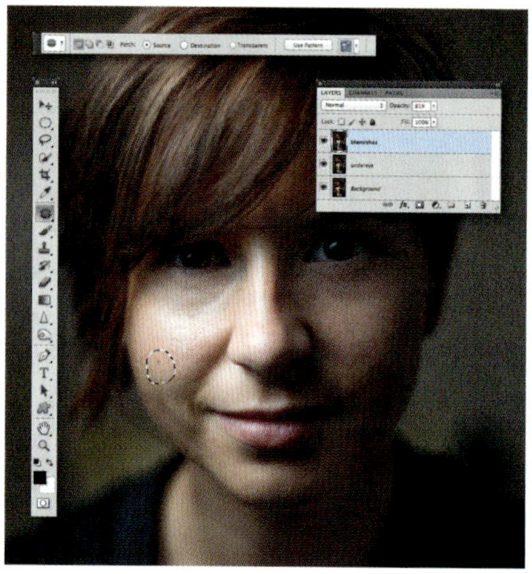

2 Remove blemishes Duplicate your new layer by dragging it down to the ***Add new layer mask*** icon at the bottom of the Layers palette and name it 'Blemishes'. Select the ***Patch Tool*** from the toolbar and select ***Source*** in the top toolbar. Now draw around a blemish and then click and drag that selection to an area of skin that you want to replace it with. As you release the mouse/stylus, the selection will blend with the pixels, hiding the blemish. Repeat for all spots, scars and wrinkles.

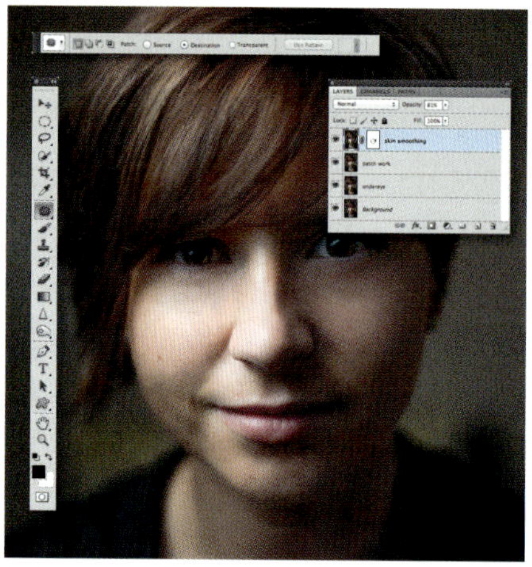

3 Smooth the skin Duplicate the 'Blemishes' layer and name it 'Skin Smoothing'. Use the ***Patch Tool*** again, but this time change ***Source*** to ***Destination*** in the top toolbar. Now select an area of skin that's of even tone and smooth texture, then click and drag that selection on top of areas that show visible pores and redness. If the result looks patchy, try reducing the layer's ***Opacity*** slider to around ***85%*** and use a Layer Mask (***Layer>Layer Mask***) with a very low opacity brush to smooth the skin's surface.

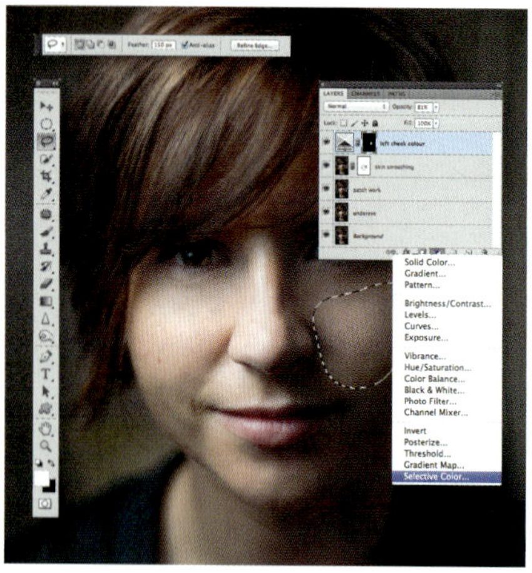

4 Start being selective This stage can take many Adjustment Layers, so try to keep organised by naming the various layers if necessary. On your last image layer, select the ***Lasso Tool*** and set the ***Feather*** to ***150px*** and loosely select an area of skin of similar tone. Go to ***Layer>New Adjustment Layer>Selective Color*** to create an Adjustment Layer to target that selection. Assess your image and decide what colours are affecting the skin – is it slightly too dark, light, magenta, red or yellow?

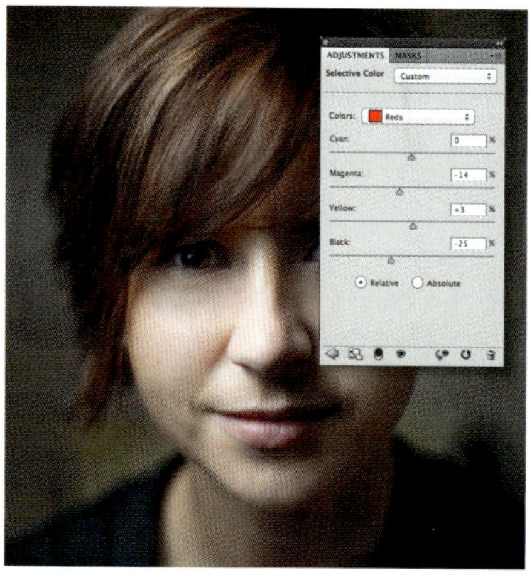

5 Target specific areas In the ***Adjustments*** panel, select the appropriate colour to target from the ***Color*** menu, using the sliders to adjust that colour and even out the skin tone. Repeat the process for different areas of the face, using the ***Lasso Tool*** to create new selections and adding new ***Selective Color*** adjustment layers. As my model's skin had a red tinge, I mainly focused on the Red and White to reduce redness using the Black slider. Also try ***Curves*** adjustment layers to adjust local contrast.

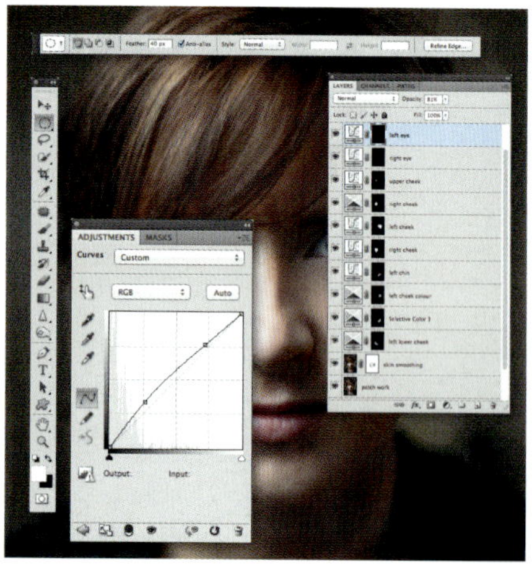

6 Finishing touch Don't rush steps four and five: be prepared to take time over perfecting the colour to ensure all areas match. Some colours will suit different areas better than others, so experiment – you can always return the sliders to 0 if needed. Once you're done, use the ***Elliptical Marquee Tool*** with its ***Feather*** set to ***40px*** and select the inner eye. Next add a ***Curves*** adjustment layer and create a soft 'S' shape with the line to pump up the contrast. Repeat for the opposite eye.

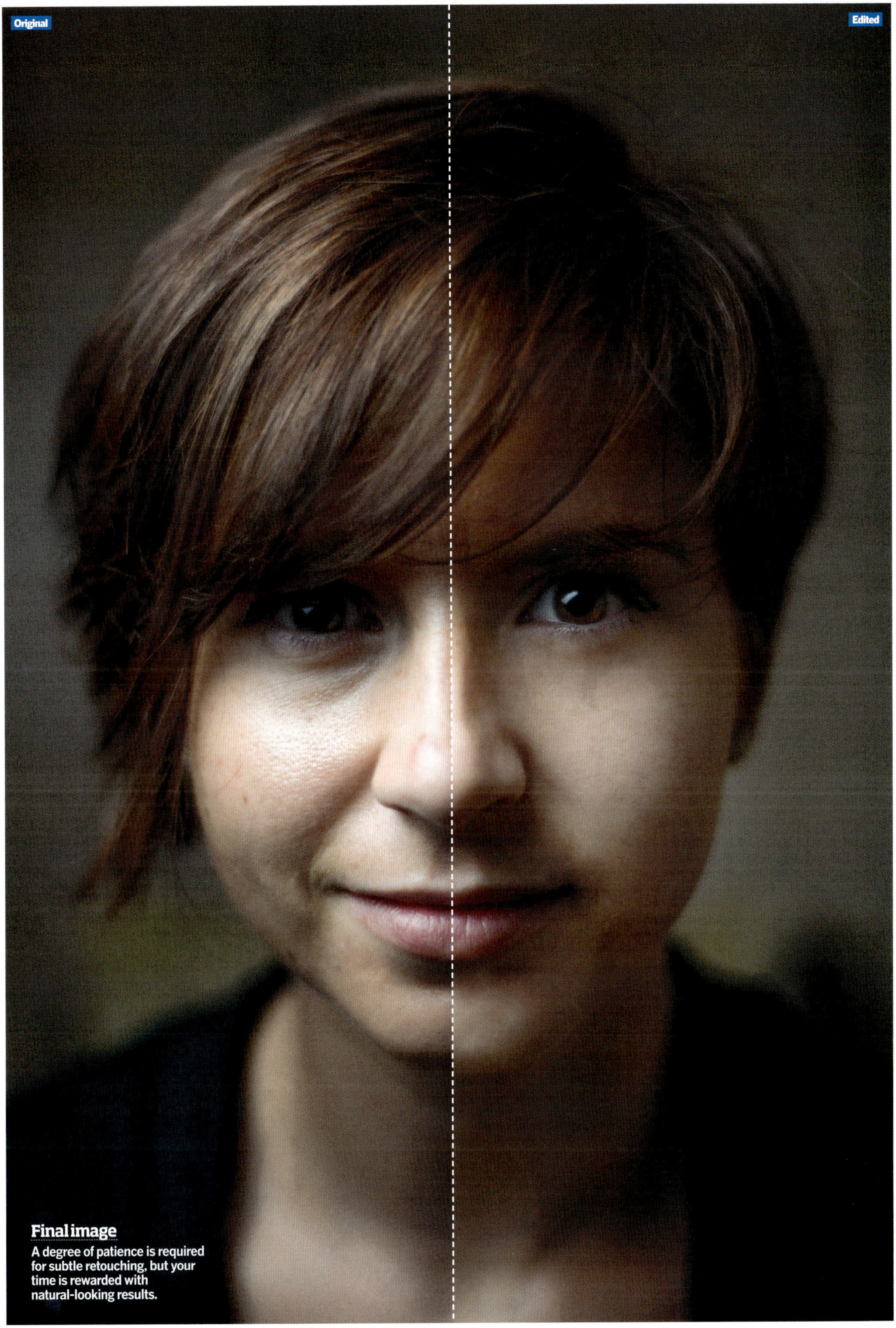

Final image

A degree of patience is required for subtle retouching, but your time is rewarded with natural-looking results.

RAW

You've grasped the basics and become familiar with the features, but now it's time to put the tools into practice and to master the power of Raw for improving the quality and creativity of your photography. Over the next 30 pages, we'll show you how to correct common in-camera errors, capture maximum detail and extend your dynamic range for terrific results

INSIDE

Want to know how to get from this to this? turn over to find out…

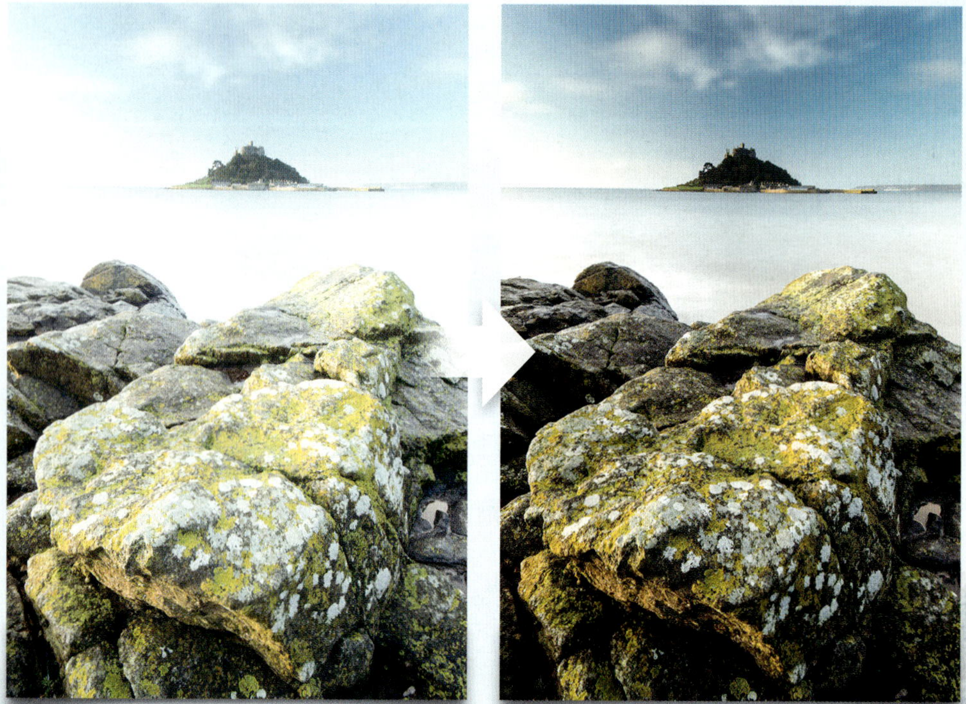

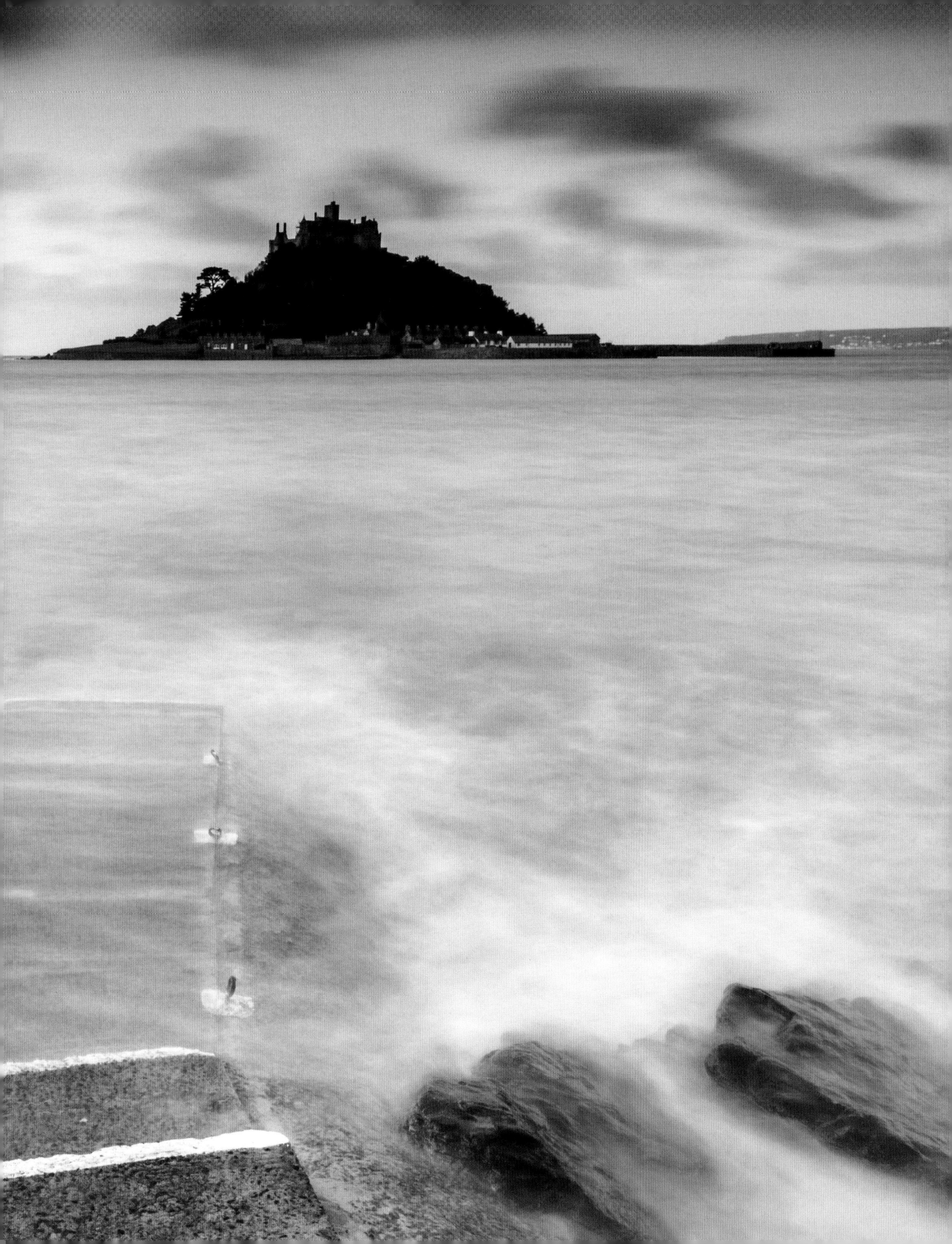

Adobe Camera Raw: the basics

Shooting in Raw has many benefits for the photographer – namely in saving all that lovely data hidden in the shadows and highlights…

WHAT WOULD YOU do if you were given one-million pounds? Buy a new house? Take a luxury holiday or two? Give up the day job to be a professional photographer? Whatever you decide, one thing you probably wouldn't do is to throw away most of that money and try to make the same dreams come true on the small fraction that's left – sounds silly, doesn't it? So why would you do this with your camera's pixels? You spend a lot of money on the latest technology with the view of getting the best image quality that your budget can buy, and then you, in effect, discard a generous proportion of this data and detail by shooting in JPEG and then wonder why your image quality is not as great as you imagined.

So what should you be using? In short – Raw. These days, digital cameras capture an extraordinary amount of image information and a large part of achieving professional-grade images is knowing how to unlock and capitalise on this detail. Some photographers believe Raw to be tricky and not a format for beginners, while others believe that if you were a good photographer and got the images right in-camera, there's no reason to not shoot JPEG. Both camps are wrong, in our opinion, and the aim of this guide is to show you why and how, with a few adjustments to your workflow, you can dramatically improve your images.

First, Raw is not difficult– it's often more involved than shooting JPEGs because you have to put more thought and time into generating the files to how you want them to look, but it's no different from shooting and processing film, which is what all great photographers did before digital. It's also the most forgiving format, making it ideal for beginners. The format allows you to make human errors without ruining a potentially great image (yes, professional photographers make mistakes too) and allows you to process the image in many different ways – just like you would with a film negative. So for creative photographers, it's really a no-brainer. If you're still not convinced that Raw is a rookies' format, too, make sure you read how our professional contributors use Raw and why they give it rave reviews.

Shoot Raw + JPEG

Not only does it allow you to save time and hard drive space by reviewing JPEGs on your monitor before having to convert the Raw files, but you can apply in-camera styles to your JPEGs, like black & white, to preview the results without affecting the Raw data, which you can then adjust later.

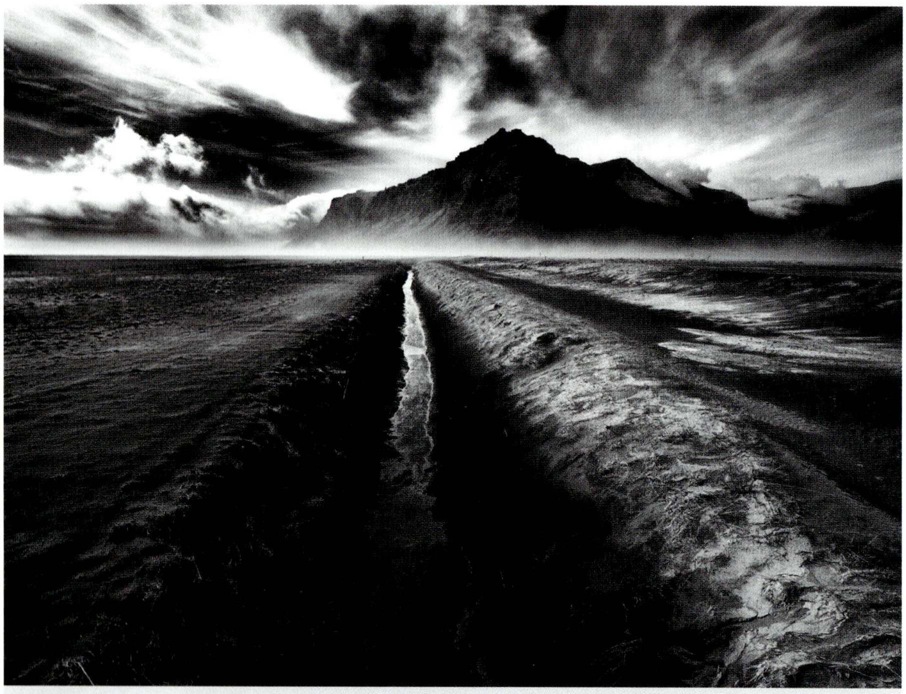

The landscape photographer: Lee Frost

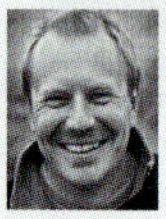

"I want to achieve optimum image quality and the Raw format does exactly that. What's the point in spending thousands of pounds on cameras and lenses, then letting the camera delete data from the images I capture before I've even had the chance to see them on my computer's monitor? A Raw file contains more data than I need, but at least by shooting in Raw I get to decide what stays and what goes. I can also save processed Raw files as 16-bit TIFF files, whereas JPEGs are 8-bit. It's easier to adjust things like colour temperature if you shoot in Raw, too, and I can batch-process Raw files to apply exactly the same settings to each image, which is useful when I shoot a sequence of images to stitch into panoramas. If I forget to specify a WB like Daylight, and instead shoot with AWB, the colour balance of each image may vary – shooting Raw allows for this margin of error." *www.leefrost.co.uk*

Set your camera for Raw

It's so easy: simply select the Image Quality setting via your camera's menu system or top plate and choose Raw or Raw + JPEG, then shoot as you normally would and take comfort in the fact that you're capturing maximum quality. There are a couple of things to be aware of, though, when shooting Raw: first, the image size (see Size matters!, page 85); second, a technique called 'exposing to the right'. As the most image information is contained in the highlights, by using your histogram as a guide to slightly overexpose your scene (not so much that you lose detail in the highlights), you can capture a lot more data and detail in a Raw file, which you can then draw out by adjusting the exposure during processing. See page 100 for a more detailed guide.

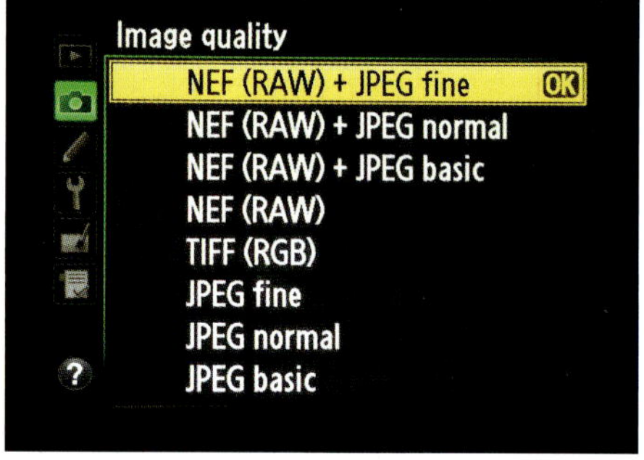

Raw software

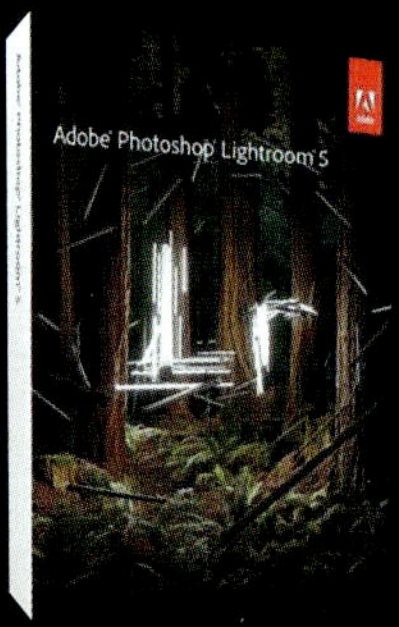

When you buy a camera, the manufacturer provides a CD-ROM with its own Raw processing software. For some, it's sufficient, but many prefer to use third-party processors and for those who already own Adobe software, they have one of the best available. Photoshop's Adobe Camera Raw (ACR) is by far the most popular and powerful editing suites, but versions of this program are also available in other Adobe products, such as Lightroom and Photoshop Elements. In fact, for the most part, the Raw editing capabilities of each are very similar or simplified versions. Apple Aperture also has a Raw converter and Capture One is another popular program for some photographers. If you're curious about how each works or how user-friendly you may find them, most can be downloaded as a free 30-day trial.

- **Lightroom 5** £103 (upgrade £58)
Free trial from www.adobe.com/products
- **Photoshop CC** Subscription only £18 per month (upgrade £9 per month)
Free trial from www.adobe.com/products
- **Elements 11** £78 (upgrade £63)
Free trial from www.adobe.com/products
- **Capture One** €229 (£146)
Free trial from www.phaseone.com/4/
- **Apple Aperture 3.4.3** £55
Free trial from www.apple.com/uk/aperture
- **Manufacturer software**
Free with your camera

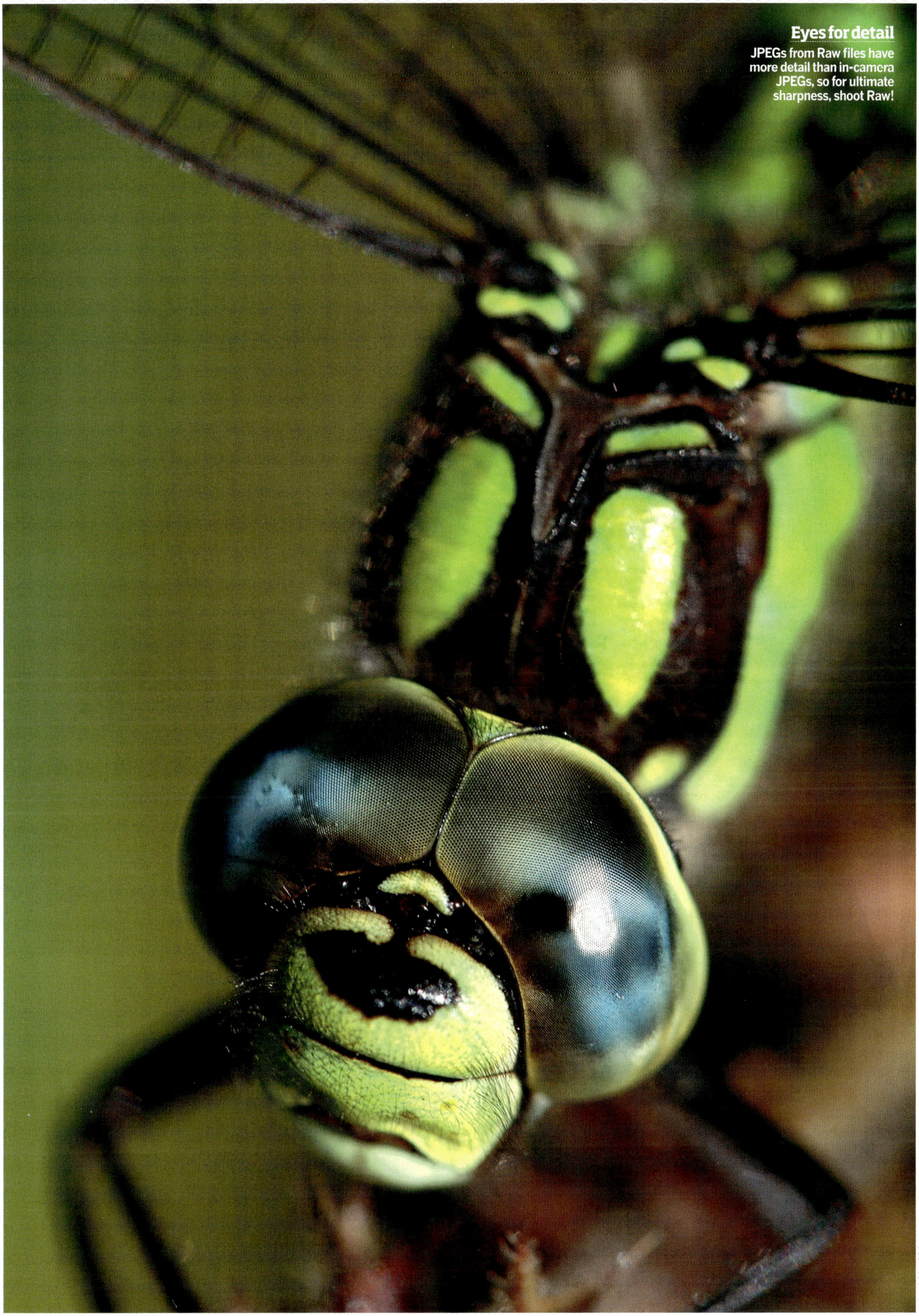

Eyes for detail

JPEGs from Raw files have more detail than in-camera JPEGs, so for ultimate sharpness, shoot Raw!

ROSS HODDINOTT

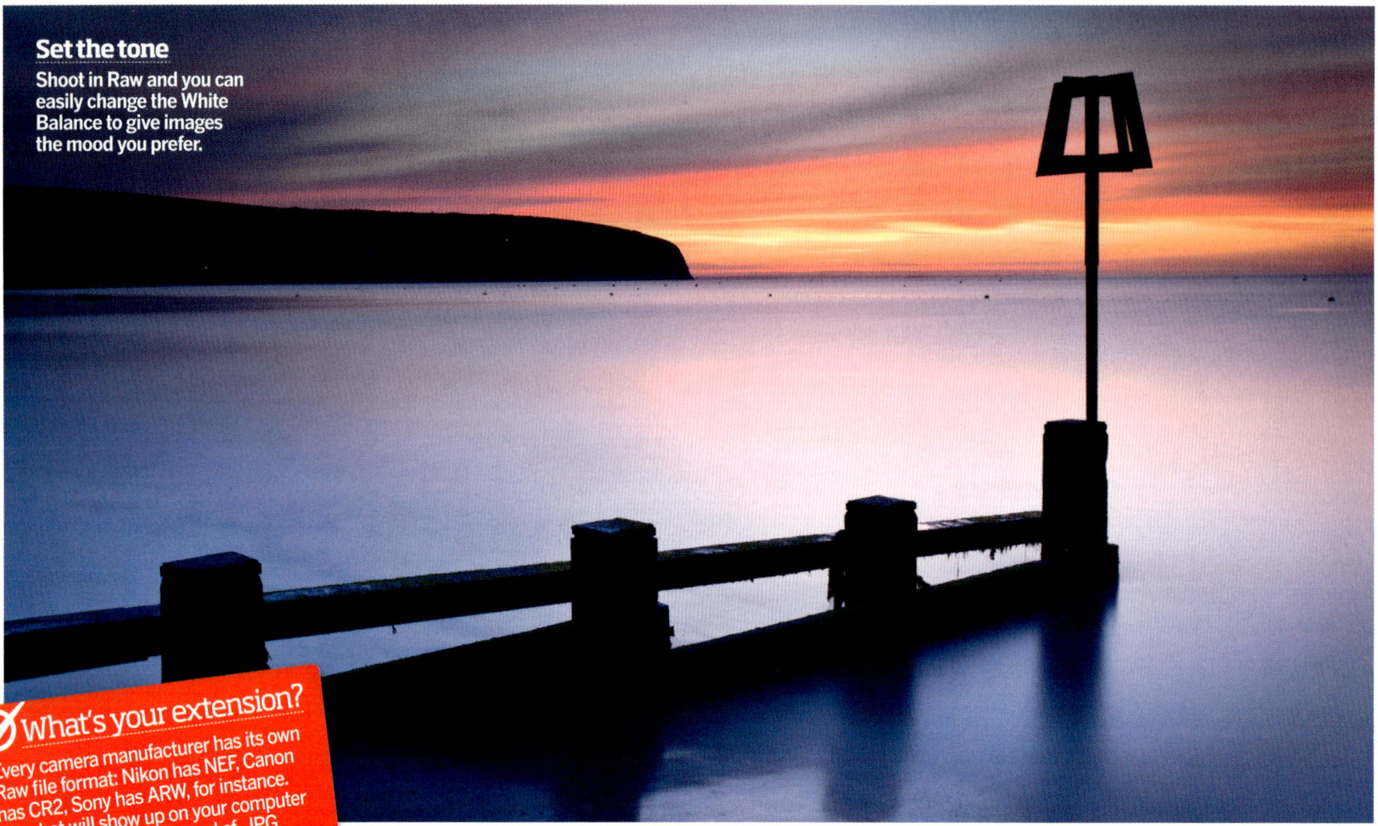

Set the tone
Shoot in Raw and you can easily change the White Balance to give images the mood you prefer.

What's your extension?
Every camera manufacturer has its own Raw file format: Nikon has NEF, Canon has CR2, Sony has ARW, for instance. It's what will show up on your computer as the file extension instead of .JPG

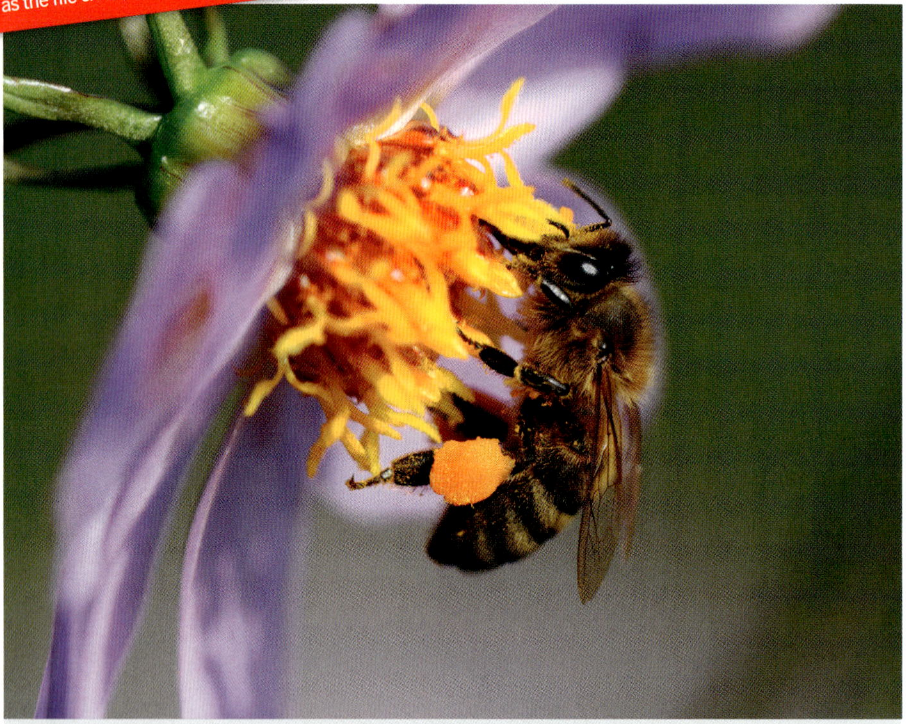

The nature photographer: Ross Hoddinott

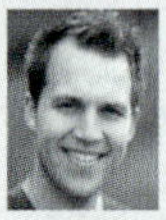

"For nature photographers, the argument for shooting Raw is overwhelming. When shooting wildlife, you have to react quickly to the subject's movement. Often, there isn't time to fine-tune all the shooting parameters, like White Balance, in-camera. However, by shooting in Raw, photographers have the luxury of being able to tweak such things later during editing, without any loss of quality. Due to a Raw file's great flexibility, nature photographers can concentrate on focusing, composition and being creative. Raw files also capture more tonal levels, so image quality is maximised. They also have greater latitude to exposure error, so if you do make a mistake, you are more likely to be able to retrieve the image. Although Raw files are larger and therefore take longer to write to the camera's card, most digital SLRs have such large buffers that shooting JPEGs offers no significant advantage to Raw, even when capturing large bursts of images." *www.rosshoddinott.co.uk*

> "Unlike a JPEG, your Raw image isn't print-ready – it's a negative waiting to be developed. it's holding a lot of potential detail for you to draw out"

Understanding the difference between Raw and JPEG might also persuade you. When you take a picture, your camera processes the data captured by the sensor, which, unaltered, is a 12-, 14- or 16-bit uncompressed Raw file (actual depth depends on the camera model you're using).

A JPEG, on the other hand, has been processed by the camera before the image is saved to your memory card, often after sharpening, colour and contrast adjustments have been applied. The camera also compresses the file down to an 8-bit image as it decides what data is needed for the best photograph and deletes the rest. If you've slightly under- or overexposed your image, chances are that you've lost valuable information that cannot be recovered or corrections made without compromising the image quality. If you had shot in Raw, however, that information would be retained and easily recovered to improve the quality of your exposure and dynamic range. Raw files contain more data than you need to create a successful image and puts you in control of all the creative decision-making. It also means you can use your computer to process your images, which has far more power and controls than a camera.

Do we have you convinced yet? Are you swapping your Quality setting from JPEG to Raw, as you read now? Great. Now what? Unlike a JPEG, your Raw image isn't print-ready – it's a

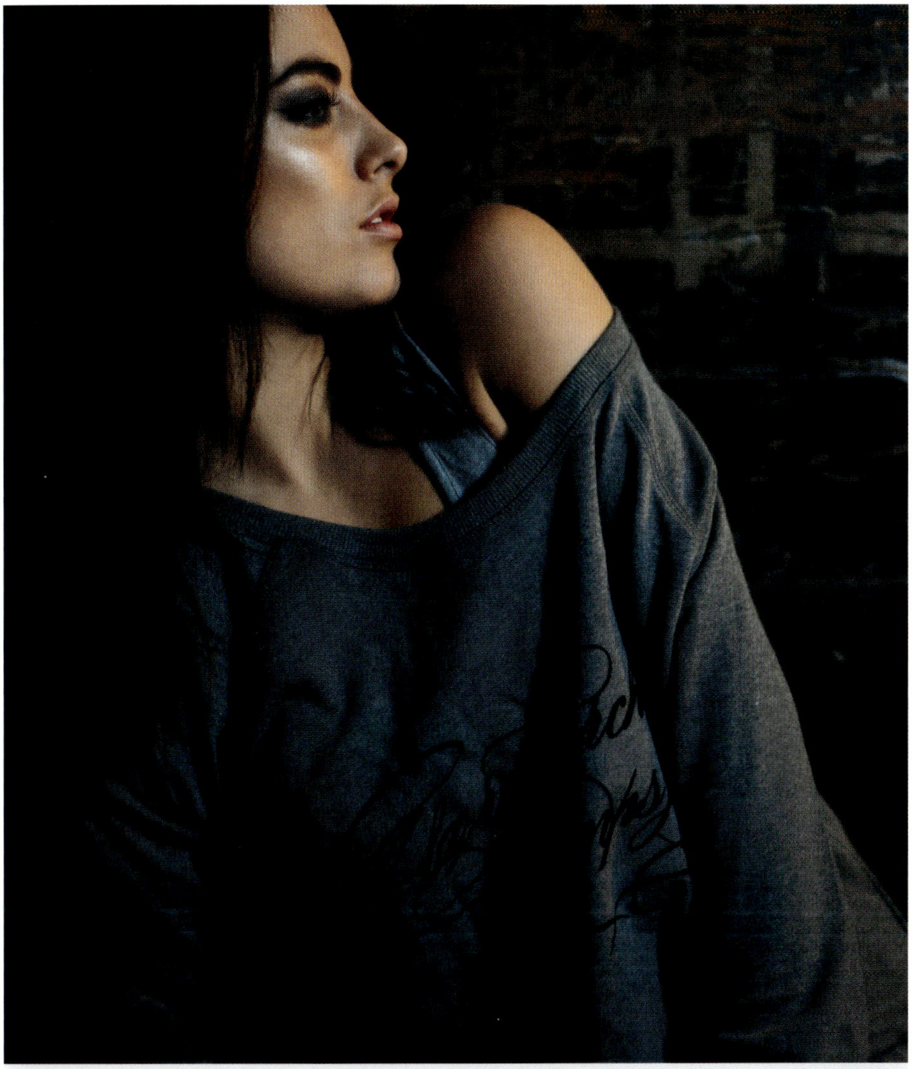

The portrait photographer: Paul Ward

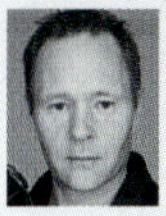

"Up until a year ago, my main priority was being able to get a lot more images on a memory card in case I made mistakes. I thought JPEGs were best. I was wrong: Raw has a lot more benefits. If you get the WB wrong, you can tweak it, whereas doing that in Photoshop on a JPEG isn't very accurate and can be hard to do. If I slightly overexpose a shot, Raw-editing software allows me to pull detail back, which is really handy. Before I moved over to the Nikon D800, whenever I tried to open up shadow areas to reveal detail, I'd get grainy images, but the D800 is amazing for revealing detail in the shadow without introducing noise. It's also useful when creating HDR images. I prefer not to take multiple exposures, as a part of the scene or the model will often move slightly between shots. With Raw I can expand the dynamic range by outputting three different exposures from a single Raw file and merging them together – it's far more controllable and the results are better." *www.paulward.net*

negative waiting to be developed. It's tonally flat, softer than it should be and holding a lot of potential detail in the highlights and shadows for you to draw out.

For many photographers, especially those new to digital editing, the idea of processing and converting Raw files can be daunting and off-putting, but it can be made as simple or as complicated as your skills permit. The beauty of Raw is that, as your skills develop, there's also no reason why you can't return to re-edit the same image again later as long you keep a file in its lossless Raw state, as the image information is never permanently altered. There are several software packages you can use, too, but our preference is Adobe: whether that be Elements, CS or Lightroom. Each have very similar Raw interfaces, borne from Adobe Camera Raw, which we'll show you exactly how to navigate over the page.

Size matters

With increasing megapixels and data collection, one modern challenge photographers are facing is massive Raw files. Depending on your camera's file size, a Raw file can take up to five or six times more space than a JPEG. Not only does this mean high-capacity memory cards, or plenty of spares, but you may eventually need a bigger hard drive and faster processor if your computer is to manage downloading and editing these mammoth images. Add to this that the file size increases as you edit the images until they're compressed, plus the fact that you might want to keep the original Raw file as well as the JPEG, and you'll be needing a lot more storage space than if you stuck with JPEG only. But let's face it, though – the pros of Raw still far outweigh these cons.

Raw FAQs

Q When I open my Raw files in ACR I get areas flashing red and blue. It's really distracting. What does it mean and how can I get rid of it?

A Don't worry, it's only the highlight and shadow warnings! If any of the shadow areas are clipped (pure black with no detail recorded), they will flash blue to let you know and if any of the highlights are blown (white with no detail recorded), the affected areas flash red. It's handy to have these warnings on so that you can identify if the clipped shadows and blown highlights improve as you're making adjustments to the image. If you do want to turn them off, though, just click on the small triangles at the top-right and left corners of the histogram in the ACR window.

Q I've got Photoshop CS, Lightroom 5 and Nikon Capture NX, which came with my Nikon D700. They can all process Raw files - which should I use?

A It's entirely up to you, but you're better off sticking with one of the three so you get used to it, rather than chopping and changing between them all. Many Nikon fans use Capture NX, but Lightroom and Photoshop are more streamlined because they allow you to do much more with your images using a single application. Don't forget you have Elements, too, for a simpler and cheaper version of Photoshop if the bigger softwares intimidate you.

Q I've just bought a new DSLR and ACR won't open my Raw files. Do I need to upgrade my version of Photoshop?

A Not necessarily. When manufacturers bring out new camera models, the Raw format used by those cameras usually won't be recognised by the version of ACR you're using in Photoshop as it predated the launch of the camera. When you try to open a Raw file, a message says: 'Could not complete your request because Photoshop doesn't recognise this type of file'.

Adobe issues free updates for ACR that allow you to open Raw files from specified new camera models – you can download them from www.adobe.com. However, whether or not this will solve your problem depends on the version of Photoshop you're using and if the DSLR you bought is a new model or one that has been around for a while. If you're running CS3 or CS4 and your camera is a recent launch, then you'll probably find that the last ACR update issued doesn't include your camera on the list of models covered. If you're running CS5, you'll probably be okay and if you're running CS6 then you'll almost definitely be able to download an ACR update for your camera.

If there is no suitable ACR update available for your version of Photoshop, you could either upgrade to Photoshop CC or, alternatively, buy Adobe Lightroom 5 – which will allow you to process Raw files from your new camera and still import into Photoshop after.

Q How should I save my image from Adobe Camera Raw?

A Before you save your image, click on Workflow Options (blue writing at the bottom of ACR) and set the Size, Depth, Space and 300 pixels/inch as the Resolution (see page 88 for full details).

If you're not opening your image into Photoshop, click Save Image... and preferably select TIFF as your Format as it retains more information than a JPEG, and set Compression to None.

Navigating the Adobe Camera Raw interface

New to ACR and confused by all its features? No fear, we make CS5 clear...

The toolbar

Zoom: Magnify the image to see it in more detail by clicking on the preview image.

Hand: Navigate around the magnified image by clicking and dragging the Hand Tool.

White Balance: By clicking on an image area that's white or grey, ACR can determine the colour of the light the image was taken in.

Color Sampler: Allows you to select a colour that you want to adjust by clicking on that area of the image.

Targeted Adjustment: Instead of using the sliders to make adjustments, drag this tool on the image to make edits.

Crop: Perhaps one of the most useful tools, use Crop to change the aspect ratio, to recompose your image or simply remove elements from the edges.

Straighten: Correct a wonky horizon or rotate your image.

Spot Removal: Get rid of sensor spots, dust marks and other unwanted blemishes.

Red-Eye Removal: Click on the subject's pupil to get rid of red-eye in portraits.

Adjustment Brush: Use this tool to make localised edits to your image. See page 88 for more details.

Graduated Filter: Draw a line across your image to apply a graduate effect. You can then adjust Exposure, Brightness, Contrast, Clarity, Saturation, Sharpness and Color of the graduate to suit your picture.

Preferences: Click here to access the Camera Raw Preferences dialogue box.

Rotate counterclockwise & Rotate clockwise: Click on the tools to rotate in either direction by 90°.

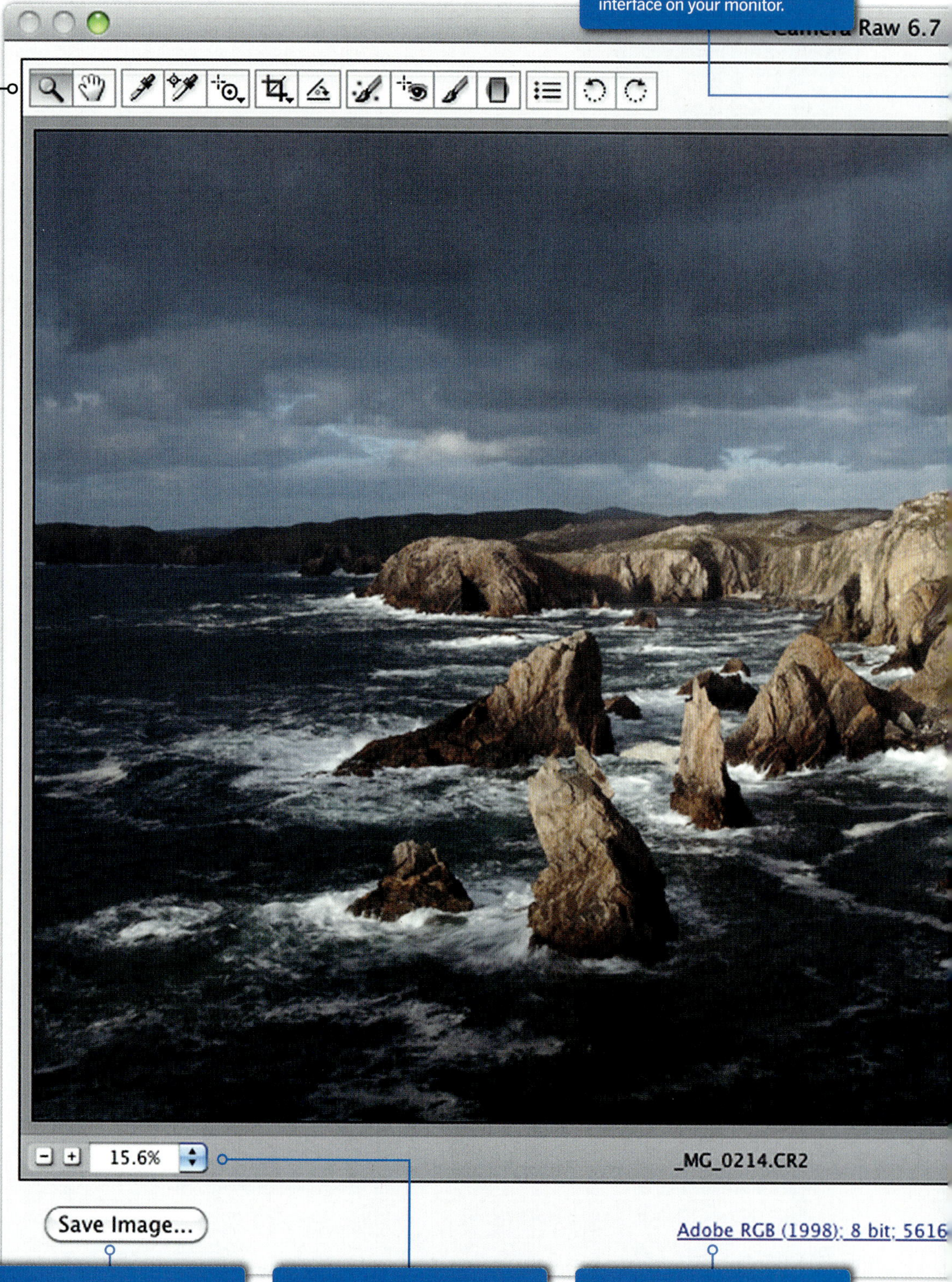

☑ PREVIEW OPTIONS

To see how your adjustments affect your image, make sure this Preview box is ticked. The button to the right expands or reduces the size of your interface on your monitor.

☑ SAVE IMAGE...

Click here to open your Save Options. From here you can select your image Format, File Extension and level of Compression before naming and saving the file.

☑ ZOOM

As an alternative to using the Zoom Tool, you can make more precise enlargements by selecting a percentage from this drop-down menu or using the + or - buttons.

☑ WORKFLOW OPTIONS

By clicking on this blue information line, you can select the best image space, resolution, size and depth to ensure optimum quality. *See page 88 for details.*

☑ CLIPPING WARNINGS

Clipping is where detail is lost at the extreme ends of the histogram spectrum – these black and white triangle buttons, when pressed, activate warnings to indicate where clipping has occurred. Areas with lost shadow detail (right triangle) flash blue, while highlights (left triangle) flash red.

☑ HISTOGRAM

Just like on your camera, the ACR histogram shows you the distribution of your exposure information from pure blacks to pure whites. It's a good reference for determining what adjustments you need to make. As you move the sliders, you'll notice the histogram changes its distribution.

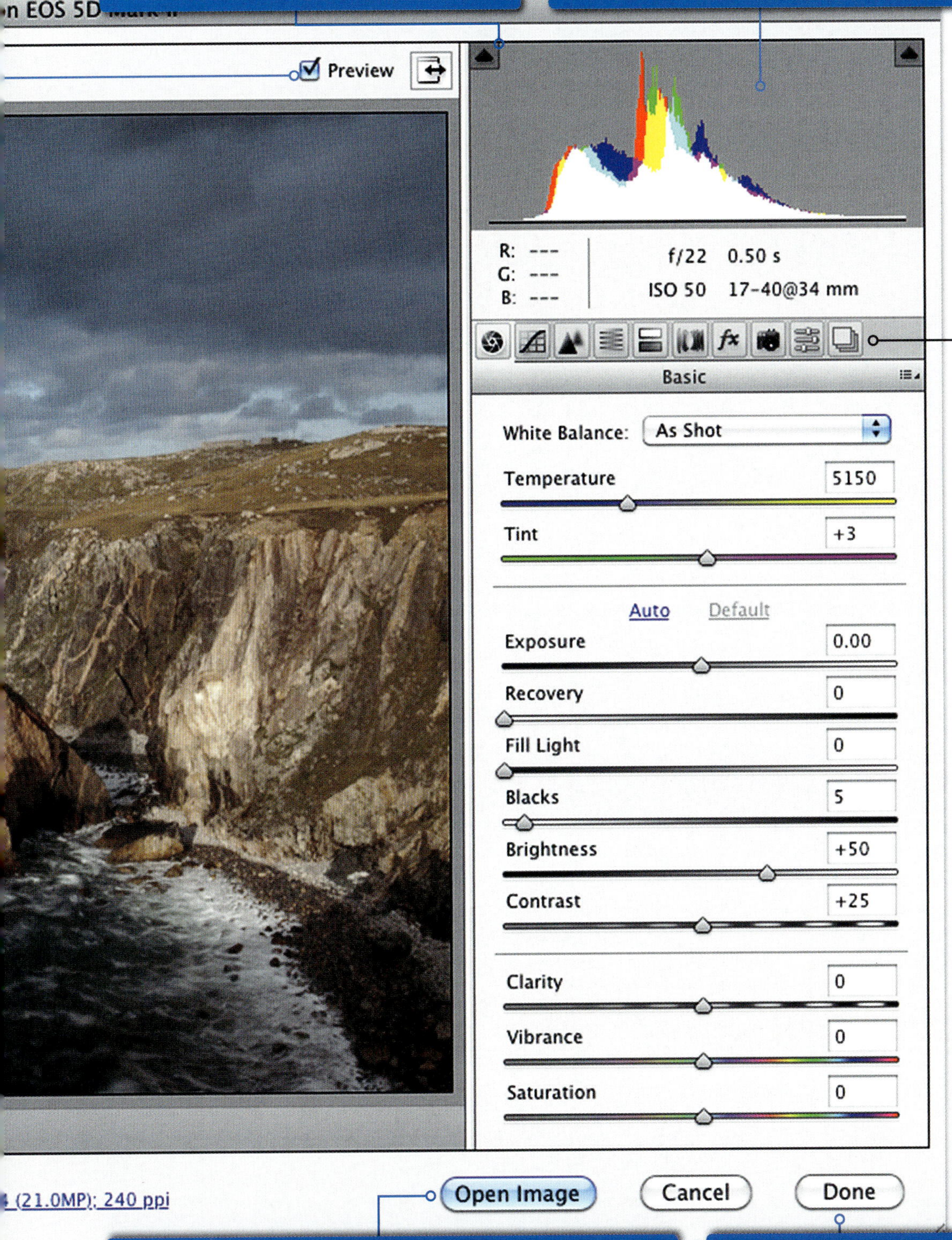

☑ OPEN IMAGE

When you've done all the editing you want to in ACR, you have the option to open the image in Photoshop for further processing. Instead of clicking Open Image, hold ***alt*** to open the image as a copy – it's useful if you want to apply different techniques to the same Raw file in Photoshop. You can also press ***alt*** to change the Cancel button to Reset, reverting all sliders to default settings.

☑ THE ACR INTERFACE

Adobe softwares have very similar interfaces and capabilities for using Raw, so whether you use Elements 10 or Lightroom 4, the tools and techniques will mostly translate.

Adjustments

Basic: Arguably the control room of ACR, these tools for the most part are all you need to dramatically transform your Raw images – turn over to find out exactly how.

Tone Curve: It functions in a similar way to Photoshop's Curves adjustment, allowing you to manually manipulate the tonal graph to affect your image's contrast.

Detail: You can access the Sharpening and Noise Reduction features of ACR via this tab. They're quite straightforward to use, but for more information and tutorials, turn to page 94.

HSL/Grayscale: This tab holds most of the controls you need to alter colour. You have HSL (Hue, Saturation and Luminance adjustments) as well as a Convert to Grayscale box that allows you to use the Grayscale Mix sliders to adjust the various grey tones in your image to improve contrast.

Split Toning: Want to be a bit more creative with colour? The Split Toning tab enables you to adjust the Hue and Saturation of the highlights and shadows separately for duotone results.

Lens Corrections: A really useful feature and one tab we recommend visiting before you do any editing, especially if you've shot with a wide-angle lens and your image has barrel or pincushion distortion, fringing or vignetting.

FX: The Effects tab features the more creative adjustments. You can add grain and apply a vignette for artistic results. See page 108 for details.

Camera Calibration: Use this tab to apply your in-camera styles, like Vivid and Landscape. You can use the Camera Profile sliders to help calibrate your on-screen image to match your LCD view, if needed.

Presets: Create your own presets so you can apply creative or routine tweaks with one click. Simply click ***New Preset*** and then record the adjustments.

Snapshots: Take 'snapshots' of your editing as you go along to compare the results or to quickly and easily return to an earlier state.

Getting started in Adobe Camera Raw

Master Basic adjustments and we promise the quality of your photographs will never be the same again

IF YOU NORMALLY SHOOT JPEGs, you won't have to know much to notice a dramatic difference to the quality of your edited images once you start working with Raw. Just being able to navigate a few basic settings in your chosen software guarantees better results, simply because you not only have a lot more image information, and therefore scope for better improvement, but you call the shots based on each image's needs rather than letting the camera apply the same blanket adjustments, like sharpening and colour saturation, to all your pictures.

The best part of editing in ACR is that it doesn't matter how many errors you make, no amount of editing you do to your Raw file degrades the image quality – unlike a JPEG – so you're free to experiment with consequence until you convert the image to a JPEG or TIFF. And even if you do save your edits to the Raw file, the edits you've made are still completely reversible. Brilliant isn't it!

Most of your key editing tools are housed under the Basic tab and are adjustable using sliders, making them fast and easy to use. If you're only interested in making minimal edits to every Raw file, then this page has all you need to know, and more: Basic is the powerhouse of ACR.

While it has more than enough to get you by, and should keep the learning curve relatively shallow, you and your images would be missing out if you left it there. There is so much more to learn about the way ACR can improve your results and so many techniques that we want to tell you about. But before we get ahead of ourselves, here's a breakdown of what the Basic panel offers and how you can use it to process your best ever pictures.

White Balance

As the pros have already plugged, this is one of the most useful tools in your Raw editing arsenal. While the White Balance Tool is great, these controls make correcting any in-camera White Balance errors a doddle once you get the hang of it: simply select a WB preset or use the sliders for a custom WB.

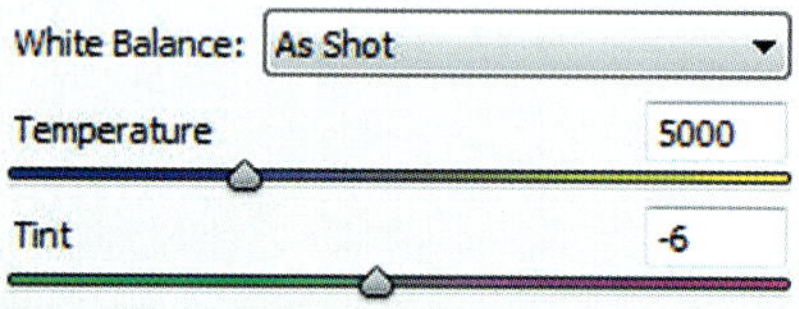

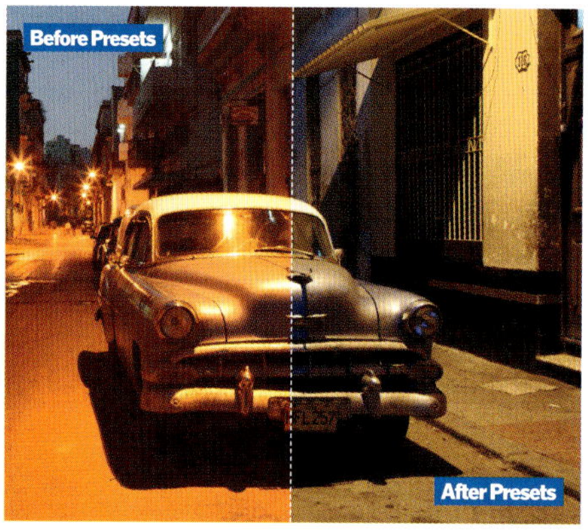

LEE FROST

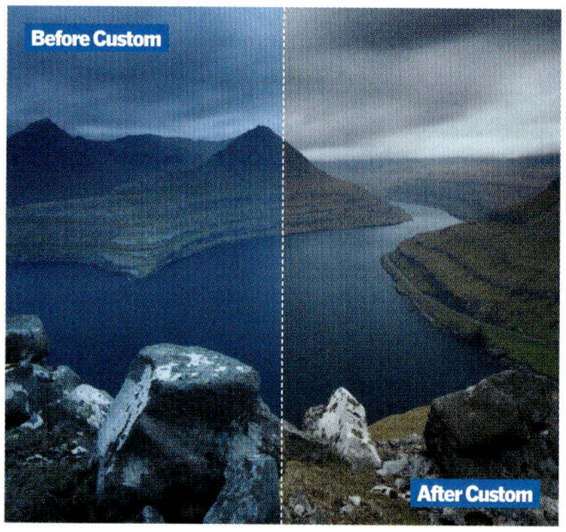

ADAM BURTON

Workflow options

If you click on the blue text below your preview image in the ACR window, a Workflow Options box opens. Make sure you have ***Space*** set to ***Adobe RGB (1998)*** and ***Depth*** to ***16 Bits/Channel***. Click ***Size*** to see various options: most of which have a – (minus) symbol after them, one that has no symbol and one or two that have a + (plus) symbol at the end. The option with no symbol is the optimum one for your camera and saves your images at maximum resolution. Choose that one. You've paid for those megapixels so you might as well use them. There's no point, generally, in choosing a lower resolution option, and if you choose one that's higher than the resolution of your camera, the files will be interpolated, which you don't usually need – increase the file size later, in Photoshop, if necessary. Also, make sure ***Resolution*** is set to ***300 pixels/inch***.

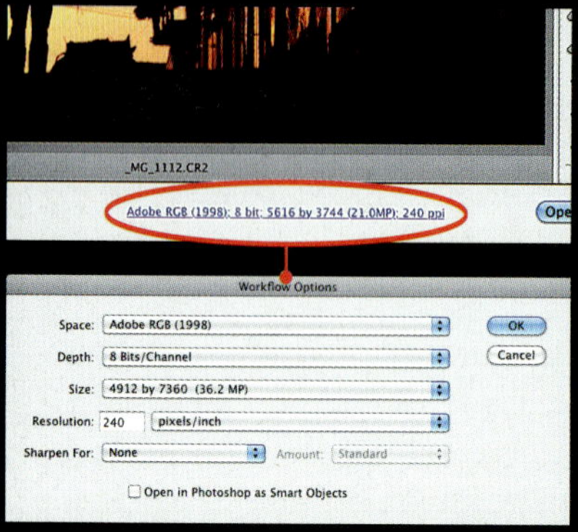

Exposure

Out of all the controls in the Basic panel, ***Exposure*** is the one you're likely to use every time you make edits. Move the slider to the right to increase or left to decrease the exposure: much the same way as adding exposure compensation to your camera. You can also type in an exposure value, like 2 for two stops, in the box. If your image is dramatically under- or overexposed, combine Exposure with other sliders for the best results and be careful of introducing noise.

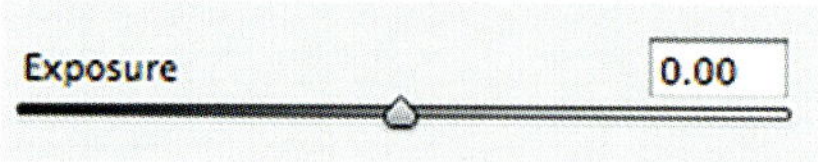

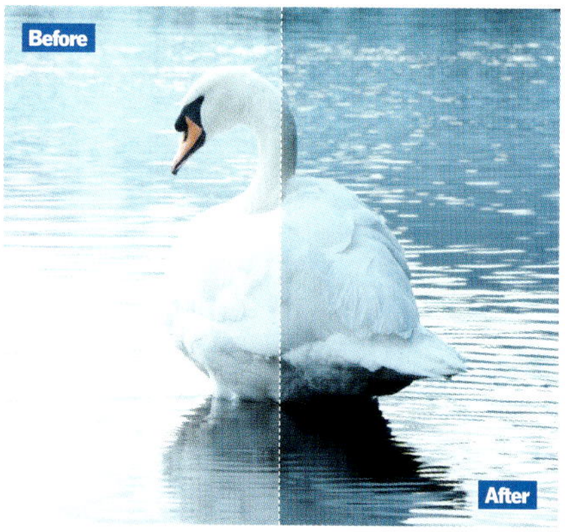

ROSS HODDINOTT

Recovery (Up to CS5)

If you overexposed your image in-camera, then this tool will be your fail-safe option; use it to recover detail that's hidden in the highlights. If you've not clipped your highlights, you can use the slider as generously as you need to, but if you've overexposed to the point where there's no detail to recover, ACR will attempt to reconstruct the detail where two or more colour channels are present. Be watchful of highlights turning grey as a result of trying to retrieve lost detail.

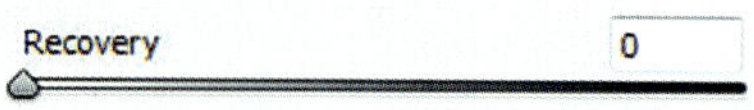

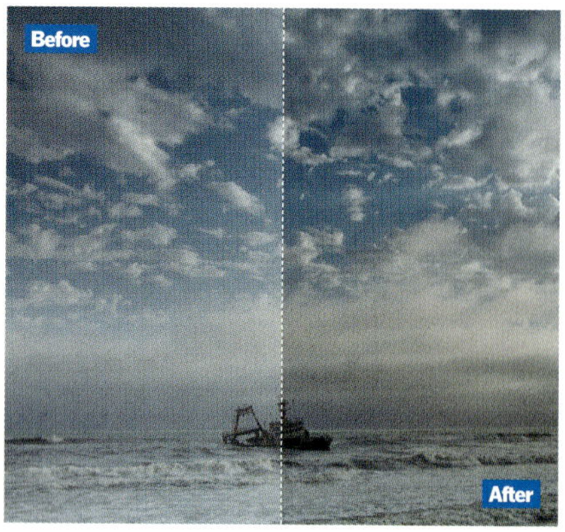

LEE FROST

Fill Light (Up to CS5)

Underexposed your image slightly and want to reveal detail in your shadows? Then this is the tool you'll need to go to after tweaking the Exposure. It works in a similar way to if you had used a burst of fill flash when taking the shot, opening up the shadows for a brighter image. Use in conjunction with the ***Blacks*** slider to improve contrast, but don't overdo it or you'll start to introduce noise, halos and the resemblance of an image with ugly hyperreal dynamic range.

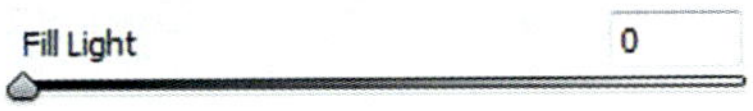

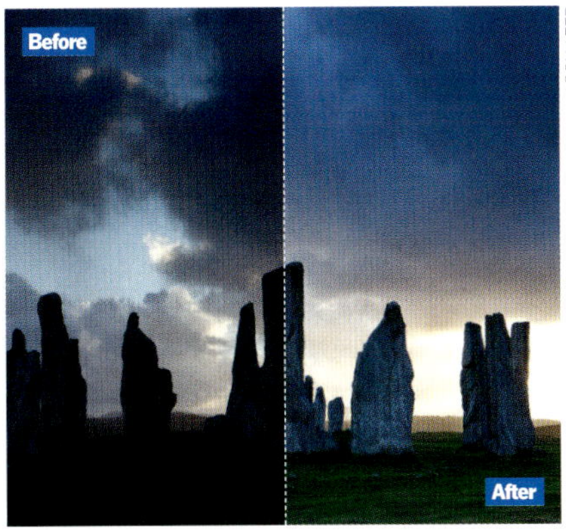

LEE FROST

Contrast

Manipulate the mid-tones, without affecting the pure whites or blacks in your image, to add a little extra punch or to soften tones. Contrast adjustments are best left to the end of your editing process. Be mindful of pushing the slider too far to the left, as this will wash out your image, or too far to the right, as this can cause clipping of shadows and highlights.

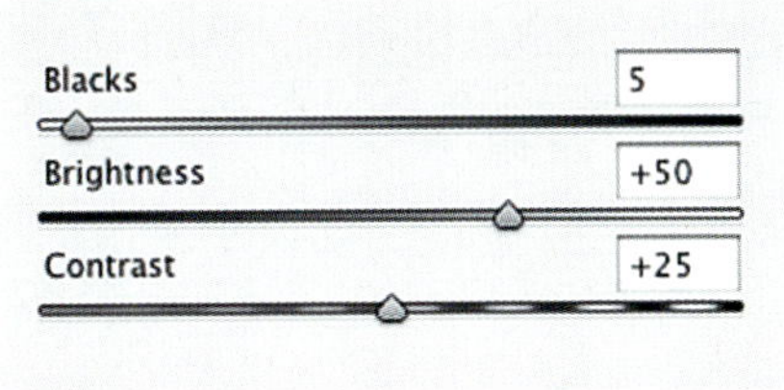

Brightness (Up to CS5)

Quite simply, it does what it says on the tin. Adjust the slider to affect the overall brightness of your image. ACR has more effective tools for doing this, like Exposure, which may be why it's not been featured in the latest version, CS6.

Blacks

Target only your darkest areas to add depth to your shadows by increasing the amount of pure blacks in your image. Watch the histogram and the preview images for areas that flash blue to avoid clipping detail.

Clarity

Fantastic for increasing the level of detail in your image, ***Clarity*** is a tool to be loved and loathed. As it targets edge contrast, use it with caution as excess can result in halos and artefacts. CS6, however, has transformed this tool so halos are now much less of a problem. Zoom in to the image for a better view of your adjustments, which are best made as a final tweak. Combine Clarity with moderate sharpening for the best results: too much of either may hinder image quality.

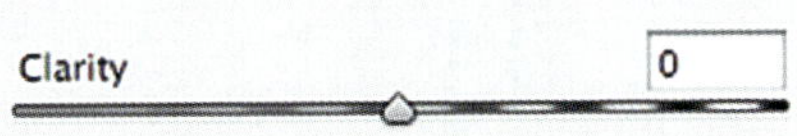

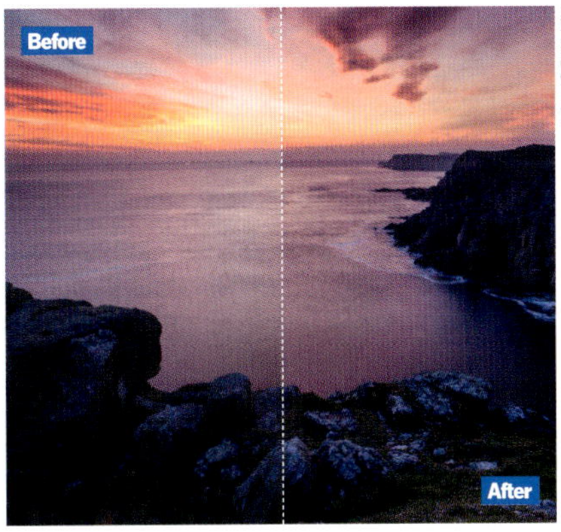

ADAM BURTON

Vibrance & Saturation

Wondering why ACR has both these sliders? It's simple: ***Vibrance*** targets areas that are not already saturated, while ***Saturation*** enhances all colours equally.

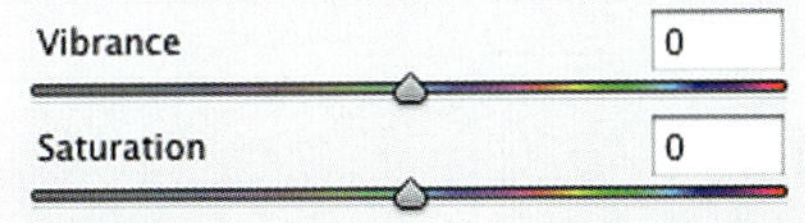

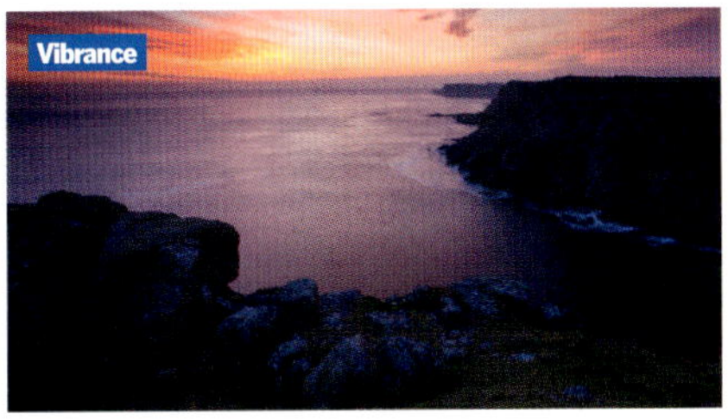

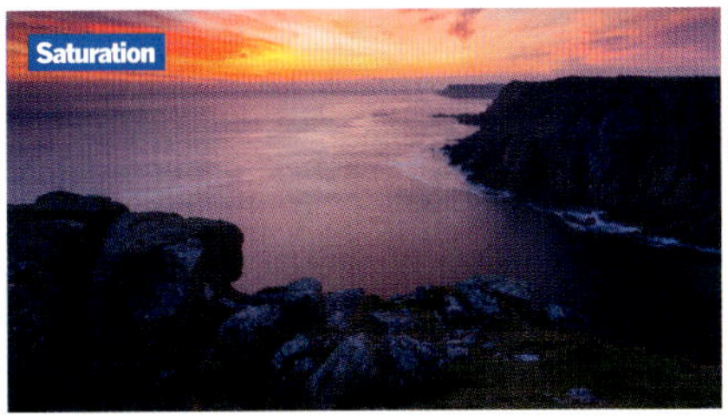

ADAM BURTON

Adjustment Brushes

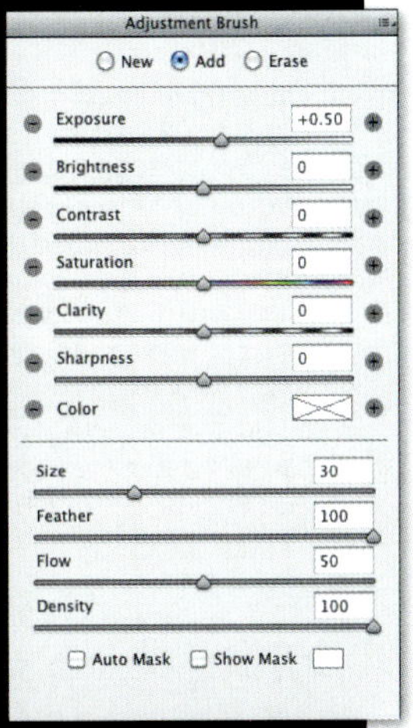

While the Basic tab holds the key to your fundamental editing tools, every adjustment you make to your image using the sliders affects your Raw file globally. But what if, after you've made all of your adjustments, there are areas of the image that are in need of further work? Do you open it in Photoshop to destruct the pixels using the Dodge/Burn Tools or arduously use Adjustment Layers with Layer Masks for selective editing? Well, while the latter option is still a preference over the former, you don't even have to leave ACR to make these localised changes – that's what the Adjustment Brush is for.

Once you select the ***Adjustment Brush*** from the toolbar, the Basic panel converts to the Adjustment Brush panel, featuring some of the same sliders: Exposure, Brightness, Contrast, Saturation, Clarity, Sharpness and Color. In CS6, you also have the benefit of Noise Reduction, Moire Reduction, Defringe, Clarity, Saturation, Shadows, Highlight, Tint and Temp.

In CS5 and CS6, there's also a sub-category that affects the brush's properties such as Size, Feather, Flow and Density. You can use the brush to target specific areas of your image and then the required adjustment slider to edit that section without interfering with the rest of your image.

The ***Auto Mask*** feature is useful for helping you to isolate areas of your image. For every new area you want to target or adjustment you want to make, click ***New*** at the top of the panel. If you want to delete an adjustment at any point, hover over the adjusted area to reveal the pin (a green node) – if it's not visible, just click ***Show Pins*** at the bottom of the panel. Click on the ***pin*** and then ***backspace*** to delete. Alternatively, you can press ***Erase*** and brush over the area again to remove the adjustment.

New to CS6

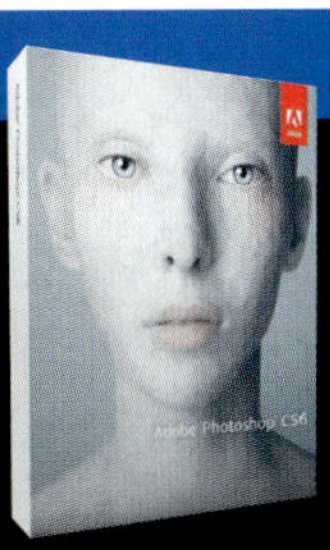

✔**HIGHLIGHTS** This new tool is incredibly powerful: drag it to the left to recover highlight detail – like Recovery in CS5 – or the right to brighten highlights with minimal clipping. Use in combination with the ***Whites*** slider for extra punch.

✔**SHADOWS** Use this slider by moving it to the right or left to brighten or darken shadows and mid-tones, respectively, and to recover detail in the shadows.

✔**WHITES** Drag this new slider to the left to reduce any clipping to the highlights – similarly to Recovery in earlier CS versions – or the right to introduce specular highlights.

Advance your skills with these top tools

Want to know how to use the other highly effective features in ACR? Here are a few…

HAVING COVERED THE basics, you should at least be able to now dabble with processing your Raw files and start to notice the difference to your images. Some photographers, after making basic ACR exposure and contrast adjustments, prefer to open their image in the main Photoshop suite to apply any distortion correction and sharpening, rather than continuing to edit in ACR. It's really a matter of choice.

If you do choose to make some, or all, of your extra adjustments in Photoshop, we strongly advise not compressing your Raw file first, but to open your Raw image as a copy or object to ensure the best results – otherwise you'll lose data and quality.

Depending on your preferred ACR workflow, some of the tools featured in this section, such as Camera and Lens Correction, defringing and vignette removal, might become your first port of call before making any edits in the Basic panel. Whatever your preference is, it's worth knowing what they do and how they work.

Further reading

For monthly in-depth tutorials on how to apply these tools and Raw processing techniques in Lightroom and ACR, read Digital SLR Photography magazine.

Lens Corrections

Different lenses exhibit various defects depending on factors like f/stop and focal length, one of which is distortion. But this is simple to correct in ACR. Select the ***Lens Corrections*** tab and click ***Profile***, then ***Enable Lens Profile Corrections*** for automatic adjustments based on the lens you've used. You can also use the ***Distortion*** slider if it's not sufficient. See Vignetting and Fixing Fringing for more information on further common corrections.

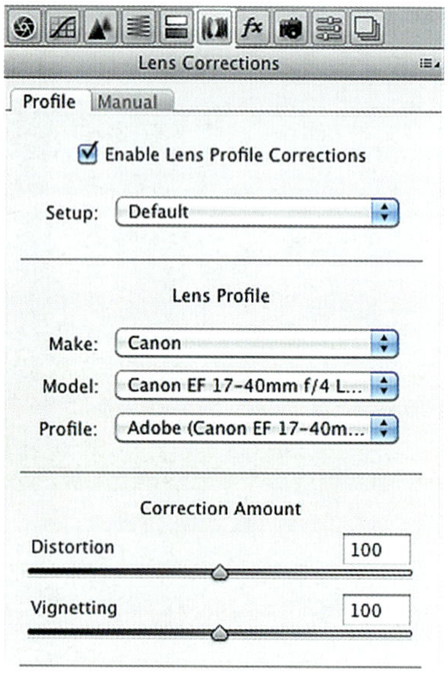

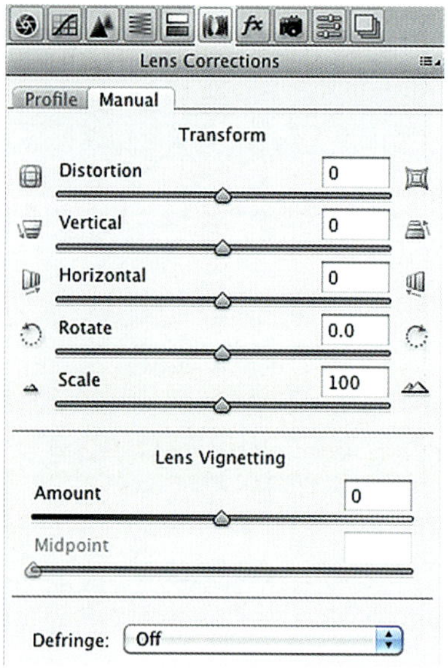

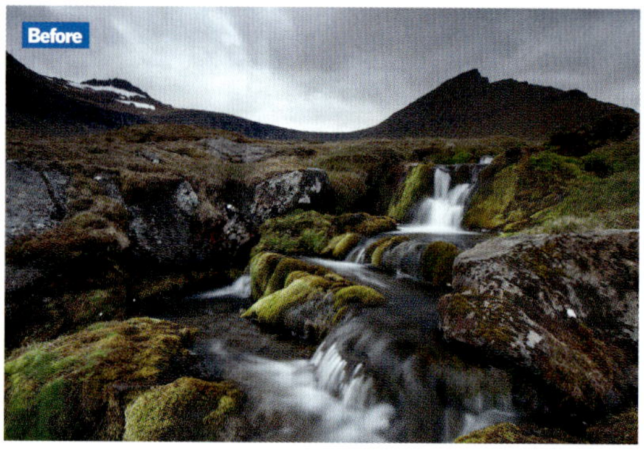

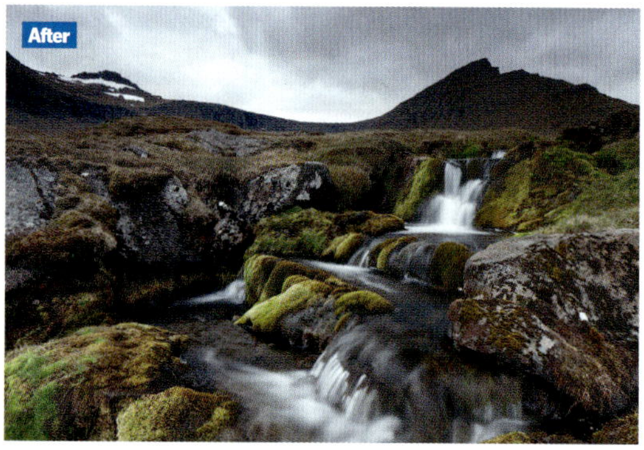

ADAM BURTON

Sharpening

A lot of photographers prefer to leave sharpening to Photoshop, or at least after all other editing has been done, as it arguably offers more control and allows you to alter the level of sharpening depending on the output (ie web or print). ACR's sharpening, however, located in Detail, is based on the same algorithm as Photoshop's Unsharp Mask, so is very effective. Sharpening in ACR also has the benefit of being nondestructive and reversible, whereas in Photoshop this is a lot more difficult to achieve. However you decide to sharpen, know that it's an essential step as, unlike a JPEG, no in-camera sharpening has been applied to a Raw file.

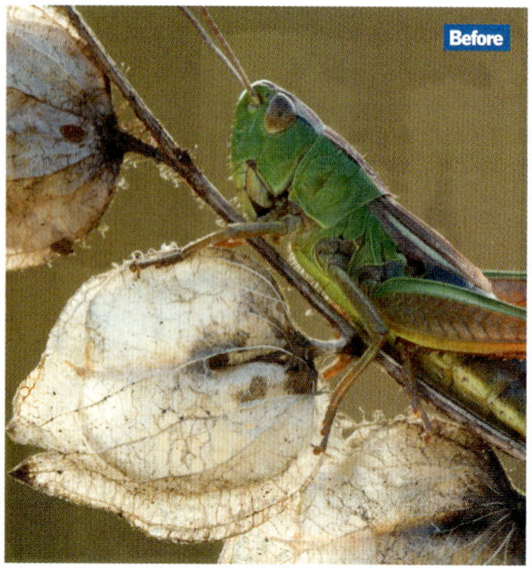

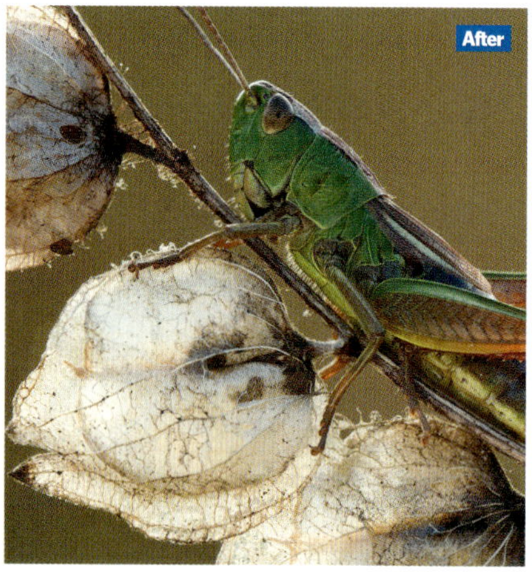

ROSS HODDINOTT

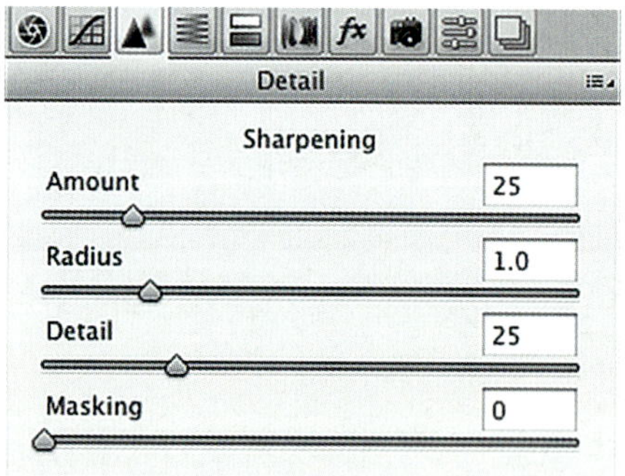

Amount: Affects edge definition. The higher the Amount, the more edges are sharpened. Be careful of adding artefacts by going too far as it can be detrimental to your image.

Radius: Adjust the size of the details that sharpening is applied to. Use a high ***Radius*** for large details and a low ***Radius*** for fine details.

Detail: Use to sharpen high-frequency data. Set it low to remove blur around edges and high for making texture much more pronounced.

Masking: Leave set to ***0*** so the other slider affects the whole image or ***100*** to restrict tweaks to the strongest edges. Press ***alt/opt*** to see the areas masked.

Tone Curve

The next tab along from Basic is Tone Curve, and it works in a similar way to Curves in Photoshop. As Raw files are notoriously flat, this section can become really useful and an alternative to some of the Basic sliders once you've got the hang of it. You have two options: Parametric and Point. Under the ***Point*** sub-tab you can select a preset that affects the brightness and contrast, or you can adjust the line intersecting the histogram manually, like you would in Curves. If Levels was more your style, stick with the default ***Parametric*** sub-tab as it allows you to use the sliders, which can be more manageable, to target ***Highlights***, ***Lights***, ***Darks*** and ***Shadows***. Move the sliders to the left to lighten, or right to darken those specific tonal bands. You'll notice as you change the sliders that the graph line changes shape – the higher you set the contrast, the steeper the curve will create an 'S' shape. In Lightroom 4 and Photoshop CS6, you can also select specific colour channels to edit – great if you only want to affect the contrast of Red, Green or Blue, or apply a creative cross-processing technique to your images.

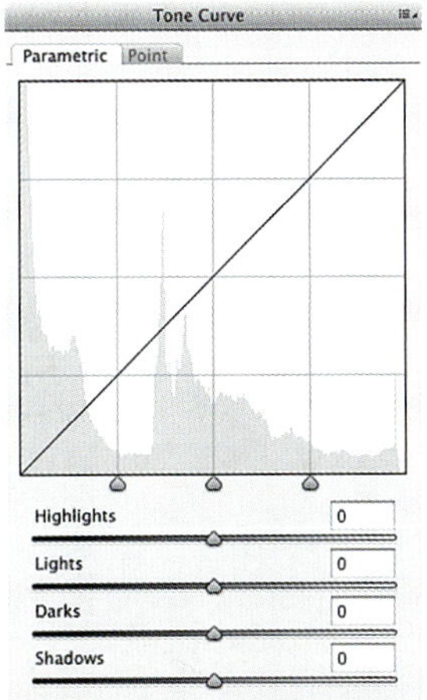

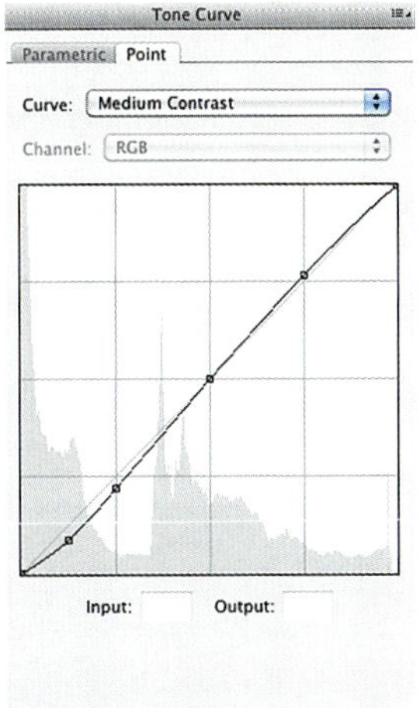

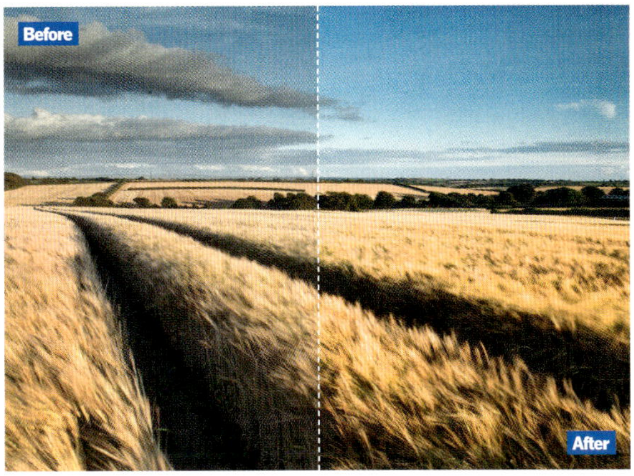

Fixing fringing

ACR makes fixing colour fringing incredibly easy: click on ***Lens Corrections*** then the ***Manual*** tab and select ***Defringe: All Edges***. If grey lines appear, select ***Highlight Edges*** instead as this is where most fringing appears. Zoom in to your image to at least ***100%*** to judge the results.

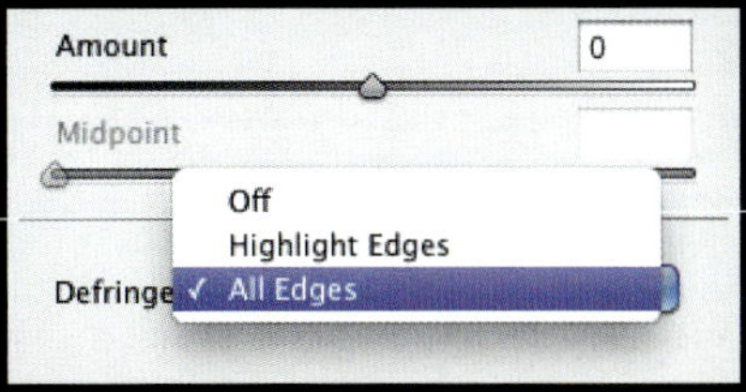

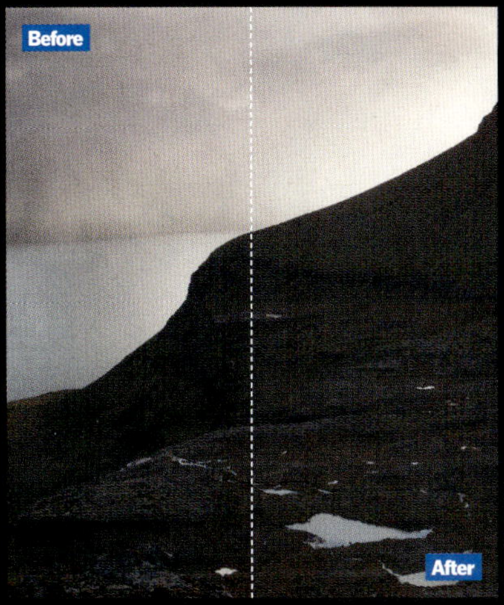

Vignetting

Lens corrections: Often if you've used a wide-angle lens, your image may suffer from slight vignetting (darkening of the corners). To correct this, click on the ***Lens Correction*** tab and use the ***Amount*** slider under ***Lens Vignetting*** to lighten or darken the edges to reduce the amount of cropping you may need to do. The ***Midpoint*** slider is useful if your vignette encroaches beyond the corners.

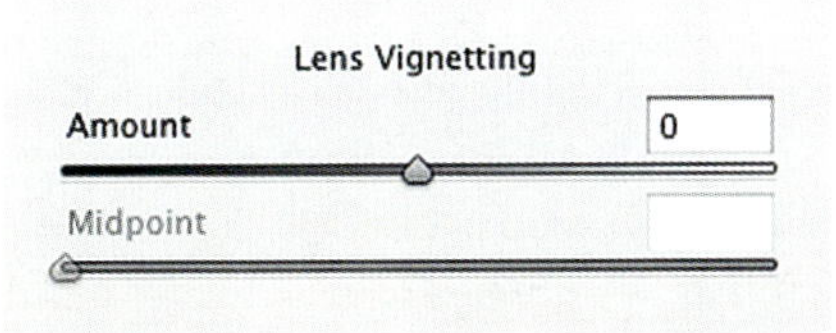

Artistic effect: Vignetting, when controlled, can be an artistic finishing touch. In this case, use ***Post Crop Vignetting*** under the ***Effects*** tab. Choose a ***Style***: ***Highlight Priority*** to protect your highlights; ***Color Priority*** to preserve hues; ***Paint Overlay*** to blend the original colours with the vignette. You can then adjust the following settings: the ***Amount*** to lighten or darken the corners; ***Midpoint*** to affect the spread of the vignette; ***Roundness*** to decide its shape; ***Feather*** to adjust the softness; and ***Highlights*** to control contrast.

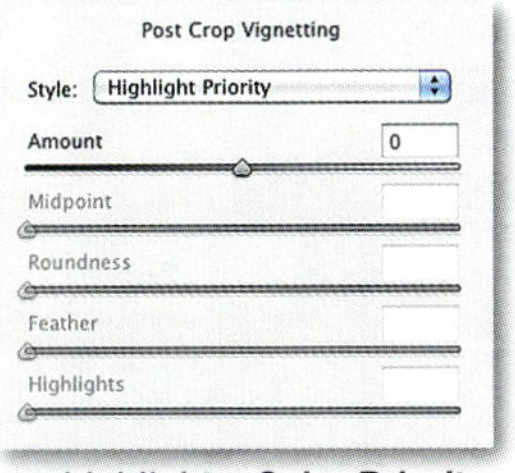

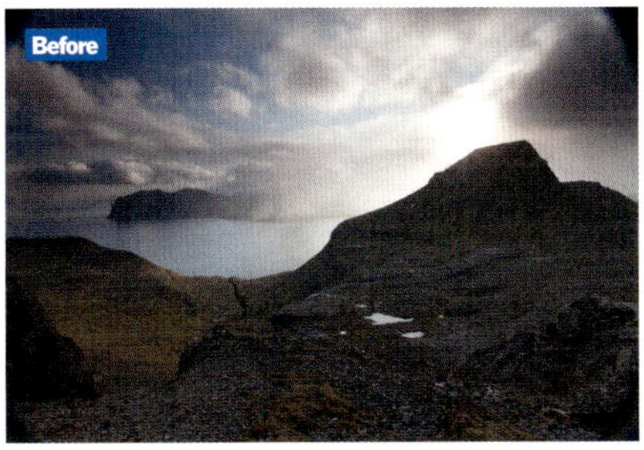

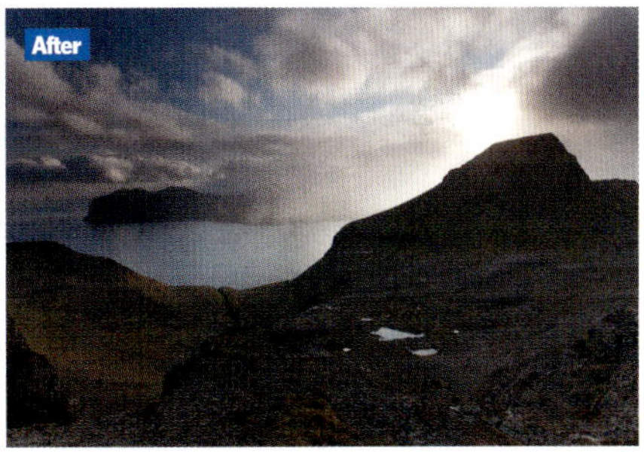

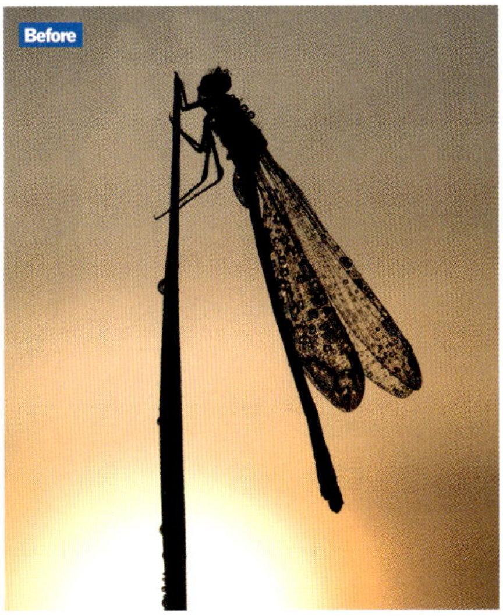

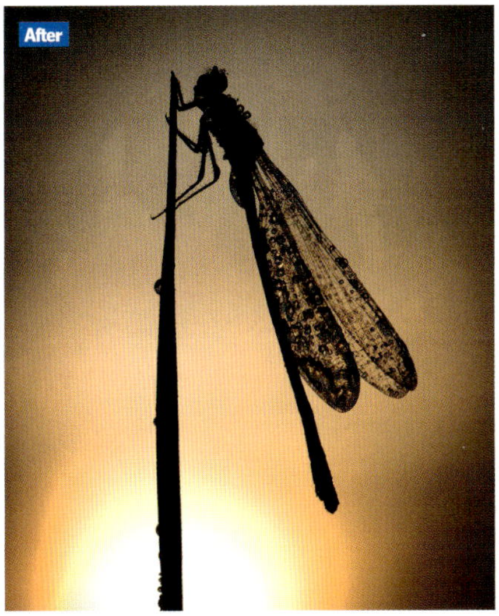

Basics of batch processing

The curse and cure of digital is being able to shoot lots of images at no additional cost, but what's the best way to manage all the files?

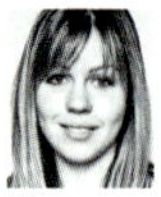

Caroline Wilkinson: You've got files upon files of Raw images and you're not sure what to do with them or how to sort them out. The beauty of Raw is that you may have a hidden gem among pictures that appear to have little potential, due to the wide parameters that software, like Adobe Camera Raw, gives you for retrieving detail and correcting exposure. Before you can assess how usable your shots are, you need to do a few basic adjustments to eek out the weak from the strong and the salvageable from print-ready. Thankfully, you can do this quite quickly in Adobe Camera Raw by batch-processing images. Most of these steps can be expanded upon – for instance, White Balance, exposure and colour – depending on how much work your images need, but for the sake of what to do to get your images ready as quickly as possible, follow this step-by-step guide.

Save in stages

If you want to save some images and continue working on others in Photoshop or Adobe Camera Raw (ACR), select the images you want while holding ***cmd/option***, then ***Save*** or ***Open***. If you click ***Done***, your nondestructive adjustments will be retained in the Raw format for you to work on again later in ACR.

UNDO YOUR REJECTS

Want to retain any files that you've rejected in ACR? No problem – simply press the ***backspace*** key again to remove the red cross that you'll find in the top-left corner of the image thumbnail.

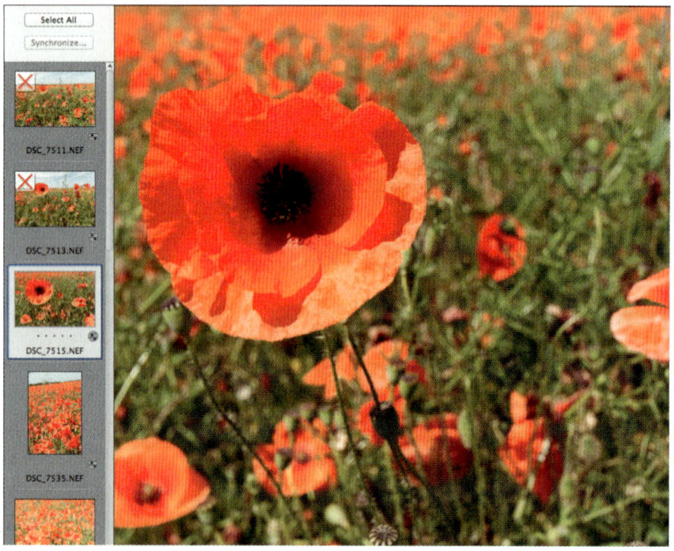

1 Load up your images Organise your files into batches, divided by what lighting conditions they were shot in/White Balance used. In Photoshop CS, go to ***File>Open*** and then select a batch of images by holding ***shift*** and clicking the first and last image. Click ***Open*** to transfer into ACR. Flick through the images on the big screen and select ***backspace*** to reject any that are out of focus; a red cross will appear in the corner of the image and it won't be affected by any other edits.

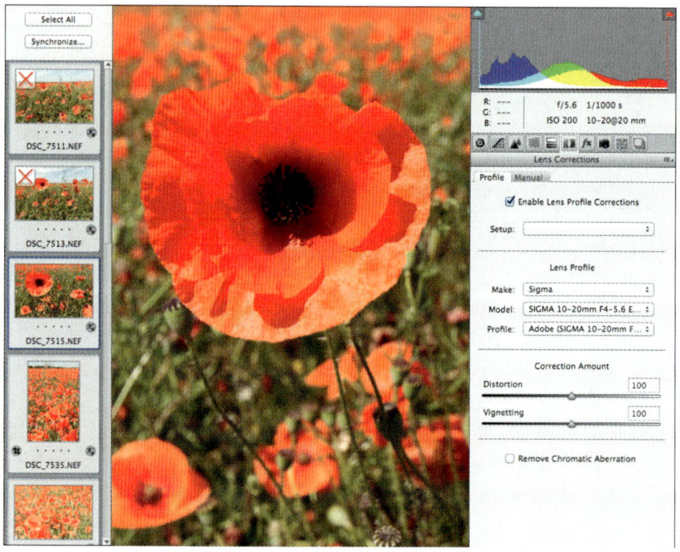

2 Correct lens distortion This step is much easier if all your images have been shot with the same lens. If they've not, you will have to adjust each image individually. Click ***Select All*** at the top of the thumbnail palette and then select the ***Lens Corrections*** tab and tick ***Enable Lens Profile Corrections***. If the details under Lens Profile are incorrect or the vignetting needs further adjustments, use the sliders under the ***Manual*** tab. Under Manual, select ***Defringe: All Edges***.

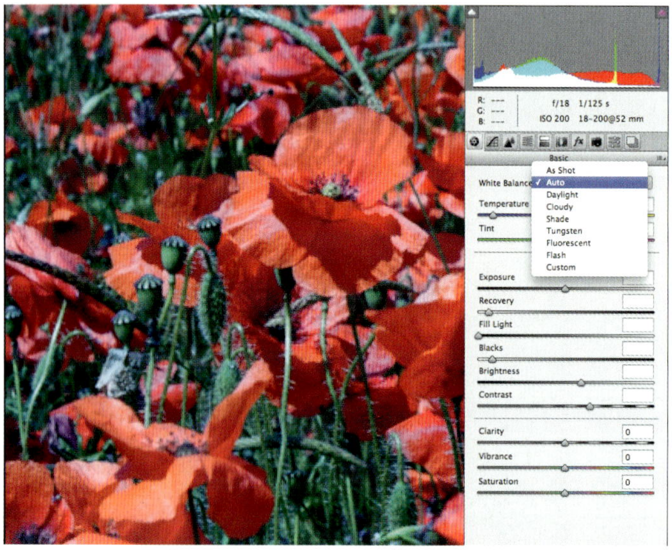

3 Adjust tonality and colour With all the images still selected, click on to the ***Basic*** tab and press ***Auto*** (just above Exposure) to correct the images' tonality. Next, click on the ***White Balance*** drop-down menu and select your correct WB setting – I picked Auto. While this is the quickest way to batch-process a large amount of images taken in the same lighting, you can always return to these settings later to refine the tonality and even pick a different WB preset for creative effect.

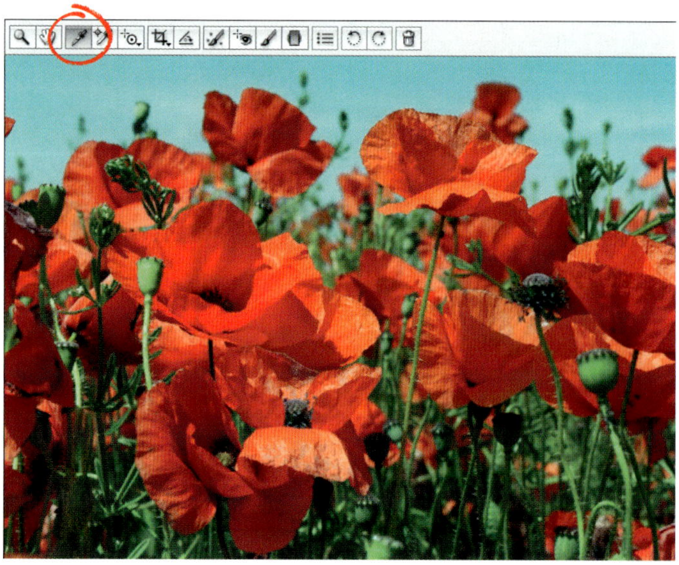

4 Selective White Balance Being able to correct colour casts with a click of a button is one of the biggest assets of working with Raw images. Note that you can also set a custom WB using the ***White Balance Tool*** in the toolbar. Click on a white area of the image to set the correct WB (even better, take a shot of a white sheet of paper as part of your batch of images and click on this to set the WB for the rest of the batch). Try clicking on a different area of the image to see what colour effects you can achieve, too.

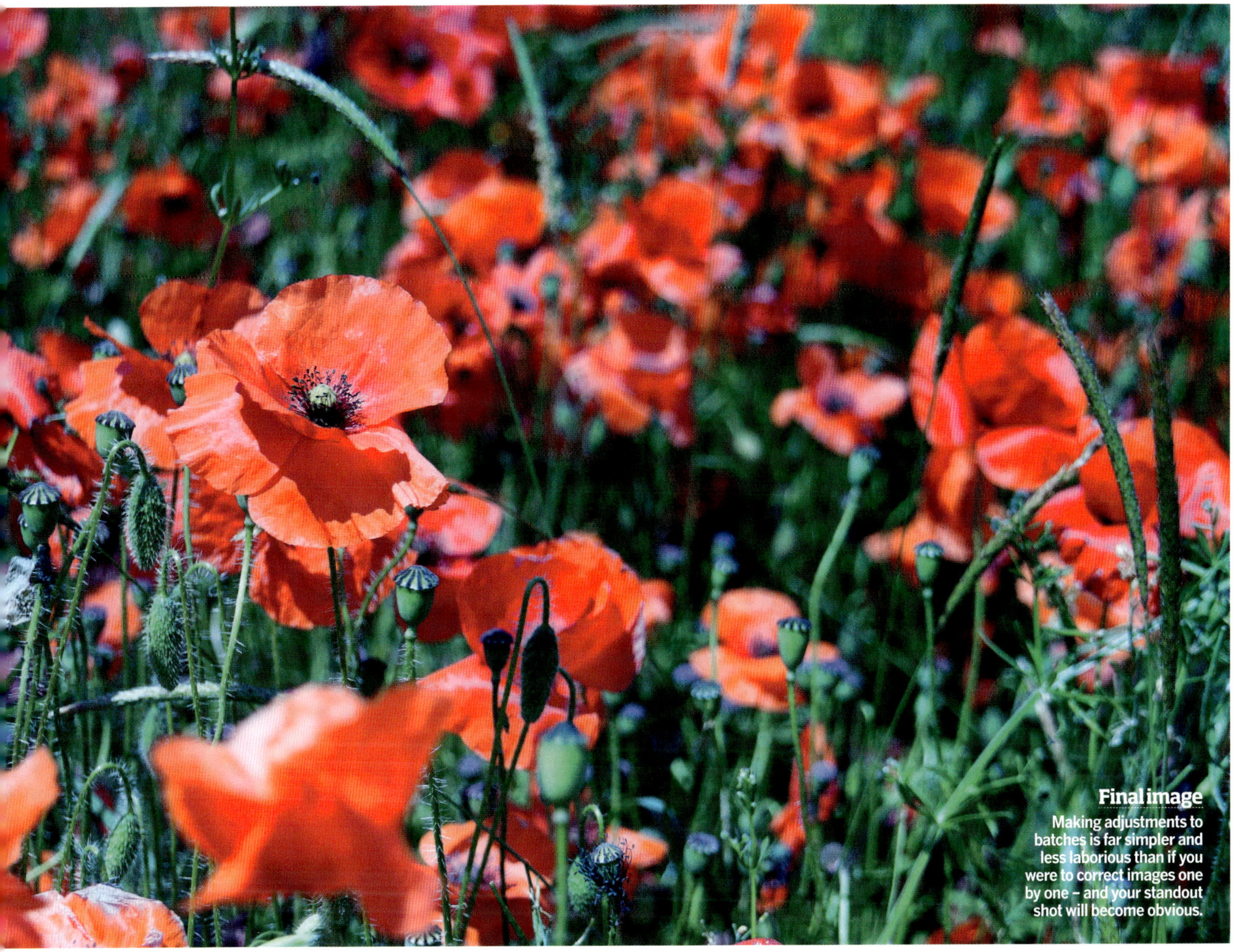

Final image
Making adjustments to batches is far simpler and less laborious than if you were to correct images one by one – and your standout shot will become obvious.

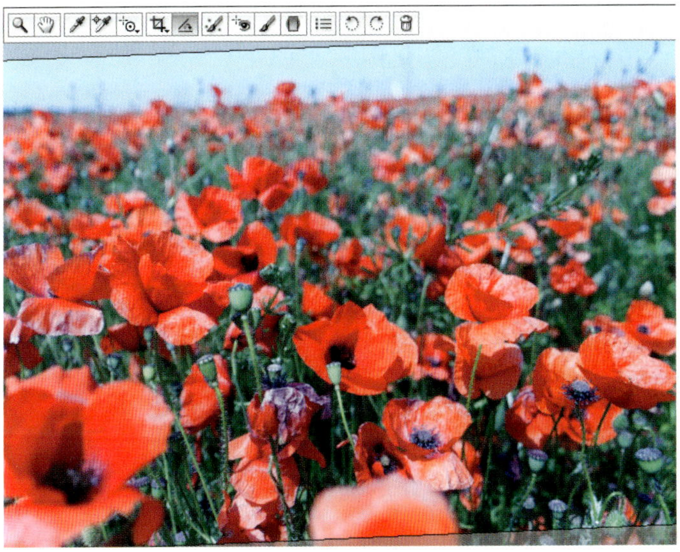

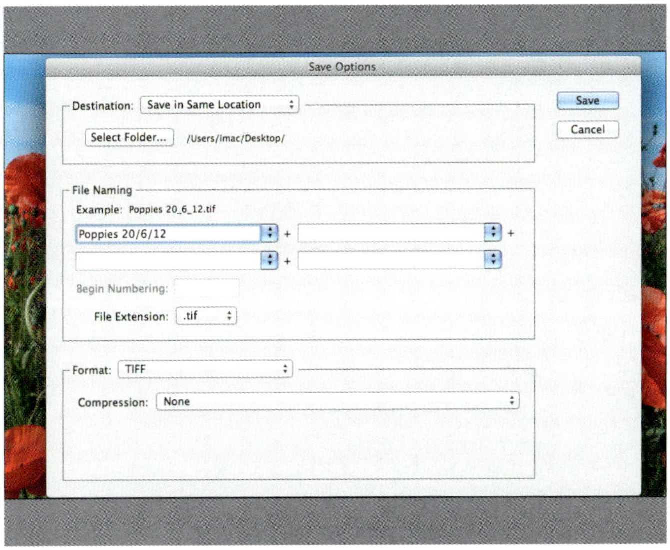

5 Straighten and crop At this stage, I recommend flicking through the images once again and rejecting any images you're sure you don't want by pressing the ***backspace*** key. It's now time to address the images individually. If an image needs to be realigned, select the ***Straighten Tool*** from the toolbar and click and drag it along the horizon and release. Then press ***enter*** to confirm the crop. You can use the ***Crop Tool***, too, if you need to refine the composition of any of your images.

6 Save images At this stage, you can either work on the images that need more attention in ACR, open in Photoshop by clicking ***Select All*** and ***Open***, or if this blitz of basic adjustments was enough, you can save the files. To do this, click ***Select All*** then ***Save Images...*** In the dialogue box, select the folder you want to save the images to and then give the batch a name, eg 'Poppies 20/6/12'. To keep the maximum amount of data for editing in Photoshop, select ***TIFF*** as a ***Format*** and ***Compression: None***.

Focus on the detail for improved images

Raw images are untouched by in-camera presets – before you hit print, know the basics…

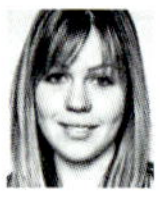

Caroline Wilkinson: When shooting Raw, there are two editing techniques worth knowing if nothing else. Even if you have perfect exposure and colour rendering, the first of these two things needs to be done to every image. The second is optional and if you've not underexposed your image or shot at a high ISO rating, you may not even need to use it. Know what they are yet?

Noise Reduction and Sharpening enable you to draw out maximum detail from your images. Some cameras are better at handling noise than others at mid to high ISOs, but if yours isn't one of them, this is a really useful feature. Noise also lives in shadow detail, so if you underexpose your image and then use ACR to open up the shadows – say, using the Fill Light or Exposure slider under the Basic tab – you may introduce noise and degrade the image quality. You can also get coloured noise during a long exposure, as you heat up the pixels. By its nature, Noise Reduction softens image detail to try to hide visible artefacts, which is why we're covering Sharpening, too. Even if you don't need Noise Reduction, though, Sharpening is a feature you should know about. The tools are brilliant in ACR, but some photographers prefer the flexibility of layers and using the Sharpen filters in Photoshop CS (see pages 68-69 for more information), though working with an uncompressed Raw file gives you loads more detail to work with. If you shot in JPEG, your images would have some sharpening applied in-camera, but in Raw you have nothing and it's up to you to draw the detail out. The trick is not to overdo it – this guide will show you how.

Noise Reduction

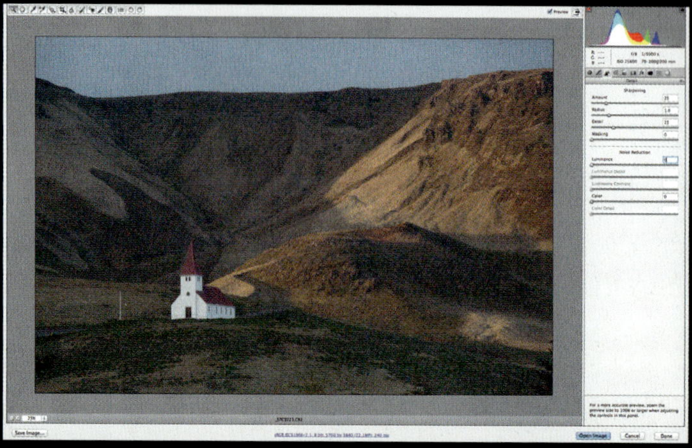

1 Assess your image Click on the ***Noise Reduction*** section of the ***Detail*** tab. Now assess your image for the type of noise you have to reduce – is it luminance; black and white pixels that make the image look grainy? Or chroma; colour noise that's denoted by coloured artefacts? This will help you decide if you need to use the Luminance or Color sliders.

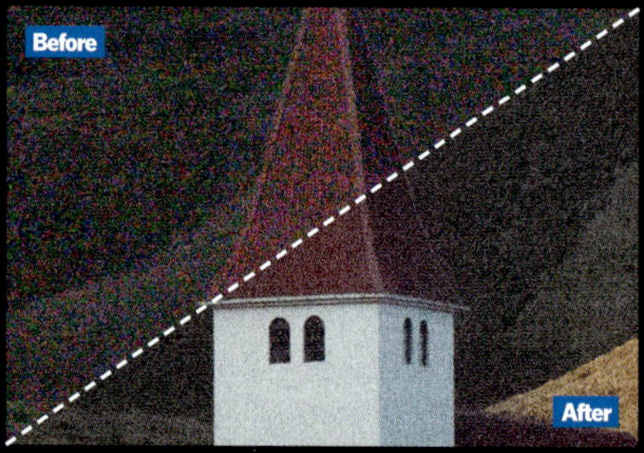

2 Target the colour noise Adjusting the ***Color*** and ***Color Detail*** sliders should preserve colour detail while you're reducing any artefacts. Use the ***Color*** slider to reduce the noise and the ***Color Detail*** slider to control the threshold. Set it to a high value to protect the edges between colours, but be watchful of introducing specks of colour: a lower setting reduces speckles but can also cause colours to blend.

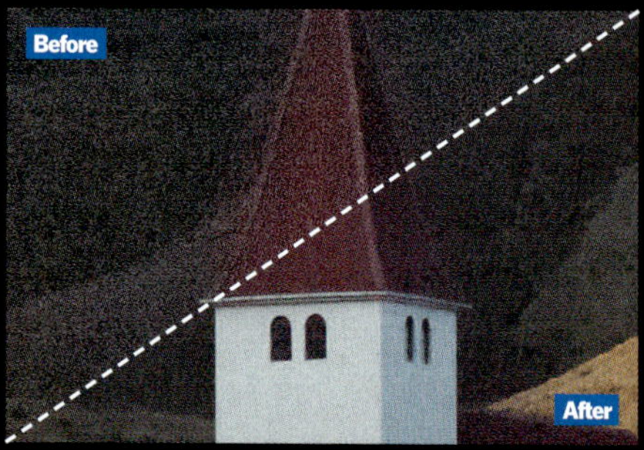

3 Target black & white noise This is the most common type of noise, usually caused by working at high ISOs. Use the ***Luminance Detail*** slider to control the threshold: set it high to preserve detail but to compromise on the level of Noise Reduction; and lower to produce cleaner images at the cost of detail. Luminance Contrast is best kept low as higher values can cause more damage than good.

Sharpening

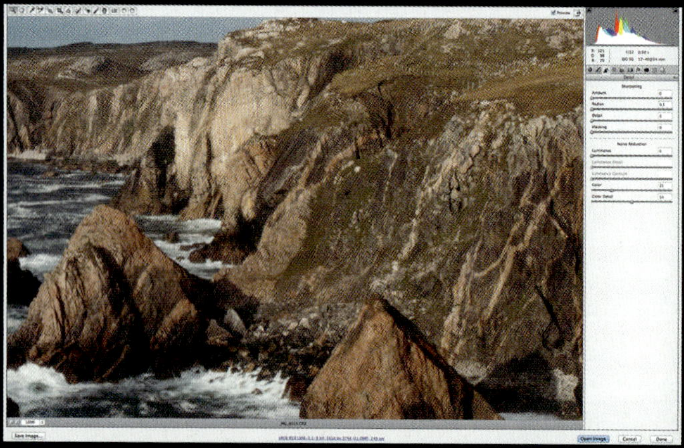

1 Zoom in to your image Sharpening is best applied as a final step. It might even help you bring back some detail lost from Noise Reduction, too, but be careful not to introduce noise back into the image. Click on the ***Detail*** tab to access ***Sharpening***. Use the ***Zoom Tool*** in the top toolbar to enlarge your image to at least ***100%*** to assess the effect: this is the only way to determine whether you're introducing artefacts.

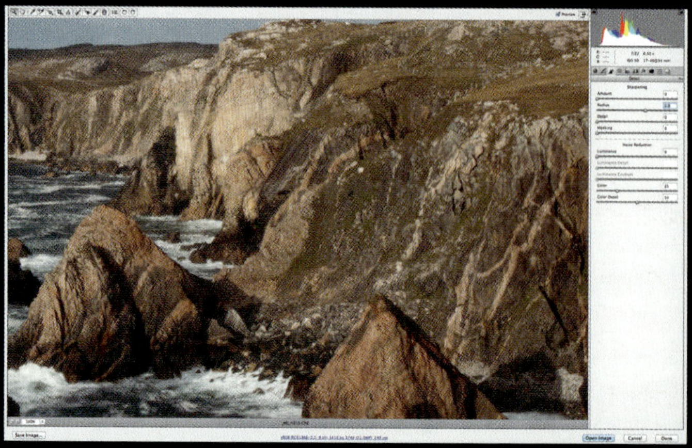

2 Adjust the Radius Look at your image and decide the average size of the details that need sharpening: the larger the details, the higher the Radius setting needs to be. If your image has fine details, set a low ***Radius*** of below ***1.0***, or for large details, a higher ***Radius*** of around ***2.0***, but be careful that you don't make your image look unnatural. You may need to adjust this slider as you work with the ***Amount*** later.

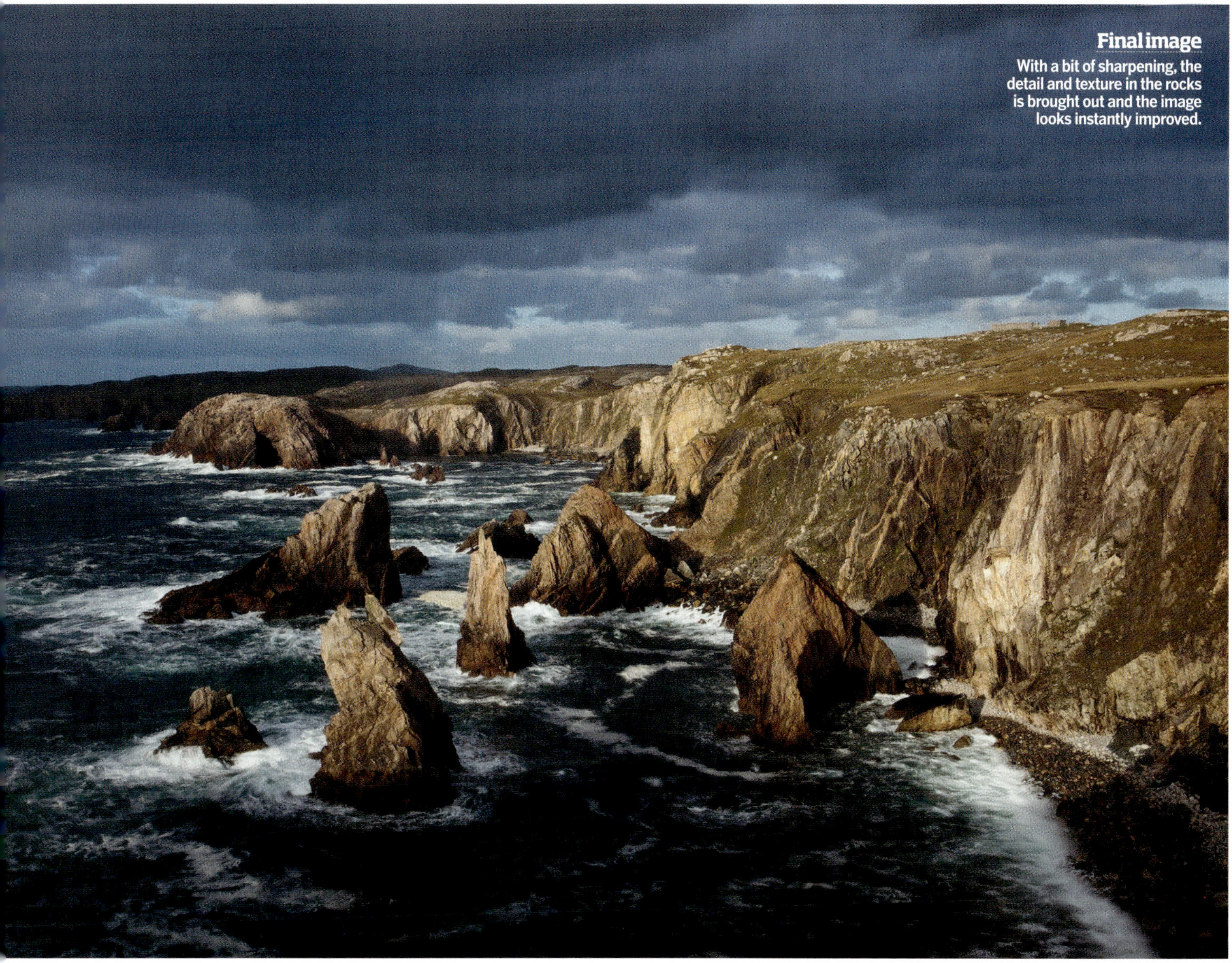

Final image
With a bit of sharpening, the detail and texture in the rocks is brought out and the image looks instantly improved.

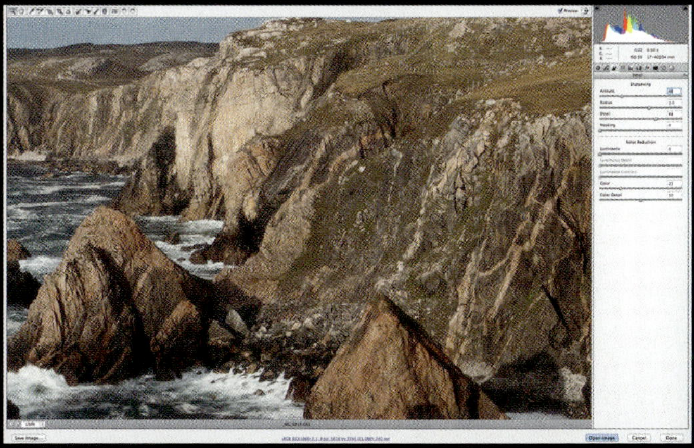

3 Concentrate on the Amount Use the ***Detail*** slider to target edge detail: to reduce blurring, set a low value (***30*** or less); and a higher value to emphasise textures. You'll see the results of the other sliders once you adjust the ***Amount***. It works much like Photoshop CS's Unsharp Mask filter, but ACR calculates the threshold to set for you based on the camera model and ISO. Move the ***Amount*** slider to adjust the edge sharpness.

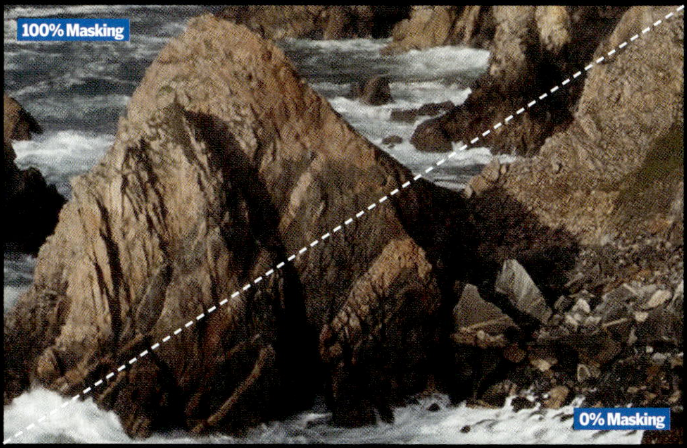

4 Use Masking Keep ***Masking*** set to ***0*** so all the adjustments you make will affect the whole image, or move the ***Masking*** slider towards ***100*** to only target the larger edges. Zoom into the image to ***200%*** or more to see the effect better. When applying Sharpening, you need to be careful of introducing artefacts: tiny dots around the areas that you've sharpened. As soon as they start to appear, you know you've gone too far.

How to manage colour with Camera Calibration

Perfect Photoshop's colour rendering and take control of your Raw editing process with a more efficient workflow

Caroline Wilkinson: It's one area of Adobe Camera Raw that often gets ignored, but it holds a few tricks and treats you might be interested to know about – especially if you like your in-camera presets or your shadows often have a colour cast. The eighth tab along the editing suite in ACR, Camera Calibration, offers a few practical and creative profiles for adjusting and improving the colour rendering of your pictures. Each profile is calibrated to get the best from your camera or to correct its unwanted colour behaviour, so it can be a really useful tool if you know how to use it. Your default profile is Adobe Camera Standard, which is excellent and very rarely – if ever – will you need to change from it. But if you want to experiment with your colour rendering, this article should show you how. Plus, if you routinely apply the same settings and treatments to images in Adobe Camera Raw, you might be interested in the section on creating and applying Presets in order to save you valuable editing time.

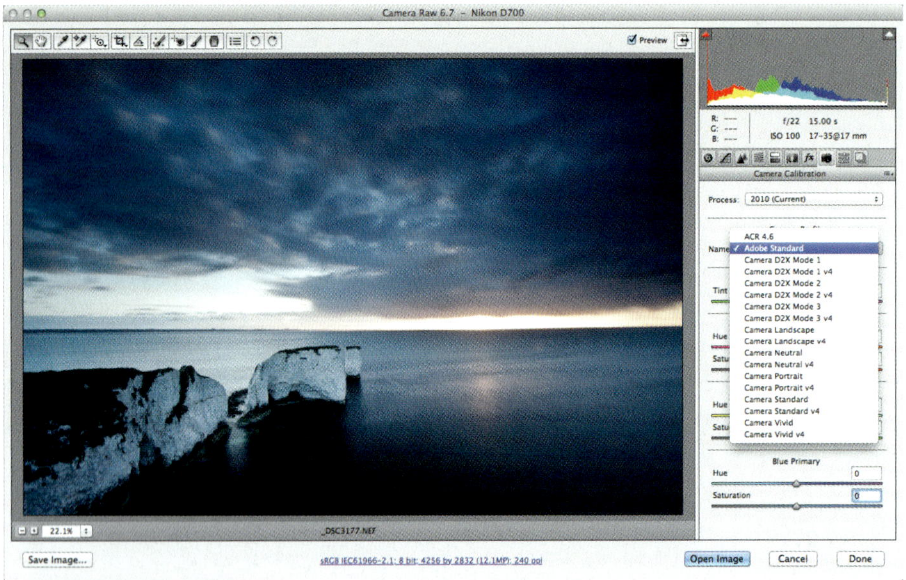

Applying profiles

If you previously shot in JPEG and liked the look of some of your camera's built-in colour profiles, you may be missing them now you've converted to Raw processing. These profiles (otherwise known as Picture Styles or Picture Controls on your camera) can be accessed via the Camera Profile section and affect your Raw file's saturation, colour and contrast to varying degrees. Depending on your camera, there may be many to choose from: some familiar, others not; some effective for making your images richer and colours punchier, while others simply ruin them. Just experiment with the different profiles – there's no harm in clicking on them as any adjustments made in ACR are nondestructive – but you'll probably find the best results come from your camera's more familiar Picture Styles.

For the example image opposite, shot on a Nikon D800, there are the following options: Landscape, Neutral, Portrait, Standard and Vivid, plus an alternate version for each. You could apply these settings in-camera if shooting in JPEG, but with Raw, all colour, contrast and sharpening adjustments are discarded, requiring you to specify the look using the controls in ACR.

The beauty of being able to apply profiles after capture, rather than in-camera, is that you can use them as a base to be refined by other settings. It also means that you can process the same image multiple times to different effect. If you create a style you like, you can always save it as a Preset, to be applied to future images with a click of a button (see below for details).

Saving a Preset

After trying the profiles on different images, shot in various lighting environments and of different subjects, you might find that you want to use one of these in-camera profiles as your new default to apply to all images imported into ACR. If that's the case, select that profile from the ***Camera Profile*** drop-down menu and then click on the drop-down menu in the top right of the ***Camera Calibration*** panel. Scroll down and click on ***Save New Camera Raw Preset***.

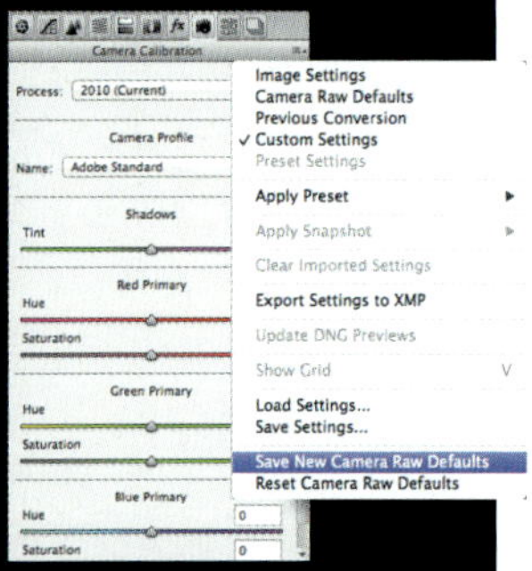

Saving a Preset

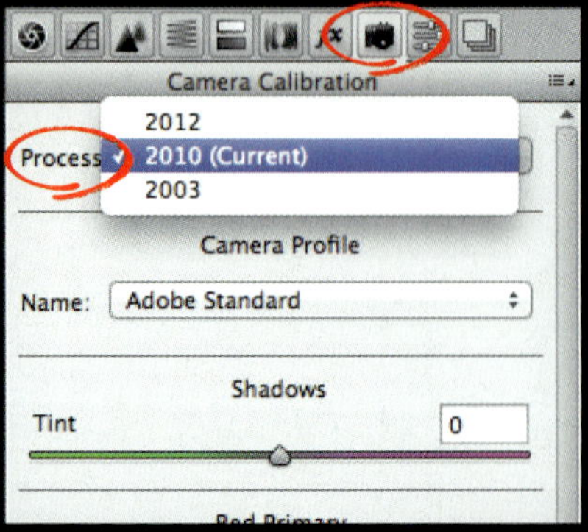

PROCESS These profiles are compatible with older versions of Camera Raw. Choose a different ACR profile if you want new images to maintain a consistent look to match with older photos.

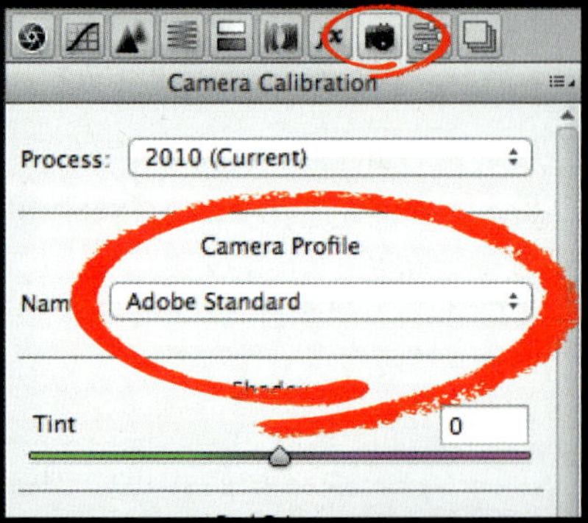

CAMERA PROFILE Sets the profile you want to use for your image.

ADOBE STANDARD This profile improves the colour rendering of your camera – especially warm tones such as reds, yellows and oranges. There's an Adobe Standard profile available for every camera.

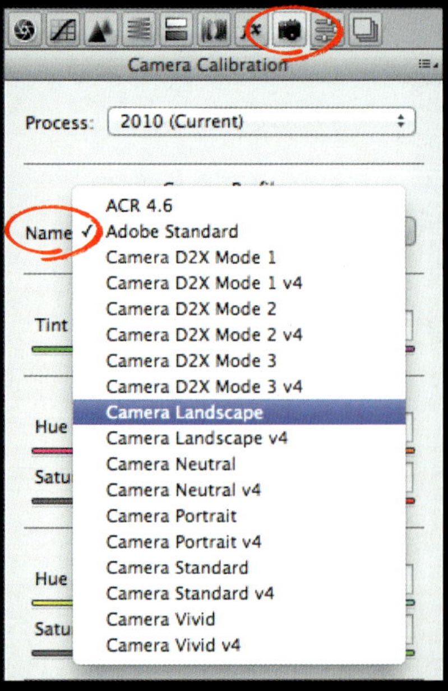

OTHER PROFILES These profiles attempt to match the camera manufacturer's in-camera Presets as closely as possible.

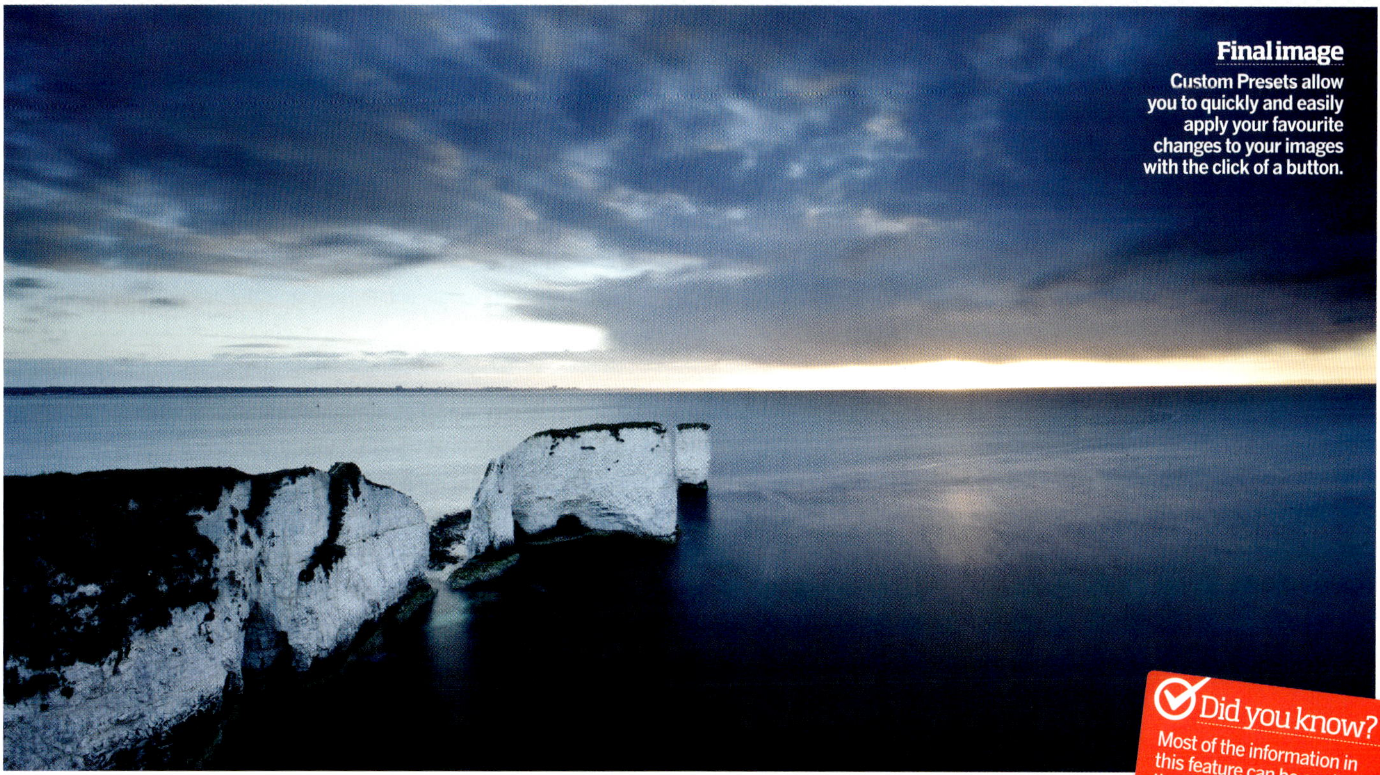

Final image
Custom Presets allow you to quickly and easily apply your favourite changes to your images with the click of a button.

Did you know?
Most of the information in this feature can be applied in the Camera Calibration panel in Lightroom 5, too – the profiles are the same for both Adobe softwares

Adding and applying Presets

Whether you're creating a new colour style, calibration profile or want to be more efficient by saving your basic or creative editing process to apply to future images, the Presets panel in ACR is just what you need. Here's how to make the most of it…

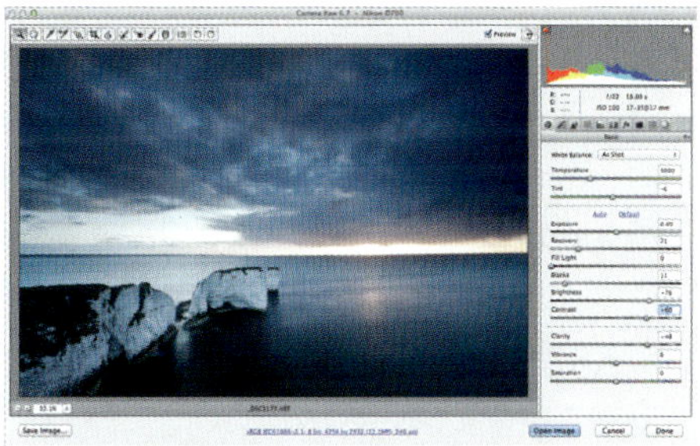

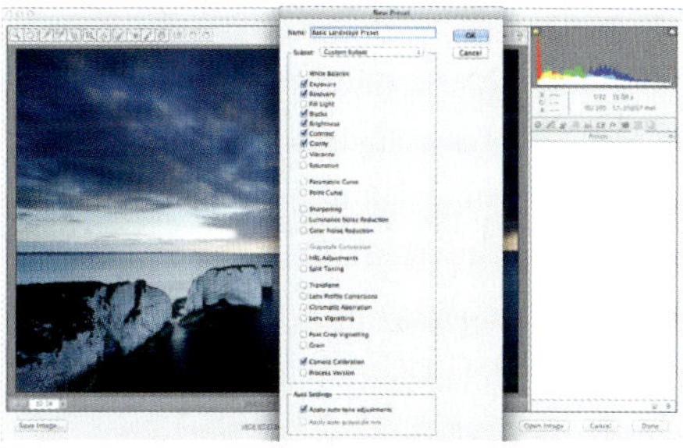

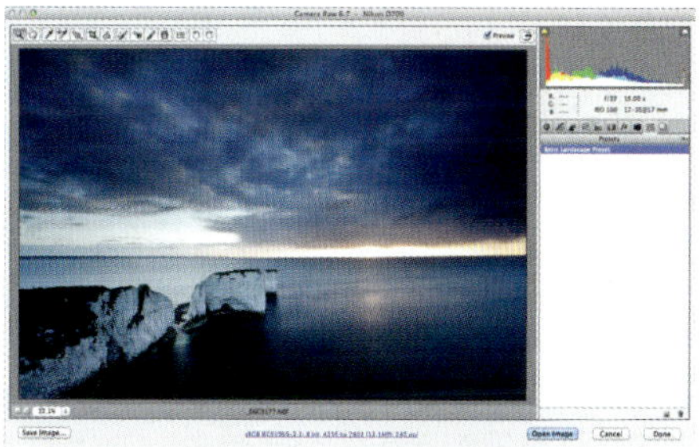

1 Make adjustments In your usual fashion, make all the adjustments that you want to apply to your future Raw files. It could be as basic as correcting exposure by a couple of stops, a combination of sharpening and improved clarity, a complete colour overhaul or a black & white style treatment – whatever you want.

2 Create the Preset Click on the ***Preset*** panel in ACR – this will be a blank panel until you add a preset. Down in the bottom right-hand corner of this panel is a ***New Preset*** icon, click on it to open the control panel. You can now select all the adjustments that you'd like to save within this preset. Give it a name and click ***OK***.

3 Apply the Preset You should now see that your new Preset is visible in the panel, ready to use. To check it works, open a new Raw file and then apply your Preset by clicking on it in the ***Preset*** panel. You can create as many Presets as you want and delete any Preset by clicking on the ***trash can*** icon in the bottom of the panel.

Fine-tune colour

You can adjust how Photoshop interprets the colours captured by your camera by using the controls in the Camera Calibration panel and saving it as a Preset (see panel on opposite page). Some images from certain models of camera can have a slight magenta or green tint to the shadows, which can be corrected here using the ***Shadows*** slider to adjust the colour and make it more neutral.

Keep the ***Camera Profile*** set to ***Adobe Standard*** for the best colour rendering for your particular camera. If that doesn't do the trick, you'll need to refer to the ***Red, Green*** and ***Blue Primary*** sliders to change the hue and saturation of that individual channel. If your picture has a green cast, pull the ***Hue*** slider away from ***Green*** until the image looks neutral. Adjust the ***Saturation*** slider afterwards, too, if required. If the tint is consistent across your images, you can save these settings as a Preset so you can apply it to all subsequent Raw files, saving you valuable time in editing.

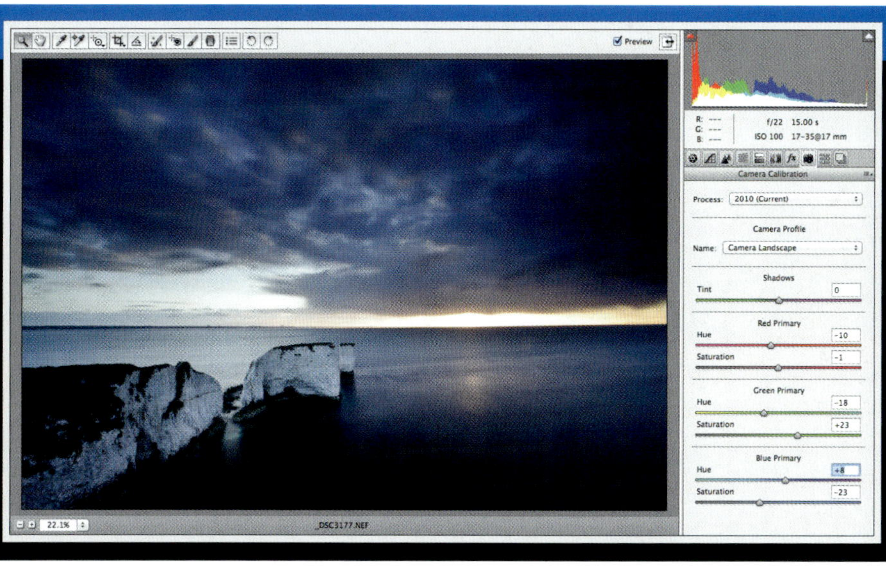

Recovering your exposure

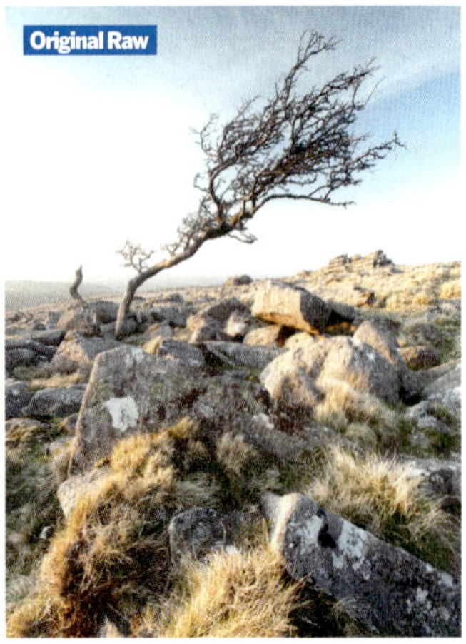

It's rarely too late to give your ill-exposed Raw shots some TLC – here's how to take those images from bland to beautiful using your histogram as a guide…

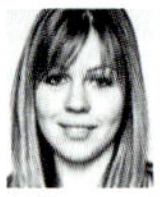

Caroline Wilkinson: Part of the pleasure of shooting in Raw format is its flexibility and forgiveness. If you mess up the exposure, ACR is there to help and maybe even salvage an image from the scrapheap: it's a photographer's safety net. Even though I'd never imagine that our readers wouldn't try to get a shot right in-camera, accidents do happen: you forget to alter settings between shots, you don't have the right ND grad filters to hand or maybe your camera's playing up (we find it's always best to blame your gear for an ill-exposed image) – but now there's no excuses really. As long as you don't overexpose an image too much, 'blowing out' detail in the highlights to the point that it's irretrievable, ACR can save your image. In fact, by exposing to the right slightly (overexposing by a stop or two) and using Raw conversion software, you can end up with an image containing far more detail as it's the brightest end of the tonal range that contains the most information. The best way to keep on top of this is to turn on your highlight warning facility on your camera's histogram, so if you have overexposed an image too much, these areas should flash red on the LCD screen. You can also check via Adobe Camera Raw. Here's how…

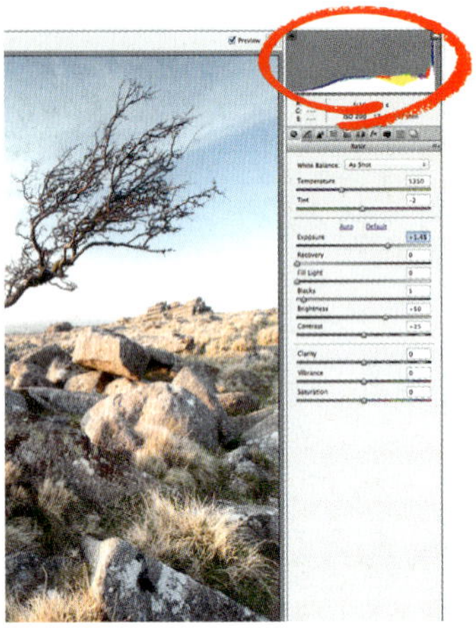

1 Open your file When you first open your image in ACR, study the histogram to see how it's exposed. Assess what types of adjustments need to be made. In this image, you can see that the colours and tones are quite light, with the histogram weighted to the right, so it's likely that some detail in the highlights needs to be recovered and the Exposure slider reduced a stop or two.

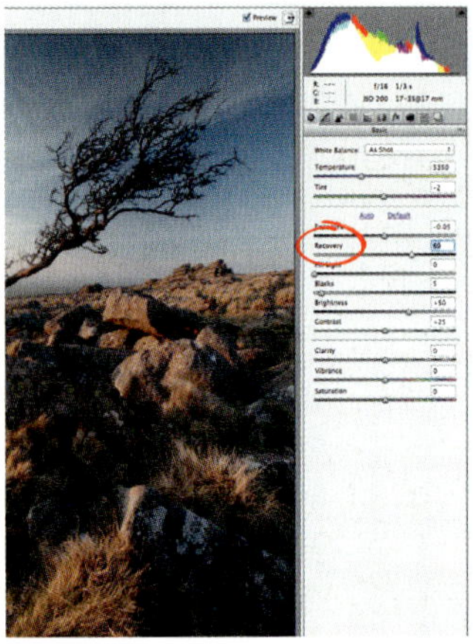

2 Recover highlights Click on the ***warning*** symbol (yellow triangle in top right) to see where and how many highlights have been clipped, identifiable by the areas flashing red. Move the ***Recovery*** slider to retrieve as much detail as possible in the highlight regions, but be aware that this slider reduces image contrast so don't overuse it at the expense of the rest of the image.

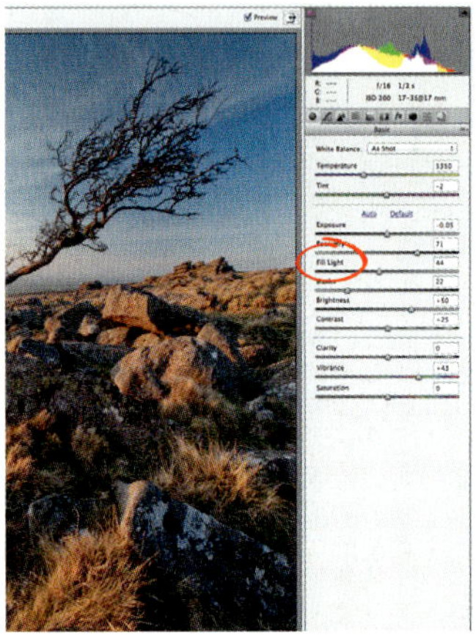

3 Exposure adjustment You may find that adjusting the ***Exposure*** slider by a stop or two can help correct most exposure errors. But if you've underexposed your image, be aware that if you add too much exposure you'll reveal noise hidden in the shadows. Try balancing the ***Exposure*** slider with the ***Fill Light*** slider to reveal detail in the darker tones and to brighten mid-tones.

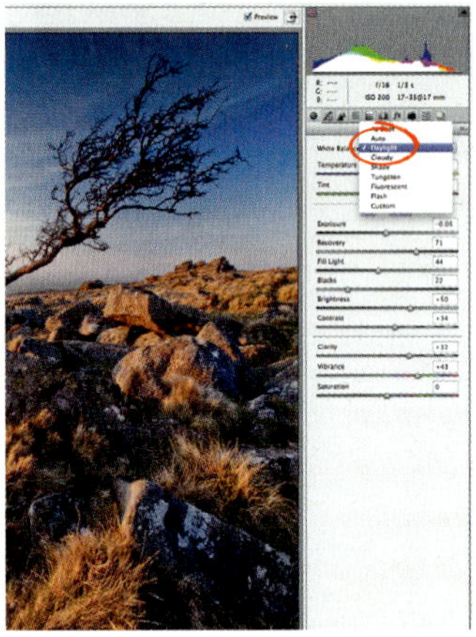

4 Boost colour & contrast Combine ***Fill Light*** with ***Blacks*** to improve contrast (you can also use the ***Contrast*** slider – just be aware of clipping any highlights if you do). Next, adjust the ***Vibrance*** slider to pump up the colour. Use the ***White Balance Tool*** or ***White Balance presets*** to correct any colour casts or to change the temperature for creative effect.

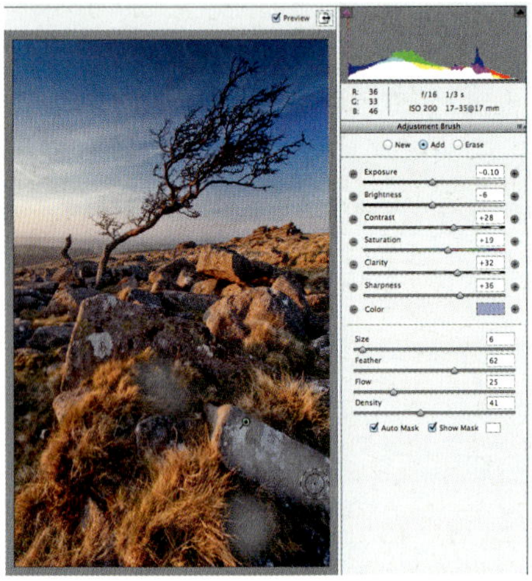

5 Make selective adjustments If there are areas of shadow or highlights that require more help to reveal detail, but you don't want to affect the image globally, use the ***Adjustment Brush***. Located in the top toolbar, this feature is great for non-destructive dodging and burning. To target shadows, click ***New*** to create a new brush and then ***Show Mask***. Brush over the area you want to affect, using the mask as a guide.

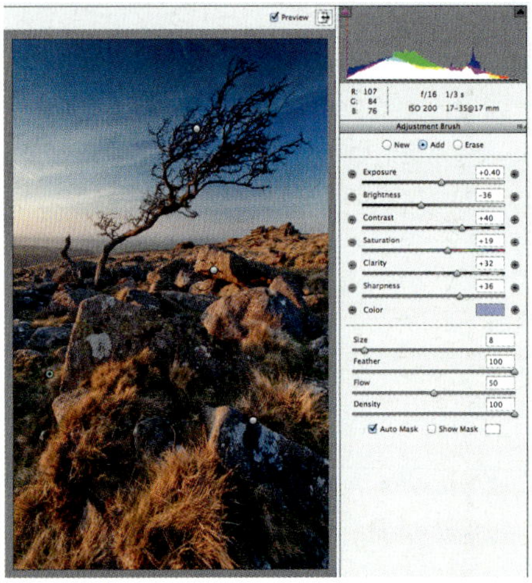

6 Repeat the process Once you're happy, click on ***Show Mask*** again to see your edits and use the various sliders to adjust the look of that area, such as ***Sharpness, Exposure*** and ***Contrast***. You can then use the same brush to apply these adjustments to other areas of the image. Use the ***Size*** and ***Feather*** sliders to change the features of the brush. To create a new adjustment, say for the highlights, click ***New*** and repeat the process.

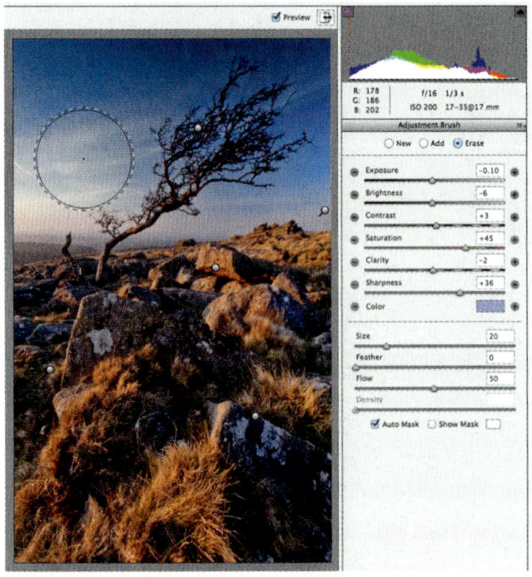

7 Edit your adjustments You can add as many new adjustment brushes as you need to target any size area of your image. To re-edit an adjustment, click on the corresponding pin on your image and adjust the sliders. To remove an adjustment, click ***Erase*** and brush over that particular area. Once happy, save as a TIFF to edit in Photoshop if needed. Click ***Done*** to keep the edited file or ***Cancel*** to keep it in its original state.

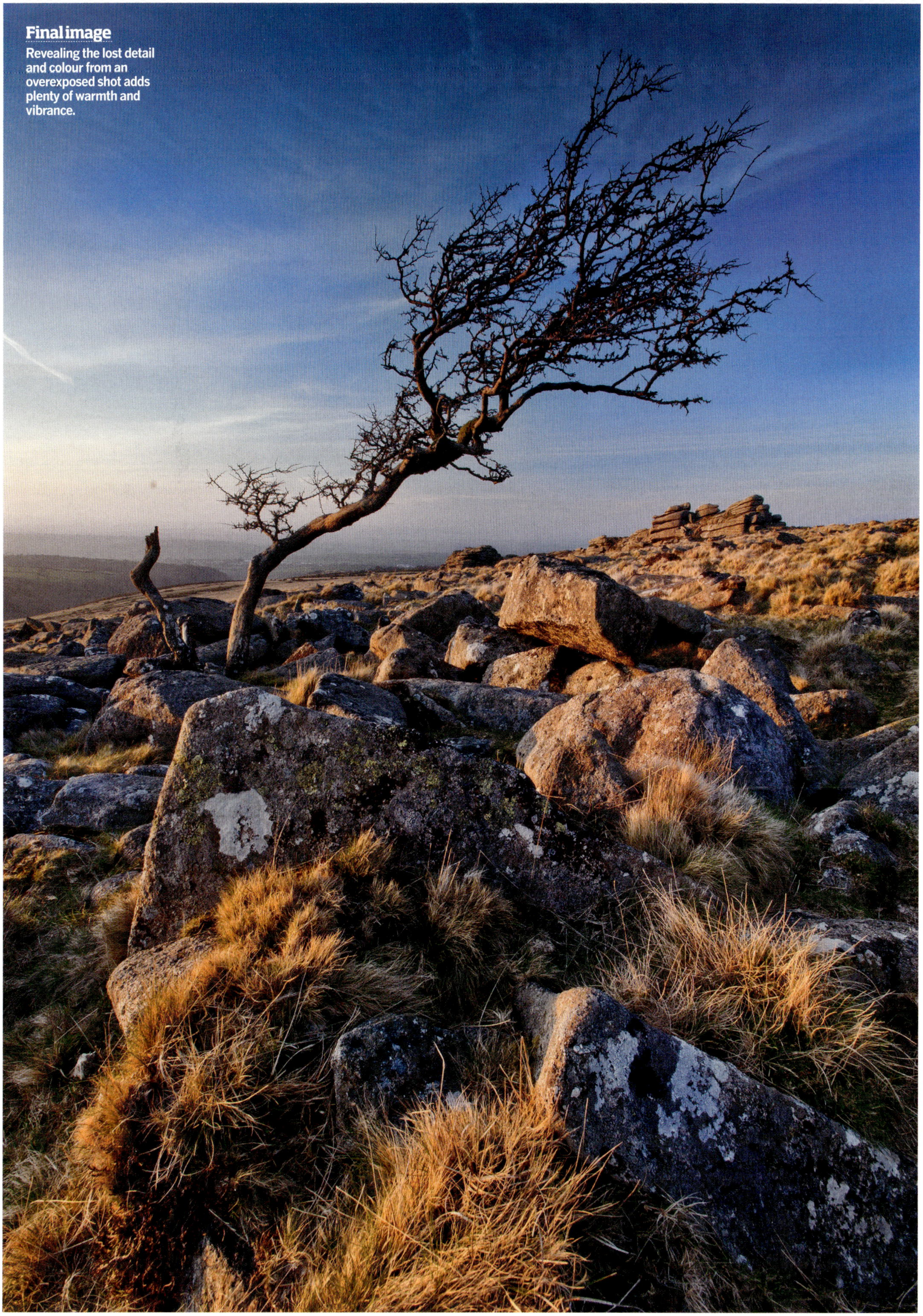

Final image
Revealing the lost detail and colour from an overexposed shot adds plenty of warmth and vibrance.

How to 'expose to the right'

Maximise the detail in your Raw data with this professional technique

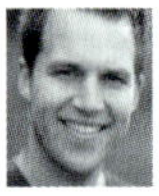

Ross Hoddinott: If you're not familiar with the term 'exposing to the right' (ETTR), despite sounding like something you could get arrested for doing, it is actually a Raw-only technique designed to help you maximise image quality. The principle is to push your image as far towards overexposure as possible, without clipping highlight areas. You do this by increasing the exposure length until the majority of pixels are grouped to the right of the histogram's mid-point – with the brightest pixels nuzzled to the far right. While ETTR images look awful initially – too bright and lacking in contrast, and require more time, thought and effort to process – the final result is an image boasting more tonal information and smoother tonal transitions.

Most digital sensors have a usable dynamic range of around six stops and can – at the very least – capture a 12-bit image, capable of recording 4,096 tonal levels. The more tonal levels available, the smoother the transition between the tones in an image will be. However, these tonal levels are not spread evenly throughout the brightness range of the sensor. So, while you might assume that each stop in the six-stop range is capable of recording an equal number of tones, in fact, each stop records half the light of the previous one. Half of the tonal levels are devoted to the brightest stop (2,048), half of the remainder (1,024 levels) are devoted to the next stop, and so on. As a result, the last and darkest of the six stops boasts just 64 levels. Therefore, if you do not utilise the right of the histogram you are wasting a large percentage of the data your camera is capable of recording.

Underexposed images contain less detail and data than a 'correctly' exposed image, and while you can attempt to lighten them during processing, the tonal transitions will not be as smooth and the risk of posterisation (abrupt changes in tone and shading) is greatly enhanced. In contrast, if you intentionally do the opposite – exposing to the right so that more data is recorded in the sensor's brighter stops – you will capture far more tonal information and image quality will be maximised. This is easy to illustrate by taking two images: one shot at a 'correct' exposure and the other exposed to the right (see below). The difference in file size can be several MB as the ETTR image has more data recorded. Even though many sensors are now 14-bit, giving photographers more tonal levels to play with, the principle is exactly the same – the sensor's brightest stop contains the most quality.

Secrets unlocked

HIGHLIGHT WARNING

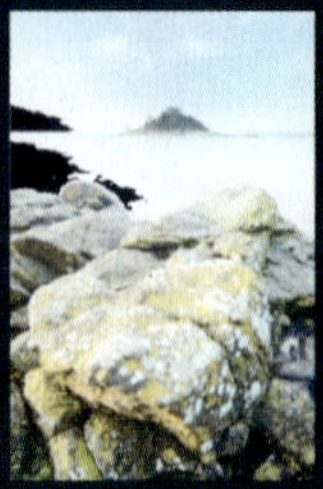

To help ensure you don't actually clip the highlights when practising exposing to the right, switch on your camera's highlights warning. This is designed to warn you if any pixels are overexposed. Affected areas will flash. If this happens, adjust exposure accordingly – selecting a faster shutter speed – and reshoot so that no clipping occurs.

To get the most out of an ETTR file, a good processing technique is essential, but it's not difficult. All you need to do is adjust the Raw file's Exposure, Brightness and Contrast until the image faithfully represents the original scene. Another benefit of ETTR is less noise. Noise is most obvious in the shadow areas of an image, but by biasing exposure towards the highlights, it is kept to a minimum.

So, while it remains important not to actually overexpose images to the degree where the highlights are blown, the benefits of exposing to the right are impossible to refute for Raw shooters. Here's a quick guide to how…

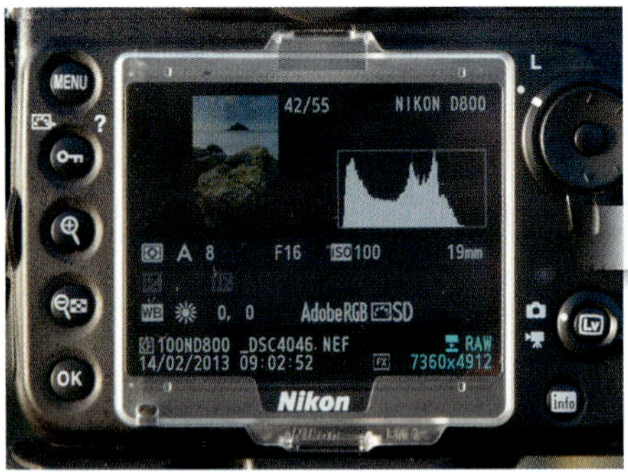

'CORRECTLY' EXPOSED This image and its histogram look fine: taken in aperture-priority, the camera has achieved a technically 'correct' exposure. However, the gap to the right of the graph indicates that the brightest stop of the sensor isn't being fully utilised, meaning valuable data is being wasted. The original Raw file is 43MB in size.

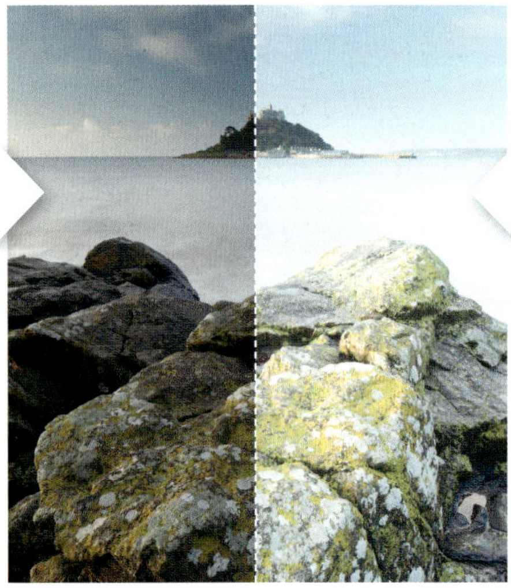

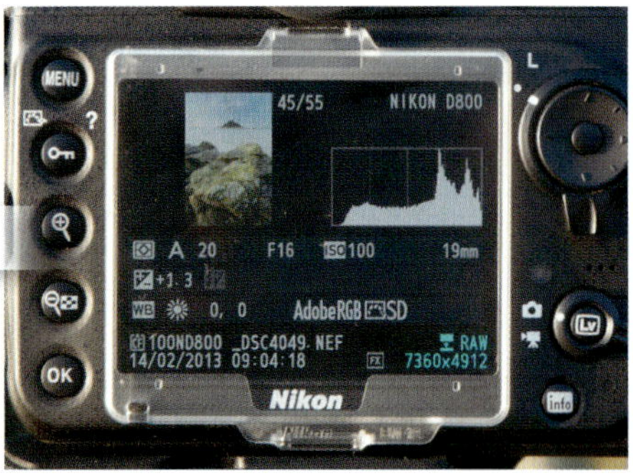

OVEREXPOSED Exposed-to-the-right images might look too bright and washed out, but valuable data has been recorded, maximising image quality. In this case, the ETTR image is 43.3MB in size – more than 0.3MB larger than the 'correctly' exposed image. The extra data helps to prevent posterisation and noise is also kept to a minimum.

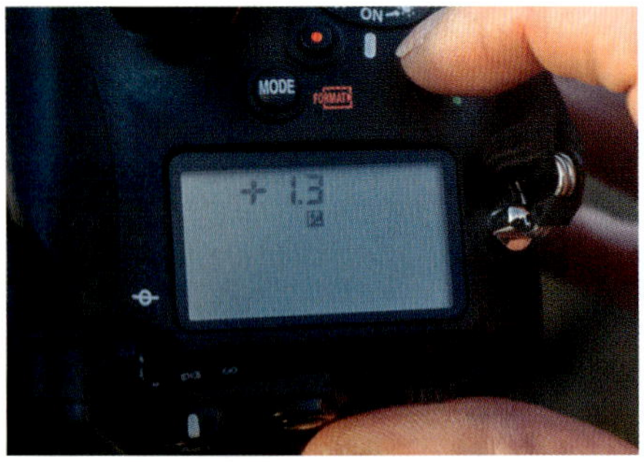

1 Achieve the result In order to push the exposure to the right to capture more tonal levels, you need to apply positive exposure compensation. How much depends on the scene and its level of contrast: apply it in 1/3-stop increments until the pixels reach the right-hand edge of the histogram. In this instance, I applied +1.3EV to achieve this.

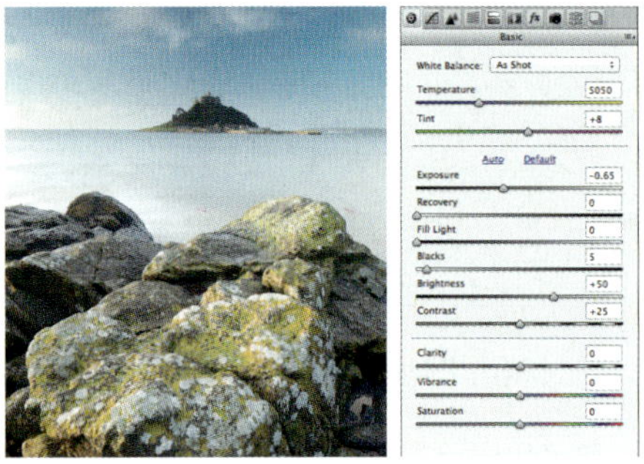

2 Recover detail Every ETTR image needs processing. In ACR, use the ***Exposure*** slider under ***Basic*** or ***Tone Curve*** to ensure the tones in the image are spread evenly across the full range of the histogram. Doing this should help restore the image's natural contrast. You may also find you need to use the ***Recovery*** and ***Blacks*** slider to retrieve highlight detail.

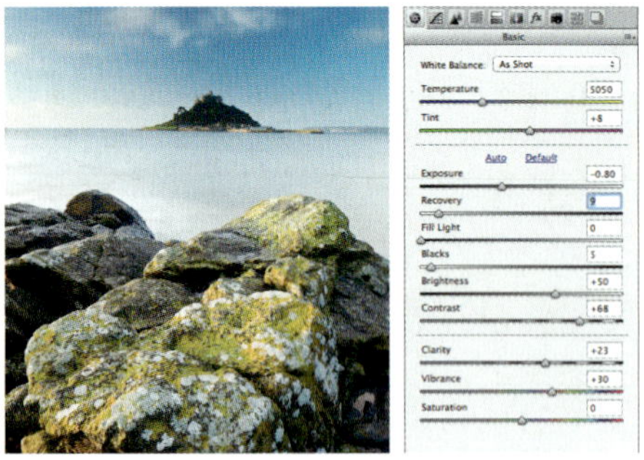

3 Boost the colour ETTR images rarely need many further adjustments. However, a small degree of ***Vibrance*** and tweak to the ***Contrast*** slider might help give your final result a little more punch. Although ETTR files do require the photographer to spend more time working on a computer, the high image quality of the final result makes it an essential and worthwhile technique.

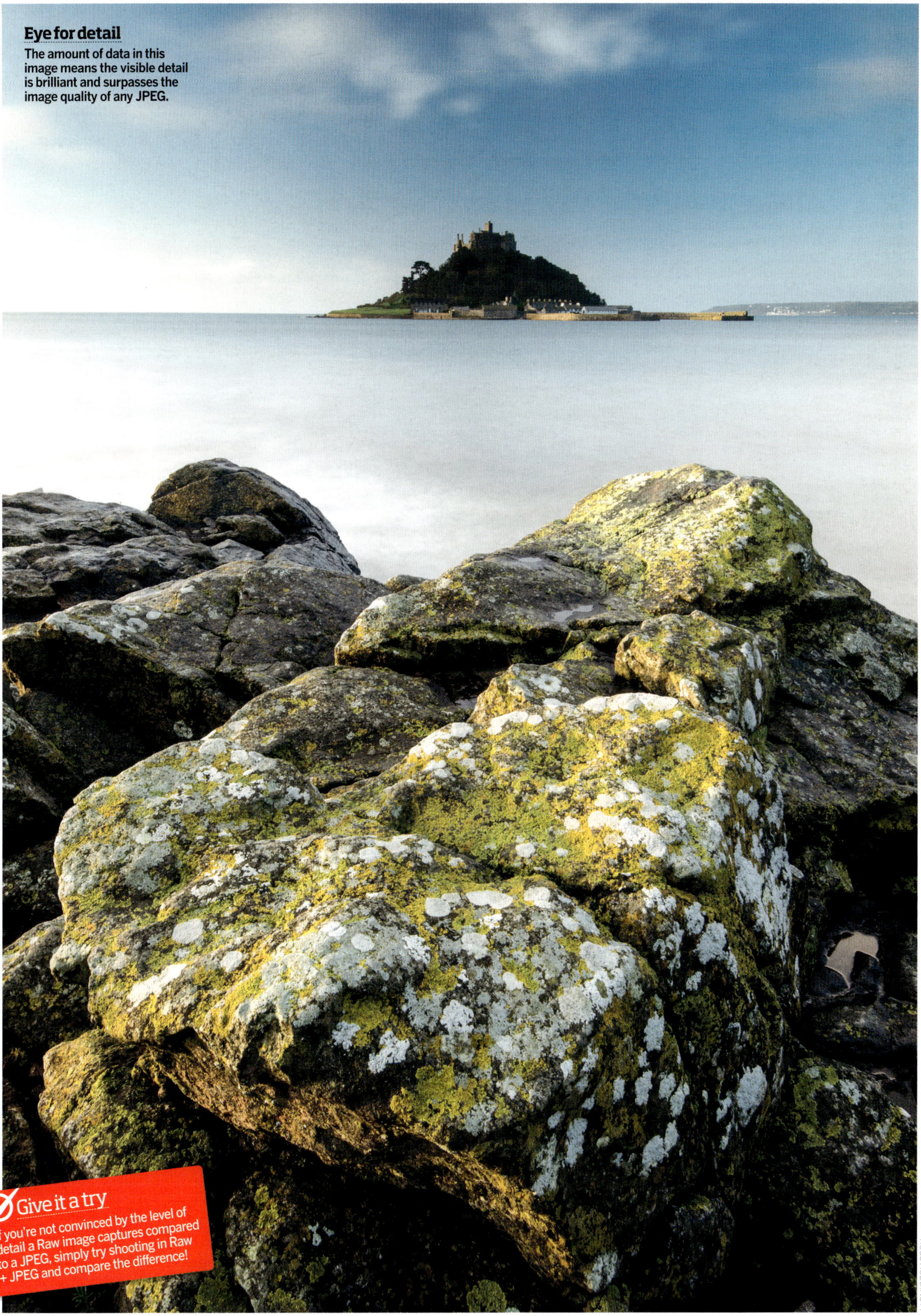

Eye for detail

The amount of data in this image means the visible detail is brilliant and surpasses the image quality of any JPEG.

Give it a try

If you're not convinced by the level of detail a Raw image captures compared to a JPEG, simply try shooting in Raw + JPEG and compare the difference!

ROSS HODDINOTT

Solving common problems

Rescue your images easily with ACR's simple adjustment tools…

SO FAR WE'VE SHOWN you around Adobe Camera Raw. You now know why Raw is superior to JPEGs, why it's the preferred format of the pros and how to use certain tools and key editing features.

The bottom line is that Raw is amazing – just like shooting on film gave you all the naked data to mould how you saw fit, a Raw file is the digital equivalent: it can revolutionise your photography if you normally shoot JPEG. And with our help, even if you already shoot Raw, you should be able to pick up a technique or two. Not only do you have more flexibility for creativity and for improving image quality, but also as long as your composition and focusing are spot-on, shooting in Raw lets you correct almost any in-camera mistake with very few images being beyond repair.

In this section, we've selected four of the most common errors and provided solutions for you to see how you can quickly and efficiently rectify them with Raw.

Lightroom 5

Adobe Lightroom 5 is a really popular alternative to Photoshop's Adobe Camera Raw – it's a lot cheaper, with a similar interface, and more features than ACR in Elements. You'll also find a lot of the same recovery and creative techniques covered here using ACR can also be done in Lightroom.

✗PROBLEM: You forgot a Neutral Density graduated filter and overexposed the sky

✓SOLUTION: Use the Gradient Tool

You know the story: you get to a location only to find you've forgotten your ND grad filter. You have no choice but to take a multiple exposure or an average exposure for the scene and hope you don't 'blow out' too much highlight detail in the sky. Your sky will probably be several stops brighter than the foreground, so regular global adjustments won't cut it. Select the *Gradient Tool* and click and drag from the top of the image to below the horizon. Use the settings in the Adjustment panel to tweak the sky's exposure, colour and clarity. You may also need to use the *Adjustment Brush Tool*, located in the top toolbar, to return intersecting objects, like rocks and trees, to their original state if the Gradient Tool has caused them to underexpose.

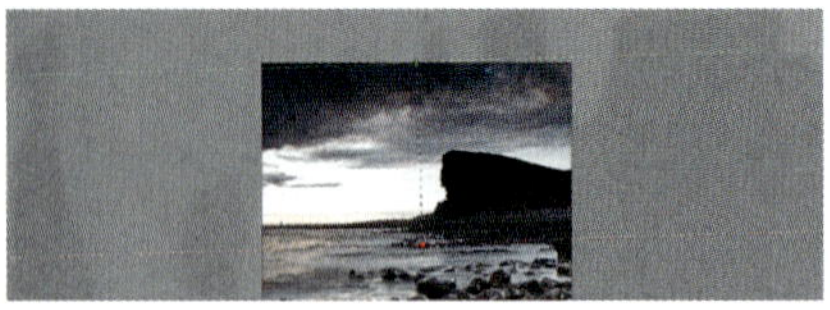

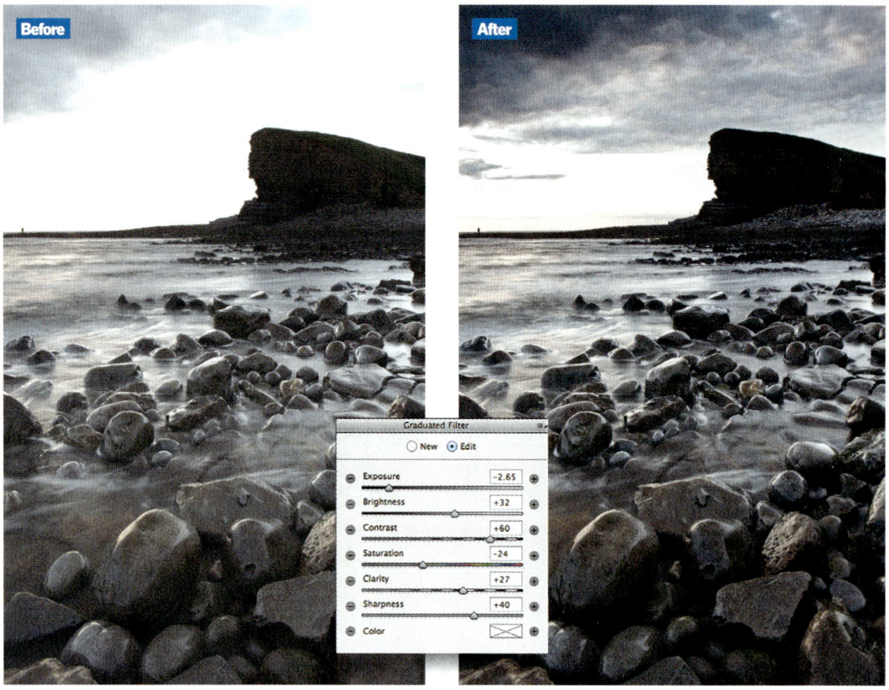

LEE FROST

✗PROBLEM: By using a very long exposure, you've introduced digital noise

✓SOLUTION: Use Noise Reduction

Noise hiding in the shadows can be caused by high ISOs and long exposures, but can be easily minimised in ACR. Noise Reduction is simple to use, but you may find the higher the camera's megapixel count, the more heavily you need to adjust the sliders. Zoom in to the image *100-200%* to better see the noise and the effect of your adjustments. You have two types of noise: Luminance and Color, which the Detail tab in ACR tackles. Luminance addresses grayscale noise (a salt and pepper effect). Color takes care of chroma noise (red, green and blue specks). In most cases, you want to reduce both but you need to strike a balance between eradicating noise and retaining image detail as the stronger the noise reduction, the more detail it will take with it. As most noise is in the Luminosity channel, we advise that you target this first to get rid of grain-like patterns, and then move the *Color* slider to reduce chroma noise. Use the *Detail* and *Contrast* sliders to retrieve some detail and edge clarity lost from Noise Reduction: stop when you notice that you're starting to reintroduce noise.

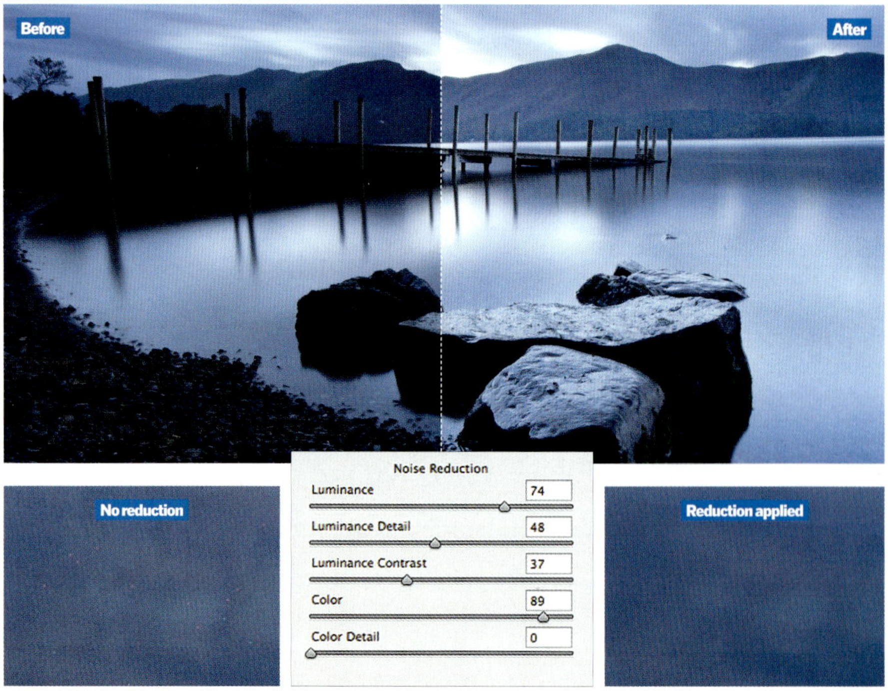

LEE FROST

✖PROBLEM: Underexposed scene due to shooting into the sun

✔SOLUTION: Use a mixture of Exposure, Fill Light and Blacks

While exposing to the right captures maximum detail, exposing to the left – often caused by shooting into a light source – can have the opposite effect. While the scope for correcting an underexposed image is much broader than with a JPEG, if you're not careful, opening up the shadows can introduce digital noise and an unnatural high-dynamic range that diminishes image quality. Look out for halos appearing, which indicate that you're using the Fill Light and Blacks slider too heavily. If you're using Lightroom 4 onwards or Photoshop CS6, instead of Exposure, Fill Light and Blacks, use *Exposure*, *Shadows* and *Contrast* for similar results. For selective adjustments, use the *Adjustment Brush Tool*.

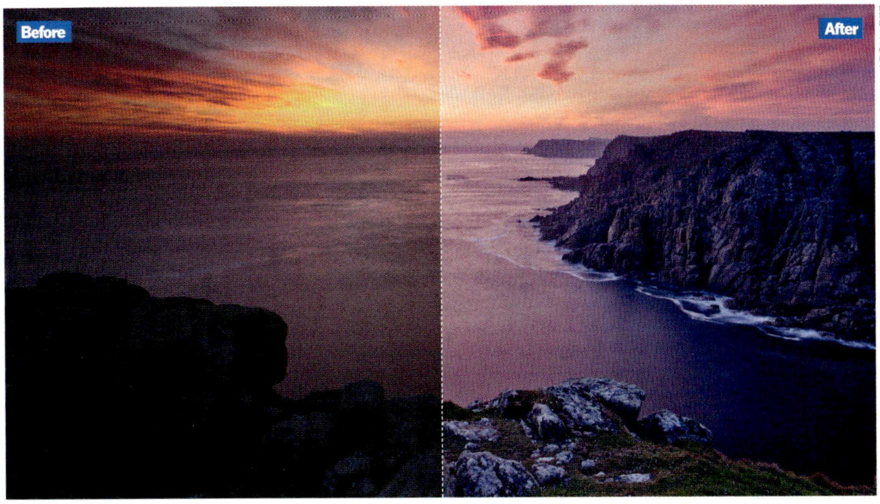

LEE FROST

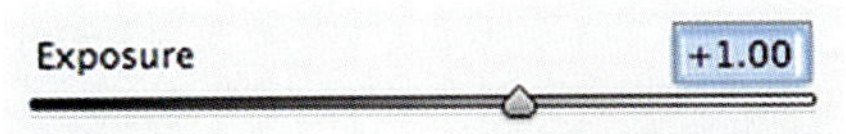

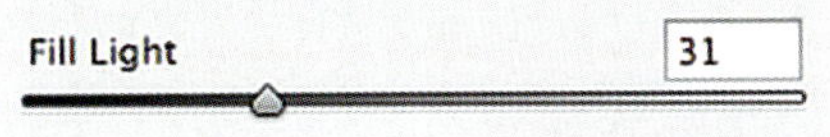

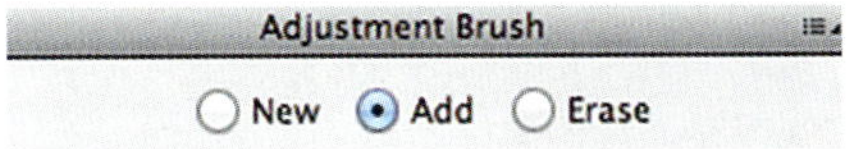

1 Exposure By letting the sunset dictate the exposure, the foreground is grossly underexposed. Turn on the shadow clipping warning (press the left triangle above the histogram). If no areas flash blue, it should be easy to improve. Adjust *Exposure* by a stop or two to the right and the *Recovery* slider to restore any highlight detail the exposure change may cause.

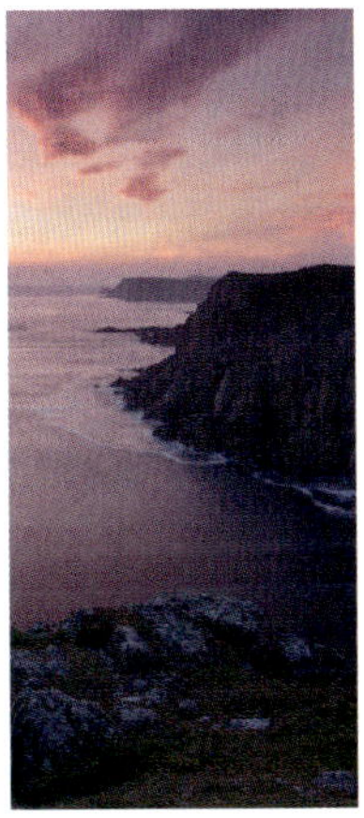

2 Fill light To open up the shadows, use Fill Light in conjunction with a little bit of Blacks to reintroduce contrast. Be careful not to create halos around objects or to reveal too much noise when using Fill Light or to lose shadow detail when adjusting Blacks: it's a balancing act. At this point you may also want to increase *Vibrance* for colour and *Clarity* for sharpening and contrast.

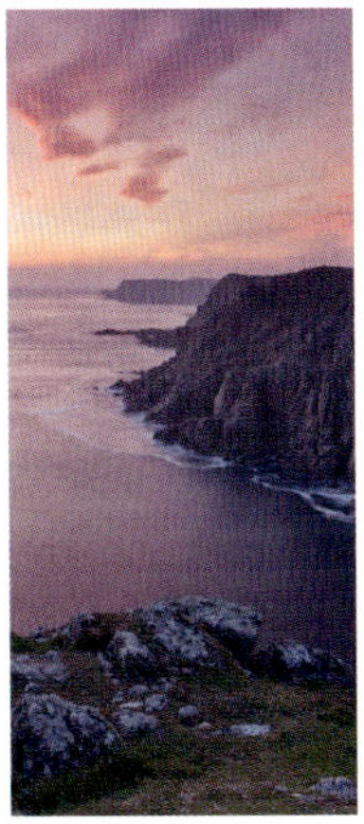

3 Selective adjustments All your adjustments so far have been global. For areas that still look underexposed, use the *Adjustment Brush Tool* to target them separately. Set the *Size* appropriate to what you want to edit and a large *Feather* to soften the edges. Brush over the area and adjust the sliders to suit. For every area you adjust independently, click *New* first.

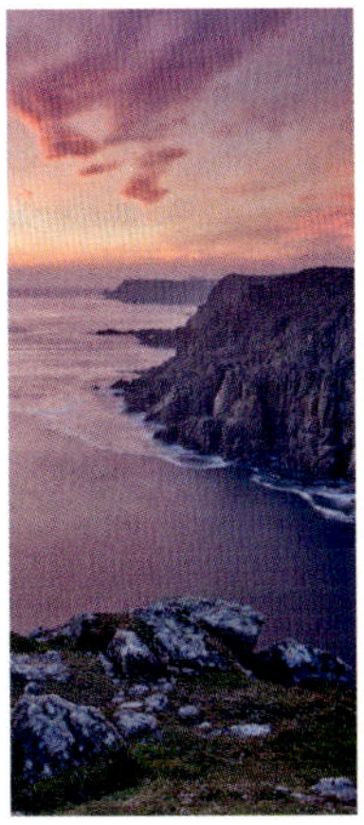

✖PROBLEM: Colour cast

✔SOLUTION: White Balance sliders

When you're working fast and in mixed or changing light, it's likely that the colour temperature of your image may not be what you want. With JPEGs, this could be an unsolvable problem post-capture, but thankfully with Raw there are the parameters to correct unwanted colour casts or to add one for creative effect.

You could use the White Balance Tool to click on a neutral area, like a grey rock or cloud, to set the appropriate WB for the lighting it was shot in, though it doesn't offer a lot of control. The preferred method is to use the WB presets under the Basics tab. Here you can select an in-camera preset such as Daylight, Shade or Auto. It's also great to try out the wrong WB settings – in some cases it can completely change the atmosphere of your picture to make a cool scene warmer and vice versa: sometimes being so wrong is just right. For total control, use the manual tools for a *Custom WB: Temperature* and *Tint*. Concentrate on the Temperature slider as it fine-tunes the Kelvin colour temperature scale. When working with JPEG, TIFF and PSDs, your scale for colour adjustment is far more limited than the Kelvin scale Raw offers. Tint should be a last move to compensate for an image's lack of greens or magenta.

If you have a series of images shot in the same lighting, you can batch-edit them by selecting all the files in ACR and making these WB adjustments. Or take a shot of an 18% grey card in the same conditions and click on it using the *White Balance Tool* to neutralise selected images.

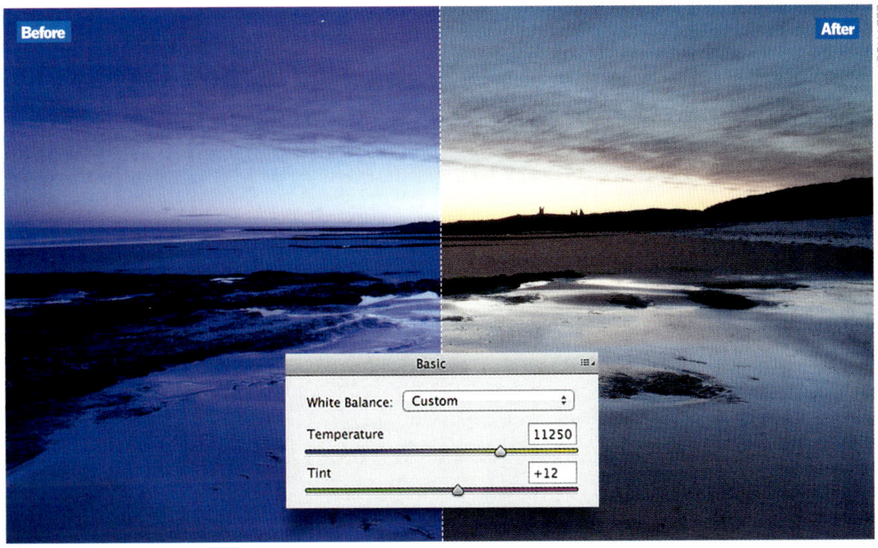

LEE FROST

Create a High Dynamic Range image

Use a single Raw file to create multiple exposures and expand your image's dynamic range…

Jordan Butters: As Raw files capture an extraordinary amount of data, it's possible to use one file to create several different exposures, which when combined can create images that extend dynamic range beyond that of the camera's sensor. Aside from creative effects, it's a handy technique for drawing out detail in the highlights and shadows, and for getting around difficult exposures. If you want a dramatic HDR result, we'd recommend using ACR to split your Raw file into multiple exposures and then import them in to a dedicated HDR software, such as Photomatix, rather than Photoshop, for more options and control.

Before you divide your Raw file, use ACR to make any corrections to the original image, such as dust removal, lens correction, cropping and straightening. These changes will then be applied every time you open that Raw file, saving you time when combining the exposures. For this tutorial, we assume you've captured a fairly balanced exposure as your base image. If the camera has under- or overexposed the scene excessively, you might struggle to get a decent set of exposures from the file.

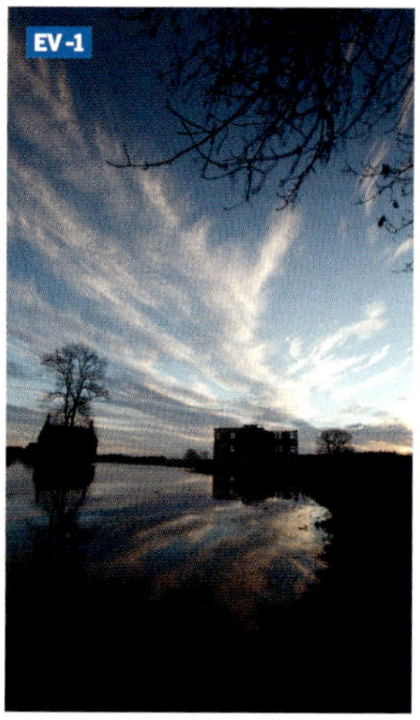

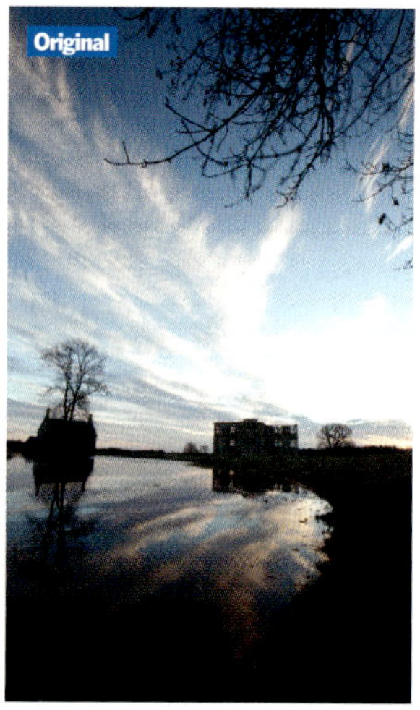

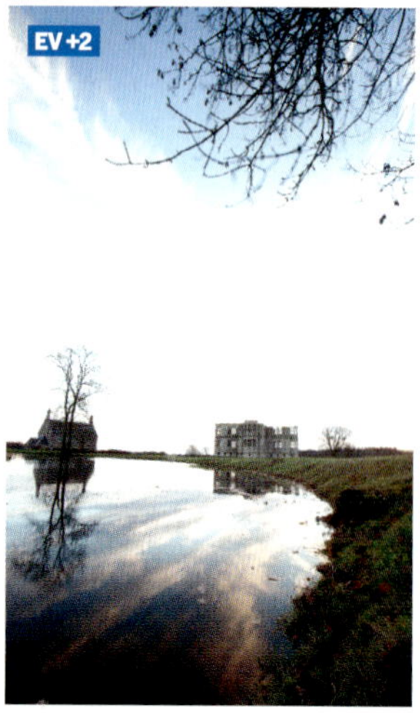

Use the Histogram clipping warning

Turn on the Histogram clipping warning when creating your different exposures. The clipping warning will highlight any shadow areas in blue that are severely underexposed, or overexposed highlights in red to indicate a loss in detail. Ideally, your darker exposure should have no overexposed areas and your lighter exposure no underexposed areas.

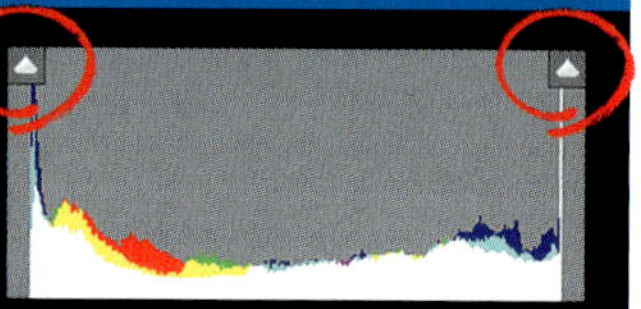

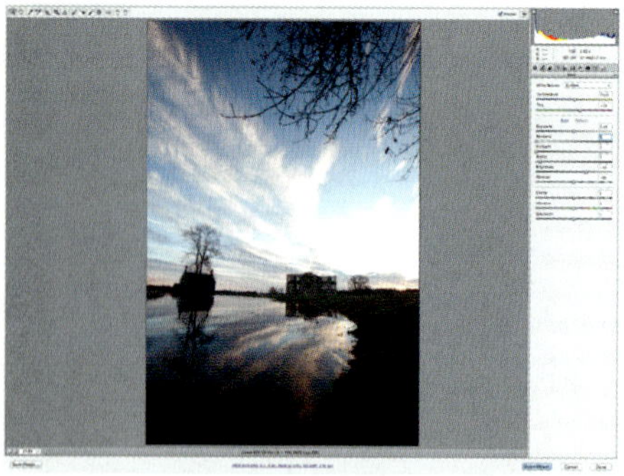

1 Open your base exposure With your fundamental changes made and a balanced exposure achieved, click the ***Open Image*** button. You've now got your middle exposure open in Photoshop. To create exposures either side of this image, locate the Raw file on your computer and open it again in ACR.

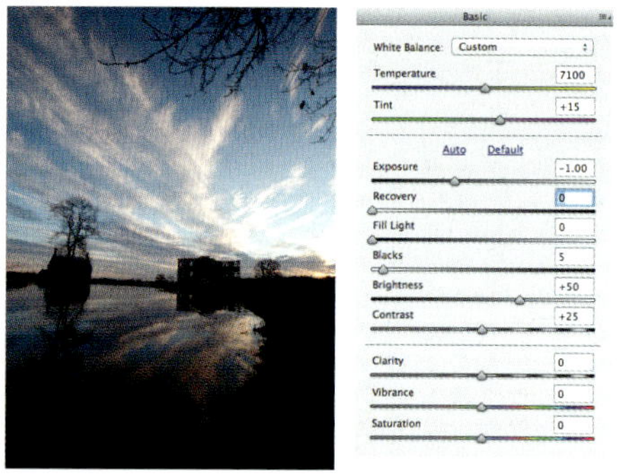

2 Create dark and light exposures Use the ***Exposure*** slider to expose for the brightest part of the image – that will usually be the sky. Then click ***Open Image***. Repeat this step with the Raw file again, and this time adjust the ***Exposure*** slider to retrieve detail from the shadows. Click on the ***Open Image*** button again.

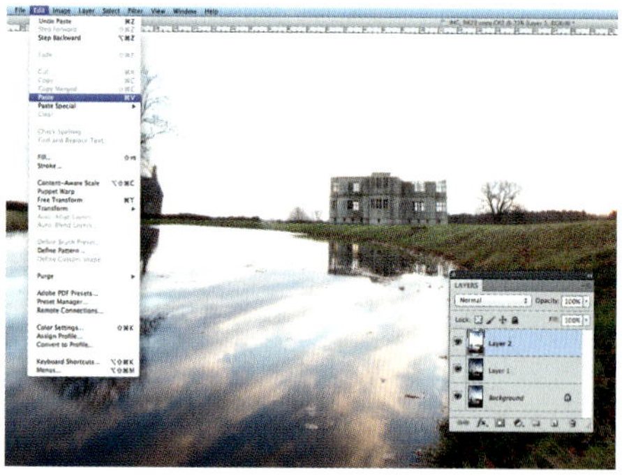

3 Consolidate the files You should now have three separate files open. Consolidate these into one by going to ***Select>All*** and ***Edit>Copy*** on the lighter exposure file before selecting your middle exposure and going to ***Edit>Paste***. Repeat this for the darker exposure. You can now close the lighter and darker exposure files.

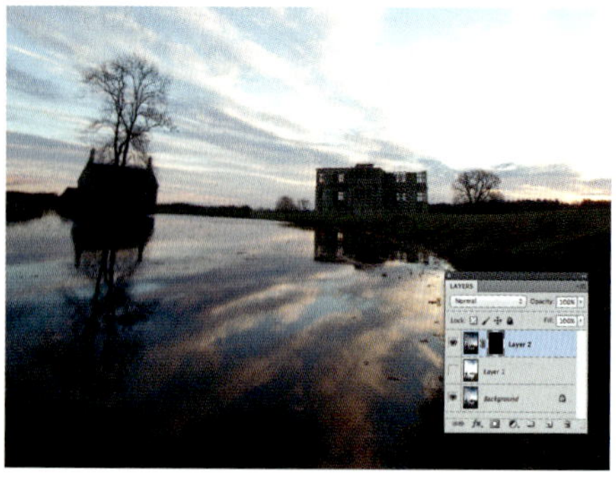

4 Apply a Layer Mask Click on the ***eye*** icon on the lighter exposure layer in the Layers palette to hide it for now. Select the darker exposure layer and hold down the ***option*** (Mac) or ***alt*** key (PC) before clicking on the ***Add new layer mask*** button in the Layers palette – this will hide the layer using a Layer Mask.

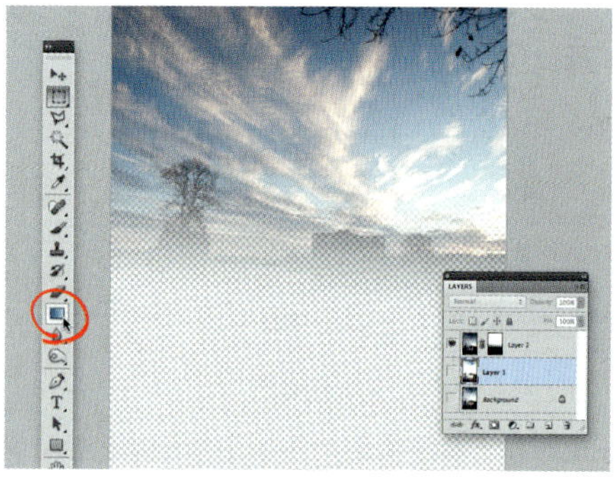

5 Add a gradient Select the ***Gradient Tool*** from the sidebar and press the ***D*** key to reset your colour palette. Click and drag on the image to reveal the sky in the darker exposure. You can click and drag multiple times until you're happy. You may find it easier to hide the Background layer, too, to judge where to place the gradient.

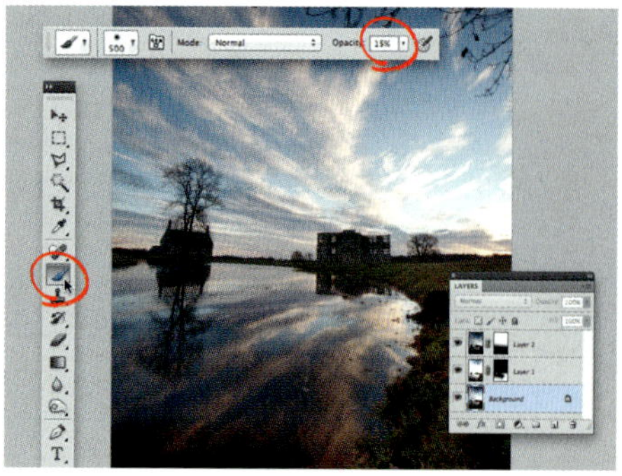

6 Rescue shadow detail Click on the eye icon to reveal the lighter layer. Select the layer in the Layers palette, hold down the ***alt*** key and click on the ***Add new layer mask*** button. Choose the ***Brush Tool*** and set the ***Opacity*** to around ***15%***. With your ***Foreground Color*** set to ***White***, brush over the shadows to reveal detail.

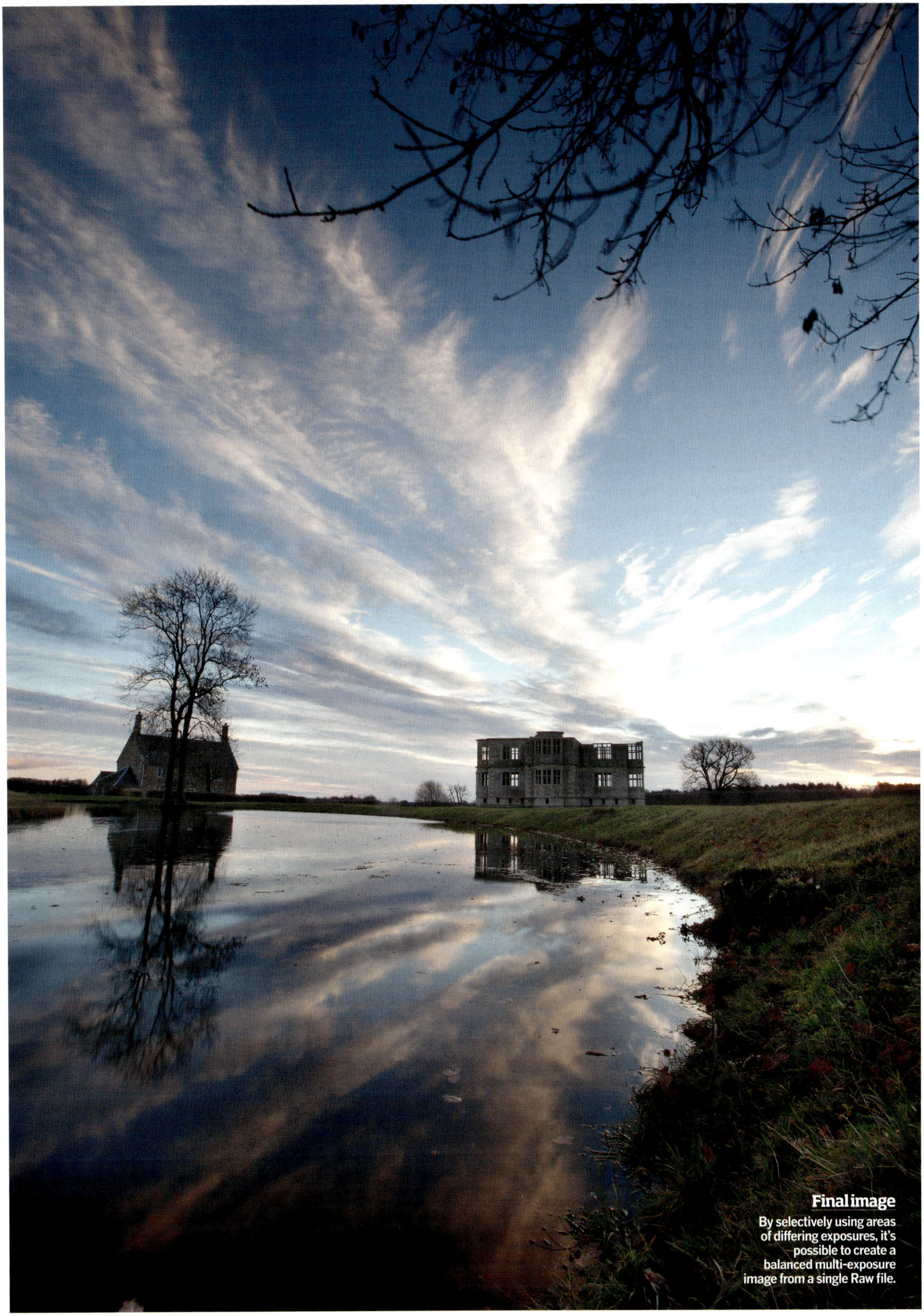

Final image

By selectively using areas of differing exposures, it's possible to create a balanced multi-exposure image from a single Raw file.

Creative effects & techniques

For simple monochrome adjustments, Adobe Camera Raw may be all the software you need. Read on for our favourite quick and creative techniques…

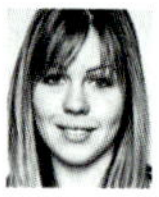

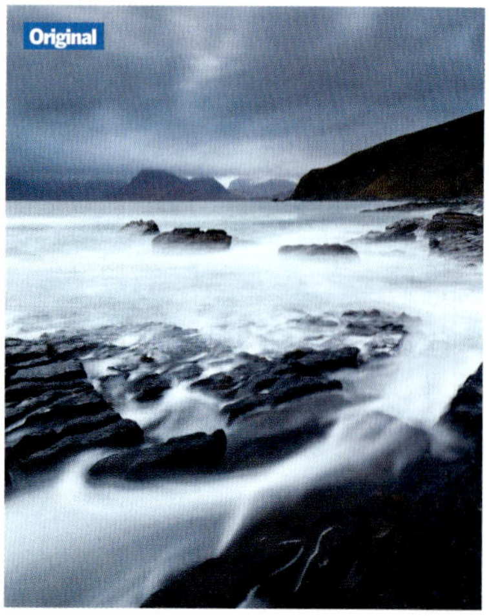

Caroline Wilkinson: Editing your Raw files to create printable images or to prepare them for Photoshop is one thing, but did you know that ACR holds several tools that can be used to enhance your images for creative results, too?

Typically, if your image is suited to colour you'll find Saturation and Vibrance are all you need, along with the adjustments already profiled in this guide. But you can also download presets into ACR from companies like OnOne Software (www.ononesoftware.com) if you want special and creative colour effects.

It's at the other end of the spectrum, when you want a punchy black & white conversion, that ACR naturally provides all you need and a few extras for the finishing touches, too. You may not even find a need to open your images in Photoshop afterwards, simply click Save Image… and you're done.

Here we cover a simple black & white conversion, before we delve deeper into ACR's more creative features over the page. From adding grain and a vignette, to split-toning and cropping effectively, you'll find everything you need to give your mono images the extra oomph that they need, all from within Adobe Camera Raw.

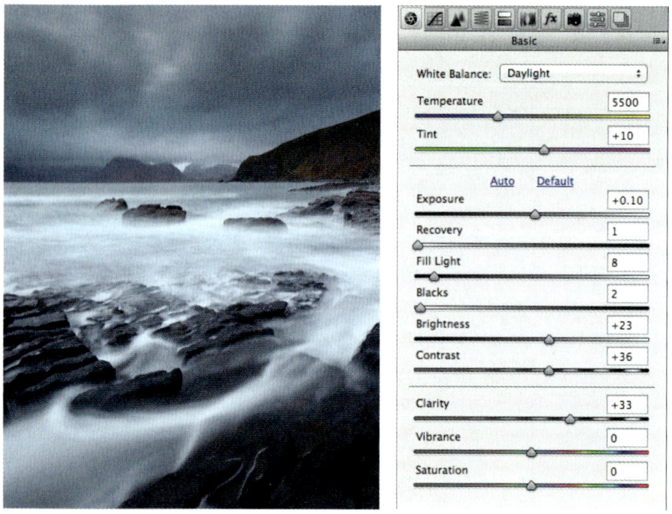

1 Make your routine edits first Take some time to perfect your colour image first using the tools under the ***Basic*** panel – the better the starting image, the stronger the conversion will be. Here, Fill Light is used to open up the shadows in the rocks, Contrast is slightly increased and Clarity is improved. Most importantly, though, via the ***Lens Corrections*** panel, click ***Enable Lens Profile Corrections***, ***Remove Chromatic Aberration*** and ***Remove Fringing*** to correct any abnormalities.

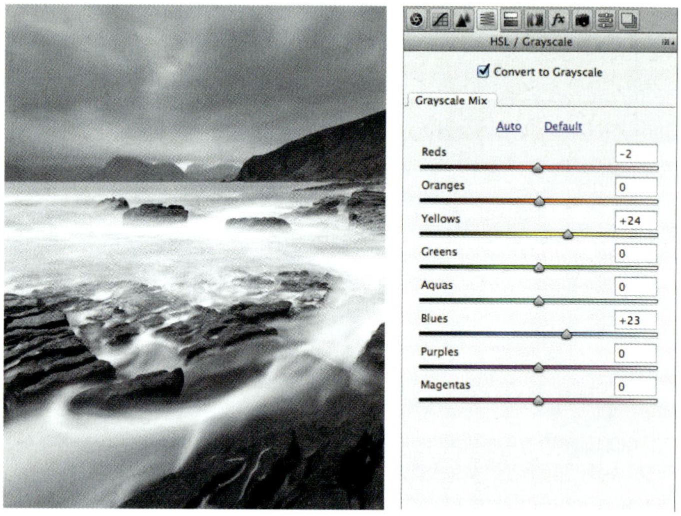

2 Turn it black & white Click on the ***HSL/Grayscale*** tab and click ***Convert to Grayscale*** for an instant monochrome conversion. To get the best out of your file, you need to adjust the tones. To avoid ACR making tonal decisions for you, click ***Default*** above the sliders to set them all to ***0***. You can now use the colour sliders to lighten or darken specific colour tones nondestructively – just like a Black & White adjustment layer in Photoshop. Try it to see the results. Here, the Blue slider has the strongest impact.

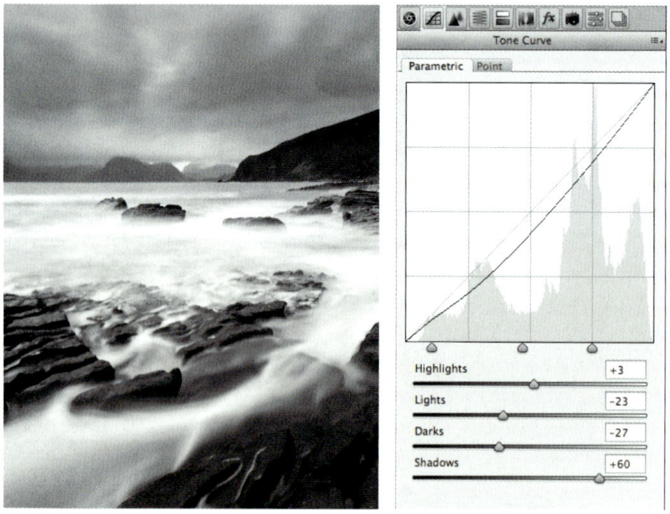

3 Adjust the contrast To enhance the contrast further, click on the ***Tone Curve*** tab and select ***Parametric*** or ***Point***, depending on your method preference. Parametric works like Levels in that you can use the sliders to target Highlights, Lights, Darks and Shadows, so it's much easier to control than Point, which works like Curves. When adjusting the sliders, be watchful of the histogram to make sure you don't clip any highlights or shadows; keep the clipping warnings switched on if you're not sure.

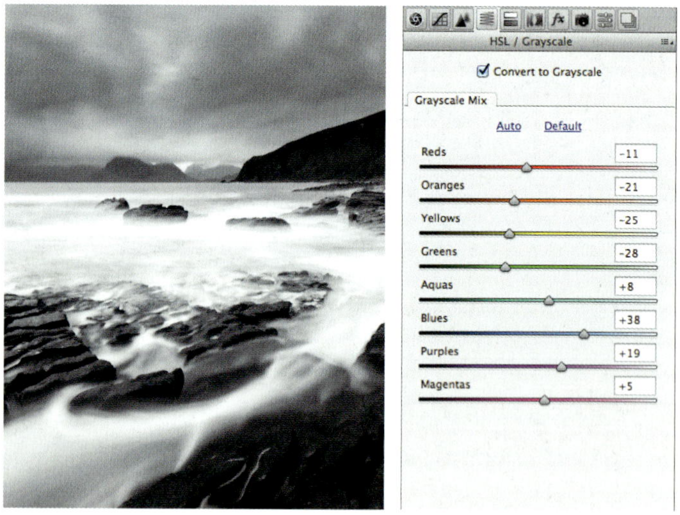

4 Assess the image You may want to go back to the ***Grayscale Mix*** and adjust the colour sliders again with a fresh approach after Tone Curve as the strength of colour tones would likely have changed. Or, if you prefer, instead of using the sliders, you could use the ***Targeted Adjustment Tool*** at the top of ACR. With Grayscale Mix still active, click on the area of your image you want to adjust, then click and drag it up and down on the image to lighten or darken the surrounding tones.

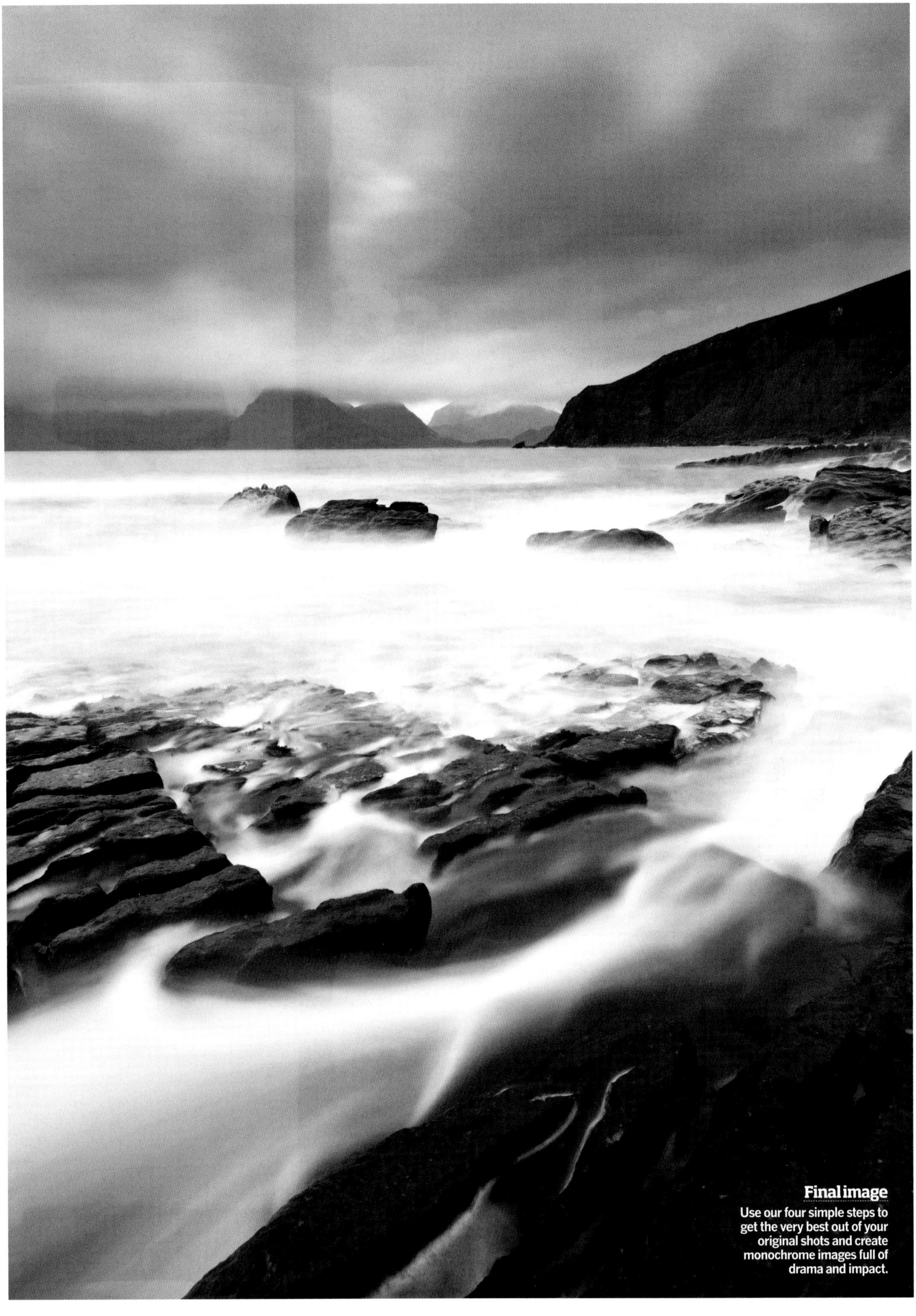

Final image

Use our four simple steps to get the very best out of your original shots and create monochrome images full of drama and impact.

LEE FROST

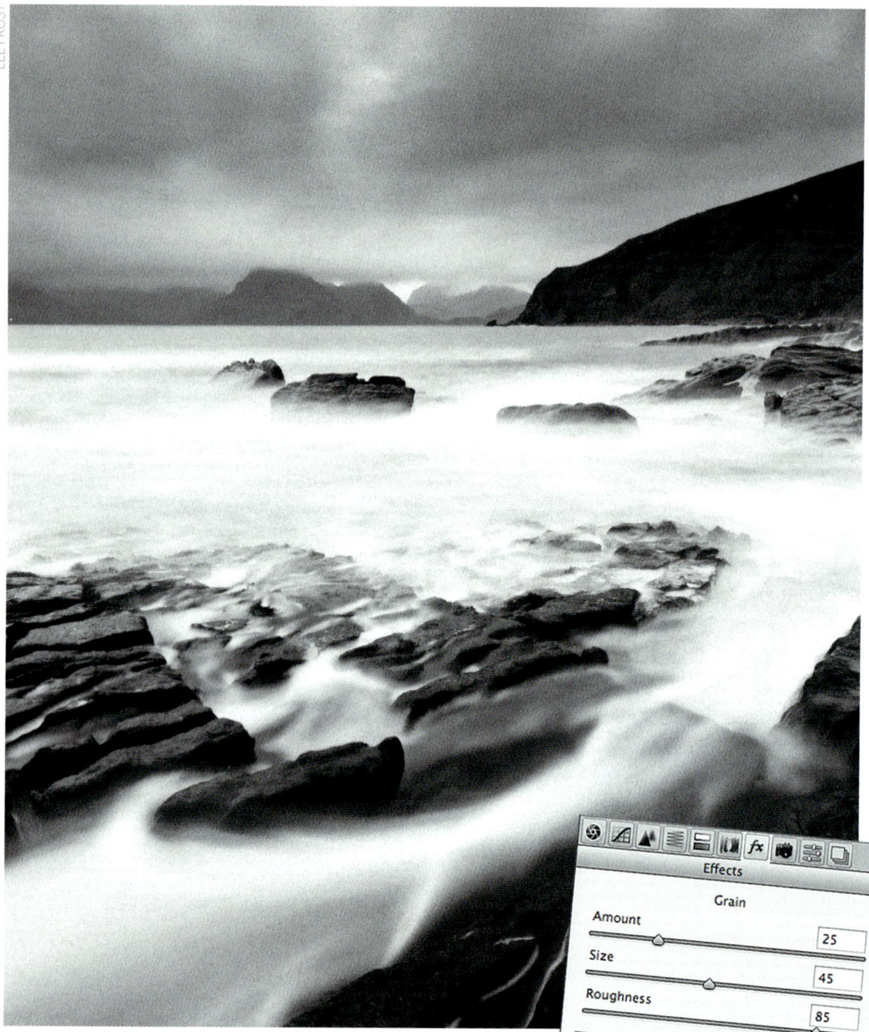

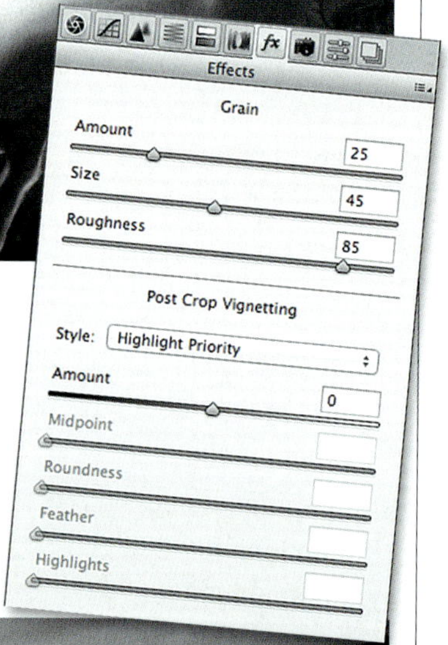

Grain

Once your image is black & white, you could simulate some grain for a high-ISO-film effect. Don't worry – as usual, all treatments in ACR are nondestructive and temporary until you save them, so there's nothing to lose in trying. Click on the ***Effects*** tab and under ***Grain*** you can select the ***Amount, Size*** of the grain and ***Roughness***. There's no right or wrong way for applying this effect, go with what suits your picture: generally, for more texture set ***Roughness*** high and, to avoid disturbing too much detail, set the ***Amount*** low.

Post-Crop Vignetting

This feature, accessible via the ***Effects*** panel, creates an attractive finishing touch so do all of your other editing first, including any cropping, before you apply the effect. If working on a mono image, select ***Style*** as ***Highlight Priority*** so you don't muddy your brights. Then adjust the ***Amount*** to darken or lighten the corners, ***Feather*** to affect the softness and ***Highlights*** to control contrast. You may also want to adjust the ***Midpoint*** to change the spread and ***Roundness*** for the shape. Watch your shadow detail around the edges as you darken corners so you don't hide too much detail.

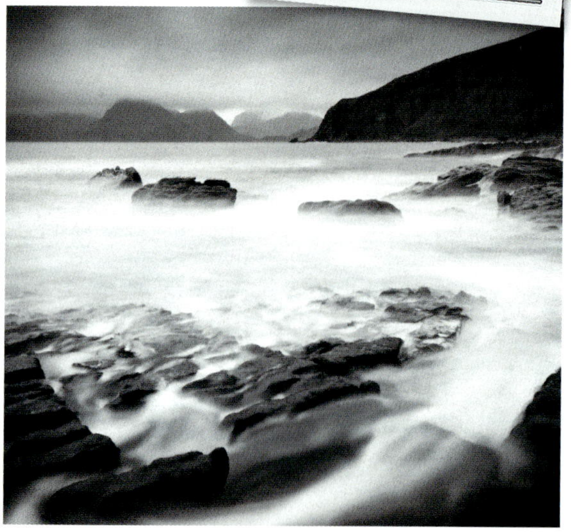

Presets

Lightroom has the same set of black & white conversion tools as Photoshop's ACR but with the bonus of lots of presets. You can compound the effect of the presets by layering them or using them in conjunction with the Black & White Mix sliders and Basic adjustments. You have a choice of a series of B&W Filter Presets, which replicate the effects you get if you were to use a coloured filter with film, such as Blue, Green, Infrared, Red and Yellow filters. You also have different contrast 'looks' and B&W Toned Presets, such as Split Tone, Creamtone and Antique to pick from for fuss-free solutions. Alternatively, create your own presets or download them – a favourite of ours has to be Pretty Presets, visit www.lightroompresets.com for more information.

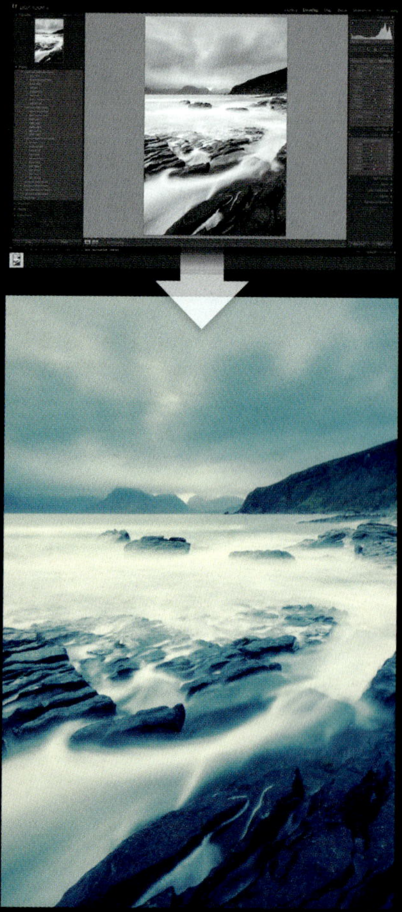

Saturation or Vibrance?

If you want to improve the colours in a Raw file you have the choice of Saturation or Vibrance. Most photographers prefer Vibrance as it only increases the strength of colours that aren't already sufficiently saturated so the effect is more subtle. Saturation, on the other hand, affects all colours and can very easily look over the top. Try both out on the same image to see how they differ.

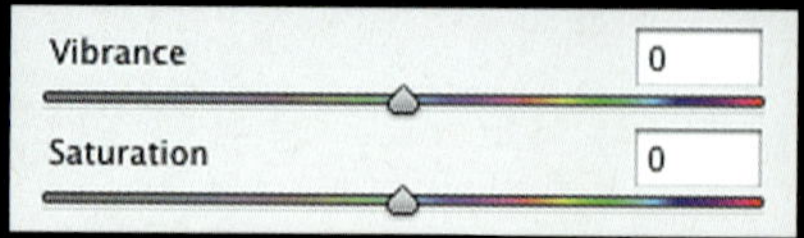

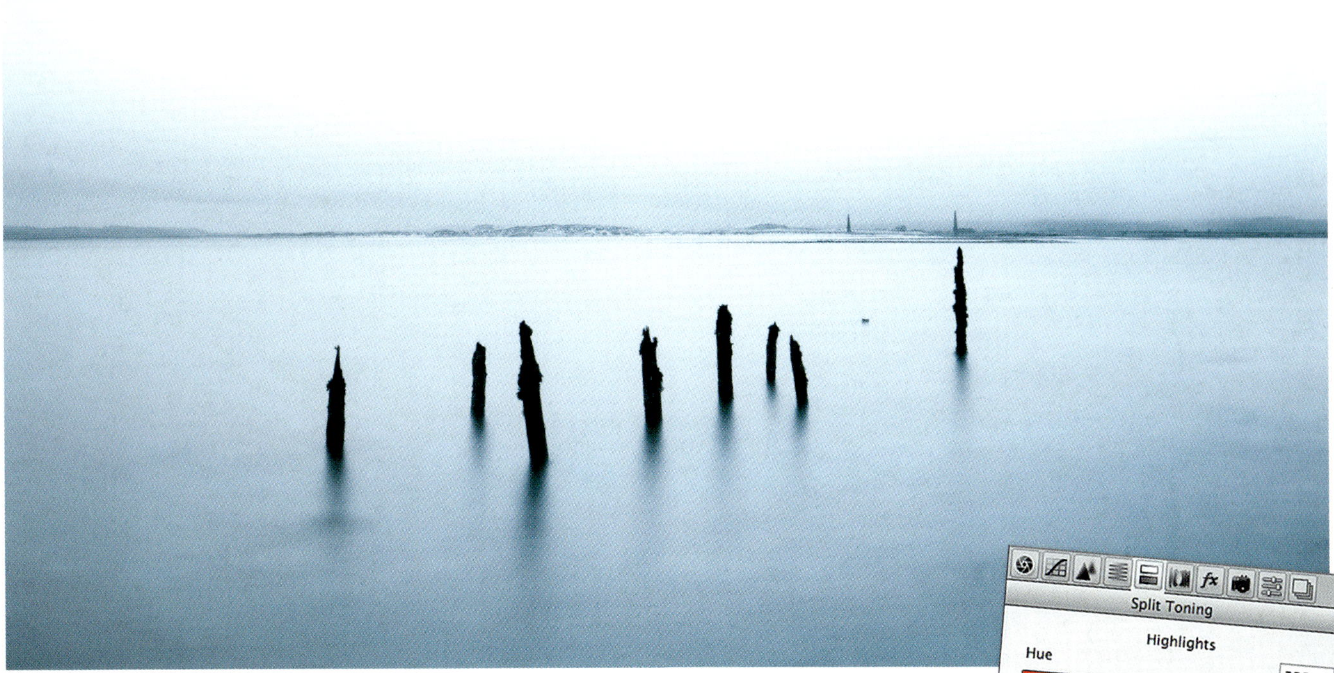

LEE FROST

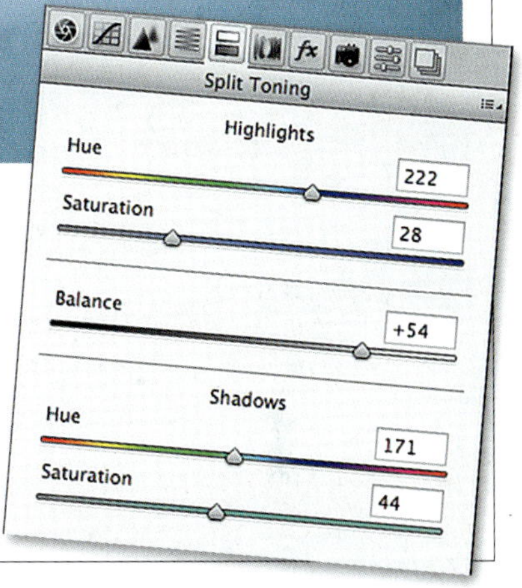

Split Toning

Sometimes a simple black & white conversion just isn't enough for giving your image a bit of pizzazz. Split-toning, on the other hand, lets you tint the highlights and shadows separately, reintroducing colour. You can also try it on your colour images for colour-toning effects, too. The tools under the Split Toning tab are quite easy to manage: you have a Hue and Saturation slider for both the Shadows and the Highlights, and a Balance slider that controls the effect's bias to the highlights or shadows. You can single-tone the shadows or highlights by adjusting one or the other, or duotone by targeting both. As default, the Saturation sliders are set to 0, which means no effect will be visible until you start to move the slider: the further to the right you move it, the stronger the tint will be. Move the ***Hue*** slider to change the colour of the tint and then the ***Balance*** slider to affect which tint is more prominent: shadows or highlights. Follow the principle of less being more to avoid overpowering the picture.

Crop Tool

You'll often find you need do nothing more than crop to vastly improve your image. Adobe Camera Raw's Crop Tool is as effective as Photoshop's, but it comes with the added benefit of being able to undo any crop at any point during your editing process. To crop your shot, first select the ***Crop Tool*** from the top toolbar and click and drag on your image, using the bounding box as a guide for your crop. When you're happy, press ***enter*** to confirm the crop. We suggest holding down the Crop Tool icon to select ***Constrain to Image and Show Overlay*** which will help with attaining the correct crop. You could also select a ***Custom Crop*** which will constrain proportions: here 1 to 1 was used for a square crop, using the bounding box corners to expand or contract the crop within these proportions.

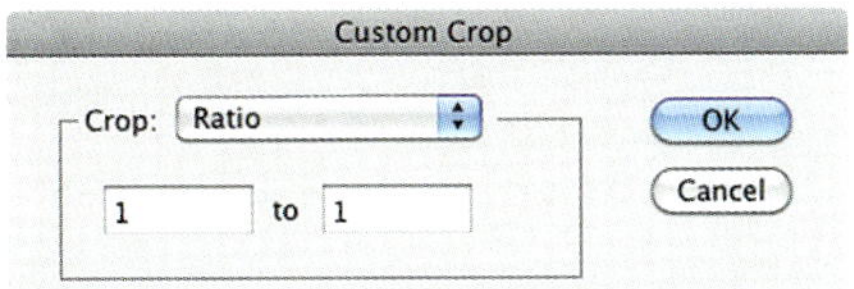

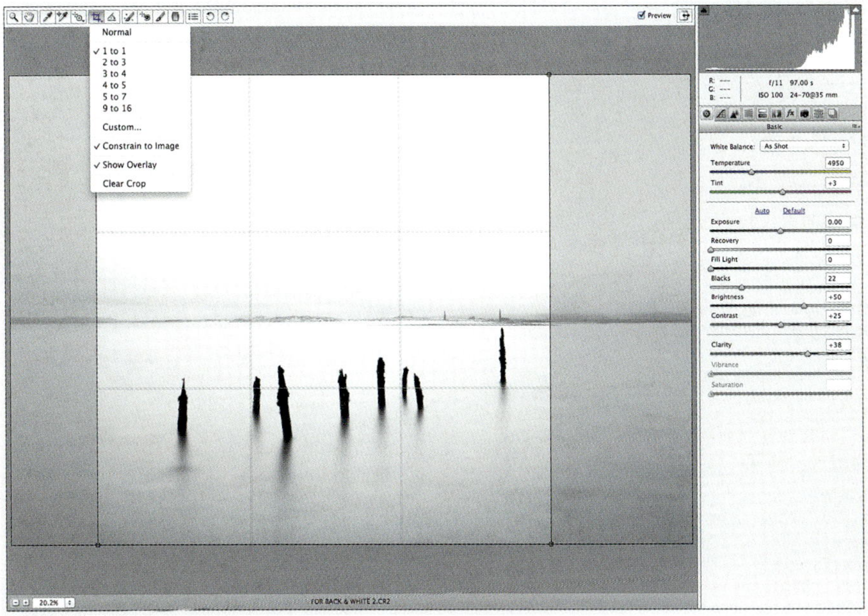

Skin softening

When time is of the essence and your image needs a finishing touch, utilise these retouching steps to perfect your subject's complexion using the Adjustment Brush. Et vôila! One beautiful portrait…

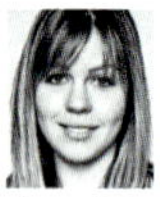

Caroline Wilkinson: When it comes to portraits, everyone wants to look their best, but few of us have the time to arduously remove every flaw, blemish or stray hair from a snapshot. If you're aspiring to professional standards, it's worth spending hours attending to intricate details, but for a photograph of friends or family, a quick solution is often in order.

If you shoot in Raw, which we can't emphasise enough that you should, your first port of call is often Adobe Camera Raw and there's really no need to go any further unless major manipulation is needed. Adobe Camera Raw has all the tools you need to tweak exposure for a dazzling smile, remove blemishes and soften skin, which is what I'll show you how to do here in only a few steps.

As you're working with a lot of image data, ACR offers you wider parameters for enhancements, enabling you to achieve more natural and realistic results than if you were to, say, edit a JPEG in Photoshop. When smoothing skin, you want to try striking a balance between reducing pores and evening out skin tone, and keeping the texture visible: less plastic-fantastic and more flawless beauty. You may want to go heavier on the skin retouching with females than men, who often suit a more rugged appearance anyway.

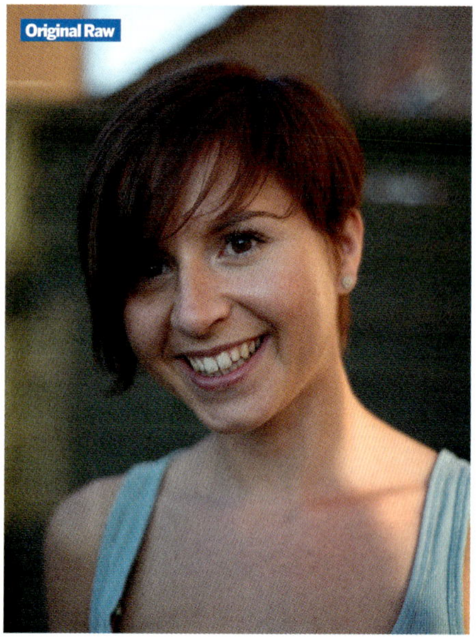

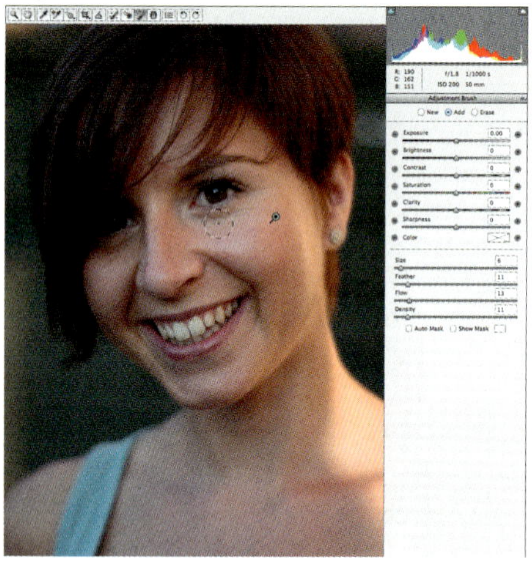

1 Remove blemishes If you need to, use the ***Spot Removal Brush*** to hide any spots or marks on the skin. Our model has quite a clear complexion anyway, which means I could jump straight into skin softening. In ACR, click on the ***Adjustment Brush*** in the top toolbar and then select the brush ***Size*** from the options bar on the right. Set all the sliders in the ***Adjustment*** panel to ***0*** before you begin.

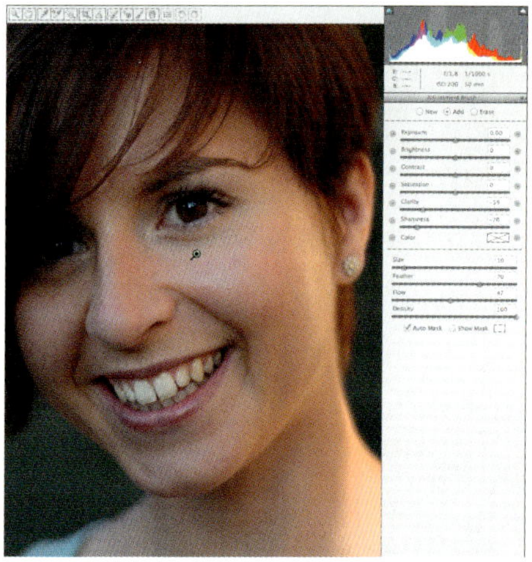

2 Reduce Clarity Set your brush's ***Density***, ***Flow*** and ***Feather*** to around ***11*** as a starting point. You might want to increase the Density depending on how strong you want the effect. Drop the ***Clarity*** slider to ***-59*** and the ***Sharpness*** slider to ***-70*** and brush over the skin. You should see the skin soften instantly. Before tackling smaller areas, apply this adjustment to all visible skin, avoiding features.

Retouching skills

✔ BRIGHTEN EYES AND SMILE

Once you've finished removing blemishes and softening the skin, you might want to consider brightening the whites of the eyes and teeth. It's easy to do: Select ***New*** under ***Adjustment Brush*** and set the ***Size*** to no bigger than the front tooth or white of the eye. Brush over each area individually and then either adjust the ***Exposure*** or ***Brightness*** sliders ever so slightly. Don't over-bleach them as they'll look fake: try to keep some of the natural tint present. You might also want to try adding a new adjustment to sharpen the eyes using the ***Clarity*** slider, too.

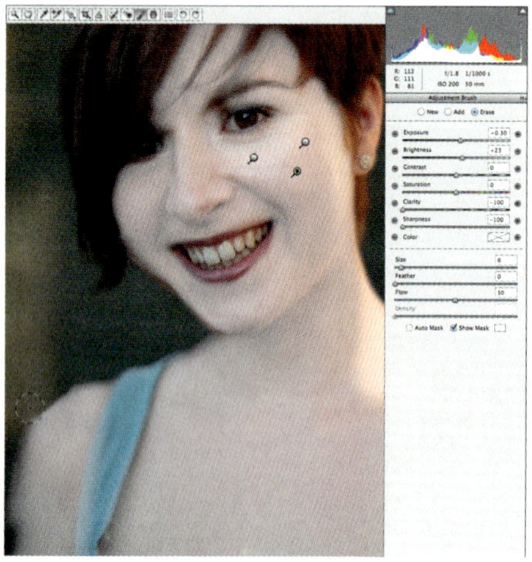

3 Use the Mask To help you judge where you are applying the adjustment, click on the ***Show Mask*** box in the bottom-right corner. You can then double-click on the adjacent coloured box and select your mask's colour. Here I've kept it white. To remove areas of the adjustment, simply click ***Erase*** at the top of the Adjustment panel and brush over the areas you want to return to their original state.

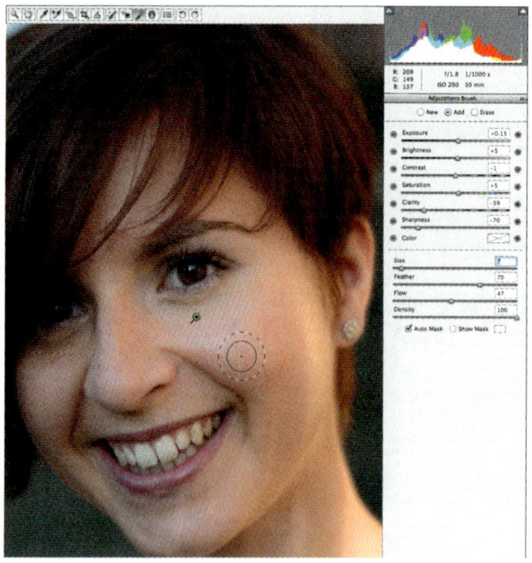

4 Adjust Exposure Once the mask is applied to your image, uncheck the ***Show Mask*** box to reveal the skin. You may find you need to alter the ***Clarity*** at this point if the skin looks over-softened or too crisp. You also may need to adjust the ***Exposure***, ***Brightness*** and ***Saturation*** sliders, too, to affect skin tone and colour – every image is different, so experiment with what looks best.

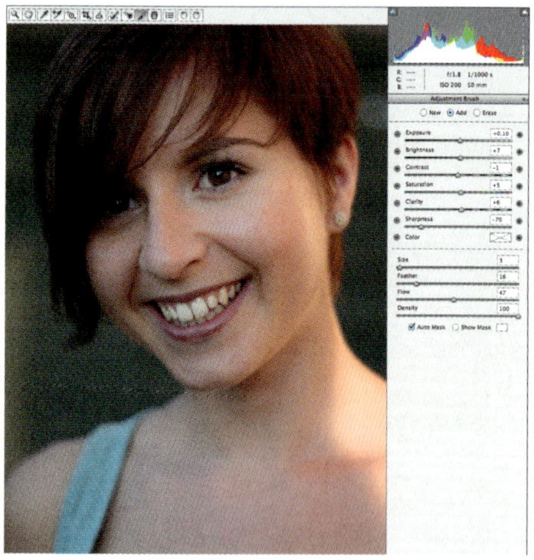

5 Open in Photoshop If you do plan to do further retouching in Photoshop, instead of clicking ***Open Image***, hold down ***shift*** to change the button to ***Open Object***. This will let you open your image as a ***Smart Object***. The benefit of this is that you can double-click on this layer at any point in Photoshop to reopen your Raw file in ACR to refine your nondestructive skin softening and raw edits.

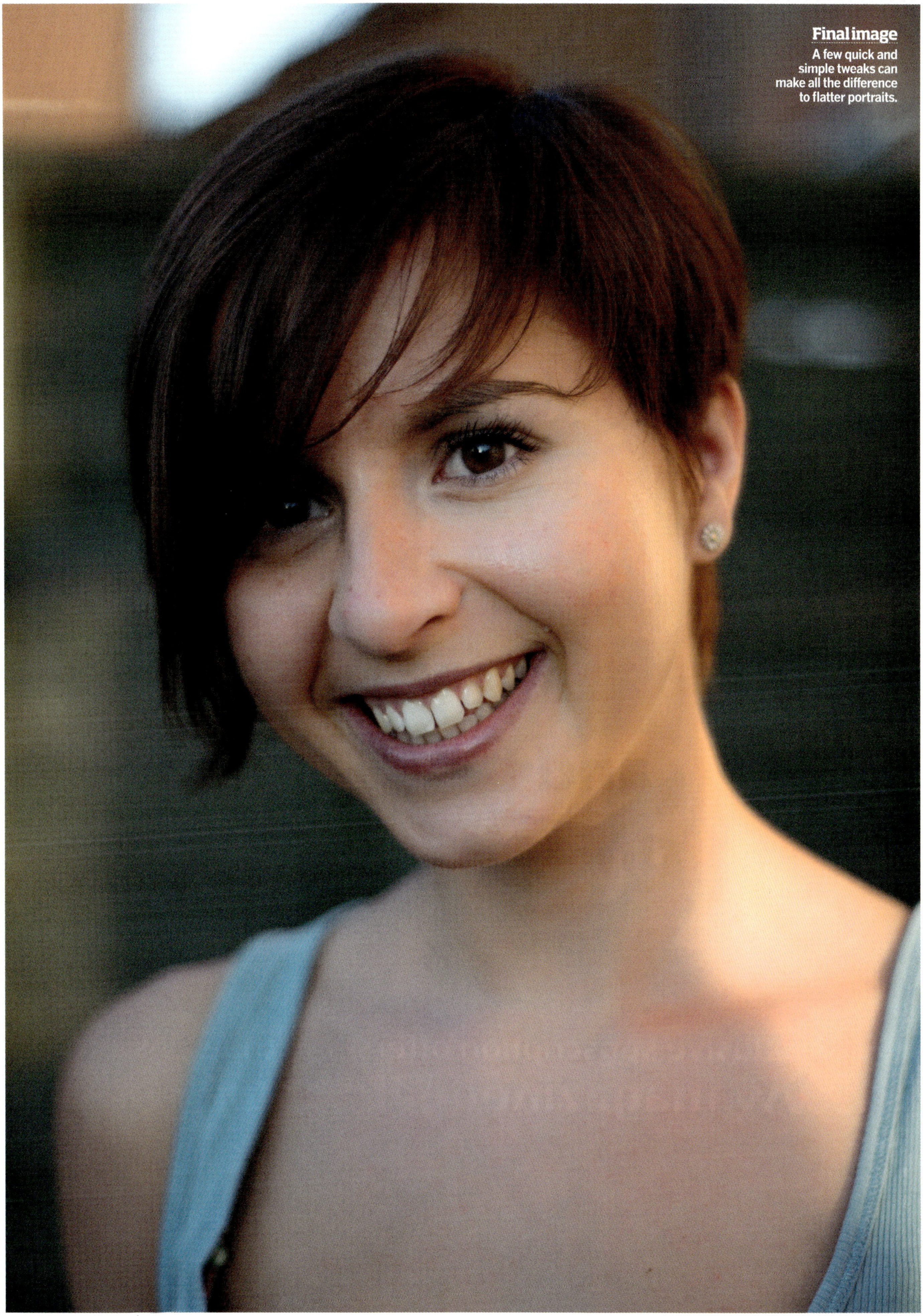

Final image
A few quick and simple tweaks can make all the difference to flatter portraits.

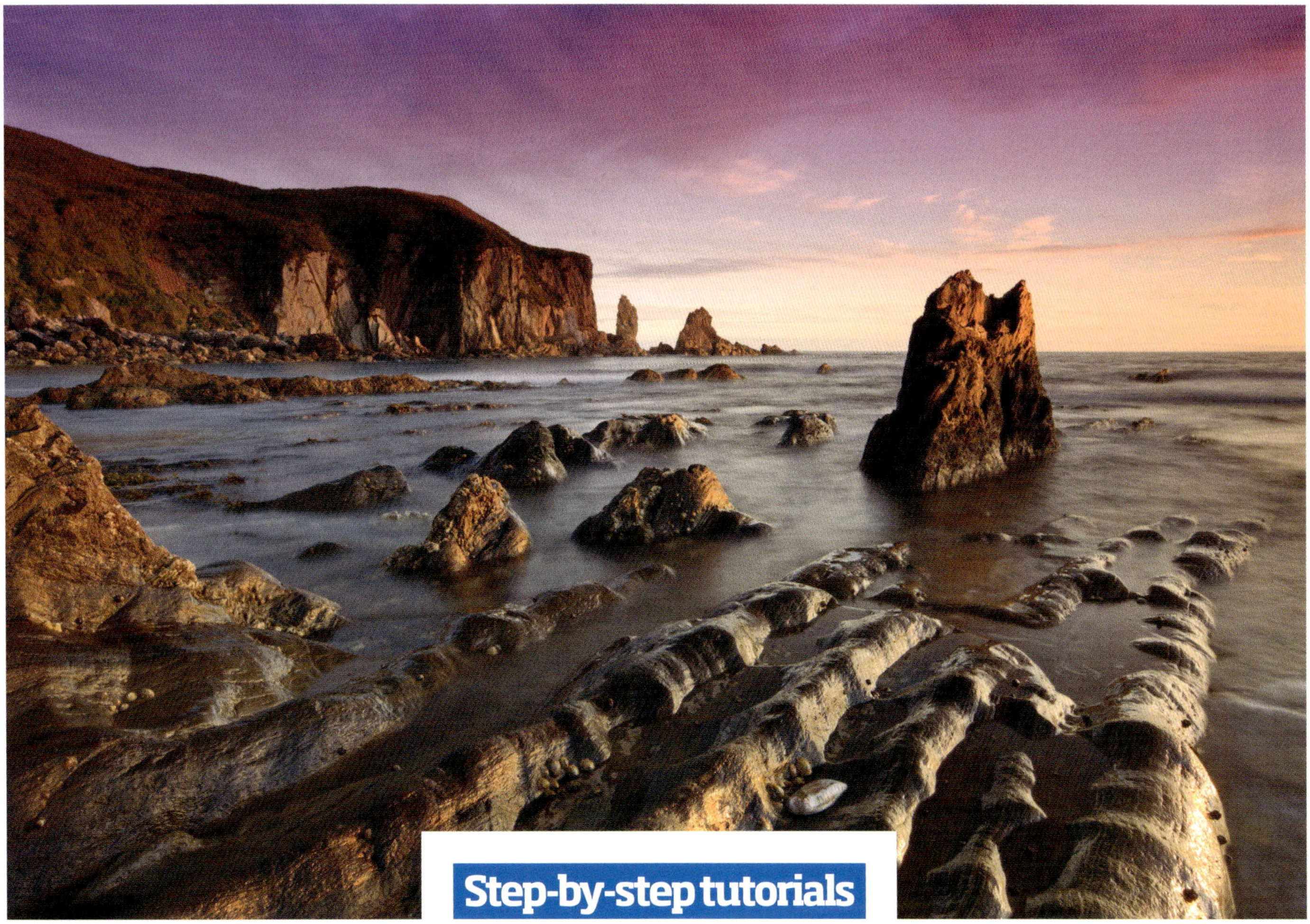

Step-by-step tutorials

CREATIVE EFFECTS

Our top choices for creative effects that help add an extra dimension to your images

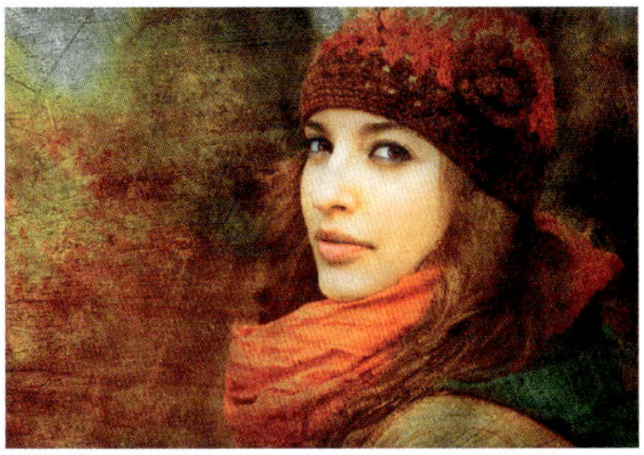

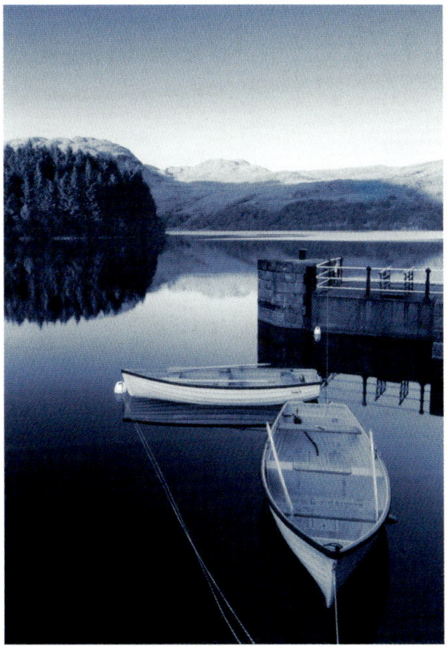

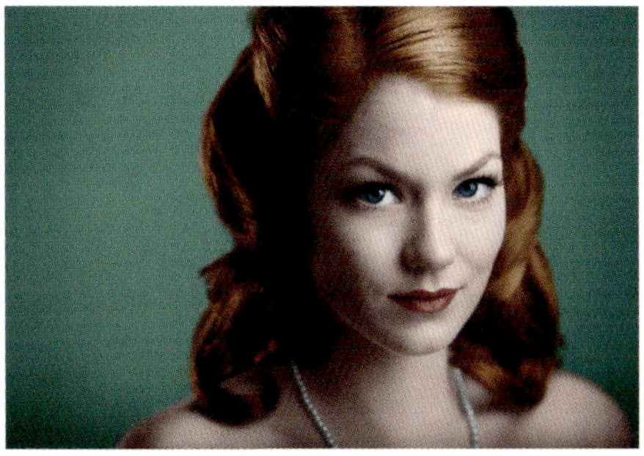

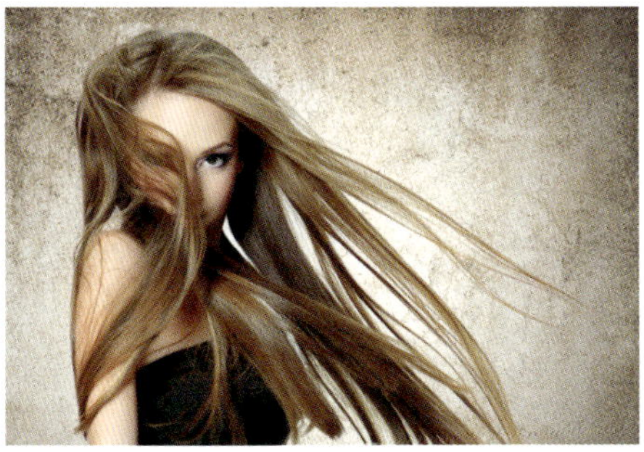

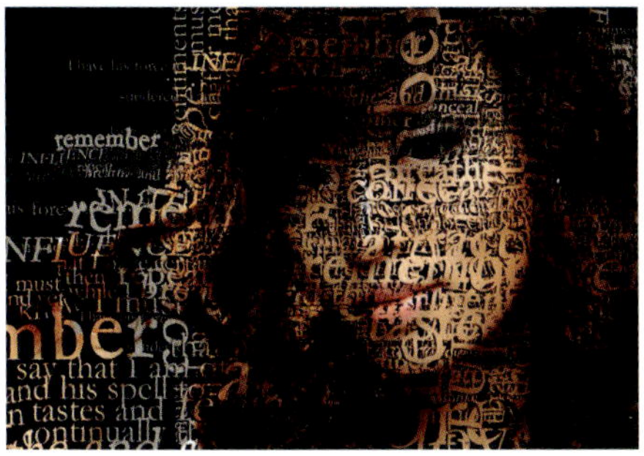

Add a colour graduated filter

Learn how to control Photoshop's gradients to create a colour graduated filter effect and transform ordinary skies into something glorious

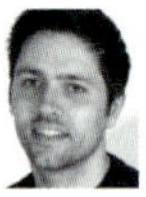

Jordan Butters: In an ideal world, landscape photographers would always have an array of ND grad filters close to hand; one for every conceivable situation and effect that you want to create. In reality, however, this isn't always practical. Thankfully there are a range of effects in Photoshop that simulate the results of using filters, even the coloured graduated variety. This technique is great for emphasising existing colours in the sky or completely changing the mood of your image by emulating a different time of day to when the image was taken.

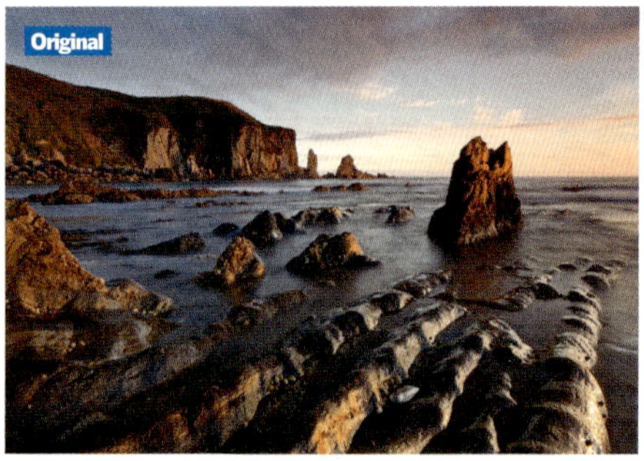

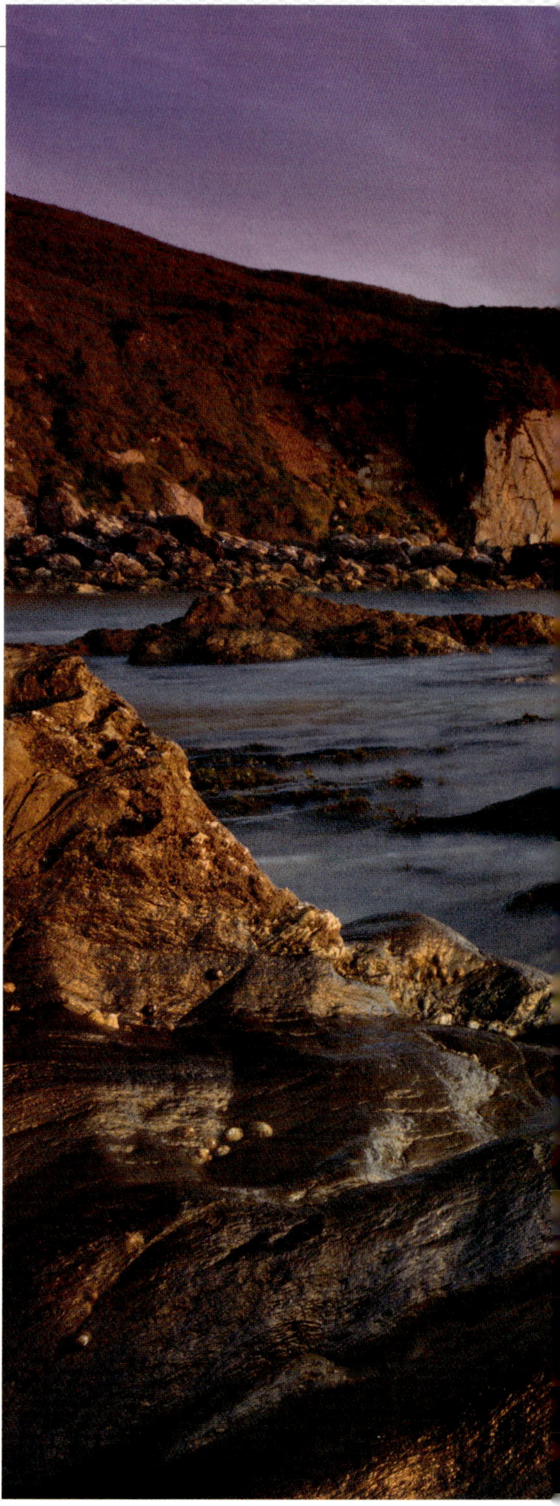

Secrets unlocked

✔ MULTIPLE FILTERS

You could always try adding more than one colour filter to your image. Simply duplicate your Gradient layer by selecting it in the Layers palette and going to ***Layer>Duplicate Layer*** and change the gradient colour as we do in steps three through to five below. Try placing the gradients at different angles using the ***Angle*** dial in the ***Gradient Fill*** menu for different effects.

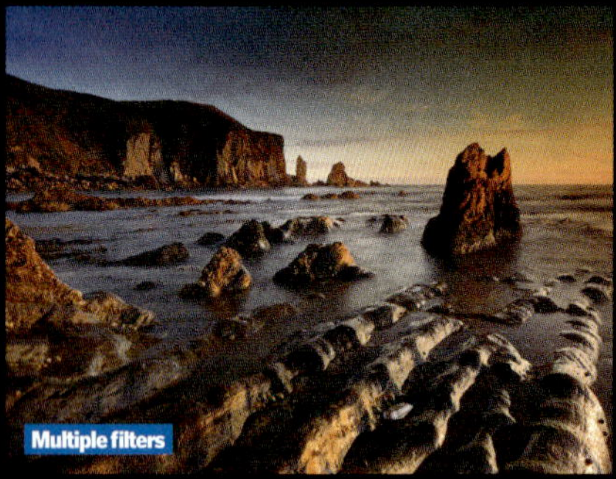

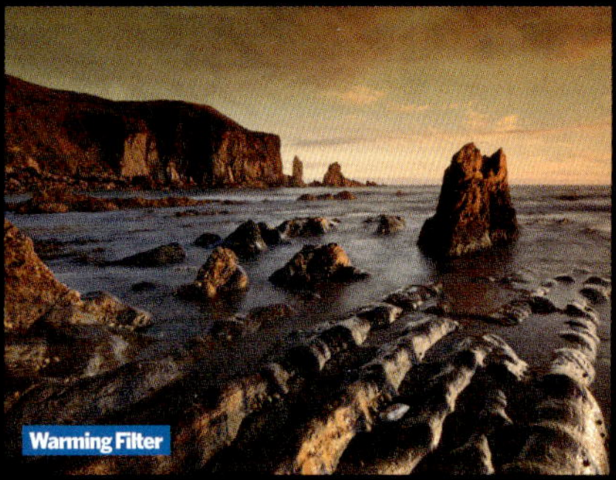

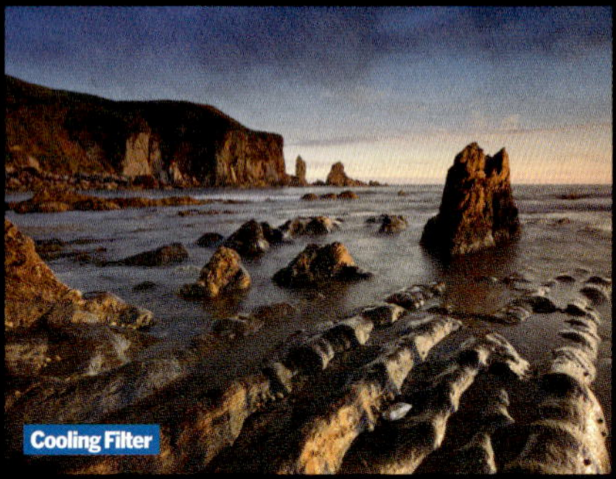

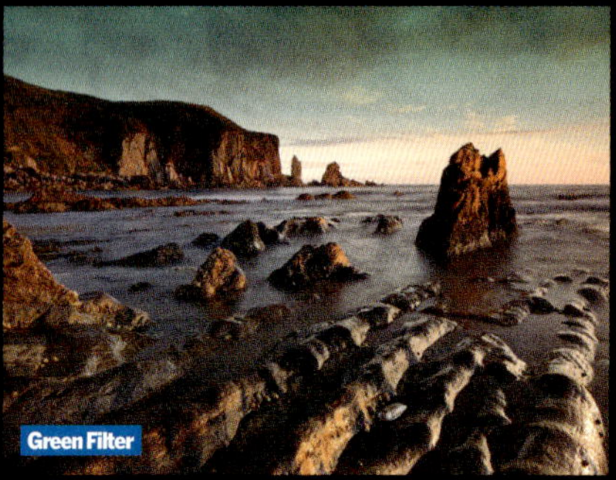

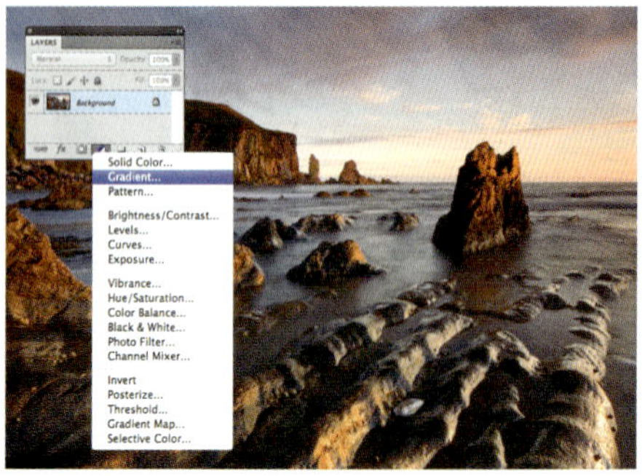

1 Add the gradient Before we begin, press the ***D*** key on your keyboard to reset your colour palette to default. Click on the ***Add new fill or adjustment layer*** button in the Layers palette and select ***Gradient*** from the drop-down menu.

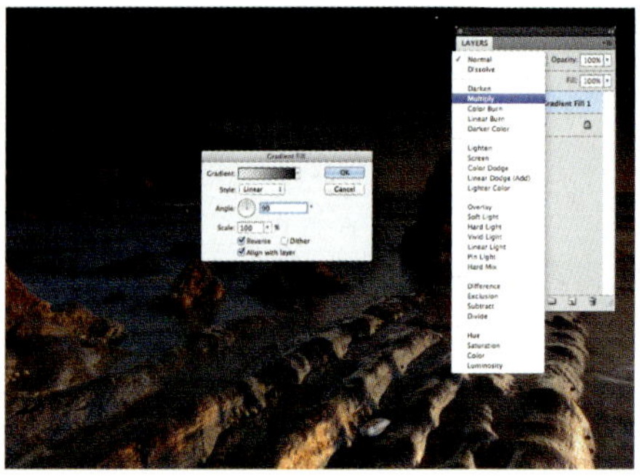

2 Adjust the gradient In the dialogue box, click on the ***Reverse*** tick-box to place the gradient at the top of the image as opposed to the bottom and then click ***OK***. Back in the Layers palette, change the ***Blend Mode*** of the ***Gradient layer*** to ***Multiply***.

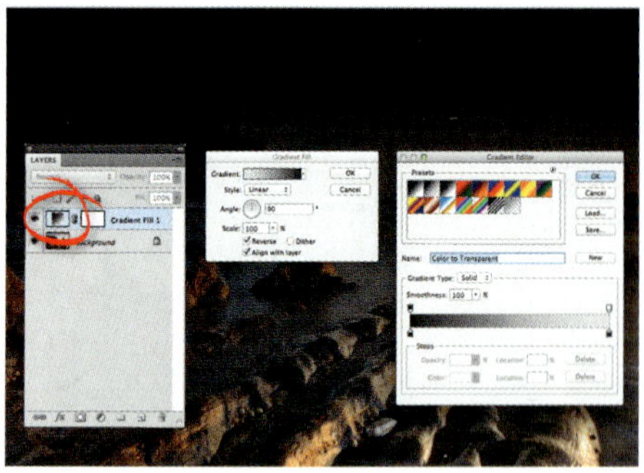

3 Open the Gradient Editor Double-click on the thumbnail on the ***Gradient layer*** in the Layers palette to open the ***Gradient Fill*** menu again and click on the ***Gradient*** thumbnail at the top to open the ***Gradient Editor*** palette.

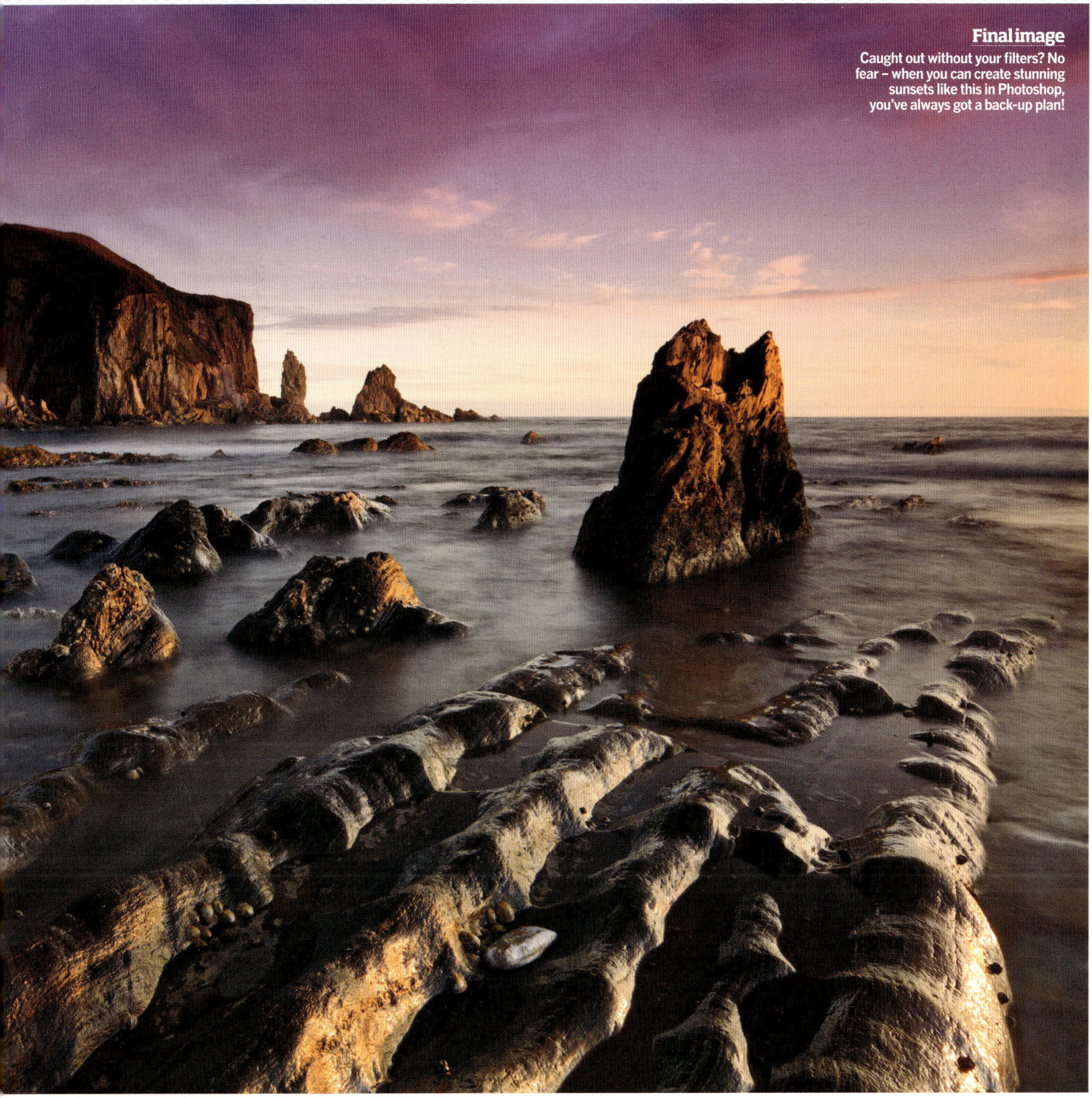

Final image

Caught out without your filters? No fear – when you can create stunning sunsets like this in Photoshop, you've always got a back-up plan!

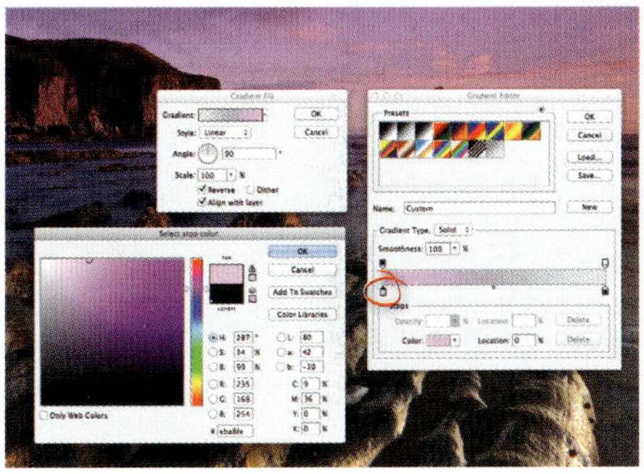

4 Change the colour Click on ***Black Color Stop*** in the bottom-left corner of the gradient. Then click on the ***Color*** thumbnail below to open the ***Color Picker*** window. Select your colour – I chose pink to emulate the sky at dusk. Click ***OK***.

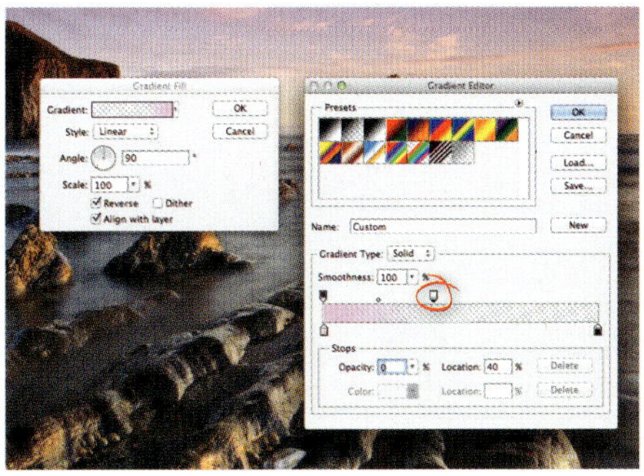

5 Alter the opacity The two ***Color Stops*** above the gradient scale control the opacity of the gradient. Move the ***White Color Stop*** in the top-right corner to control the depth and hardness of the gradient to suit your image. Once done, click ***OK***.

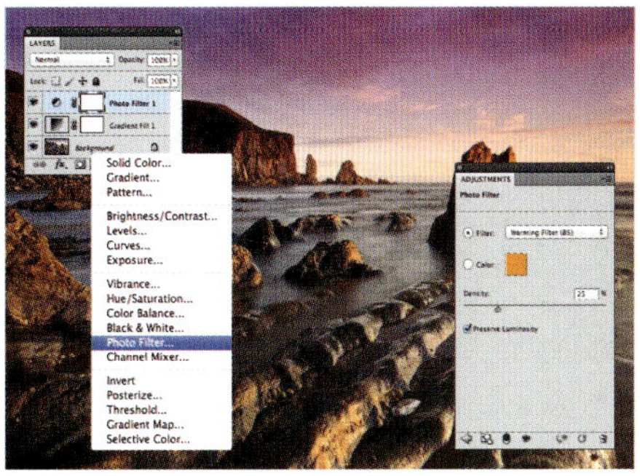

6 Add a Photo Filter Back in the Layers palette, click on the ***Add new fill or adjustment layer*** button again and this time select ***Photo Filter***. Select one of the ***Warming Filters*** and click ***OK*** – this will warm the entire image to suit the dusk colours.

Duotone your black & white photographs

We reveal how to add colour to your shadows and highlights

Caroline Wilkinson: There is so much you can do with a black & white photograph to alter its look, but one traditional technique that's still increasingly popular is colour-toning. All too often it's a technique that's done horrendously badly: images look like they've been dipped in a purple or magenta wash, or like they've been taken using the wrong White Balance.

Subtly altering the temperature of the highlights or shadows with a yellow/orange hue or blue tint can add warmth or a contemporary coolness respectively. So, as a rule of thumb with this technique, err on the side of caution: you want the tint to work with the scene, not overpower it. We're going to split-tone, otherwise known as duotone, a mono image here, which requires you to separately tone the shadows and highlights. The difficulty comes from finding colours that work well together: putting complementary colours in the mix is a good place to start and after that, experimentation.

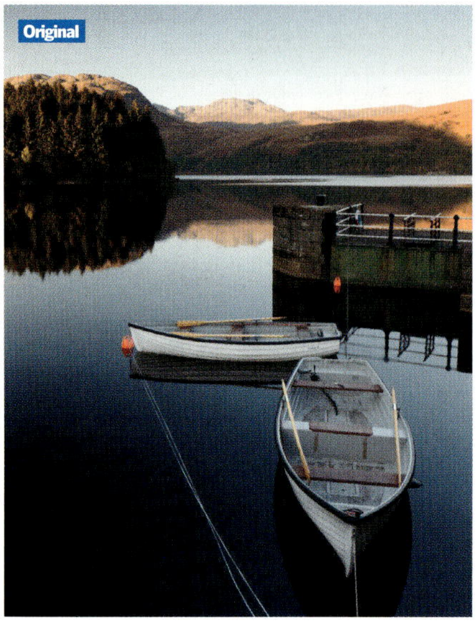

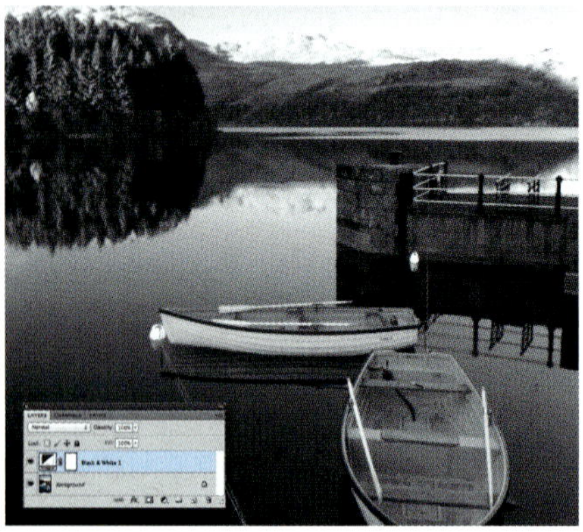

1 Convert to monochrome Add a Black & White adjustment layer (***Layer>New Adjustment Layer>Black & White***...) and adjust the colour sliders until you reach the level of contrast that best suits your image. You can also select one of the options under ***Preset*** for one-click effects. Here, I decide to opt for the High Contrast Red Filter.

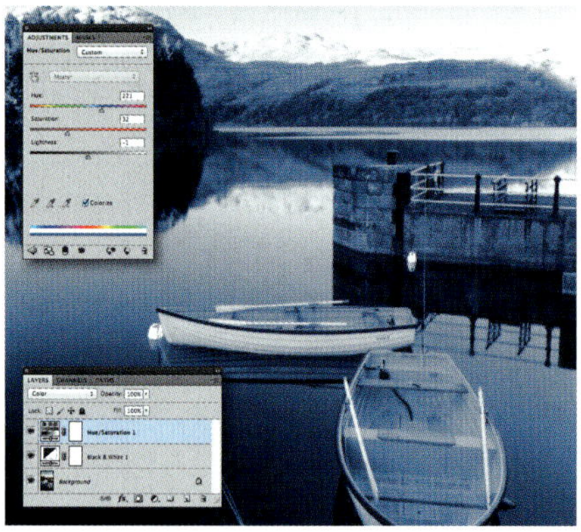

2 Apply colour Add a Hue/Saturation adjustment layer the alternative way by clicking on the ***Add new fill or adjustment layer*** icon at the bottom of the Layers palette. With the adjustment panel open, click on the ***Colorize*** box and drag the ***Hue*** slider to pick the tint for the shadows, ignoring the effect on the rest of the image for now.

Common errors

✔ HOW NOT TO DO IT

It can be tempting to take the easy route and colourwash your pictures using a Hue/Saturation adjustment layer or to be too heavy-handed with applying colour. You'll know you've gone too far as you'll start to lose details and will have very little graduation in tone. Often the best results come from picking a colour that isn't so vibrant that it overpowers the scene. You want viewers to see the beautiful photograph first, and then the tint.

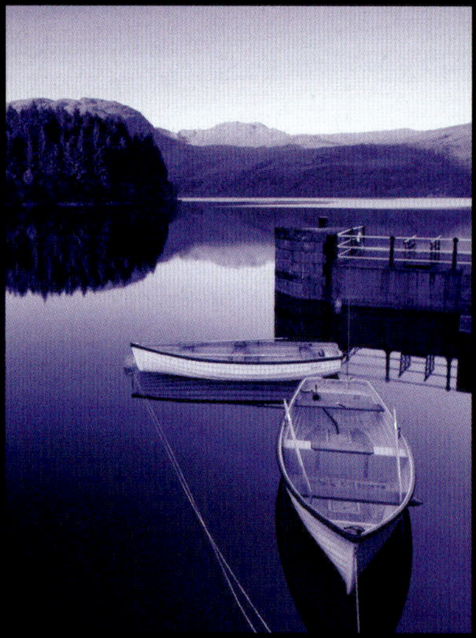

Secrets unlocked

✔ COLOR BALANCE ADJUSTMENT LAYER

A quick but less effective way to split-tone is to use a Color Balance adjustment layer on a black & white image. You can control the tones using the Shadows, Midtone and Highlight settings all in one place.

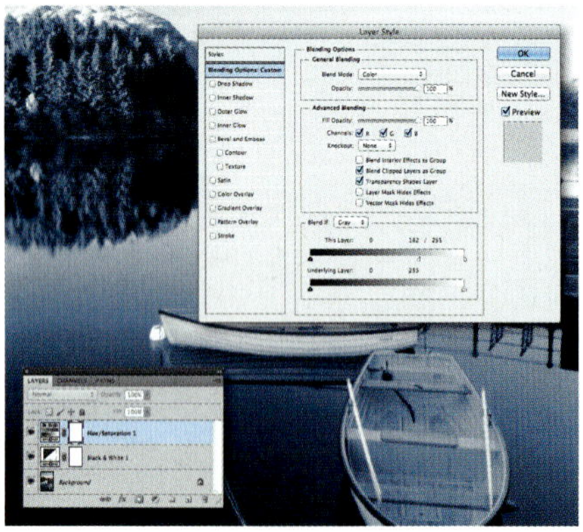

3 Tone the shadows In the Layers palette, change the Hue/Saturation layer's ***Blend Mode*** to ***Color***. Now go to ***Layer>Layer Style>Blending Options***. Hold ***alt*** and click the white triangle to split it in two and drag them until you find the balance between excluding highlights from the tint and a smooth graduation in tones. Best positions here are around ***100*** and ***200***.

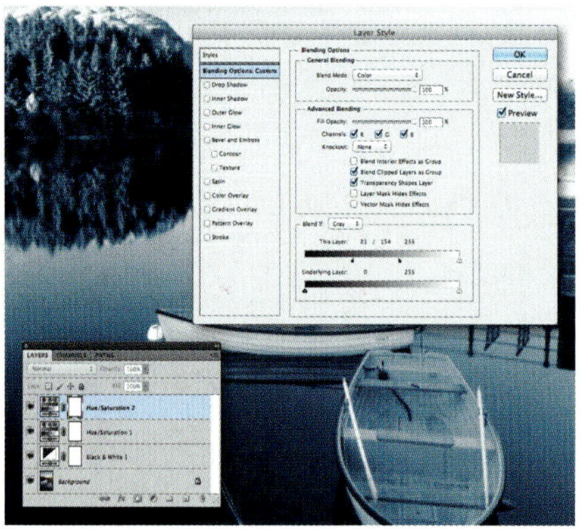

4 Tone the highlight Repeat step three, but focus on the shadows. Add a ***Hue/Saturation*** adjustment layer, change its ***Blend Mode*** to ***Color***, click ***Colorize*** and adjust the ***Hue*** slider to tone the highlights – ignoring the shadows. Access ***Blending Options*** and split the black sliders to remove the tint from the shadows. Good positions here are around ***80*** and ***155***.

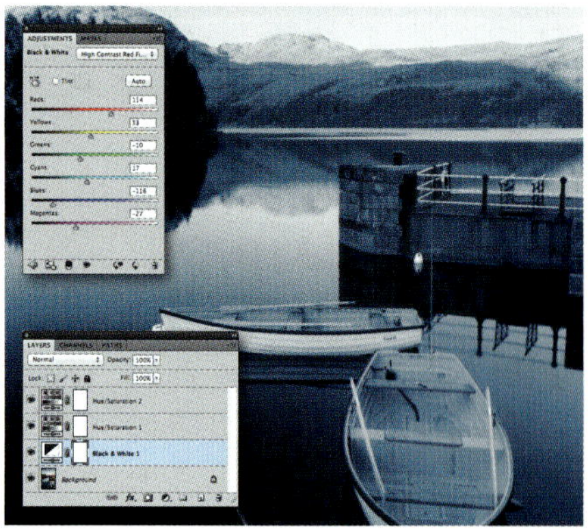

5 Tweak your contrast One of the reasons for working with Adjustment Layers is so you can revert back to previous adjustments and tweak them once you've finished. The contrast in your black & white conversion greatly affects the duotone treatment, so double-click on the ***Black & White*** adjustment layer to re-edit the sliders and see if you can improve the results.

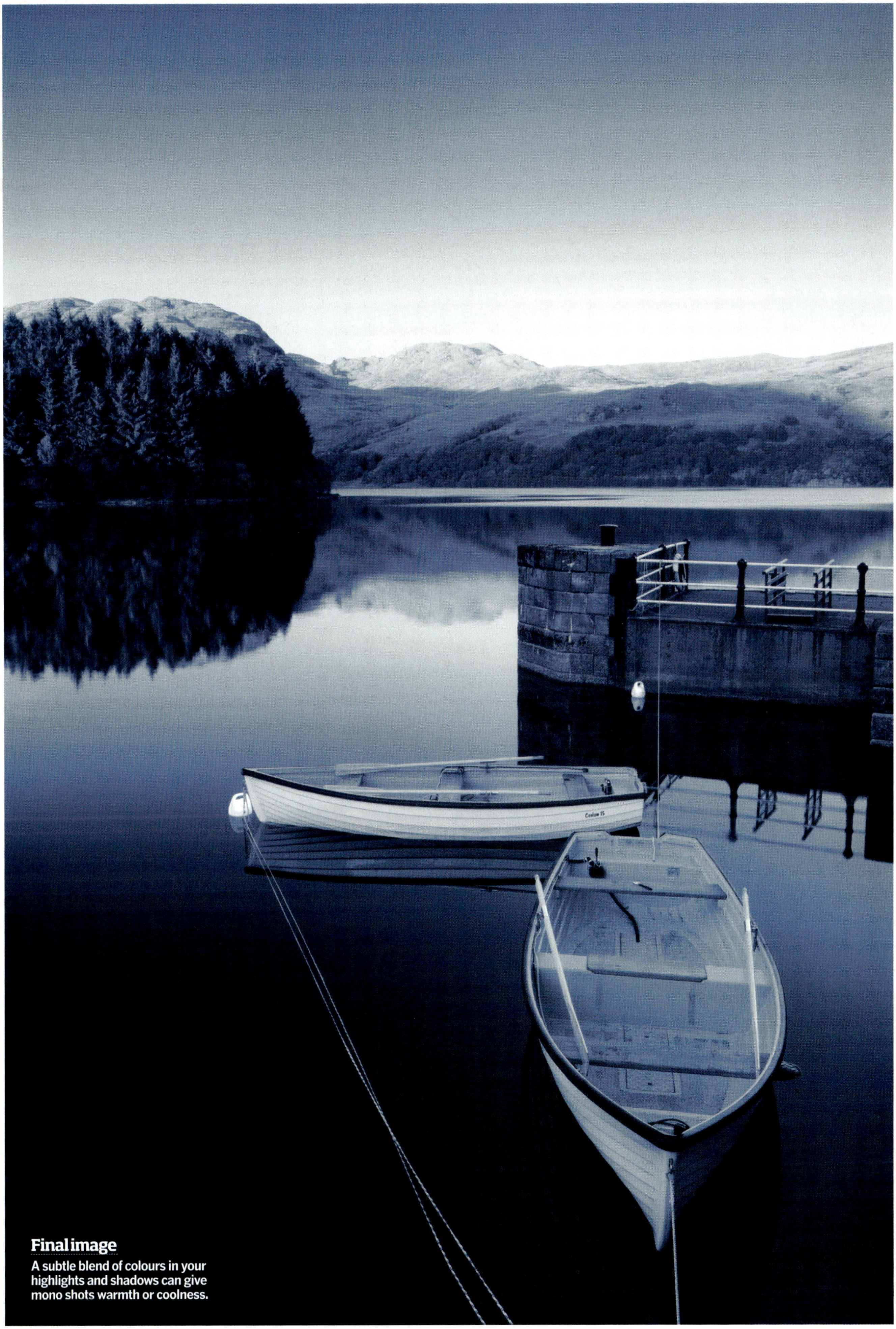

Final image

A subtle blend of colours in your highlights and shadows can give mono shots warmth or coolness.

Add a creative lens flare effect

Captured a shot that's missing that extra bit of punch? See how adding a faux lens flare in Photoshop can add interest to your images

Jordan Butters: Lens flare is caused by harsh light entering your lens and bouncing between the lens elements. The results vary from colourful circles of light scattered across your image to reduced contrast, overexposed areas and colour casts. On the surface they all sound like the kind of thing we strive to avoid in our photographs, but half the fun of photography is in bending the rules.

Lens flare can add great atmosphere and a summer feel to an image. Capturing flare intentionally in-camera is relatively straightforward – however, controlling flare so that it doesn't detract from your image is another matter altogether. Thankfully, lens flare is relatively straightforward to recreate using Photoshop.

Lens flare is one of those elements that very much depends on the type of image it is being applied to; it certainly won't work for all pictures. It is a warm, soft effect so tends to suit outdoor portraits of women and children very well. It's also an effect that has to be applied with caution, as incorrect placement of the flare can completely spoil an image. It works best when applied to photographs whereby your light source is above and behind your subject – for example, when the sun is low in the sky, such as during early morning or late afternoon. If you apply lens flare to an image in which the sun is directly overhead, the direction of the shadows in the image will contradict the direction that the flare is coming from, instantly discrediting the effect. Therefore, before you start editing your image, the most important step is to identify the direction that the light is coming from. Look at the direction of any shadows for clues or for areas of light and dark on your subject. Always apply the flare to complement the direction of the natural light.

Furthermore, this is one of those effects that should be applied with restraint. The temptation is always there to crank the sliders all the way across for the most dramatic effect, but the further you push the parameters, the less realistic the effect will appear. If done right, the viewer shouldn't be able to tell that the flare isn't all natural.

Original

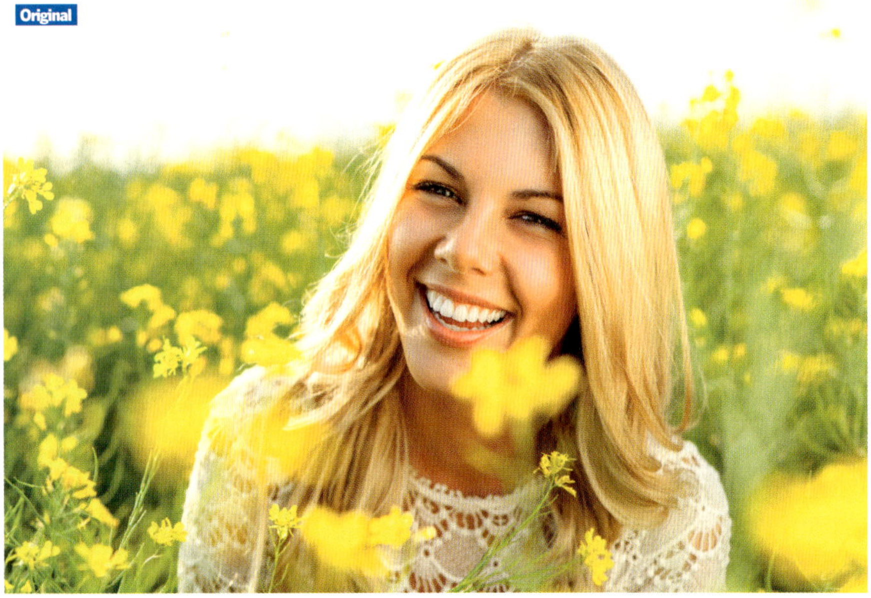

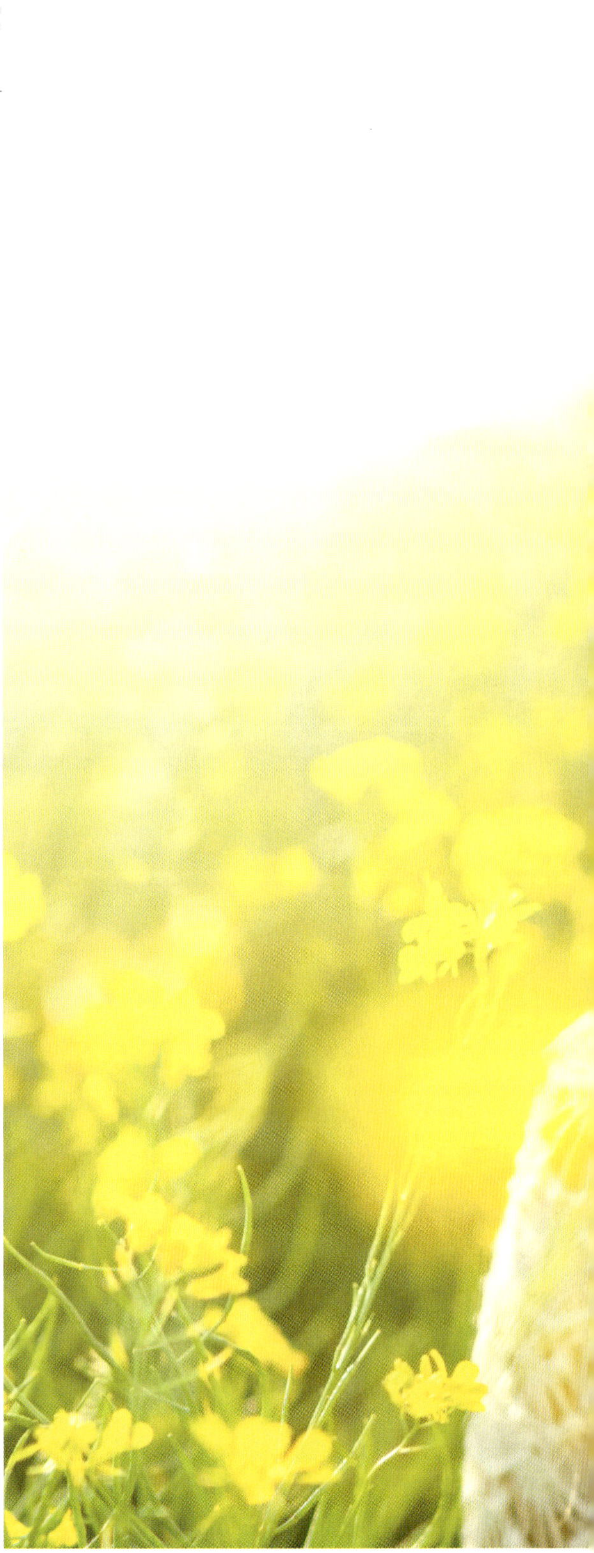

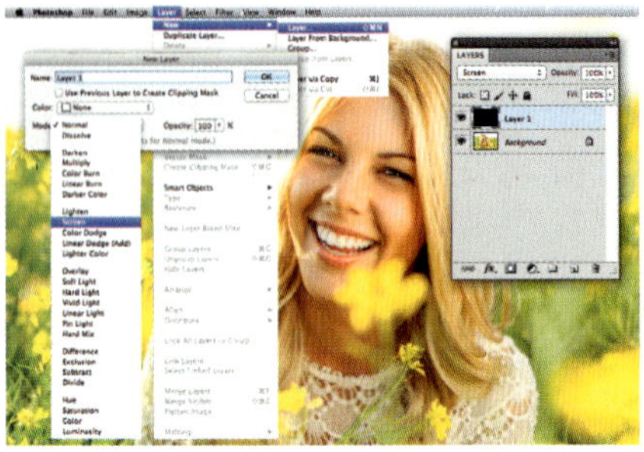

1 Create a layer for the flare Create a blank new layer for your flare by going to ***Layer>New>Layer***. In the New Layer dialogue box that opens, change the ***Blend Mode*** to ***Screen*** and tick the ***Fill with Screen-neutral colour*** (black) checkbox. Click ***OK*** to create the layer.

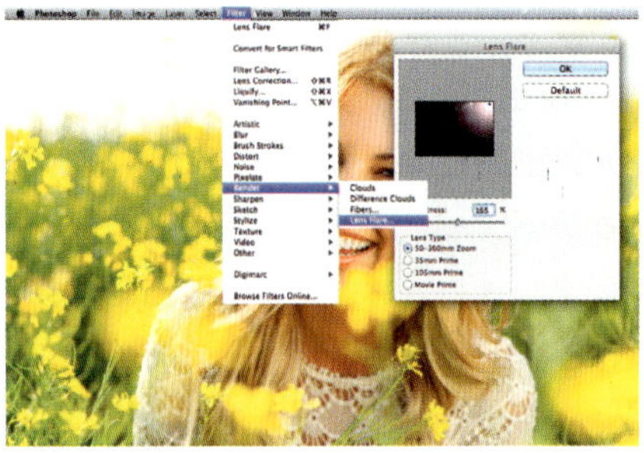

2 Add the flare Go to ***Filter>Render>Lens Flare*** to open the Lens Flare dialogue box. Click on the black thumbnail window to set the position of the flare in relation to your image and select your choice of ***Flare*** and ***Brightness***. I have chosen 50-300mm Zoom at 165%. Click ***OK***.

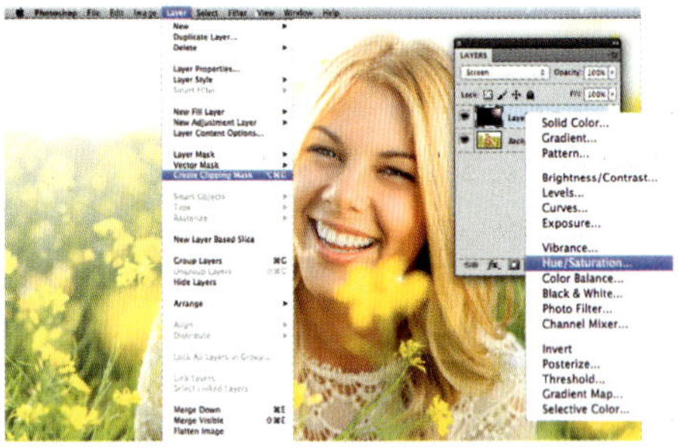

3 Create an Adjustment Layer In the Layers palette, click on the ***Add new fill or adjustment layer*** button and select ***Hue/Saturation***. Go to ***Layer>Create Clipping Mask*** to clip the Adjustment Layer to the lens flare layer only.

Final image

Tweak the effect by adjusting the *Opacity* slider of the flare layer in the Layers palette.

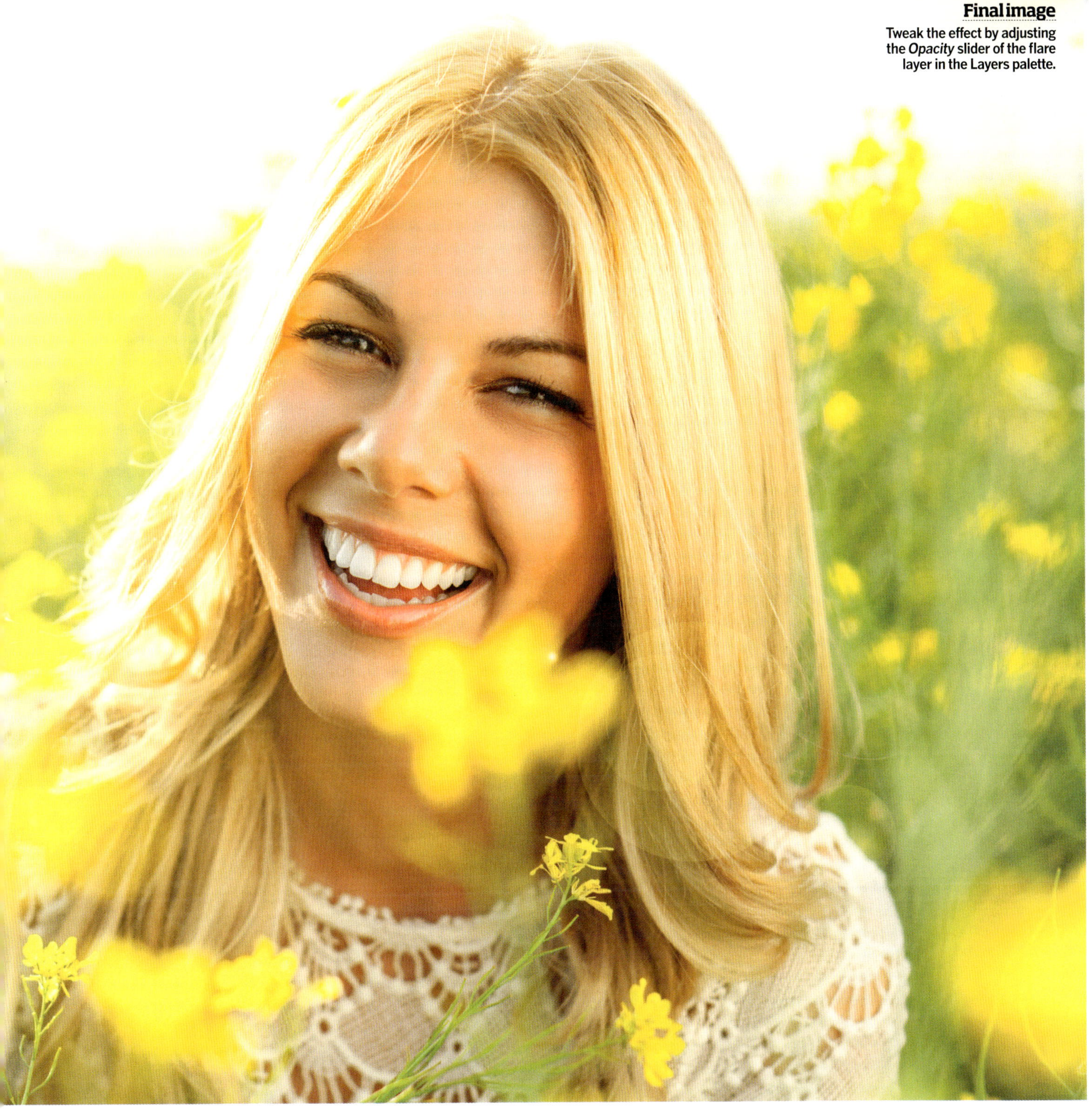

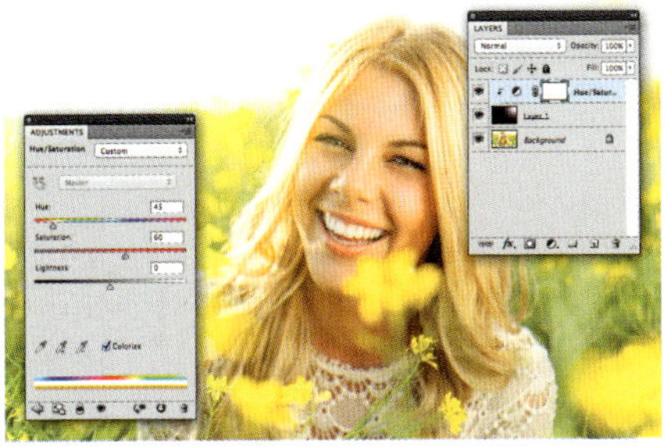

4 Adjust the Hue In the Adjustments palette, click the ***Colorize*** check box and change the ***Hue*** and the ***Saturation***. I found setting the Hue to around 45 and Saturation to around 60 gives the flare a warmer, more realistic cast.

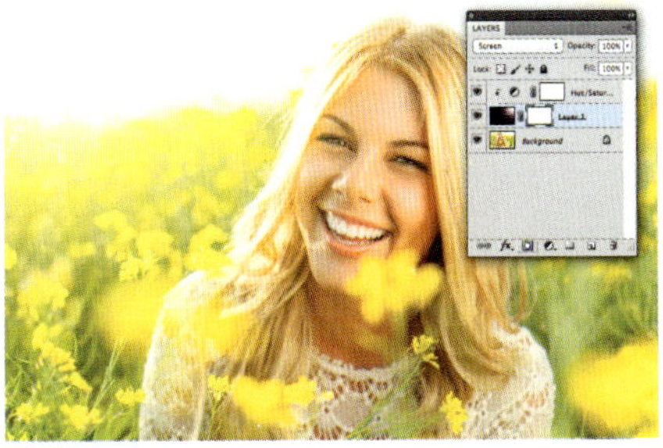

5 Add a Layer Mask If any flare artefacts are distracting or cover important areas of your image, click on the flare layer in the Layers palette before clicking on the ***Add layer mask*** button. Select the ***Brush Tool*** and adjust the ***Opacity*** to ***50%*** at the top menu bar.

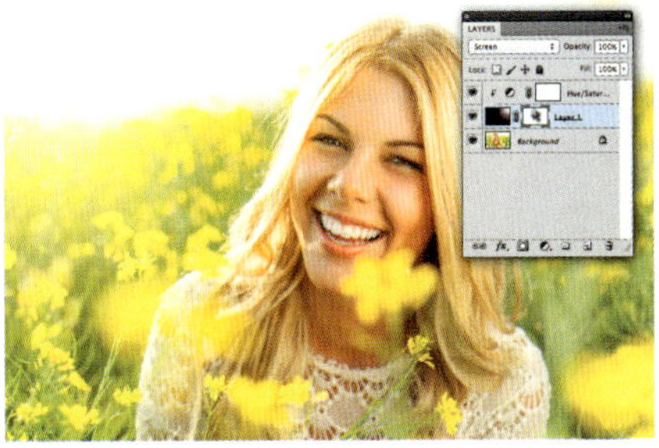

6 Remove distractions Make sure that your ***Foreground Color*** is set to ***Black*** and paint over any areas of flare that you wish to remove from the image. If you go a step too far, switch your ***Foreground Color*** to ***White*** and brush back over.

Composite subjects with fine hair

Wispy strands of hair are a headache to select even for the seasoned Photoshop user, but this simple step-by-step technique should make the process a lot smoother and give a really good result

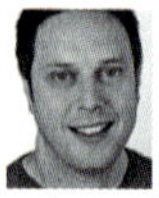

Luke Marsh: If you've ever tried to composite a person on to a different background, then you'll know that the hair can be the hardest area to select. Extracting the fine, flyaway strands can be frustrating and time-consuming, but crucial if you want your composite to look seamless and not like a hard-edged helmet.

The success of this technique depends on the type of background you're extracting from and it's a lot easier if the subject is against a grey or white backdrop, or one that's uniform and light in tone. If it's not uniform, you could use the Brush Tool to paint the background white.

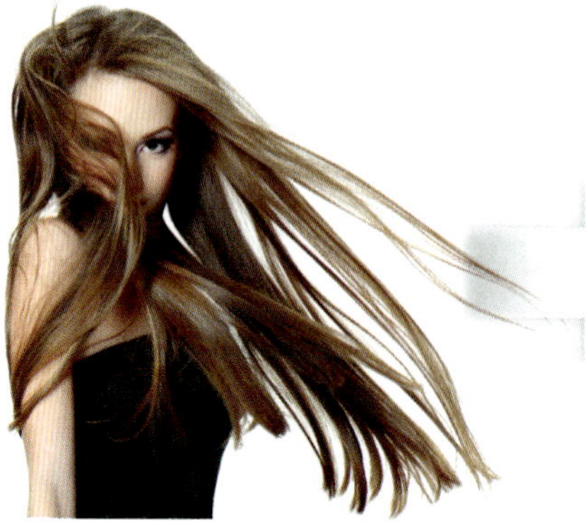

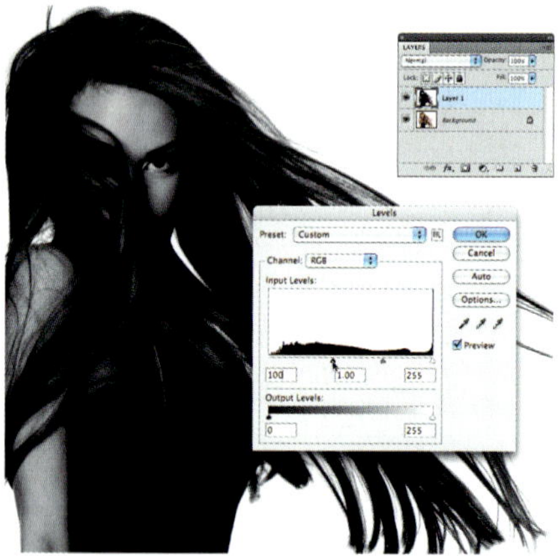

1 Duplicate layer Create a copy of your image layer (***Layer>New>Layer via Copy***), then go to ***Image>Adjustments>Desaturate*** to remove the colour from this new layer. Next, go to ***Image>Adjustments>Levels...*** and move the black slider right to no more than ***100*** for lighter hair or no more than ***50*** for dark or black hair. This process is to darken the hair significantly, the hair strands don't need to be perfectly black at this stage.

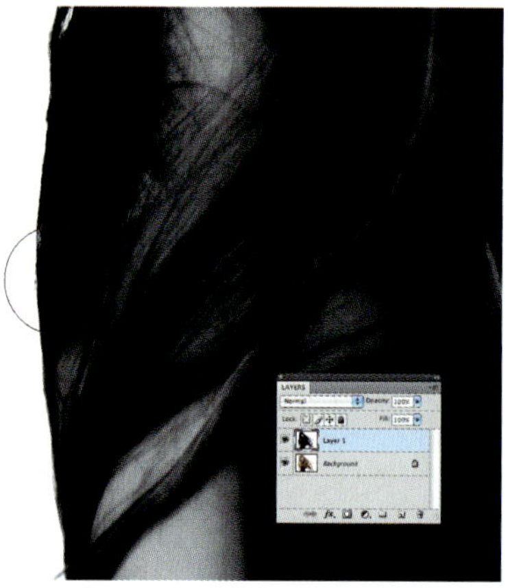

2 Brush the edges Select the ***Brush Tool*** set to ***Black***, with a medium-sized, soft edge and with the ***Mode*** set to ***Overlay*** in the Options bar. Now brush around the edge of the model to darken areas missed by Levels. The brush will darken areas of the subject while the white background will remain unaffected. Don't go over any areas of fine hair yet as this is best done gradually with reduced opacity to avoid problems.

Workflow tools

✔DIFFERENT BACKGROUNDS

Creating a Layer Mask that works well with fine hair can be time-consuming, but once it's done, pretty much any background can be dropped in without the need for further editing. Simply reveal the silhouette layer hidden in step seven by clicking on the eye icon, then repeat the instructions from step five to step eight, using your replacement background accordingly.

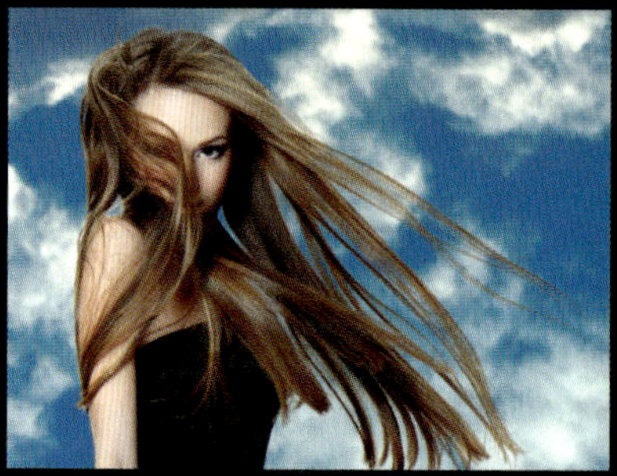

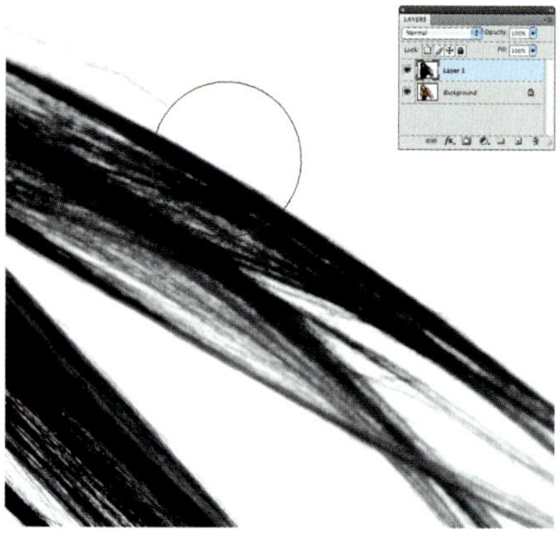

3 Darken the fine hair Reduce the brush ***Opacity*** to ***50%*** in the Options bar then, using the same principle as before, work over the hair strands to darken them. The reduced opacity will help to build up the effect, especially on very fine hair strands. Don't attempt to get the strands completely black at this stage as this can thicken them irreversibly. Once the background is added, final tweaks can be made to perfect the strands.

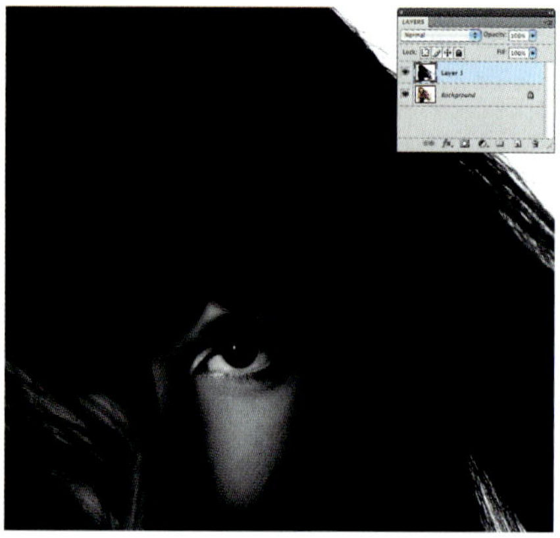

4 Fill the gaps Now the edges of the image have been darkened, it's time to fill in detail in the centre. Change the brush's ***Mode*** to ***Normal*** and ***Opacity*** to ***100%***, and begin to fill any areas of detail that remain. As the brush is now set to Normal, be sure to work at the centre of the subject, and prevent your strokes from overlapping into the white areas of the image. You should now have a perfect silhouette of your hair image.

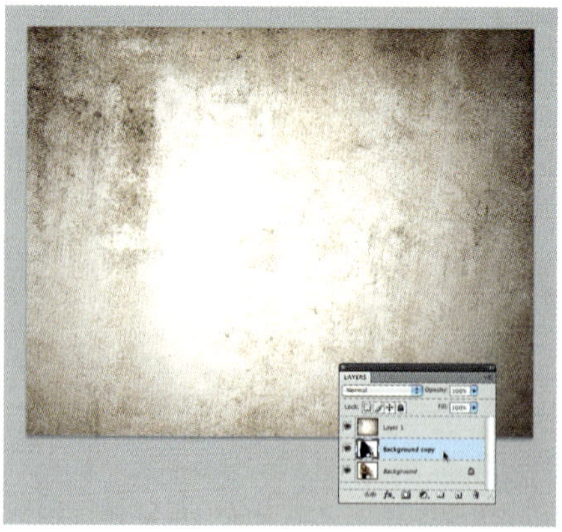

5 Add a background Open your background file and go to ***Select>All*** then ***Edit>Cut*** to copy the image. Go back to your hair file and click ***Edit>Paste*** to place the background image at the top of the Layers palette and resize the image if necessary. Click on the hair silhouette layer beneath, go to ***Select>All*** and then ***Edit>Copy*** to place the silhouette on to the pasteboard. Now click back on the background image layer above.

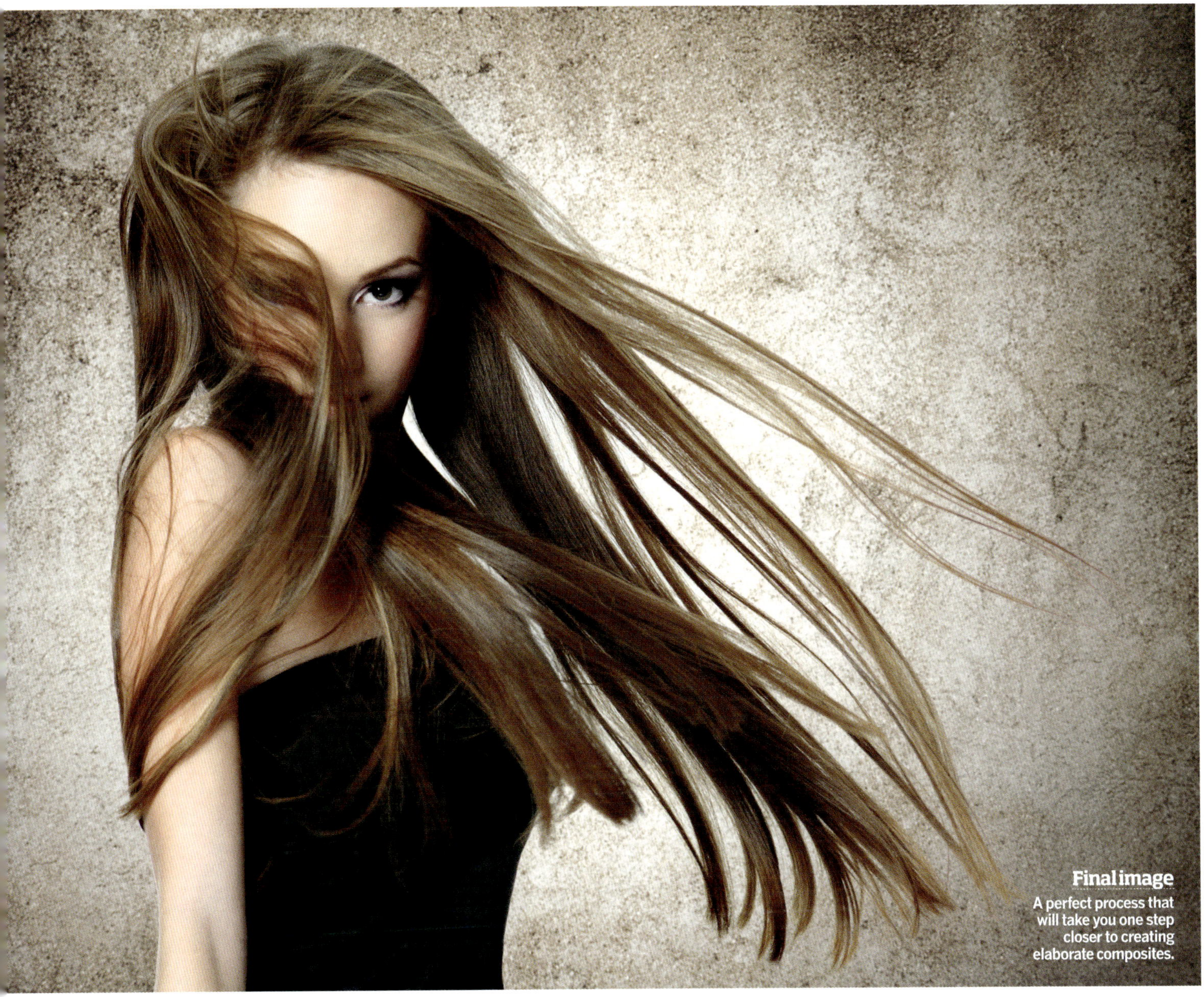

Final image
A perfect process that will take you one step closer to creating elaborate composites.

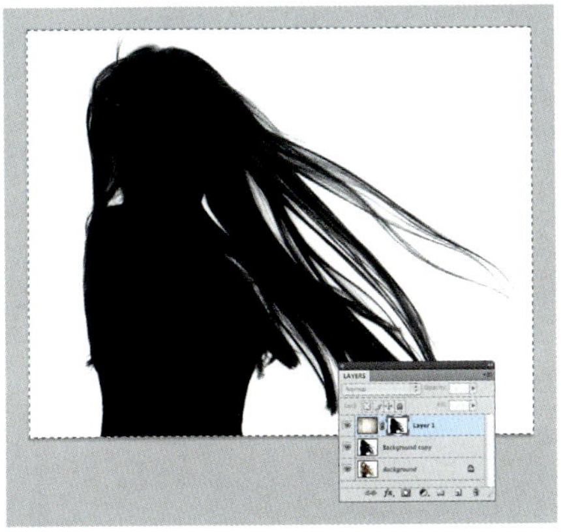

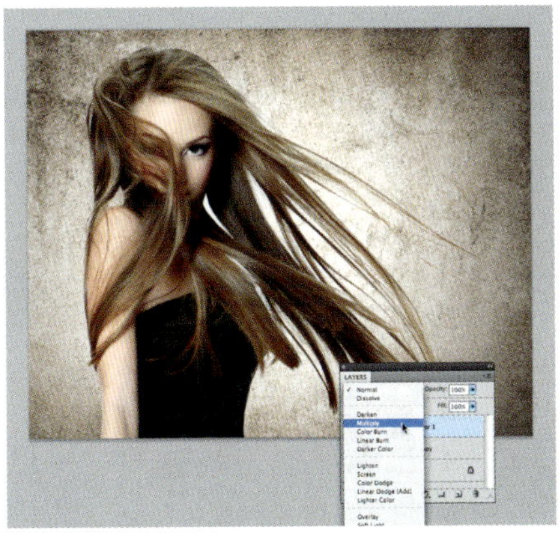

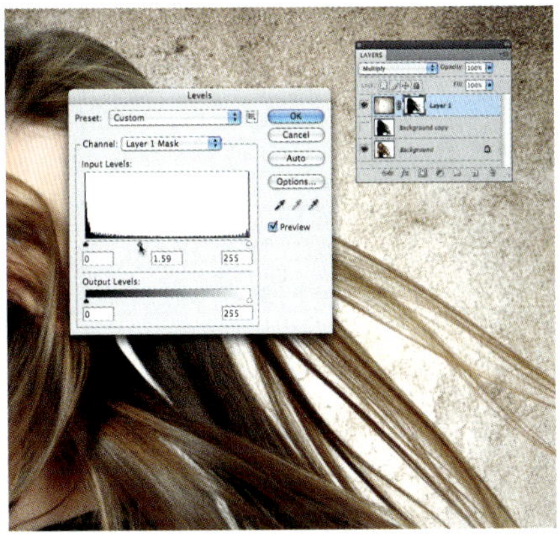

6 Add a Layer Mask Add a Layer Mask to the background image by going to ***Layer>New Layer Mask>Reveal All*** – the Layer Mask will appear next to the image thumbnail in the Layers palette. Hold the ***alt*** key and click on the ***Layer Mask***: the screen will go blank to show that the content of the mask is empty. Now go to ***Edit>Paste*** to place the hair silhouette into the Layer Mask. It will also appear on the blank screen.

7 View the effect The original silhouette layer has served its purpose so hide it by clicking on its eye icon in the Layers palette. Hold down ***alt*** and click on the ***Layer Mask*** attached to the background layer to hide the preview. You will now see a rough composite of the hair and background image. The hair at this stage is looking good but by no means perfect. Change the ***Blend Mode*** to ***Multiply*** to improve the composite further.

8 Final tweaks With the Layer Mask active, open ***Image>Adjustments>Levels...*** and move the grey slider left while previewing the results on the image. Stop when you feel the hair strands are almost perfect without any halos appearing around them. Finally, using the ***Brush Tool***, with the ***Mode*** set to ***Overlay*** and the colour to ***Black***, work over any remaining imperfections, which tend to be in areas of very fine hair.

Add texture to photographs

Mastering the fundamentals of Layers, Layer Masks and Blend Modes creates new possibilities for post-production. Find out how to combine all three to apply textures and add impact to your pictures

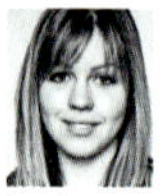

Caroline Wilkinson: Adding texture to a photograph can produce beautifully artistic effects and, while the results may look complicated, it's relatively simple to achieve a strong finish. The principle behind it is mastering how to blend layers together by becoming accustomed with the various methods of doing so, as each one produces a different end result.

Textures aren't something that should be used recklessly: it's easy to allow them to overwhelm a perfectly good picture. Your choice of texture should work with the image to enhance its mood, colour and, ultimately, impact. However, picked carefully they can add character to an ordinary snapshot and improve a picture's appeal tenfold.

To truly understand how this technique works, the *Photoshop Fundamentals* section at the front of this MagBook explains in-depth how Layers, Layer Masks and Blend Modes work together. As an outline, though, when applying a texture, make sure it's on top of the image layer in the Layers palette for it to affect the image. You can then use the Opacity slider at the top of the Layers palette to control the transparency of the texture and/or apply a Blend Mode from the drop-down menu at the top of the Layers palette. In general, we've found that Multiply, Screen, Soft Light and Overlay work the best when merging layers. There are no rules for how many layers you should use, but the more you do apply, the more the original character of the image will be altered.

HOW TO USE

Layer Masks

A Layer Mask allows you to hide detail from the layer it's applied to, revealing the image beneath without erasing it. When the Layer Mask is selected, simply add the colour ***Black*** to the mask to hide image detail and change to the colour ***White*** to restore the detail. Use the ***X*** key to quickly switch between the colours.

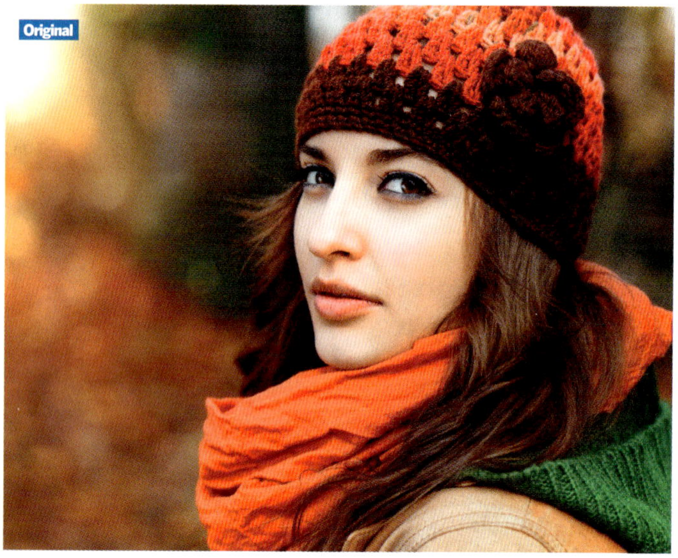

Original

ISTOCKPHOTO

HOT KEY

Changing Blend Modes

To quickly apply Blend Modes, hold down ***shift*** and press **+** and **–** keys to move up and down the list respectively. Or, for an even quicker way, press ***alt/ option+shift*** and the letter for that particular Blend Mode, eg ***O*** for Overlay or ***S*** for Soft Light.

Final image

Choosing textures that enhance the warm colours of the original image complement the image, creating a painterly effect.

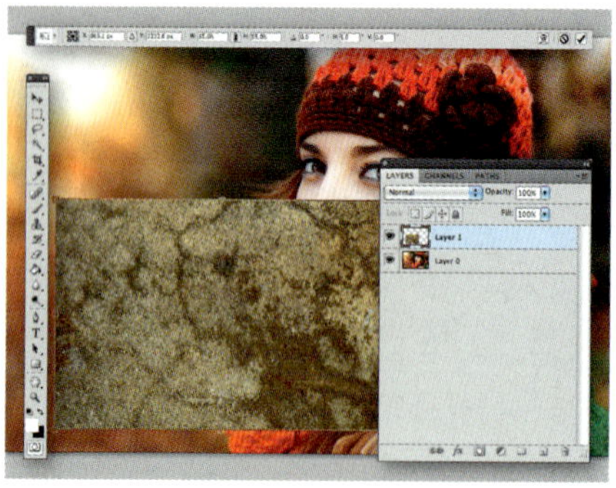

1 Open your image Duplicate your photograph (***Layer>Duplicate Layer***) and open your first textured layer. I've used a picture of sandstone as the colour complements the autumn tones and the cracks make good texture. Click on and drag the textured image layer on to the image layer using the ***Move Tool***.

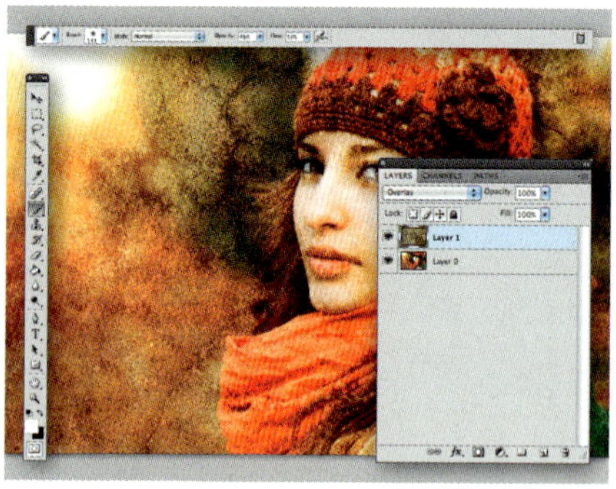

2 Transform the texture Go to ***Edit>Free Transform***, hold ***shift*** to constrain the proportions and drag a corner widget outwards to meet the sides of your image. Press the ***tick*** to commit to the adjustment. Change the texture layer's ***Blend Mode*** to merge it with the image layer. Here, Overlay was used to boost saturation.

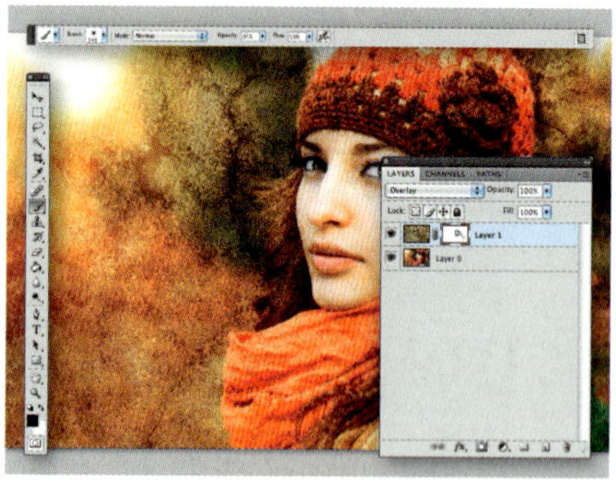

3 Add a Layer Mask As the texture flows over the face, it can start to obscure the features. Apply a Layer Mask to the texture layer by clicking on ***Create layer mask*** at the bottom of the Layers palette. Select the ***Brush Tool*** and set a soft-edge brush with a low ***Opacity***, then brush over the face using ***Black*** paint to reduce the texture.

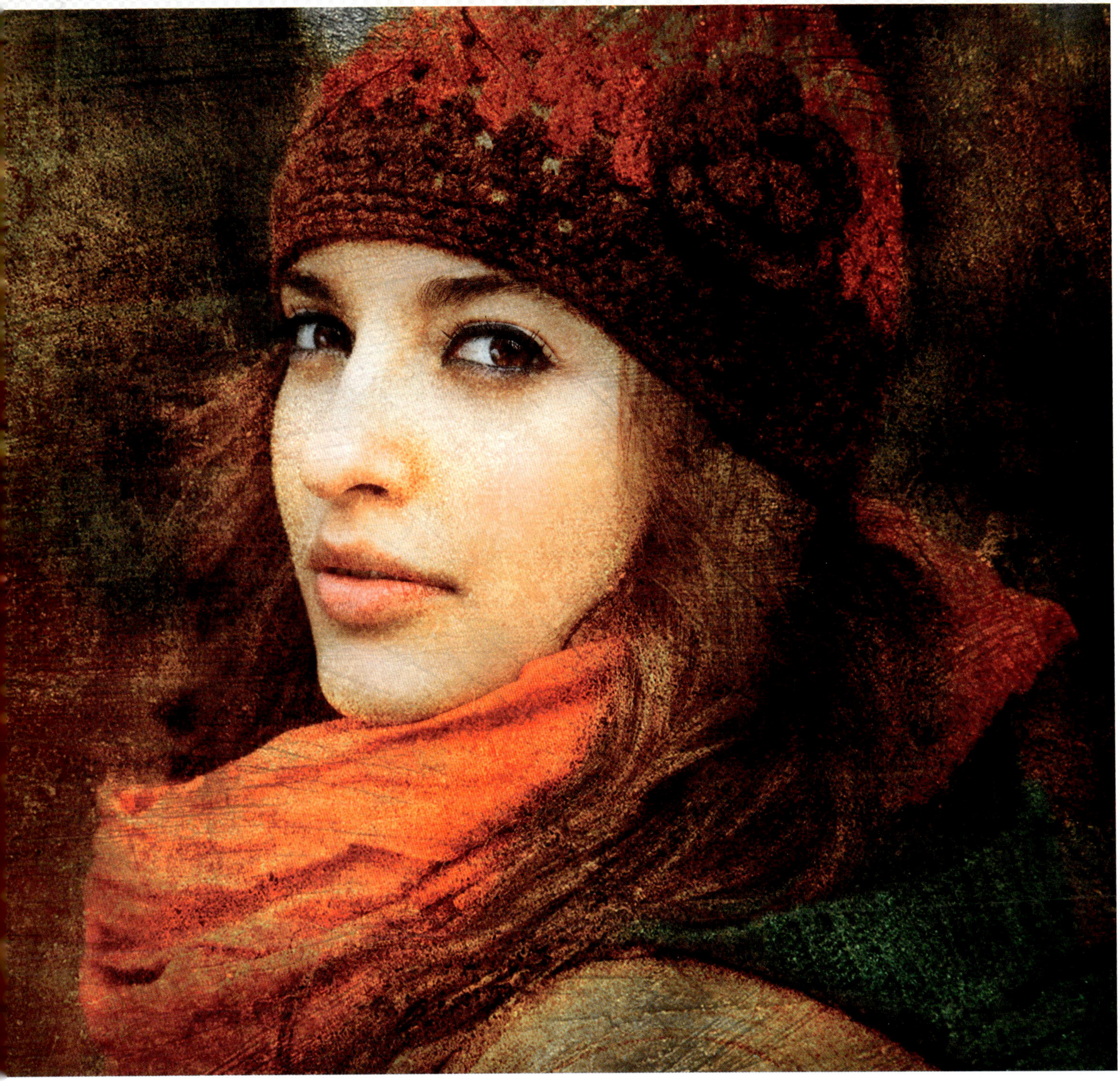

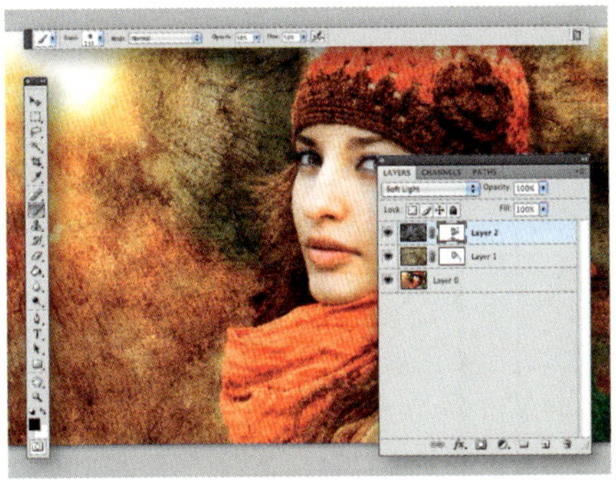

4 Add more texture Repeat steps one to three with another texture and try out the different Blend Modes to see their effects. Here, Multiply was used to emphasise the lines in the tree texture. If the resulting texture is still slightly too strong, try reducing the layer's ***Opacity*** using the slider at the top of the Layer's palette.

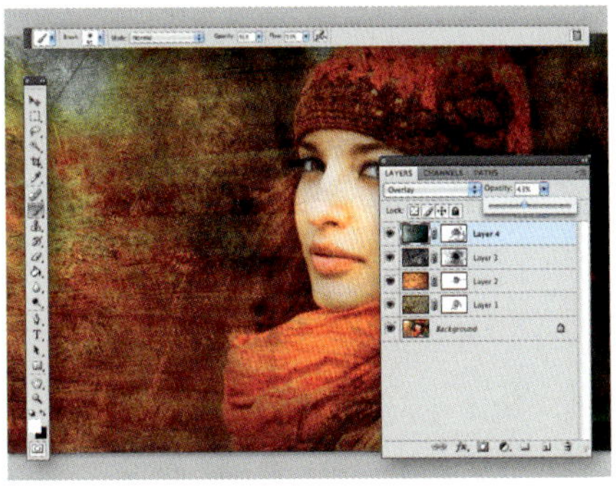

5 Repeat the steps There's no rule for what textures work and how many you should use; the key is trial and error and building up the effect gradually. Here, four textures are layered, each with different Blend Modes and varying opacity. Moving the layers in different positions within the Layers palette can also change the result.

Secrets unlocked

WHERE CAN I GET TEXTURES?

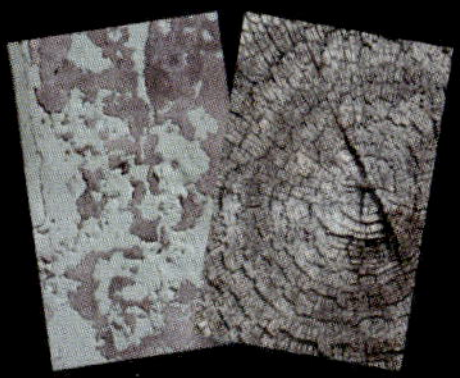

The easiest way to get texture images is to photograph them yourself: it's so easy to do and you can find them anywhere, be it a brick wall, granite table top, scrunched-up paper or flaky paint on a wall. Textures are everywhere. Your other option is to download them from the internet. Sites such as deviantart.com, textureking.com and amazingtextures.com are good sources, but a quick Google search will uncover hundreds of options.

Control your viewer's gaze by adding a vignette

Maximise the impact of your pictures by rounding off with this classic technique – a very simple trick to make your subject stand out…

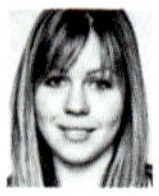

Caroline Wilkinson: How to take your images from good to great, quite frankly, could simply be a few tweaks in Photoshop. A test of a great picture is how well it contains your eye within the frame: the longer you can control the viewer's gaze, the more engaging the image. While composition plays a big part in this, adding a vignette can help, too. Essentially, the technique is to gradually reduce the image's brightness from the centre (focal point), fading off toward the edges, creating a border around the subject and drawing the eye towards the point of interest.

While some photographers do whatever they can to avoid lens vignetting, if the effect is controlled for creative effect and used on an appropriate picture – like this one where the focal point is central in the frame – it can have massive impact. It can be as subtle or as strong as you like, but some of the most appealing vignettes have a very soft graduation and edges that blend with the image for a natural finish.

Anyone that worked in the darkroom will know that vignetting is not a digital technique – in fact, it's been around since the dawn of photography – though there are now countless methods of creating one, each with differing effects. For now, try this modern version of the darkroom classic – you'll be surprised at what a difference it makes.

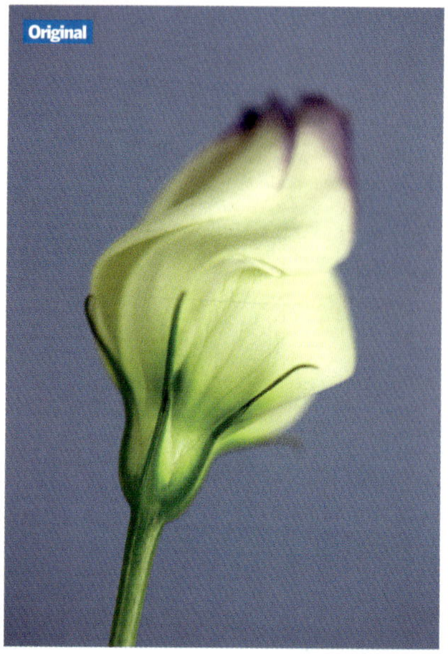

HELEN DIXON

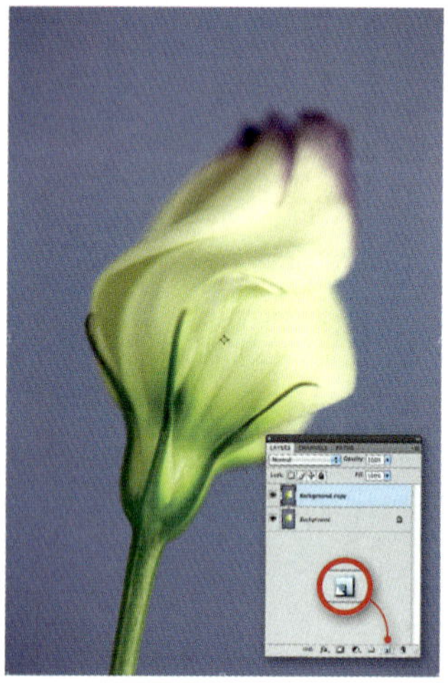

1 Create a copy Make any adjustments you need to before finishing the image with a vignette. First, copy the image by going to ***Layer>Duplicate Layer*** or drag the ***Background Layer*** down to the ***Create a new layer*** icon at the bottom of the Layers palette.

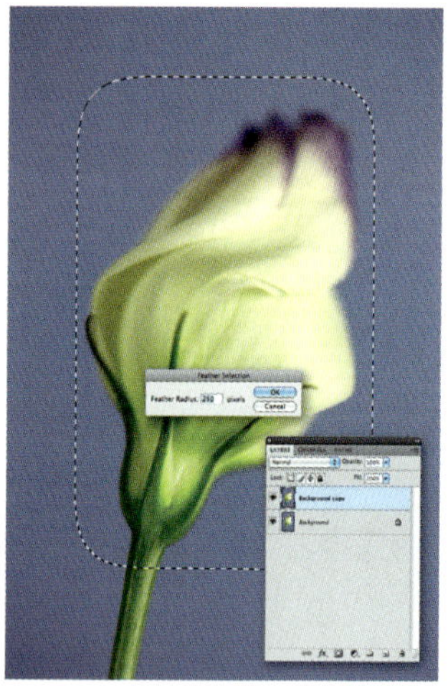

2 Draw your vignette Select the ***Rectangular Marquee Tool*** and click and drag the marquee over the area you want to frame, or, in other words, your focal point. To soften the edge of the vignette, go to ***Select>Modify>Feather*** and type in ***250px***, then click ***OK***.

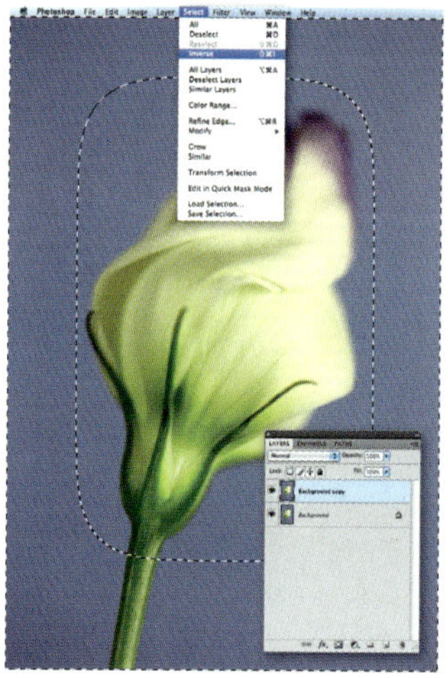

3 Invert the selection At the moment, any adjustments you make will affect the area within the marquee selection, which is not what you want. To target the area outside of the marquee, creating a frame around your focal point, go to ***Select>Inverse***.

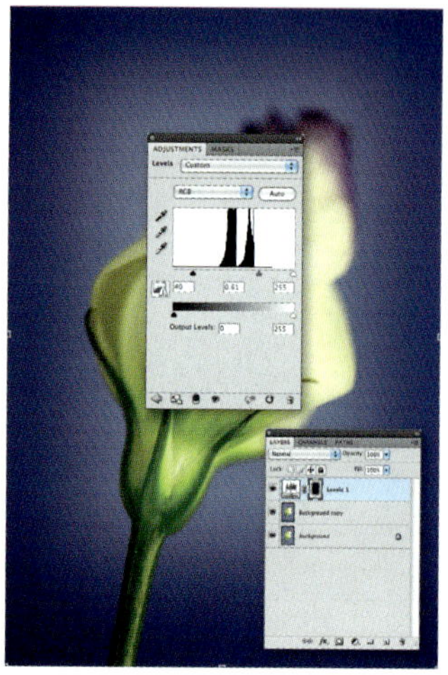

4 Darken the edges Add a Levels adjustment layer (***Layer>New Adjustment Layer>Levels***) and slowly drag the black and grey triangle sliders to the right to darken the corners until you reach your desired effect. Once you're done, go to ***Select>Deselect***.

Blend Modes

Try changing the Blend Mode of your Levels adjustment layer for different results. Click on the ***Levels*** adjustment layer in the Layers palette and select the ***Blend Mode*** drop-down menu at the top of the Layers palette. Experiment with the different modes and try reducing the strength of the effect by reducing the ***Opacity*** slider for the Levels layer. Here are three of our favourite Blend Modes…

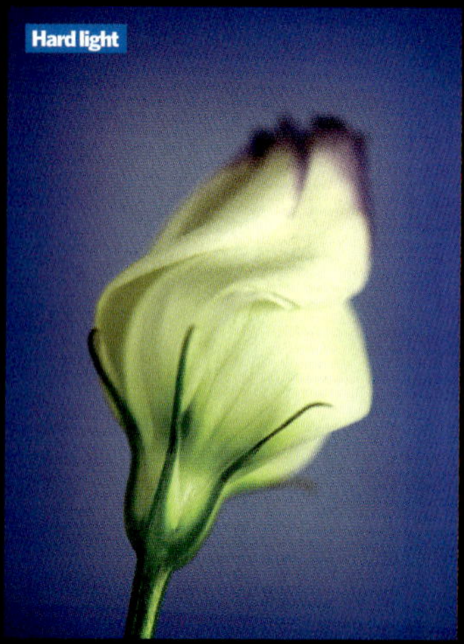

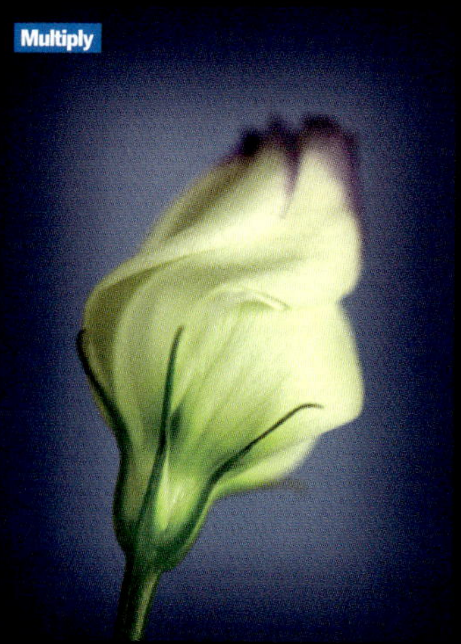

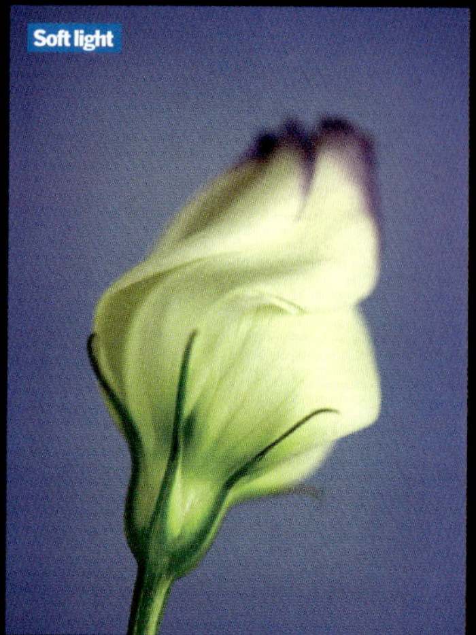

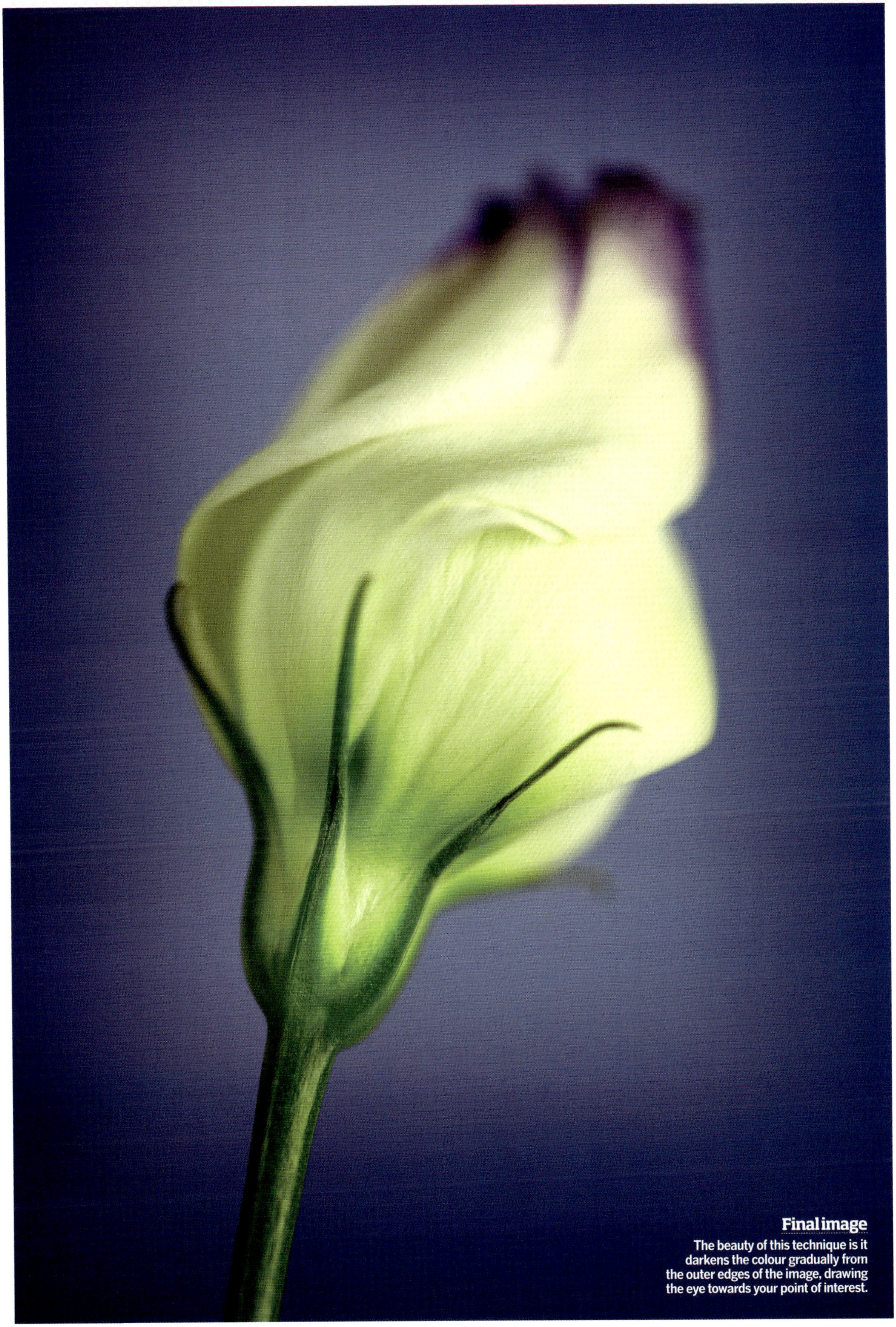

Final image

The beauty of this technique is it darkens the colour gradually from the outer edges of the image, drawing the eye towards your point of interest.

Create a photo mosaic

Photo mosaics are often time-consuming to put together, but five minutes is all you need when you follow our simple guide…

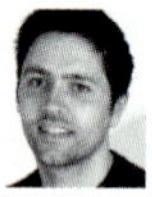

Jordan Butters: A mosaic is an image made up of lots of smaller images. A true mosaic image is created by matching the colours of hundreds or thousands of smaller pictures to the tones of the final image. It's a complicated process that requires you to possess a huge library of pictures to pull from. Thanks to Photoshop's Blend Modes, however, creating a mosaic effect couldn't be easier and you only need a small selection of images to choose from. You can apply this effect using just a single image, but the effect tends to look more pleasing the more you use. You might find it easier if you put them all in one folder to keep everything organised.

Secrets unlocked

✓ MOSAIC SOFTWARE

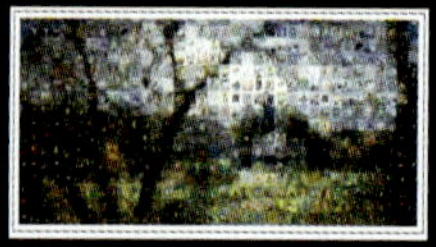

There are various standalone photo mosaic software options available online – ideal if you are planning on putting mosaics together regularly. Two popular software packages are Mosaic Creator and AndreaMosaic. Mosaic Creator is available as a 30-day trial with the full version starting from around £20. Visit www.aolej.com to download.

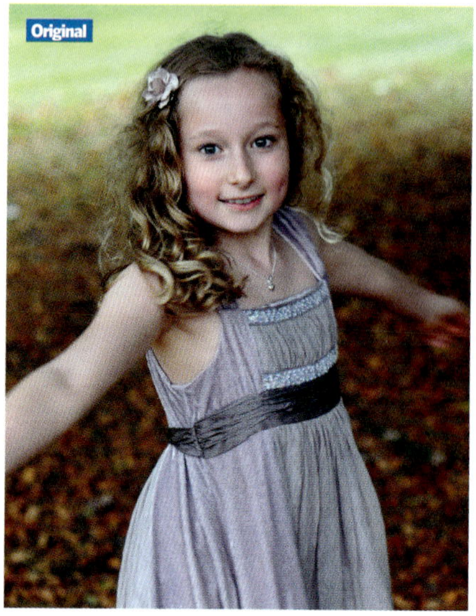

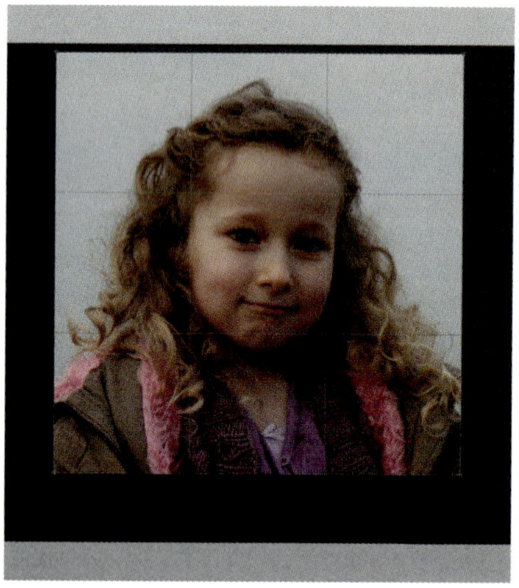

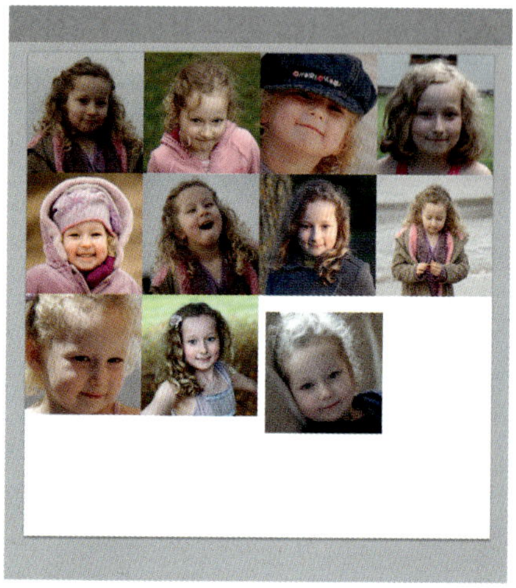

1 Crop your images First make each of your mosaic images the same size. Open your first image and select the ***Crop Tool***. In the top toolbar, enter a value of ***250px*** in both the ***Width*** and the ***Height***. Click and drag to select the area that you wish to include. Press the ***Enter*** key or the ***tick*** in the top toolbar to commit to the crop.

2 Paste in your images Go to ***Select>All*** and ***Edit>Copy***. Go to ***File>New*** to create a blank document. Set both the ***Width*** and ***Height*** to ***1,000*** pixels and click ***OK***. In the ***View*** menu, ensure ***Snap*** is turned on, then click on ***Edit>Paste*** to paste in your image. Using the ***Move Tool***, lock the image in the top-left corner.

3 Repeat and arrange Repeat the first two steps for each of your images, cropping, resizing and copying before pasting them into the new document. Use the ***Move Tool*** to lock each image into place alongside the previous image. If you have any gaps you may need to duplicate some images to fill the page.

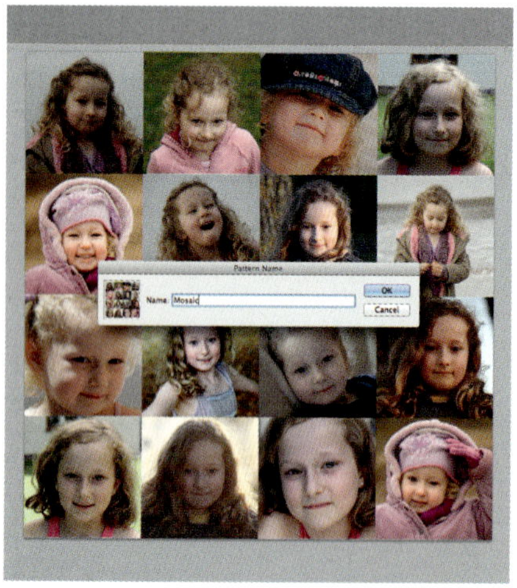

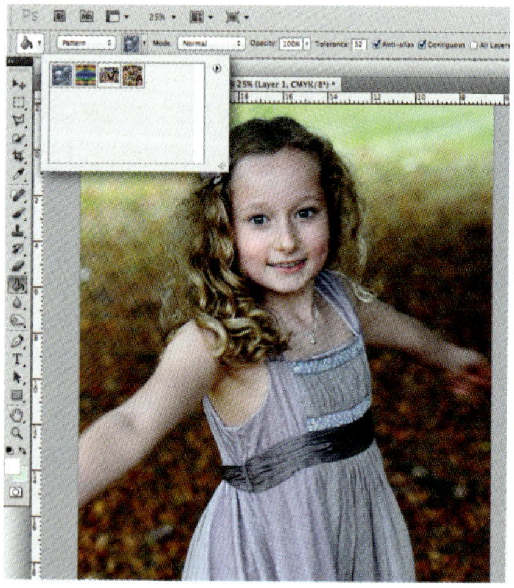

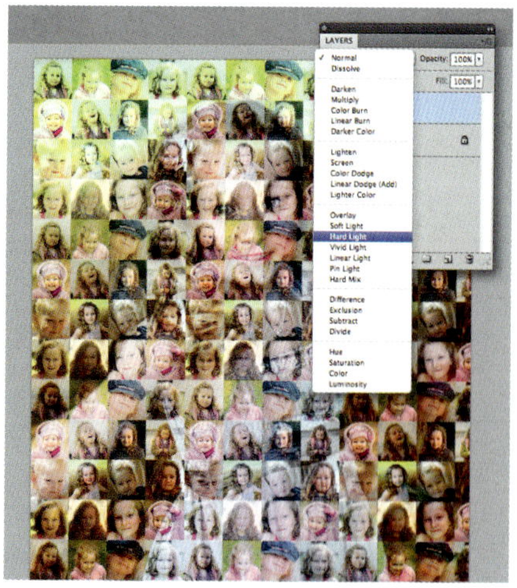

4 Create a pattern Once complete, go to ***Layer>Flatten Image*** to combine all of your images in to a single layer. Go to ***Edit>Define Pattern***, name your pattern 'Mosaic' and click ***OK***. Your pattern is now saved for future use. Close your image without saving and open the file that you wish to use as your final image.

5 Insert your pattern Click on the ***Create new layer*** button in the Layers palette. Select the ***Paint Bucket Tool*** and in the top toolbar click on the ***Foreground*** menu and select ***Pattern***. Click on the thumbnail to the right and select your new ***Mosaic*** pattern. Insert the pattern onto the image by clicking anywhere on the picture.

6 Change the Blend Mode In the Layers palette, change the ***Blend Mode*** to ***Hard Light***. Use the ***Opacity*** slider to reduce the opacity of the mosaic layer. The final opacity depends on how clear you want the original image to show through – I found around 60% was the perfect amount for this image.

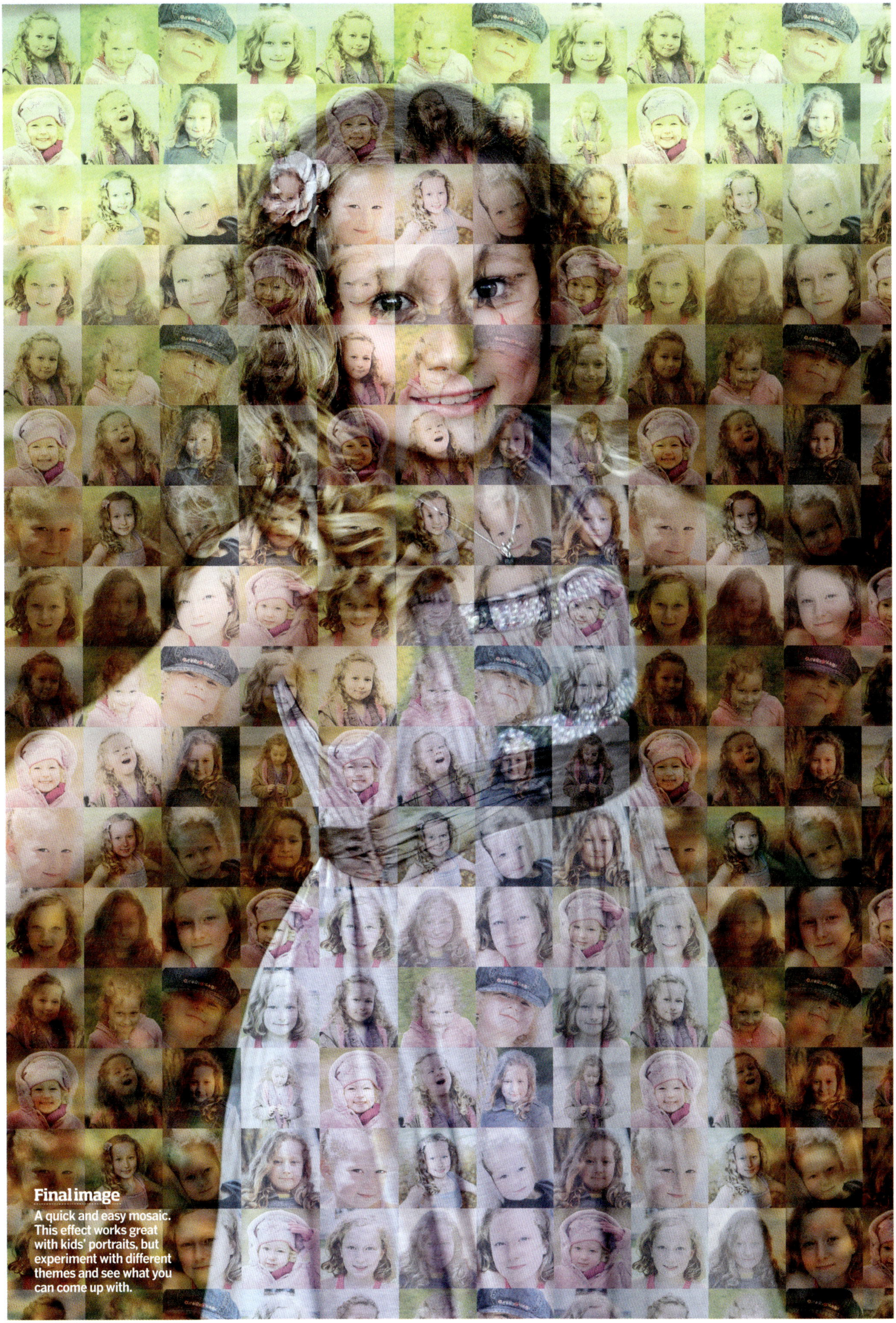

Final image

A quick and easy mosaic. This effect works great with kids' portraits, but experiment with different themes and see what you can come up with.

Create sepia images

Give your images a nostalgic twist with this easy way to sepia tone

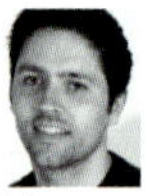

Jordan Butters: Sepia toning has been around since the early days of film photography. Its original purpose being to prolong the lifespan of the print, as images that weren't treated with sepia tended to fade and degrade more quickly.

Today, sepia toning is still one of the most popular and long-standing photographic effects. Now used for purely aesthetic rather than archival reasons, sepia toning can add a romantic bygone feel to an image. It has power to add drama and atmosphere in much the same way as black & white photography, while retaining a warmth rarely present in the cold tones of a greyscale image.

For this reason, sepia is suited to portrait and wedding photography. There are several ways to sepia tone images and each gives slightly different results. Sepia has no defined shade or hue as it is simply a warm brown tint applied to a mono image, so look to create your own favourite shades.

I've added a twist in the final two steps by reintroducing a little of the original colour – if you prefer a traditional sepia image, save your work after the fourth step.

Secrets unlocked

✔ SEPIA IN LIGHTROOM

Thanks to the various presets available in Adobe Lightroom, users can also apply this effect in a few easy steps. Load your image into the ***Develop*** module, click on the ***Presets tab*** on the left-hand side and then, under ***B&W Toned Presets***, select ***Sepia Tone***. To bring a hint of colour back, click on ***Treatment: Color*** at the top of the ***Basic*** tab and drag the ***Saturation*** slider down until you reach the desired effect. You can also adjust the ***Vibrance*** slider to affect how much colour shows through. Have a play until you find a result you like.

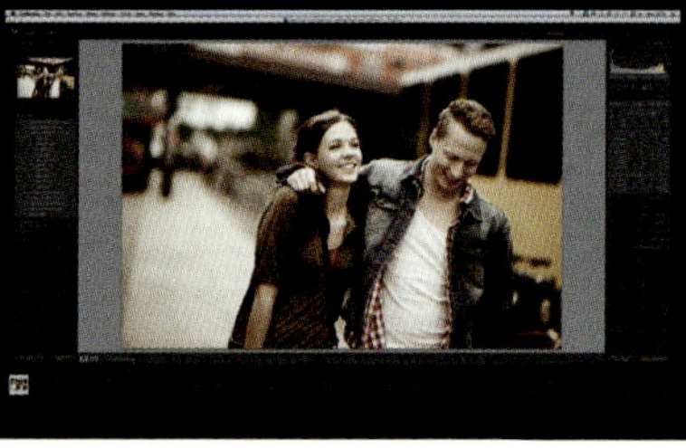

Final image

A sepia tint with a hint of colour suits this romantic shot perfectly.

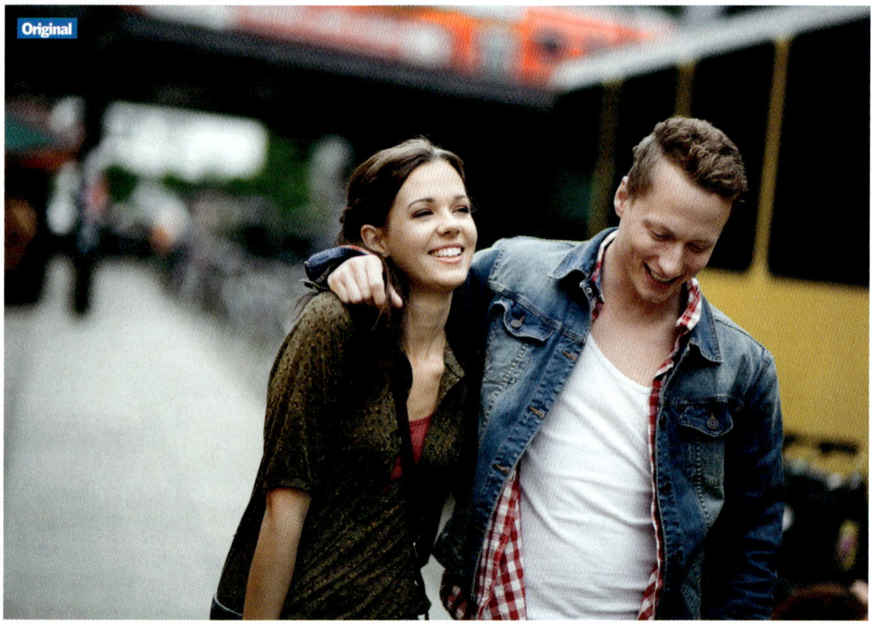

Original

ISTOCK PHOTO

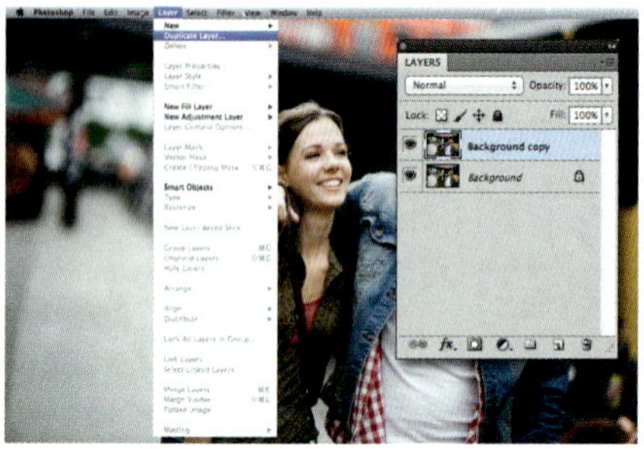

1 Create a duplicate Work nondestructively by opening your image and clicking on ***Layer>Duplicate Layer*** to create a copy of your main image layer. In doing so, if you make a mistake or want to start over, your original image remains intact.

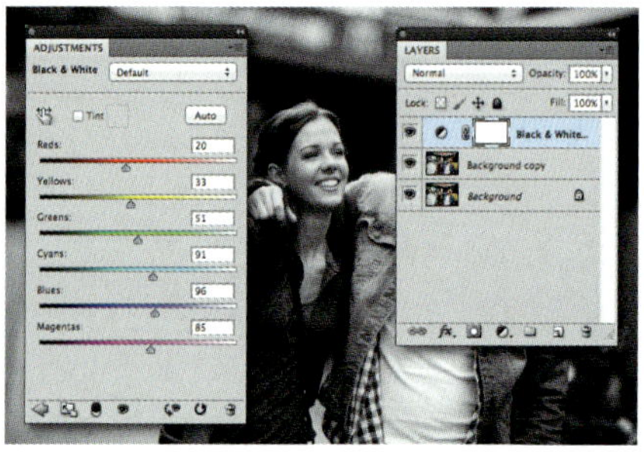

2 Convert to monochrome In the Layers palette, click on the ***Create new fill or adjustment layer*** button and select ***Black & White***. In the Adjustments palette, tweak the respective colour sliders to tune the effect and suit your image.

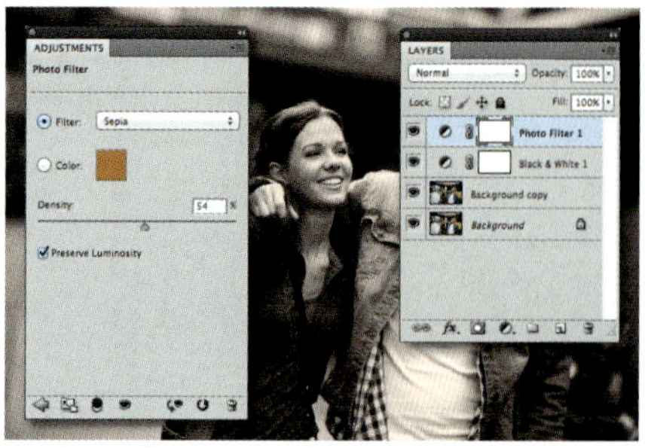

3 Add the sepia Create another Adjustment Layer, this time selecting ***Photo Filter***. In the Adjustment palette make sure that ***Preserve Luminosity*** is checked and select the ***Sepia*** filter. Use the ***Density*** slider to adjust the effect's strength; I chose 55%.

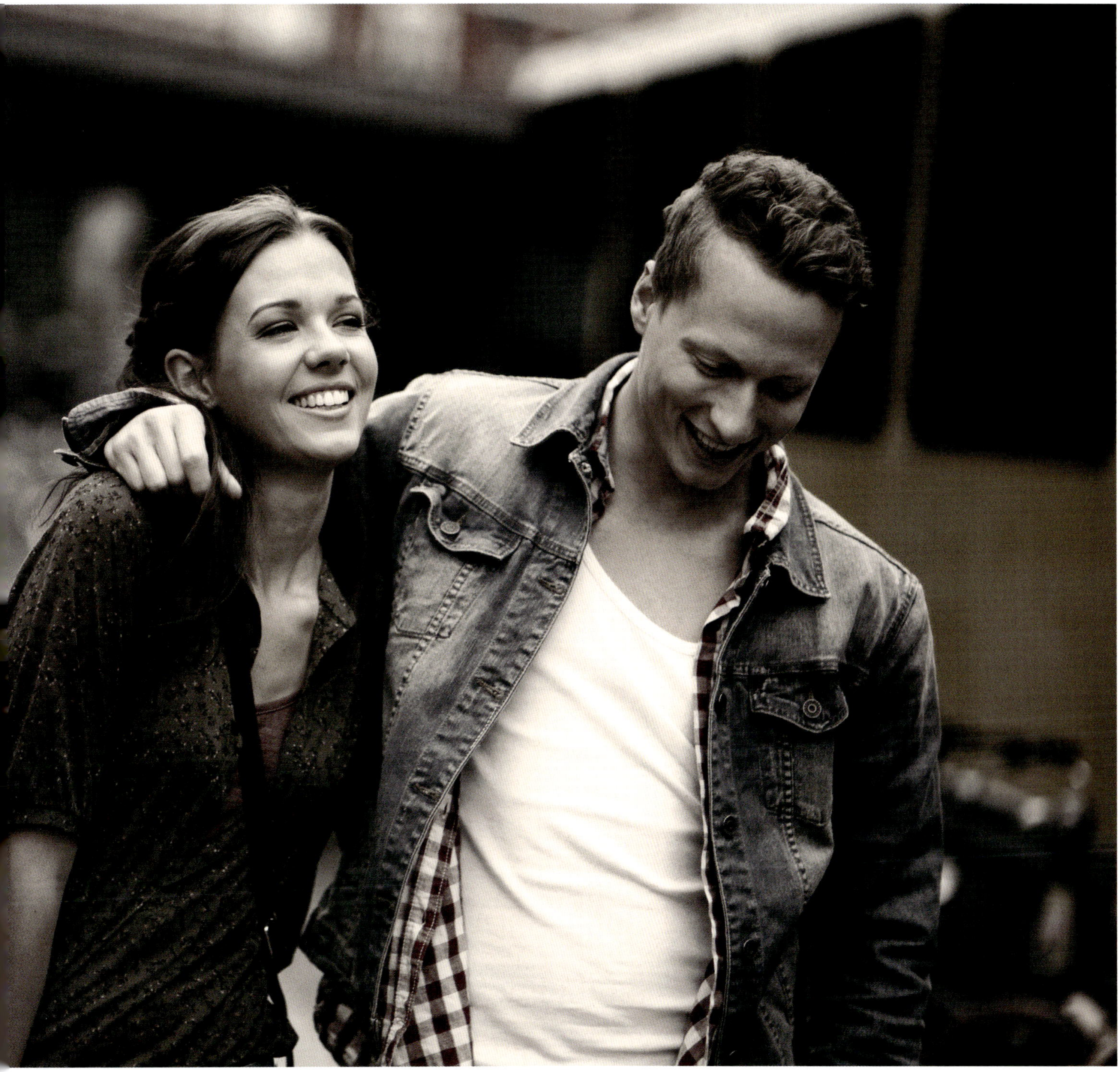

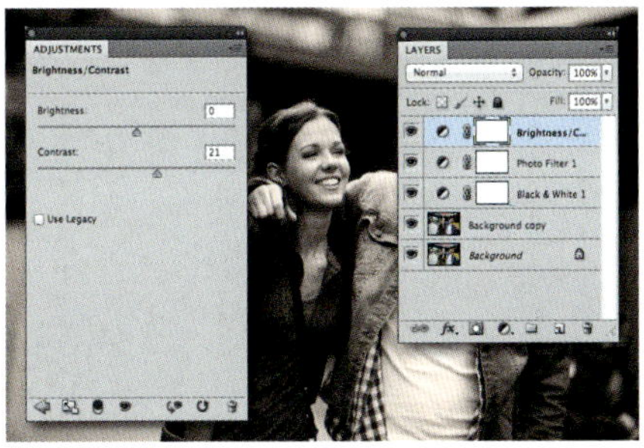

4 Boost contrast Create another Adjustment Layer and select ***Brightness/Contrast***. Use the sliders to fine-tune the contrast of your image. You can either stop here and save your image or continue to bring back a hint of colour to your image with the following two steps.

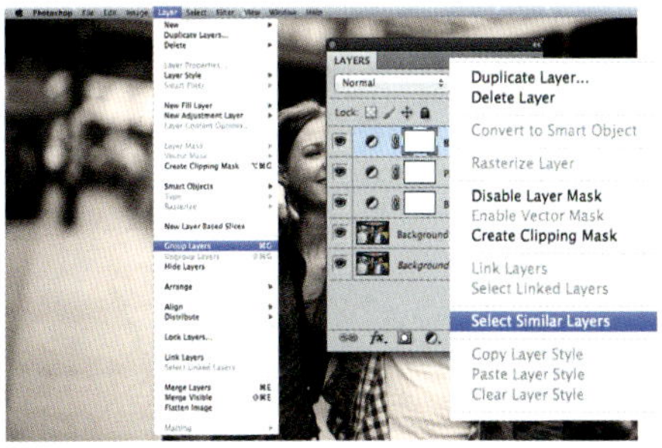

5 Group the layers Group your Adjustment Layers together by right-clicking on one of your Adjustment Layers in the Layers palette and choosing ***Select similar layers***. Then go to ***Layer>Group Layers*** to put them into a Group folder.

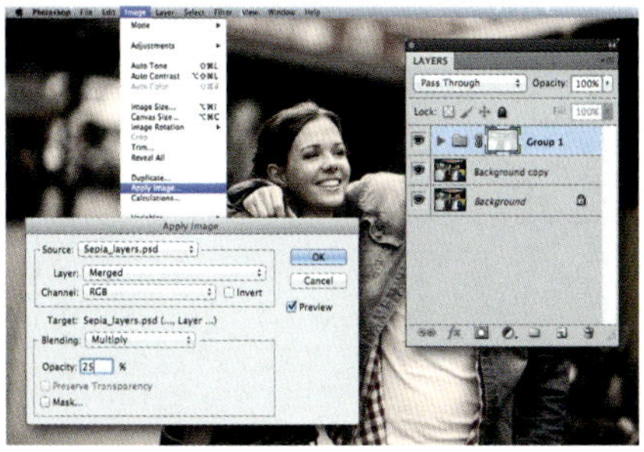

6 Bring back some colour Click on the ***Add layer mask*** button before going to ***Image>Apply Image***. In the dialogue box that appears, you can check or uncheck the ***Invert*** box to alter the effect as well as change the ***Blend Mode*** and ***Opacity***.

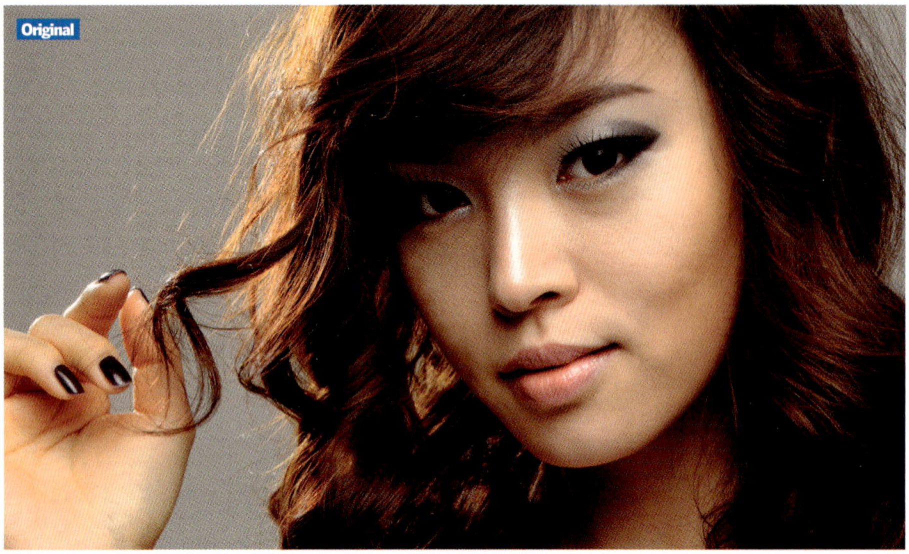

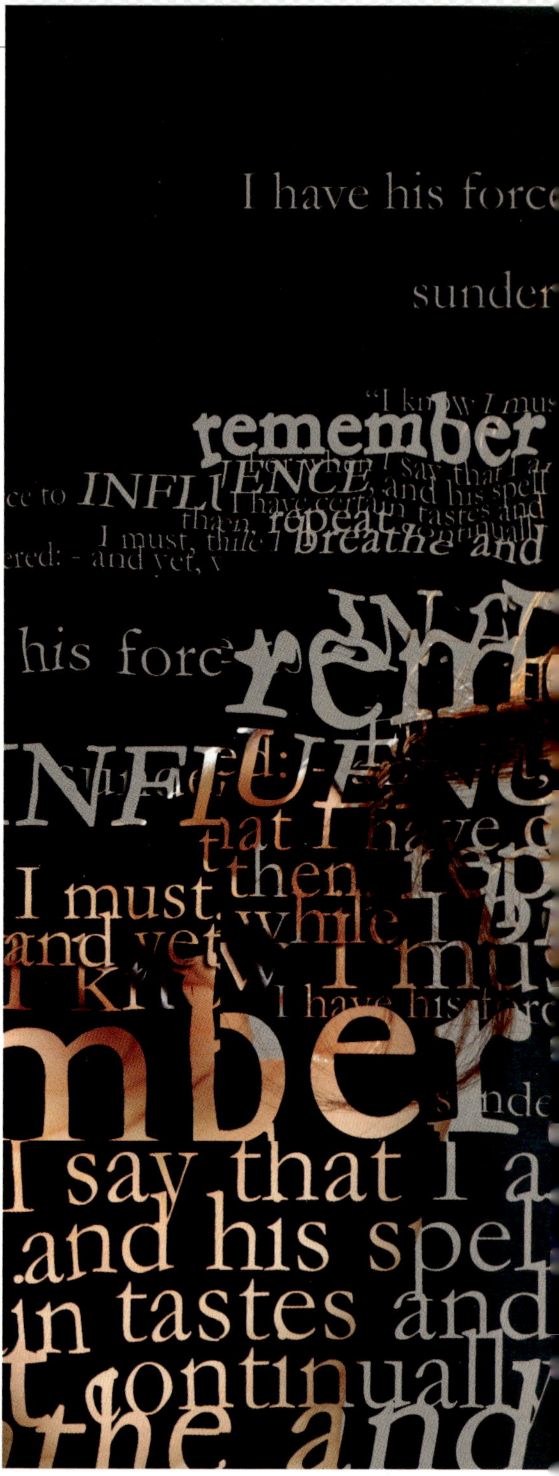

Create a typography portrait

Combine photography and typography to create a stylish and unusual abstract portrait which also incorporates a message about your subject

Jordan Butters: An important part of portrait photography is communicating your subject's attitude, ethos or style. This can be done via their clothes, surroundings, or simply their look or pose. Using Photoshop's Type Tool you can further communicate this message by overlaying your image with a stylish verse. The words you choose can be a few lines describing your subject's outlook, a poem or song, or verse from a book that has influenced them. Find out how below…

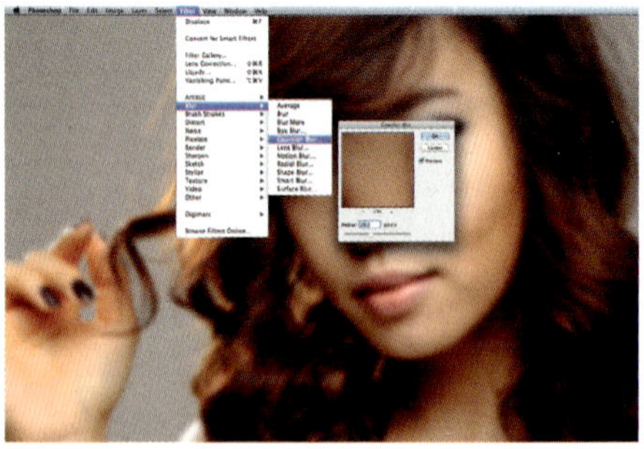

1 Save as a .psd file Open your image and go to ***Filter>Blur>Gaussian Blur***. Select a ***Radius*** of ***10.0 pixels*** and click ***OK***. Save your file by going to ***File>Save As*** and in the box set the ***Format*** to ***Photoshop***. Choose an easy-to-find location for the file and click ***OK***. Close this file and reopen your original image.

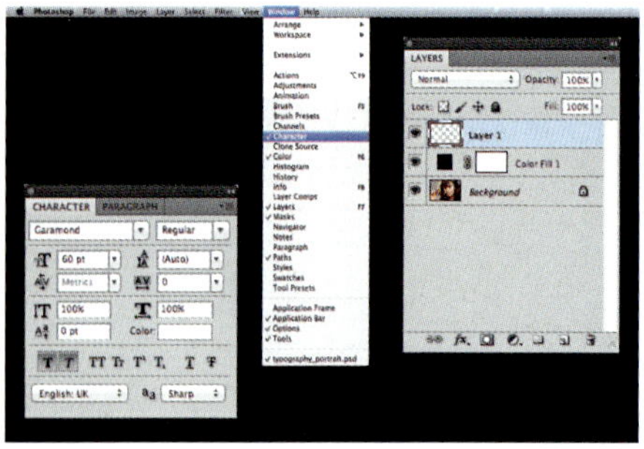

2 Create a blank layer Go to ***Layer>New Fill Layer>Solid Color*** and click ***OK***. Select the colour as ***Black*** and press ***OK*** again. Next, add a new layer with ***Layer>New>Layer*** and select the ***Horizontal Type Tool***. Go to ***Window>Character*** to show the Character palette. Pick your ***Font Style*** and ***Size*** and set the text colour to ***White***.

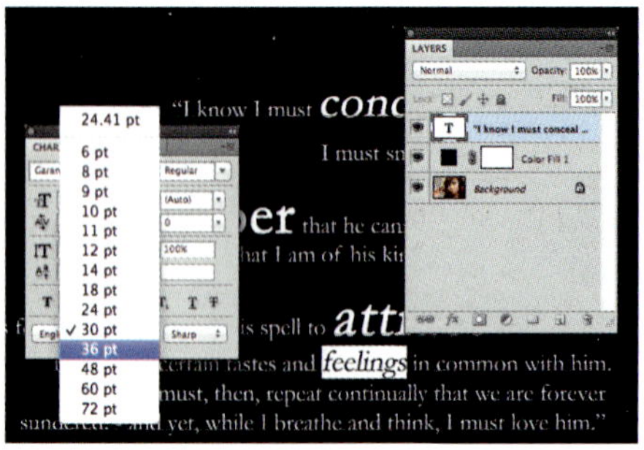

3 Add the text Click on the image and type in your text. Alternatively, you can copy and paste in a body of text from elsewhere. Click and drag over key words to highlight them, then use ***Font Size, Faux Bold*** and ***Faux Italics*** in the Character palette to stylise the words. Alter the size and style from word to word for variety.

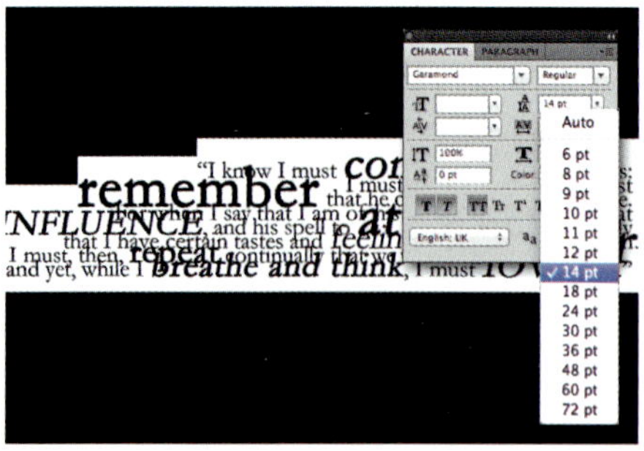

4 Overlap the text Highlight all of the text and reduce the ***Leading*** via the Character palette until the letters overlap. Click on the ***tick*** in the top menu bar to confirm. Right-click on your text layer in the Layers palette and select ***Blending Options***. Select ***Drop Shadow*** and click ***OK***, then go to ***Layer>Duplicate Layer***.

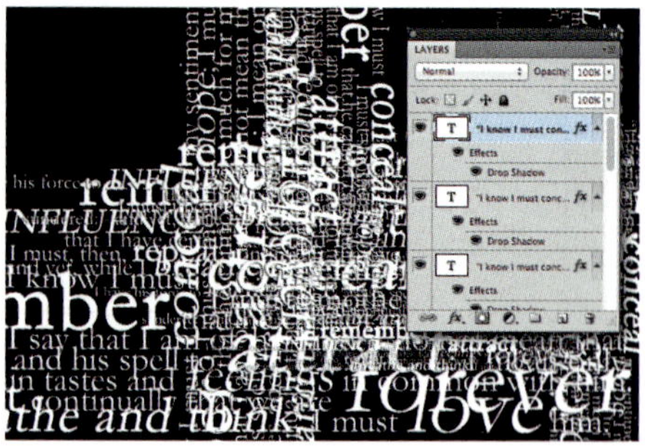

5 Duplicate the text To fill the portrait with text, use ***Edit>Free Transform*** to rotate and scale your text. Duplicate this layer again, as before, and rotate and scale this new layer. Position each layer to reduce any gaps. Repeat until the majority of your image is filled with text at seemingly random angles and sizes.

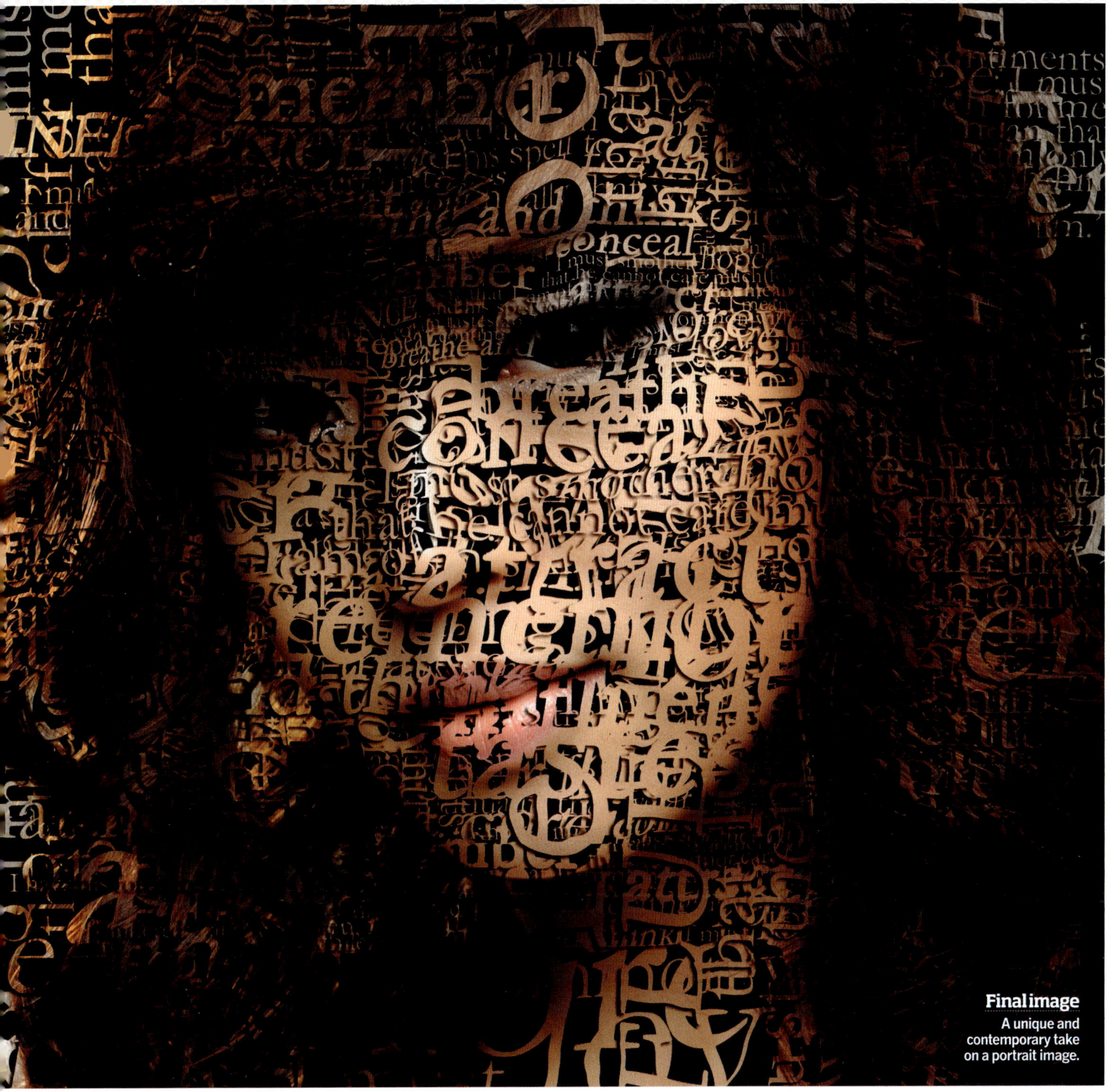

Final image

A unique and contemporary take on a portrait image.

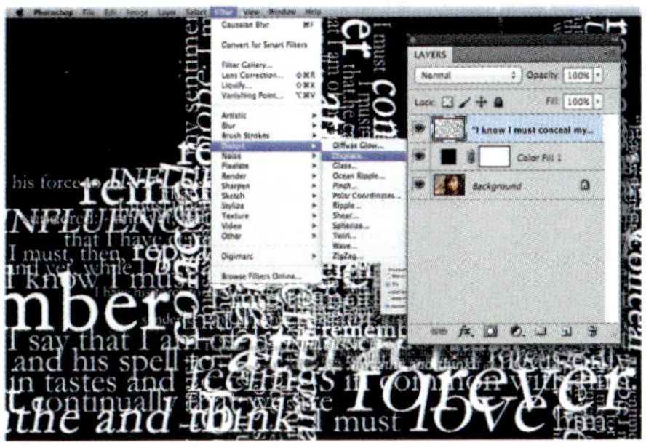

6 Distort the text To select all of the text layers in the Layers palette, hold down ***cmd*** (Mac) or ***ctrl*** (PC) and click on each of the layers. Then go to ***Layer>Merge Layers***. Go to ***Filter>Distort>Displace*** and set both ***Vertical*** and ***Horizontal Scales*** to ***15***, ***Displacement Map*** to ***Tile*** and ***Undefined Areas*** to ***Repeat Edge Pixels***.

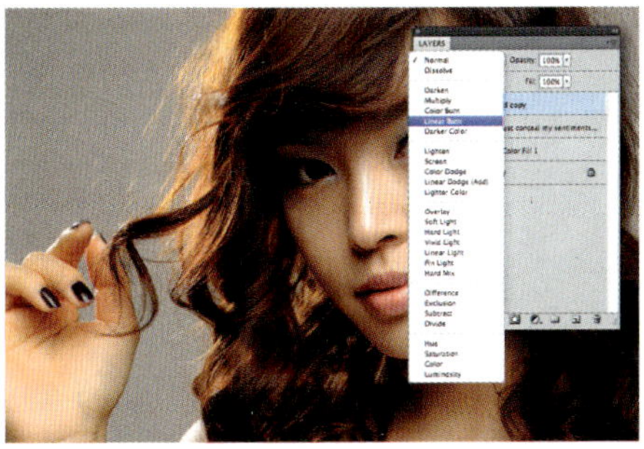

7 Add the portrait Click ***OK*** and, in the window that appears, find and select the Photoshop file that you saved earlier and click ***OK*** again. Select your ***Background layer*** in the Layers palette and go to ***Layer>Duplicate Layer*** – drag this new layer to the top of the other layers and change its ***Blend Mode*** to ***Linear Burn***.

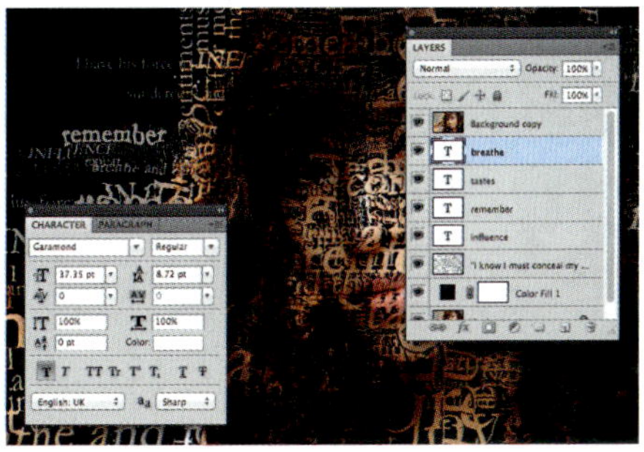

8 Tweak the text to suit The text should be showing through the image now. If there are any large or distracting gaps in the text, simply click on the text layer in the Layers palette and use the ***Horizontal Type Tool*** to add some extra words or lines of text wherever required to fill the gaps. Once you are done, save your image.

Quick guide to colour swapping

Replacing one colour for another is a useful trick that can completely transform an image. Here's your simple guide to colour swapping…

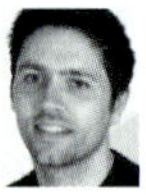

Jordan Butters: Capturing an aesthetically pleasing range of colours and hues is an essential part of colour photography, and Adobe Photoshop and Elements presents you with an array of tools to adjust, correct and replace colours to suit your needs. There are several scenarios whereby you may want to replace the colour of one element of an image with an alternative hue; there might be a distracting item in the background of your image that you want to tone down, or you may want to change an item of clothing or object to a more pleasing colour. You can even use it to give a vehicle a new paint job without the hassle of actually having it resprayed. Yellow London buses, green skies, pink elephants or purple grass: only your imagination is the limit.

One of the easiest methods is using the Replace Color Tool. This allows you to specify the colour that you wish to replace using the Eyedropper Tool, adjust the tolerance of this selection to encompass the full range of hues and shades, and choose the colour you want to replace it with all within a single dialogue box before committing to the changes.

It's worth noting that the tool isn't foolproof; the colour you replace needs to be of a similar lightness and saturation to the colour you introduce. For example, if you are trying to swap a bright yellow for a dark red, you may notice that the end result isn't as realistic as you might have hoped. The good thing is that the changes aren't applied until you click OK, so you can tweak the various parameters until you are happy with the final result.

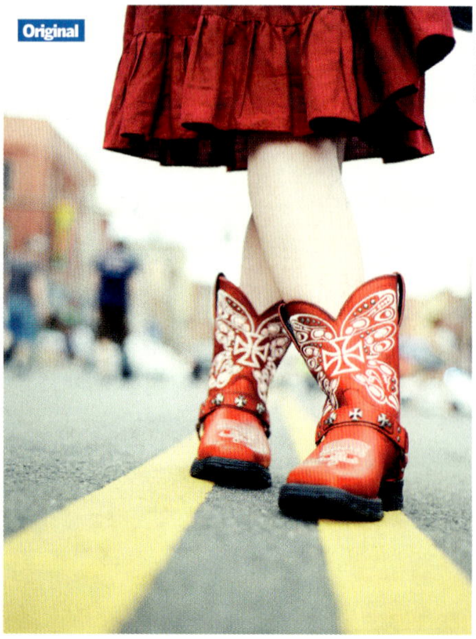

ISTOCK PHOTO

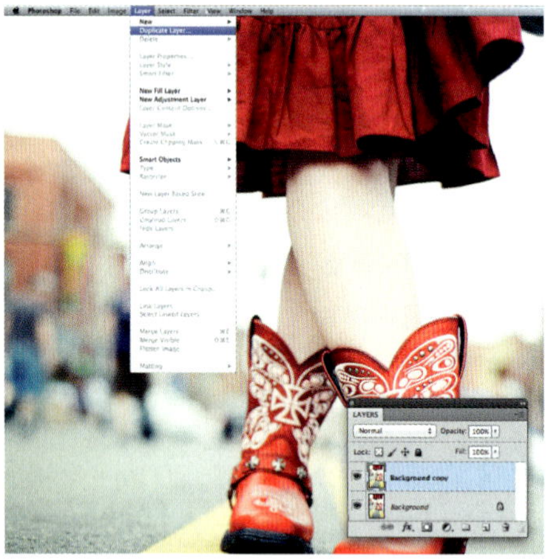

1 Prepare your image Before beginning to edit, it's good practice to create a duplicate layer so any work you do is nondestructive. Doing this will also help when tidying the image in the later stages of the process. Go to ***Layer>Duplicate Layer*** and make sure that this new layer is selected in the Layers palette.

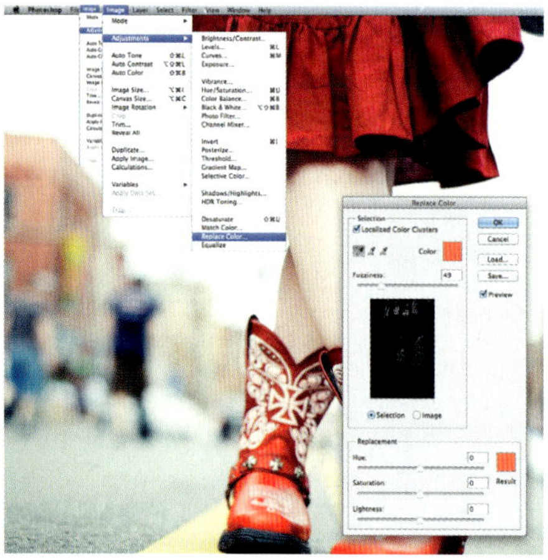

2 Pick your colour Go to ***Image>Adjustments>Replace Color*** to bring up the Replace Color dialogue box. Check the ***Localized Color Clusters*** box. The Eyedropper Tool will be selected, so simply click on the colour in your image that you wish to replace; this will highlight the area in white in the thumbnail preview.

Useful tools

As an alternative to the Replace Color menu, you can use the Color Replacement Tool. Click and hold on the ***Brush Tool*** to reveal the ***Color Replacement Tool***. Set your ***Foreground Color*** to the colour you want to introduce and brush over the area of colour you wish to replace. The small crosshair in the centre of your brush is the area the tool will sample from, so keep this within the colour you are replacing. You can use the top menu bar to adjust how the tool works, including the brush ***Size*** and ***Shape***, how often it samples the area and the tolerance of the sample colour.

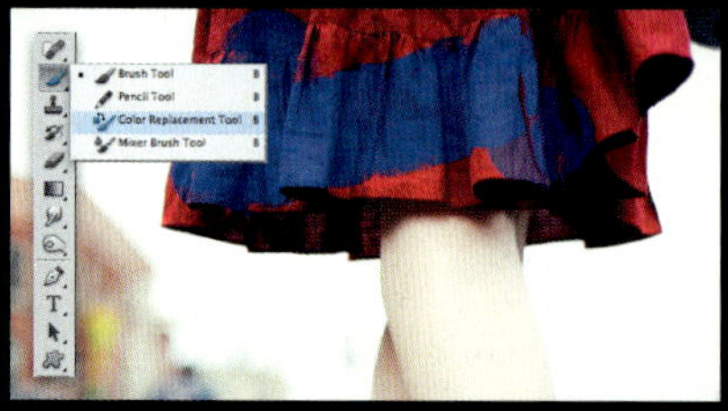

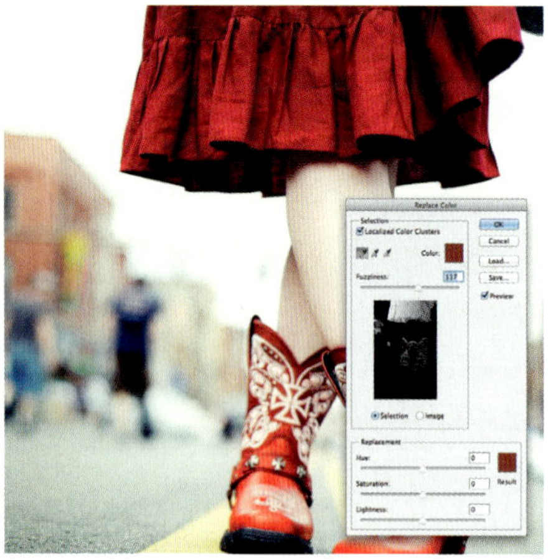

3 Adjust the range Hold down the ***shift*** key and click on the image to add further shades of the colour to the selection. If you happen to select an area by mistake, holding down the ***alt*** key and clicking on that area will remove it from the selection. Use the ***Fuzziness*** slider to adjust the edges of the selection.

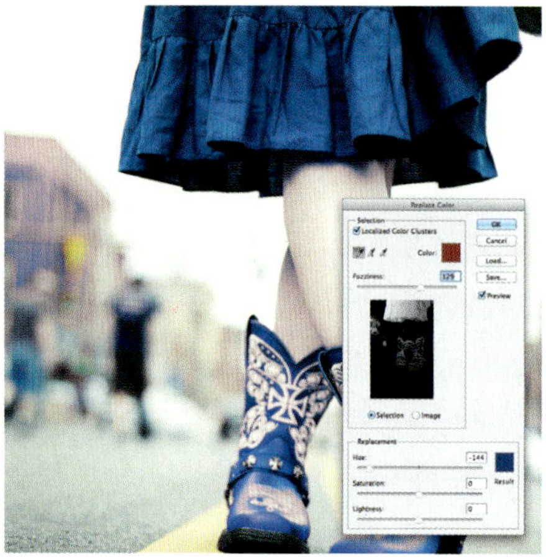

4 Swap the colour Use the ***Replacement Hue*** slider to introduce your new colour. You can then use the ***Saturation*** and ***Lightness*** sliders to tweak the colour's intensity and shade. You may need to readjust the ***Fuzziness*** slider to adjust the effect. Click ***OK*** once you're happy with the replacement colour.

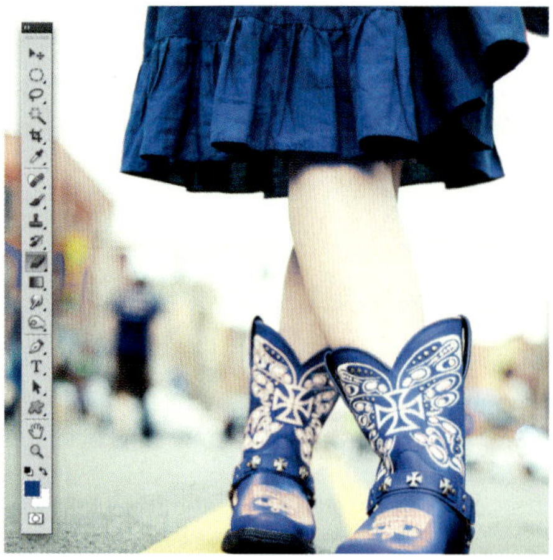

5 Tweak the results Depending on your image, you may find that some other elements within your shot have changed colour without you wanting them to. Select the ***Eraser Tool***, adjust your brush ***Size*** and ***Hardness*** in the top menu bar and brush over these areas, which will return them to their original colour.

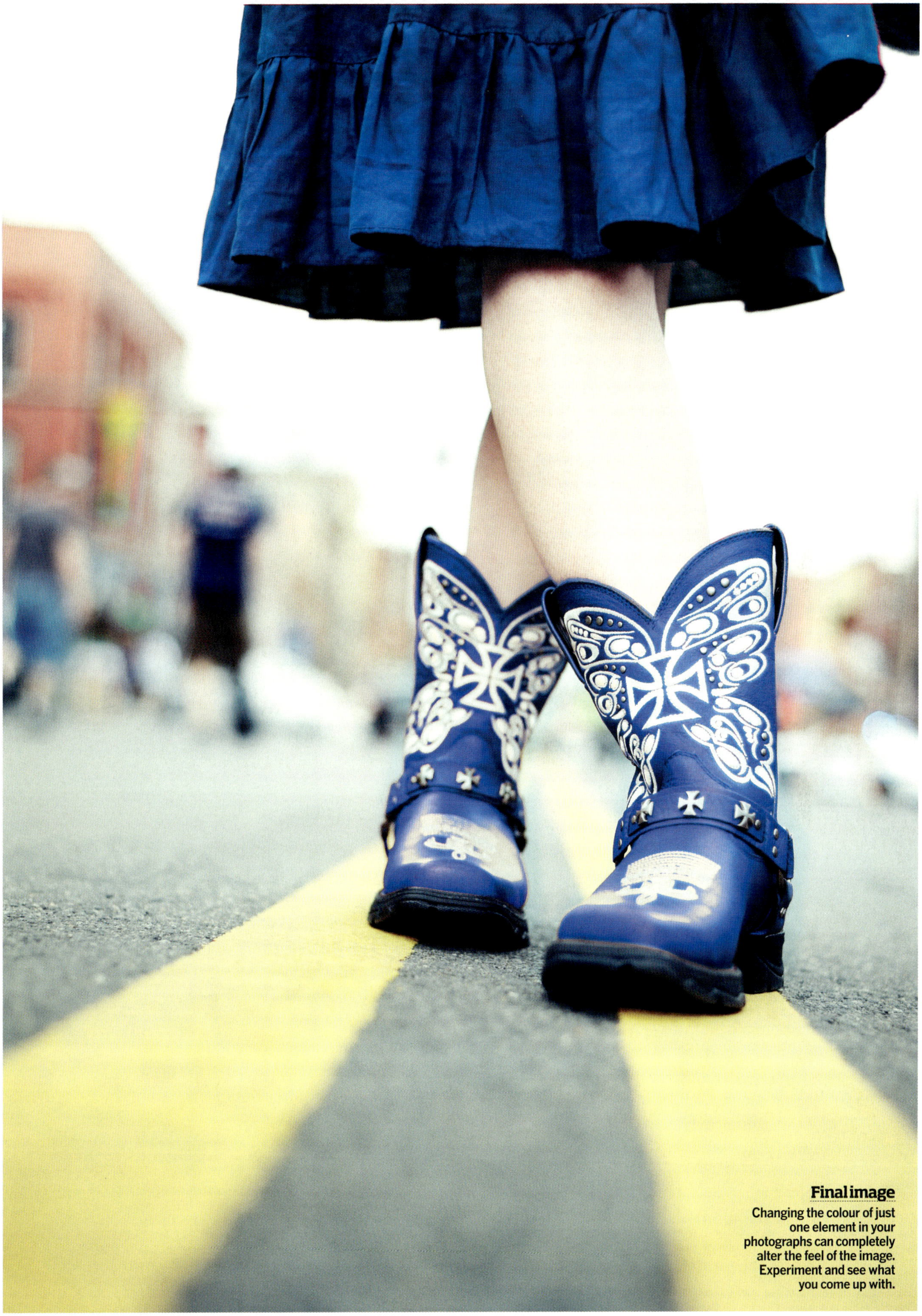

Final image

Changing the colour of just one element in your photographs can completely alter the feel of the image. Experiment and see what you come up with.

Retro toy camera

Vintage effects are all the rage in photography at the moment: follow our guide to apply a retro toy camera treatment to your images

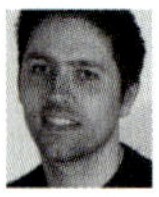

Jordan Butters: In the past few years, retro photography has taken off in a big way. For many, shooting with film has a nostalgic romance attached to it and so people are seeking to emulate the film look in their digital images. There are apps available for smartphones, such as the popular Hipstamatic and Instagram, which allow you to quickly and easily apply any number of filters to your camera phone snaps – however, as expected, shots from your digital SLR require a little more effort in Photoshop. The benefits of shooting on your DSLR are a higher image quality and more control over both the shot you take and the processing you apply afterwards.

The term 'toy camera' refers to a film camera made almost entirely of plastic, lens included. They are cheap to buy and easy to shoot with, but offer very little in the way of control. Images shot on toy cameras tend to display traits such as oversaturated colours, a sharp image centre with soft edges, heavy vignetting and maybe the occasional light leak. Ironically, the very traits that improvements in technology over the years have eradicated are the ones that the retro photography trend aims to reproduce. The results are visually appealing and the nice thing about this look is that it can be applied to pretty much any kind of photograph, from portraits to cityscapes. Surprisingly, images with visual imperfections such as noise or slight misfocusing often suit the effect better, as this adds to the authenticity of the shot.

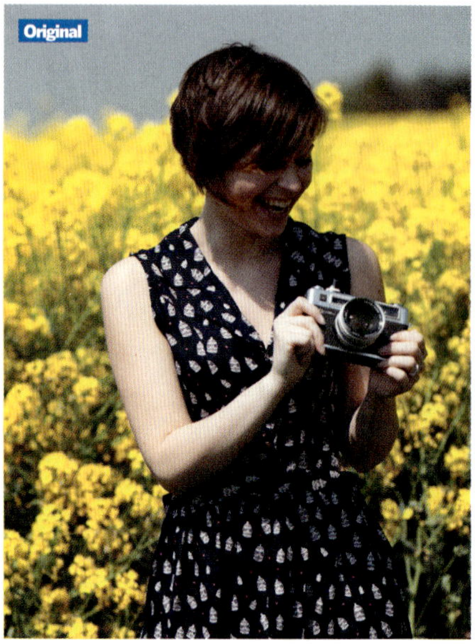

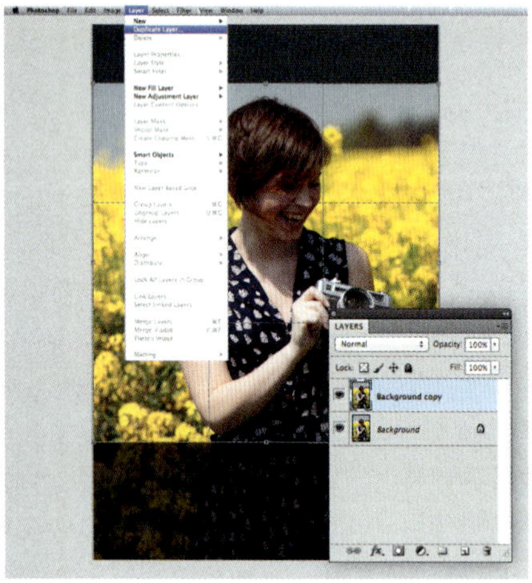

1 Crop your image Start by going to ***Layer>Duplicate Layer***. Next, crop your image into a square format by selecting the ***Crop Tool*** and holding down the ***Shift*** key while selecting an area of your image. Once happy, click on the ***tick*** in the top menu bar or press the ***enter*** key to commit to the crop.

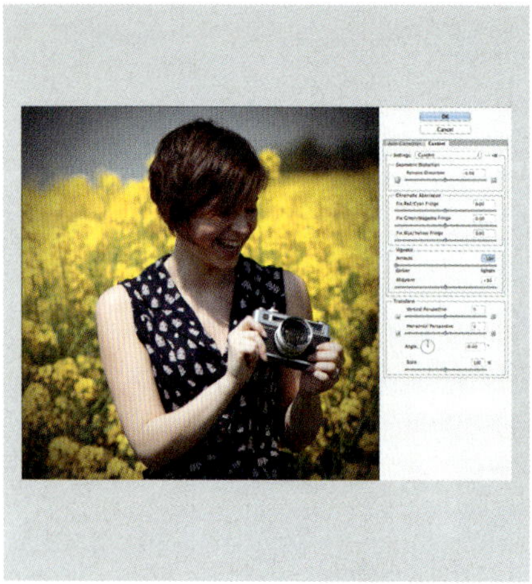

2 Add a vignette In the Layers palette, right-click on your duplicate layer and then select ***Convert to Smart Object***. Select ***Filter>Lens Correction*** and, in the dialogue box that opens, click on the ***Custom*** tab at the top. In the ***Vignette*** section, move the ***Amount*** slider to ***-100*** and click ***OK***.

Workflow tools

✔ USING THE CURVES TOOL

Photoshop's Curves tool is powerful, but at first glance it can be quite intimidating. Not only does it allow you to tweak contrast as per the Levels tool, but with it you can also adjust how the red, green and blue channels appear independent of one another; perfect for mimicking film effects. The Curves window presents you with a grid with a diagonal line running from the black point of the image in the bottom left to the white point in the top right. The points at which the diagonal line intersects with the grid controls the shadows, the mid-tones and the highlights of your image. The suggestions in our step-by-step are a good start in replicating a retro film effect – however, experimentation is the key. Adjustments to the shape of the curves can completely change the appearance of your image. Thankfully, by using Adjustment Layers, none of the changes are destructive, allowing you to try different settings before settling on one.

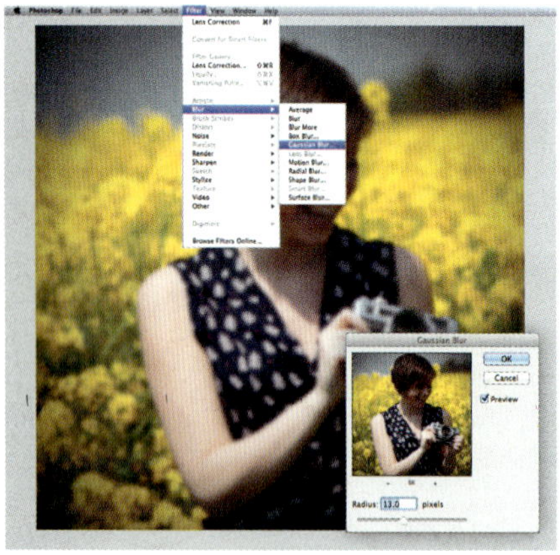

3 Add some blur Once back in your main window, go to ***Filter>Blur>Gaussian Blur*** and, in the Gaussian Blur window that's just opened, set the ***Radius*** to ***13.0*** pixels before clicking ***OK***. This will blur your entire image. Back in the Layers palette, click on the ***Add layer mask*** button. Click and hold on the ***Paint Bucket Tool*** icon to select the ***Gradient Tool*** and make sure that your ***Foreground color*** is set to ***Black***.

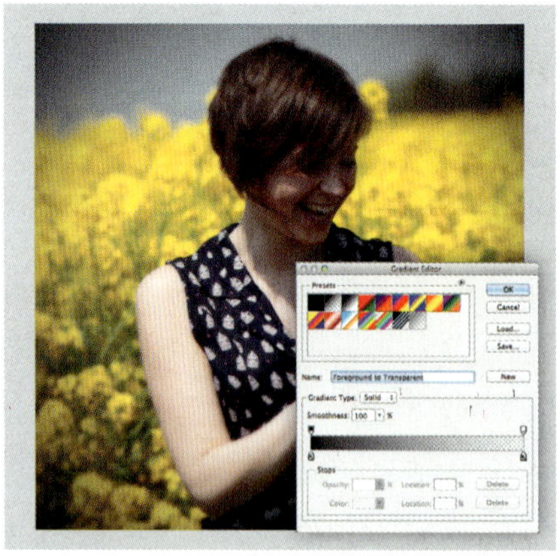

4 Add the edge effects In the menu bar at the top of the screen, click on the ***Click to edit the gradient*** button and set your gradient as ***Foreground to Transparent*** from the thumbnail list before clicking ***OK***. Select the ***Radial Gradient*** from the top menu, and click and drag from the centre of your image to one of the corners. You can choose to repeat this action again to create a stronger fall-off in sharpness.

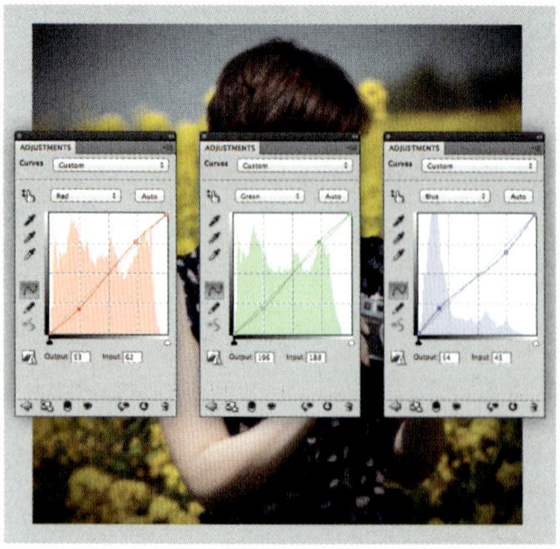

5 Tweak the colours Click on the ***Create a new fill or adjustment layer*** button in the Layers palette and select ***Curves***. In the Adjustments palette, click on the ***RGB*** menu and select the ***Red*** channel. Create a shallow 'S'-shaped curve in the Curves window. Select the ***Green*** channel and apply the same curve. Select the ***Blue*** channel and create an inverted 'S' curve, as per the image above.

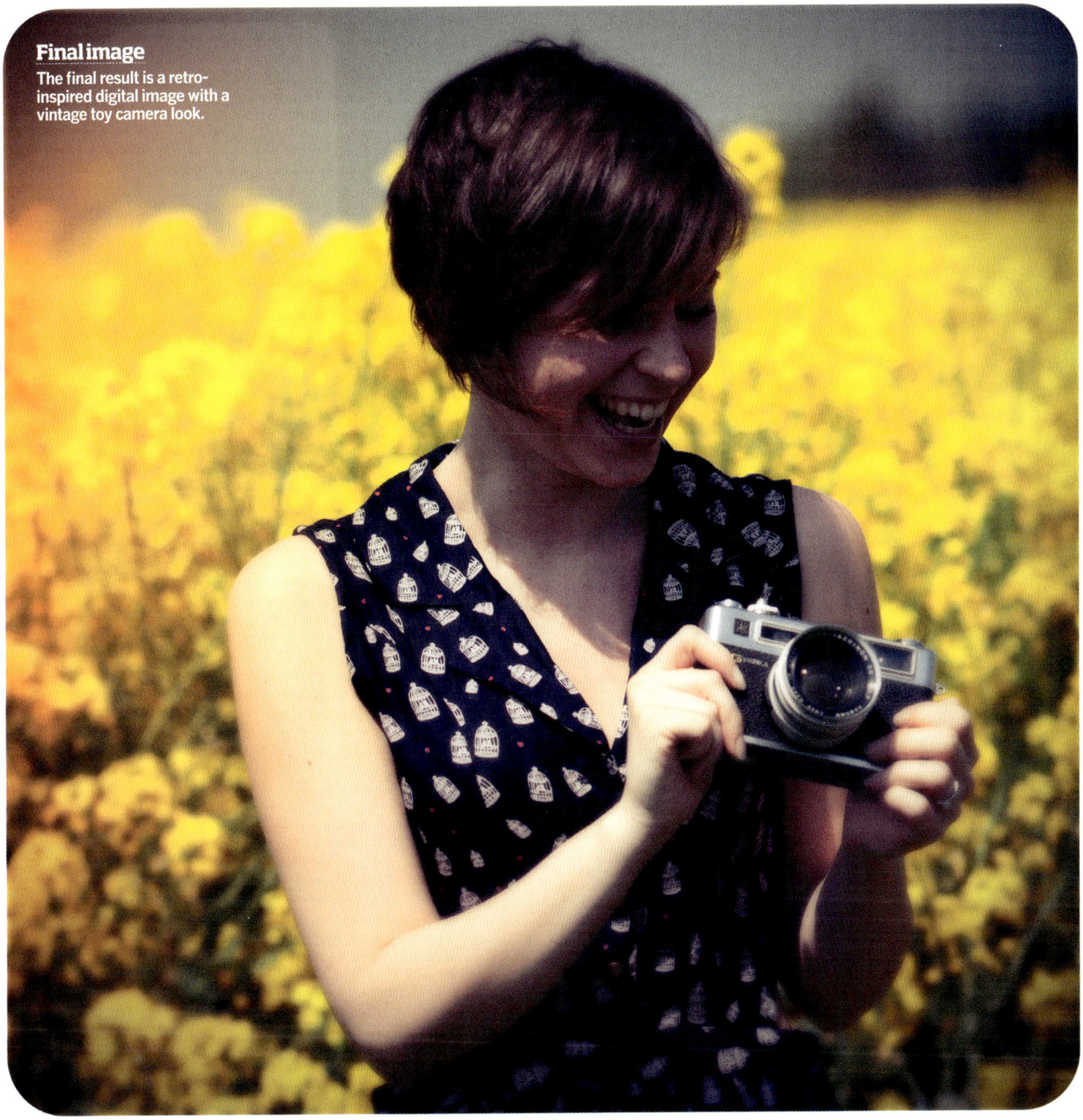

Final image

The final result is a retro-inspired digital image with a vintage toy camera look.

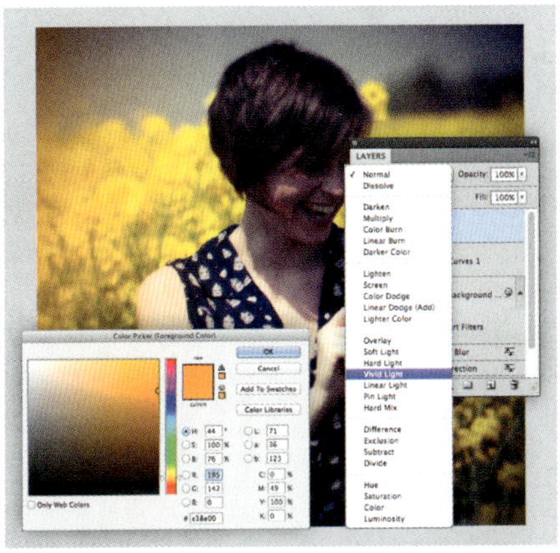

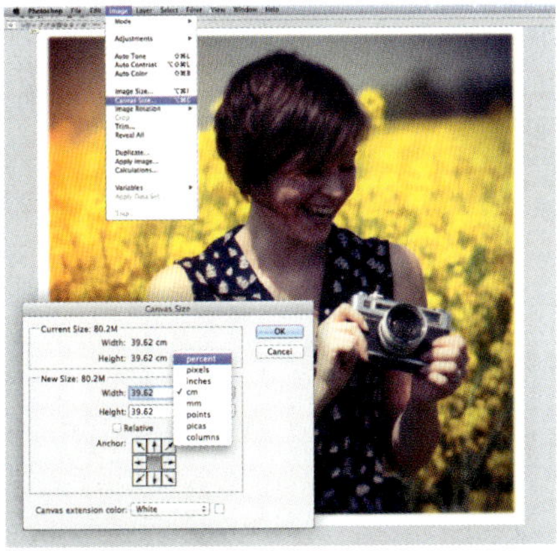

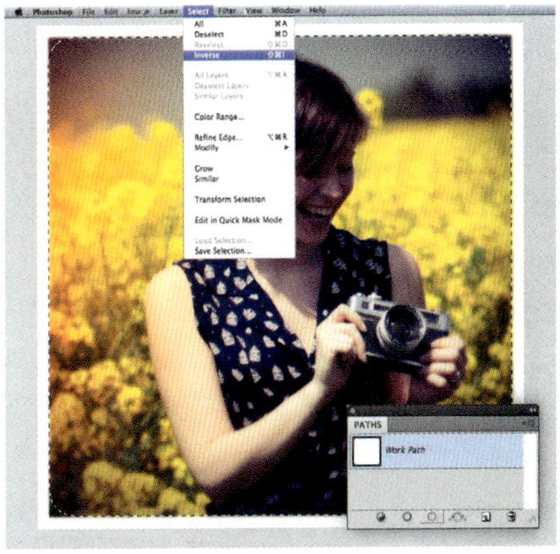

6 Add light leaks Click on the ***Create new layer*** button in the Layers palette, choose the ***Gradient Tool*** once more and select ***Orange*** as your ***Foreground color.*** Click and hold on the artboard off the edge of your image and drag the line into the image to create the gradient. Finally, in the Layers palette, change the ***Blend Mode*** for the layer to ***Vivid Light*** and reduce the opacity using the ***Opacity*** slider.

7 Draw the border Go to ***Image>Canvas Size*** and change the units to ***percent***. Set both the ***Width*** and ***Height*** to ***105*** and click ***OK*** – this will create a border around your image. Click and hold on the ***Rectangle Tool*** to select the ***Rounded Rectangle Tool***. In the top menu bar, first make sure that the ***Paths*** icon is selected and then set the ***Radius*** to ***200px***. Click and drag from one corner of your image to the other.

8 Fill the border Click on ***Layer>Flatten Image.*** Go into the Paths palette (***Window>Paths***) and click on the ***Load path as a selection*** button at the bottom to highlight your rounded rectangle selection. Go to ***Select>Inverse*** before pressing the ***Backspace*** key to delete the contents of the selection. In the Fill window that opens, set the ***Contents*** to ***White*** before clicking ***OK***. Finally, click ***Select>Deselect***.

Add colour to mono images

Dust off your colouring book skills to transform black & white images

Jordan Butters: Most of us are not strangers to converting images to monochrome. The process can be completed in a matter of seconds with just a few clicks of your mouse. Performing the conversion in the opposite direction is not quite as straightforward unfortunately, but it is still easily achievable. The main issue is that the colour information is no longer present in the image and therefore the only way to achieve this is to reintroduce the colours manually into parts of it. This may sound a complicated process, but don't worry – you don't have to be Van Gogh to make this technique work, thanks to the different Blend Modes in Photoshop and Elements. The colouring process can be done in a few simple steps – however, the more care taken, the more convincing the final effect will be. You can apply this technique to images that were shot on black & white film, too – just scan in the photo and use the Dust & Scratches filter and the Healing Brush Tool to tidy up any marks first. As you'll discover, there's something enchanting about seeing an old image converted to colour and given a new lease of life.

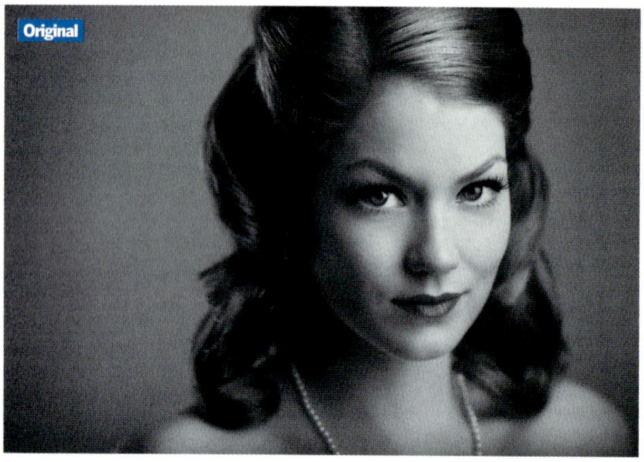

TOP TIP...

Blend Modes

Your choice of Blend Mode will affect how each layer of colour is applied to your image. The most useful Blend Modes for this technique are Soft Light and Color. Some experimentation is often required when it comes to applying Blend Modes, as no two modes will offer the exact same effect when applied.

Final image

Adding different hues can make an image feel incredibly fresh and vibrant.

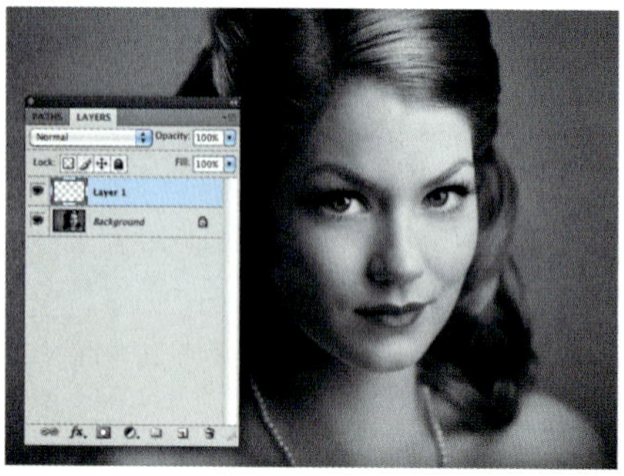

1 Create a new layer To begin, click on the ***Create new layer*** button in the Layers palette. This layer will contain the base colour for our subject's skin tone. Click on the ***Foreground Color*** icon in the toolbar and use the colour map to choose a suitable skin tone.

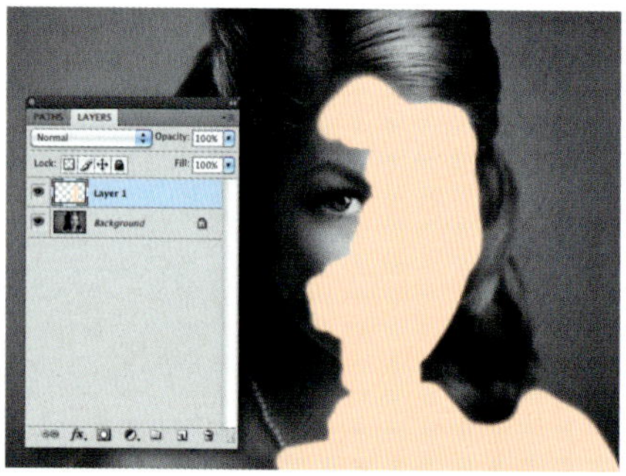

2 Add skin colour Select the ***Brush Tool*** and, in the brush options at the top, set the ***Hardness*** to ***50%*** and pick an appropriate brush ***Size***. Begin painting over your subject's skin. Do not worry if you go outside of the edges or over facial features as we will correct this later.

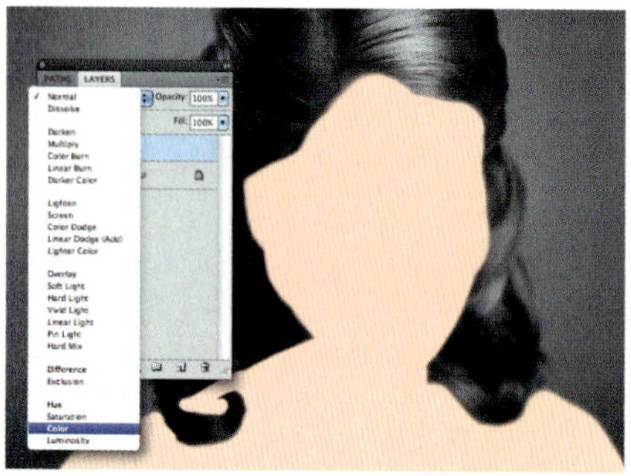

3 Change Blend Mode In the Layers palette, change the ***Blend Mode*** to ***Color***. If the skin tone doesn't look realistic, adjust the ***Opacity*** slider in the Layers palette to desaturate the tone slightly. If this doesn't correct it, try a different foreground colour and repeat the previous step.

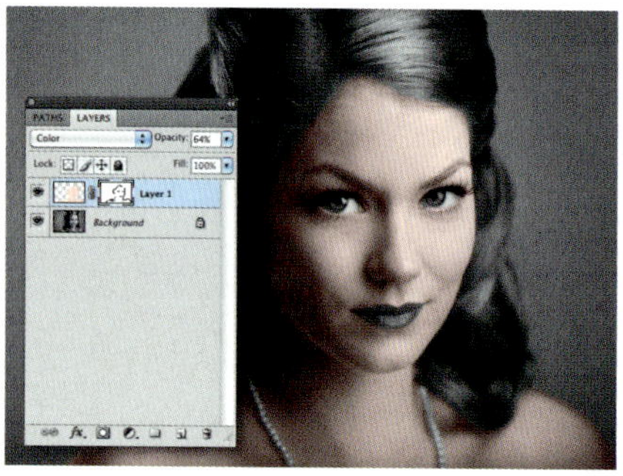

4 Add a Layer Mask Create a Layer Mask by clicking on the ***Add layer mask*** button and make sure that your ***Foreground Color*** is set to ***Black***. Use the ***Brush Tool*** on the Layer Mask to paint over any areas where you have coloured outside of the lines, including the eyes and mouth.

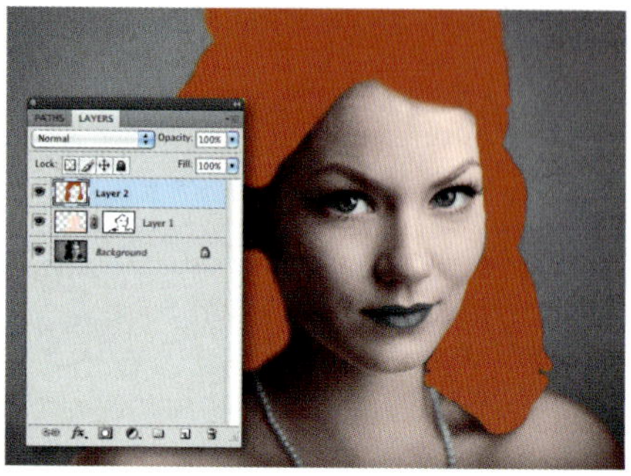

5 Paint in hair colour Click on ***Create a new layer*** again in the Layers palette and choose a ***Foreground Color*** to suit your subject's hair. Once again, use the ***Brush Tool*** to paint the hair colour onto your image, again not worrying too much about going outside of the edges.

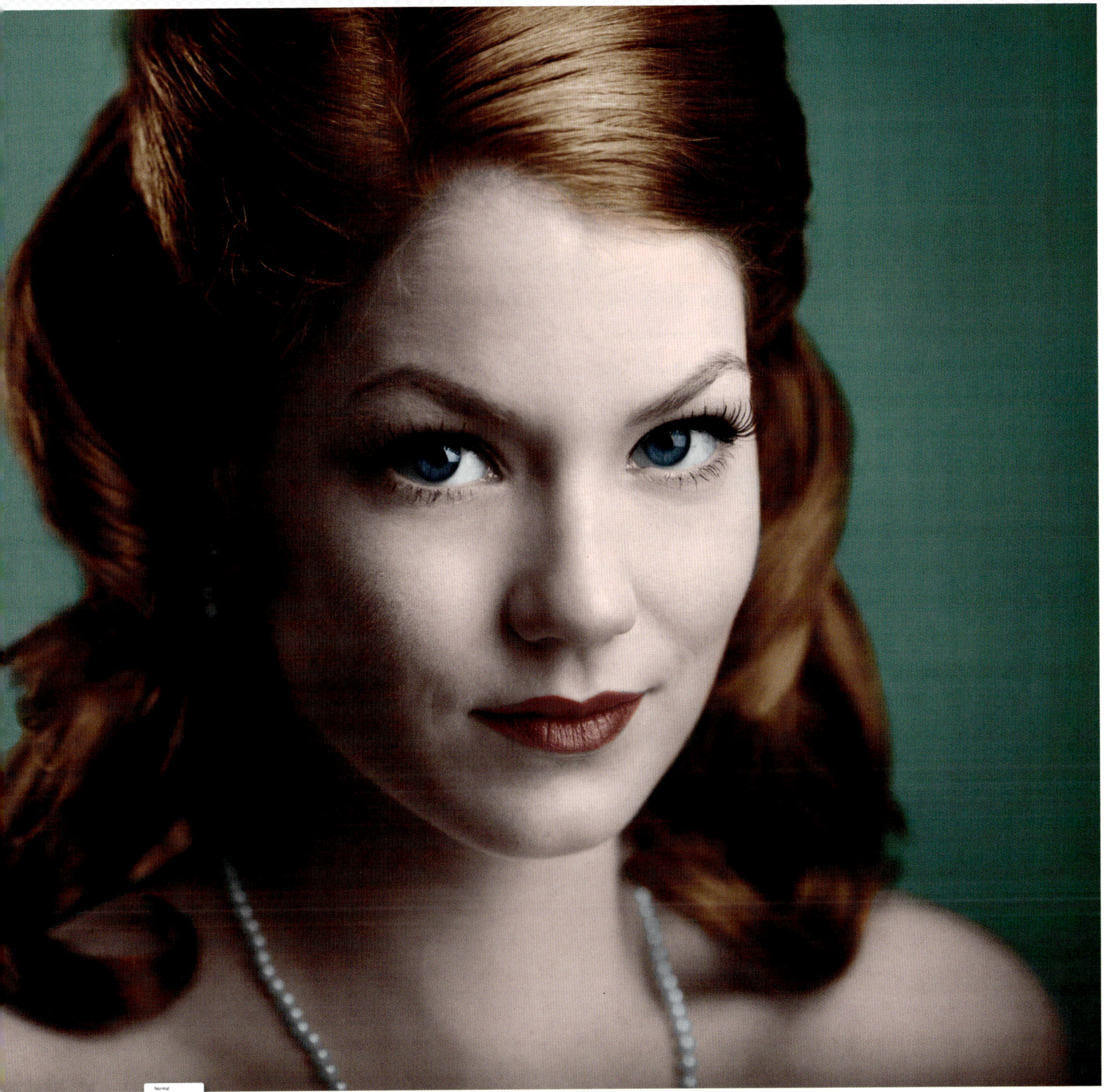

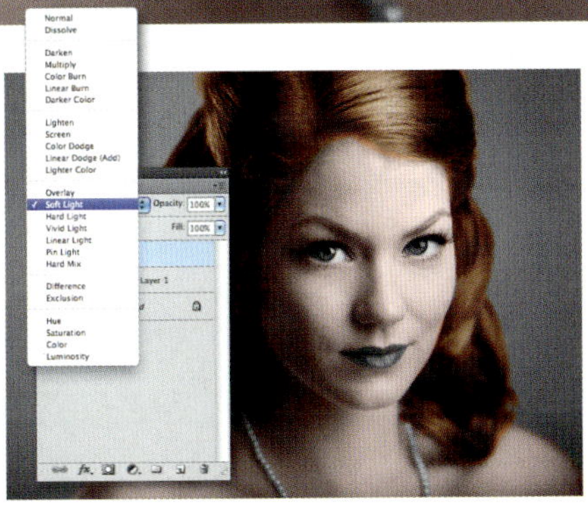

6 Change Blend Mode In the Layers palette, change the ***Blend Mode*** of this layer. The Blend Mode will depend on the colour of your subject's hair. It's worth trying both ***Color*** and ***Soft Light*** to see which produces the nicest effect, again adjusting ***Opacity*** if needed.

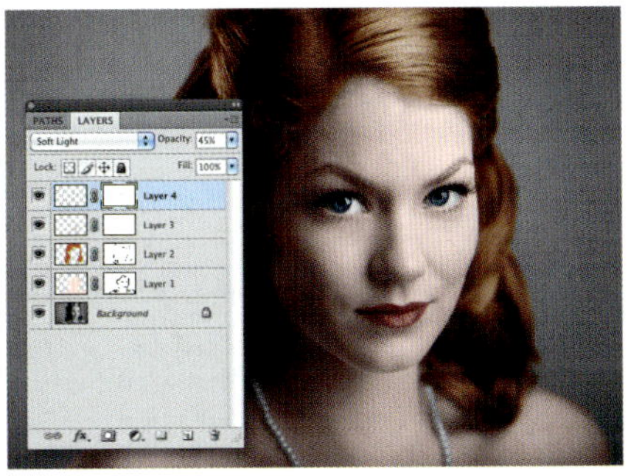

7 Add a Layer Mask Add a ***Layer Mask*** to the same layer and brush out any areas of overspill. Repeat these steps for each section of colour, starting on a new layer each time and experimenting with the ***Blend Mode*** and ***Opacity*** for each layer until you're happy with the finish.

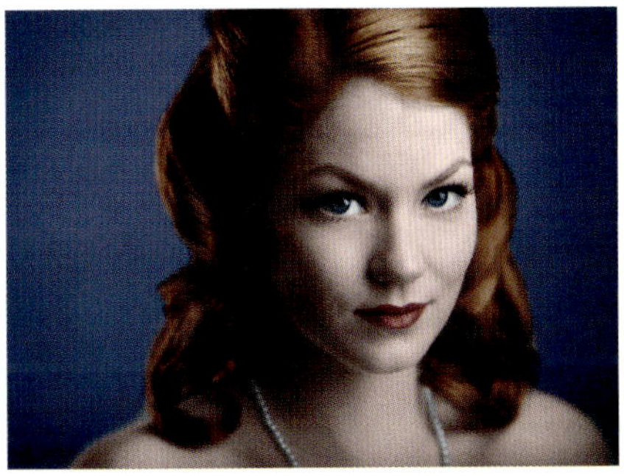

8 Experiment with colour Don't be afraid to have fun with the colours that you choose. Obviously certain things have to be the correct colour to look right, but there's no reason why you can't spice things up by experimenting with different background or clothing colours.

Turn pictures into a sketch

Eager to try artistic effects on your images, but not sure how? Follow this tutorial to see your photograph transform into a detailed drawing

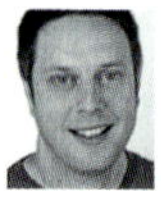

Luke Marsh: Post-production of photographs needn't be limited to a clean-up or colour and tonal adjustments. CS and Elements have a host of filters that can use the information in the image to convert the picture into different styles, even mediums, for creative effect. For instance, unless you're talented with a pencil, chances are you wouldn't be able to create a detailed sketch of this standard from a photograph without the help of Photoshop. Try it for yourself with a portrait that has a simple, blurred background so as not to distract from the subject and sketch detailing.

Useful tools

THE FILTER GALLERY

If you go to ***Filter>Filter Gallery...*** you'll be presented with many creative filters. The filters are categorised into sections such as Artistic, Distort, Sketch and Texture, and by clicking on the section folders, you can access the filters. Click on a filter icon and you are presented with a large preview of your image along with a set of controls allowing you to fine-tune the filter's effect. Take time to experiment with them all.

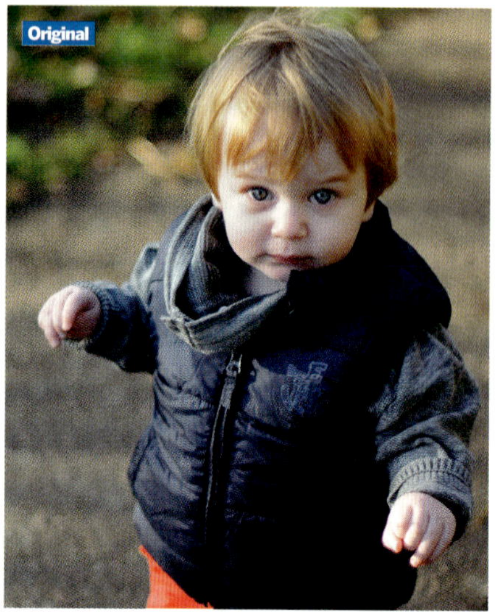

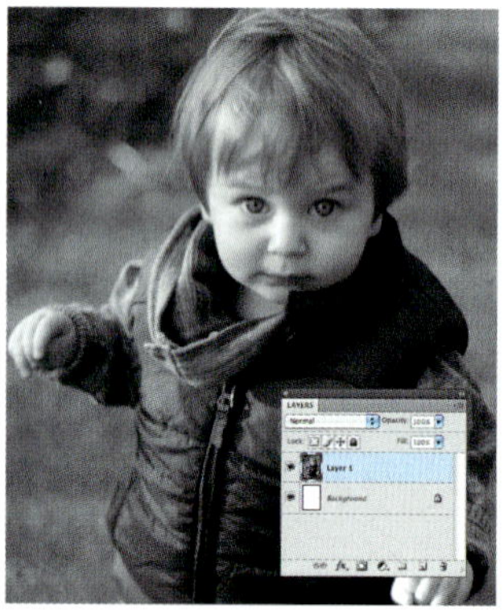

1 Desaturate The first thing to do is desaturate the image. Go to ***Image>Adjustments>Hue/Saturation*** and move the ***Saturation*** slider to ***-100%***. With the ***Foreground*** and ***Background Colors*** set to ***Black*** and ***White***, go to ***Select>All***. Now go to ***Edit>Cut*** then ***Edit>Paste*** to remove the image from the background and paste onto a new layer.

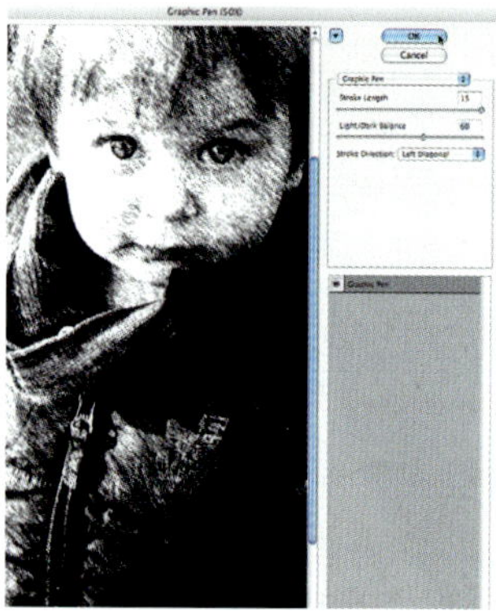

2 Apply Graphic Pen Create a duplicate from the original image by going to ***Layer>Duplicate Layer*** and name the layer 'Graphic Pen'. Next, go to ***Filter>Sketch>Graphic Pen...*** and enter the ***Stroke Length*** as ***15*** and ***Light/Dark Balance*** as ***60***, then set the ***Direction*** to ***Left Diagonal***, and click ***OK***. Change the layer's ***Blend Mode*** to ***Multiply*** and the layer's ***Opacity*** to ***40%***.

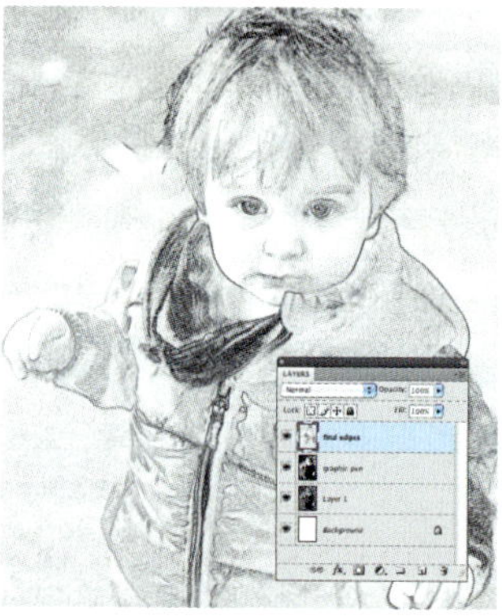

3 Find the edges Duplicate the original image layer once more, this time naming the layer 'Find Edges', then drag the layer above the 'Graphic Pen' layer in the Layers palette. Next, go to ***Filter>Stylize>Find Edges*** to recreate the appearance of a pencil outline. As before, change the layer's ***Blend Mode*** to ***Multiply*** and reduce the ***Opacity***, this time to ***70%***.

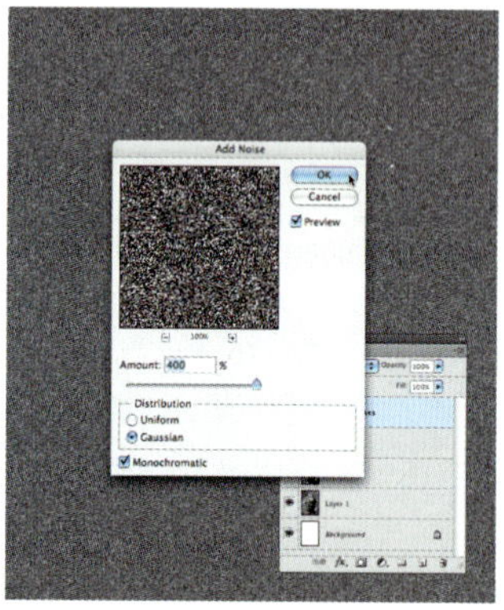

4 Add pencil strokes To create drastic pencil strokes, first create a new layer by going to ***Layer>New>Layer...***, naming the layer 'Pencil Strokes' and moving this new layer to the top of the Layers palette. Now go to ***Edit>Fill...*** and change ***Use*** to ***Black*** and click ***OK***. Finally, add some noise with ***Filter> Noise>Add noise***, entering the maximum value and ensuring ***Monochromatic*** is ticked.

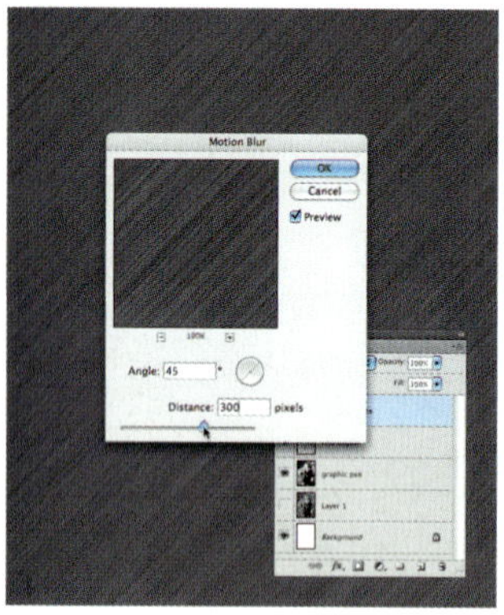

5 Refine the strokes Open ***Image>Adjustments>Levels...*** and adjust the black and white sliders until the preview shows white dots on solid black. Next, go to ***Filter>Blur>Motion Blur...*** and change the ***Angle*** to ***45°*** and the ***Distance*** to around ***300*** pixels and click ***OK***. Finally, change the layer's ***Blend Mode*** to ***Overlay*** and reduce the ***Opacity*** to ***85%***.

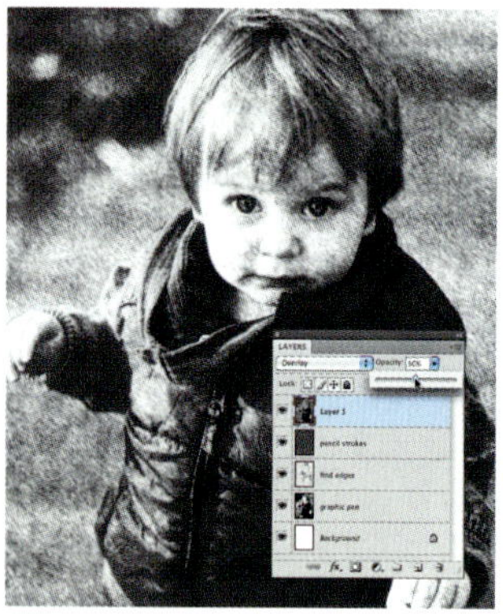

6 Boost the contrast To increase the image's overall contrast without losing any sketch detailing, drag the remaining original image layer to the top of the Layers palette. Change the layer ***Blend Mode*** to ***Overlay*** and you'll see a vast improvement in contrast. The effect will appear harsh, so adjust the ***Opacity*** slider to between ***40-50%*** to reduce its strength.

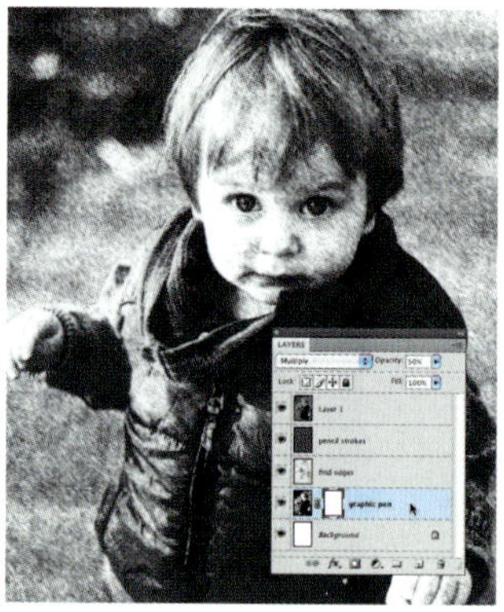

7 Add a Layer Mask The problem at this stage is that the sketch is almost too perfect. Rectify this by spending some time hand-painting areas on a Layer Mask, making the image seem more like it's been drawn. The bulk of the image detail is stored on the 'Graphic Pen' layer, so click the layer and go to ***Layer>New>Layer Mask>Reveal All*** to add the Layer Mask.

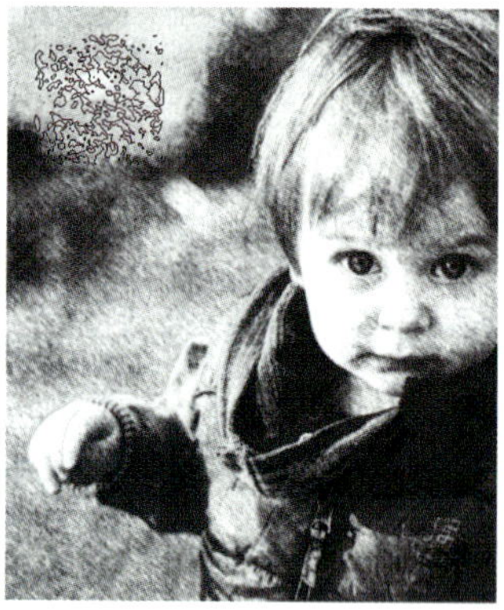

8 Hide detail Select the ***Brush Tool*** and load the ***Dry Media Brushes*** set from the Brushes panel. Ensuring the ***Foreground Color*** is ***Black***, work around the edges, often reducing the ***Opacity*** slider of the brush to around ***50%*** for a more subtle effect. I also work on the jacket area and eyes, changing the brush colour back to White if I need to restore any areas.

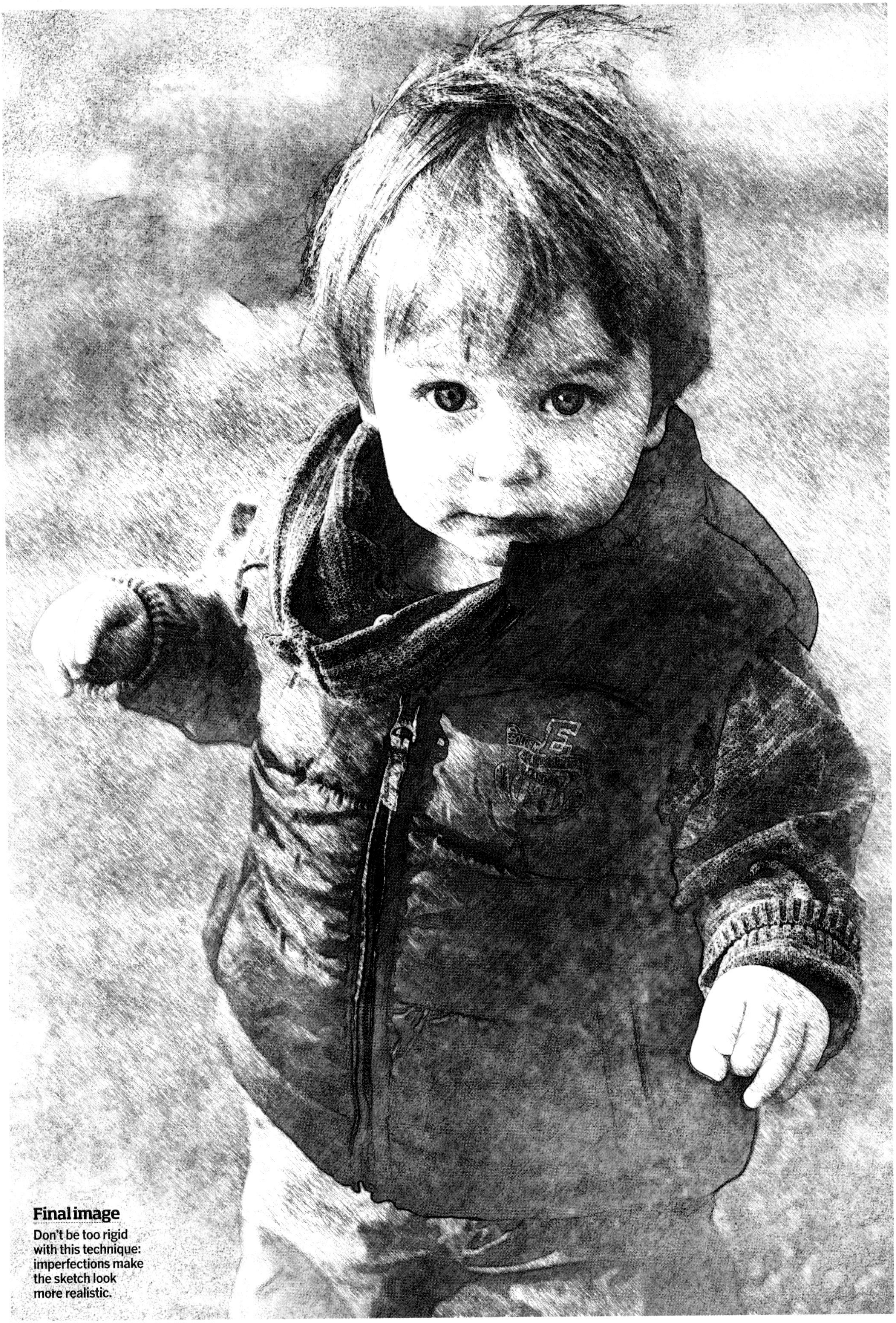

Final image

Don't be too rigid with this technique: imperfections make the sketch look more realistic.

Turn pictures into paintings

Want to make your image fit for an art gallery? Follow this tutorial to see your picture transform into a stunning watercolour masterpiece...

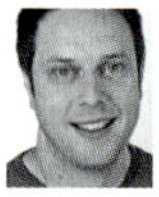

Luke Marsh: Photoshop has a plethora of filters and artistic presets that most of us have probably dabbled with out of curiosity. Few of us know how to get the best out of these filters, though, and quite often get deterred by disappointing results. Clicking on Filter>Artistic>Watercolor... is usually the first and only step most people take when trying to convert one of their photographs into a pseudo painting, and while this can create an acceptable finish, combining it with other artistic filters can produce more convincing images that might have people questioning whether the image is indeed a photograph or a print of a painting. Here we show you how to do this using four different effects and the best way of applying the Watercolor filter. You might want to look for further brushes online – see the panel (right) to find out how to download some for free.

Useful tools

✔ BRUSH DOWNLOADS

If after investigating Photoshop's pre-installed brushes you feel there's nothing that quite works, search online for brush sets to download. Sites like www.brusheezy.com and www.myphotoshopbrushes.com have loads of categorised brush sets that are free to download for personal use. Downloading a set will give you a .abr file – to use it, simply place this file into the Photoshop brushes folder: ***User>Library>Application Support>Adobe>Adobe Photoshop>Presets>Brushes*** (Mac), or ***C:\>Program Files>Adobe>Photoshop>Presets>Brushes*** (PC). Open Photoshop and select your new brush sets via ***Windows> Brush Panel*** and you're ready to begin painting.

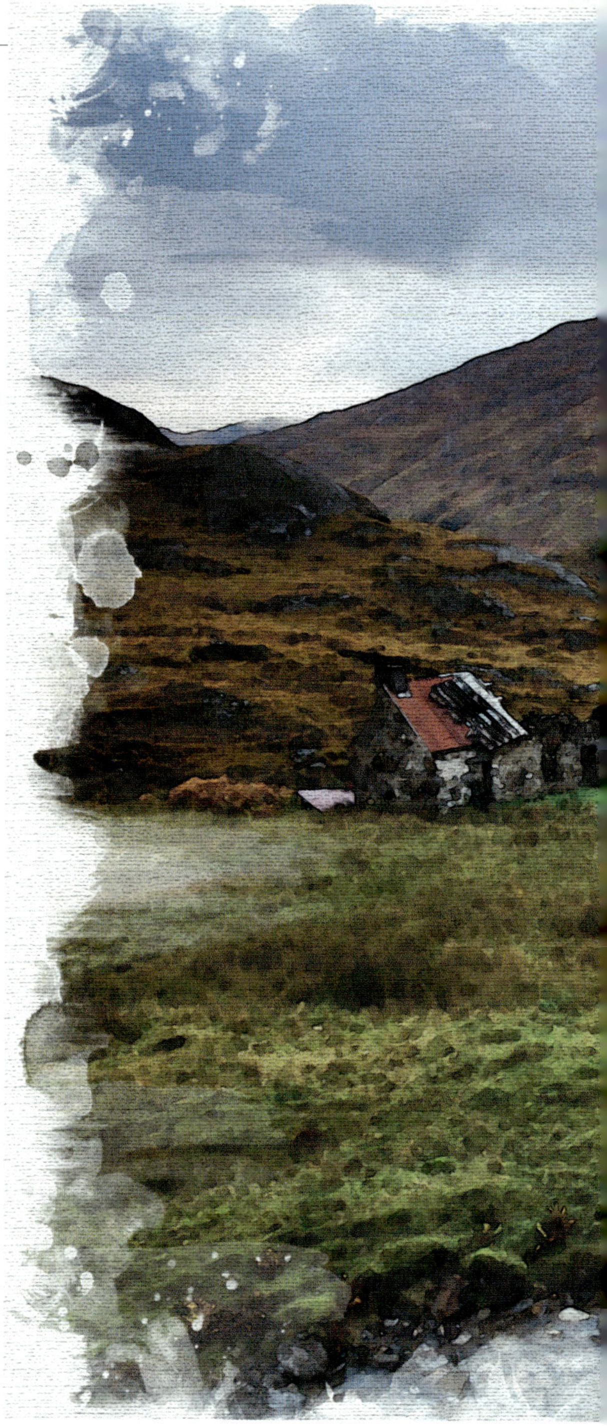

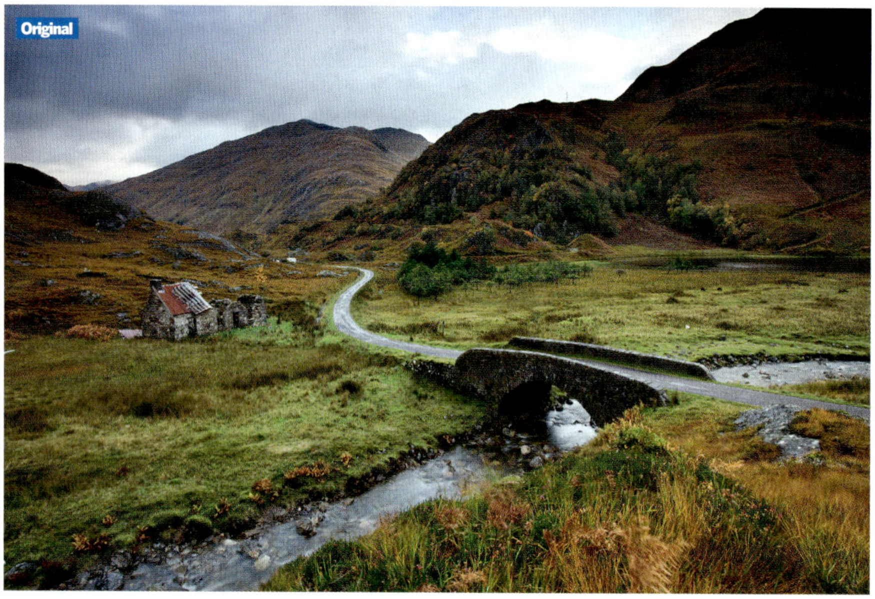

ADAM BURTON

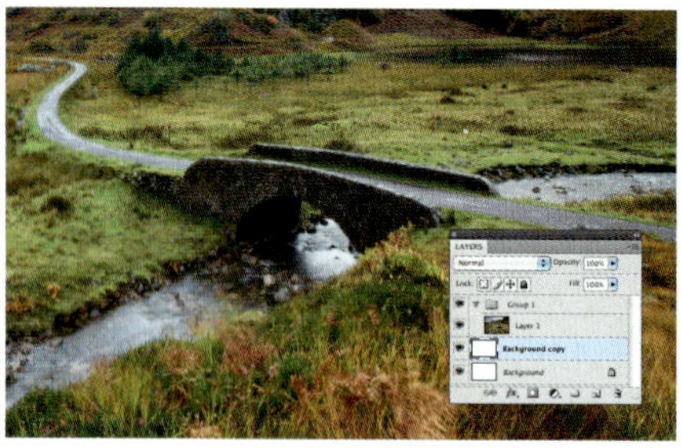

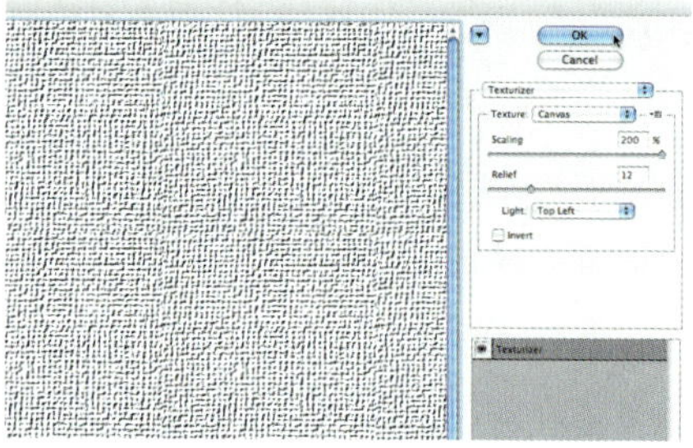

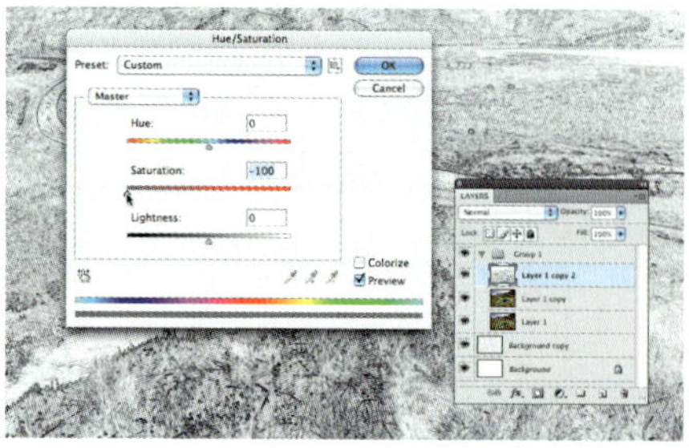

1 Prepare the layers Open your chosen image and go to ***Select>All*** and then ***Edit>Cut***, followed by ***Edit>Paste*** to cut the entire image area from the background, placing it on its own layer. Next, go to ***Layer>New>Group...***, creating a folder icon in the Layers palette. Drag the image layer into this folder. A Layer Mask will be added to this group later on, allowing all layers within it to be edited as one. Now click the ***Background layer*** and go to ***Layer>New>Layer via Copy***, creating a layer above the background but below the group.

2 Add texture On the background copy layer, go to ***Filter>Texture>Texturizer...*** and in the preview window, select ***Canvas*** as the ***Texture***, increase ***Scaling*** to maximum value (***200%***), set ***Relief*** to between ***10*** and ***15***, and ***Light*** to ***Top Left***, then click ***OK***. Now change the ***Opacity*** of the layer to around ***50%***. Click on the image layer in the group folder and go to ***Layer>Duplicate Layer***, creating a duplicate of the layer above it. Repeat this once more so there are three identical image layers within the group folder.

3 Apply pencil outline Click on the top layer in the folder to activate it. Go to ***Filter>Stylize>Find Edges***. Next, go to ***Image>Adjustments>Hue/Saturation*** and move the ***Saturation*** slider to ***-100*** to remove the colour so that the edges in the image look like they've been drawn by pencil. Finally, change the layer ***Blend Mode*** to ***Multiply*** and reduce the ***Opacity*** to ***50-60%***. Once complete, hide the layer by clicking on the ***eye*** icon next to the layer's thumbnail in the Layers palette.

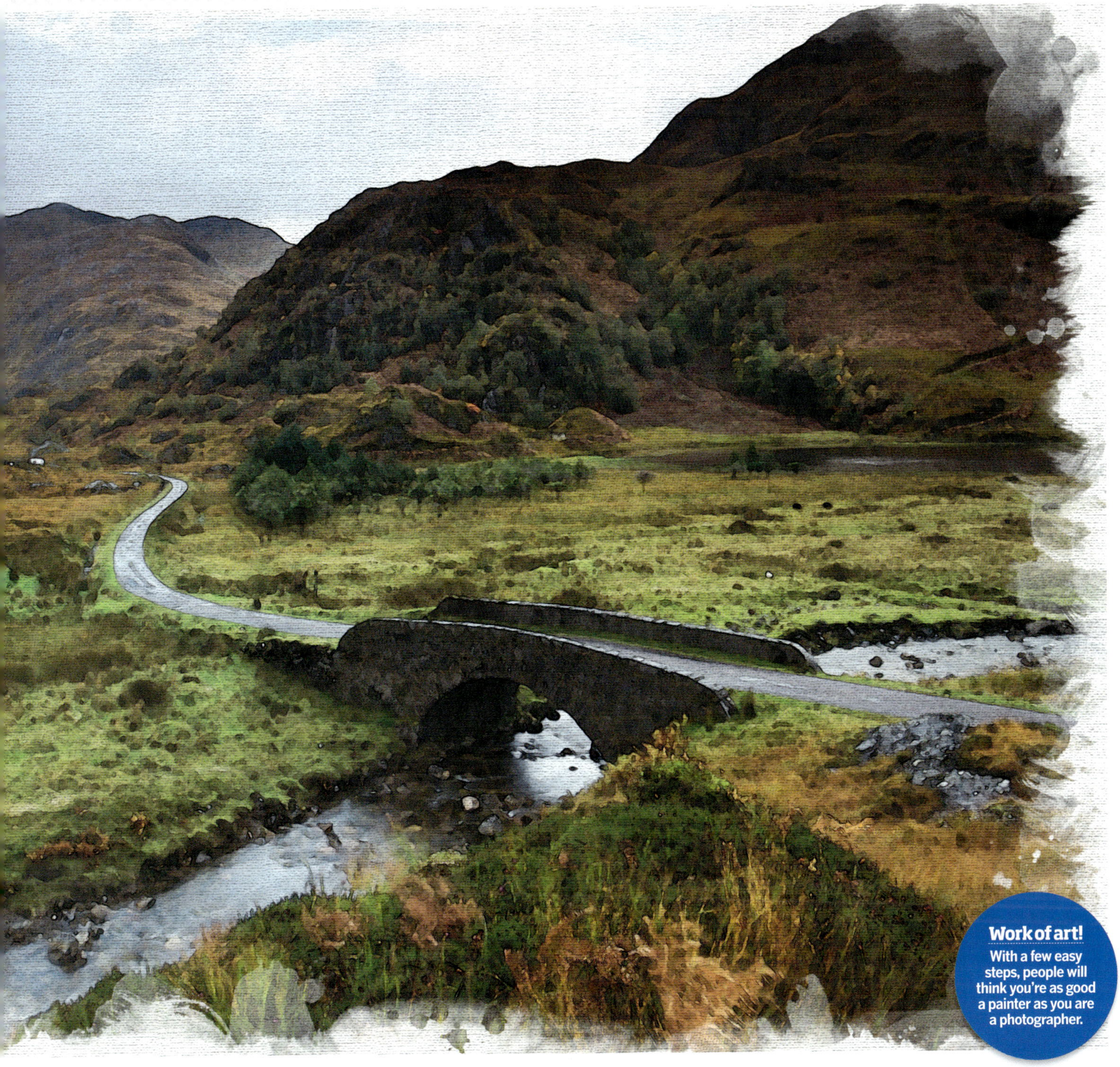

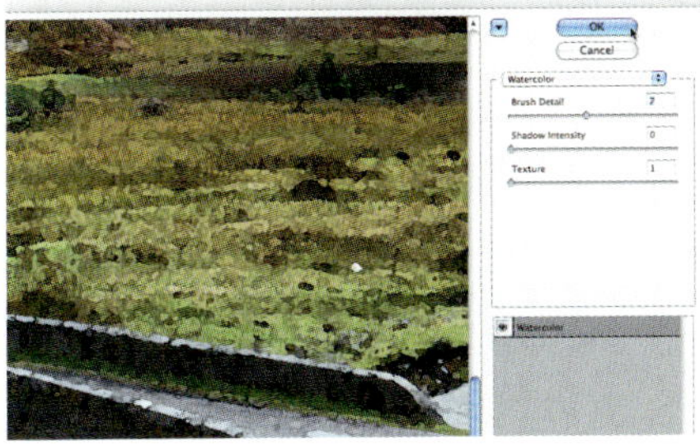

4 Add the watercolour The watercolour effect is built up from the other two layers in the group folder. First, click on the middle layer and go to ***Filter>Artistic>Watercolor...*** and enter ***Brush Detail*** as *7*, ***Shadow Intensity*** as *0* and ***Texture*** as *1*. Change the layer ***Blend Mode*** to ***Overlay*** and reduce the ***Opacity*** to ***50%***, then hide the layer. Click on the bottom layer and go to ***Filter>Brush Strokes>Accented Edges...*** and enter ***Edge Width*** as *2*, ***Edge Brightness*** as ***15*** and ***Smoothness*** as ***8***. Finally, change the layer ***Opacity*** to ***80%***.

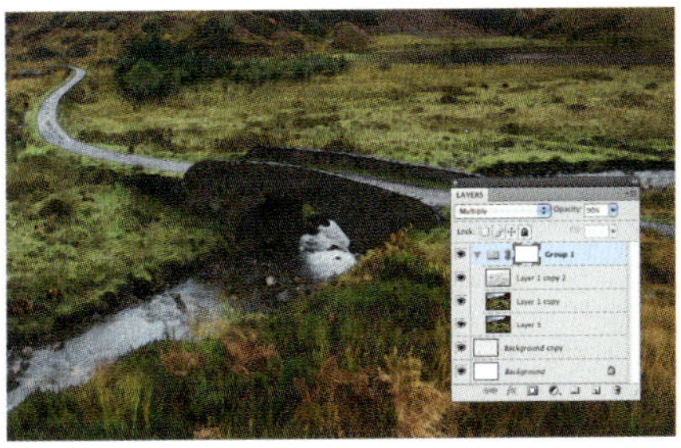

5 Edit the effect Make all three layers visible by clicking the ***eye*** icons to see the complete watercolour effect. To give the impression that this is a real painting on canvas, you will need to add a hand-brushed border. To do this, first click on the ***folder*** icon and go to ***Layer>Layer Mask>Reveal All***. Applying a Layer Mask to the group rather than individual layers allows all the layers to be edited at once. Change the group ***Blend Mode*** to ***Multiply*** and its ***Opacity*** to ***90%***, allowing the canvas texture to show through.

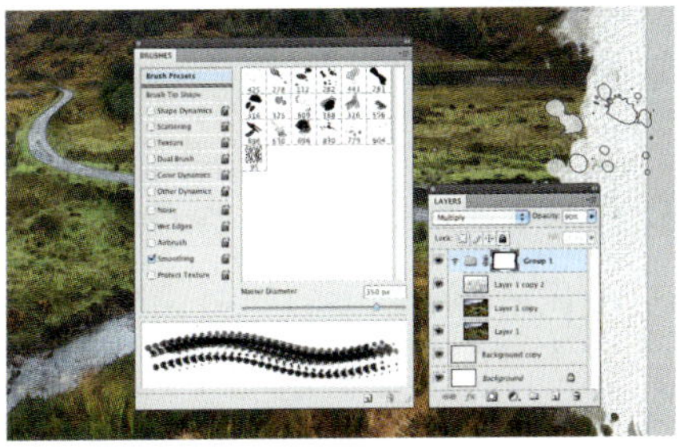

6 Create an art border With the Layer Mask selected, paint over the image with the ***Brush Tool***. Choose from the default brushes or download artistic brushes (see panel) – for this step-by-step I downloaded a set of free watercolour brushes. Change the brush ***Color*** to ***Black***, set an appropriate ***Size***, then work around the edge of the image, using artistic licence, to build up the border. Whenever you think you've overdone it, simply change the brush colour to ***White*** and work over the area to restore the detail.

Create a rainy-day portrait

Today we forecast a heavy downpour! Give your images the illusion of rain with a few tweaks using Noise and Motion Blur…

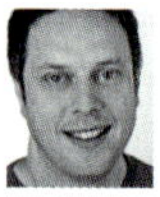

Luke Marsh: For most photographers, shooting in the rain isn't their favourite pastime, but it can add a different dimension to your pictures. So how can you create the appearance of rain without having to actually get you or your camera gear wet? Easy, follow this technique!

Its success lies in trying to make the scene look authentic, so if your starting image is of a street scene, make sure it was taken just after it's rained, when the ground is still wet. Similarly, have your subject/s hold an umbrella for the same reasons – if it's pouring with rain, they'd be soaking wet without one. An umbrella is the perfect cover-up, quite literally.

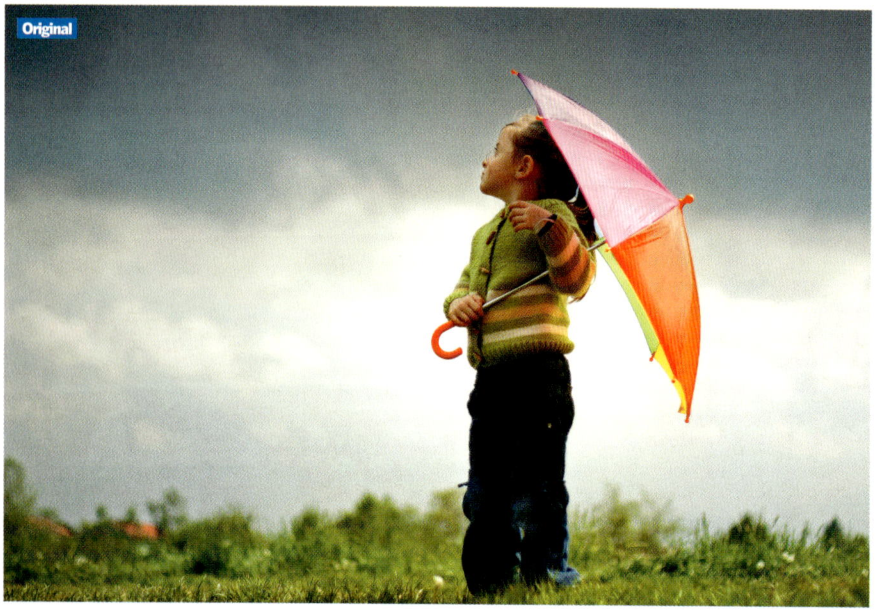

ISTOCK PHOTO

Secrets unlocked

✔ LET IT SNOW, LET IT SNOW!

You can also adapt this rain technique to create a great snow effect! In step four, when using Motion Blur, reduce the ***Distance*** down to less than ***10*** pixels to give the appearance of drifting snow, as opposed to heavy rain. Also, having different sized flakes adds extra dimension to the scene, so go to ***Layer>New>Layer via Copy*** to duplicate the layer. Then ***Edit>Transform>Scale*** to increase the size of the new snow layer by holding ***shift*** and dragging a corner widget.

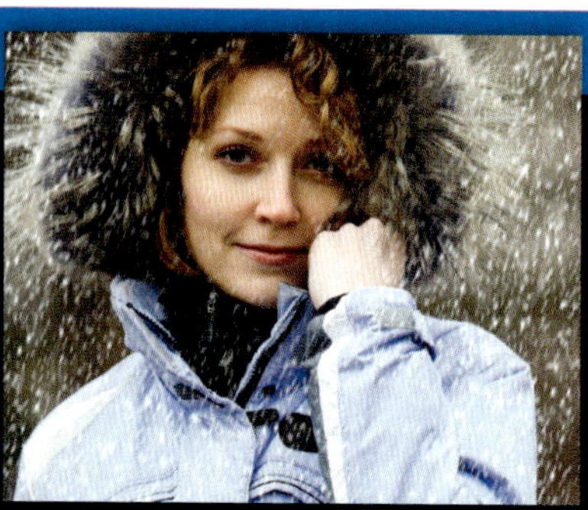

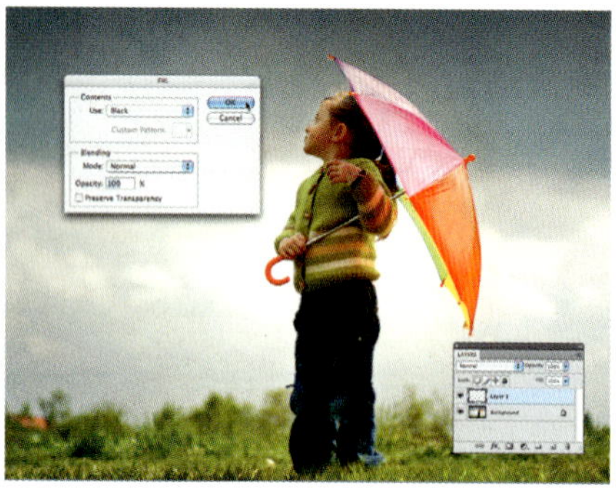

1 Open your image Create a new layer above the original by going to ***Layer>New Layer...*** and clicking ***OK*** in the pop-up window. To be able to affect this layer, you need to put content into it. For this, go to ***Edit>Fill...*** and, under Contents, change ***Use*** to ***Black*** and ensure ***Mode*** is ***Normal*** and ***Opacity*** is ***100*** under the Blending Options.

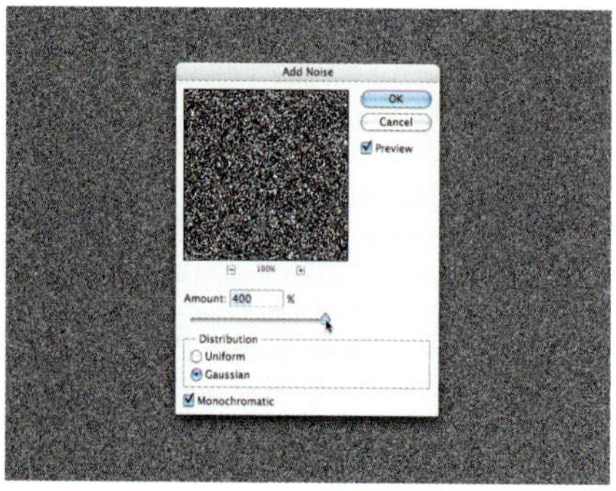

2 Add some noise Now add noise to the new black layer by going to ***Filter>Noise>Add noise...*** Select ***Gaussian*** under ***Distribution***, and ensure that ***Monochromatic*** is ticked. The ***Amount*** of noise you need to enter will depend on the image's resolution. For large files, you will need to enter the maximum amount of ***400%***.

3 Scale the noise Even though the maximum amount of noise was used, the noise 'dots' need to be bigger (the higher the image resolution and size, the more this will be the case). Go to ***Edit>Transform>Scale***, enter ***400%*** in the horizontal scale field and click the ***link*** icon to scale in proportion. Double-click to apply.

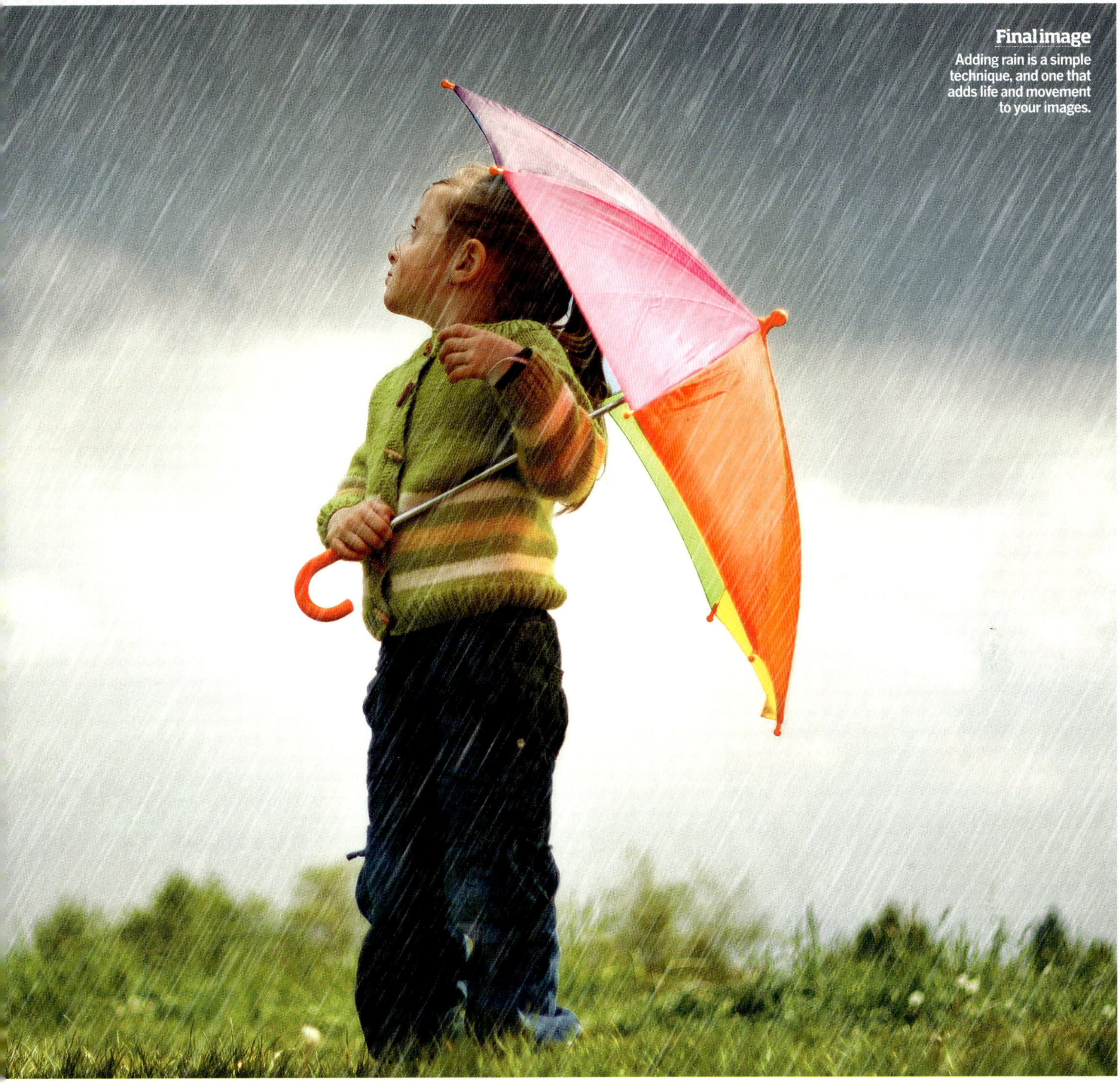

Final image

Adding rain is a simple technique, and one that adds life and movement to your images.

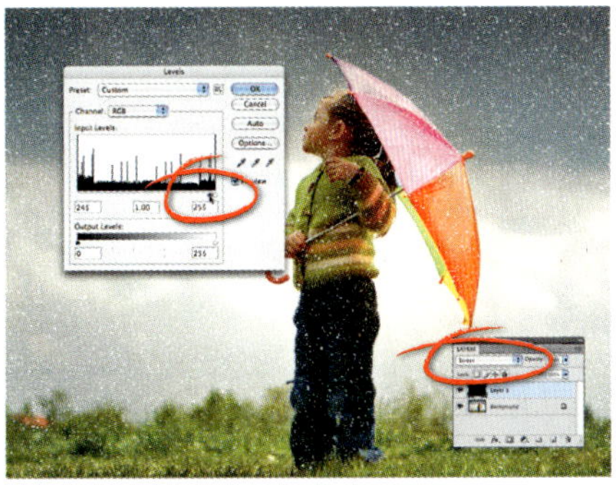

4 Create raindrops Now change the noise layer's ***Blend Mode*** to ***Screen***, making the image beneath visible. The noise needs editing to create fine raindrops, so go to ***Image>Adjustments>Levels...*** and drag the ***black slider*** all the way to the right, making the drops smaller and allowing a better interaction with the image.

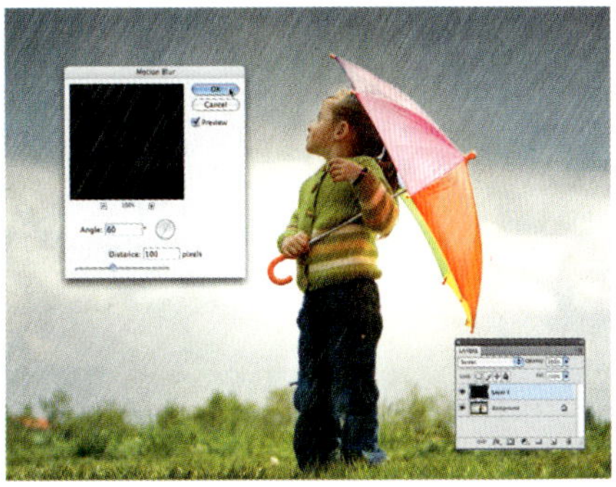

5 Blur the raindrops Use ***Filter>Blur>Motion Blur...*** to add the effect of moving rain. In the control panel, enter an ***Angle*** that suits your particular image. Here, 60° was used to reflect the position the little girl holds her umbrella. Then enter a ***Distance*** that gives intermittent streaks rather than solid lines running across the image.

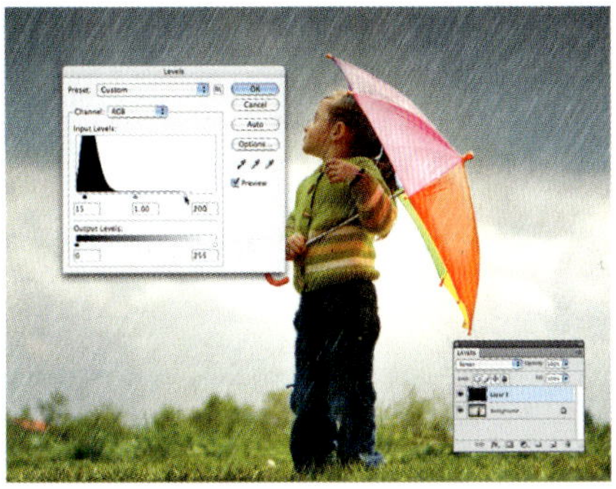

6 Perfect the storm The final tweaks are done using Levels (***Image>Adjustments>Levels...***). Move the ***black*** and ***white*** sliders to change the rain's appearance depending on your image. The black slider reduces the appearance of rain from sheets to drizzle, whereas the white slider improves the contrast of the rain.

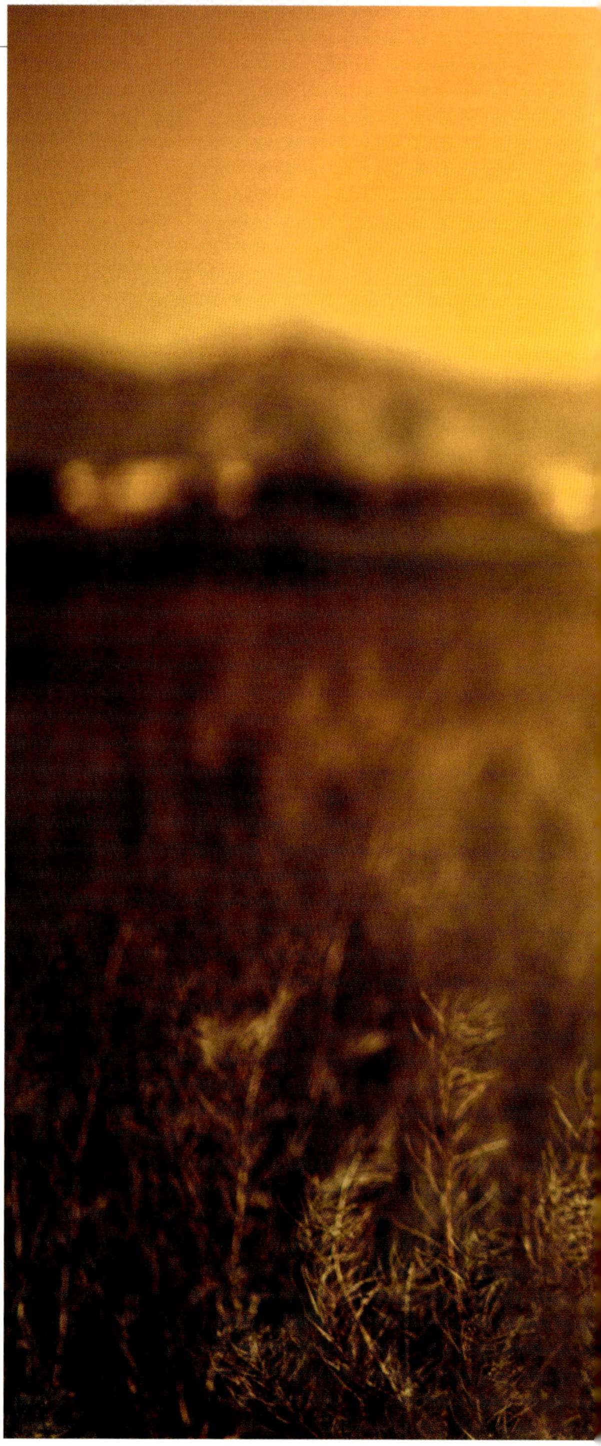

Create 'golden hour' light

A balmy summer's evening can give a supremely flattering glow to your subject. Recreate the look using Curves and the Burn Tool…

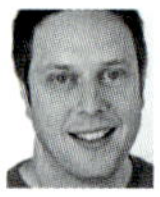

Luke Marsh: There's nothing quite like a glorious summer sunset to add ambience and colour to your portrait images. However, capturing such a backlit effect can be technically challenging with tricky metering and flare posing problems, but with this simple step-by-step you can transform daytime portraits with minimal effort.

You can try this technique on any outdoor portrait, but the effect will be more dramatic the cooler the original image tones are. You rarely see clouds when there's a burning sunset so, if you can, pick an image with a generous expanse of clear blue sky in a summery location such as a flower-filled field or one with plenty of lush greenery. An image with shallow depth-of-field can also enhance the final hazy warmth of the image, though it's not essential.

Getting the Photoshop effect correct relies on you working well with Layer Masks, but the beauty of them is that they're fully editable so you can refine and retry the technique without damaging your original image. Use Black paint and a soft brush on a Layer Mask to hide effects and White paint to reveal them again, altering the Opacity for better control.

QUICK FIND

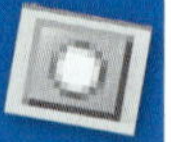

Layer Masks Click the ***Add a mask*** icon at the bottom of the Layers palette. A thumbnail appears on the active layer in the palette.

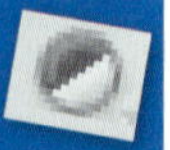

Adjustment Layers Click and hold on the ***New Adjustment Layer*** icon at the bottom of the Layers palette, then scroll down to select the adjustment.

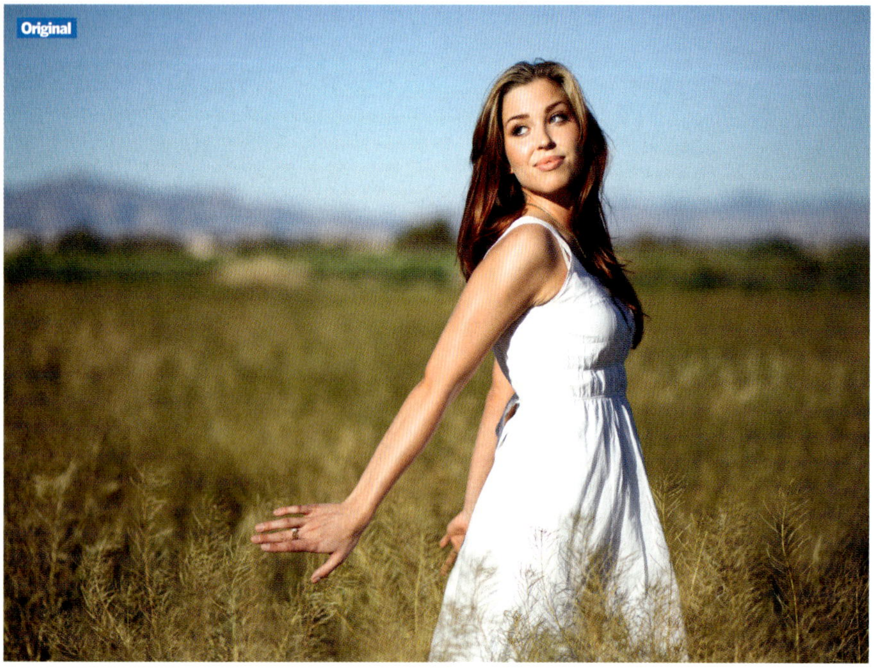

ISTOCKPHOTO

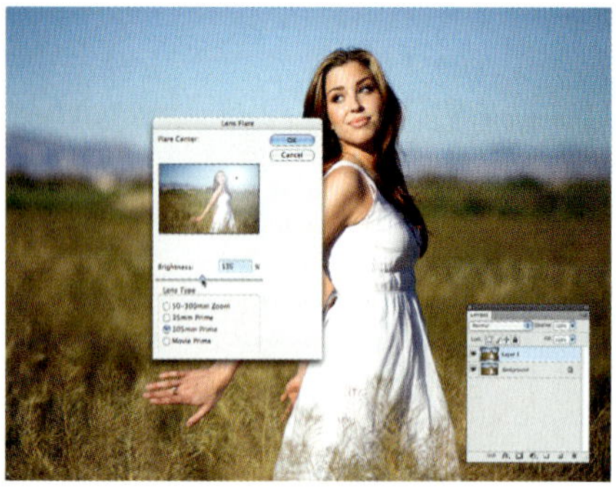

1 Create the sun First, add the sun. To do this, create a duplicate of the original image: go to ***Layer>New>Layer via Copy***, then open ***Filter>Render>Lens Flare...*** Select ***105mm Prime*** from ***Lens Type*** and position the small cross hairs on the thumbnail preview. Finally, enter an appropriate ***Brightness*** amount for the image.

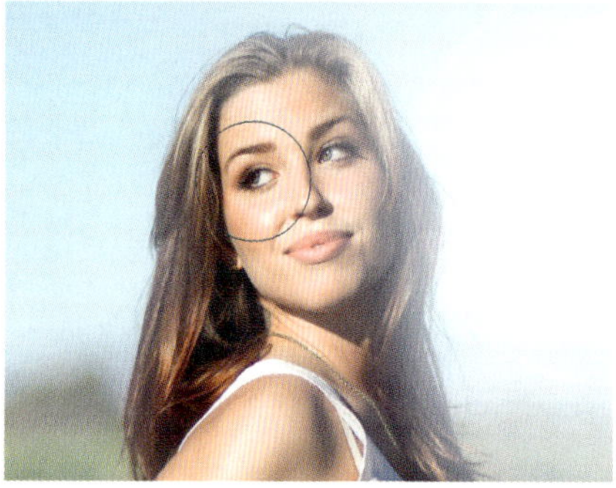

2 Improve the face The flare strength means the subject's face appears very burnt out. To solve this, add a ***Layer Mask*** by clicking the icon in the Layers palette. Select a soft-edged brush, set to ***Black***, with an ***Opacity*** of around ***20%***, and paint over the subject to reduce the effects of the flare, without removing it completely.

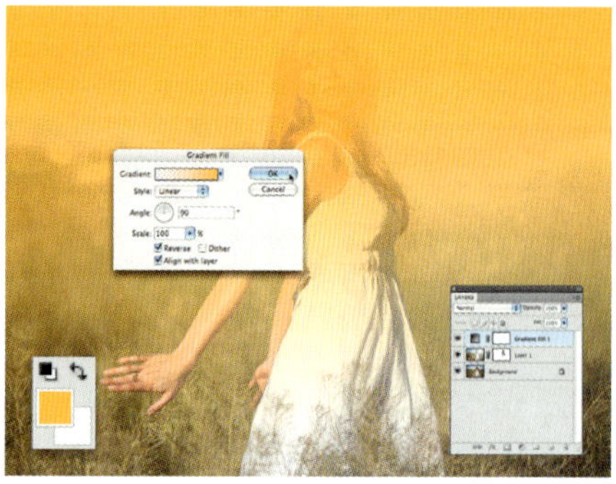

3 Sunset gradient In the toolbar, make sure the ***Background Color*** is ***White***, then click on the ***Foreground Color*** icon. In the Color Picker, change to a sunset colour. Now click on the ***Add new adjustment layer*** icon in the Layers palette and select ***Gradient...*** Set ***Style*** to ***Linear*** and tick ***Reverse***, so the gradient runs from top to bottom.

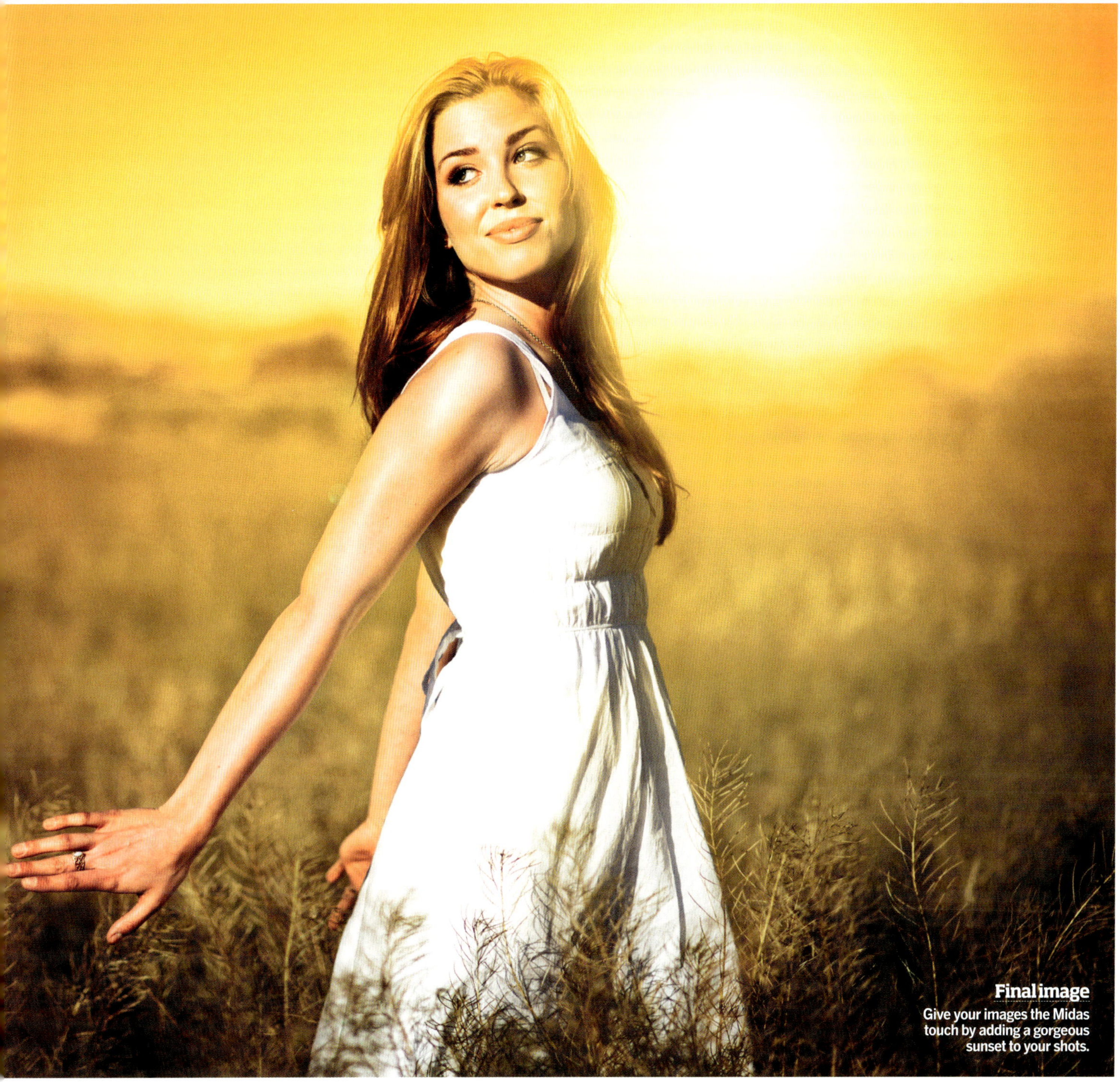

Final image
Give your images the Midas touch by adding a gorgeous sunset to your shots.

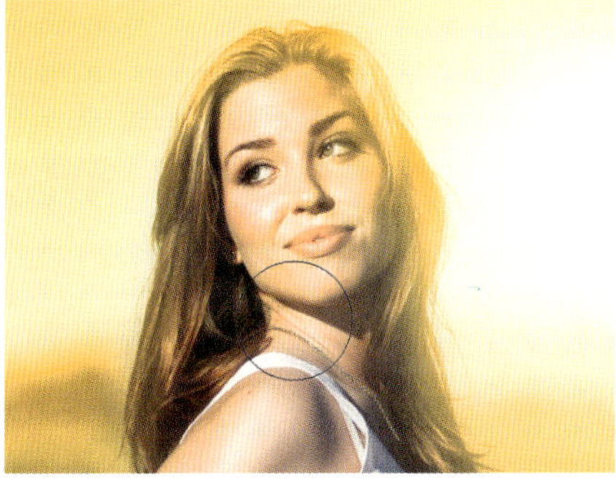

4 Tweak the gradient Change the ***Blend Mode*** to ***Color***. To reduce the colour tint on the subject, use a ***Layer Mask***, as in step two. A Gradient adjustment layer has a Layer Mask by default, so click on it in the Layers palette, select a medium soft-edged brush, set to ***Black***, with ***Opacity*** at ***20%***, and begin work on the subject.

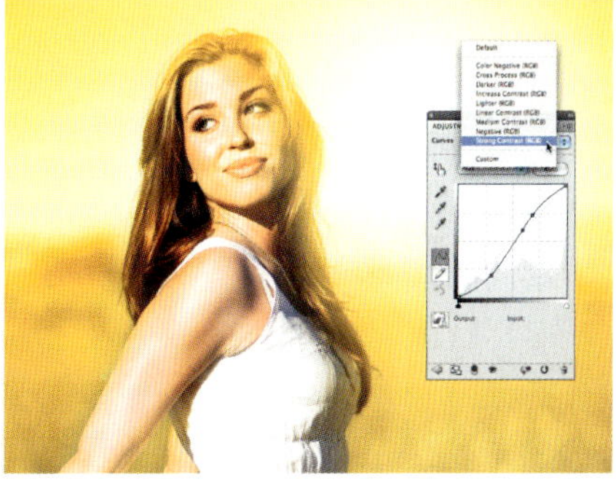

5 Use Curves Click the ***Add new adjustment layer*** icon and choose ***Curves***... Now you can create an 'S' curve or choose ***Strong Contrast*** from the ***Preset*** menu and click ***OK***. The effect can be harsh on the subject's face, so add a ***Layer Mask*** and reduce the effects by using the ***Brush Tool*** set to ***Black***, as in the previous step.

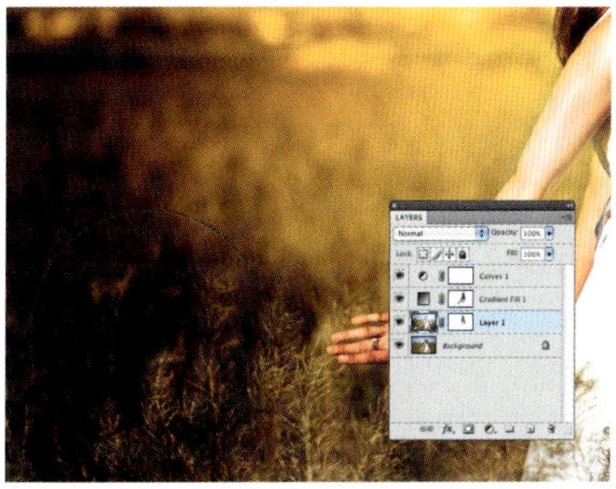

6 Burn the foreground To finish, click on the duplicate image layer that holds the flare, ensuring the image thumbnail is active and not the Layer Mask. Select the ***Burn Tool*** and, using a large soft-edged brush with ***Opacity*** set to about ***20%***, begin to work around the foreground of the image to darken it off, adding depth to the image.

Apply body art

Make your portraits a little more edgy and interesting with this simple step-by-step

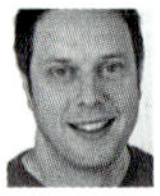

Luke Marsh: Tattoos are one of those artistic accessories that you either love or you hate, but whatever camp you sit in, one thing you can't dispute is that they add visual interest and a focal point to a picture. Tattoos are statement pieces, so applying one to a simple image, like this one, allows it to have unbridled impact. Careful consideration should be given to picking a suitable picture and the placement of the tattoo as you want to enhance, not distract from, the rest of the image.

While the technique for applying the tattoo is quite simple, it'll be much easier if your tattoo image is on a white background first as, if not, you'll need to cleanly select it before placing it on the body, which can be tricky with intricate designs.

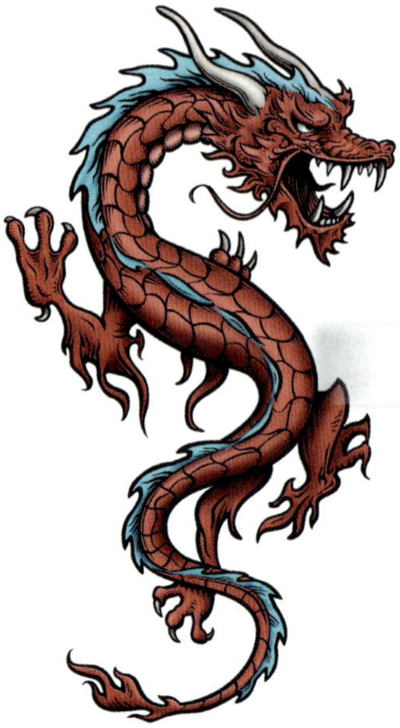

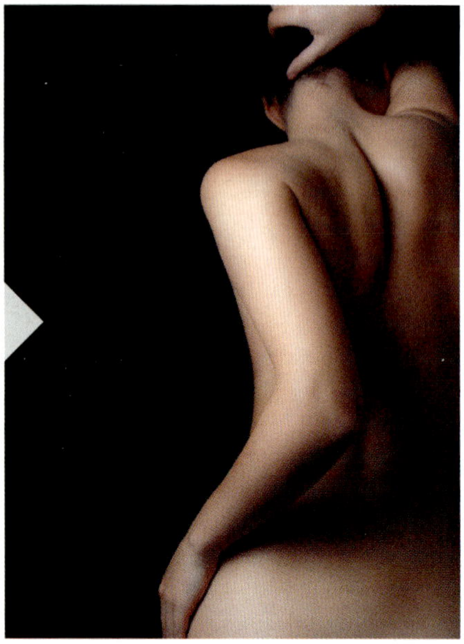

IMAGES: ISTOCKPHOTO

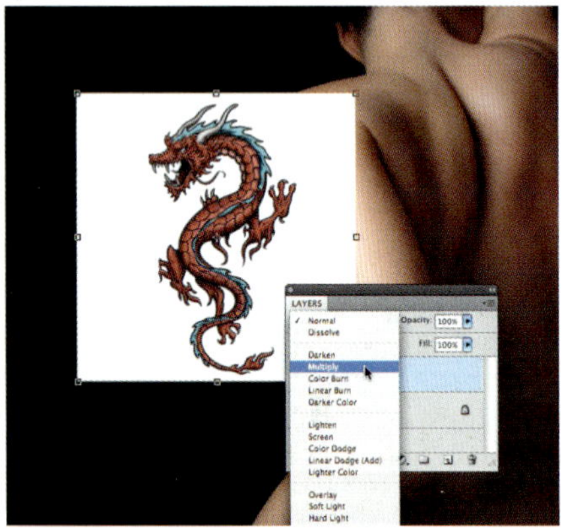

1 Combine the files The first thing to do is combine the two files you've chosen. With the tattoo image open, choose ***Select>All*** then go to ***Edit>Copy***, copying the image to the pasteboard. Close the file and open your body image, and go to ***Edit>Paste***, placing the tattoo image onto a new layer, above the body image. Now change the layer's ***Blend Mode*** to ***Multiply***, making the white in the tattoo transparent.

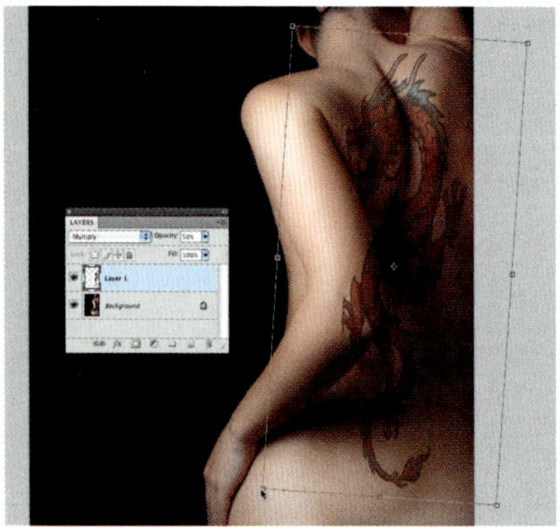

2 Resize the tattoo Change the tattoo layer's ***Opacity*** to around ***50%*** to give the tattoo a far more subtle and realistic appearance. Now select the ***Move Tool*** and position the tattoo where you want it on the subject. Go to ***Edit>Free Transform*** and use the centre and corner tabs to resize the tattoo to suit your subject. Placing the cursor just outside any of the corner tabs will allow you to rotate the tattoo, should you wish to do so.

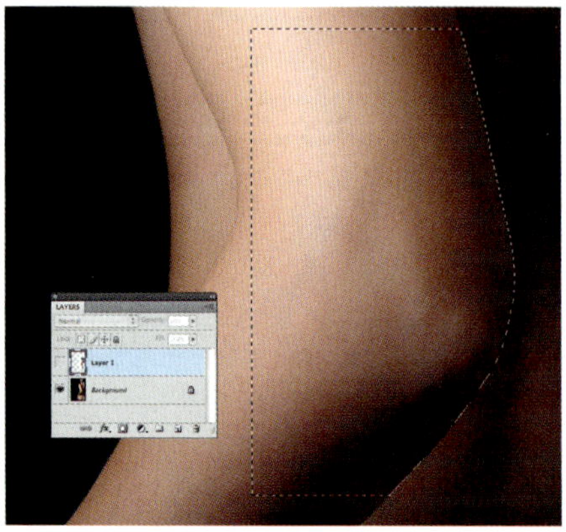

3 Edit the tattoo Limbs that overlap the tattoo can add depth to an image and realism to the effect. To help view the body clearly, hide the tattoo layer by clicking on the eye icon in the Layers palette. Here, the elbow area needs to be selected in order to isolate it from the tattoo. To do this, use the ***Polygonal Lasso Tool*** to work around the elbow, taking your time to get an accurate selection.

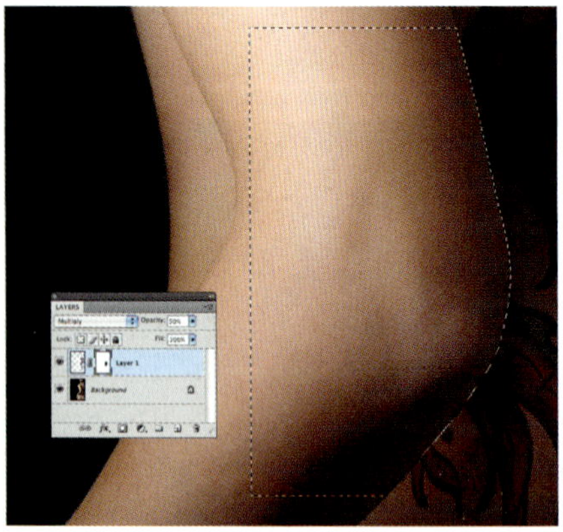

4 Add a Layer Mask Once the selection is made, add a ***Feather*** to ***1*** pixel (***Select>Modify>Feather...***). Now create a Layer Mask by going to ***Layer>Layer Mask>Reveal All***, then go to ***Edit>Fill...*** and select ***Use as Black*** and click ***OK***. These commands fill the selection with black on the Layer Mask and, subsequently, any of the tattoo underneath the black area is hidden, giving the illusion that the elbow passes in front of it.

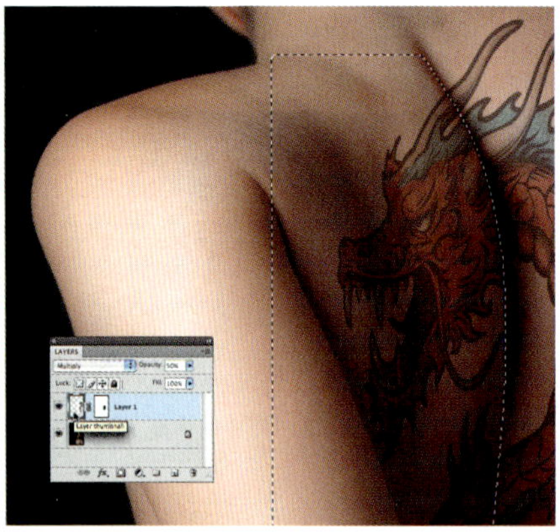

5 Shape the tattoo To edit the tattoo image rather than its Layer Mask, click on the image thumbnail in the Layers palette. The main body contour on this image is the crease in the model's back, so this is where you'd expect to see the most distortion. Using the ***Polygonal Lasso Tool***, make a rough selection along the crease and ***Feather*** the selection to ***5*** pixels to soften the transition of the Liquify effect you are about to apply.

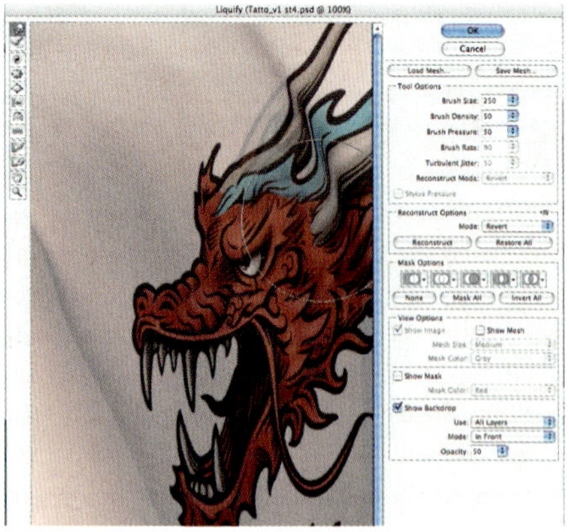

6 Use Liquify Open the Liquify control panel (***Filter>Liquify...***) where you'll preview the image selection. Ensure ***Show Backdrop*** is ticked to see the body layer, then select the ***Forward Warp Tool*** in the top-left corner. Set the ***Brush Size*** to ***250***, then both ***Brush Density*** and ***Brush Pressure*** to ***50***. Now move the brush down along the crease to distort the tattoo, using ***Edit>Undo*** if you want to try again. Click ***OK*** when done.

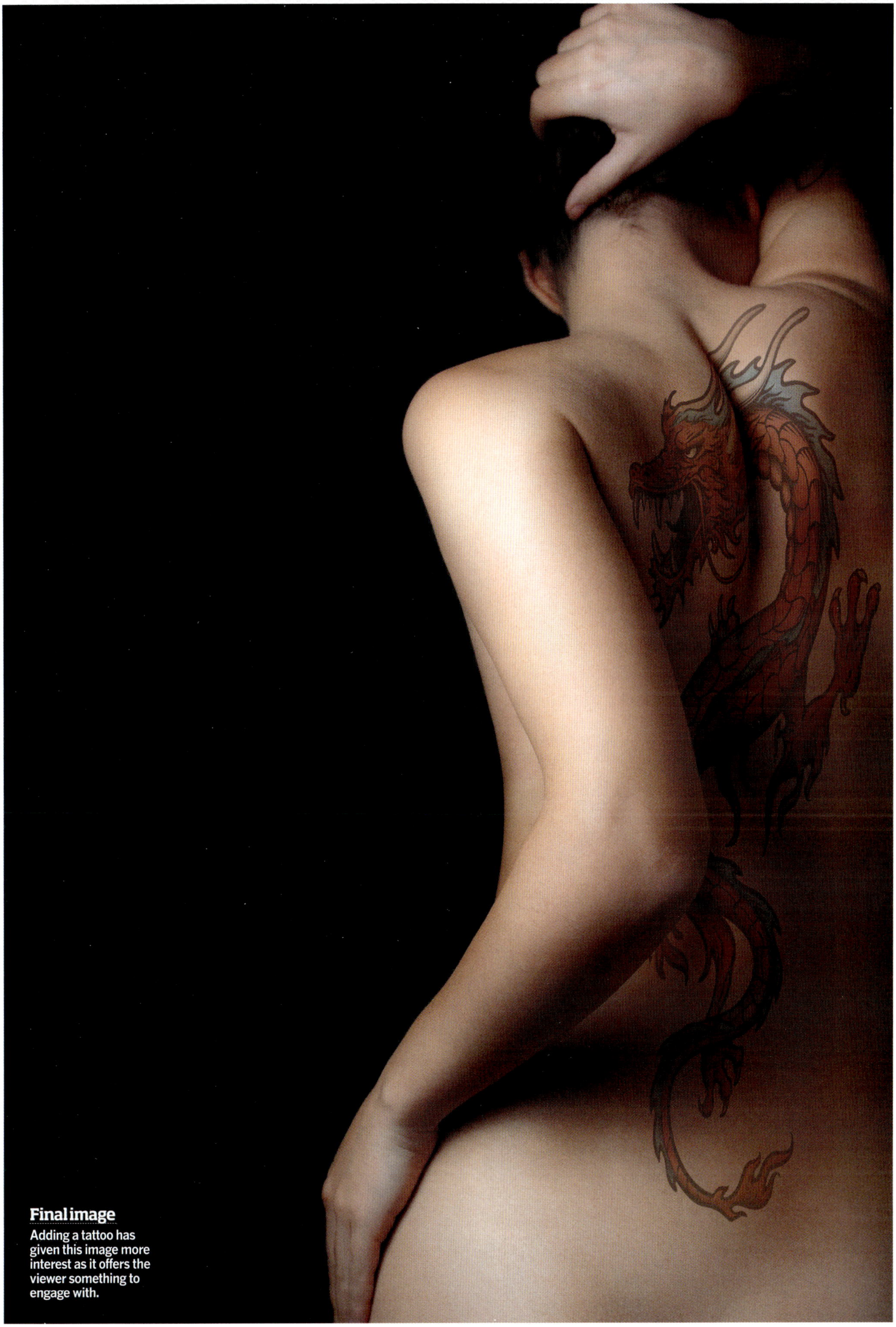

Final image

Adding a tattoo has given this image more interest as it offers the viewer something to engage with.

Add a dispersion effect

Make your subject dissipate using this easy yet impactful technique to manipulate motion and make your action shots far more artistic

Jordan Butters: A fun part of editing and manipulating images is taking a picture beyond the boundaries of reality and this dispersion effect does just that. It allows you to make a moving person or object seem as if they are moving so quickly that they leave trails of colour and particles behind.

An important part of this technique relies on you picking, or shooting, the right type of image. For effective results, pick a picture with motion; it could be as simple as an action shot, someone jumping or hair blowing in the wind. You'll find the selection stage easier if your subject is set against a clean backdrop, too, such as a white wall or blue sky. You'll also need a selection of splat Photoshop brushes, which can be downloaded free from an online brush library, such as www.brusheezy.com.

Workflow tools

✓ BRUSHES PALETTE

The Brushes palette window allows you to tweak and manipulate preset brushes to suit your application. From the Brushes palette, you can change the direction and shape of the brush tip, vary the spacing, scatter, shape dynamics and texture, and even apply dual brushes at once. There is a handy preview window at the bottom of the palette for you to see how the adjusted settings affect the brush and its effect.

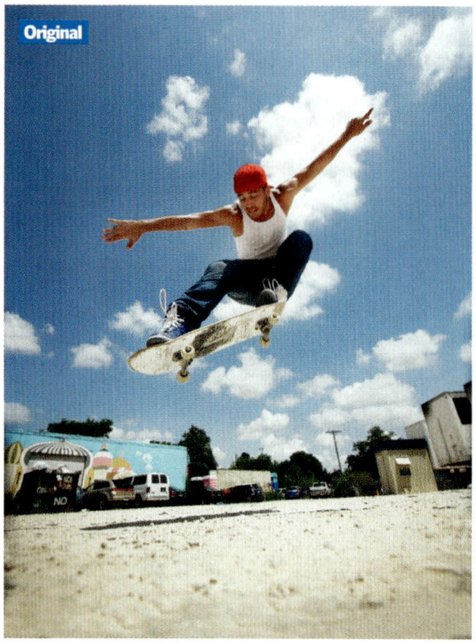

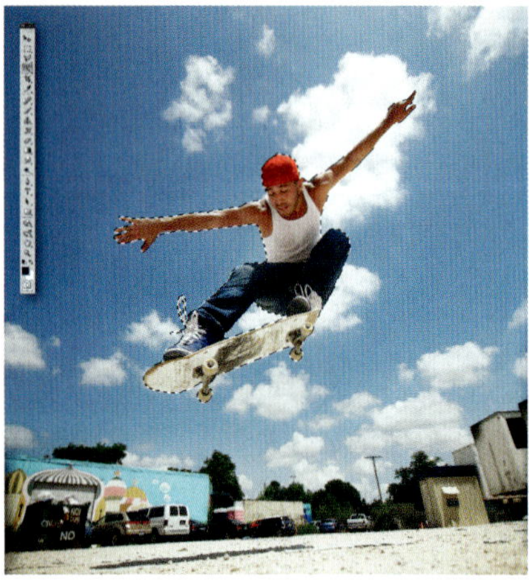

1 Separate your subject Using the ***Quick Selection Tool***, draw around your subject to select the background behind them. If the tool picks out an area you don't want selected, hold down the ***alt*** key and go back over the area to deselect. Zoom in and reduce the brush ***Size*** for detailed areas. Once happy, go ***Select>Inverse***.

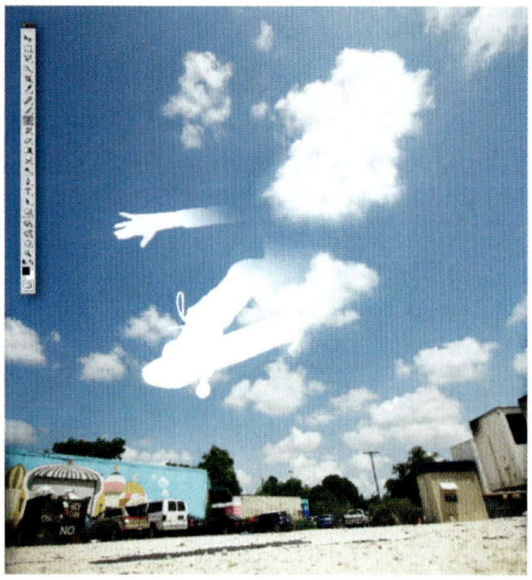

2 Remove your subject Go to ***Edit>Cut*** to remove your subject. Select the ***Clone Stamp Tool*** and hold down the ***alt*** key to set your reference point. Begin cloning out the silhouette until you are left with a clean backdrop; it need not be perfect, but the closer the better. Go to ***Edit>Paste*** to paste your subject onto a new layer.

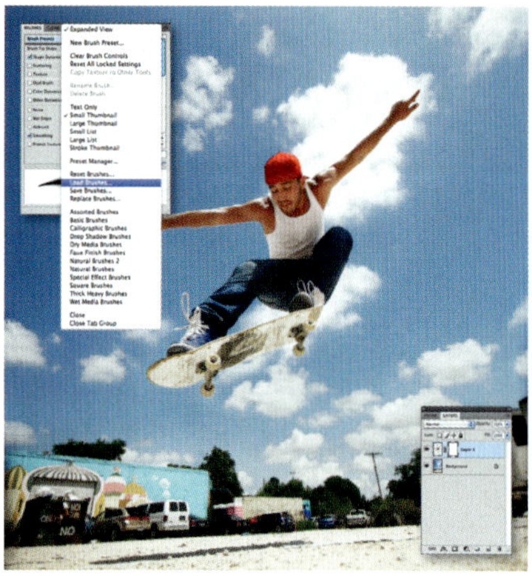

3 Load the brushes Click on the ***Add layer mask*** button and select the ***Brush Tool***. Go to ***Window>Brushes*** to bring up the Brushes palette and click on the small menu button at the top right to select ***Load Brushes***. Locate the splatter brush set that you have downloaded on your computer and click ***Load***.

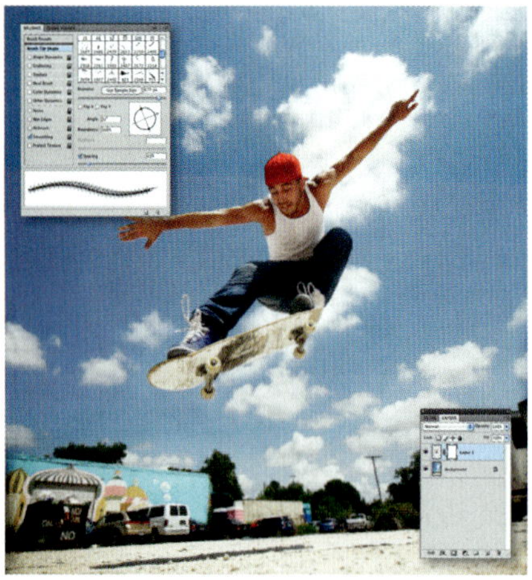

4 Customise your brushes Scroll down to choose one of the new splatter brushes and select ***Brush Tip Shape*** on the left. Set the brush size using the slider and the angle of your brush by rotating the compass on the right. The angle of your brush should match the direction that your subject is moving in.

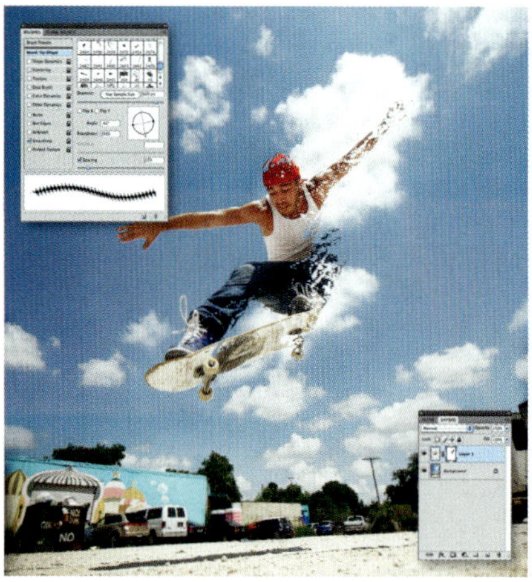

5 Start masking Making sure that your ***Foreground Color*** is set to ***Black***, begin clicking to mask areas of your subject, revealing the background behind. Repeat the previous step after each click to change the brush and vary the effect. Once happy with this stage, click on the ***Create new layer*** button in the Layers palette.

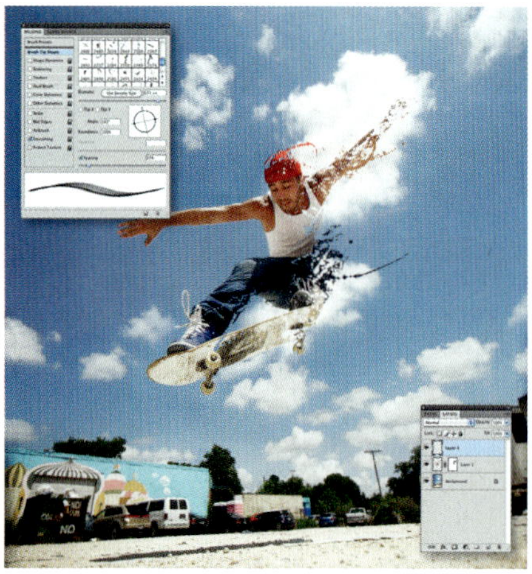

6 Add splats and trails Select the ***Brush Tool*** and once again go into the Brushes palette. Choose a splatter and set the ***Angle*** of your brush. Before you apply each splat, use the ***Eyedropper Tool*** to pick a colour sample from your subject. Select the ***Brush Tool*** again and apply the splat, starting from the area of colour you selected.

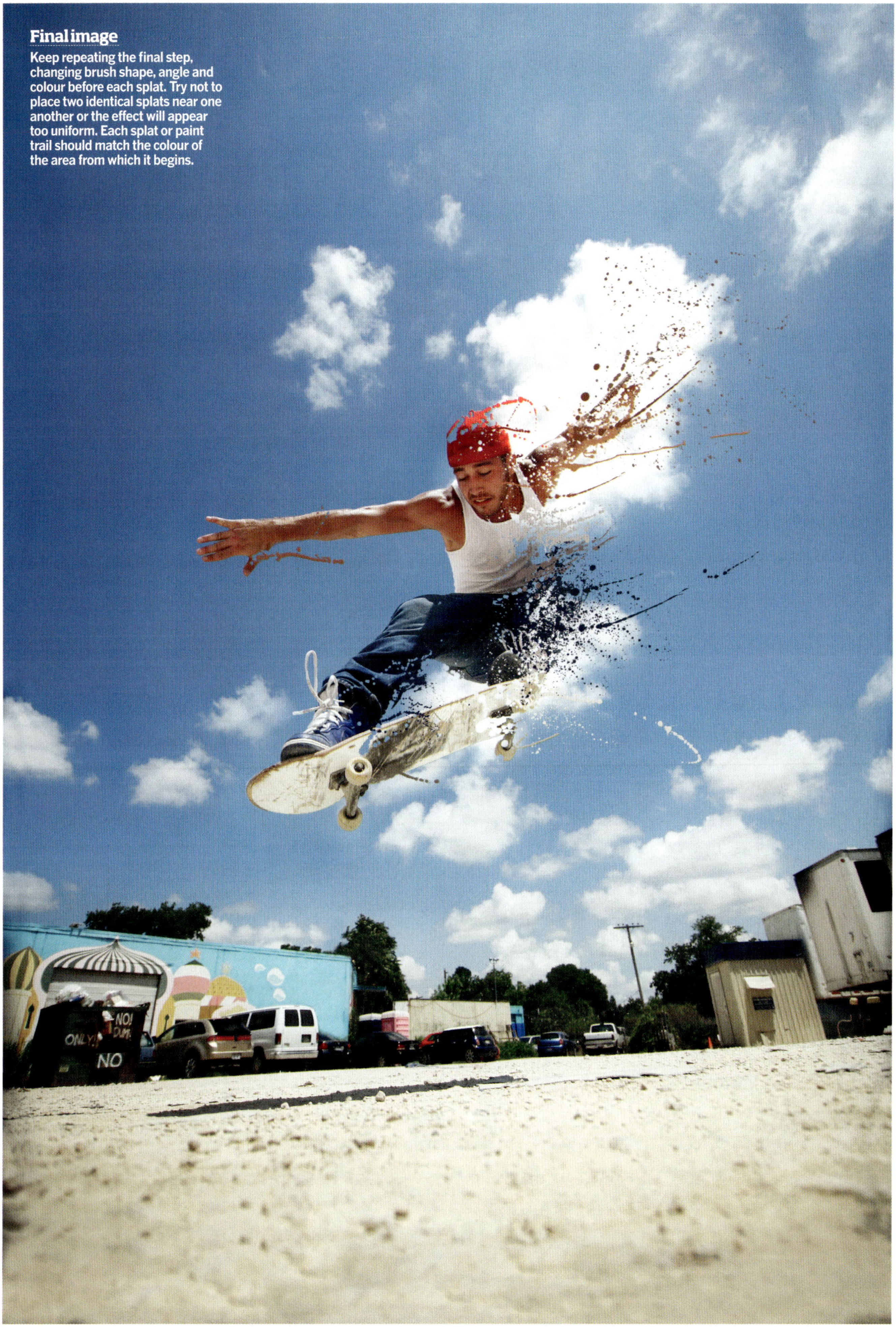

Final image

Keep repeating the final step, changing brush shape, angle and colour before each splat. Try not to place two identical splats near one another or the effect will appear too uniform. Each splat or paint trail should match the colour of the area from which it begins.

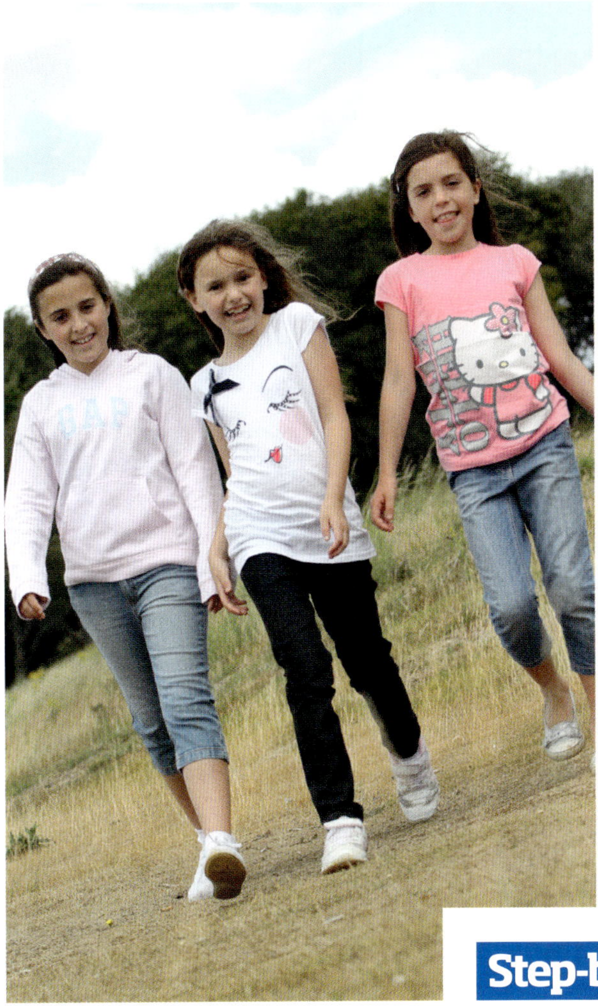
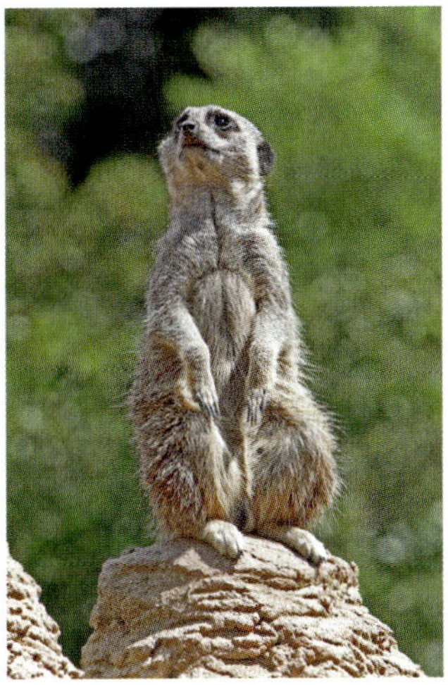
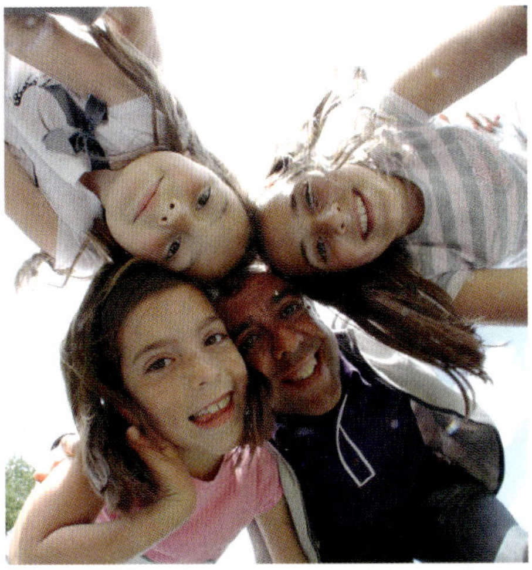
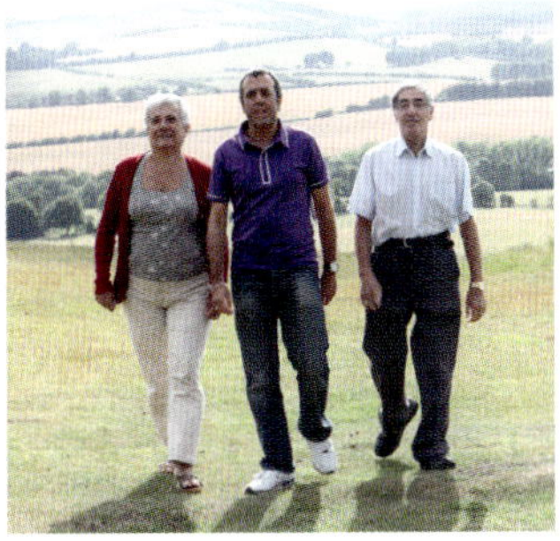
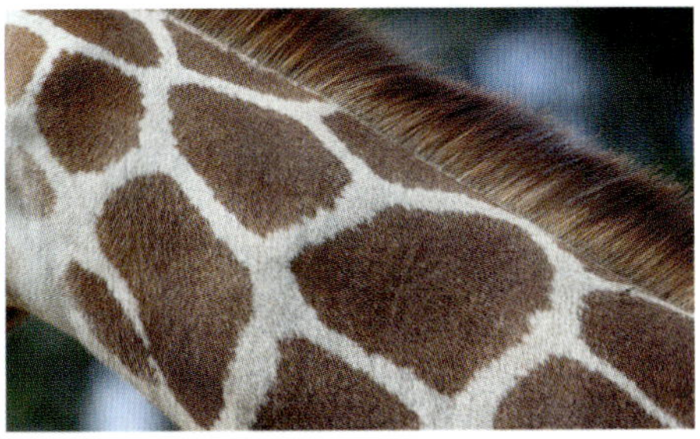
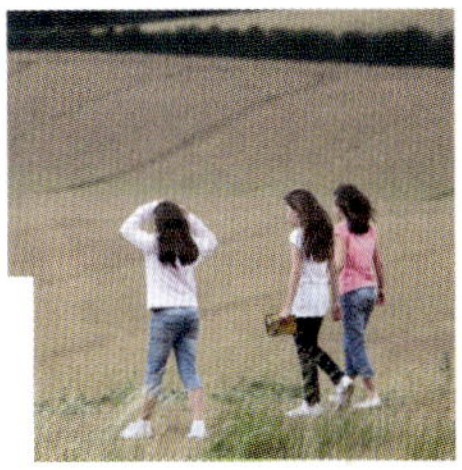
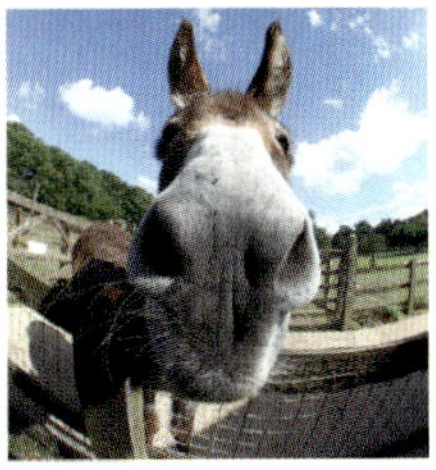

Step-by-step tutorials

PRESENTATION

Add a finishing touch to your images with our favourite ways to present your photos

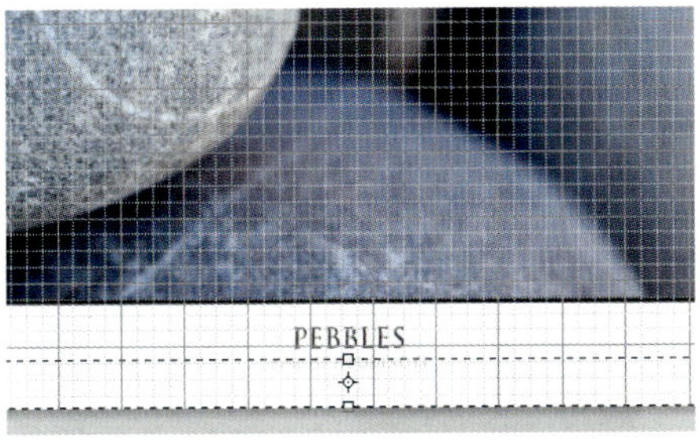

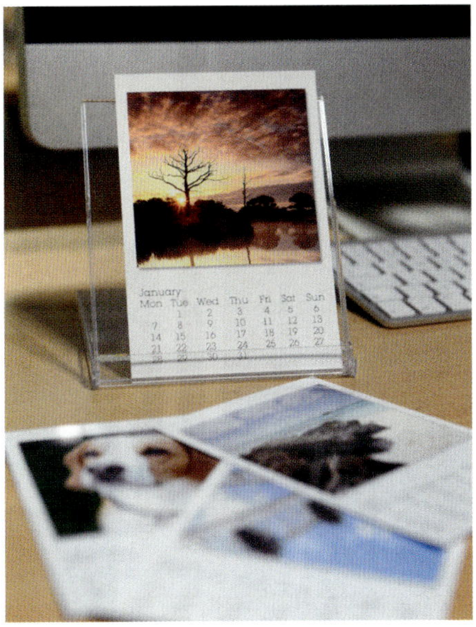
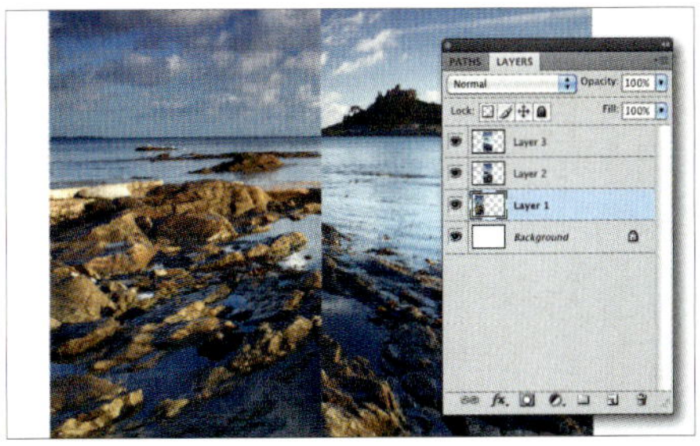
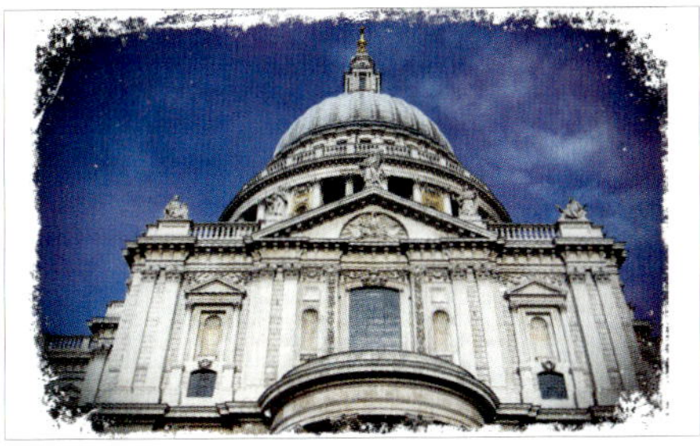
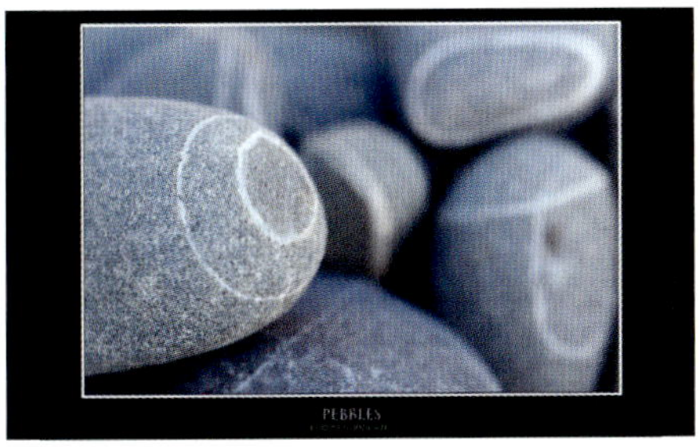

Create a photo collage

Combine a collection of images to tell a story by getting to grips with Clipping Masks to create a funky photo collage

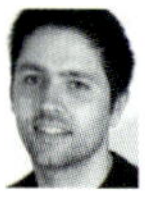

Jordan Butters: A collage is a collection of two or more images within a single image file. They are becoming increasingly popular with wedding and lifestyle photographers, as they're a great way to creatively tell a story through a series of related images.

Collages tend to work best when there is an underlying theme running throughout – this could be a holiday, day out or even a colour. To maximise interest, try to include a variety of different images within the collage that show various subjects, techniques, compositions or types of image such as a portrait combined with a close-up and a scenic landscape.

The long-winded way to piece it together is to manually copy and paste each image onto one document, before using the Transform tools to resize and shift them into position. However, Photoshop's preset shapes and Clipping Mask feature makes it a lot quicker and easier – here we show you how.

Other ideas to try

You don't have to stick to rectangular shapes when creating your collage. Use the ***Custom Shape Tool*** to create unique shapes within your collage, or to frame a single image. You can change the colour of the frames between the images by selecting the ***Background layers*** in the Layers palette and using the ***Paint Bucket Tool*** equipped with the colour of your choosing. Alternatively, why not fill the Background layer with a pattern?

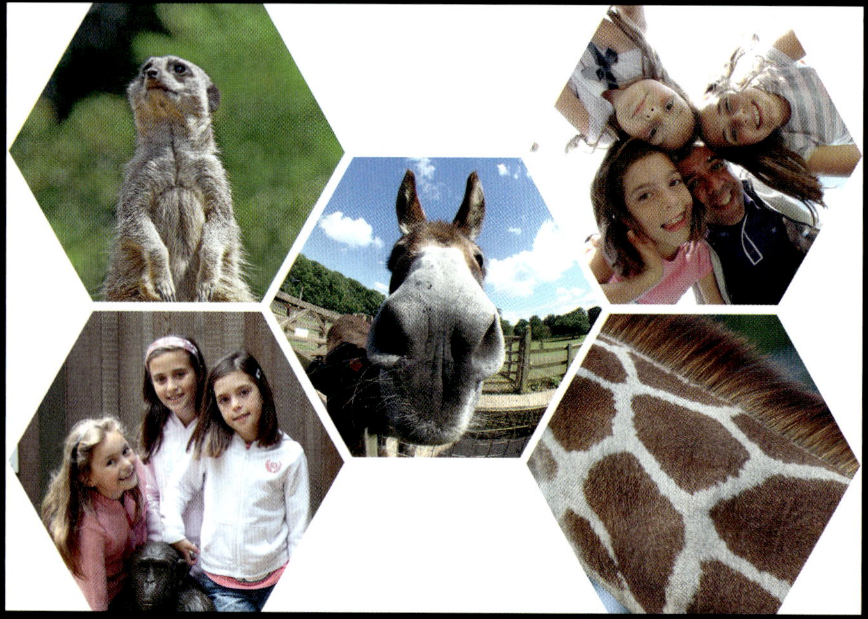

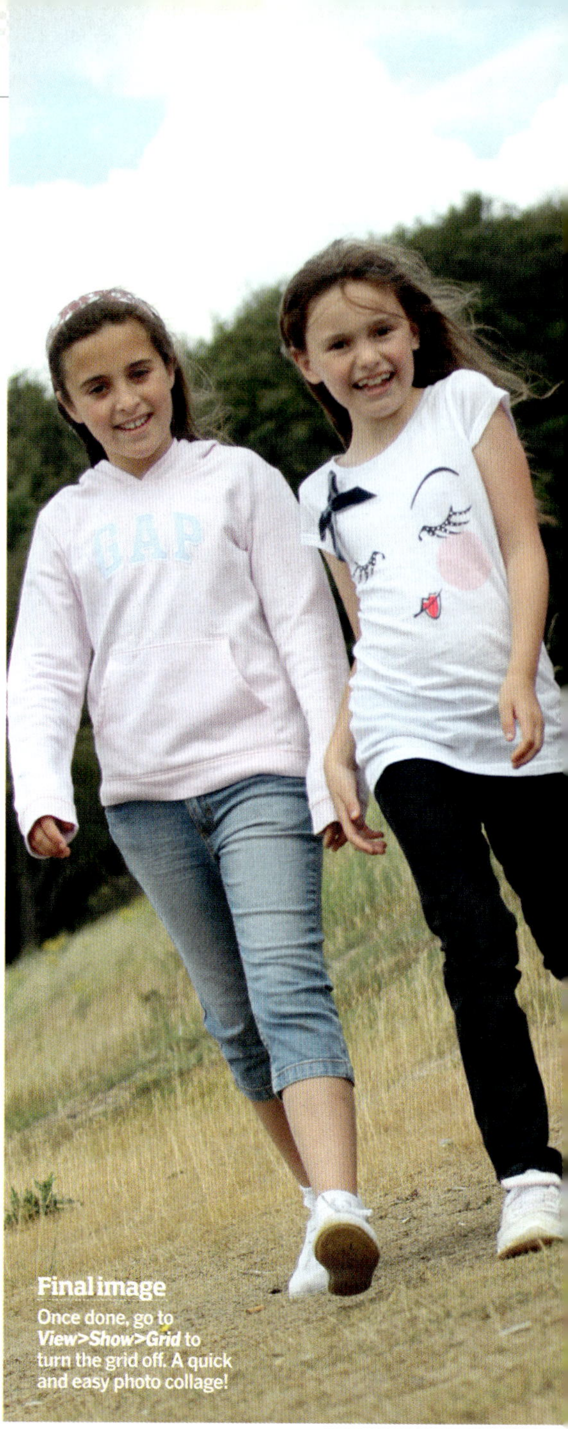

Final image
Once done, go to ***View>Show>Grid*** to turn the grid off. A quick and easy photo collage!

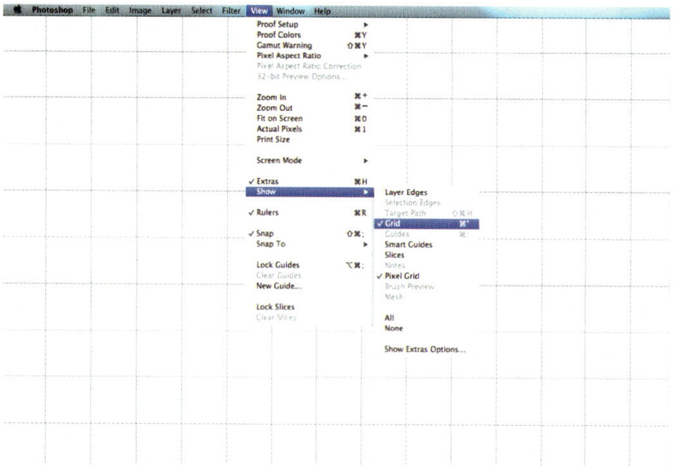

1 Create your document Go to ***File>New*** and select your image dimensions of your new document. Click ***OK***. Now go to ***View>Show*** and make sure that ***Grid*** is selected. Also in the ***View*** menu, make sure that ***Snap To>Grid*** is enabled as this will make placing images easier.

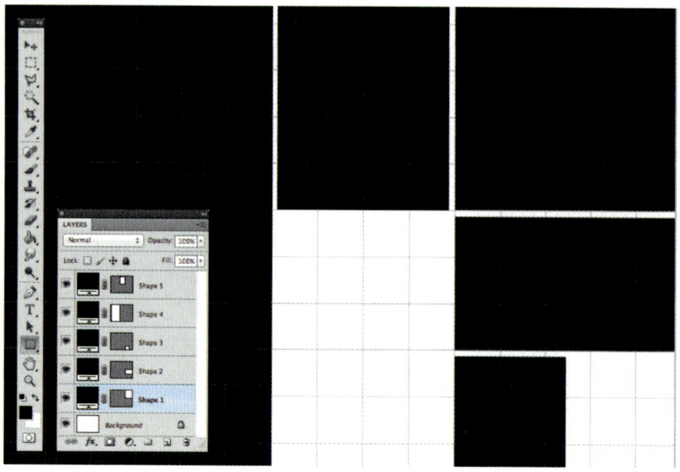

2 Mark out the layout Select the ***Rectangle Tool*** and, with your images in mind, create rectangles on your image to mark your layout. Pay close attention to the grid – the collage will look more aesthetically pleasing if the gaps between the rectangles are the same size throughout.

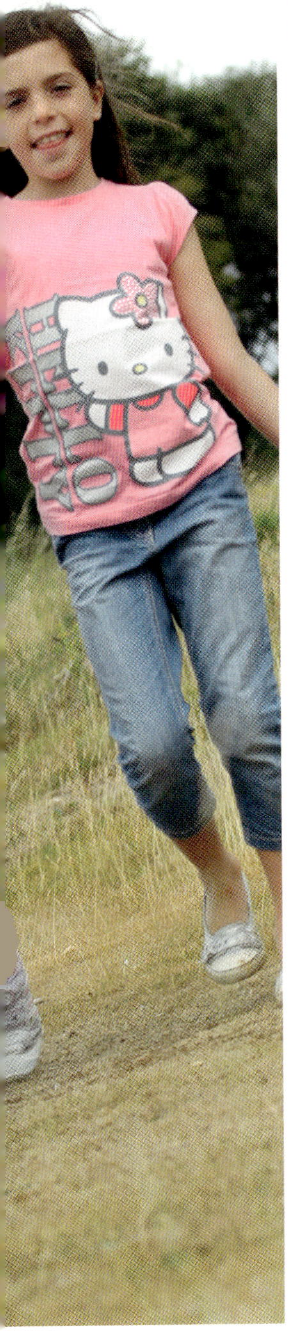
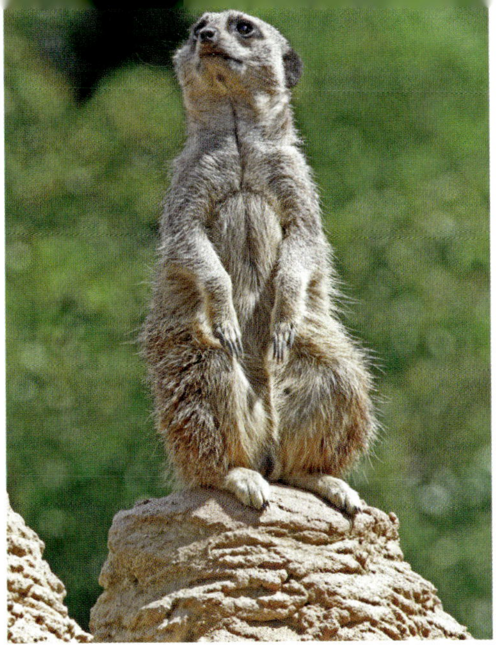
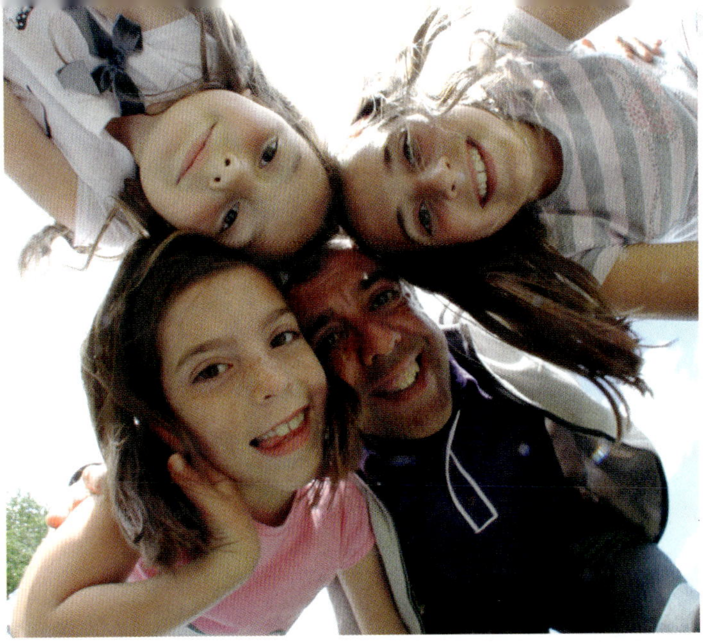
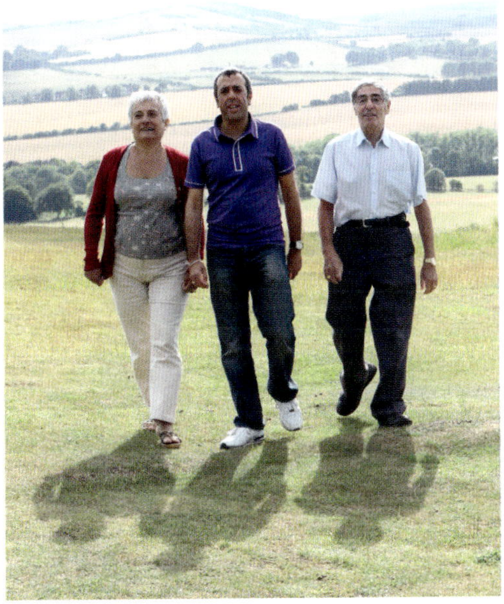
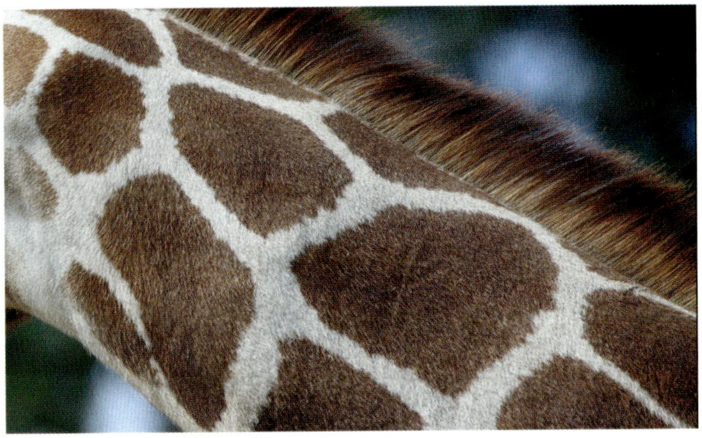
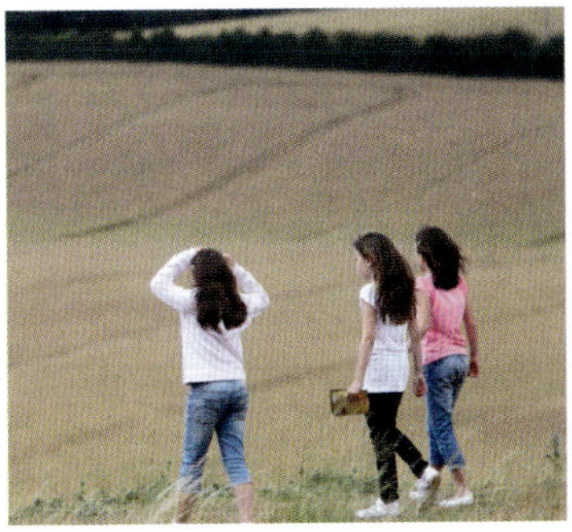
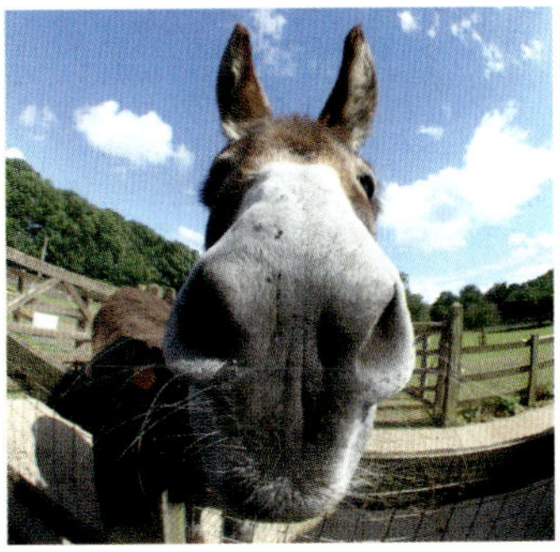
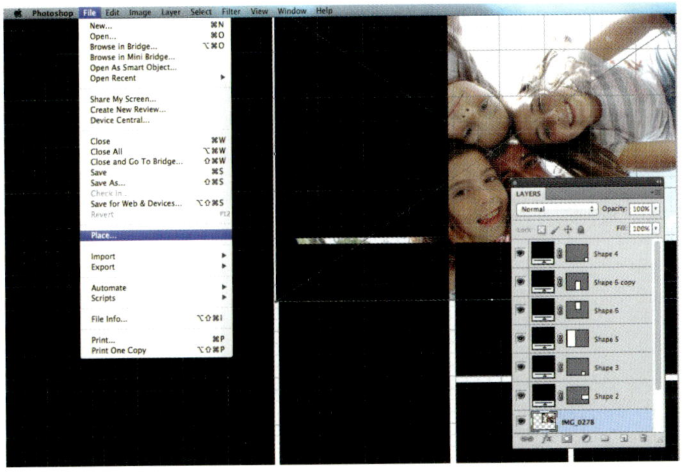

3 Place the image In the Layers palette, select one of your shape layers and go to ***File>Place***. Locate the first image on your computer and click ***OK***. Move the image into place, using the anchor points in the corners, if necessary, to scale the image before pressing the ***enter*** key.

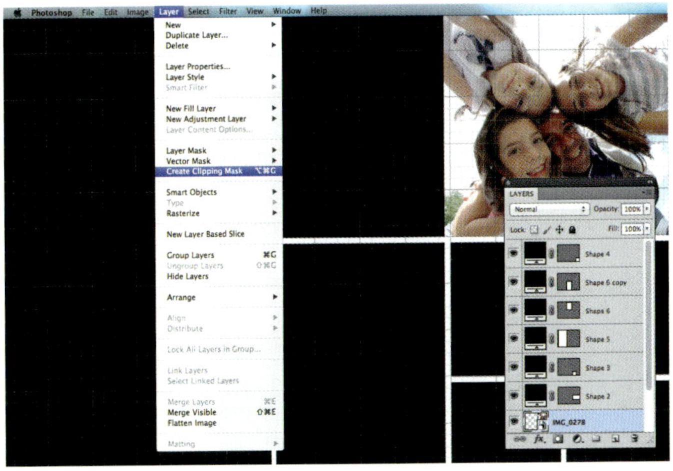

4 Create a Clipping Mask Go to ***Layer>Create Clipping Mask*** to clip the image to the rectangle shape. You can then use the ***Move Tool*** to reposition the image within that space. Repeat steps three and four, selecting a new shape layer before placing each image.

Learn how to frame your prints

Finish off your photographs with a classic framing and title technique

Caroline Wilkinson: We spend a long time deliberating over how to take our best photographs, but little time considering how to translate them to print. Nowadays, the choices for ways to present your pictures are endless: at-home inkjet prints, speciality lab prints, canvas prints, acrylic prints, art posters or simply just showcased on a website. However you decide to present your images, you should make sure it looks its best and that doesn't stop with Photoshop adjustments. Preparing a picture for output is probably the most overlooked part of post-production but spending a little bit of time framing and titling your image gives it a professional finish and elevates it from a pretty picture to a saleable product. Simply take a look in art stores, or even IKEA, and you'll be hard-pressed not to find a print without these finishing touches. Follow these simple steps to find out how to do it...

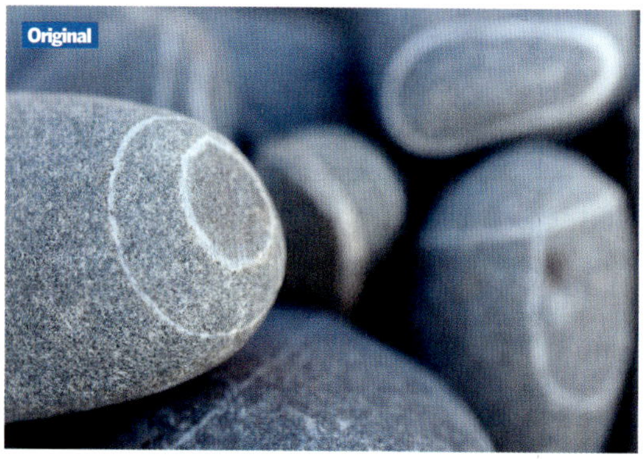

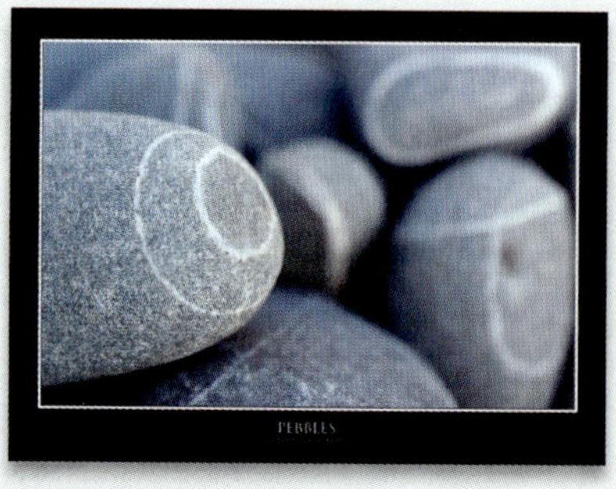

TIP: ALTERNATIVE FRAMING

Instead of a white border, why not choose another colour that complements your image. An easy way to change the colour of the border after you've created it is to select it using the ***Magic Wand Tool***, then use the ***Paint Bucket Tool*** to fill the border with your chosen colour. You may need to change the colour of the ***Stroke*** border too, as explained in step three.

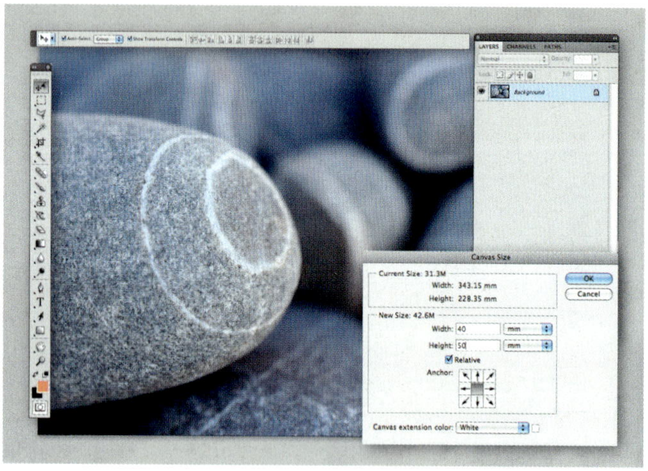

1 Create the border The first thing to do is add a white frame around the image. Go to ***Image>Canvas Size*** and add an extra ***40mm*** to the ***Width*** and ***50mm*** to the ***Height***. The extra 10mm is to allow room for the text to be added later. Leave the ***Anchor*** centred, select the ***Relative*** box and set the ***Canvas*** extension colour to ***White***.

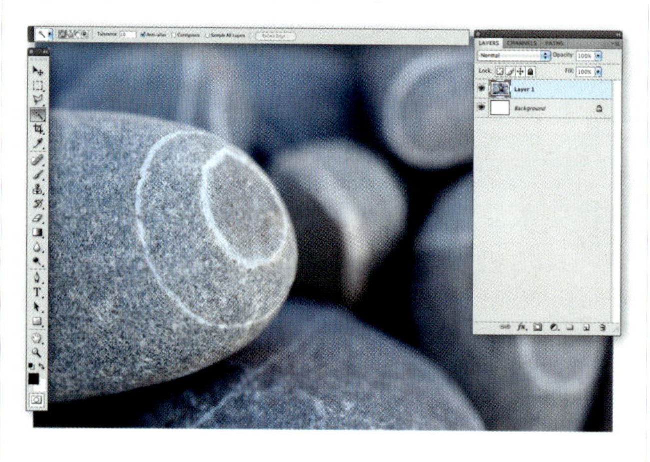

2 Extract the image Select the ***Magic Wand Tool*** from the toolbar and click on the white border. If part of the image is selected too, decrease the ***Tolerance*** level in the Options bar. Go to ***Select>Inverse*** to select the image and then choose ***Layer>New>Layer via Cut*** to extract the image and paste it on to a new empty layer.

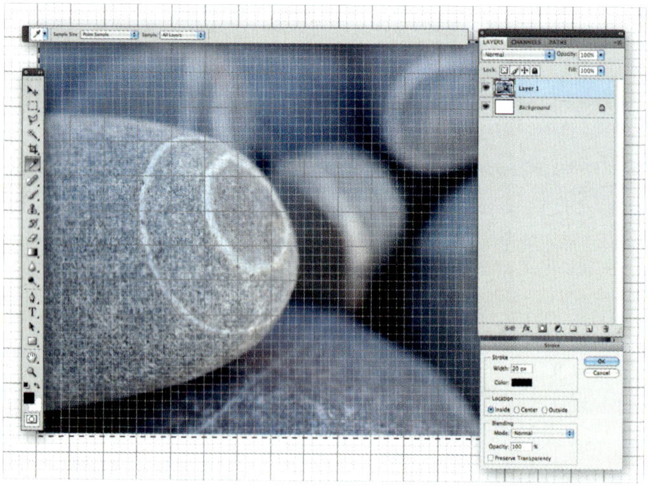

3 Position the image To help with alignment, go to ***View>Show>Grid*** and then ***View>Snap to>Grid.*** Using the ***Move Tool***, drag the image so the edges are equal width on the top, left and right side – using the grid as a guide. Next, using the ***Rectangular Marquee Tool,*** select the image, then go to ***Edit>Stroke*** to add a thin black border. Set the ***Width*** to ***20px***.

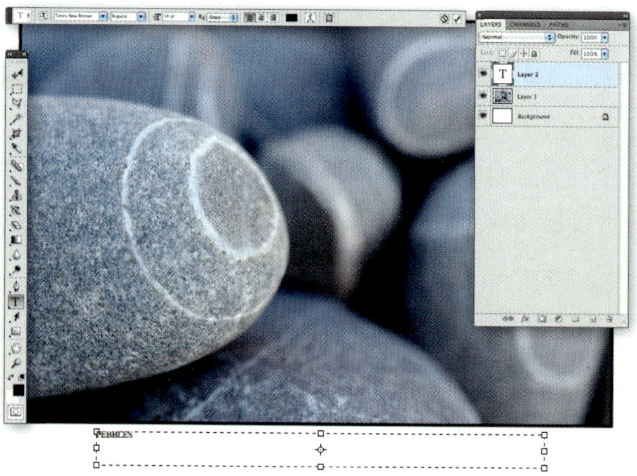

4 Add a title Go to ***Select>Deselect*** to remove the selection and turn off the grid (***View>Show>Grid***) so it is easier to read the text you'll be writing. Using the ***Horizontal Type Tool***, create a text box on the white border below the image and type out your title. Use the Options bar to select the text size, type, weight and colour.

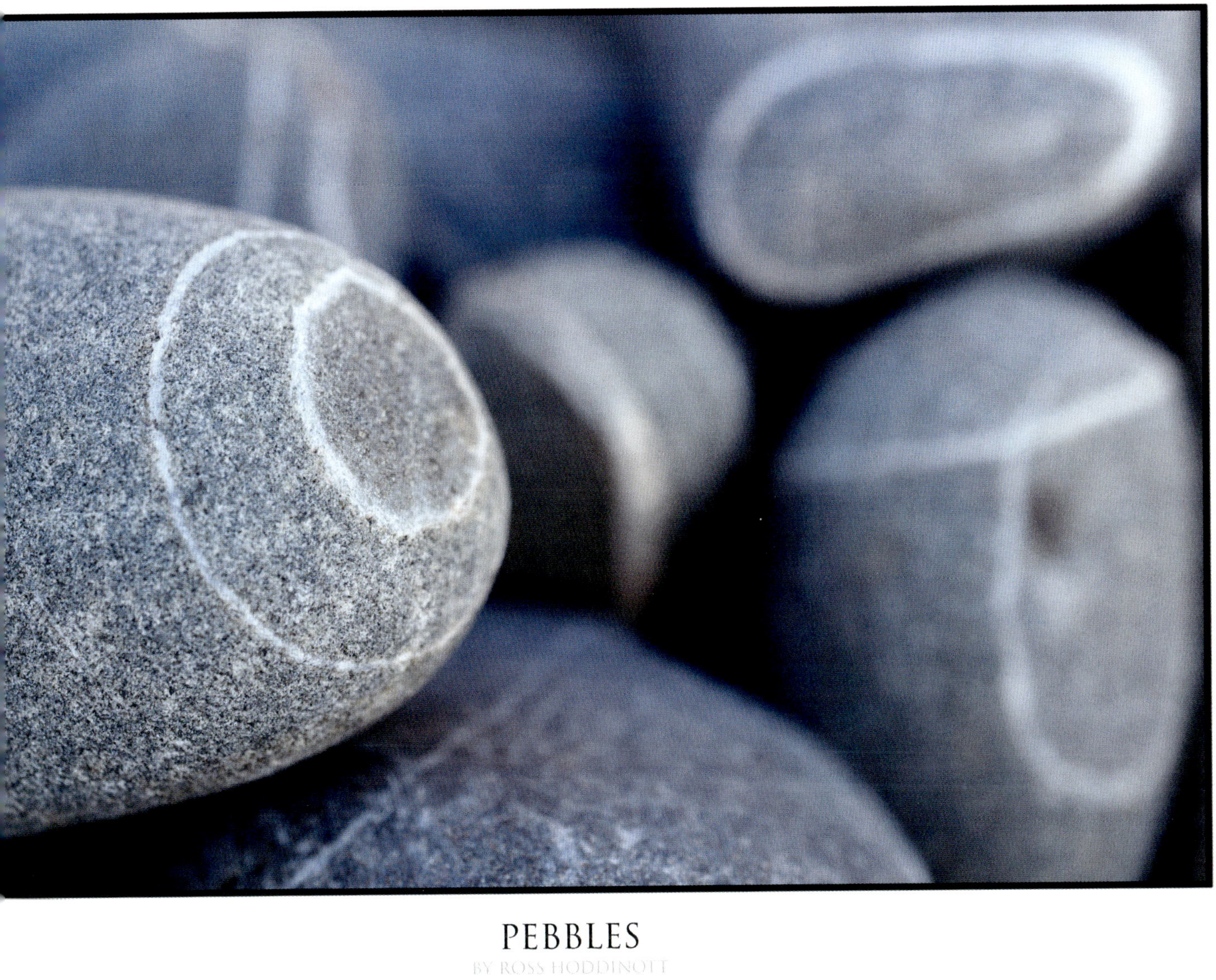

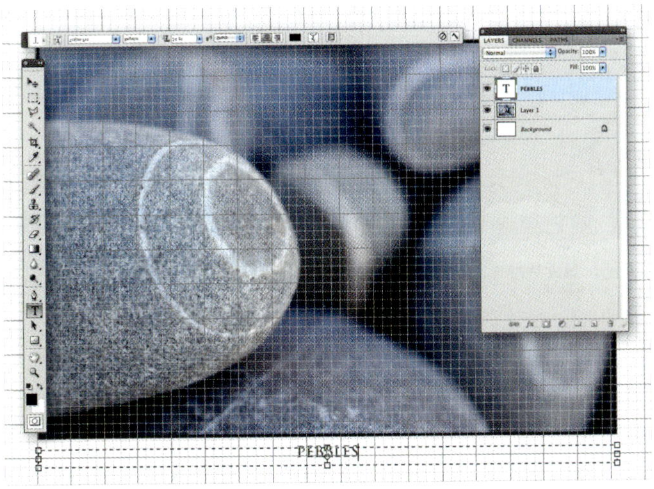

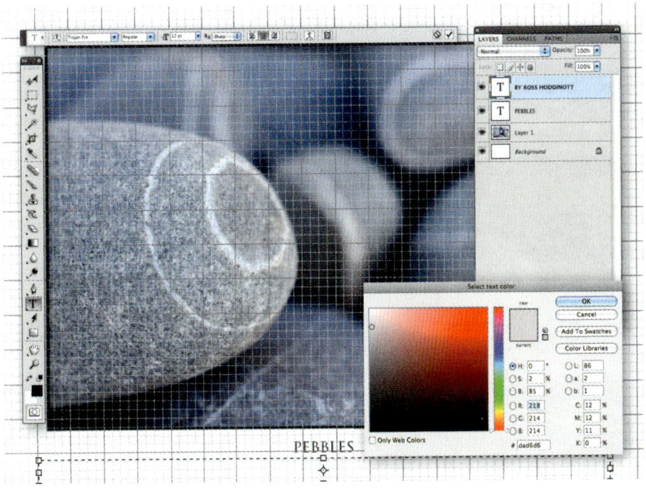

5 Perfect the alignment Once you're happy with the text, click on the ***Center Text*** icon in the Options bar to centrally align the text box with the image. Activate the grid lines again to help with this step (***View>Show>Grid***) and using the ***Move Tool***, drag the text box over until it snaps to the centre of the image/middle grid line.

6 Finishing touch Repeat steps four and five to add a credit line beneath the title. It aesthetically looks better if you make the credit smaller than the title and alter its colour so it's less prominent than the main heading. To change the colour, select the right layer in the Layers palette and click on the coloured box in the Options bar to access the colour picker.

Add a modern grunge frame

Framing a picture is the perfect finishing touch before printing. Find out how to apply unconventional frames for highly creative results

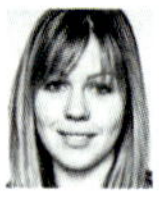

Caroline Wilkinson: Adding a frame to a photograph is really simple: in fact, it took longer to write this article than it did to create the effect. Typically, frames in Photoshop tutorials are plain, straight borders, sometimes with a title added at the bottom: classic, but arguably a little boring for edgier pictures. Grunge borders, on the other hand, add to the character of a photograph and you don't have to create them either – simply blend them with your image. Finding creative frames is fairly easy as you can download many for free or buy certain designs over the internet. There's not much to explain for this tutorial: it's that easy and the results speak for themselves. Pick a frame and give it a go…

Did you know?

If you have a frame from an old photograph or a Polaroid, you can scan it in to Photoshop and follow our step-by-step for applying it to a digital image. You can also find loads of borders by doing an internet search for 'free grunge borders' or download vector borders for a small fee at istockphoto.com

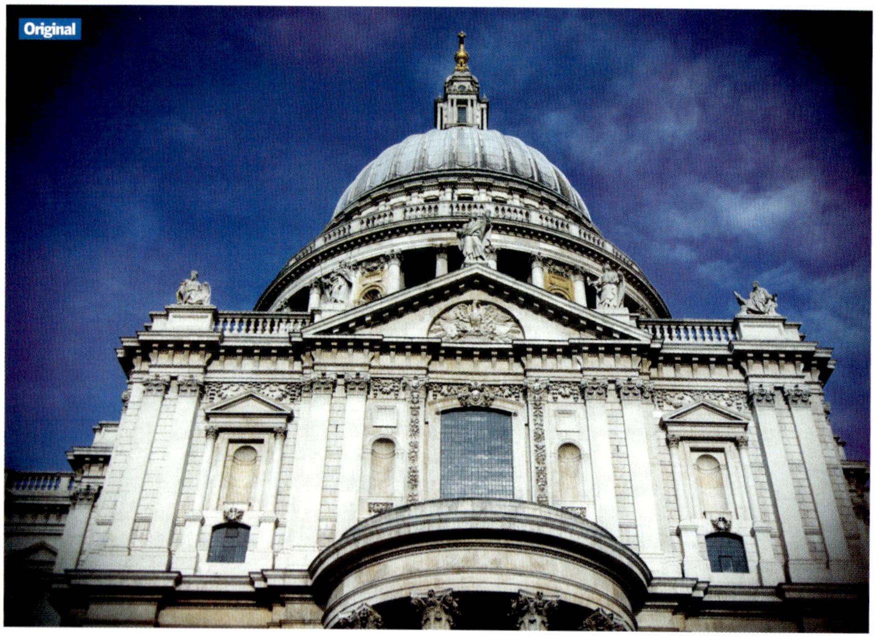

Three simple steps to creating a frame

Draw your own Photoshop, especially CS5, has an extensive brush panel (***Window>Brushes***) which features a plethora of brush types and controllable characteristics. One way to create your own border is to draw it on to your picture. It's not the cleanest method and will look rough around the edges, but this can add character to an image. Have a play and see what effects you can create, but we suggest you combine different brush effects and work on an empty layer (***Layer>New Layer***) rather than the image, in case you want to edit or delete the border without affecting the original image.

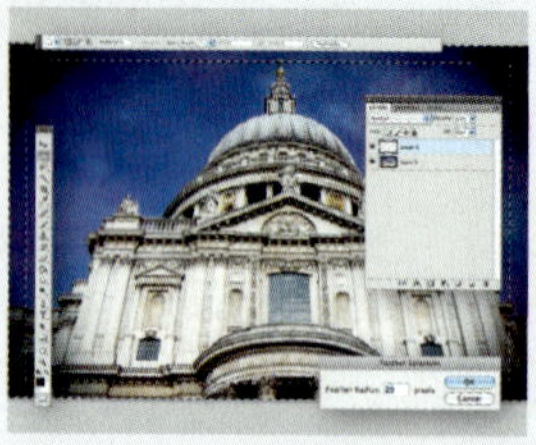

1 Use the ***Rectangular Marquee Tool*** to select the inside of your image, leaving the width of the border you want from the edge. Then go to ***Select>Inverse*** and then ***Select>Modify>Feather***, adding a feather of about ***20px***.

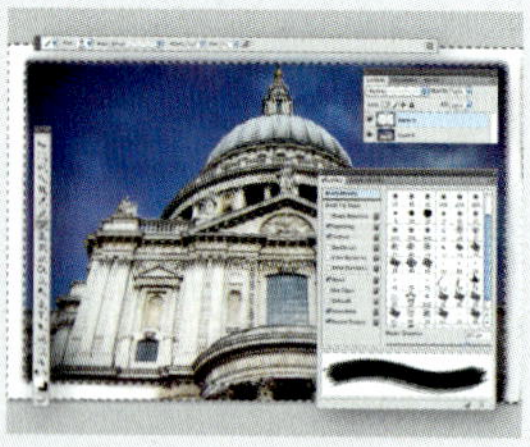

2 Access the Brushes panel (***Window>Brushes***) and pick your style. We advise making the brush ***Diameter*** a bit larger than the width of your border so you can create it in a single stroke. Once you're done, go to ***Select>Deselect***.

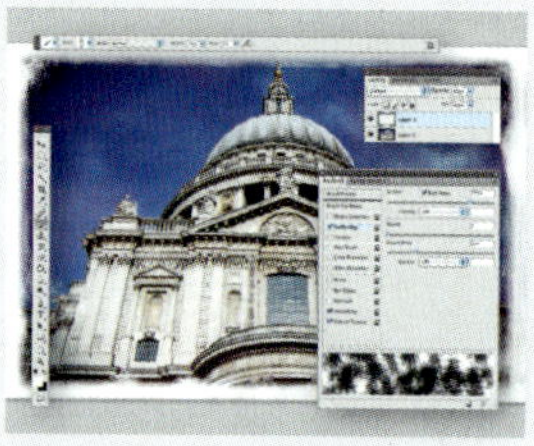

3 The border will probably be fairly clean at this point, which is fine if that's what you want. But if you want to make it look a little grungy, select a brush with ***Scattering*** and dirty up the edges slightly to get your desired effect.

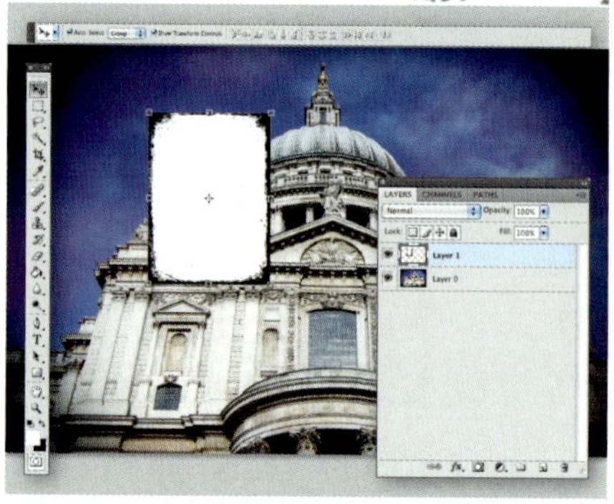

1 Open your image Once you've completed the editing of your image, keep the file open. This type of frame works particularly well on images with a Lomo or vintage toy-camera look, like this one. Now open your chosen frame image and, using the ***Move Tool***, drag the image on top of your processed photo. You'll see it automatically creates a new layer.

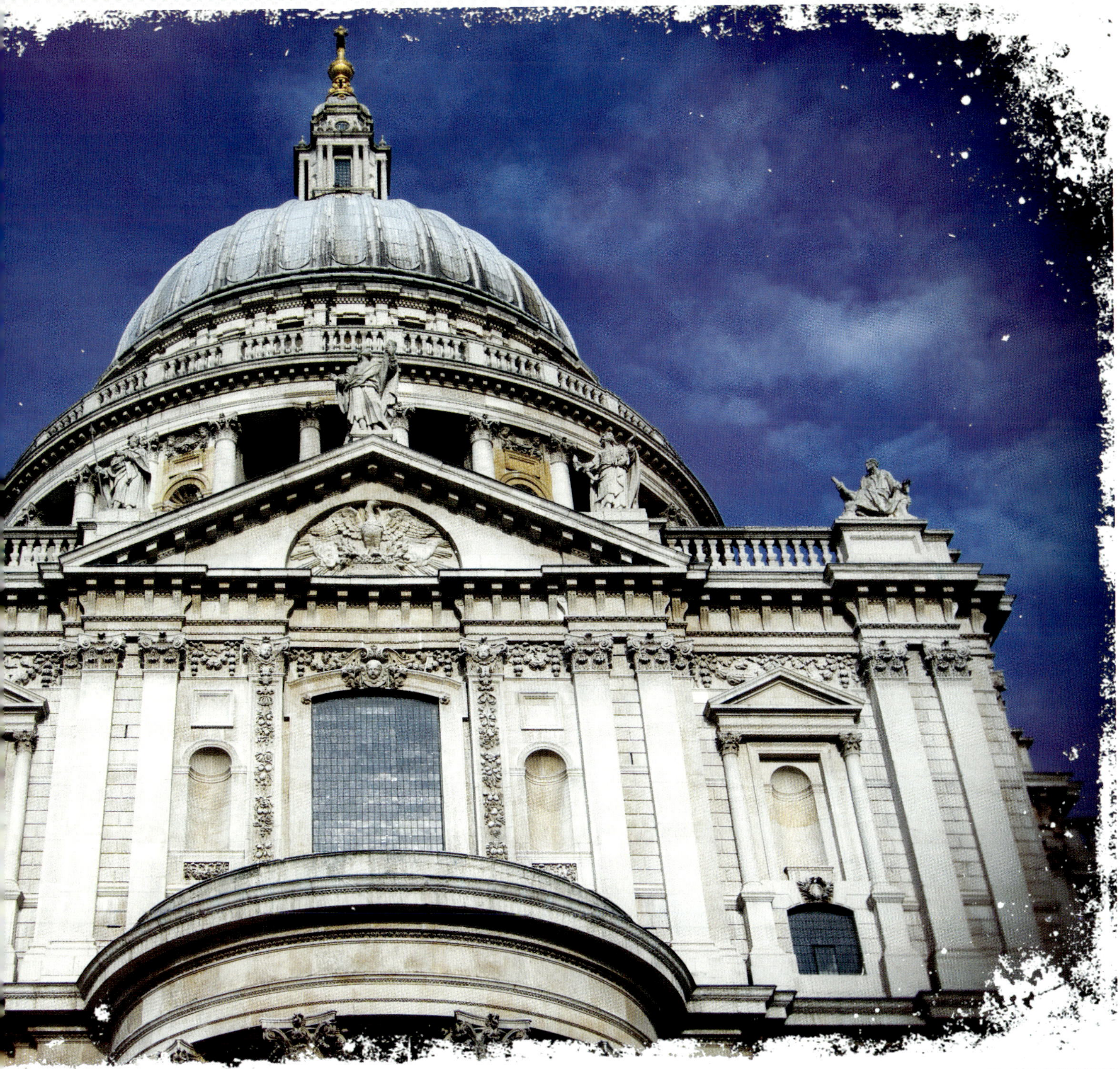

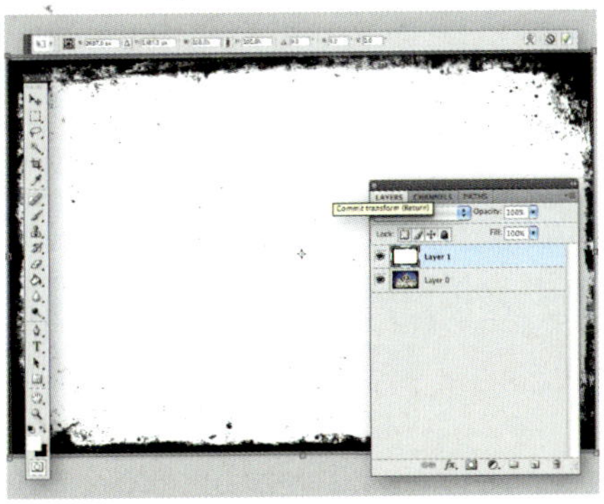

2 Transform your frame Go to ***Edit>Free Transform*** and, if you need to rotate your frame, hover the cursor over the corner widget until it bends, then click, hold and rotate. Next, to resize the frame, hold ***shift*** to constrain the proportions and drag a corner widget outwards to meet the sides of your image. Press the ***tick*** button to commit to the adjustment.

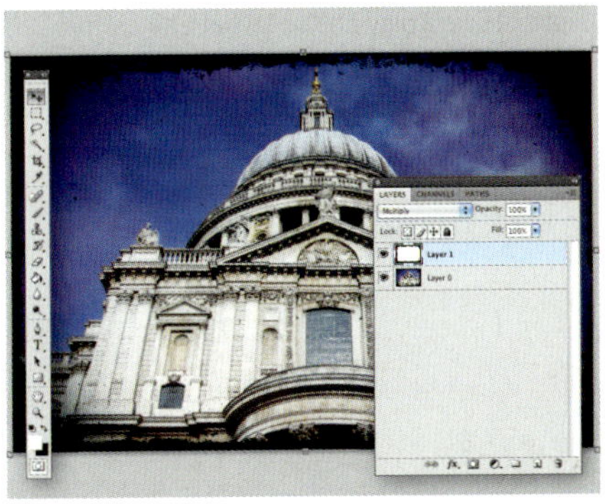

3 Reveal the image Now your frame fits your image, if you want to keep the frame black, change the layer ***Blend Mode*** to ***Multiply*** to eliminate any white in the layer, allowing the picture to show through the frame. You could leave it there if you want, but turning the frame white can sometimes add more impact. Go to the next step to see how.

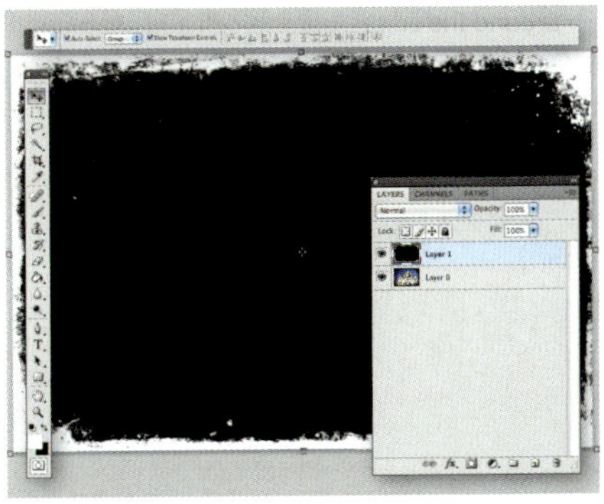

4 Turn it white If you've changed the ***Blend Mode*** to ***Multiply***, change it back to its default ***Normal***. Select the frame layer and go to ***Layer>Adjustments>Invert*** to change it from black to white. Change the ***Blend Mode*** to ***Lighten*** to reveal the image. If the centre of your frame layer isn't filled with black or white, there's no need to use a Blend Mode.

How to create a stylish triptych from one image

Get the most from your images using these simple steps to divide a single shot into three for a creative way of presenting your work

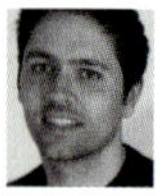

Jordan Butters: Unfortunately fewer and fewer photographers are printing their images and it's such a shame, especially since there are some very creative ways to present pictures these days – with one popular choice being the triptych. In simple terms, a triptych is a series of three images that are either separate pictures linked by a common theme or a single image divided into three sections. It's the latter version we'll show you how to do here. While we've opted to divide our image sections into equal widths, you can make some panels more prominent than others.

There are no rules, only guidelines for how a triptych should look. For instance, if you are creating your triptych from an single photo, consider your choice of image. This finish tends to work best if the original photograph has a point of interest in each section. You can also use images where parts of the scene lead your eye from one panel in to the next, as the curved sea wall does in our example. If your image doesn't have enough interest to divide it into thirds, consider dividing it into two sections for a diptych or four sections for a quadtych using the same technique. Or, rather than a horizontal triptych, make it a vertical sectioning. You can then print them on a single sheet or individually and hang them together. Easy!

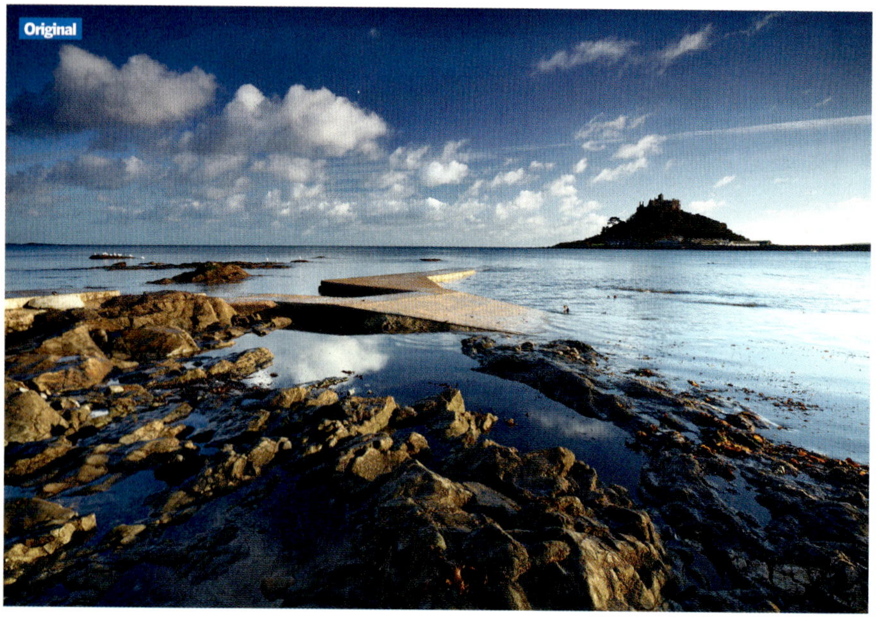

HELEN DIXON

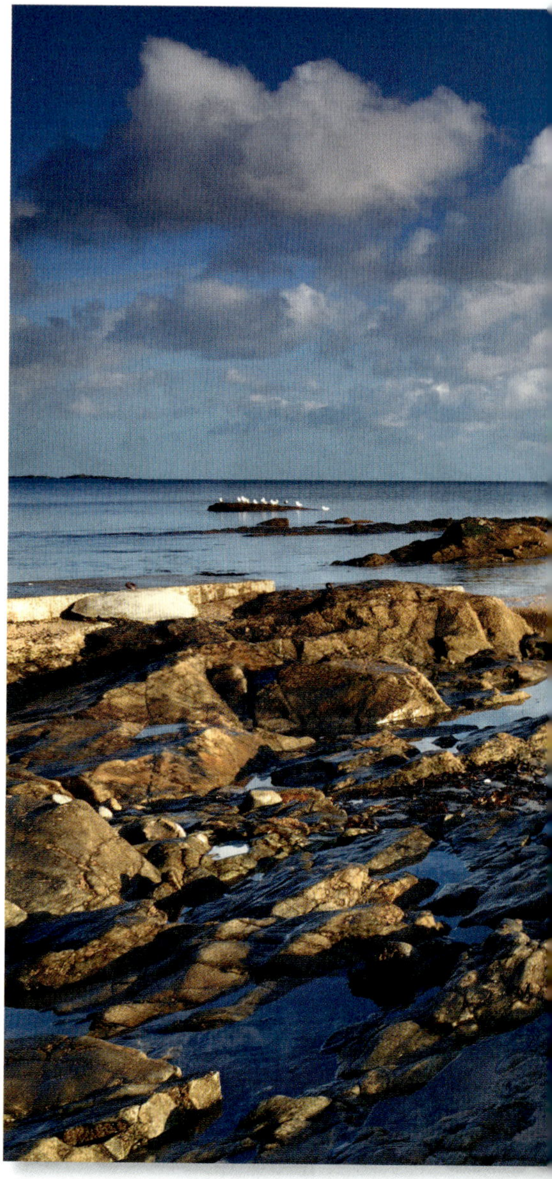

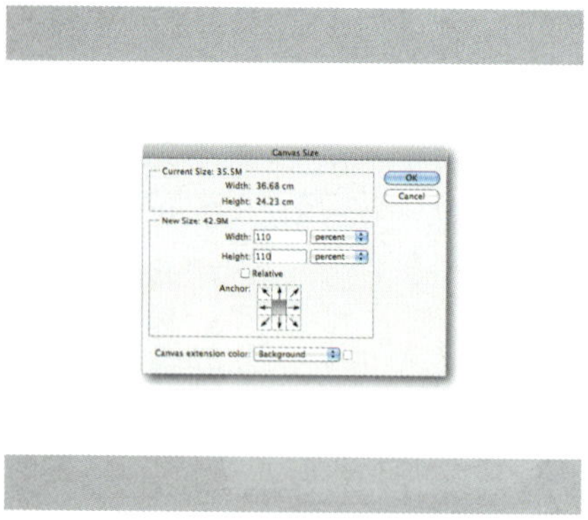

1 Create a blank canvas Open your image and go to ***Select>All*** and ***Edit>Copy***. This not only copies the image, but its dimensions. Create a blank document by going to ***File>New***. Leave the dimensions as they are for now and click ***OK***. With your blank document open, go to ***Image>Canvas Size***. Change the units of measurement from ***cm*** to ***Percent*** and change both the ***Width*** and ***Height*** to ***110***. Click ***OK***.

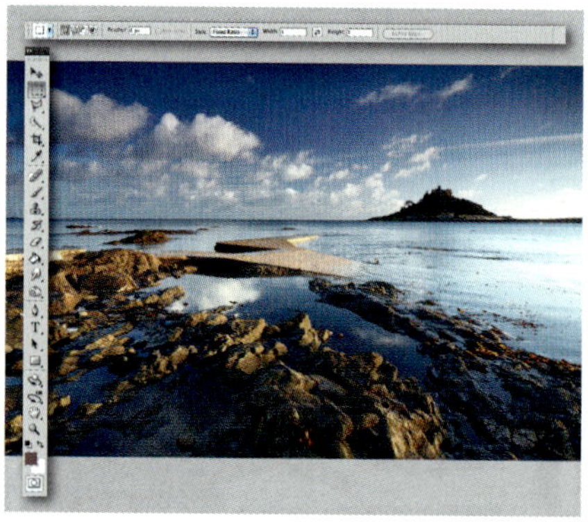

2 Set up the selection tool Open your original image and go to ***Select>Deselect Layers***. Pick the ***Rectangular Marquee Tool***. Alter the ratio of the rectangle by changing the ***Width*** to ***1*** and the ***Height*** to ***2*** in the top menu bar. Go to ***View>Zoom Out*** and zoom out until you can see the full image on screen. Grab the lower-right corner of the window and drag it to leave some grey space around your image.

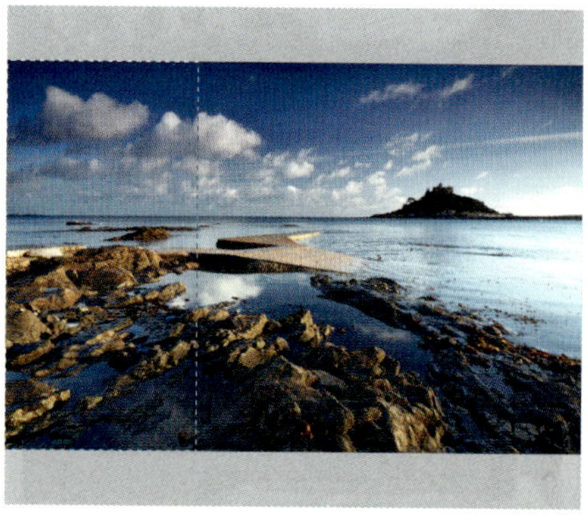

3 Select your first panel Click to the top left of the image, within the grey border, and drag the selection box down past the bottom of the image. Starting and ending your selection outside of the image ensures that you leave no gaps at the top and bottom. This selection will form the first part of your triptych. Go to ***Edit>Copy***, open your blank canvas again and go to ***Edit>Paste***. The first part of your triptych will appear in the centre.

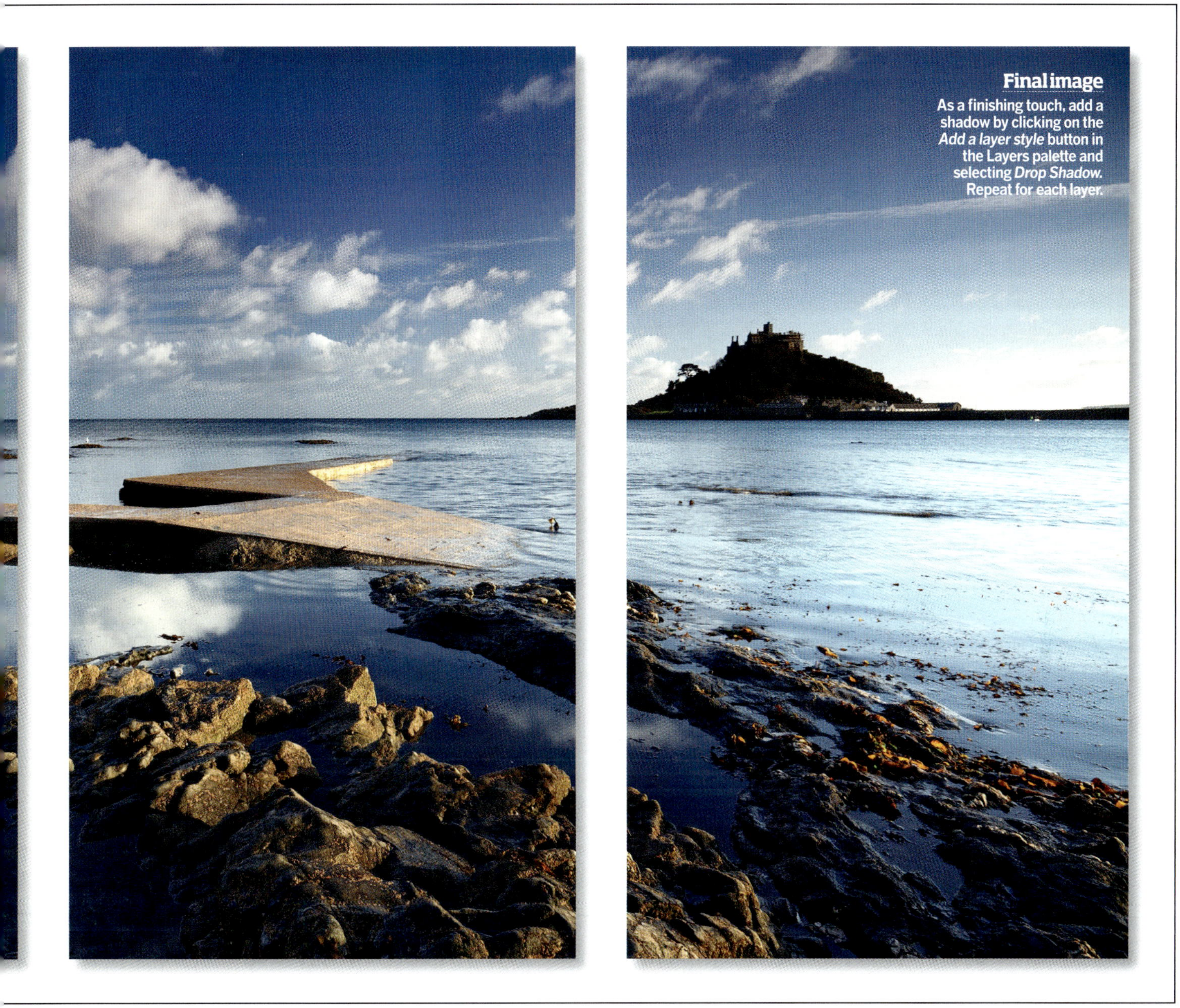

Final image

As a finishing touch, add a shadow by clicking on the *Add a layer style* button in the Layers palette and selecting *Drop Shadow*. Repeat for each layer.

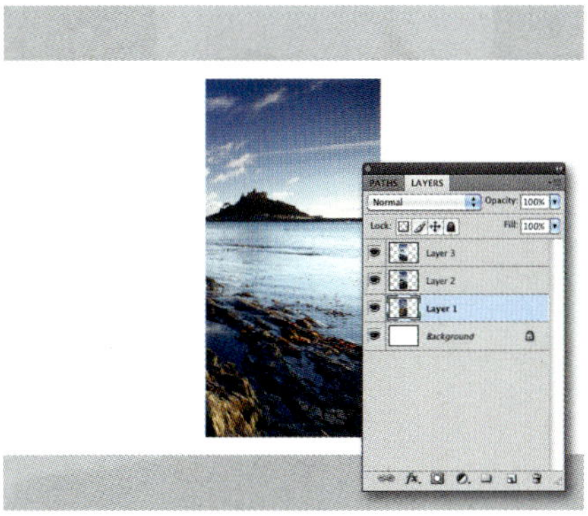

4 Add the other panels Head back over to your image and select the next panel, starting your selection from the top right of your current selection and dragging down to the bottom of the image again. Go to ***Edit>Copy***, open your canvas again and go to ***Edit>Paste***. Repeat this step for the final part of your image. All three parts of your triptych will be stacked on top of each other on the blank canvas, so it's time to space them out.

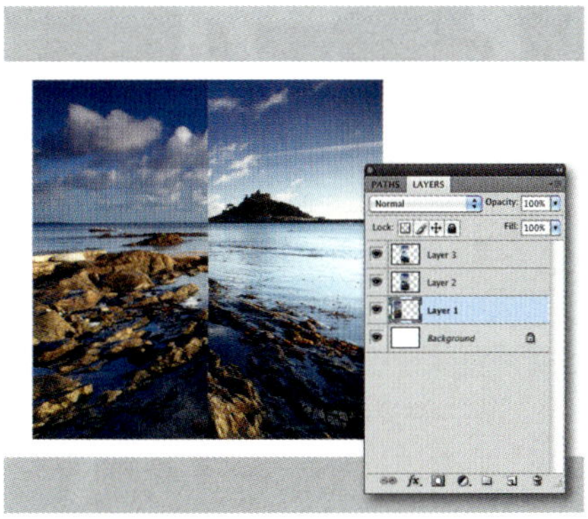

5 Space out the images Close your main image without saving and work on your new canvas. Making sure that ***Layer 1*** is selected in the Layers palette, select the ***Move Tool***. Hold down the ***shift*** key, and click and drag the layer to the left until it locks on to the side of the other layers. Select ***Layer 3*** in the Layers palette and repeat, this time dragging to the right until it locks into place. It will look similar to your original image.

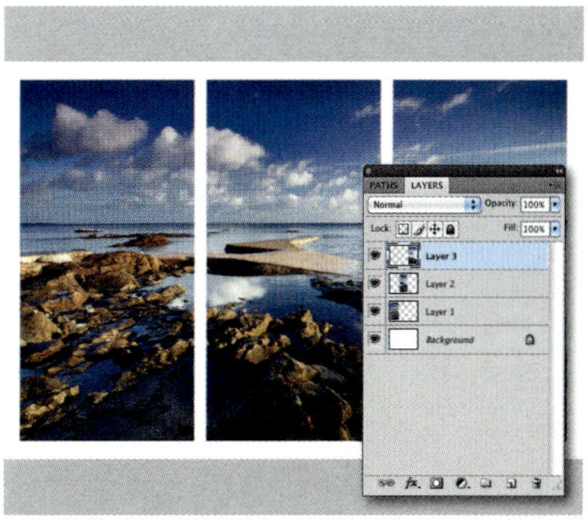

6 Create borders With Layer 3 still selected, hold down the ***shift*** key again and tap the ***right arrow*** key to create a border. Count the number of times you tap the key. Select ***Layer 1*** in the Layers palette and, holding down the ***shift*** key again, tap the ***left arrow*** key an equal number of times to create an equal-size gap on the other side. Holding down the ***shift*** key moves your image five pixels at a time.

Create a calendar

One of the first purchases of the New Year has to be a new calendar. But don't rush out and buy one – make your own!

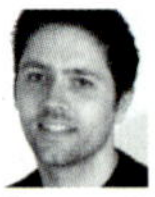

Jordan Butters: As one year comes to an end and a new year rolls around, we can start to plan all of the exciting things that the New Year has in store for us. Of course, to do this we need a calendar and the shelves are packed with choices to suit everybody's taste. Whatever your hobby or interest, you can be sure there's a calendar out there for you – from Dalmatians to David Beckham, helicopters to Heidi Klum – there's something for everyone. But why should you look at someone else's images each month when you can make up a calendar using your own photographs and enjoy your favourite images throughout the whole year?

Follow this guide to create a simple calendar that looks great all year round. We've given you the basics here, but there's no reason why you can't tweak the design to make it work for you. Why not add a section for notes at the bottom of each sheet? Or highlight important dates such as holidays and birthdays?

Before you begin, revisit your photo library and choose 12 images for your calendar. I'd suggest matching each image to the seasons or time of year for each month, or an important event or date during that month. Rename each image using the month for which it will be used and move the 12 images into a new folder so you can find them easily.

Presentation

When you're done, you can print each page on photo paper to display in a desktop stand or send the design to a local or online printer to have it printed and ring-bound. Or why not size your document to match your computer's desktop resolution? You can use it as your home screen and never miss a date again!

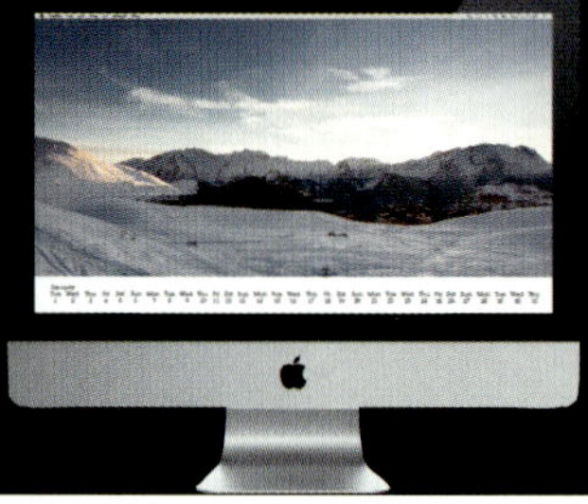

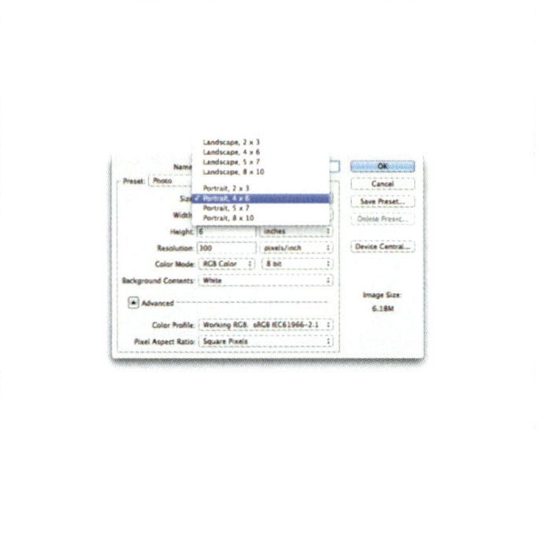

1 Create a blank document Open Photoshop and create a new document by going to ***File>New***. In the dialogue box that opens up, use the ***Preset*** menu to select a paper size for your calendar. Once you have selected a preset, use the ***Size*** menu below to set the size. This will depend on how you want to display your calendar, but I've chosen the Photo preset and set the size to Portrait, 4x6in.

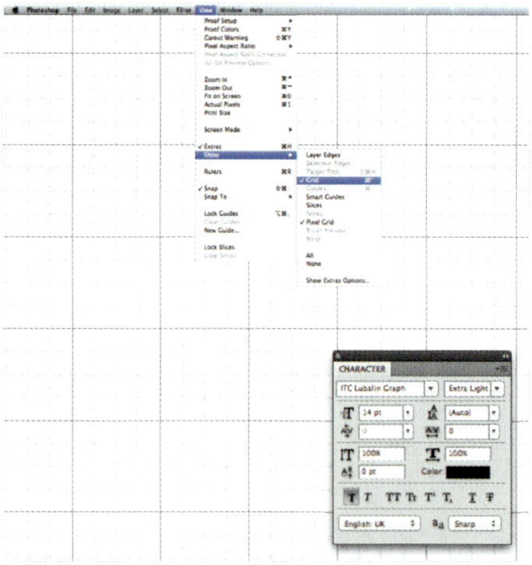

2 Display the Grid Enable the Grid, which will help you align the text, by going to ***View>Show>Grid***. Then ensure that the Character palette is visible by going to ***Window>Character***. Pick the ***Horizontal Type Tool*** and select your choice of font and colour from the Character palette. Set the size to ***14pt*** as a starting point – we will adjust the size in the next step if needed.

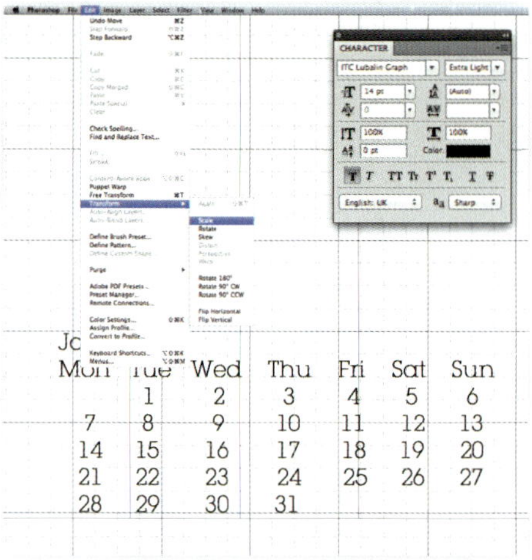

3 Insert the dates Type out the dates, leaving equal spaces between each date. Use the ***Grid*** to line them all up, adding or omitting extra spaces where needed. Once complete, click on the ***tick*** in the top menu bar to confirm and apply the text. Then go to ***Edit>Transform>Scale*** and, holding down the ***shift*** key, click and drag one of the corner anchor points to scale your calendar diary to size.

4 Create space for your image Click on the ***Rectangular Marquee Tool*** and click and drag on your document to select a square or rectangle in which your image will sit. Use the grid as a reference and leave equal space on each side between the image area and the edge of the document. Open your first image and go ***Select>All*** and ***Edit>Copy***. Close this image without saving.

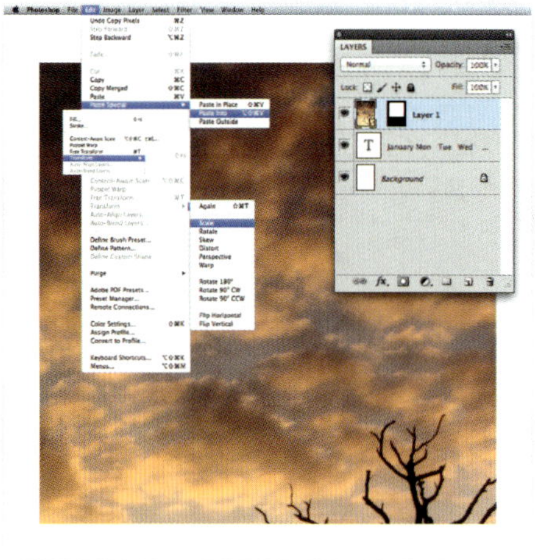

5 Paste in your image Back on your calendar document, go to ***Edit>Paste Special>Paste Into***. Use the ***Move Tool*** to move your image into place and use the ***Edit>Transform>Scale*** tool to scale your image to size. If you need to change the size or shape of your image area, click on the right-hand thumbnail on the active layer in the Layers palette and again use ***Transform*** to adjust the rectangle.

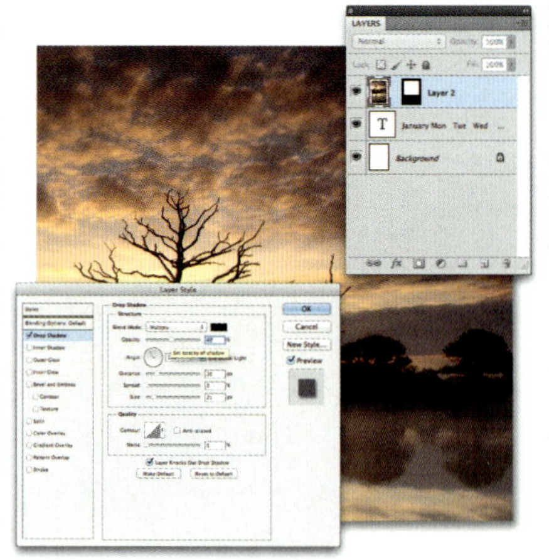

6 Add a border effect Double-click on the top layer in the Layers palette to open the ***Blending Options*** menu. From here you can add a border effect to your image. I have opted for a ***Drop Shadow***, but you can add a ***Stroke*** outline as an alternative. Click on the ***Drop Shadow*** tab and use the sliders to adjust the ***Opacity, Distance, Spread*** and ***Size*** until you are happy with the effect.

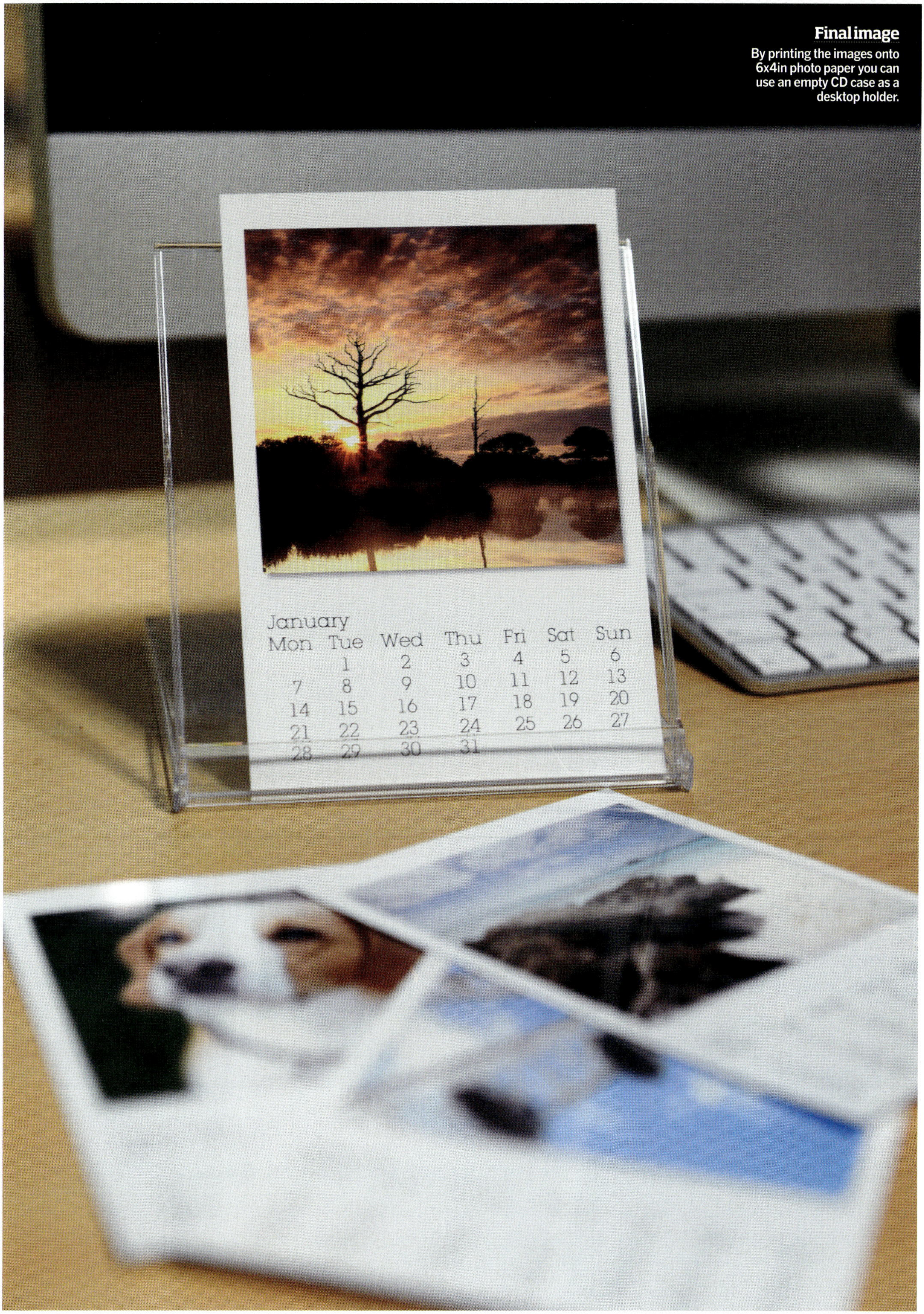

Final image
By printing the images onto 6x4in photo paper you can use an empty CD case as a desktop holder.

Useful Photoshop shortcuts for PC & Mac

General	PC-Windows	Apple Mac
New file	<ctrl> N	<cmd> N
Open file	<ctrl> O	<cmd> O
Close file	<ctrl> W	<cmd> W
Save file	<ctrl> S	<cmd> S
Save file as	<shift> <ctrl> S	<shift> <cmd> S
Print file	<ctrl> P	<cmd> P
Step backward (undo)	<ctrl> Z	<cmd> Z
Step forward (redo)	<ctrl> Y	<cmd> Y
Free Transform	<ctrl> T	<cmd> T
Apply Transform	<enter>	<return>
Copy selection	<ctrl> C	<cmd> C
Cut selection	<ctrl> X	<cmd> X
Paste selection as new layer	<ctrl> V	<cmd> V
Image size	<alt> <ctrl> I	<option> <cmd> S
Levels	<ctrl> L	<cmd> L
Select default colours	D	D
Swap background / foreground colours	X	X
Repeat last filter used	<ctrl> F	<cmd> F
Adjust Hue / Saturation	<ctrl> U	<cmd> U
Show / hide rulers	<shift> <ctrl> R	<shift> <cmd> R
Toggle Quick Mask mode	Q	Q

Auto Adjustments	PC-Windows	Apple Mac
Auto Smart Fix	<alt> <ctrl> M	<option> <cmd> M
Auto Levels	<shift> <ctrl> L	<shift> <cmd> L
Auto Contrast	<alt> <shift> <ctrl> L	<option> <shift> <cmd> L
Auto colour	<shift> <ctrl> B	<shift> <cmd> B
Auto red-eye fix	<ctrl> R	<cmd> R

Selections	PC-Windows	Apple Mac
Select all	<ctrl> A	<cmd> A
Deselect	<ctrl> D	<cmd> D
Invert selection	<shift> <ctrl> I	<shift> <cmd> I
Feather selection	<alt> <ctrl> D	<option> <cmd> D
Add to selection	<shift> and selection tool	<shift> and selection tool
Remove from selection	<alt> and selection tool	<option> and selection tool
Show / hide selection boundary	<ctrl> H	<cmd> H
Constrain marquee (circle or square)	<shift> and shape tool	<shift> and shape tool
Draw marquee from centre	<alt> and shape tool	<option> and shape tool
Exit crop tool	<esc>	<esc>

Layers	PC-Windows	Apple Mac
New Layer	<shift> <ctrl> N	<shift> <cmd> N
Copy Layer	<ctrl> J	<cmd> J
Group layers	<ctrl> G	<cmd> G
Ungroup layers	<shift> <ctrl> G	<shift> <cmd> G
Merge layers	<ctrl> E	<cmd> E
Merge all visible layers	<shift> <ctrl> E	<shift> <cmd> E

Zooming	PC-Windows	Apple Mac
Zoom in	<ctrl> +	<cmd> +
Zoom out	<ctrl> –	<cmd> –
Fit on screen	<ctrl> 0	<cmd> 0
Actual pixels (100% zoom)	<alt> <ctrl> 0	<option> <cmd> 0
Scroll using hand tool	<spacebar> use mouse	<spacebar> use mouse

Drawing tools	PC-Windows	Apple Mac
Eyedropper	<alt> in painting or shape tool	<option> in painting or shape tool
Fill with background colour	<ctrl> <backspace>	<cmd> <delete>
Increase brush size	]	]
Decrease brush size	[	[
Increase brush hardness	<shift>]	<shift>]
Decrease brush hardness	<shift> [	<shift> [